FOUNDATIONS *of*

C++

AND Object-Oriented

PROGRAMMING

PROGRAMMERS PRESS

NAMIR C. SHAMMAS

Foundations of C++ and Object-Oriented Programming

Published by
IDG Books Worldwide, Inc.
An International Data Group Company
919 E. Hillsdale Blvd.
Suite 400
Foster City, CA 94404

Library of Congress Catalog Card No.: 95-83094

ISBN: 1-56884-709-2

Printed in the United States of America

10 9 8 7 6 5 4 3 2 1

1B/SX/RR/ZV

Distributed in the United States by IDG Books Worldwide, Inc.

Distributed by Macmillan Canada for Canada; by Computer and Technical Books for the Caribbean Basin; by Contemporanea de Ediciones for Venezuela; by Distribuidora Cuspide for Argentina; by CITEC for Brazil; by Ediciones ZETA S.C.R. Ltda. for Peru; by Editorial Limusa SA for Mexico; by Transworld Publishers Limited in the United Kingdom and Europe; by Al-Maiman Publishers & Distributors for Saudi Arabia; by Simron Pty. Ltd. for South Africa; by IDG Communications (HK) Ltd. for Hong Kong; by Toppan Company Ltd. for Japan; by Addison Wesley Publishing Company for Korea; by Longman Singapore Publishers Ltd. for Singapore, Malaysia, Thailand, and Indonesia; by Unalis Corporation for Taiwan; by WS Computer Publishing Company, Inc. for the Philippines; by WoodsLane Pty. Ltd. for Australia; by WoodsLane Enterprises Ltd. for New Zealand.

For general information on IDG Books Worldwide's books in the U.S., please call our Consumer Customer Service department at 800-762-2974. For reseller information, including discounts and premium sales, please call our Reseller Customer Service department at 800-434-3422.

For information on where to purchase IDG Books Worldwide's books outside the U.S., contact IDG Books Worldwide at 415-655-3021 or fax 415-655-3295.

For information on translations, contact Marc Jeffrey Mikulich, Director, Foreign & Subsidiary Rights, at IDG Books Worldwide, 415-655-3018 or fax 415-655-3295.

For sales inquiries and special prices for bulk quantities, write to the address above or call IDG Books Worldwide at 415-655-3200.

For information on using IDG Books Worldwide's books in the classroom, or ordering examination copies, contact Jim Kelly at 800-434-2086.

For authorization to photocopy items for corporate, personal, or educational use, please contact Copyright Clearance Center, 222 Rosewood Drive, Danvers, MA 01923, or fax 508-750-4470.

are trademarks under exclusive license to IDG Books Worldwide, Inc., from International Data Group, Inc.

From the Publisher

The *Foundations* series is designed, written, and edited *by* working programmers *for* working programmers. We asked you what you needed from a book to become productive using a programming tool, technique, or language. You told us to publish a book that:

- Is written from the perspective of a professional programmer

- Provides great coding examples that can be readily applied to your programs

- Serves as a tutorial that facilitates mastery of complex techniques, features, and concepts

- Serves as a comprehensive reference, achieving "dog-eared" status on your short-shelf of must-have books

- Provides a comprehensive index (programmers always go to the index first!)

- Includes either a fully indexed and linked electronic reference for quick and portable reference or valuable software that helps you get your job done better.

Our goal is to deliver all of this and more. We offer no gimmicks; no promise of instant proficiency through repetition or oversimplification. Sure, it's okay to learn the basics of driving a car doing 20 MPH with your dad in an empty parking lot. But if you're competing the next day in the Indy 500, you need entirely different preparation. You need to know the capabilities of your machine, the idiosyncrasies of the course, and how to translate that knowledge into a competitive advantage.

Like all Programmers Press books, this book is written by professionals. It is meticulously edited for technical accuracy, completeness, and readability. It is a book you will come to trust and rely on.

Thank you for choosing our product.

Christopher J. Williams

Christopher J. Williams
Publisher

Welcome to the world of IDG Books Worldwide.

IDG Books Worldwide, Inc., is a subsidiary of International Data Group, the world's largest publisher of computer-related information and the leading global provider of information services on information technology. IDG was founded more than 25 years ago and now employs more than 7,700 people worldwide. IDG publishes more than 250 computer publications in 67 countries (see listing below). More than 70 million people read one or more IDG publications each month.

Launched in 1990, IDG Books Worldwide is today the #1 publisher of best-selling computer books in the United States. We are proud to have received 8 awards from the Computer Press Association in recognition of editorial excellence and three from Computer Currents' First Annual Readers' Choice Awards, and our best-selling ...*For Dummies*® series has more than 19 million copies in print with translations in 28 languages. IDG Books Worldwide, through a joint venture with IDG's Hi-Tech Beijing, became the first U.S. publisher to publish a computer book in the People's Republic of China. In record time, IDG Books Worldwide has become the first choice for millions of readers around the world who want to learn how to better manage their businesses.

Our mission is simple: Every one of our books is designed to bring extra value and skill-building instructions to the reader. Our books are written by experts who understand and care about our readers. The knowledge base of our editorial staff comes from years of experience in publishing, education, and journalism — experience which we use to produce books for the '90s. In short, we care about books, so we attract the best people. We devote special attention to details such as audience, interior design, use of icons, and illustrations. And because we use an efficient process of authoring, editing, and desktop publishing our books electronically, we can spend more time ensuring superior content and spend less time on the technicalities of making books.

You can count on our commitment to deliver high-quality books at competitive prices on topics you want to read about. At IDG Books Worldwide, we continue in the IDG tradition of delivering quality for more than 25 years. You'll find no better book on a subject than one from IDG Books Worldwide.

John J. Kilcullen

John Kilcullen
President and CEO
IDG Books Worldwide, Inc.

IDG Books Worldwide, Inc., is a subsidiary of International Data Group, the world's largest publisher of computer-related information and the leading global provider of information services on information technology. International Data Group publishes over 250 computer publications in 67 countries. Seventy million people read one or more International Data Group publications each month. International Data Group's publications include: **ARGENTINA:** Computerworld Argentina, GamePro, Infoworld, PC World Argentina; **AUSTRALIA:** Australian Macworld, Client/Server Journal, Computer Living, Computerworld, Digital News, Network World, PC World, Publishing Essentials, Reseller; **AUSTRIA:** Computerwelt, PC TEST; **BELARUS:** PC World Belarus; **BELGIUM:** Data News; **BRAZIL:** Annuário de Informática, Computerworld Brazil, Connections, Super Game Power, Macworld, PC World Brazil, Publish Brazil, SUPERGAME; **BULGARIA:** Computerworld Bulgaria, Networkworld/Bulgaria, PC & MacWorld Bulgaria; **CANADA:** CIO Canada, ComputerWorld Canada, InfoCanada, Network World Canada, Reseller World; **CHILE:** Computerworld Chile, GamePro, PC World Chile; **COLUMBIA:** Computerworld Colombia, GamePro, PC World Colombia; **COSTA RICA:** PC World Costa Rica/Nicaragua; **THE CZECH AND SLOVAK REPUBLICS:** Computerworld Czechoslovakia, Elektronika Czechoslovakia, PC World Czechoslovakia; **DENMARK:** Communications World, Computerworld Danmark, Macworld Danmark, PC World Danmark, PC World Danmark Supplements, TECH World; **DOMINICAN REPUBLIC:** PC World Republica Dominicana; **ECUADOR:** PC World Ecuador, GamePro; **EGYPT:** Computerworld Middle East, PC World Middle East; **EL SALVADOR:** PC World Centro America; **FINLAND:** MikroPC, Tietoverkko, Tietoviikko; **FRANCE:** Distributique, Golden, Info PC, Le Guide du Monde Informatique, Le Monde Informatique, Reseaux & Telecoms; **GERMANY:** Computer Business, Computerwoche, Computerwoche Extra, Computerwoche Focus, Electronic Entertainment, GamePro, I/M Information Management, Macwelt, PC Welt; **GREECE:** GamePro, Macworld & Publish; **GUATEMALA:** PC World Centro America; **HONDURAS:** PC World Centro America; **HONG KONG:** Computerworld Hong Kong, PCWorld Hong Kong, Publish in Asia; **HUNGARY:** ABCD CD-ROM, Computerworld Szamitastechnika, PC & Mac World Hungary, PC-X Magazine; **INDIA:** Computerworld India, PC World India, Publish in Asia; **INDONESIA:** InfoKomputer PC World, Komputek Computerworld, Publish in Asia; **IRELAND:** ComputerScope, PC Live!; **ISRAEL:** PC World 32 BIT, People & Computers; **ITALY:** Computerworld Italia, Computerworld Italia Special Editions, Lotus Italia, Macworld Italia, Networking Italia, PC Shopping, PC World Italia, PC World/Walt Disney; **JAPAN:** Macworld Japan, Nikkei Personal Computing, SunWorld Japan, Windows World Japan; **KENYA:** East African Computer News; **KOREA:** Hi-Tech Information/Computerworld, Macworld Korea, PC World Korea; **MACEDONIA:** PC World Macedonia; **MALAYSIA:** Computerworld Malaysia, PC World Malaysia, Publish in Asia; **MEXICO:** Computerworld Mexico, GamePro, Macworld, PC World Mexico; **MYANMAR:** PC World Myanmar; **NETHERLANDS:** Computable, Computer! Totaal, LAN Magazine, Macworld, Net Magazine; **NEW ZEALAND:** Computer Buyer, Computerworld New Zealand, MTB, Network World, PC World New Zealand; **NICARAGUA:** PC World Costa Rica/Nicaragua; **NIGERIA:** PC World Africa; **NORWAY:** Computerworld Norge, Computerworld Privat, CW Rapport Klient/Tjener, CW Rapport Nettverk & Telecom, CW Rapport Offentlig Sektor, IDG's KURSGUIDE, Macworld Norge, Multimedia World, PC World Ekspress, PC World Nettverk, PC World Norge, PC World's Produktguide, Windows Spesial; **PAKISTAN:** Computerworld Pakistan, PC World Pakistan; **PANAMA:** GamePro, PC World Panama; **PARAGUAY:** PC World Paraguay; **P. R. OF CHINA:** China Computerworld, China Infoworld, Computer & Communication, Electronic Product World, Electronics Today, Game Camp, PC World China, Popular Computer Week, Software World, Telecom Product World; **PERU:** Computerworld Peru, GamePro, PC World Profesional Peru, PC World Peru; **POLAND:** Computerworld Poland, Computerworld Special Report, Macworld, Networld, PC World Komputer; **PHILIPPINES:** Computerworld Philippines, PC Digest, Publish in Asia; **PORTUGAL:** Cerebro/PC World, Correio Informático/Computerworld, Mac•In/PC•In Portugal; **PUERTO RICO:** PC World Puerto Rico; **ROMANIA:** Computerworld Romania, PC World Romania, Telecom Romania; **RUSSIA:** Computerworld Rossiya, Network World Russia, PC World Russia; **SINGAPORE:** Computerworld Singapore, PC World Singapore, Publish in Asia; **SLOVENIA:** MONITOR; **SOUTH AFRICA:** Computing S.A., Network World S.A., Software World; **SPAIN:** Computerworld España, COMUNICACIONES WORLD, Dealer World, Macworld España, PC World España; **SWEDEN:** CAP&Design, Computer Sweden, Corporate Computing, MacWorld, Maxi Data, MikroDatorn, Nätverk & Kommunikation, PC/Aktiv, PC World, Windows World; **SWITZERLAND:** Computerworld Schweiz, Macworld Schweiz, PCtip; **TAIWAN:** Computerworld Taiwan, Macworld Taiwan, PC World Taiwan, Publish Taiwan, Windows World; **THAILAND:** Thai Computerworld, Publish in Asia; **TURKEY:** Computerworld Monitör, MACWORLD Turkiye, PC WORLD Turkiye; **UKRAINE:** Computerworld Kiev, Computers & Software Magazine, PC World Ukraine; **UNITED KINGDOM:** Acorn User, Amiga Action, Amiga Computing, Amiga, Appletalk, CD Powerplay, CD-ROM Now, Computing, Connexion, GamePro, Lotus Magazine, Macaction, Macworld, Open Computing, Parents and Computers, PC Home, PC Works, The WEB; **UNITED STATES:** Cable in the Classroom, CD Review, CIO Magazine, Computerworld, Computerworld Client/Server Journal, Digital Video Magazine, DOS World, Electronic, InfoWorld, I-Way, Macworld, Maximize, MULTIMEDIA WORLD, Network World, PC World, PUBLISH, SWATPro Magazine, Video Event, WebMaster; **URUGUAY:** PC World Uruguay; **VENEZUELA:** Computerworld Venezuela, GamePro, PC World Venezuela; and **VIETNAM:** PC World Vietnam   10/17/95

About the Author

Namir C. Shammas is a software engineer living in Midlothian, Virginia. He is a self-employed technical writer and an expert in object-oriented programming who has authored over 50 computer titles, including *Windows Programmer's Guide to Object Windows Library*, *Advanced C++*, and *Teach Yourself Visual C++ in 21 Days*. Namir has also contributed articles to such publications as *BYTE*, *Dr. Dobb's Journal*, and *Computer Language*.

Dedication

To my very special friend, Emily Rennie

Credits

**Group Publisher
and Vice President**
Christopher J. Williams

Publishing Director
John Osborn

Senior Acquisitions Manager
Amorette Pedersen

Managing Editor
Kim Field

Editorial Director
Anne Marie Walker

Production Director
Beth Jenkins

Production Assistant
Jacalyn L. Pennywell

**Supervisor of
Project Coordination**
Cindy L. Phipps

Supervisor of Page Layout
Kathie S. Schnorr

Production Systems Specialist
Steve Peake

Pre-Press Coordination
Tony Augsburger
Patricia R. Reynolds
Theresa Sánchez-Baker

Media/Archive Coordination
Leslie Popplewell
Kerri Cornell
Michael Wilkey

Project Editor
Ralph E. Moore

Manuscript Editor
Bob Campbell

Technical Editor
Elham Moradeshaghi

**Associate Project
Coordinator**
J. Tyler Connor

Graphics Coordination
Shelley Lea
Gina Scott
Carla Radzikinas

Production Page Layout
Cameron Booker
Dominique DeFelice
Maridee V. Ennis
Angela F. Hunckler

Proofreaders
Gwenette Gaddis
Christine Meloy
Dwight Ramsey
Carl Saff
Robert Springer

Indexer
Liz Cunningham

CD-ROM Production
The Komando Corporation

Cover Photo
Rio C.

Cover Design
Draper and Liew, Inc.

Acknowledgments

This book is the fruit of the labor of many people. I would like to thank the publishing director, Amorette Pedersen, project editor Ralph Moore, technical editor Ellie Moradeshaghi, manuscript editor Bob Campbell, and many others at IDG Books who have contributed to this book. I also would like to thank my literary agent, Carol McLyndon of Waterside Productions, for her encouragement to pursue this project.

(The publisher would like to give special thanks to Patrick McGovern, without whom this book would not have been possible.)

CONTENTS OVERVIEW

To introduce you to the exciting world of C++, Part I offers an overview of structured and object-oriented programming and gives you a taste of the various aspects of this highly useful language.

The two major paradigms for programming today are *structured* and *object-oriented* programming. This chapter discusses both and highlights the differences between these two methods.

To get you familiar with the C++ language features and to begin to understand its constructs, this chapter briefly introduces the components of C++.

Your real journey into the world of C++ begins in Part II, where you will understand in detail the response to object-oriented programming embodied in C++.

This chapter demonstrates the organization of simple C++ programs while introducing you to comments, data types, variables, and constants.

Operators and expressions allow your programs to query conditions, update information, and assign new values. This chapter discusses various kinds of each and shows you how to manipulate data using these constructs.

Functions contain the executable statements that drive a program, as well as provide the data interface between various parts of the program. This chapter will help you understand C++ functions, thereby empowering you to write robust applications.

Object-oriented programming (OOP) fosters a new and exciting way to craft, maintain, update, and reuse software. This chapter looks at how C++ supports OOP through classes.

C++ does not define console input and output statements as part of the language. Instead it relies on libraries to perform console I/O. This chapter focuses on managing input and output using the stream libraries.

Decision-making constructs allow programs to examine conditions and take appropriate action. This chapter takes an in-depth look at this all-important feature.

The ability to repeat operations virtually endlessly was among the most prominent features of the first computers. This chapter discusses loops, which make that repetition possible.

Arrays are the simplest yet most powerful data structures supported by many programming languages. This chapter takes an in-depth look at how C++ handles this universal programming construct with single-dimensional arrays.

The support for arrays in C++ extends to multidimensional arrays as well. This chapter presents a smaller selection of the methods used for sorting and searching single-dimensional arrays and shows you how to apply them to multidimensional arrays.

Some of the more advanced C++ components are presented in Part III, including user-defined types, pointers, and class hierarchies.

TABLE OF CONTENTS

Introduction

*T*his book, *Foundations of C++ and Object-Oriented Programming,* will give you a solid grounding in the emerging paradigm of object-oriented programming (OOP) as it teaches you generic C++, allowing you to learn this language with the compiler of your choice and in the operating system of your choice. It includes straightforward and useful examples, explained in step-by-step detail, for every aspect of the language, building chapter by chapter from basic to advanced topics. This book assumes that you have previous programming experience in common languages such as BASIC, Pascal, and C. It also assumes that you know how to edit, compile, link, and run programs on your machine. I have included special comments to readers who already program in C, Pascal, and BASIC, pointing out important differences between these languages and C++.

This book consists of four parts that make up 18 chapters, presenting the C++ language from the ground up. The accompanying CD contains the entire *Foundations of C++ and Object-Oriented Programming* in easy-to-use hypertext form. It also contains copies of all the source code used in the book.

Part I, which includes Chapters 1 and 2, presents an introduction to C++. Chapter 1 offers an overview of structured programming and how it differs from object-oriented programming. The chapter presents the basic notions of object-oriented programming. Chapter 2, an overview of the C++ language, gives a you taste of what C++ code looks like and very briefly presents the main constructs of the language.

Part II, including Chapters 3 through 11, presents the basics of C++. Chapter 3 demonstrates the organization of simple C++ programs as it introduces you to comments, data types, variables, and constants.

Chapter 4 discusses various kinds of operators (such as arithmetic, logical, and relational operators) and expressions and shows you how to manipulate data using these constructs. The chapter also shows you how to write expressions that allow you to test conditions, display values, and assign values.

Chapter 5 discusses C++ functions, which are the placeholders for executable statements. The chapter discusses declaring and calling functions. It also covers local variables and various kinds of functions, such as inline functions.

Chapter 6 discusses the basic principles of object-oriented programming and presents C++ classes. The chapter discusses how to declare C++ classes, the components of a class, and the creation of class instances.

Chapter 7 discusses console input and output. The text covers the basics of the C++ stream library and the standard input and output stream objects. The chapter also covers the **printf** function and shows you how to incorporate the stream output operator in your own classes.

Chapter 8 discusses decision-making constructs in C++ and covers the various kinds of **if** statements and the **switch** statement.

Chapter 9 discusses loops and covers the fixed-iteration **for** loop and the conditional-iteration **do-while** and **while** loops. The text also discusses nesting loops, exiting from loops, and skipping loop iterations.

Chapters 10 and 11 cover single- and multidimensional arrays, showing you how to declare, initialize, and access such arrays. Chapter 10 additionally presents various methods for sorting and searching single-dimensional arrays. Chapter 11 presents a smaller selection of such methods and shows you how to apply them to multidimensional arrays.

Part III, including Chapters 12 through 14, presents advanced components of C++. Chapter 12 discusses user-defined types and shows you how to define enumerated types, structures, and unions. The chapter also discusses how to define function parameters using user-defined types.

Chapter 13 presents pointers and discusses how to access existing variables and manage dynamic variables using pointers. The chapter also discusses using pointers to access arrays and structures and how to declare pointers to various types as function parameters.

Chapter 14 discusses class hierarchies and shows you how to create descendant classes from existing classes. The chapter discusses constructors of descendant classes, virtual member functions, virtual destructors, operators as member functions, friend functions, friend operators, and friend classes.

Part IV, including Chapters 15 through 18, presents advanced topics. Chapter 15 presents the basic stream file I/O. The chapter discusses the stream library functions that allow you to support text file I/O, binary file I/O, and random access file I/O.

Chapter 16 presents exception (runtime error) handling and discusses the C++ metaphor of throwing and catching exceptions. The chapter presents the C++ syntax for these operations and shows you how to manage exceptions.

Chapter 17 presents templates; it shows you how to use function templates and class templates to write generic functions and classes, respectively. The chapter discusses the syntax for declaring function templates and also illustrates how to declare class templates, define their member functions, and instantiate the classes.

Chapter 18 covers new developments in C++. These include the Standard C++ Libraries, such as the Standard Template Library (STL). The text discusses new features such as the new include format, namespaces, and template parameter arguments.

I hope that this book is instrumental in your learning of C++, a language that is gaining popularity, especially in programming GUI applications.

Happy Programming,

Namir Clement Shammas

September 1995

I

Introducing C++

*T*he C programming language is the most popular structured programming language, especially among software developers. The success of C has encouraged Bell Labs, where C was created, to create C++ as a successor for C. The main difference between C and C++ is the support of classes and object-oriented programming in C++.

The first part of this book consists of two chapters that introduce you to C++. The first chapter looks at structured programming and compares it to object-oriented programming. Basically, this first chapter takes a philosophical look at our programming roots as well as where we are all heading. The second chapter in this book gives an overview, or a taste if you prefer, of C++. This overview briefly presents selected components of C++. The approach of this chapter is to present material by examples. The remaining chapters in the book present material in more depth and offer the general syntax for the various language components.

CHAPTER 1

Structured and Object-Oriented Programming

Welcome to the world of C++! Your journey with this exciting programming language begins with a general discussion about programming language trends. This brief chapter then describes the two major paradigms for programming today—*structured* and *object-oriented* programming (OOP)—and highlights the basic differences between these two programming methods. By the end of this chapter, you'll be acquainted with the main features of the OOP paradigm, including the central role within it of the "object" itself.

Structured Programming

Structured programming evolved during the '60s and '70s as the need arose to implement well-coded programs. Unstructured programs are hard to read, update, and maintain. Designers of languages such as FORTRAN IV recognized early on the need to define separate and reusable subroutines and functions. These subroutines and functions enjoyed a certain level of autonomy, making them reusable in multiple applications. While FORTRAN gained popularity among scientists, mathematicians, and engineers as a number-crunching language, BASIC was also gaining popularity among general novice programmers. The early implementations of BASIC severely lacked the formal support of structured programming constructs. Many programming language teachers complained that BASIC fostered bad programming language techniques. After all, these BASIC implementations did not support semi-independent routines (that is, routines that have their own constants and variables), and all the variables were global! The lack of BASIC routines caused problems when translating the BASIC code to other languages. In addition, using global variables was recognized to be undesirable, because of side effects that may occur when different sets of statements use these variables for different purposes.

BASIC's major rival in the '70s and '80s was the Pascal programming language. Pascal supported procedures and functions to structure the code, the mandatory declaration of variables and constants, and the declaration of user-defined types. Moreover, Pascal evolved to support library units containing reusable code. These library units could export constants, data types, variables, procedures, and functions. Moreover, programmers could use an already-defined library unit to build other units. Although Pascal succeeded as a champion of structured programming, Pascal's designers felt the need to develop a successor language, Modula-2, a structured programming language that stressed the use of modules to build programs. The modules in Modula-2 were somewhat more sophisticated than Pascal library units, and Modula-2 itself offered many constructs suitable for developing operating system software. Modula-2 fizzled out due to the lack of de facto standards among vendors.

The popularity of Pascal as a structured programming language was paralleled by the advent of C, from Bell Labs. C was initially intended as a portable high-level assembler to be used for systems programming. However, C demonstrated that it could do whatever Pascal did and do it better! To begin with, C compilers have historically been designed to produce tight and fast code suitable for systems programming. By contrast, Pascal compilers were not under the same constraints. Moreover, the core C language is smaller than the core Pascal language. C relies on standard libraries for file I/O, string manipulation, math operations, and so on. By contrast, Pascal has many of these language components built in. In a nutshell, Pascal offers structured programming with a guardrail, whereas C does not. The advent of the ANSI standard for C has forced C to offer additional protection and code verification.

Today, the C programming language is the most popular general-purpose structured programming language. C modularizes the source code by using functions as code placeholders. In addition, C allows you to create source code libraries. Typically, each library has a header file (with the .H file extension) and an implementation file (with the .C file extension). The header file declares constants, data types, global variables, and prototype declarations of functions exported by the library. The implementation file contains the actual definitions of the exported functions. The same file may contain local constants, data types, variables, and functions.

Structured programming with C consists in defining data types to store the targeted information and using the various functions that manipulate that information. The manipulation includes input, output, and processing. The primary focus is the function, which manipulates the data. The secondary focus is the data types. You can write additional functions (in separate library files) to manipulate the data types defined in existing libraries. This programming feature may seem convenient at first. However, the predefined data are fair game, open to whatever happens! In large-scale software projects, this open-ended data manipulation can lead to chaos.

Another weak point of structured programming is the limits it places on code reuse. Expanding on existing data types requires that you define a new data type that contains the existing data type. For example, consider the following C structure, **Cylinder**, which defines a cylinder:

```
struct Cylinder {
  double radius;
  double height;
};
```

To define a hollow-cylinder structure, **hollowCylinder**, which uses the structure **Cylinder**, you need to declare the following nested structure:

```
struct hollowCylinder {
  Cylinder cyl;
  double innerRadius;
};
```

The field **innerRadius** is not on the same access level as the nested fields **radius** and **height**. For example, suppose you have a variable **CylVar** declared as follows:

```
hollowCylinder CylVar;
```

To access the fields **radius**, **height**, and **innerRadius**, you need the expressions **CylVar.cyl.radius**, **CylVar.cyl.height** and **CylVar.innerRadius**, respectively. These expressions show the awkwardness of accessing the fields **radius** and **height**.

How do you make the functions that you write for the structure **Cylinder** work for the structure **hollowCylinder**? For example, suppose you have a function **getVolume**, which returns the total volume of the cylinder:

```
double getVolume(Cylinder aCylinder);
```

To use the function **getVolume** with the structure **hollowCylinder**, you need to declare a structure of the same type and pass the field **cyl** from the structure **hollowCylinder** to the **getvolume** function:

```
hollowCylinder CylVar;
double vol;
...
vol = getVolume(CylVar.cyl);
...
```

You *cannot* write the following statement:

```
hollowCylinder CylVar;
double vol;
...
vol = getVolume(CylVar); // error!
...
```

Thus, structured programming does not support sophisticated ways to expand on data types and to associate them with functions.

Enter C++! The idea behind C++, which Bjarne Stroustrup developed at Bell Labs, is to build on C in order to use the standard C libraries and salvage the investments many companies have made in C. C++ has evolved out of the C language and has inherited many of the structured programming aspects of C. Object-oriented programming (OOP) purists point out that C++ is not a pure OOP language, like Smalltalk. Instead, they say that C++ supports OOP language extensions. Personally, I agree with this statement. However, this does not mean that C++ is not a serious contender in object-oriented programming.

The "Object" Is the Focal Point

If you have not been exposed to an object-oriented programming language (or a structured programming language with OOP extensions, such as Borland's Object Pascal), then learning C++ requires a new way of thinking. The basic approach in writing good object-oriented programs in C++ is to focus on *objects*. Just look around you! The computer you are using is an object; the chair you are sitting on is an object; the radio you may be listening to is an object. You and I live in a world of objects, each of which has its own attributes and possible operations. Some objects are animated, and some are not. Many objects are made up of smaller objects. A good example is your computer system—the monitor is an object, the keyboard is an object, the hard disk is an object, and so on. Each object is unique because it has a unique state. You and I may own the same calculator make and model, but the data in each calculator (which define the state of the calculator as an object) are different.

Similarly, there are different kinds of calculators that vary in features and operations. You can think of the more advanced calculators as classes derived from the simple calculators. Thus, the collection of different calculator models forms a class hierarchy that models calculators.

Object-Oriented Programming

This section discusses basic object-oriented programming concepts and offers a few examples in C++. My aim is to introduce you (or expose you, if you prefer) to these concepts. I will discuss these concepts, including the specifics of C++ classes, in more detail in Chapter 6, "Object-Oriented Programming."

CLASSES

Object-oriented programming fosters an approach to software design that differs significantly from that of structured programming. Instead of supporting data types with an open-ended set of functions, OOP looks at the real world as made up of objects. Each object belongs to a *class* of objects. For example, a simple four-function calculator belongs to the class of calculators. Each class models a specific kind of object by encapsulating the data that describe the object and the routines that manipulate that kind of object. Thus, you can use a class to model a simple calculator and define components (that is, members) that describe the state and operation of the calculator. Therefore, the encapsulation does away with the open-ended access to the object's data using functions written by someone other than the author of the class. Here is an example in C++ for a class that models a rectangle:

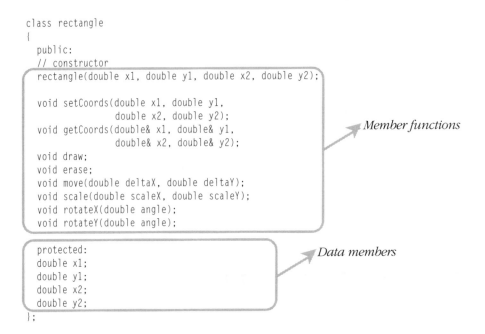

```
class rectangle
{
  public:
  // constructor
  rectangle(double x1, double y1, double x2, double y2);

  void setCoords(double x1, double y1,
                 double x2, double y2);
  void getCoords(double& x1, double& y1,
                 double& x2, double& y2);        Member functions
  void draw;
  void erase;
  void move(double deltaX, double deltaY);
  void scale(double scaleX, double scaleY);
  void rotateX(double angle);
  void rotateY(double angle);

  protected:                                     Data members
  double x1;
  double y1;
  double x2;
  double y2;
};
```

This class defines four *data members* (x1, y1, x2, y2), which specify the upper-left and lower-right corners of a rectangle. The class also defines a set of *member functions* to create, draw, erase, move, scale, and rotate the rectangle. In addition, the class has member functions to query and set the rectangle's coordinates. Conceptually, the class **rectangle** encapsulates all the data members and member functions needed to manipulate a rectangle for a specific kind of application.

Once you define a class, you can create objects that are *instances* of that class. Each object is a unique instance that has its own copies of the data members and can access the public member functions of the class. You can think of the data members as the placeholders for the object's state. In addition, you can think of the member functions as *methods* to set and query the object's state. Here are examples of creating instances of class **rectangle**:

```
rectangle histogram1(0.0, 0.0, 100.0, 100.0);
rectangle histogram2(10.0, 10.0, 30.0, 50.0);
```

These declarations create the objects **histogram1** and **histogram2** as separate instances of class **rectangle**. Each object has its own copies of data members **x1**, **y1**, **x2**, and **y2**. The different arguments used to create each instance supply different sets of data to these data members.

METHODS AND MESSAGES

What about manipulating the objects? The object-oriented programming language Smalltalk uses the term *method* to refer to the routines encapsulated in the class. Applying the Smalltalk concept, you can say that member functions **draw, erase, move, scale,** and so on are methods of class **rectangle**. A *method* specifies *how* to manipulate an object. As for invoking a method with an object, Smalltalk uses the term *sending a message*. A *message* specifies *what* happens to an object. Here is a sample code fragment showing the C++ messages sent to the object **histogram1**:

```
histogram1.draw();
myWait;
histogram1.erase();
histogram1.move(10.0, 5.0);
histogram1.draw();
```

The first statement sends the C++ message **draw** to the object **histogram1**. The runtime system resolves this message by invoking the method (that is, the member function) **draw** defined in class **rectangle**. The third statement sends the C++ message **erase** to the object **histogram1**. The runtime system resolves this message by invoking the method **erase** defined in class **rectangle**. The last two statements send the C++ messages **move** and **draw** to the object **histogram1**. These messages result in invoking the methods **move** and **draw**, respectively.

This introduction of the Smalltalk terms *method* and *message* are not unique to this C++ book. I have noticed other authors using these terms, and I also have used them in other C++ books that I have written. I feel that using these terms to describe C++ code is very appropriate, since it reflects and favors OOP thinking over structured programming thinking.

INHERITANCE

Object-oriented programming supports code reuse in a manner not available in structured programming. In OOP, you can create a new class as a child of an existing class. The new class *inherits* the data members and member functions of the parent class (and all the other ancestor classes); it typically defines additional data members and member functions to support the refined behavior. The child class can also override inherited member functions with new ones to support the correct response. Thus *inheritance* is an important part of object-oriented programming, since it supports a more sophisticated form of code reuse.

To give a quick and simple example, consider the class **rectangle** presented earlier in this chapter. You can declare class **autoRect** as a child of class **rectangle** to automatically erase and redraw the current rectangle after you manipulate its coordinates. Here is the C++ declaration of class **autoRect**:

```
class autoRect : public rectangle
{
  public:
  // constructor
  autoRect(double x1, double y1, double x2, double y2);
  void setRedrawOn();
  void setRedrawOff();
  int getRedrawState();

  protected:
  int redraw;
};
```

The class **autoRect** inherits the data members and member functions of class **rectangle** and adds the data member **redraw** and the member functions **setRedrawOn**, **setRedrawOff**, and **getRedrawState**.

POLYMORPHISM

Another powerful aspect of object-oriented programming is *polymorphism*, a term that suggests the capability to assume several shapes. Polymorphism allows the objects in a class *hierarchy* to offer consistent behavior in an abstract manner. For example, consider a class hierarchy that models geometric shapes. Each class defines its own version of member function **drawIt** (or may inherit the function from a parent or ancestor class) to correctly draw the instances of that class. As a result, when you send the C++ message **drawIt** to an object that is an instance of a shapes class, you need not worry about how the object responds.

Object-oriented programming invites you to study the objects you wish to model in a program. Each object requires that you define a class with attributes and operations. Often you can easily define a hierarchy of classes that describe a set of refined objects. Moreover, you can define classes that contain data members that are themselves instances of other classes (this is called *containment*). You may also end up writing an application in which objects communicate with each other—one object sends a C++ message to another object, and so on.

The next step in your journey into C++ presents an overview of the language. Chapter 2 looks at selected aspects of C++, just to give you a taste!

Summary

Over the last few decades, software engineering evolution has been driven by the need to create programs and libraries that are easy to maintain, update, and reuse. Structured programming offers techniques that focus on the routines first and the data second. By contrast, object-oriented programming invites you to focus on the data—to design classes that describe objects by defining their attributes and the methods that alter these attributes. Thus classes present small software packages that support robust models of objects. The power of object-oriented programming comes from the features of inheritance and polymorphism, which allow you to create class hierarchies. The benefit of these hierarchies is the ability to reuse the inherited parts of a parent class and to focus on the data members and member functions that introduce a new feature in a child class. Using parent and child classes allows better modeling of real-world objects, which are seen as successive levels of refinement of generic concepts.

The next chapter will bring some of these OOP concepts down to earth by giving you an overview of the C++ programming language, which includes a brief introduction to C++ classes.

2

C++: an Overview

*T*his chapter introduces you to C++ by giving you a taste of the various aspects of this programming language. I highly recommend that you read this chapter to get a good idea of the programming features of C++. Keep in mind that this chapter presents a general example-oriented overview. The details start in the next chapter. In this chapter you will learn about C++ comments, predefined data types, declaring and using constants and variables, simple input and output, making decisions, looping, user-defined data types, functions, and classes.

Introduction to C++

Bjarne Stroustrup developed C++ at Bell Labs as a version of C that incorporates classes and supports object-oriented programming. Thus, many of the non-OOP aspects of C++ have evolved from their roots in C, and others simply maintain their earlier forms.

The basic philosophy behind C++ is to maximize the use of tried-and-true C libraries while introducing the programmer to object-oriented programming thinking and software development. The lineage of C++ empowers C programmers to migrate to C++ without having to learn a new language from the ground up.

Although C++ is not a pure object-oriented programming language like Smalltalk, its OOP features are by no means trivial. C++ offers powerful and sophisticated object-oriented programming features that empower developers to create robust and complex applications.

Getting Familiar with Your C++ Compiler

This book presents C++ in a manner independent of any specific software vendor's product. Learning any programming language requires practice. For this reason, the companion CD-ROM contains all of the source code in this book, but you still need to use a C++ compiler package to compile, link, and execute these programs. Several software vendors, such as Microsoft, Borland, Symantec, and Watcom, sell C++ compilers for various operating systems, such as MS-DOS, Windows 3.1, Windows95, Windows NT, and UNIX.

Since dealing with the various compiler packages is beyond the scope of this book, I recommend that you become familiar with using a C++ compiler. If you don't have one yet, you need to purchase a package from your local software store, a mail-order catalog, or a C++ compiler vendor. Appendix C lists some of these vendors. Depending on the operating system and environment you are using to run the C++ compiler package, you need to read the compiler's manuals and learn the following aspects of its operation:

- Learn the general operations provided by the C++ integrated development environment (IDE)—opening files, saving files, and so on.
- Learn how to work with the text editor that may be part of the C++ integrated development environment. Such editors may have special features, such as the ability to display various syntactical elements of code in different colors (also called *syntax coloring*).
- Learn how to set the switches for the compiler, the linker, the project, and other components in your C++ compiler package that contribute to creating executable files.
- Learn how to create the project files that allow you to list the implementation files used to create the executable files.
- Learn how to compile, link, and run C++ source code.

Keep in mind that a single vendor may alter the operational aspects of a C++ compiler package from one version to the next. This kind of change is often made as part of improving the operations of the integrated development environment.

A Simple C++ Program

Let's look at a very simple, but not too trivial, C++ program. Listing 2-1 shows the source code for the C++ program SIMPLE1.CPP. The program prompts you to enter your name and then your age. The program then displays your name and your age. Here is a sample session with the program SIMPLE1.CPP (user input is underlined):

Enter your name : <u>Namir Shammas</u>
Enter your age : <u>41</u>
Namir Shammas is 41 years old

Listing 2-1
The source code for the C++ program SIMPLE1.CPP.

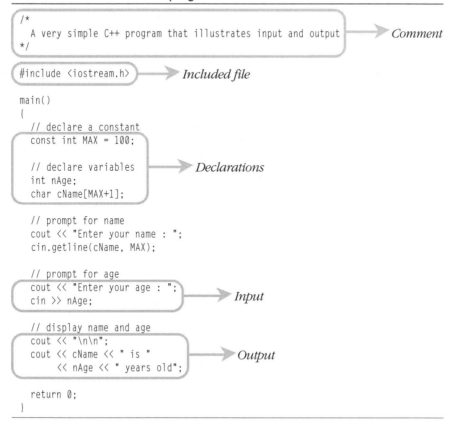

```
/*
  A very simple C++ program that illustrates input and output
*/                                                                  Comment

#include <iostream.h>                                               Included file

main()
{
  // declare a constant
  const int MAX = 100;

  // declare variables                                              Declarations
  int nAge;
  char cName[MAX+1];

  // prompt for name
  cout << "Enter your name : ";
  cin.getline(cName, MAX);

  // prompt for age
  cout << "Enter your age : ";                                      Input
  cin >> nAge;

  // display name and age
  cout << "\n\n";                                                   Output
  cout << cName << " is "
       << nAge << " years old";

  return 0;
}
```

Listing 2-1 contains the function **main**. In C++, the name of this function specifies the default starting point for the code execution. Thus, every C++ program must have one and only one function **main**. The function **main** contains statements that declare variables, prompt for input, obtain the input, and display data in variables. Notice that each statement ends with the semicolon character.

Comments

C++ supports two kinds of comments. The first one uses the pairs of characters /* and */ to define the comment's range. This range can be confined within the same line, or it can span several lines. The second kind of comments in C++ uses the // character pair to mark the beginning of a comment that strictly runs to the end of the same line. Listing 2-2 shows the source code for the C++ program SIMPLE1B.CPP, which is a version of the source code in SIMPLE1 but with more comments. The listing uses both kinds of C++ comments.

Listing 2-2
The source code for the C++ program SIMPLE1B.CPP, which illustrates the two types of comments in C++.

```
/*
   Very simple C++ that illustrates input and output
   Version B: heavily commented source code
*/

#include <iostream.h>            // include stream library header
                                 // file to support stream input
                                 // and output

main()                          // main function where default
{                                // program execution starts

  const int MAX = 100;           // declare a constant

  int nAge;                      // declare a simple variable
  char cName[MAX+1];             // declare a simple array

  cout << "Enter your name : ";  // prompt for name
  cin.getline(cName, MAX);       // input name
```

```
cout << "Enter your age : ";      // prompt for age
cin >> nAge;                      // input age

cout << "\n\n";                   // output two blank lines
cout << cName << " is "           // output name
     << nAge << " years old";     // output age

return 0;                         // return function value
}
```

Notice that Listing 2-2 has more comments, most of which are right justified, than its predecessor. Additionally, it illustrates alternative styles for commenting your source code.

Predefined Data Types

C++ supports several predefined data types for characters, integers, and floating-point numbers. The most popular data types are **char** (the character type), **int** (the basic integer type), **long** (the long integer type), and **double** (the double-precision floating-point type).

We'll next offer examples of literal values for these predefined types. First, here is a set of characters:

```
'a'
'A'
'!'
```

Next, here is a set of integers:

```
33
-455
3200
```

And here is a set of long integers:

```
33L
-455L
50000
-123456
3200L
```

Finally, here is a set of double-precision floating-point numbers:

```
3.3
-45.5
-2.3e+12
+3.4-03
2.14e+02
3200.
```

C++ also supports string literals, treating them as arrays of characters:

```
"Hello"
"Here is an empty string"
""
"!"
```

It's important to point out from the start that C++ does not have a predefined data type for strings. C++ treats a string as an array of characters that ends with the null character (ASCII 0). This kind of string is also called an *ASCIIZ string*.

C++ allows you to declare constants, variables, arrays, and pointers using defined data types (either the ones predefined in C++ or the ones you or other programmers have already defined). In Listing 2-2 the following statement declares a constant:

```
const int MAX = 100;            // declare a constant
```

The keyword **const** tells the compiler that the statement defines the constant **MAX** that has the type **int** and the associated value of 100.

Listing 2-2 also declares the variable **nAge**:

```
int nAge;                       // declare a simple variable
```

The statement declares the variable **nAge** to have the integer type **int**. Notice that, like declaring a constant, declaring a variable specifies the data type before the name of the identifier (in the example, the name of the variable). C++ allows you to declare and initialize variables in one statement. Thus for example, you can write:

```
int nNumElements = 100;
```

By contrast with declarations of constants, you can alter the value of initialized variables in subsequent statements.

Listing 2-2 declares the array **cName**:

```
char cName[MAX+1];              // declare a simple array
```

The basic data type associated with this array is the character type, **char**. The square brackets that follow the array's name define the number of array elements. The statement uses the expression **MAX+1** to specify that the array stores **MAX** + 1 characters. Why store **MAX** + 1 characters instead of just **MAX** characters? The additional array cell ensures that the string can store **MAX** characters plus the null terminating character. C++ assigns 0 as the index of the first array element. Thus the elements of array **cName** have indices in the range of 0 to **MAX**.

C++ supports *pointers,* which are special variables that store addresses for other variables. C++ requires that you associate a data type with a pointer to permit the pointer to interpret the data it accesses. To declare a pointer, include the * character after the data type. Here are examples of pointers:

```
char* pszStr; // pointer to a string
double* pfX;  // pointer to a double
int* pnN;     // pointer to an int
long* plH;    // pointer to a long
```

This code snippet declares the **char**-type pointer **pszStr**, the **double**-type pointer **pfX**, the **int**-type pointer **pnN**, and the **long**-type pointer **plH**.

Pointers must be initialized before they can be used. C++ offers the address-of operator, **&**, to take the address of an existing variable. Here is a simple example:

```
double fX = 123.456; // declare variable
double* pfX = &fX;   // pointer to a variable fX
```

These statements define the **double**-type variable **fX** and the **double**-type pointer **pfX**. The statement that declares the pointer **pfX** also initializes that pointer by assigning it the address of the variable **fX**.

To access the data using a pointer, use the pointer access operator, *****. Here is an example:

```
double fX = 123.456; // declare variable
double* pfX = &fX;   // pointer to a variable fX
*pfX = 33 + *pfX;    // add 33 to number in variable
                     // fX using pointer pfX
cout << *pfX;        // display value in fX using pointer
```

This example assigns the address of the **double**-type variable **fX** to the **double**-type pointer **pfX**. The last two statements manipulate the value in variable **fX** using the pointer **pfX**. The expression ***pfX** accesses the data in the variable **fX**.

Simple Output

C++ is a programming language that does not have built-in functions for input and output. This lack of built-in I/O actually makes the language more adaptable, since it relies on libraries to provide the console and file I/O operations. In this book I use the standard libraries to perform console and file I/O. C++ uses a collection of stream I/O libraries to support a diverse set of input/output operations. The header file IOSTREAM.H allows C++ programs to perform console input/output—that is, keyboard input and screen output.

Listing 2-2 shows the output using the standard output stream, **cout**:

```
cout << "Enter your name : ";    // prompt for name
```

The stream uses the *inserter* operator, **<<**, to display output to the standard output object. The flexibility of using **cout** comes from the fact that you can chain output of multiple values. Listing 2-2 contains the following statement, which displays string constants, the variable **nAge**, and the array of characters **cName**:

```
cout << cName << " is "        // output name
     << nAge << " years old";  // output age
```

Notice that the statement uses the inserter operator between each item to chain the output.

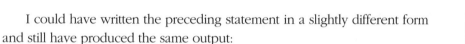

I could have written the preceding statement in a slightly different form and still have produced the same output:

```
cout << cName << " is ";        // output name
cout << nAge << " years old";   // output age
```

I could even have used a separate **cout** statement to display each item!

Simple Input

The basic stream I/O library in C++ offers the **cin** object and the *extractor* operator, **>>**, as the data entry counterparts of the **cout** object and the inserter operator, **<<**.

Listing 2-2 contains a statement that allows you to type in an integer value:

```
cin >> nAge;                    // input age
```

The preceding statement takes the input and stores it in the variable **nAge**. What about string input? Listing 2-2 contains a statement that allows you to key in a string:

```
cin.getline(cName, MAX);        // input name
```

The statement uses the *member function* **getline** to obtain a string of characters. This member function stores the input characters in the **char**-type array **cName**. The argument **MAX** specifies the maximum number of input characters when the statement is being executed.

Decision-Making Constructs

C++ offers the **if** and **switch** statements to support decision making.

THE IF STATEMENT

The **if** statement is available in different forms. First, there is the single-alternative **if** statement, as shown here:

```
if (nValue > 10)
  nValue = 10;
```

Then, there is the dual-alternative **if-else** statement, as shown next:

```
if (nValue > 10)
  nResult = 5;
else
  nResult = nValue * nValue - 2;
```

Listing 2-3 shows the source code for the C++ program IF1.CPP. This listing shows the dual-alternative **if-else** statement. The program first prompts you for your name and age. It then determines if you are at least 18 years old. If you are, the program displays a message saying that you can vote. Otherwise, it displays a message telling you that you are too young to vote (but never too young to learn C++).

Here is a sample session with the program:

```
Enter your name : Joe Shanes
Enter your age : 21
Joe Shanes can vote
```

Listing 2-3
The source code for the C++ program IF1.CPP.

```
// A C++ program that illustrates
// the dual-alternative if-else statement

#include <iostream.h>

main()
{
  // declare a constant
  const int MAX = 100;

  // declare variables
```

```
    int nAge;
    char cName[MAX+1];

    // prompt for name
    cout << "Enter your name : ";
    cin.getline(cName, MAX);

    // prompt for age
    cout << "Enter your age : ";
    cin >> nAge;

    // test if age is 18 and above
    if (nAge > 17) {
      cout << cName;
      cout << " can vote!";                          if statement
    }
    else {
      cout << "Sorry! ";
      cout << cName;
      cout << " can't vote";
    }

    return 0;
}
```

Listing 2-3 uses the **if-else** statement to compare the value in variable **nAge** with 17. If the value in variable **nAge** exceeds 17, the program executes the statement block (C++ encloses statement blocks in braces) right after the tested condition. Otherwise, the program executes the statement block located after the keyword **else**.

In addition to the kinds of **if** statements just described, C++ supports the multiple-alternative **if-else** statement. This statement allows you to examine the value (or expressions based on the value) stored in a variable and to determine the course of action. Listing 2-4 shows the source code for the C++ program IF2.CPP. This program uses the multiple-alternative **if-else** statement to translate an integer day number that you type into the corresponding day name. Here is a sample session with the program:

```
Enter weekday number (1 to 7) : 6
The day is Friday
```

Listing 2-4

The source code for the C++ program IF2.CPP.

```cpp
// A C++ program that illustrates
// the multiple-alternative if-else statement

#include <iostream.h>

main()
{
  // declare a variable
  int nDayNum;

  // prompt for day number
  cout << "Enter weekday number (1 to 7) : ";
  cin >> nDayNum;

  cout << "The day is ";
  if (nDayNum == 1)
    cout << "Sunday";
  else if (nDayNum == 2)
    cout << "Monday";
  else if (nDayNum == 3)
    cout << "Tuesday";
  else if (nDayNum == 4)
    cout << "Wednesday";
  else if (nDayNum == 5)
    cout << "Thursday";
  else if (nDayNum == 6)
    cout << "Friday";
  else if (nDayNum == 7)
    cout << "Saturday";
  else
    cout << "an invalid day";

  return 0;
}
```

The first stream output statement **cout** in Listing 2-4 prompts you to enter an integer day number. The following stream input statement **cin** stores your input in the variable **nDayNum**. The listing uses the multiple-alternative **if-else** statement to compare the value in variable **nDayNum** with the integers 1 through 7. If any one of these seven tested conditions is true, the program executes the output statement in the corresponding **if** or **if else** clause. Otherwise, the program executes the output statement in the catch-all **else** clause.

THE SWITCH STATEMENT

C++ also offers the multiple-alternative **switch** statement, which allows you to compare the value of an integer-type or character-type expression with a set of similarly typed constants.

The **switch** statement is equivalent to certain forms of the multiple-alternative **if-else** statement. Listing 2-5 shows the source code for the C++ program SWITCH1.CPP. This program performs the same tasks as IF2.CPP, except that it uses the **switch** statement instead of the **if-else** statement.

Listing 2-5
The source code for the C++ program SWITCH1.CPP.

```
// A C++ program that illustrates
// the multiple-alternative switch statement

#include <iostream.h>

main()
{
  // declare a variable
  int nDayNum;

  // prompt for day number
  cout << "Enter weekday number (1 to 7) : ";
  cin >> nDayNum;

  cout << "The day is ";
  switch (nDayNum) {                    switch starts here
    case 1:
      cout << "Sunday";
      break;
    case 2:
      cout << "Monday";
      break;
    case 3:
      cout << "Tuesday";
      break;
    case 4:
      cout << "Wednesday";
      break;
```

```
   case 5:
     cout << "Thursday";
     break;
   case 6:
     cout << "Friday";
     break;
   case 7:
     cout << "Saturday";
     break;
   default:
     cout << "an invalid day";
   }

  return 0;
}
```

Notice that in Listing 2-5, the program selects the variable **nDayNum** as the variable to be examined. The **switch** statement uses a set of **case** labels, each with a value to be compared with the one in variable **nDayNum**. The case value that matches the value in variable **nDayNum** results in the execution of the statements associated with that **case** value. Each **case** label ends with the **break** keyword to prevent further comparisons. The **switch** statement uses the catch-all **default** clause to execute the statements when the value in variable **nDayNum** has no match in the **case** labels.

Loops

C++ supports fixed and conditional loops. The **for** loop somewhat parallels FOR loops in other programming languages. I use the word *somewhat* because it is far more versatile than typical FOR loops in languages such as Pascal and BASIC. C++ also supports the **while** and **do-while** conditional loops.

THE FOR LOOP

The **for** loop typically uses a loop control variable to manage the loop's iteration. The loop contains three parts: the initialization, the loop continuation test, and the increment/decrement. Here is a sample of an upward-counting **for** loop:

```
for(i = 1; i <= 10; i++)
```

This loop uses the loop control variable i to control the loop's iterations. The initialization sets the variable i to 1. The continuation test checks that i is less than or equal to 10. The increment/decrement increments the variable i by 1 (the C++ operator ++ increments a variable by 1). The **for** loop iterates for the values 1 to 10 in variable i. In other words, the loop iterates 10 times. A more typical way for writing such a **for** loop is

```
for(i = 0; i < 10; i++)
```

Notice that this version of the **for** loop also iterates ten times, with the values in variable i increasing from 0 to 9.

C++ allows you to use multiple loop control variables, which may appear in any of the loop's three parts. Moreover, C++ does not require that each part contain an expression. Thus, this **for** loop constitutes an open loop:

```
for(;;)
```

Let's look at an example that shows an upward-counting **for** loop, a downward-counting **for** loop, and a **for** loop with multiple loop control variables. The program uses **for** loops to perform the following successive tasks:

■ Initialize the elements of an **int**-type array
■ Display the array elements in a normal sequence
■ Display the array elements in a reversed sequence
■ Reverse the sequence of the array elements
■ Display the array elements in a normal sequence

Here is the output of the program in Listing 2-6:

```
Array is:
10 9 8 7 6 5 4 3 2 1
Reversed array (using downward-counting loop) is:
1 2 3 4 5 6 7 8 9 10
Reversed array (after actually reversing the order of elements) is:
1 2 3 4 5 6 7 8 9 10
```

Listing 2-6

The source code for the C++ program FOR1.CPP.

```cpp
// A C++ program that illustrates different for loops

#include <iostream.h>

main()
{
  const int MAX = 10;
  int nArr[MAX];
  int nSwap;
  int i,j;

  // assign values to the array elements
  for(i = 0;      // initialize loop control variable
      i < MAX;    // test for loop continuation
      i++)        // increment loop control variable
    nArr[i] = MAX - i;

  cout << "Array is:\n";
  // display the array elements
  for (i = 0; i < MAX; i++)
    cout << nArr[i] << ' ';
  cout << "\n";

  cout << "Reversed array (using "
       << "downward-counting loop) is:\n";
  // display the array elements
  for (i = MAX - 1; i >= 0; i--)
    cout << nArr[i] << ' ';
  cout << "\n";

  // reverse the order of the array elements
  for (i = 0, j = MAX - 1; // initialize loop control variables
       i < j;              // test for loop continuation
       i++, j--) {         // increment loop control variable i and
                           // decrement loop control variable j
    nSwap = nArr[i];
    nArr[i] = nArr[j];
    nArr[j] = nSwap;
  }

  cout << "Reversed array (after actually "
       << "reversing the order of elements) is:\n";
  // display the array elements
  for (i = 0; i < MAX; i++)
    cout << nArr[i] << ' ';

  return 0;
}
```

Listing 2-6 has several **for** loops. The first **for** loop initializes the elements of array **nArr**. The loop initializes its control variable **i** with 0, the index of the first element in array **nArr**. The loop's continuation test verifies that the value in variable **i** is less than the value of the constant **MAX**. This condition ensures that during the last loop iteration the variable **i** stores **MAX − 1**. This value is the index of the last element in array **nArr**. The loop increment/decrement increments the variable **i** by 1 to access the next element in array **nArr**. This first loop is an upward-counting loop. I could have used the following downward-counting loop to initialize the elements of array **nArr**:

```
for(i = MAX - 1;   // initialize loop control variable
    i >= 0;        // test for loop continuation
    i--)           // decrement loop control variable
```

The listing uses the second **for** loop to display the elements of array **nArr**. This is an upward-counting **for** loop that iterates over the indices of the elements in array **nArr**. The three parts of this second **for** loop are identical to those in the first **for** loop.

The third **for** loop in Listing 2-6 displays the elements of array **nArr** in a reverse sequence by counting downward. The loop initializes its control variable with the value **MAX − 1**, which is the index of the last array element. The loop's continuation condition causes the loop to iterate as long as the variable **i** stores a non-negative integer. The increment/decrement part of the loop decrements the loop control variable **i**.

The fourth **for** loop in Listing 2-6 uses the loop control variables **i** and **j** to reverse the order of the elements in array **nArr**. The variable **i** accesses the leading array elements (that is, those elements with the lower index values), whereas variable **j** accesses the trailing array elements (that is, those elements with the higher index values). The loop initializes the variables **i** and **j** using 0 and **MAX − 1**, respectively. The condition for the loop's iteration is **i < j**. This condition tells the loop to continue iterating as long as the element swapping has not reached the median element. The last part of the loop increments the variable **i** and decrements the variable **j**. Thus, the loop first swaps the elements located at the array's head and tail and then moves inward.

The last **for** loop in Listing 2-6 displays the newly rearranged elements of array **nArr**. This **for** loop is identical to the second **for** loop in the listing.

NESTED FOR LOOPS

C++ supports nested loops—you can nest the different kinds of loops to various levels. Nested loops often manipulate multidimensional arrays. Listing 2-7 is the source code for the C++ program FOR2.CPP, which illustrates nested **for** loops. These loops perform the following tasks:

- Store random numbers (in the range of 100 to 999) in an **int**-type matrix
- Display the matrix of integers
- Search for the smallest elements in each matrix column
- Search for the largest elements in each matrix column

FOR2.CPP uses a **for** loop to display the smallest and largest elements in each matrix column. Here is sample output for the program (remember that using random numbers generates an output that is different each time the program runs):

```
787 673 793 358 588
535 262 297 324 597
186 237 715 175 350
791 368 771 546 304
814 332 494 170 526

Column # 0 : smallest value is 186 and largest value is 814
Column # 1 : smallest value is 237 and largest value is 673
Column # 2 : smallest value is 297 and largest value is 793
Column # 3 : smallest value is 170 and largest value is 546
Column # 4 : smallest value is 304 and largest value is 597
```

Listing 2-7
The source code for the C++ program FOR2.CPP.

```
// A C++ program that illustrates nested for loops

#include <iostream.h>
#include <stdlib.h>
#include <time.h>

main()
{
  const int MIN_NUM = 100;
```

```
const int MAX_NUM = 899;
const int MAX_ROWS = 5;
const int MAX_COLS = 5;
int nMat[MAX_ROWS][MAX_COLS];
int nBig[MAX_COLS];
int nSmall[MAX_COLS];
int i,j;

// reseed random-number generator
srand((unsigned)time(NULL));

// assign random values (range from 100 to 999)
// to the matrix elements
for (i = 0; i < MAX_ROWS; i++)
  for (j = 0; j < MAX_COLS; j++)
    nMat[i][j] = rand() % MAX_NUM + MIN_NUM;

// display matrix
for (i = 0; i < MAX_ROWS; i++) {
  for (j = 0; j < MAX_COLS; j++)
     cout << nMat[i][j] << " ";
  cout << "\n";
}
cout << "\n";

// find the smallest elements in each column
for (j = 0; j < MAX_COLS; j++) {
  nSmall[j] = MAX_NUM + 1;
  for (i = 0; i < MAX_ROWS; i++)
     if (nSmall[j] > nMat[i][j])
       nSmall[j] = nMat[i][j];
}

// find the largest elements in each column
for (j = 0; j < MAX_COLS; j++) {
  nBig[j] = MIN_NUM - 1;
  for (i = 0; i < MAX_ROWS; i++)
     if (nBig[j] < nMat[i][j])
       nBig[j] = nMat[i][j];
}

// display smallest and largest values
for (j = 0; j < MAX_COLS; j++) {
  cout << "Column # " << j << " : ";
  cout << "smallest value is " << nSmall[j];
  cout << " and largest value is " << nBig[j] << "\n";
}

  return 0;
}
```

Listing 2-7 contains four sets of nested **for** loops. The first set assigns random numbers to the elements of array **nMat**. The outer **for** loop uses the control variable **i** to iterate over the rows of the matrix. The inner **for** loop uses the control variable **j** to iterate over the columns of the matrix. The expression **nMat[i][j]** accesses row number **i** and column number **j** of the matrix **nMat**.

The second set of nested **for** loops displays the values in the matrix **nMat**. The nested **for** loops iterate in the same order and over the same range of values as the first set.

The third and fourth sets of **for** loops search for the smallest and largest column elements. In each one of these nested **for** loops, the outer loop uses the variable **j** to access the various columns, and the inner loop uses the variable **i** to access the various rows. The first statement after the outer loop initializes the element that will store the smallest or largest value. The inner loop contains an **if** statement that searches for and updates the smallest or largest values stored in arrays **nSmall** and **nBig**, respectively.

THE WHILE LOOP

C++ supports the **while** loop, which operates like typical WHILE loops in other programming languages. The keyword **while** is followed by a tested condition enclosed in parentheses. The **while** loop iterates as long as the tested condition is true. Here is an example of a **while** loop:

```
int i = 4;
while(i < 40) {
  cout << i << "n";
  i = i + 2;
}
```

Let's look at a simple program that uses a **while** loop to count the number of characters and words that you type in. Listing 2-8 contains the source code for the C++ program WHILE1.CPP. The program prompts you to enter a string. It then scans the input characters (stored in an array) to count them and also to count the space characters. To keep the code simple, the program *assumes* that you will not enter a sequence of multiple spaces (so please don't!). The program then displays the number of input characters and the number of words (which is equal to the number of spaces plus one). Here is a sample session with the program in Listing 2-8:

```
Enter a string : C++ programming language
You typed 24 characters
You typed 3 words
```

Listing 2-8
The source code for the C++ program WHILE1.CPP.

```
// A C++ program that illustrates while loops

#include <iostream.h>

main()
{
  const int MAX = 100;
  char cName[MAX+1];
  int nLen;
  int nNumWords;

  cout << "Enter a string : ";
  cin.getline(cName, MAX);

  nLen = 0; // initialize string length
  nNumWords = 1;  // initialize word count
  while (cName[nLen] != '\0') {
    if (cName[nLen] == ' ')
      nNumWords++;
    nLen++;
  }

  cout << "You typed " << nLen << " characters\n";
  if (nLen > 0)
    cout << "You typed " << nNumWords << " words";
  else
    cout << "You typed 0 words";

  return 0;
}
```

Listing 2-8 declares the array of characters **cName** to store the input string. The listing also declares the variables **nLen** and **nNumWords** to store the number of characters and words, respectively. The listing contains statements to prompt you for a string and to store your input in array **cName**. Remember that C++ strings terminate with the null character. The listing contains a **while** loop that is preceded by two statements that initialize the variables **nLen** and **nNumWords** with the values 0 and 1, respectively.

The **while** loop iterates as long as the current character in array **cName** is not the null character (that is, as long as variable **nLen** does not access the end of the input string). The **while** loop contains an **if** statement that increments the variable **nNumWords** if character number **nLen** is a space. The **while** loop also increments the variable **nLen**, which acts as a loop control variable. The listing contains statements that display the values in variables **nLen** and **nNumWords**.

The do-while Loop

In addition to the **while** loop, C++ offers the **do-while** loop. This conditional loop tests the iteration condition at its end. Consequently, the **do-while** loop iterates at least once. Here is a sample **do-while** loop:

```
int i = 4;
do {
  cout << i << "n";
  i = i + 2;
} while(i < 40)
```

The loop iterates as long as the value in variable **i** is less than 40.

The WHILE1.CPP program does not reprompt you to enter a string if you simply press the Enter key. Listing 2-9 shows the source code for DOWHILE1.CPP, which uses a **do-while** loop to detect the end of user input. This program will, in fact, reprompt you to enter a string (with at least a single character). Here is a sample session with the program in Listing 2-9 (the character ↵ indicates that the user simply presses the Enter key):

```
Enter a string : ↵
Enter a string : ↵
Enter a string : C++ is the best language
You typed 24 characters
You typed 5 words
```

Listing 2-9
The source code for the C++ program DOWHILE1.CPP.

```
// A C++ program that illustrates do-while loops

#include <iostream.h>
```

```
main()
{
  const int MAX = 100;
  char cName[MAX+1];
  int nLen;
  int nNumWords;

  do {
    cout << "Enter a string : ";
    cin.getline(cName, MAX);
  // test if the first character in cName is
  // the null character (that is, user just pressed
  // the Enter key
  } while (cName[0] == '\0');

  nLen = 0; // initialize string length
  nNumWords = 1;  // initialize word count
  while (cName[nLen] != '\0') {
    if (cName[nLen] == ' ')
      nNumWords++;
    nLen++;
  }

  cout << "You typed " << nLen << " characters\n";
  if (nLen > 0)
    cout << "You typed " << nNumWords << " words";
  else
    cout << "You typed 0 words";

  return 0;
}
```

Listing 2-9 contains a **do-while** loop that in turn contains the prompt and input statements. The loop determines if the character at index 0 of array **cName** is a null character. This condition is true when you simply press the Enter key, causing the function **getline** to store the null character at index 0 of array **cName**. This loop iterates as long as you simply press the Enter key.

User-Defined Data Types

C++ empowers you to declare user-defined data types. Such data types include enumerated types, structures, and unions. I'll cover the first two types in this chapter. Chapter 12, "User-Defined Types," discusses unions.

ENUMERATED TYPES

Enumerated data types allow you to define a set of identifiers that have integer values associated with them. The associated values can be implicit (that is, automatically assigned by the compiler) or explicit (that is, you assign the numeric constants to some or all of the enumerated values). Using enumerated values replaces a set of integers with a more meaningful set of identifiers called *enumerators*. Here is an example of an enumerated type that represents colors:

```
enum fewColors { clBlack, clWhite, clRed, clBlue,
                 clGreen, clYellow };
```

The keyword **enum** starts the declaration of an enumerated type. The code snippet declares the enumerated type **fewColors** and specifies the enumerators **clBlack**, **clWhite**, **clRed**, **clBlue**, **clGreen**, and **clYellow**. The compiler assigns the value 0 to **clBlack**, 1 to **clWhite**, 2 to **clRed**, and so on. You can explicitly assign values to the enumerators as shown in the next example:

```
enum moreColors { mclBlack = 10, mclWhite, mclRed = 20, mclBlue,
                  mclGreen, mclYellow };
```

This code snippet declares the enumerated type **moreColors** and includes explicit value assignments to some of the enumerators. The compiler assigns the value 10 to **mclBlack**, 11 to **mclWhite**, 20 to **mclRed**, 21 to **mclBlue**, 22 to **mclGreen**, and 23 to **mclYellow**.

Let's look at an example that uses the enumerated data type to represent the days of the week. Listing 2-10 shows the source code for the C++ program ENUM1.CPP. This program performs the following tasks:

- Generate five random integers between 1 and 7
- Translate the generated integer into an weekday enumerated value
- Display the name of day for that enumerated value as well as the names of the subsequent and preceding days

Here is sample output for the program in Listing 2-10:

```
Day # 1
Today is Sunday
```

```
Tomorrow is Monday
Yesterday was Saturday

Day # 2
Today is Monday
Tomorrow is Tuesday
Yesterday was Sunday

Day # 3
Today is Wednesday
Tomorrow is Thursday
Yesterday was Tuesday

Day # 4
Today is Wednesday
Tomorrow is Thursday
Yesterday was Tuesday

Day # 5
Today is Tuesday
Tomorrow is Wednesday
Yesterday was Monday
```

Listing 2-10
The source code for the C++ program ENUM1.CPP.

```cpp
// A C++ program that illustrates enumerated types

#include <iostream.h>
#include <stdlib.h>
#include <time.h>

enum weekDay { Sunday, Monday, Tuesday, Wednesday,
               Thursday, Friday, Saturday };

main()
{
  const int MAX = 5;
  weekDay Day;
  int i, n;

  // reseed random-number generator
  srand((unsigned)time(NULL));
  for (i = 0; i < MAX; i++) {
    // get random day number
    n = rand() % 8 + 1;
    // translate integer day number
    // into enumerated value
    switch (n) {
      case 1:
        Day = Sunday;
        break;
```

```
      case 2:
        Day = Monday;
        break;

      case 3:
        Day = Tuesday;
        break;

      case 4:
        Day = Wednesday;
        break;

      case 5:
        Day = Thursday;
        break;

      case 6:
        Day = Friday;
        break;

      case 7:
        Day = Saturday;
        break;
    }

    // display today
    cout << "Day # " << i+1 << "\n";
    cout << "Today is ";
    switch (Day) {
      case Sunday:
        cout << "Sunday\n";
        break;

      case Monday:
        cout << "Monday\n";
        break;

      case Tuesday:
        cout << "Tuesday\n";
        break;

      case Wednesday:
        cout << "Wednesday\n";
        break;

      case Thursday:
        cout << "Thursday\n";
        break;

      case Friday:
        cout << "Friday\n";
        break;
```

```
    case Saturday:
      cout << "Saturday\n";
      break;
}

// display tomorrow
cout << "Tomorrow is ";
switch (Day) {
  case Sunday:
    cout << "Monday\n";
    break;

  case Monday:
    cout << "Tuesday\n";
    break;

  case Tuesday:
    cout << "Wednesday\n";
    break;

  case Wednesday:
    cout << "Thursday\n";
    break;

  case Thursday:
    cout << "Friday\n";
    break;

  case Friday:
    cout << "Saturday\n";
    break;

  case Saturday:
    cout << "Sunday\n";
    break;
}

// display yesterday
cout << "Yesterday was ";
switch (Day) {
  case Sunday:
    cout << "Saturday\n";
    break;

  case Monday:
    cout << "Sunday\n";
    break;

  case Tuesday:
    cout << "Monday\n";
    break;
```

```
        case Wednesday:
          cout << "Tuesday\n";
          break;

        case Thursday:
          cout << "Wednesday\n";
          break;

        case Friday:
          cout << "Thursday\n";
          break;

        case Saturday:
          cout << "Friday\n";
          break;
      }
    cout << "\n";
  }

  return 0;
}
```

Listing 2-10 declares the enumerated type **weekDay**. The declaration lists the names for **weekDay**—**Sunday** through **Saturday**—as enumerators. The compiler automatically assigns 0 to the enumerator **Sunday**, 1 to **Monday**, and so on. The program uses a **for** loop to display five randomly selected weekdays. The loop contains a statement that assigns a random number between 1 and 7 to the variable **n**. It then uses the first **switch** statement to translate the value in that variable into an enumerator stored in the enumerated variable **Day**. The loop uses a second **switch** statement to examine the value in variable **Day** and display the name (as a string) of the corresponding day. The loop uses two more similar **switch** statements to display the names of the days that come after and before the day stored in variable **Day**.

STRUCTURES

C++ supports the **struct** user-defined type, which defines *structures*. These structures are similar to records used in other programming languages. A structure contains data members that either have a predefined data type or are themselves previously defined structures. Let's look at a few examples. Here is a simple structure that defines the x-y coordinates of a point:

```
struct Point {
  int x;
  int y;
};
```

The declaration defines the structure **Point** with the **int**-type data members **x** and **y**. Here is a structure that represents a complex number:

```
struct Complex {
  double x;
  double y;
};
```

The declaration defines the structure **Complex** with the **double**-type data members **x** and **y**. Here is a structure that represents personal data:

```
struct Personal {
  char cFirstName[11];
  char cMiddleInit;
  char cLastName[16];
  char SocialSecurity[11];
  char cStreet[31];
  char cCity[21];
  char cState[3];
  char cZip[11];
  char cPhone[15];
  char cFax[15];
  int nAge;
  double fWeight;
  double fSalary;
};
```

This declaration defines the structure **Personal** and declares a rich set of data members, which describe a name, an address, a phone number, a fax number, an age, a weight, and a salary. Many of the data members in structure **Personal** are arrays of characters, which store ASCIIZ string data. Here is another example, one that uses nested structures:

```
struct Rectangle {
  Point ulc; // upper-left corner;
  Point lrc; // lower-right corner;
};
```

This declaration defines the structure **Rectangle**, which contains the data members **ulc** and **lrc**, themselves previously defined structures.

Accessing a data member of a structure involves using the dot access operator for a structure variable. Here is an example:

```
Point pointX;

pointX.x = 10;
pointX.y = 200;
```

In the case of a pointer to a structure, use the pointer access operator **->** to access the data members. Here is an example:

```
Point pointX;
Point *ptrX = &pointX;

ptrX->x = 10;
ptrX->y = 200;
```

Let's look at an example that uses a structure to process data. Listing 2-11 shows the source code for the C++ program STRUCT1.CPP. The program generates 100 random numbers in the range of 1 to 1000. The program then calculates the mean and standard deviation for the random numbers. Statistics tell us that the mean and standard deviation should be near the values 500 and 280, respectively. The program uses a structure to store the statistical summations and basic statistics. Here is sample output for the program in Listing 2-11:

```
Number of observations = 100
Mean = 500.66
Standard deviation = 293.693
```

Listing 2-11
The source code for the C++ program STRUCT1.CPP.

```cpp
// A C++ program to illustrate structures

#include <iostream.h>
#include <stdlib.h>
#include <time.h>
#include <math.h>

// declare the structure for basic statistical data
struct BasicStat {
  int nNumData;
  double fSumOfX;
  double fSumOfXSqr;
```

```
  double fMean;
  double fSdev;
};

main()
{
  const int MAX = 100;
  const int MIN_NUM = 1;
  const int MAX_NUM = 1000;
  double fData[MAX];
  int i;
  // declare a structure
  BasicStat StatData;
  // declare a pointer to structure StatData
  BasicStat* pStatData = &StatData;

  // reseed random-number generator
  srand((unsigned)time(NULL));

  for (i = 0; i < MAX; i++)
    fData[i] = double(rand() % MAX_NUM + MIN_NUM);

  // initialize some of the data members
  StatData.nNumData = MAX;
  StatData.fSumOfX = 0;
  StatData.fSumOfXSqr = 0;
  // obtain statistical summations
  for (i = 0; i < MAX; i++) {
    StatData.fSumOfX += fData[i];
    StatData.fSumOfXSqr += fData[i] * fData[i];
  }

  // calculate mean value using pointer pStatData
  pStatData->fMean = pStatData->fSumOfX / pStatData->nNumData;
  // calculate standard deviation using pointer pStatData
  pStatData->fSdev =
      sqrt((pStatData->fSumOfXSqr -
          pStatData->fSumOfX * pStatData->fSumOfX /
          pStatData->nNumData) /
          (pStatData->nNumData - 1));

  cout << "Number of observations = "
      << StatData.nNumData << "\n"
      << "Mean = " << StatData.fMean << "\n"
      << "Standard deviation = "
      << StatData.fSdev;

  return 0;
}
```

Listing 2-11 declares the structure **BasicStat** with the **int**-type data member **nNumData** and the **double**-type data members **fSumOfX**, **fSumOfXSqr**, **fMean**, and **fSdev**. The function **main** declares the constants to define the size of the array that stores the random numbers and the range of the random numbers. The function also declares the structure variable **StatData** and the **BasicStat**-type pointer **pStatData**, initializing this pointer with the address of the structure variable **StatData**. Further statements generate the random numbers and store them in array **fData**. The function uses the structure **StatData** to initialize the statistical summations, accumulate data in them, and display the results. It uses the pointer **pStatData** to access the structure's data members in order to calculate the mean and standard deviation statistics. The code offers examples of both common methods of accessing structure members. For example, some statements access the structure's data members through the structure variable's own name, **StatData**, and so use the dot operator—for example, by using the expression **StatData.fSumOfX** to access member **fSumOfX**. Other statements access the structure's data members through pointer **pStatData** by using the -> operator—for example, by using the expression **pStatData->fSumOfX** to access the same structure member, **fSumOfX**.

Functions

Functions (including member functions, which are presented in the next section) play an important role in C++, since they are placeholders for executable statements. In fact, C++ does not support formal procedures or subroutines. In other words, C++ does not use the keyword **procedure** or **sub** to declare a routine that returns no value. That is why C++ does not even use the keyword **function** in declaring routines, since they are all functions! Every C++ program must have at least the function **main** to execute. Nontrivial programs use other functions to perform various tasks, such as obtaining input, processing data, and displaying output.

Essentially, C++ functions have the same basic form as functions found in other common programming languages such as BASIC and Pascal. A C++ function has a *parameter list* and returns a value. The function caller supplies the *arguments* for the parameters. C++ allows you to discard the function's return value after calling that function. C++, like other common programming languages, allows you to write a wide variety of functions, ranging from very simple to complex. As a matter of good programming practice, refrain from having the same function perform multiple tasks. Instead, use a separate function for each task.

The next subsections look at different kinds of functions, starting with very simple C++ functions.

SIMPLE FUNCTIONS

Let me first present simple functions to give you a clear idea of the underlying form. Listing 2-12 contains the source code for the C++ program FN1.CPP, which illustrates a set of simple functions. The program uses these functions to perform the following tasks:

- Obtain the lowercase form of the character 'a', apply a character conversion function, and then display the uppercase equivalent

- Calculate the factorial of 5, using a factorial function, and then display the argument and result

- Calculate the cube of 2.5, using a number-cubing function, and then display the argument and result

- Calculate the fifth power of 2.5, using a power function, and then display the arguments and result

Here is the output of the program in Listing 2-12:

```
Uppercase of a is A
Factorial of 5 = 120
Cube of 2.5 = 15.625
2.5 raised to power 5 = 97.6563
```

Listing 2-12
The source code for the C++ program FN1.CPP.

```
// A C++ program that illustrates simple C++ functions

#include <iostream.h>
#include <stdlib.h>
#include <ctype.h>
```

```
// declare prototype of functions
double cube(double x);
double factorial(int n);
char uppcaseChar(char c);
double power(double fBase, int nExponent);

main()
{
  double fX = 2.5;
  int nNum = 5;
  char cChar = 'a';

  cout << "Uppercase of " << cChar
       << " is " << uppcaseChar(cChar) << "\n";

  cout << "Factorial of " << nNum
       << " = " << factorial(nNum) << "\n";

  cout << "Cube of " << fX << " = " << cube(fX) << "\n";

  cout << fX << " raised to power " << nNum
       << " = " << power(fX, nNum) << "\n";

  return 0;
}

double cube(double x)
{
  return x * x * x;
}

double factorial(int n)
{
  double fResult = 1;
  for (int i = n; i > 0; i-)
    fResult *= (double)i;

  return fResult;
}

char uppcaseChar(char c)
{
  return char(toupper(c));
}

double power(double fBase, int nExponent)
{
  double fResult = 1;

  // process positive exponent
  if (nExponent > 0)
    for (int i = 1; i <= nExponent; i++)
```

```
        fResult *= fBase;
   // process negative exponent
   else if (nExponent < 0)
      for (int i = nExponent; i < 0; i++)
        fResult *= fBase;

   return fResult;
}
```

Listing 2-12 contains the advance declarations of the functions **cube**, **factorial**, **uppcaseChar**, and **power**. This kind of declaration is called a *prototype*. The listing defines first function **main** and then the functions prototyped above **main**. The sequence of how the functions appear is important. Since function **main** uses the other functions in the listing, the prototypes give the compiler an idea about the functions' parameters and return types. There is no need to prototype these functions if their bodies appear before function **main**.

The function **cube** is a simple function with a single **double**-type parameter. It also returns a **double**-type. The function returns its result using this statement:

```
return x * x * x;
```

All functions that yield a non-**void** data type (more about the **void** data type in Chapter 3, "Getting Started") must return a value.

The function **factorial** calculates the factorial for its single **int**-type parameter **n**. It uses the local variable **fResult** and a **for** loop to calculate the factorial value; it finally returns a **double**-type value using the statement

```
return fResult;
```

The function **uppcaseChar** converts the arguments of its **char**-type parameter **c** into the equivalent uppercase character and returns that character. It uses the result of the standard C function **toupper**.

The function **power** raises the value of the **double**-type parameter **fBase** to the power specified by the **int**-type parameter **nExponent**. It uses an **if-else** statement to calculate the power for positive and negative exponents. Each part of the **if-else** statement contains a **for** loop that calculates the power using the local variable **fResult**. The function returns the value in that same variable.

The function **main** declares and initializes the local variables **fX**, **nNum**, and **cChar**. It then displays the following output:

- The character in variable **cChar** and its uppercase equivalent. The function **main** calls function **uppcaseChar** to obtain the uppercase character. The argument for this function call is the variable **cChar**.

- The argument for function **factorial** (the value in variable **nNum**) and the factorial value. The function **main** calls function **factorial** to obtain the result. The argument for this function call is the variable **nNum**.

- The floating-point number in variable **fX** and its cubed value. The function **main** calls function **cube** to obtain the result. The argument for this function call is the variable **fX**.

- The base value (stored in variable **fX**), the exponent value (stored in variable **nNum**), and the result of raising the base value to the exponent value. The function **main** calls function **power** to obtain this result. The arguments for this function call are the variables **fX** and **nNum**.

OVERLOADED FUNCTIONS

Overloaded functions in C++ are a valuable feature that allows you to declare functions in sets of versions that have the same name but different parameters. These parameters form each version's *signature*. Using an overloaded function empowers you to use the same name for a set of function versions that performs similar tasks on different data types. For example, you can define the function **Square** to obtain the squares of parameters that have the types **int**, **long**, **float**, and **double**. Here are the declarations of the overloaded function **Square**:

```
double Square(int i);
double Square(long m);
double Square(float x);
double Square(double x);
```

Each version of function **Square** has a different parameter list. When you call the function **Square**, the compiler examines the data type of the argument to decide which version of function **Square** to call.

Let's look at an example that displays various data types using an overloaded function. Listing 2-13 shows the source code for the C++ program FN2.CPP, which illustrates overloaded functions. The program's overloaded function displays values for variables that have the types char, int, long, double, and char*.

Here is the output of the program in Listing 2-13:

```
Demonstrating overloaded functions
The character is F
The integer value is 23
The long integer value is 70000
The double value is 3.14
The string is 'C++ is really cool!'
```

Listing 2-13
The source code for the C++ program FN2.CPP.

```cpp
// A C++ program that illustrates overloaded functions

#include <iostream.h>

// declare prototype of functions
void show(const char* pszMsg);
void show(const char* pszMsg, char c);
void show(const char* pszMsg, int i);
void show(const char* pszMsg, long m);
void show(const char* pszMsg, double x);
void show(const char* pszMsg, const char* pszStr);


main()
{
  char cChar = 'F';
  int nAnInt = 23;
  long lALong = 70000;
  double fX = 3.14;
  char* pszStr = "C++ is really cool!";

  show("Demonstrating overloaded functions");
  show("The character is ", cChar);
  show("The integer value is ", nAnInt);
  show("The long integer value is ", lALong);
  show("The double value is ", fX);
  show("The string is ", pszStr);

  return 0;
}
```

```
void show(const char* pszMsg)
{
   cout << pszMsg << "\n";
}

void show(const char* pszMsg, char c)
{
   cout << pszMsg << c << "\n";
}

void show(const char* pszMsg, int i)
{
   cout << pszMsg << i << "\n";
}

void show(const char* pszMsg, long m)
{
   cout << pszMsg << m << "\n";
}

void show(const char* pszMsg, double x)
{
   cout << pszMsg << x << "\n";
}

void show(const char* pszMsg, const char* pszStr)
{
   cout << pszMsg << "'" << pszStr << "'\n";
}
```

Listing 2-13 contains the prototypes of the overloaded function **show**, the function **main**, and the definitions of the different versions of function **show**. As you look at the prototype declarations for **show**, notice that the parameter lists each include two parameters, except that the list for the first version has only one. Also notice that the first parameter is identical in all versions, but that each version has a different second parameter (or none). The number of parameters need not be the same in the different versions of an overloaded function.

The implementation of the different versions of function **show** is straightforward—each function uses a single output statement. The function **main** declares and initializes the local variables **cChar**, **nAnInt**, **lALong**, **fX**, and **pszStr**, which have the types **char**, **int**, **long**, **double**, and **char***, respectively. The function **main** then invokes the overloaded function **show** several times, each time with a different argument list. The first call to function **show** has a single argument, a string literal. The compiler resolves this call by using the first version of function **show**, which has a matching single parameter of the type **const char***.

The second call to function **show** has two arguments: a string literal and a **char**-type variable. The compiler resolves this call by using the second version of the function, which has two parameters with the data types **const char*** and **char**.

The third call has two arguments: a string literal and an **int**-type variable. The compiler resolves this call by using the third version of the function, which has two parameters with the data types **const char*** and **int**. Similarly, the third, fourth, and fifth calls to function **show** end up invoking the third, fourth, and fifth versions, respectively.

DEFAULT ARGUMENTS

C++ allows you to assign default arguments to the parameters of a function. You will normally supply these default arguments to represent the values most likely to be passed to the associated parameters. Here is an example of a function with a default argument:

```
double power(double fBase, int nExponent = 2);
```

This function has the default argument of 2 assigned to the second parameter **nExponent**. To use the default argument, omit from the call the argument for the parameter with the default value. Thus, to use the default argument of function **power**, I can write the following statement:

```
cout << "Square of " << x << " = " << power(x);
```

Since the call to function **power** has only one argument, the compiler resolves this call by using the default argument of 2 for parameter **nExponent**. Consequently, the function **power** returns the square of a number when you don't specify the exponent value.

Using default arguments also empowers you to reduce the number of overloaded functions. Consider the declaration of the following function with default arguments assigned to its three parameters (the code fragment assumes that the enumerated data types **boolean** and **charState** are already defined):

```
void show(const char* pszStr = "Greetings!",
          boolean bEmitCR = true,
          charState state = asIs);
```

The function replaces the following four versions of overloaded function **Show** that use no default arguments:

```
void Show();
void Show(const char* pszStr);
void Show(const char* pszStr,
          boolean bEmitCR);
void Show(const char* pszStr,
          boolean bEmitCR,
          charState state);
```

The first version of the overloaded function **Show** parallels calling function **show** with no arguments. The second version parallels calling function **show** with one argument. The third and fourth versions continue paralleling the effect of calling function **show** with successively greater numbers of arguments.

Let's look at an example that implements and uses the preceding function **show**. Listing 2-14 contains the source code for the C++ program FN3.CPP. The function **main** in the program invokes the function **show** several times, each time with a different number of arguments or different argument values. Here is the output of the program in Listing 2-14:

```
Greetings!
Object-Oriented Programming
Object-Oriented Programming
OBJECT-ORIENTED PROGRAMMING
object-oriented programming
```

Listing 2-14
The source code for the C++ program FN3.CPP.

```
// A C++ program that illustrates
// default arguments in functions

#include <iostream.h>
#include <string.h>

enum boolean { false, true };
enum charState { asIs, toUpper, toLower };
```

```
// declare prototype of function
void show(const char* pszStr = "Greetings!",
          boolean bEmitCR = true,
          charState state = asIs);


main()
{
  char* pszStr = "Object-Oriented Programming";

  // call show with all default arguments
  show();

  // call show with two default arguments
  show(pszStr);

  // call show with one default argument
  show(pszStr, false);
  cout << "\n";

  // call show with no default arguments
  show(pszStr, true, toUpper);
  show(pszStr, true, toLower);

  return 0;
}

void show(const char* pszStr,
          boolean bEmitCR,
          charState state)
{
  char cStr[100];

  switch (state) {
    case asIs:
      cout << pszStr;
      break;

    case toUpper:
      strcpy(cStr, pszStr);
      strupr(cStr);
      cout << cStr;
      break;

    case toLower:
      strcpy(cStr, pszStr);
      strlwr(cStr);
      cout << cStr;
      break;
  }

  if (bEmitCR)
    cout << "\n";
}
```

Listing 2-14 declares the enumerated types **boolean** and **charState**. The latter type defines the enumerators **asIs**, **toUpper**, and **toLower**. The function **show** uses type **charState** to possibly alter the output's character case.

The listing declares the function **show** and assigns default arguments to its three parameters. The first parameter has the type **const char*** and the default argument "Greetings!" The second parameter has a **boolean** type and the default argument of **true** (to emit a carriage return). The third parameter has a **charState** type and the default argument **asIs** (to display the characters of parameter **pszStr** without changing their character case).

The function **main** invokes the function **show** several times. The first call to function **show** supplies no arguments. The compiler resolves this function call by using all of the default arguments in function **show**. The result is that the function call emits the string "Greetings!" followed by a newline.

The second call to function **show** supplies one argument, namely, the string pointer **pszStr**. The compiler resolves this function call by using the default arguments for the last two parameters in function **show**. The result is that the function call emits the string "Object-Oriented Programming" followed by a newline.

The third call to function **show** supplies two arguments: the string pointer **pszStr** and the enumerator **false**. The compiler resolves this function call by using the default argument for the last parameter in function **show**. The result is that the function call emits the string "Object-Oriented Programming" without a following newline, although one is supplied by a separate statement in **main**.

The last two calls to function **show** use three arguments for each call. The compiler resolves these calls by using the supplied arguments for the function's three parameters.

C++ functions enjoy many other features. Chapter 5, "Functions," discusses these features and the ones that I presented previously, but in more detail.

Classes

Classes are undoubtedly the highlight of C++ as a programming language and the major difference between C++ and its parent language, C.

The next subsections look at simple classes and small class hierarchies.

SIMPLE CLASSES

Let's look at a simple class that gives you a general feel for the declaration of a class and the definition of its components. Listing 2-15 shows the source code for the C++ program CLASS1.CPP, which illustrates a simple class that models a rectangle, defining it by its length and width. The class operations allow you to set the length and width and query the length, width, and area of the rectangle. Here is the output of the program in Listing 2-15:

```
Length = 10.212
Width  = 20.543
Area   = 209.785

Length = 5.142
Width  = 15.453
Area   = 79.4593
```

Listing 2-15
The source code for C++ program CLASS1.CPP.

```cpp
// A C++ program that illustrates simple classes

#include <iostream.h>

class Rectangle
{
  public:
    // constructor
    Rectangle(double fLength = 0, double fWidth = 0);

    // query data members
    double getLength();
    double getWidth();
```

```
    // set data members
    void setLength(double fLength);
    void setWidth(double fWidth);

    // return calculated attribute
    double getArea();

  protected:
    double m_fLength; // length
    double m_fWidth;  // width
};


Rectangle::Rectangle(double fLength, double fWidth)
{
  m_fLength = fLength;
  m_fWidth = fWidth;
}

double Rectangle::getLength()
{
  return m_fLength;
}

double Rectangle::getWidth()
{
  return m_fWidth;
}

void Rectangle::setLength(double fLength)
{
  m_fLength = fLength;

}

void Rectangle::setWidth(double fWidth)
{
  m_fWidth = fWidth;
}

double Rectangle::getArea()
{
  return m_fLength * m_fWidth;
}

main()
{
  Rectangle rect(10.212, 20.543);

  // display current dimensions and area
  cout << "Length = " << rect.getLength() << "\n";
  cout << "Width  = " << rect.getWidth() << "\n";
```

```
cout << "Area   = " << rect.getArea() << "\n";
cout << "\n";

// set new dimensions
rect.setLength(5.142);
rect.setWidth(15.453);

// display current dimensions and area
cout << "Length = " << rect.getLength() << "\n";
cout << "Width  = " << rect.getWidth() << "\n";
cout << "Area   = " << rect.getArea() << "\n";

return 0;
}
```

Listing 2-15 declares the class **Rectangle**. The declaration uses the keyword **class** and declares the *member functions* and the *data members*. The member functions are the methods that manipulate the class instances. The listing shows that class **Rectangle** declares public and protected members. These members differ in how the class instances can access them. Class instances can access only **public** members. For example, the instance **rect** accesses the public member functions **setLength** and **setWidth**. The member functions can access all **public**, **protected**, and **private** members (note that class **Rectangle** has no **private** section). Chapter 6, "Object-Oriented Programming," explains the differences between the public, protected, and private sections.

The protected section contains the **double**-type data members **m_fLength** and **m_fWidth**, which store the length and width of a rectangle, respectively. Since these members are protected, the instances of class **Rectangle** cannot access them directly. Instead, the class instances must use the member functions **getLength** and **getWidth**.

The public section contains the following members:

- The constructor, which is a special member function that has the same name as the class and has no return type. C++ uses constructors to initialize class instances automatically.

- The member functions **getLength** and **getWidth**, which return the values in the data members **m_fLength** and **m_fWidth**, respectively.

- The member functions **setLength** and **setWidth**, which assign new values to the data members **m_fLength** and **m_fWidth**, respectively.

- The member function **getArea**, which calculates and returns the area of the rectangle based on the values in data members **m_fLength** and **m_fWidth**.

The declaration of class **Rectangle** does not define any protected member function. Instead, the listing places all of the definitions for the constructor and other member functions outside the class declaration. Notice that the definitions of the constructor and member functions use the class name identifier followed by two colons to qualify the definitions. The code that defines the constructor and member functions is simple and suggests that these members have automatic access to the data members of the class.

The function **main** declares the object **rect** as an instance of class **Rectangle**. The declaration includes the initial values of 10.212 and 20.543, which define the length and width, respectively, of object **rect**.

The first set of output statements in function **main** display the length, width, and area of object **rect**. These statements obtain their output by sending the C++ messages **getLength**, **getWidth**, and **getArea**, respectively, to this object. These messages invoke the methods **Rectangle::getLength**, **Rectangle::getWidth**, and **Rectangle::getArea**, again respectively.

The function **main** assigns new dimensions to the object **rect** by sending it the C++ messages **setLength** and **setWidth**. The message **setLength** has the argument of 5.142, whereas the message **setWidth** has the argument 15.453. These messages invoke the methods **Rectangle::setLength** and **Rectangle::setWidth**, respectively.

After function **main** assigns new dimensions to the object **rect**, it displays these dimensions and the new area. This output obtains the sought values by sending the C++ messages **getLength**, **getWidth**, and **getArea**, respectively, to the object **rect**. These messages invoke the methods **Rectangle::getLength**, **Rectangle::getWidth**, and **Rectangle::getArea**, respectively.

C++ permits you to define member functions inside the class declaration. Typically, this kind of *inline* definition involves single statements and results in generating inline code for that member function (that is, the compiled code consists of the member function's statements instead of a call to the member function itself). Listing 2-16 shows the source code for the C++ program CLASS1B.CPP, which illustrates simple classes with inline definitions of member functions. This listing declares the same class **Rectangle** as did Listing 2-15. The main difference is that the new class version uses inline definitions for all the member functions except the constructor. The source code for function **main** is the same as in Listing 2-15. The output of the program in Listing 2-16 matches that of Listing 2-15.

Listing 2-16
The source code for the C++ program CLASS1B.CPP.

```
// A C++ program that illustrates classes with
// inline definitions of member functions

#include <iostream.h>

class Rectangle
{
  public:
    // constructor
    Rectangle(double fLength = 0, double fWidth = 0);

    // query data members
    double getLength() { return m_fLength; }
    double getWidth() { return m_fWidth; }

    // set data members
    void setLength(double fLength) { m_fLength = fLength; }
    void setWidth(double fWidth) { m_fWidth = fWidth; }

    // return calculated attribute
    double getArea() { return m_fLength * m_fWidth; }

  protected:
    double m_fLength; // length
    double m_fWidth;  // width
};


Rectangle::Rectangle(double fLength, double fWidth)
{
  m_fLength = fLength;
  m_fWidth = fWidth;
}

main()
{
  Rectangle rect(10.212, 20.543);

  // display current dimensions and area
  cout << "Length = " << rect.getLength() << "\n";
  cout << "Width  = " << rect.getWidth() << "\n";
  cout << "Area   = " << rect.getArea() << "\n";
  cout << "\n";
```

```
// set new dimensions
rect.setLength(5.142);
rect.setWidth(15.453);

// display current dimensions and area
cout << "Length = " << rect.getLength() << "\n";
cout << "Width  = " << rect.getWidth() << "\n";
cout << "Area   = " << rect.getArea() << "\n";

return 0;
}
```

CHILD CLASSES

C++ allows you to declare a new class as a *child* of another class. The child class inherits the members of its *parent* class (and all those of the parents of the parent class, and so on). The child class, which represents a refinement over its parent class, declares new data members (if needed), new member functions, and member functions that override inherited ones.

Let's look at an example. The last section presented the class **Rectangle**, which models a rectangle. The next example builds on the class **Rectangle** to create the class **Solid**, which represents a solid tetrahedron. A tetrahedron has a length, a width, and a height. Since the base area of the solid is a rectangle, the class modeling the solid is a good candidate to be a child of class **Rectangle**. Listing 2-17 shows the source code for the C++ program CLASS2.CPP, which illustrates a small class hierarchy. The program displays the dimensions, base area, and volume of the solid. Here is the output of the program in Listing 2-17:

```
Length = 3.5
Width  = 2.5
Height = 1.5
Area   = 8.75
Volume = 13.125

Length = 5.5
Width  = 7.5
Height = 4.5
Area   = 41.25
Volume = 185.625
```

Listing 2-17

The source code for the C++ program CLASS2.CPP, which illustrates a small class hierarchy.

```cpp
// A C++ program that illustrates child classes

#include <iostream.h>

class Rectangle
{
  public:
    // constructor
    Rectangle(double fLength = 0, double fWidth = 0);

    // query data members
    double getLength() { return m_fLength; }
    double getWidth() { return m_fWidth; }

    // set data members
    void setLength(double fLength) { m_fLength = fLength; }
    void setWidth(double fWidth) { m_fWidth = fWidth; }

    // return calculated attribute
    double getArea() { return m_fLength * m_fWidth; }

  protected:
    double m_fLength; // length
    double m_fWidth;  // width
};

class Solid : public Rectangle
{
  public:
    // constructor
    Solid(double fLength = 0,
          double fWidth = 0,
          double fHeight = 0);

    // query data members
    double getHeight() { return m_fHeight; }

    // set data members
    void setHeight(double fHeight) { m_fHeight = fHeight; }

    // return calculated attribute
    double getVolume() { return m_fHeight * getArea(); }


  protected:
    double m_fHeight;
};
```

```
Rectangle::Rectangle(double fLength, double fWidth)
{
  m_fLength = fLength;
  m_fWidth = fWidth;
}

Solid::Solid(double fLength, double fWidth, double fHeight)
{
  m_fLength = fLength;
  m_fWidth = fWidth;
  m_fHeight = fHeight;
}

main()
{
  Solid Brick(3.5, 2.5, 1.5);

  // display current dimensions, area, and volume
  cout << "Length = " << Brick.getLength() << "\n";
  cout << "Width  = " << Brick.getWidth() << "\n";
  cout << "Height = " << Brick.getHeight() << "\n";
  cout << "Area   = " << Brick.getArea() << "\n";
  cout << "Volume = " << Brick.getVolume() << "\n";

  cout << "\n";

  // set new dimensions
  Brick.setLength(5.5);
  Brick.setWidth(7.5);
  Brick.setHeight(4.5);

  // display current dimensions, area, and volume
  cout << "Length = " << Brick.getLength() << "\n";
  cout << "Width  = " << Brick.getWidth() << "\n";
  cout << "Height = " << Brick.getHeight() << "\n";
  cout << "Area   = " << Brick.getArea() << "\n";
  cout << "Volume = " << Brick.getVolume() << "\n";

  return 0;
}
```

Listing 2-17 declares the classes **Rectangle** and **Solid**. The declaration of class **Rectangle** is identical to that in Listing 2-16. The listing declares class **Solid** as a descendant of class **Rectangle**. The declaration of class **Solid** contains declarations for the constructor, the protected data member **m_fHeight** (which stores the height), and the member functions **getHeight**, **setHeight**, and **getVolume**. The class **Solid** inherits all of the data members and member functions of class **Rectangle**. Table 2-1 lists all of the members of class **Solid** as they relate to the parent class **Rectangle**. The table indicates which members are inherited and which ones are not.

Table 2-1

The Members of Class Solid As They Relate to the Parent Class Rectangle

Member Type	Member	Inherited from Class Rectangle?
data member	m_fLength	Yes
data member	m_fWidth	Yes
data member	m_fHeight	No
member function	getLength	Yes
member function	getWidth	Yes
member function	getHeight	No
member function	setLength	Yes
member function	setWidth	Yes
member function	setHeight	No
member function	getLength	Yes
member function	getArea	Yes
member function	getVolume	No

The function **main** declares the object **Brick** as an instance of class **Solid**. The declaration includes the initial values of 3.5, 2.5, and 1.5, which define the length, width, and height, respectively, of object **Brick**.

The first set of output statements in function **main** displays the length, width, height, area, and volume of object **Brick**. These statements obtain their output by sending the object **rect** the C++ messages **getLength**, **getWidth**, **getHeight**, **getArea**, and **getVolume**, in turn. These messages invoke the methods **Rectangle::getLength**, **Rectangle::getWidth**, **Solid::getHeight**, **Rectangle::getArea**, and **Solid::getVolume**, respectively.

The function **main** assigns new dimensions to the object **Brick** by sending it the C++ messages **setLength**, **setWidth**, and **setHeight**. The message **setLength** has the argument of 5.5, the message **setWidth** has the argument 7.5, and the message **setHeight** has the argument 4.5. These messages invoke the methods **Rectangle::setLength**, **Rectangle::setWidth**, and **Solid::setHeight** respectively.

After function **main** assigns new dimensions to the object **Brick**, it displays these dimensions, the new area, and the new volume. This output uses the same C++ messages sent in the first set of output statements.

Summary

This chapter has offered you an overview of the various components of C++. These components include predefined data types, user-defined data types, classes, variables, decision-making constructs, loops, and functions. The chapter has given you a small taste for C++ in order to prepare you to learn about the language in more detail.

At this point you should have a feeling for the basic forms of program organization and control structures found in C++, both those that it has inherited from the C language (such as functions definitions and loop constructs) and those that have been evolved in response to the demands of OOP (most especially, classes). You should now appreciate something of C++'s place in programming language history and begin to appreciate the response to the challenge of OOP embodied in C++. In the coming chapters, you will see how this response is embodied in C++ in detail and find the answers to any questions this overview has raised.

II

The Basics of C++

*T*his part of the book looks at the basics of C++. Chapter 3 gets you started with the predefined data types in C++, as well as showing you how to declare variables and constants. Chapter 4 discusses most of the C++ operators and shows you how to build various kinds of expressions in program statements. Chapter 5 looks at functions, which are the cornerstone of executable code. You will learn to declare different kinds of functions and to handle various aspects of declaring parameters and local variables. Chapter 6 ushers you into the world of object-oriented programming by presenting classes. It discusses the basics of C++ classes, such as data members, member functions, constructors, and destructors. Chapter 7 discusses how to manage stream input and output. Chapter 8 looks at the C++ constructs for decision making, which include the versatile `if` statement and the `switch` statement. Chapter 9 looks at the various kinds of loops in C++ and how to master their use. The last two chapters in this part present single-dimensional and multidimensional arrays in C++. There, you will learn how to declare, access, initialize, sort, and search arrays in C++.

3

Getting Started

*T*he first two chapters in this book offered a general introduction to object-oriented programming and C++. Your real journey into the world of C++ begins in this chapter, which looks at the predefined data types, naming C++ identifiers, compiler directives, and declarations for variables and constants.

Predefined Data Types

Typically, programming languages offer predefined data types to manage fundamental kinds of data, such as characters, integers, floating-point numbers, and strings. Such data types represent the building blocks for user-defined data types.

Table 3-1 shows the predefined data types in C++. Your particular compiler may support additional types. Notice that some of the examples in Table 3-1 show numbers that start with the characters 0x. This is how hexadecimal numbers are represented in C++. For example, the decimal integers 1241 and the hexadecimal integer 0xf1 are equivalent.

Table 3-1

Predefined Data Types in C++

Data Type	Byte Size	Range	Examples
bool	1	false and true	false, true
char	1	−128 to 127	'A', '@'
signed char	1	−128 to 127	23
unsigned char	1	0 to 255	250, 0x1c
int (16-bit)	2	−32768 to 32767	3200, −6000
int (32-bit)	4	−2147483648 to 2147483647	−1000000, 345678
unsigned int (16 bit)	2	0 to 65535	0x00aa, 32769
unsigned int (32-bit)	4	0 to 4294967295	0xffea, 65535
short int	2	−32768 to 32767	234
unsigned short int	2	0 to 65535	0x1e, 52000
long int	4	−2147483648 to 2147483647	0xaffaf, −64323
unsigned long int	4	0 to 4294967295	167556
float	4	3.4E−38 to 3.4E+38 and −3.4E−38 to −3.4E+38	−15.443, 22.35, 2.45e+24
double	8	1.7E−308 to 1.7E+308 and −1.7E−308 to −1.7E+308	−2.5e+100, −78.32544
long double	10	3.4E−4932 to 1.1E+4932 and −1.1E−4932 to −3.4E+4932	8.5e−3000, −9.345e+2341

The data types in Table 3-1 include such keywords as **short, long,** and **unsigned,** which are really *type modifiers.* For the sake of shortening type names, however, some of these type modifiers have become synonymous with the fuller versions of the data type names. For example, the types **long, short,** and **unsigned** are equivalent to **long int, short int,** and **unsigned int,** respectively.

CODING NOTES

The bool Type

The ANSI C++ Standard Committee is proposing to define the Boolean type **bool** as part of the C++ language. Up until now, C++, like its parent language C, has handled Boolean values using integers—the integer 0 is equivalent to the Boolean false, and any nonzero integer value is equivalent to the Boolean true. When upcoming versions of C++ compilers begin to support the **bool** type, the integer values that represent Boolean values in old C++ source code will be converted to the type **bool** by the compiler.

CODING NOTES

C++ Strings

You may have noticed that Table 3-1 does not include a type that supports *strings*. C++ treats a string as an array of characters that ends with the null character. C++ compilers support string literals, such as "Hello World!"—they do not support a formal string type.

Languages such as BASIC and Pascal support formal string types and the use of the operator + (some BASIC dialects use the operator &) to concatenate strings and characters. C++, like its parent language C, does not support the operator in the same way. Concatenating strings requires the use of functions that are declared in the standard header library STRING.H (see Chapter 14, "Strings").

Naming Items in C++

When naming items in C++, you need to observe the following rules:

1. The first character of a name must be a letter or an underscore (_).

2. Subsequent characters may be underscores, letters, or digits.

3. Identifiers in C++ are case-sensitive. For example, the names **volume**, **VOLUME**, **VOLume**, and **Volume** are four different identifiers.

4. You cannot use reserved words, such as **int**, **double**, or **static**, as identifiers.

Here are examples of valid identifiers:

```
y
X
myString
HOURS_PER_DAY
HexNumber1
hex_number_1
hex1Number3
_Length
_length_
```

Beyond these rules, C++ does not impose on you a style rule for naming identifiers. However, there are several customary styles for naming identifiers that range from simple to sophisticated. Here are some suggestions for different style name conventions you may wish to choose among:

- Use lowercase names. In the case of a multiple-word name, separate the two names by an underscore. This style is popular in Pascal and C. Here are examples for this style:

```
first_occurrence
next_element
number_of_elements
hours_per_day
number_of_zeros_in_array
```

- Use lowercase names. In the case of a multiple-word name, start each embedded word with an uppercase character. This style is sometimes called the Smalltalk style, after the Smalltalk programming language. Here are examples for this style:

```
firstOccurrence
nextElement
numberOfElements
hoursPerDay
numberOfZerosInArray
```

- Use uppercase to specify constants. In the case of a name containing multiple words, separate the various words with the underscore character. Here are examples for this style:

```
MAX_ARRAY_SIZE
MINUTES_PER_HOUR
HOURS_PER_DAY
BASE_ZERO
ONE
TWO
MAX
ONE_HUNDRED
```

- Start the name of an identifier with a special character that hints at the data type associated with the name of that variable or data member. This *Hungarian notation* is a popular way to clarify the types associated with variables and data members. Table 3-2 shows a partial list of identifier prefixes and includes examples.

Table 3-2

A Partial List of Identifier Prefixes Used in the Hungarian Notation

Data Type	Prefix Characters	Examples
char	c	cDriveName
int	n	nIndex
long	l	lFileSize
double	f	fVolume
char*	psz	pszMyString
ASCIIZ string	sz	szName
long pointer	lp	lpszDirName
data member	m_	m_nIndex

The #include Directive

In order for a programming language to perform sophisticated tasks (especially those required by operating systems, complex programs, and mission-critical applications), the source code must be able to incorporate special *directives* to the compiler. These directives guide and fine-tune the actions of the compiler.

The first, and perhaps most widely used, compiler directive you'll come across is **#include**. This directive instructs the compiler to read a source code file and treat it as though you had typed its contents where the directive appears. The general syntax for the **#include** directive is:

```
// form 1
#include <filename>
// form 2
#include "filename"
```

The first identifier *filename* represents the name of the file to be included. The two forms of **#include** vary in how they lead a program to conduct searches for the include file. The first form searches for the file in the special directory for include files. The second form expands the search to incorporate the current directory.

Here are examples of using the **#include** directive:

```
#include <iostream.h>
#include "myarray.hpp"
```

The first example includes the header file IOSTREAM.H by searching for it in the directory of include files. The second example includes the header file MYARRAY.HPP by searching for it in the directory of include files as well as in the current directory.

The #define Directive

The **#define** directive defines macros. C++ has inherited this directive from C for the sake of software compatibility. The general syntax for the **#define** directive is:

```
// form 1
#define identifierName
// form 2
#define identifierName literalValue
// form 3
#define identifierName(parameterList) expression
```

The first form of the **#define** directive is typically used to indicate that a file has been read or to flag a certain software state. In this case, the **#define** directive need not associate a value with the *identifierName*. The main point for such use is to determine whether or not an identifier has been defined. Here are examples of using the **#define** directive to define state-related identifiers:

```
#define _IOSTREAM_H_
#define _DEFINES_MINMAX_
```

These examples define the identifiers **_IOSTREAM_H_** and **_DEFINES_MINMAX_**. The first example may indicate that the file IOSTREAM.H has been read. The second example might, for example, flag the compiler to define or not define certain functions. Using uppercase identifiers is a common convention and is not enforced by the compiler.

The second form of the **#define** directive defines the names of constants and associates literal values (numbers, characters, strings, and so on) with these names. The preprocessor (which automatically runs before the compiler) replaces the name of the defined identifier with its associated value. Here are examples of using the **#define** directive to declare constants:

```
#define MAX 100
#define ARRAY_SIZE 20
#define MINUTE_PER_HOUR 60
```

These examples define the constants **MAX, ARRAY_SIZE**, and **MINUTE_PER_HOUR** and associate the values 100, 20, and 60 with these constants, respectively.

The third form of the **#define** directive defines pseudo-inline functions. In this way, the directive can create macros with arguments. The preprocessor replaces the name of the defined identifier and its arguments with the associated expression. Here are a few examples:

```
#define Square(x) ((x) * (x))
#define Reciprocal(x) (1/(x))
#define Lowercase(c) (char(tolower(c)))
#define Uppercase(c) (char(toupper(c)))
```

These examples define the pseudo-inline functions **Square, Reciprocal, Lowercase**, and **Uppercase**.

CODING NOTES

Avoid Using #define to Create Pseudo-Inline Functions

C++ gurus advise that you avoid using the **#define** directive to create pseudo-inline functions. Instead, you should use the formal inline functions. These C++ gurus have cited problems with expanding macro expressions. Moreover, the gurus argue that these pseudo-inline functions perform no type checking on their argument—basically anything goes!

Other Directives

In addition to the directives **#define** and **#include**, C++ supports other directives. This section looks at the ones that you are most likely to use in the near future.

THE #UNDEF DIRECTIVE

The **#undef** directive counteracts the **#define** directive by removing the definition of an identifier. The general syntax for the **#undef** directive is:

```
#undef identifierName
```

Here is an example of using the **#undef** directive:

```
#define ARRAY_SIZE 100
int nArray[ARRAY_SIZE];
#undef ARRAY_SIZE
```

This code snippet performs the following tasks:

- Define the identifier **ARRAY_SIZE** with the **#define** directive
- Use the identifier **ARRAY_SIZE** to define the number of elements of array **nArray**
- Undefine identifier **ARRAY_SIZE** using the **#undef** directive

You need not use the directive **#undef** to undefine an identifier before redefining it with another **#define** directive. Simply use the second **#define** directive to redefine an identifier. The following code snippet demonstrates this idea:

```
// first definition of ARRAY_SIZE
#define ARRAY_SIZE 100
int nArray1[ARRAY_SIZE];
#undef ARRAY_SIZE
// second definition of ARRAY_SIZE
#define ARRAY_SIZE 10
int nArray2[ARRAY_SIZE];
```

These statements define, use, undefine, redefine, and then reuse the identifier **ARRAY_SIZE**. The next code snippet, however, which lacks the **#undef** directive, yields the same array declarations as the earlier one:

```
// first definition of ARRAY_SIZE
#define ARRAY_SIZE 100
int nArray1[ARRAY_SIZE];
// second definition of ARRAY_SIZE
#define ARRAY_SIZE 10
int nArray2[ARRAY_SIZE];
```

THE #IFDEF AND #IFNDEF DIRECTIVES

The **#ifdef** and **#ifndef** directives determine if an identifier is currently defined or not currently defined, respectively. The general syntax for the **#ifdef** directive is:

```
// form 1
#ifdef identifierName
   // statements
#endif
// form 2
#ifdef identifierName
   // statements set #1
#else
   // statements set #2
#endif
```

The **#ifdef** directive yields true (a nonzero value) if *identifierName* is currently defined and yields false (0) if it is not. In form 1 of the directive's syntax, if the directive returns true, the compiler processes the statements between the **#ifdef** and **#endif** directives. In form 2, the compiler processes the first set of statements if the **#ifdef** directive returns true or the second set of statements if the directive returns false.

The general syntax for the **#ifndef** directive is:

```
#ifndef identifierName
    // statements
#endif
// form 2
#ifndef identifierName
    // statements set #1
#else
    // statements set #2
#endif
```

The **#ifndef** directive works in a manner opposite the **#ifdef** directive.

Let's look at a simple program that illustrates the **#ifdef** and **#ifndef** directives. Listing 3-1 contains the source code for the program IFDEF1.CPP, which uses the **#ifdef** and **#ifndef** directives, along with the **#define** and **#undef** directives. The program defines the identifier **DEBUG** and uses the **#ifdef** directive to display a message letting you know whether or not the **DEBUG** identifier is currently defined. The program then undefines **DEBUG** and uses the **#ifndef** directive to let you know whether or not the **DEBUG** identifier is currently undefined. Here is the output of the program in Listing 3-1:

```
Testing the #ifdef directive
DEBUG is currently defined
Testing the #ifndef directive
DEBUG is not currently defined
```

Listing 3-1
The source code for the program IFDEF1.CPP.

```
// A C++ program that demonstrates the #ifdef and
// #ifndef directives

#include <iostream.h>

#define DEBUG
```

```
main()
{
  cout << "Testing the #ifdef directive\n";

#ifdef DEBUG
  cout << "DEBUG is currently defined\n";
#else
  cout << "DEBUG is not currently defined\n";
#endif

#undef DEBUG

  cout << "Testing the #ifndef directive\n";

#ifndef DEBUG
  cout << "DEBUG is not currently defined\n";
#else
  cout << "DEBUG is currently defined\n";
#endif

  return 0;
}
```

Listing 3-1 contains the **#ifdef** and **#ifndef** directives located inside the function **main**. The program uses the **#define** directive to define the identifier **DEBUG**. When the compiler examines the **#ifdef** directive, it finds that the expression in the directive returns true. Therefore the compiler processes the stream output statement right after that directive and ignores the output statement after the **#else** directive.

The **#undef** statement undefines **DEBUG** and causes the **#ifndef** directive to return true. Consequently, the compiler processes the stream output statement right after that directive and ignores the output statement after the **#else** directive.

THE #IF AND #ELIF DIRECTIVES

The **#if** and **#elif** directives allow you to offer the compiler the choice of compiling one of multiple sets of statements depending on tested conditions. The general syntax for **#if** and **#elif** is:

```
#if expression1
  // statement set #1
[#elif expression2
  // statement set #2 ]
```

```
    . . .
[#else
    // statement set #N]
#endif
```

If **expression1** returns true (a nonzero integer), the compiler processes
the first set of statements and ignores the other statements after the **#elif** and
#else directives. By contrast, if **expression1** is false, the compiler examines
the conditions of the **#elif** directives starting with the first one. When the
compiler finds an **#elif** directive whose expression returns true, it processes
the statements associated with that directive. If the expressions of the **#if**
and **#elif** directives are all false, the compiler processes the statements after
the **#else** clause (if one is used).

The tested expressions may evaluate to a constant, and they may
include logical operators and the operator **defined** (this operator returns true
if its argument is a currently defined identifier). However, you cannot use
the operator **sizeof**, type casts, floating-point types, or enumerated types.

Let's look at an example that uses the **#if** and **#elif** directives. Listing 3-2
shows the source code for the program IFDEF2.CPP. The program defines
the identifiers **DEBUG1**, **DEBUG2**, and **DEBUG3** and uses the test directives
to determine which statements to compile. The compiled statements display
output that comments on the state of the program's identifiers. Here is the
output of Listing 3-2:

```
DEBUG1 is currently defined
DEBUG1, DEBUG2, and DEBUG3 are currently defined
```

Listing 3-2
The source code for the program IFDEF2.CPP.

```
// A C++ program that demonstrates the #if and
// #elif directives

#include <iostream.h>

main()
{

#define DEBUG1
#define DEBUG2
#define DEBUG3
```

```
#if !defined(DEBUG1)
  cout << "DEBUG1 is not currently defined\n";
#else
  cout << "DEBUG1 is currently defined\n";
#endif

#if defined(DEBUG1) && defined(DEBUG2) && !defined(DEBUG3)
  cout << "DEBUG1 and DEBUG2 are currently defined. "
       << "DEBUG3 is not defined\n";
#elif defined(DEBUG1) && defined(DEBUG3) && !defined(DEBUG2)
  cout << "DEBUG1 and DEBUG3 are currently defined. "
       << "DEBUG2 is not defined\n";
#elif defined(DEBUG2) && defined(DEBUG3) && !defined(DEBUG1)
  cout << "DEBUG2 and DEBUG3 are currently defined. "
       << "DEBUG1 is not defined\n";
#else
  cout << "DEBUG1, DEBUG2, and DEBUG3 are currently defined\n";
#endif

  return 0;
}
```

Listing 3-2 defines the identifiers **DEBUG1**, **DEBUG2**, and **DEBUG3** using the **#define** directive located inside function **main**. The listing uses the first **#if** directive to determine whether or not the identifier **DEBUG1** is defined. I chose to use the expression **!defined(DEBUG1)** to test if the identifier **DEBUG1** is not defined. Since that identifier is defined, the expression **!defined(DEBUG1)** returns false. Consequently, the compiler processes the output statement after the **#else** directive.

The second **#if** directive in the listing illustrates a more elaborate scheme for conditional compilation. The **#if** directive and the first two **#elif** directives use expressions that determine whether or not only two of the three identifiers **DEBUG1**, **DEBUG2**, and **DEBUG3** are defined. Since all three identifiers are indeed defined, all the tested conditions return false. Consequently, the compiler processes the output statement after the **#else** directive.

THE #ERROR DIRECTIVE

The **#error** directive makes the compiler display a message on the standard error stream and also yield a nonzero integer code when the compiler terminates. The general syntax for the **#error** directive is:

```
#error message
```

After the compiler encounters an **#error** directive, it scans the remaining part of the program for other syntax errors but does not generate an object file. Here is an example of the **#error** directive:

```
#if defined(DEBUG_MODE)
#error Need to turn off debug mode!
#endif
```

This code snippet generates the error message "Need to turn off debug mode!" if the identifier **DEBUG_MODE** is currently defined.

Declaring Variables

C++ requires that you declare variables before you use them. Typically, you declare variables at the beginning of a function's body. The general syntax for declaring a variable is:

```
// form 1
type variableName;
// form 2
type variableName = initialValue;
```

The first form allows you to declare an uninitialized variable by specifying first its data type and then its name. The second form allows you to declare and initialize a variable in one statement. This feature allows you to reduce the number of statements in your source code. Here are examples of declaring variables:

```
int nCount;
double fSum = 0.0;
```

The first example declares the **int**-type variable named **nCount**. The second example declares the **double**-type variable **fSum** and initializes this variable with the value 0.

C++ allows you to declare multiple variables in the same statement. You can even initialize some or all of the declared variables. Here are a few examples:

```
int i, j, k;
unsigned uIndex, uCount = 0;
double fSum = 0.0, fSumX = 0.0, fSumXSqr = 0;
```

The first example declares the uninitialized **int**-type variables **i**, **j**, and **k**. The second example declares the **unsigned**-type variables **uIndex** and **uCount**, initializing the variable **uCount**. The third example declares the **double**-type variables **fSum**, **fSumX**, and **fSumXSqr** and initializes each variable to 0.

Let's look at a simple C++ program that declares and initializes variables. Listing 3-3 shows the source code for the program VAR1.CPP, which declares simple variables. The program requires no input from you. Instead, it displays the following three characters:

```
!
#
#
```

Listing 3-3

The source code for the program VAR1.CPP.

```cpp
// A C++ program that illustrates declaring variables
// at the beginning of a function

#include <iostream.h>

main()
{
  char cChar1;
  char cChar2 = '#';
  char cChar3 = cChar2;

  cChar1 = '!';

  cout << cChar1 << "\n"
       << cChar2 << "\n"
       << cChar3 << "\n";

  return 0;
}
```

Listing 3-3 declares the **char**-type variables **cChar1**, **cChar2**, and **cChar3**. The declaration of variable **cChar1** does not include initialization. The function **main** assigns the character literal '!' to variable **cChar1**. By contrast, the function **main** declares the variable **cChar2** and initializes it with the character literal '#'. As for the variable **cChar3**, the function **main** declares it and initializes it using the value in variable **cChar2**. The output of the program confirms that variables **cChar2** and **cChar3** store the '#' character.

C++ allows you to declare variables throughout the body of a function. I can write the source code for Listing 3-3 such that I can place the declaration of some of the variables further down in function **main**. Listing 3-4 contains the source code for the program VAR2.CPP, which distributes variable declarations more widely than did its predecessor.

Listing 3-4
The source code for the program VAR2.CPP, which declares simple variables in a more scattered fashion.

```
// A C++ program that illustrates declaring variables
// in the course of a function

#include <iostream.h>

main()
{
  // declare first variable
  char cChar1;

  // initialize variable
  cChar1 = '!';
  // display contents of cChar1
  cout << cChar1 << "\n";

  // declare second variable
  char cChar2 = '#';
  // display contents of cChar2
  cout << cChar2 << "\n";

  // declare third variable
  char cChar3 = cChar2;
  // display contents of cChar3
  cout << cChar3 << "\n";

  return 0;
}
```

Listing 3-4 declares the variable **cChar2** in the middle of function **main** and declares variable **cChar3** in the latter part of function **main**. The programs in Listings 3-3 and 3-4 generate the same output.

BASIC

Declare Every Variable

C++ requires that you declare every variable before you use it. The older implementations of BASIC create variables on the fly as they appear in BASIC statements. Some of the new BASIC implementations support a special version of the OPTION statement to force you to declare every variable; by using such a setting, you will better appreciate C++ usage.

Declaring Constants

C++ allows you to declare constants either using the **#define** directive or using the formal constant syntax. The general syntax for declaring a formal constant is:

```
const type constantName = constantValue;
```

The declaration of a constant resembles the declaration of an initialized variable. Declaring a constant requires the keyword **const**. If you omit the constant's type, the compiler uses the **int** data type.

Here are examples of constants:

```
const int MAX_NUM = 1000;
const int MIN_NUM = 1;
const SEC_PER_MINUTE = 60;
const char FIRST_DRIVE = 'A';
const double MIN_RATE = 0.023;
```

The first two examples declare the constants **MAX_NUM** and **MIN_NUM** and explicitly associate the **int** type with these constants. By contrast, the third example, which contains the declaration of constant **SEC_PER_MINUTE**, has the **int** type by omission. The fourth and fifth examples declare constants that have the types **char** and **double**, respectively. Using uppercase with these constants is a common convention and is not enforced by the compiler.

PASCAL

Note Where Variables May Be Declared

C++ has a more relaxed approach than Pascal to placement of variable declarations. In C++, local variables appear anywhere inside a function's body. By contrast, Pascal variables are declared in the VAR section of a function or procedure. Moreover, C++ allows you to declare and initialize variables in a single statement.

Let's look at a simple example. Listing 3-5 shows the source code for the program CONST1.CPP, which illustrates C++ constants. The program declares a character constant and uses that constant to initialize a **char**-type variable. The program also displays the values associated with the constant and the variable. Here is the output of the program in Listing 3-5:

```
Character variable is ?
Character constant is ?
```

Listing 3-5
The source code for the program CONST1.CPP.

```cpp
// A C++ program that illustrates declaring constants

#include <iostream.h>

main()
{
  const char QUESTION_MARK = '?';
  char cChar = QUESTION_MARK;

  cout << "Character variable is " << cChar << "\n"
       << "Character constant is " << QUESTION_MARK << "\n";

  return 0;
}
```

Listing 3-5 declares the **char**-type constant QUESTION_MARK. This constant is associated with the question mark character. The listing also declares the **char**-type variable cChar and initializes it using the constant QUESTION_MARK. The program then displays the values in both the constant QUESTION_MARK and the variable cChar.

Summary

This chapter has introduced you to the basics of C++ related to data types, variables, constants, and compiler directives. The topics in this chapter have led you on the first steps in creating C++ source code. Learning about the predefined C++ data types offers you an understanding of the data type basics in C++. You've learned, for example, that C++ does not support a formal predefined string type. This is important, especially if you are coming from BASIC or Pascal. The chapter has also shown you how to declare constants and variables—the cornerstone of managing data. It has also presented the compiler directives that are most relevant to you as a novice C++ programmer.

The next chapter introduces C++ operators and expressions. You will learn how to use operators and expressions to manipulate and query information in variables.

4 Operators and Expressions

*T*his chapter looks at the C++ operators and expressions. Operators and expressions allow your programs to query conditions, update information, and assign new values. In this chapter you will learn about arithmetic, increment, assignment, relational, logical, bit-manipulation, comma, and **sizeof** operators. You will also learn about arithmetic and Boolean expressions, as well as about typecasting and operator precedence.

Arithmetic Operators

Arithmetic operators support the manipulation of integers and floating-point numbers. Table 4-1 shows the arithmetic operators in C++.

Table 4-1
The Arithmetic Operators in C++

C++ Operator	Role	Data Type	Example
+	unary plus	numerical	z = +h − 2
−−	unary minus	numerical	z = −1 * (z+1)
+	add	numerical	h = 34 + g
−−	subtract	numerical	z = 3.4 − t
/	divide	numerical	d = m / v
*	multiply	numerical	area = len * wd
%	modulus	integers	count = w % 12

Let's look at a program that applies the arithmetic operators to variables having the integer and floating-point types. Listing 4-1 shows the source code for the OPER1.CPP program, which illustrates the arithmetic operators. The program performs the following tasks:

- Prompt you to enter two nonzero integers
- Apply the operators +, −, *, /, and % to your input
- Display the integer operands and the results of the operations just described
- Prompt you to enter two nonzero floating-point numbers
- Apply the operators +, −, *, and / to your input
- Display the floating-point operands and the results of the operations just described

Here is the input and output of a sample session with the program in Listing 4-1 (user input is underlined):

```
Enter a nonzero integer : 342
Enter another nonzero integer : 23


342 + 23 = 365
342 - 23 = 319
342 * 23 = 7866
342 / 23 = 14
342 % 23 = 20

Enter a nonzero floating-point number : 4.56
Enter another nonzero floating-point number : 12.34

4.56 + 12.34 = 16.9
4.56 - 12.34 = -7.78
4.56 * 12.34 = 56.2704
4.56 / 12.34 = 0.36953
```

Listing 4-1

The source code for the OPER1.CPP program, which illustrates the arithmetic operators.

```
// A C++ program that demonstrates arithmetic operations

#include <iostream.h>

main()
{
  int nNum1, nNum2;
  long lAdd, lSub, lMul, lDiv, lMod;
  double fX, fY;
  double fAdd, fSub, fMul, fDiv;

  // prompt for two integers
  cout << "Enter a nonzero integer : ";
  cin >> nNum1;
  cout << "Enter another nonzero integer : ";
  cin >> nNum2;
  cout << "\n";

  // apply arithmetic operators
  lAdd = nNum1 + nNum2;
  lSub = nNum1 - nNum2;
  lMul = nNum1 * nNum2;
  lDiv = nNum1 / nNum2;
  lMod = nNum1 % nNum2;
  // display operands and results
  cout << nNum1 << " + " << nNum2 << " = " << lAdd << "\n";
  cout << nNum1 << " - " << nNum2 << " = " << lSub << "\n";
  cout << nNum1 << " * " << nNum2 << " = " << lMul << "\n";
  cout << nNum1 << " / " << nNum2 << " = " << lDiv << "\n";
  cout << nNum1 << " % " << nNum2 << " = " << lMod << "\n";
  cout << "\n";

  // prompt for two floating-point numbers
  cout << "Enter a nonzero floating-point number : ";
  cin >> fX;
  cout << "Enter another nonzero floating-point number : ";
  cin >> fY;
  cout << "\n";

  // apply arithmetic operators
  fAdd = fX + fY;
  fSub = fX - fY;
  fMul = fX * fY;
  fDiv = fX / fY;
```

```
// display operands and results
cout << fX << " + " << fY << " = " << fAdd << "\n";
cout << fX << " - " << fY << " = " << fSub << "\n";
cout << fX << " * " << fY << " = " << fMul << "\n";
cout << fX << " / " << fY << " = " << fDiv << "\n";

return 0;
}
```

Listing 4-1 declares three sets of variables in function **main**. The first set comprises the **int**-type variables **nNum1** and **nNum2**. The second set of variables is made up of the **long**-type variables **lAdd**, **lSub**, **lMul**, **lDiv**, and **lMod**. The third set of variables includes the **double**-type variables **fX**, **fY**, **fAdd**, **fSub**, **fMul**, and **fDiv**.

The function **main** prompts you to enter two integers, which it then stores in variables **nNum1** and **nNum2**. The function then uses the values in these variables as the operands of the tested operators. It assigns the results of the integer operations to the **long**-type variables. I chose to use **long**-type variables (which have a wider range of values than **int**-type variables) to store the results of the operations in order to fend off possible arithmetic overflow, especially with the **+**, **−**, and ***** operators. The function **main** then displays the integer operands and results.

As for applying the arithmetic operators to the floating-point numbers, function **main** also prompts you to enter two numbers. The function stores your input in variables **fX** and **fY**. It then uses the values in these variables as the operands of the tested operators. It assigns the results of the floating-point operations to the **double**-type variables **fAdd**, **fSub**, **fMul**, and **fDiv**. The function **main** then displays the floating-point operands and results.

Arithmetic Expressions

Listing 4-1 demonstrates the arithmetic operators using simple expressions. The following program statements contain expressions that appear on the right-hand side of the assignment operator:

```
lAdd = nNum1 + nNum2;
lSub = nNum1 - nNum2;
lMul = nNum1 * nNum2;
```

```
1Div = nNum1 / nNum2;
1Mod = nNum1 % nNum2;
fAdd = fX + fY;
fSub = fX - fY;
fMul = fX * fY;
fDiv = fX / fY;
```

Each expression in these statements is made up of two simple terms (the operands) and an operator. C++ supports more complicated expressions that implement more advanced mathematical equations. For example, you can write expressions such as:

```
fZ = (((3 + 2 * fX) * fX - 5) * fX - 3) * fX - 20;
fH = (2 + fX + fY) * (34.2 - fX) / (fX * fX + fY * fY);
fD = (11 + (22 + fX) * (56 - fY)) / (fX * fX + fY * fY);
```

The last section in this chapter discusses the order of executing the operators. This order is fairly consistent in most programming languages, including BASIC, Pascal, and C. Therefore, you need not learn a new way to write expressions in C++.

Increment Operators

C++ offers the increment operators **++** and **--** to support a shorthand syntax for adding or subtracting 1 from the value in a variable, respectively. The general syntax for the operator **++** is:

```
// form 1: preincrement
++variableName
// form 2: postincrement
variableName++
```

The preincrement version of the operator **++** increments the value in its operand **variableName** *before* that variable supplies its value to the host expression. By contrast, the postincrement version increments the value in its operand **variableName** *after* that variable supplies its value to the host expression. If you use the increment operator in a statement that has no other operators (not even an assignment operator), then it makes no difference which form of the operator you use. Thus, these two statements have the same effect:

```
nCount++;
++nCount;
```

Here are examples of using the increment operator:

```
int nCount = 1;
int nNum;
nNum = nCount++; // nNum stores 1 and nCount stores 2
nNum = ++nCount; // nNum stores 3 and nCount stores 3
```

In this code snippet the variable **nCount** has the initial value of 1. The first statement that uses the increment operator employs the postincrement version. Consequently, the statement assigns the value in variable **nCount** to variable **nNum** and then increments the value in variable **nCount**. The result is that variable **nNum** stores 1 and variable **nCount** contains 2. The second statement that uses the increment operator employs the preincrement version. Consequently, the statement first increments the value in variable **nCount** and then assigns the value in variable **nCount** to variable **nNum**. The result is that both variables **nNum** and **nCount** store 3.

As for the decrement operator, the general syntax for this operator is:

```
// form 1: pre-decrement
--variableName
// form 2: post-decrement
variableName--
```

The predecrement version of the operator -- decrements the value in its operand **variableName** *before* that variable supplies its value to the host expression. By contrast, the postdecrement version of the same operator decrements the value in its operand *after* that variable supplies its value to the host expression. If you use the decrement operator in a statement that has no other operators (including the assignment operator), then it makes no difference which form of the operator you use. Thus, the following two statements have the same effect:

```
nCount--;
--nCount;
```

Here are examples of using the decrement operator:

```
int nCount = 10;
int nNum;
nNum = nCount--; // nNum stores 10 and nCount stores 9
nNum = --nCount; // nNum stores 8 and nCount stores 8
```

In this code snippet the variable **nCount** has the initial value of 10. The first statement that uses the decrement operator employs the postdecrement version. Consequently, the statement assigns the value in variable **nCount** to variable **nNum** and then decrements the value in variable **nCount**. The result is that variable **nNum** stores 10 and variable **nCount** contains 9. The second statement that uses the decrement operator employs the predecrement version. Consequently, the statement first decrements the value in variable **nCount** and then assigns the value in variable **nCount** to variable **nNum**. The result is that both variables **nNum** and **nCount** store 8.

Let's look at a program that illustrates somewhat nontrivial use of the operators **++** and **−−**. Listing 4-2 shows the source code for the OPER2.CPP program, which illustrates the two forms of increment and decrement operators. Each part of the test displays the initial value of a variable, the value of the variable after using an increment or decrement operator, and the result of multiplying that variable by 4. The result depends on the operator used and its pre- or post- form. Here is the output of the program in Listing 4-2:

```
j = 22 (initial value)
j = 23
i = 88

j = 22 (initial value)
j = 23
i = 92

j = 22 (initial value)
j = 21
i = 88

j = 22 (initial value)
j = 21
i = 84
```

Listing 4-2
The source code for the OPER2.CPP program.

```
// A C++ program that demonstrates the increment
// and decrement operators

#include <iostream.h>

main()
{
  int i, j = 22;

  cout << "j = " << j << " (initial value)\n";
  // test postincrement operator
  i = 4 * j++;
  cout << "j = " << j << "\n";
  cout << "i = " << i << "\n\n";
  j--; // reset j

  // test preincrement operator
  cout << "j = " << j << " (initial value)\n";
  i = 4 * ++j;
  cout << "j = " << j << "\n";
  cout << "i = " << i << "\n\n";
  --j; // reset j

  // test postdecrement operator
  cout << "j = " << j << " (initial value)\n";
  i = 4 * j--;
  cout << "j = " << j << "\n";
  cout << "i = " << i << "\n\n";
  j++; // reset j

  // test predecrement operator
  cout << "j = " << j << " (initial value)\n";
  i = 4 * --j;
  cout << "j = " << j << "\n";
  cout << "i = " << i << "\n\n";

  return 0;
}
```

In Listing 4-2, function **main** declares the **int**-type variables i and j. The function initializes the variable j by assigning the value 22 to that variable.

First, the function **main** tests the postincrement operator **++** by performing the following sequence of tasks:

- Display the initial value in variable j

- Execute the assignment statement that multiplies 4 by j++. This statement first multiplies 4 by 22 (the value in variable j), then assigns the result 88 to variable i, and finally increments the variable j.

- Display the current value in variable j (which is 23)
- Display the value in variable i (which is 88)
- Reset the value in variable j by using the postdecrement operator −−. You can use the predecrement operator to obtain the same overall result for this task.

Second, the function **main** tests the preincrement operator ++ by performing the following tasks:

- Display the initial value in variable j
- Execute the assignment statement that multiplies 4 by ++j. This statement first increments the value in variable j (from 22 to 23), then multiplies 4 by 23 (the new value in variable j), and finally assigns the result 92 to variable i.
- Display the current value in variable j (which is 23)
- Display the value in variable i (which is 92)
- Reset the value in variable j by using the postdecrement operator −−. You can use the predecrement operator to obtain the same overall result for this task.

Third, the function **main** tests the postdecrement operator −− by performing the following tasks:

- Display the initial value (relative to testing the operator −−) in variable j
- Execute the assignment statement that multiplies 4 by j−−. This statement first multiplies 4 by 22 (the value in variable j), then decrements the value in variable j (from 22 to 21), and finally assigns the result 88 to variable i.
- Display the current value in variable j (which is 21)
- Display the value in variable i (which is 88)
- Reset the value in variable j by using the postincrement operator ++. You can use the preincrement operator to obtain the same overall result for this task.

Fourth and last, the function **main** tests the predecrement operator --
by performing the following tasks:

- Display the initial value in variable j
- Execute the assignment statement that multiplies 4 by --j. This state-
  ment first decrements the variable j, then multiplies 4 by 21 (the new
  value in variable j), and finally assigns the result 84 to variable i.
- Display the current value in variable j (which is 21)
- Display the value in variable i (which is 84)

Let's look at another program example, one in which the incremented
variable appears more than once in an expression. The next program
assigns 10 to the variable j and evaluates the following expressions:

```
j * j * j++
j * j++ * j
j++ * j * j
j * j * ++j
j * ++j * j
++j * j * j
```

According to the ANSI C specifications, this type of coding is ambiguous
and should not be used in ordinary applications. I am showing you this
code and the next example to demonstrate to you the side effects of using
the operators ++ and -- in this manner.

The OPER3.CPP program shows the effect of evaluation order on where
you place the increment operator. Listing 4-3 contains the source code. Here
is the program's output:

```
j = 10 (initial value)
j = 11
j * j * j++ = 1210

j = 10 (initial value)
j = 11
j * j++ * j = 1100

j = 10 (initial value)
j = 11
j++ * j * j = 1000
```

```
j = 10 (initial value)
j = 11
j * j * ++j = 1331

j = 10 (initial value)
j = 11
j * ++j * j = 1210

j = 10 (initial value)
j = 11
++j * j * j = 1100
```

Listing 4-3

The source code for the OPER3.CPP program, which illustrates the evaluation order and increment operators.

```cpp
// A C++ program that demonstrates the increment operators
// and how they relate to the order of evaluation of operators

#include <iostream.h>

main()
{
  const long INIT_NUM = 10;
  long i, j = INIT_NUM;

  cout << "j = " << j << " (initial value)\n";
  i = j * j * j++;
  cout << "j = " << j << "\n";
  cout << "j * j * j++ = " << i << "\n\n";

  j = INIT_NUM;
  cout << "j = " << j << " (initial value)\n";
  i = j * j++ * j;
  cout << "j = " << j << "\n";
  cout << "j * j++ * j = " << i << "\n\n";

  j = INIT_NUM;
  cout << "j = " << j << " (initial value)\n";
  i = j++ * j * j;
  cout << "j = " << j << "\n";
  cout << "j++ * j * j = " << i << "\n\n";

  j = INIT_NUM;
  cout << "j = " << j << " (initial value)\n";
  i = j * j * ++j;
  cout << "j = " << j << "\n";
  cout << "j * j * ++j = " << i << "\n\n";
```

```
j = INIT_NUM;
cout << "j = " << j << " (initial value)\n";
i = j * ++j * j;
cout << "j = " << j << "\n";
cout << "j * ++j * j = " << i << "\n\n";

j = INIT_NUM;
cout << "j = " << j << " (initial value)\n";
i = ++j * j * j;
cout << "j = " << j << "\n";
cout << "++j * j * j = " << i << "\n";

return 0;
}
```

Listing 4-3 declares the **long**-type constant **INIT_NUM** and the **long**-type variables **i** and **j** inside the function **main**. The source code in function **main** uses a set of statements that performs the following tasks:

- Initialize the variable **j**
- Display the value in that variable
- Evaluate the tested expression with the increment operator **++** and assign the result to variable **i**
- Display the text that represents the expression and the value in variable **i**

The program output indicates that each expression is evaluated from right to left. Table 4-2 shows the values supplied by the different occurrences of variable **j** in each expression. The table shows the pre- and postincrement values of variable **j**—10 and 11, respectively—and how they contribute to the result.

Table 4-2
The Values Supplied by the Different Occurrences of Variable j in Each Expression

Expression	Evaluated As	Result
j * j * j++	11 * 11 * 10	1210
j * j++ * j	11 * 10 * 10	1100
j++ * j * j	10 * 10 * 10	1000
j * j * ++j	11 * 11 * 11	1331
j * ++j * j	11 * 11 * 10	1210
++j * j * j	11 * 10 * 10	1100

Assignment Operators

If you have programmed in BASIC, Pascal, or another structured programming language, then you have probably written expressions such as these:

```
sum = sum + x;
diff = diff - x;
scale = scale / factor;
factorial = factorial * x;
```

Each statement contains the same variable on both sides of the assignment operator. C++ supports assignment operators that combine arithmetic and bitwise operations with the assignment operator. Thus, you can write the preceding statements as:

```
sum += x;
diff -= x;
scale /= factor;
factorial *= x;
```

Table 4-3 lists the arithmetic assignment operators in C++. The table also contains examples of using these operators, in addition to the long-form versions of the statements in the examples.

Table 4-3

The Arithmetic Assignment Operators in C++

C++ Operator	Example	Long-Form Example
+=	fSum += fX;	fSum = fSum + fX;
-=	fY -= fX;	fY = fY - fX;
/=	nCount /= N;	nCount = nCount / N;
*=	fScl *= fFactor;	fScl = fScl * fFactor;
%=	nBins %= nCount;	nBins = nBins % nCount;

Let's look at a simple program that uses the assignment operators with **double**-type variables. Listing 4-4 contains the source code for the OPER4.CPP program, which performs the following tasks:

- Prompt you to enter three numbers
- Display the sum of the numbers you entered
- Prompt you to enter a multiplicative scale factor
- Display the scaled value of the sum
- Prompt you to enter a division scale factor
- Display the scaled value of the sum
- Prompt you to enter two numbers to subtract from the current sum
- Display the new sum value

Here is a sample session with the program in Listing 4-4:

```
Enter first number : 10
Enter second number : 20
Enter third number : 30
Sum of numbers = 60
Enter multiplicative scale factor : 2
Scaled sum = 120
Enter dividing scale factor : 0.25
Scaled sum = 480
Enter first number to subtract from sum : 180
Enter first number to subtract from sum : 300
New sum = 0
```

Listing 4-4
The source code for the OPER4.CPP program.

```cpp
// A C++ program that demonstrates the assignment operators

#include <iostream.h>

main()
{
  double fSum = 0;
  double fX;

  cout << "Enter first number : ";
  cin >> fX;
  fSum += fX;

  cout << "Enter second number : ";
  cin >> fX;
  fSum += fX;

  cout << "Enter third number : ";
  cin >> fX;
```

```
    fSum += fX;

    cout << "Sum of numbers = " << fSum << "\n";

    cout << "Enter multiplicative scale factor : ";
    cin >> fX;
    fSum *= fX;
    cout << "Scaled sum = " << fSum << "\n";

    cout << "Enter dividing scale factor : ";
    cin >> fX;
    fSum /= fX;
    cout << "Scaled sum = " << fSum << "\n";

    cout << "Enter first number to subtract from sum : ";
    cin >> fX;
    fSum -= fX;

    cout << "Enter second number to subtract from sum : ";
    cin >> fX;
    fSum -= fX;

    cout << "New sum = " << fSum << "\n";
    return 0;
}
```

Listing 4-4 declares the **double**-type variables **fSum** and **fX** inside function **main**, where the following sequence of steps takes place:

1. The source code initializes the variable **fSum** with the value 0.

2. Three sets of statements prompt you for three numbers and add your input to the value in variable **fSum**. The operator **+=** performs this addition.

3. After entering and adding the input, the code displays the current value in variable **fSum**.

4. Next, you are prompted to enter a multiplicative scale value, which is stored in variable **fX**.

5. The assignment operator ***=** scales the value of variable **fSum** using the value in variable **fX**.

6. You are prompted to enter a dividing scale value, which is stored in variable **fX**.

7. The assignment operator /= scales the value of variable **fSum** using the value in variable **fX**.

8. You are then prompted to enter two numbers to subtract from the current value in variable **fSum**. The function uses the assignment operator -= to subtract the value of each number (stored in variable **fX**) from the value in variable **fSum**.

Finally, the function **main** displays the current value in variable **fSum**.

The sizeof Operator

C++ offers the operator **sizeof** to return the byte size of a data type or a variable. The general syntax for the operator **sizeof** is:

```
// form 1:
sizeof(dataType)
// form 2
sizeof(variableName)
```

Here are examples of using the **sizeof** operator:

```
char cDriveName;
int nCharSize = sizeof(char);
int nDriveNameSize = sizeof(cDriveName);
```

This code snippet declares the **char**-type variable **cDriveName** and the **int**-type variables **nCharSize** and **nDriveNameSize**. The declaration of variable **nCharSize** initializes this variable using the result of the expression **sizeof(char)**. The declaration of variable **nDriveNameSize** initializes this variable using the result of the expression **sizeof(nDriveName)**.

Let's look at a simple program that uses the operator **sizeof** with a set of predefined data types and variables that are of these data types. Listing 4-5 shows the source code for the OPER5.CPP program. This program displays the byte sizes for the predefined types **char**, **int**, **long**, and **double**. The program also displays the byte sizes for variables that have these types. Here is the output of the program in Listing 4-5:

```
*************** NOTE ***************
* The sizes of data types depend on  *
* the compiler and operating system. *
**************************************


char type uses 1 bytes
int type uses 2 bytes
long type uses 4 bytes
double type uses 8 bytes

char-type variable uses 1 bytes
int-type variable uses 2 bytes
long-type variable uses 4 bytes
double-type variable uses 8 bytes
```

Listing 4-5
The source code for the OPER5.CPP program.

```cpp
// A C++ program that demonstrates the sizeof operator

#include <iostream.h>

main()
{
  char cAChar = 'A';
  int nAnInt = 45;
  long lALong = 51234;
  double fADouble = 3.14;

  cout << "*************** NOTE ***************\n"
       << "* The sizes of data types depend on  *\n"
       << "* the compiler and operating system. *\n"
       << "**************************************\n\n";
  cout << "char type uses " << sizeof(char) << " bytes\n";
  cout << "int type uses " << sizeof(int) << " bytes\n";
  cout << "long type uses " << sizeof(long) << " bytes\n";
  cout << "double type uses " << sizeof(double) << " bytes\n";
  cout << "\n";
  cout << "char-type variable uses "
       << sizeof(cAChar) << " bytes\n";
  cout << "int-type variable uses "
       << sizeof(nAnInt) << " bytes\n";
  cout << "long-type variable uses "
       << sizeof(lALong) << " bytes\n";
  cout << "double-type variable uses "
       << sizeof(fADouble) << " bytes\n";

  return 0;
}
```

Your Data Type Sizes May Vary

The byte sizes for the various predefined data types vary with the compiler make and version, as well as with the operating system. Therefore, do not be surprised if running the program OPER5.CPP generates different results for you. For example, the **int** type in a 32-bit operating system typically occupies four bytes instead of two.

Listing 4-5 contains straightforward source code. The function **main** declares the variables **cAChar**, **nAnInt**, **lALong**, and **fADouble**, which have the types **char**, **int**, **long**, and **double**, respectively. The function uses the **sizeof** operator with these data types to display their byte sizes. The function **main** then uses the **sizeof** operator with the local variables.

Typecasting

Compilers for most popular programming languages, such as Pascal, BASIC, FORTRAN, and C, perform automatic data type conversions, especially in mathematical and Boolean expressions. Often, the compiler promotes an integer type into a floating-point type. C++ is no exception. Moreover, C++ supports the typecasting feature (inherited from C) to allow you to explicitly convert a value from one data type into another type. The general syntax for typecasting is:

```
// form 1
(newType)expression
// form 2
newType(expression)
```

Here are examples of using the typecasting feature:

```
char cLetter = 'A'
int nASCII = int(cLetter);
long lASCII = (long)cLetter;
```

C

A New Typecasting Format

The second form of the typecasting syntax — int(cLetter) — uses the function format. This format is new to C++.

PASCAL

Typecasting in Pascal

Typecasting is not part of the core Pascal language. However, if you have used more recent versions of the Turbo Pascal or Borland Pascal compiler, then you may have come across typecasting.

BASIC

Typecasting in BASIC

Typecasting is not supported in BASIC. Therefore, pay attention to this feature, since it empowers you to look at the value of one data type as though it were another (compatible) data type.

This code snippet declares and initializes the char-type variable cLetter. The code also declares the int-type variable nASCII and initializes it using the int typecast of variable cLetter. In addition, the code declares the long-type variable lASCII and initializes it using the long typecast of variable cLetter.

Let's look at a simple program that illustrates typecasting. Listing 4-6 shows the source code for the TYPCAST1.CPP program. This program declares a set of variables, including two char-type variables. The program assigns values to these two variables and then assigns the differences in their ASCII values to variables that have the types short, int, long, and double. The program performs these assignments three times. The first time, the assignments of the ASCII code difference use no typecasting. The second and third times, the assignments use two forms of typecasting. The program displays the values in the variables after each set of assignment statements. Here is the output generated by the program in Listing 4-6:

```
Character 1 is A
Character 2 is a
ASCII code diff. (short) = 32
ASCII code diff. (int) = 32
ASCII code diff. (long) = 32
ASCII code diff. (double) = 32

Using typecasting form 1
Character 1 is A
Character 2 is a
ASCII code diff. (short) = 32
ASCII code diff. (int) = 32
ASCII code diff. (long) = 32
ASCII code diff. (double) = 32

Using typecasting form 2
Character 1 is A
Character 2 is a
ASCII code diff. (short) = 32
ASCII code diff. (int) = 32
ASCII code diff. (long) = 32
ASCII code diff. (double) = 32
```

Listing 4-6

The source code for the TYPCAST1.CPP program.

```cpp
// A C++ program that demonstrates typecasting

#include <iostream.h>

main()
{
  char cChar1 = 'A';
  char cChar2 = 'a';
  short nAShortInt;
  int nAnInt;
  long lALong;
  double fADouble;

  // assign difference in ASCII codes without typecasting
  nAShortInt = cChar2 - cChar1;
  nAnInt = cChar2 - cChar1;
  lALong = cChar2 - cChar1;
  fADouble = cChar2 - cChar1;

  // display values
  cout << "Character 1 is " << cChar1 << "\n";
```

```
cout << "Character 2 is " << cChar2 << "\n";
cout << "ASCII code diff. (short) = " << nAShortInt << "\n";
cout << "ASCII code diff. (int) = " << nAnInt << "\n";
cout << "ASCII code diff. (long) = " << lALong << "\n";
cout << "ASCII code diff. (double) = " << fADouble << "\n\n";

// assign difference in ASCII codes with typecasting (form 1)
nAShortInt = (short)cChar2 - cChar1;
nAnInt = (int)cChar2 - cChar1;
lALong = (long)cChar2 - cChar1;
fADouble = (double)cChar2 - cChar1;

// display values
cout << "Using typecasting form 1\n";
cout << "Character 1 is " << cChar1 << "\n";
cout << "Character 2 is " << cChar2 << "\n";
cout << "ASCII code diff. (short) = " << nAShortInt << "\n";
cout << "ASCII code diff. (int) = " << nAnInt << "\n";
cout << "ASCII code diff. (long) = " << lALong << "\n";
cout << "ASCII code diff. (double) = " << fADouble << "\n\n";

// assign difference in ASCII codes with typecasting (form 2)
nAShortInt = short(cChar2 - cChar1);
nAnInt = int(cChar2 - cChar1);
lALong = long(cChar2 - cChar1);
fADouble = double(cChar2 - cChar1);

// display values
cout << "Using typecasting form 2\n";
cout << "Character 1 is " << cChar1 << "\n";
cout << "Character 2 is " << cChar2 << "\n";
cout << "ASCII code diff. (short) = " << nAShortInt << "\n";
cout << "ASCII code diff. (int) = " << nAnInt << "\n";
cout << "ASCII code diff. (long) = " << lALong << "\n";
cout << "ASCII code diff. (double) = " << fADouble << "\n";

return 0;
}
```

Listing 4-6 declares and initializes the **char**-type variables **cChar1** and **cChar2** inside function **main**. The function also declares the **short**-type variable **nAShortInt**, the **int**-type variable **nAnInt**, the **long**-type variable **lALong**, and the **double**-type variable **fADouble**.

The function **main** assigns the expression **cChar2 – cChar1** to the variables **nAShortInt**, **nAnInt**, **lALong**, and **fADouble** without using typecasting. These statements let the compiler handle the type conversion automatically. The function then displays the values in all of the local variables.

The function then assigns the expression **cChar2 – cChar1** to the variables **nAShortInt, nAnInt, lALong**, and **fADouble** using the first form of typecasting—the assignment statements use the targeted type to typecast the value in variable **cChar2**. The compiler responds by automatically updating the result to match the typecasting data type. The function once again displays the values in all of the local variables.

Next, the function assigns the expression **cChar2 – cChar1** to the variables **nAShortInt, nAnInt, lALong**, and **fADouble** using the second form of typecasting — the assignment statements use the targeted type to typecast the entire expression **cChar2 – cChar1**. The function once more displays the values in all of the local variables.

Relational and Logical Operators

Programs require relational and Boolean operators to create decision-making Boolean expressions. Since decision-making is a fundamental part of programming, all common programming languages, such as BASIC, Pascal, FORTRAN, and C, support such operators.

Table 4-4 shows the relational and Boolean operators in C++. Notice that the list lacks the logical operator XOR. You can emulate this operator using an inline function (more about inline functions in Chapter 5, "Functions"). Also notice that Table 4-4 contains the conditional assignment operator **?:**. This operator will be new to you (unless you program in C); it has the following syntax:

```
(expression) ? trueValue : falseValue
```

The operator yields the **trueValue** if the expression is true (or nonzero) and returns the **falseValue** otherwise. Consider how this statement uses the conditional assignment operator to assign a value to a variable:

```
variable = (expression) ? trueValue : falseValue;
```

The effect is similar to the following **if** statement:

```
if (expression)
  variable = trueValue;
else
  variable = falseValue;
```

Table 4-4
The Relational and Boolean Operators in C++

C++ Operator	Meaning	Example
&&	logical AND	k > 1 && k < 11
||	logical OR	k < 0 || k > 22
!	logical NOT	!(k > 1 && k < 10)
<	less than	k < 12
<=	less than or equal to	k <= 33
>	greater than	k > 45
>=	greater than or equal to	k >= 77
==	equal to	k == 32
!=	not equal to	k != 33
?:	conditional assignment	k = (k < 0)? 1 : k

BASIC

The Equality Test Relational Operator

Remember that the operator == (with two equal signs!) tests for equality. Using the assignment operator = (which is also the equality test operator in BASIC) instead does not generate a compiler error. It may generate a compiler warning, depending on the warning settings in your compiler.

In addition, C++ relational and Boolean operators do not work on string literals and string variables (that is, arrays of characters).

PASCAL

The Equality Test Relational Operator

Keep in mind that the operator == (with two equal signs!) tests for equality. If you instead apply the assignment operator =, the compiler does not generate an error. It may generate a compiler warning, depending on the warning settings in your compiler.

Also keep in mind that C++ relational and Boolean operators do not work on string literals and string variables (that is, arrays of characters).

Boolean Expressions

Boolean expressions use relational and Boolean operators to produce Boolean values. Boolean expressions can range from simple to complex. Simple expressions use single relational or Boolean operators. By contrast, complex Boolean expressions use a combination of both. Here are examples of simple Boolean expressions:

```
i < 10
nCount >= nMinLimit
nIndex == nArrayBound
bDriveFlag && bDiskFlag
bNeedFile || bNewFile
!bNewFile
```

Here are examples of more complex Boolean expressions:

```
i < 10 && i >= 100
!(nCount <= nMinLimit || nCount >= nMaxLimit)
nIndex >= nArrayBound && nIndex < 100
```

Let's look at a programming example that uses the relational and Boolean operators. Listing 4-7 contains the source code for the RELOP1.CPP program. The program generates three random numbers in the range of 1 to 100. It then tests the following conditions:

- The first number is less than the second number.
- The first number is less than or equal to the third number.
- The second number is greater than the third number.
- The first and second numbers are equal.
- The first and third numbers are not equal.
- The first number is less than the second number, and the second number is less than the third number.
- The first number is less than the second number, or the second number is less than the third number.
- The first number is not less than and not equal to the second number.

CODING NOTES

Boolean Expression Bugs

When you write a Boolean expression, make sure that such an expression is not either consistently true or consistently false. For example, consider the following expression:

```
nCount < 0 && nCount > 100
```

This Boolean expression is always false because the value in variable **nCount** cannot be negative and also exceed 100!

The program displays each test and the outcome of that test. Here is sample output for the program in Listing 4-7 (remember that since this program generates random numbers, you should very rarely get the same output shown below):

```
First number is 41
Second number is 65
Third number is 29
41 < 65 is TRUE
41 <= 29 is FALSE
65 > 29 is TRUE
41 == 65 is FALSE
41 != 29 is TRUE
41 < 65 AND 65 < 29 is FALSE
41 < 65 OR 65 < 29 is TRUE
NOT (41 <= 65 ) is FALSE
```

Listing 4-7
The source code for the RELOP1.CPP program.

```
// A C++ program that demonstrates relational
// and Boolean operators

#include <iostream.h>
#include <stdlib.h>
#include <time.h>

main()
{
  const int LO = 1;
  const int HI = 100;
```

```
int nNum1, nNum2, nNum3;

// reseed the random number generator using the system time
srand((unsigned)time(NULL));
// get the three random numbers
nNum1 = rand() % HI + LO;
nNum2 = rand() % HI + LO;
nNum3 = rand() % HI + LO;

cout << "First number is " << nNum1 << "\n"
     << "Second number is " << nNum2 << "\n"
     << "Third number is " << nNum3 << "\n";

cout << nNum1 << " < " << nNum2 << " is "
     << ((nNum1 < nNum2) ? "TRUE" : "FALSE") << "\n";
cout << nNum1 << " <= " << nNum3 << " is "
     << ((nNum1 <= nNum3) ? "TRUE" : "FALSE") << "\n";
cout << nNum2 << " > " << nNum3 << " is "
     << ((nNum2 > nNum3) ? "TRUE" : "FALSE") << "\n";
cout << nNum1 << " == " << nNum2 << " is "
     << ((nNum1 == nNum2) ? "TRUE" : "FALSE") << "\n";
cout << nNum1 << " != " << nNum3 << " is "
     << ((nNum1 != nNum3) ? "TRUE" : "FALSE") << "\n";

cout << nNum1 << " < " << nNum2 << " AND "
     << nNum2 << " < " << nNum3 << " is "
     << ((nNum1 < nNum2 && nNum2 < nNum3) ? "TRUE" : "FALSE")
     << "\n";
cout << nNum1 << " < " << nNum2 << " OR "
     << nNum2 << " < " << nNum3 << " is "
     << ((nNum1 < nNum2 || nNum2 < nNum3) ? "TRUE" : "FALSE")
     << "\n";
cout << "NOT (" << nNum1 << " <= " << nNum2 << " ) is "
     << ((!(nNum1 <= nNum2)) ? "TRUE" : "FALSE")
     << "\n";

return 0;
}
```

Function **main** in Listing 4-7 declares the **int**-type constants **LO** and **HI**, which define the range of random numbers to generate. The function also declares the three **int**-type variables **nNum1**, **nNum2**, and **nNum3**. It calls the function **srand** to reseed the random number generator and then assigns three random numbers to the variables **nNum1**, **nNum2**, and **nNum3**. The function **rand** generates the random numbers and together with the constants **LO** and **HI** provides the program with the desired range of random numbers.

The function **main** uses a set of stream output statements to display the tests for the relational and Boolean operators, and also to display the results of the tests. Notice that the output statements use the conditional operator to invoke the relational and Boolean operators. In each statement, the conditional operator yields the string "TRUE" or "FALSE" if the tested condition is true or false, respectively. The function **main** uses the following expressions in connection with the relational and Boolean operators:

- The expression **nNum1 < nNum2** to determine if the first number is less than the second number

- The expression **nNum1 <= nNum3** to determine if the first number is less than or equal to the third number

- The expression **nNum2 > nNum3** to determine if the second number is greater than the third number

- The expression **nNum1 == nNum2** to determine if the first and second numbers are equal

- The expression **nNum1 != nNum3** to determine if the first and third numbers are not equal

- The expression **nNum1 < nNum2 && nNum2 < nNum3** to determine if the first number is less than the second number and the second number is less than the third number

- The expression **nNum1 < nNum2 || nNum2 < nNum3** to determine if the first number is less than the second number or the second number is less than the third number

- The expression **!(nNum1 <= nNum2)** to determine if the first number is not less than and not equal to the second number

Bit-Manipulation Operators

In order for programming languages such as C and C++ to be used in system programming, they must be able to manipulate bits quickly and efficiently. Table 4-5 shows the bit-manipulation operators in C++. Notice that C++ supports the bitwise AND, OR, XOR, and NOT operators. Table 4-6 shows the bit-manipulation assignment operators in C++.

Table 4-5

The Bit-Manipulation Operators in C++

C++ Operator	Meaning	Example
&	bitwise AND	m & 255
|	bitwise OR	k | 122
^	bitwise XOR	i ^ 44
~	bitwise NOT	~k
<<	bitwise shift left	m << 3
>>	bitwise shift right	m >> 4

Table 4-6

The Bit-Manipulation Assignment Operators in C++

C++ Operator	Example	Long Form
&=	n &= 23	n = n & 23
|=	k |= 122	k = k | 122
^=	i ^= 44	i = i ^ 44
<<=	m <<= 3	m = m << 3
>>=	m >>= 4	m = m >> 4

Let's look at a simple program that uses the bit-manipulation operators. Listing 4-8 contains the source code for the BITSOP1.CPP program. The program generates two random numbers and applies the bitwise AND, OR, XOR, NOT, shift left, and shift right operators to these numbers. Here is sample output for the program in Listing 4-8 (remember that since this program generates random numbers, you should very rarely get the same output shown below):

```
First number is 226
Second number is 196
226 AND 196 = 192
226 OR 196 = 230
226 XOR 196 = 38
NOT 226 = -227
226 << 2 = 904
196 >> 2 = 49
```

Listing 4-8

The source code for the BITSOP1.CPP program.

```
// A C++ program that demonstrates bit-manipulation operators

#include <iostream.h>
#include <stdlib.h>
#include <time.h>

main()
{
  const int LO = 0;
  const int HI = 255;

  int nNum1, nNum2, nNum3;


  // reseed the random number generator using the system time
  srand((unsigned)time(NULL));
  // get the two random numbers
  nNum1 = rand() % HI + LO;
  nNum2 = rand() % HI + LO;

  cout << "First number is " << nNum1 << "\n"
       << "Second number is " << nNum2 << "\n";

  cout << nNum1 << " AND " << nNum2 << " = "
       << (nNum1 & nNum2) << "\n";
  cout << nNum1 << " OR " << nNum2 << " = "
       << (nNum1 | nNum2) << "\n";
  cout << nNum1 << " XOR " << nNum2 << " = "
       << (nNum1 ^ nNum2) << "\n";
  cout << "NOT " << nNum1 << " = "
       << (~nNum1) << "\n";
  nNum3 = nNum1 << 2;
  cout << nNum1 << " << " << 2 << " = " << nNum3 << "\n";
  nNum3 = nNum2 >> 2;
  cout << nNum2 << " >> " << 2 << " = " << nNum3 << "\n";

  return 0;
}
```

Listing 4-8 declares the **int**-type constants **LO** and **HI** in function **main**. These constants define the range of the random numbers generated. The function also declares the three **int**-type variables **nNum1**, **nNum2**, and **nNum3**. The function then performs the following tasks:

- Assign two random numbers to variables **nNum1** and **nNum2**

- Display the random numbers in variables **nNum1** and **nNum2**

- Perform the bitwise AND operation using the values in variables **nNum1** and **nNum2** and display the result. The output also includes the operands and the operation.

- Perform the bitwise OR operation using the values in variables **nNum1** and **nNum2** and display the result. The output also includes the operands and the operation.

- Perform the bitwise XOR operation using the values in variables **nNum1** and **nNum2** and display the result. The output also includes the operands and the operation.

- Perform the bitwise NOT operation using the value in variable **nNum1** and display the result. The output also includes the operand and the operation.

- Shift the value in variable **nNum2** to the left by two bits and then assign the result to variable **nNum3**

- Display the operands, operation, and result of the shift left operation

- Shift the value in variable **nNum2** to the right by two bits and then assign the result to variable **nNum3**

- Display the operands, operation, and result of the shift right operation

The Comma Operator

The comma operator is peculiar to both C and C++. This operator allows the evaluation of multiple expressions in a statement. This programming feature may sound odd to you if you have programmed in languages other than C. However, the comma operator has its uses. The typical example of using the comma operator is in a **for** loop that has multiple loop control variables. Here is an example:

```
for(int i= 0, j = MAX - 1; i < j; i++, j--)
```

This **for** loop declares the variables i and j to control the loop's iterations. The initialization statement uses the comma operator to initialize both loop control variables in the same statement. Likewise, the increment part of the loop increments variable i and decrements variable j. The comma operator separates the two expressions in the increment part.

Operator Precedence and Evaluation Order

This chapter has introduced you to most of the C++ operators. I did leave out a few that deal with pointers (see Chapter 13, "Pointers"). Table 4-7 shows the C++ operators and their precedence. The table shows the operators by category, the evaluation order, and the precedence. The evaluation order tells you how the compiler sets the evaluation of an expression with operators that have the same precedence. The precedence column in Table 4-7 shows precedence numbers—the smaller the number, the higher the precedence the accompanying operator has. Thus, all operators with a value of 2 in the precedence column have equal precedence, and all with a value of 3 share a lower precedence.

Here is an example of operator precedence:

```
double fX = 2.0;
double fY = 5.0;
double fZ = 10.0;
double fA;

fA = fX + fY * fZ;
cout << fA; // displays 52
```

This example calculates the value for variable fA by first multiplying the values in variables fY and fZ (to yield 50), because the multiplication has a higher precedence than addition. The runtime system then adds the value in variable fX to the result of the multiplication and assigns the final result, 52, to variable fA.

Table 4-7

The C++ Operators and Their Precedence

Category	Name	Symbol	Evaluation Order	Precedence
Monadic	Postincrement	++	Left to right	2
	Postdecrement	––	Left to right	2
	Address	&	Right to left	2
	Bitwise NOT	~	Right to left	2
	Typecast	(type)	Right to left	2
	Logical NOT	!	Right to left	2
	Negation	–	Right to left	2
	Plus sign	+	Right to left	2
	Preincrement	++	Right to left	2
	Predecrement	––	Right to left	2
	Size of data	sizeof	Right to left	2
Multiplicative	Modulus	%	Left to right	3
	Multiply	*	Left to right	3
	Divide	/	Left to right	3
Additive	Add	+	Left to right	4
	Subtract	–	Left to right	4
Bitwise Shift	Shift left	<<	Left to right	5
	Shift right	>>	Left to right	5
Relational	Less than	<	Left to right	6
	Less than or equal	<=	Left to right	6
	Greater than	>	Left to right	6
	Greater than or equal	>=	Left to right	6
	Equal	==	Left to right	7
	Not equal	!=	Left to right	7
Bitwise	AND	&	Left to right	8
	XOR	^	Left to right	9
	OR			Left to right	10

Category	Name	Symbol	Evaluation Order	Precedence
Logical	AND	&&	Left to right	11
	OR	||	Left to right	12
Ternary	Cond. express.	?:	Right to left	13
Assignment	Arithmetic	=	Right to left	14
		+=	Right to left	14
		-=	Right to left	14
		*=	Right to left	14
		/=	Right to left	14
		%=	Right to left	14
	Shift	>>=	Right to left	14
		<<=	Right to left	14
	Bitwise	&=	Right to left	14
		|=	Right to left	14
		^=	Right to left	14
Comma		,	Left to right	15

Summary

This chapter has presented the C++ operators that enable you to write mathematical and Boolean expressions. Most if not all of these operators function basically as they did in the C language, and many of them have common equivalents in other programming languages. The C++ operators permit you to perform arithmetic operations, compare values, perform Boolean math on expressions, and manipulate bits. C++ also offers assignment operators that incorporate arithmetic and bitwise operations to allow you to write terse assignment statements. These operators empower you to write expressions that query and set data. This is the heart of data processing.

The next chapter presents functions, which are the placeholders for executable statements.

5 Functions

*F*unctions are the placeholders for executable statements. That is to say, functions contain the executable statements that drive a program. In addition, functions provide the data interface between various parts of a program. Understanding C++ functions—including their data types, parameters, and other aspects—empowers you to develop robust applications. In this chapter you will learn about the syntax of declaring functions, prototyping functions, local variables in functions, static variables in functions, inline functions, void functions, recursive functions, exiting functions, default arguments of functions, constant parameters, and function overloading.

Essential Features of C++ Functions

All C++ functions have certain basic features. Each function has a name, a return type, and an optional parameter list. Functions can declare local constants and variables. Except for the function **main** you should prototype functions (that is, declare them in advance). The next subsections discuss these function features in more detail.

FUNCTION SYNTAX

C++ functions have the following syntax:

```
returnType functionName(parameterList)
{
  // declarations

  // statements

  return expression;
}
```

Every function has a *return type* that appears before the name of the
function. The *parameter list* follows the function's name and is enclosed in
parentheses. The function returns a value using the **return** statement that
typically appears at the end. A function may have more than one
return statement.

The parameter list of a function may contain one or more *parameters,*
which correspond to the *arguments* given the function when it is actually
called. The list of parameters is comma-delimited, and each parameter has
the following syntax:

```
parameterType[&] parameterName
```

You need to observe the following rules about the parameters of
a function:

1. Each parameter must have its own type. You cannot use the same type
   to declare multiple parameters (as you can when declaring variables).

2. If a function has no parameters, the parentheses that come after the
   function's name contain nothing.

3. The argument for a parameter is *passed by copy* (or, as it is sometimes
   said, "by value"), unless you insert the reference-of operator **&** after the
   parameter's type. When a parameter passes a copy of its argument, the
   function can alter only the copy of the argument used within the
   function itself. The original argument remains intact. By contrast, using
   the reference-of operator allows the argument to be *passed by reference*
   by declaring the parameter as a reference to its argument. In this case,
   the parameter becomes a special alias to its argument. Any changes the
   function makes to the parameter also affect the argument.

4. Reference parameters take arguments that are the names of variables. You cannot use an expression or a constant as an argument to a reference parameter since an expression does not have an address as a variable does.

5. Copy parameters take arguments that are constants, variables, or expressions. The type of argument must either match the type of the parameter or be compatible with it. You may use typecasting (described in Chapter 4) to tell the compiler how to adjust the type of the argument to match the type of the parameter.

Here are examples of functions:

```
double getSquare(double x) // one parameter
{
  return x * x;
}

double Square(double& x) // one parameter, modifies its argument
{
  x = x * x;
  return x;
}

int randomNumber(int nLow, int nHi) // two parameters
{
  return rand() % nHi + nLow;
}

int getMin(int nNum1, int nNum2) // two parameters
{
  return (nNum1 < nNum2) ? nNum1 : nNum2;
}

int getSmall(int nNum1, int nNum2, int nNum3); // three parameters
{
  if (nNum1 < nNum2 && nNum1 < nNum3)
    return nNum1;
  else if (nNum2 < nNum1 && nNum2 < nNum3)
    return nNum2;
  else
    return nNum3;
}

double getPI() // no parameters
{
  return 4 * atan(1);
}
```

The first function, getSquare, has the return type double and the single double-type parameter x. The function returns the squared value of the parameter x. The function getSquare contains a single statement, namely the return statement.

The second function, Square, has the return type double and the single double-type reference parameter x. The function squares the value of the reference parameter and returns the new value in x (this value also affects the argument for function Square). Therefore, the function returns the squared value in two ways: first as the function's return value, and second using the reference parameter x.

The third function, randomNumber, has the return type int and the two int-type parameters nLow and nHi. The function returns the random number in the range specified by the arguments for the parameters nLow and nHi. The function randomNumber has a single statement that returns the random number sought. This statement calls the function rand, which is declared in the STDLIB.H header file.

The fourth function, getMin, has the return type int and the two int-type parameters nNum1 and nNum2. The function returns the smaller of the values supplied by the arguments for the parameters. The function getMin has a single statement that returns the minimum number sought. This statement uses the conditional assignment operator.

The fifth function, getMin, has the return type int and the three int-type parameters nNum1, nNum2, and nNum3. The function returns the smallest value supplied by the arguments for the three parameters. The function getSmall uses a multiple-alternative if-else statement to obtain the sought-after minimum.

The last function, getPI, has the return type double and has no parameters. The function has a single statement that yields the value of pi.

CODING NOTES

Ignoring the Function's Return Value

C++ allows you to write statements that *ignore* the return value of functions. Therefore, you need not use dummy variables to receive the *ignored* values of functions. Such a statement uses the C++ function more like a subroutine—the function's action, and not its result, is important.

DECLARING AND PROTOTYPING FUNCTIONS

C++ also supports the forward declaration of functions (which is called *prototyping*). The forward declaration allows you to list the functions at the beginning of the source code. Such a list offers a convenient way to know what functions are in a source code file. In addition, using the prototypes gives the compiler advance notice of the names, return types, and parameter lists of the various functions. You can then place the definitions of the functions in any order and not worry about the compile-time errors that occur when you call a function before you either declare it or define it. The general syntax for a function prototype is:

```
returnType functionName(parameterList);
```

Notice that the semicolon at the end is needed for the prototype but does not work in the function definition.

Here are the function prototypes for the functions that I presented in the last section:

```
double getSquare(double x); // one parameter
double Square(double& x); // one parameter
int randomNumber(int nLow, int nHi); // two parameters
int getMin(int nNum1, int nNum2); // two parameters
int getSmall(int nNum1, int nNum2, int nNum3); // three parameters
double getPI(); // no parameters
```

It is worth pointing out that the names (as distinct from the *types*) of the parameters are optional in function prototypes.

Let's look at an example that uses functions and function prototypes. Listing 5-1 shows the source code for FN4.CPP. The program performs the following tasks:

- Prompt you to enter a character

- Display the input character

- Display the character that comes after the input character in ASCII sequence

- Display the character that comes before the input character in ASCII sequence

- Prompt you to enter two integers

- Display the integer average value of the input values

- Prompt you to enter two numbers
- Display the average value of the input values

Here is a sample session with the program in Listing 5-1 (user input is underlined):

```
Enter a letter : B
Input character is B
Next character is C
Previous character is A



Enter first integer : 44
Enter second integer : 56
Average integer = 50



Enter first number : 12
Enter second number : 55.5
Average number = 33.5
```

Listing 5-1
The source code for the FN4.CPP program.

```cpp
// A C++ program that illustrates simple functions

#include <iostream.h>

// declare function prototypes
char getNextChar(char c);
char getPrevChar(char c);
int showChar(const char* pszMsg, char c);

int getAverage(int nNum1, int nNum2);
int showInt(const char* pszMsg, int nNum);

double getMean(double fX1, double fX2);
int showDouble(const char* pszMsg, double fX);

main()
{
  char cLetter;
  int nN1, nN2;
  double fX1, fX2;

  cout << "Enter a letter : ";
  cin >> cLetter;
```

Prototypes

```
  showChar("Input character is ", cLetter);
  showChar("Next character is ", getNextChar(cLetter));
  showChar("Previous character is ", getPrevChar(cLetter));
  cout << "\n";

  cout << "Enter first integer : ";
  cin >> nN1;
  cout << "Enter second integer : ";
  cin >> nN2;
  showInt("Average integer = ", getAverage(nN1, nN2));
  cout << "\n";

  cout << "Enter first number : ";
  cin >> fX1;
  cout << "Enter second number : ";
  cin >> fX2;
  showDouble("Average number = ", getMean(fX1, fX2));

  return 0;
}

char getNextChar(char c)
{
  return c + 1;
}

char getPrevChar(char c)
{
  return c - 1;
}

int showChar(const char* pszMsg, char c)
{
  cout << pszMsg << c << "\n";
  return 0;
}


int getAverage(int nNum1, int nNum2)
{
  return (nNum1 + nNum2) / 2;
}

int showInt(const char* pszMsg, int nNum)
{
  cout << pszMsg << nNum << "\n";
  return 0;
}

double getMean(double fX1, double fX2)
{
  return (fX1 + fX2) / 2;
}
```

```
int showDouble(const char* pszMsg, double fX)
{
  cout << pszMsg << fX << "\n";
  return 0;
}
```

Listing 5-1 declares the prototypes of the *auxiliary* functions getNextChar, getPrevChar, showChar, getAverage, showInt, getMean, and showDouble. These prototypes allow function main to call the auxiliary (that is, supporting) functions before the compiler encounters their definitions. I can rewrite the source code in Listing 5-1 such that I remove the function prototypes and move the definitions of the auxiliary functions before function main. However, the style used in Listing 5-1 is the recommended one, since it places function main first and then defines the auxiliary functions.

The function getNextChar has the return type char and the char-type parameter c. It returns the character that comes after the parameter c, using a single statement to return the character sought.

The function getPrevChar has the return type char and the char-type parameter c. This function returns the character that comes before the parameter c. The function uses a single statement to return the character sought.

The int-type function showChar has the const char*-type parameter pszMsg and the char-type parameter c. The function displays the contents of both parameters. The first parameter displays text that comments on the value in parameter c. The function returns the dummy integer value of 0.

The function getAverage has the return type int and the int-type parameters nNum1 and nNum2. The function returns the average of the values in these parameters.

The int-type function showInt has the const char*-type parameter pszMsg and the int-type parameter nNum. The function displays the contents of both parameters. The first parameter displays text that comments on the value in parameter nNum. The function returns the dummy integer value of 0.

The function getMean has the return type double and the double-type parameters fX1 and fX2. The function returns the average of the values in these parameters.

The int-type function showDouble has the const char*-type parameter pszMsg and the double-type parameter fX. The function displays the contents of both parameters. The first parameter displays text that comments on the value in parameter fX. The function returns the dummy integer value of 0.

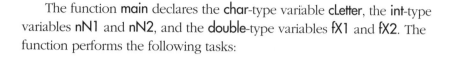

The function **main** declares the **char**-type variable **cLetter**, the **int**-type variables **nN1** and **nN2**, and the **double**-type variables **fX1** and **fX2**. The function performs the following tasks:

- Prompt you to enter a character and save the input character in the variable **cLetter**

- Display the input character by calling the function **showChar**. The arguments for this function call are the string literal "Input character is " and the variable **cLetter**. The function **main** ignores the result of function **showChar**, since the output generated by **showChar** is what function **main** needs.

- Display the character that comes after the input character by calling the function **showChar** a second time. The arguments for this function call are the string literal "Next character is " and the result of calling function **getNextChar** (the argument for calling this function is the variable **cLetter**). The function **main** ignores the result of function **showChar**.

- Display the character that comes before the input character, again by calling the function **showChar**. The arguments for this function call are the string literal "Previous character is " and the result of calling function **getPrevChar** (the argument for calling this function is the variable **cLetter**). The function **main** ignores the result of function **showChar**.

- Prompt you to enter two integers and save these integers in variables **nN1** and **nN2**

- Display the average of the input values by calling function **showInt**. The arguments for this function call are the string literal "Average integer = " and the result of calling function **getAverage** (the arguments for calling this function are the variables **nN1** and **nN2**). The function **main** ignores the result of function **showInt**.

- Prompt you to enter two numbers and save the input in the variables **fX1** and **fX2**

- Display the average of the input values by calling function **showDouble**. The arguments for this function call are the string literal "Average number = " and the result of calling function **getMean** (the arguments for calling this function are the variables **fX1** and **fX2**). The function **main** ignores the result of function **showDouble**.

Let's look at another sample program. Listing 5-2 shows the source code for the FN5.CPP program, which illustrates reference parameters. The program generates 100 random numbers between 1 and 1000 and then calculates and displays the statistical mean and standard deviation for these numbers. Based on statistical analysis the generated values yield a mean and standard deviation near 500 and 280, respectively. Here is a sample session with the program in Listing 5-2:

```
Number of observations = 100
Mean = 528.51
Std. deviation = 271.324
```

Listing 5-2
The source code for FN5.CPP.

```cpp
// A C++ program that illustrates functions
// with reference parameters

#include <iostream.h>
#include <stdlib.h>
#include <time.h>
#include <math.h>

// declare function prototypes
int updateSums(double fX, int& nSum,
               double& fSumX, double& fSumXX);
int getStats(int nSum, double fSumX, double fSumXX,
             double& fMean, double& fSdev);

main()
{
  const int LO = 1;
  const int HI = 1000;
  const int MAX = 100;
  double fX, fMean, fSdev;
  // declare and initialize statistical summations
  int nSum = 0;
  double fSumX = 0.;
  double fSumXX = 0.;

  // reseed random number generator
  srand((unsigned)time(NULL));
  for (int i = 0; i < MAX; i++) {
    fX = double(rand() % HI + LO);
    updateSums(fX, nSum, fSumX, fSumXX);
  }
  // get the basic statistics
  getStats(nSum, fSumX, fSumXX, fMean, fSdev);
```

```
    cout << "Number of observations = " << nSum << "\n"
         << "Mean = " << fMean << "\n"
         << "Std. deviation = " << fSdev;

    return 0;
}
int updateSums(double fX, int& nSum,
               double& fSumX, double& fSumXX)
{
    // update statistical summations with data
    nSum++;
    fSumX += fX;
    fSumXX += fX * fX;
    return 0;
}

int getStats(int nSum, double fSumX, double fSumXX,
             double& fMean, double& fSdev)
{
    // calculate mean
    fMean = fSumX / nSum;
    // calculate std. deviation
    fSdev = sqrt((fSumXX - fSumX * fSumX / nSum)/(nSum - 1));
    return 0;
}
```

Listing 5-2 declares the function prototypes **updateSums** and **getStats**. The function **updateSums** has the following parameters:

- The **double**-type parameter **fX**, which passes arguments to the function by value

- The reference **int**-type parameter **nSum**, which passes values between the function and its caller. This parameter keeps track of the number of observations.

- The reference **double**-type parameter **fSumX**, which passes values between the function and its caller. This parameter keeps track of the sum of observations.

- The reference **double**-type parameter **fSumXX**, which passes values between the function and its caller. This parameter keeps track of the sum of observations squared.

The function **getStats** returns the mean and standard deviation through the reference parameters. The function declares the following parameters:

- The **int**-type parameter **nSum**, which passes the number of observations to the function
- The **double**-type parameter **fSumX**, which passes the sum of observations to the function
- The **double**-type parameter **fSumXX**, which passes the sum of observations squared to the function
- The reference **double**-type parameter **fMean**, which returns the value of the statistical mean to the function's caller
- The reference **double**-type parameter **fSdev**, which returns the value of the statistical standard deviation to the function's caller

The function **main** declares a number of constants and variables, including **nSum**, **fSumX**, and **fSumXX**, which keep track of the statistical summations. The function uses a **for** loop to generate random numbers and accumulate them in the statistical summations. The loop calls function **updateSums**, passing the arguments **fX**, **nSum**, **fSumX**, and **fSumXX**. The last three arguments pass values between functions **main** and **updateSums**.

To obtain the basic statistics, function **main** calls the function **getStats**. The arguments for this call are variables **nSum**, **fSumX**, **fSumXX**, **fMean**, and **fSdev**. The last two arguments pass the values of the sought-after statistics back to function **main**. This function then displays these statistics.

LOCAL VARIABLES IN FUNCTIONS

Any function, and not just function **main**, can declare local constants and variables. The scope of these local constants and variables is limited to the host function. No function can directly and automatically access the local constants and variables of another function.

There are two types of local variables: *automatic* and *static*. The runtime system creates the automatic variables when the host function begins to execute. Likewise, when the host function ends, the runtime system removes the automatic variables. The next section discusses the static variables.

Let's look at a program that demonstrates the use of local automatic variables in auxiliary functions. Listing 5-3 shows the source code for the FN6.CPP program, which I created by modifying the source code in Listing 5-2. The new program performs several runs that test the statistical mean and standard deviation. The output for each run should generate values for the mean and standard deviation that are close to 500 and 280, respectively. Here is the output of a sample session with the program in Listing 5-3:

```
Test #1
Number of observations = 100
Mean = 514.73
Std. deviation = 279.253
Test #2
Number of observations = 100
Mean = 457.27
Std. deviation = 287.135
Test #3
Number of observations = 100
Mean = 503.74
Std. deviation = 305.265
```

Listing 5-3
The source code for the FN6.CPP program.

```cpp
// A C++ program that illustrates functions
// with local automatic variables

#include <iostream.h>
#include <stdlib.h>
#include <time.h>
#include <math.h>

// declare function prototypes
int updateSums(double fX, int& nSum,
               double& fSumX, double& fSumXX);
int getStats(int nSum, double fSumX, double fSumXX,
             double& fMean, double& fSdev);
int testRandomNumbers();

main()
{
  // reseed random number generator
  srand((unsigned)time(NULL));

  cout << "Test #1\n";
  testRandomNumbers();

  cout << "Test #2\n";
  testRandomNumbers();

  cout << "Test #3\n";
  testRandomNumbers();

  return 0;
}
```

```
int updateSums(double fX, int& nSum,
               double& fSumX, double& fSumXX)
{
  // update statistical summations with data
  nSum++;
  fSumX += fX;
  fSumXX += fX * fX;
  return 0;
}

int getStats(int nSum, double fSumX, double fSumXX,
             double& fMean, double& fSdev)
{
  // calculate mean
  fMean = fSumX / nSum;
  // calculate std. deviation
  fSdev = sqrt((fSumXX - fSumX * fSumX / nSum)/(nSum - 1));
  return 0;
}

int testRandomNumbers()
{
  const int LO = 1;
  const int HI = 1000;
  const int MAX = 100;
  double fX, fMean, fSdev;
  // declare and initialize statistical summations
  int nSum = 0;
  double fSumX = 0.;
  double fSumXX = 0.;

  for (int i = 0; i < MAX; i++) {
    fX = double(rand() % HI + LO);
    updateSums(fX, nSum, fSumX, fSumXX);
  }
  // get the basic statistics
  getStats(nSum, fSumX, fSumXX, fMean, fSdev);
  cout << "Number of observations = " << nSum << "\n"
       << "Mean = " << fMean << "\n"
       << "Std. deviation = " << fSdev << "\n";
  return 0;
}
```

Listing 5-3 is very similar to Listing 5-2. The new source code components and features in Listing 5-3 are these:

- The function **main** does not declare any variables. Instead, this function reseeds the random number generator and then performs three test runs by calling the function **testRandomNumbers** three times.

- The function **testRandomNumbers** has most of the declarations and statements of function **main** in Listing 5-2. The declarations include the constants **LO**, **HI**, and **MAX** and the automatic variables **fX**, **fMean**, **fSdev**, **nSum**, **fSumX**, and **fSumXX**. The function **testRandomNumbers** initializes the last three variables with zeros. These constants and variables come into being every time function **main** calls function **testRandomNumbers**. When the latter function terminates, the runtime system removes the constants and variables from the computer's memory.

The remaining functions in Listing 5-3 are identical to their counterparts in Listing 5-2.

STATIC VARIABLES IN FUNCTIONS

Unlike automatic variables, static variables retain their values between function calls. This feature allows a function to pick up where it left off the last time it executed. To declare a static variable, you need to place the keyword **static** before the variable's type. You may assign an initial value to the static variable. Initializing static variables allows the host function to determine whether or not it is executing for the first time in an application. Here is the general syntax for declaring a static variable:

```
static type variableName [= initialValue];
```

Here are examples of static variables declared in a function:

```
int doCalc()
{
  static int nIndex = 0;
  static int nLastIndex = 0;
  static double fLastValue;
  // other declarations
  // statements
  return 1;
}
```

This code snippet declares the initialized static variables **nIndex** and **nLastIndex**. The code also declares the uninitialized static variable **fLastValue**. These variables retain their values between calls to function **doCalc**.

Let's look at a simple program that uses a static variable in a random number-generating function. Listing 5-4 contains the source code for the FN7.CPP program, which contains a function that generates random numbers between 0 and 1 (excluded). The function stores the last-generated random number using a local static variable. It then employs that variable to generate the next random number. Using the static variable absolves the caller from keeping track of the last random number generated. The program uses the random number-generating function to generate 100 numbers. It displays every 20th random number along with the current average value for the random numbers generated so far. Here is a sample session for the program in Listing 5-4:

```
Sample random number is 0.417719
Current Average = 0.630081 (20 points)
Sample random number is 0.940495
Current Average = 0.58468 (40 points)
Sample random number is 0.857697
Current Average = 0.56166 (60 points)
Sample random number is 0.935686
Current Average = 0.568185 (80 points)
Sample random number is 0.237602
Current Average = 0.546415 (100 points)
```

Listing 5-4

The source code for the FN7.CPP program.

```cpp
// A C++ program that illustrates functions
// with local static variables

#include <iostream.h>
#include <math.h>

const double PI = 4 * atan(1);
const double INIT_SEED = 13.0;

// declare function prototypes
double getRunningSum(double x);
double random();
double cube(double x);
double fract(double x);

main()
{
  const int MAX_NUMS = 100;
  const int SHOW_INTERVAL = 20;
  double fX;

  for (int i = 0; i < MAX_NUMS; i++) {
    fX = random();
    if ((i+1) % SHOW_INTERVAL != 0)
      getRunningSum(fX);  // ignore function value
```

```
        else {
          cout << "Sample random number is "
               << fX << "\n"
               << "Current Average = "
               << getRunningSum(fX) / (i+1)
               << " (" << (i+1) << " points)\n";
        }
      }

    return 0;
    }

double getRunningSum(double x)
{
  static double fSum = 0.;

  fSum += x;
  // return running sum
  return fSum;
}

double random()
{
  static double fSeed = INIT_SEED;

  // get the next pseudo-random number
  fSeed = fract(cube(fSeed + PI));
  // return number
  return fSeed;
}

double cube(double x)
{
  return x * x * x;
}

double fract(double x)
{
  return x - double(long(x));
}
```

Static variables

Listing 5-4 declares the global constants **PI** and **INIT_SEED**. The latter constant supplies the random number-generating function with the initial seed. Change the value of this constant to generate a different sequence of random numbers.

The listing contains the prototypes for the functions **getRunningSum**, **random**, **cube**, and **fract**. The final two functions are very simple: The function **cube** returns the cubed value of its argument, and the function **fract** returns the fractional part of a floating-point number.

The function **getRunningSum** has the **double** return type and the single **double**-type parameter **x**. This function keeps track of the sum of its arguments and returns the current sum. It uses the local static variable **fSum** to maintain the running sum between calls to itself. The static variable **fSum** is initialized when it is declared. The function **getRunningSum** simply adds the argument for parameter **x** to the variable **fSum** and returns the new value in that variable.

The function **random** returns the next random number. The function has the return type of **double** and an empty parameter list. The function declares the local static variable **fSeed** and initializes it using the global constant **INIT_SEED**. It calculates the next random number by taking the fractional part of the cubed sum of **fSeed** plus pi. The function returns the new value in the local variable **fSeed**. This variable retains the last random number generated between calls to function **random**.

Special-Purpose Functions

C++ supports special-purpose functions. These include inline functions, void functions, and recursive functions. Inline functions assist in generating fast code. Void functions emulate procedures in other programming languages. Recursive functions are special kinds of functions that call themselves in order to obtain the final result. The next subsections discuss these special functions in more detail.

INLINE FUNCTIONS

Using functions enables you to modularize the source code of an application or a library. Each function should perform a specific task. However, using functions generates overhead code. This overhead consists of calling the function, passing the arguments to the function, and returning the function's result. In the case of single-statement functions that are frequently called by other functions, you can speed program execution (perhaps at the cost of program size) by declaring these functions as *inline functions*. An inline function looks like an ordinary function, but the compiler replaces any call to that inline function with a copy of its definition body. The compiler also replaces the function's parameters with its arguments. The general syntax for declaring an inline function is:

```
inline returnType functionName(parameterList)
{
  return expression;
}
```

The declaration of an inline function must begin with the keyword **inline**. An inline function should have a single **return** statement. If you place declarations and other statements in the inline function, your C++ compiler *may* elect (depending on the compiler's make and version) to simply treat the inline function as a non-inline function. In other words, don't expect a C++ compiler to replace a 100-statement inline function with 100 statements!

Here is an example of an inline function:

```
inline long square(int nNum)
{
  return nNum * nNum;
}

main()
{
  int N = 3;
  cout << square(N) << "\n";
    return 0;
}
```

This code snippet declares the inline function **square**, which returns the square of the **int**-type parameter **nNum**. When the function **main** calls function **square**, the compiler substitutes the function call with the expression N * N. In other words, the compiler replaces the function call with the function's statement and also replaces the function's parameters with the function's arguments.

C

Using Inline Functions

Formal inline functions will be new to C programmers. C programs use the **#define** directive to create inline functions. C++ programming style discourages you from using the **#define** directive because the resulting pseudo-inline functions perform no type checking. In addition, these pseudo-inline functions may not expand correctly, yielding logically erroneous expressions.

Let's look at a simple example. Listing 5-5 shows the source code for the FN8.CPP program, which illustrates inline functions. I created this program by modifying Listing 5-1, which contains program FN4.CPP. The new program interacts just as does FN4.CPP. The difference is that the program FN8.CPP uses inline functions to support the program's operations. Here is a sample session with the program in Listing 5-5:

```
Enter a letter : G
Input character is G
Next character is H
Previous character is F


Enter first integer : 45
Enter second integer : 12
Average integer = 28


Enter first number : 23.4
Enter second number : 18.6
Average number = 21
```

Listing 5-5
The source code for the FN8.CPP program.

```
// A C++ program that illustrates inline functions

#include <iostream.h>

// declare function prototypes
inline char getNextChar(char c);
```

```
inline char getPrevChar(char c);
int showChar(const char* pszMsg, char c);

inline int getAverage(int nNum1, int nNum2);
int showInt(const char* pszMsg, int nNum);

inline double getMean(double fX1, double fX2);
int showDouble(const char* pszMsg, double fX);

main()
{
  char cLetter;
  int nN1, nN2;
  double fX1, fX2;

  cout << "Enter a letter : ";
  cin >> cLetter;
  showChar("Input character is ", cLetter);
  showChar("Next character is ", getNextChar(cLetter));
  showChar("Previous character is ", getPrevChar(cLetter));
  cout << "\n";

  cout << "Enter first integer : ";
  cin >> nN1;
  cout << "Enter second integer : ";
  cin >> nN2;
  showInt("Average integer = ", getAverage(nN1, nN2));
  cout << "\n";

  cout << "Enter first number : ";
  cin >> fX1;
  cout << "Enter second number : ";
  cin >> fX2;
  showDouble("Average number = ", getMean(fX1, fX2));

  return 0;
}

char getNextChar(char c)
{
  return c + 1;
}

char getPrevChar(char c)
{
  return c - 1;
}

int showChar(const char* pszMsg, char c)
{
```

```
    cout << pszMsg << c << "\n";
    return 0;
}


int getAverage(int nNum1, int nNum2)
{
    return (nNum1 + nNum2) / 2;
}

int showInt(const char* pszMsg, int nNum)
{
    cout << pszMsg << nNum << "\n";
    return 0;
}

double getMean(double fX1, double fX2)
{
    return (fX1 + fX2) / 2;
}

int showDouble(const char* pszMsg, double fX)
{
    cout << pszMsg << fX << "\n";
    return 0;
}
```

Listing 5-5 declares the same functions as Listing 5-1. The main difference is that Listing 5-5 declares the functions **getNextChar**, **getPrevChar**, **getAverage**, and **getMean** as inline functions. Notice that the keyword **inline** appears only in the function prototypes. When the listing defines these functions, the compiler already knows that they are inline functions.

The C++ compiler generates the object code for the following statements in Listing 5-5:

```
showChar("Next character is ", getNextChar(cLetter));
showChar("Previous character is ", getPrevChar(cLetter));
showInt("Average integer = ", getAverage(nN1, nN2));
showDouble("Average number = ", getMean(fX1, fX2));
```

It is as if the source code contained the following statements:

```
showChar("Next character is ", cLetter + 1;
showChar("Previous character is ", cLetter - 1);
showInt("Average integer = ", (nN1 + nN2) / 2);
showDouble("Average number = ", (fX1 + fX2) / 2);
```

VOID FUNCTIONS

If you are a BASIC or Pascal programmer, you may ask about declaring functions that act as procedures. C++ uses the special type **void** to indicate that the function does not have a return type. Consequently, using **return** statements in a **void** function only supports an early exit from the function (see the section "Exiting Functions" later in this chapter). Moreover, you can optionally use the keyword **void** to explicitly indicate that the parameter list of a function is empty. Here are examples of void function prototypes, showing the parameter lists:

```
void updateDataBase(); // no parameters
void createNewDataBase(void); // no parameters
void sortData(int bOrder); // one parameter
void reseedRandomNumber(double fNewSeed); // one parameter
```

Looking back at the source code of programs FN4.CPP and FN8.CPP (in Listings 5-1 and 5-5), you may have noticed that each of the functions **showChar**, **showInt**, and **showDouble** has an **int** return type and returns the dummy value of 0. Moreover, you may have observed that the function **main** in each of these programs consistently ignores the results of these functions. Thus, the coding and usage of the functions **showChar**, **showInt**, and **showDouble** clearly indicate that the programs use them more as *procedures* than as functions. Consequently, these functions are perfect candidates to be declared as **void** functions. Listing 5-6 shows the source code for the FN9.CPP program, which contains the **void** functions **showChar**, **showInt**, and **showDouble**.

Listing 5-6
The source code for the FN9.CPP program.

```
// A C++ program that illustrates void functions

#include <iostream.h>

// declare function prototypes
inline void newLine();
inline char getNextChar(char c);
inline char getPrevChar(char c);
inline void showChar(const char* pszMsg, char c);

inline int getAverage(int nNum1, int nNum2);
inline void showInt(const char* pszMsg, int nNum);
```

```cpp
inline double getMean(double fX1, double fX2);
inline void showDouble(const char* pszMsg, double fX);

main()
{
  char cLetter;
  int nN1, nN2;
  double fX1, fX2;

  cout << "Enter a letter : ";
  cin >> cLetter;
  showChar("Input character is ", cLetter);
  showChar("Next character is : ", getNextChar(cLetter));
  showChar("Previous character is ", getPrevChar(cLetter));
  newLine();

  cout << "Enter first integer : ";
  cin >> nN1;
  cout << "Enter second integer : ";
  cin >> nN2;
  showInt("Average integer = ", getAverage(nN1, nN2));
  newLine();

  cout << "Enter first number : ";
  cin >> fX1;
  cout << "Enter second number : ";
  cin >> fX2;
  showDouble("Average number = ", getMean(fX1, fX2));

  return 0;
}

void newLine()
{
  cout << "\n";
}

char getNextChar(char c)
{
  return c + 1;
}

char getPrevChar(char c)
{
  return c - 1;
}

void showChar(const char* pszMsg, char c)
{
  cout << pszMsg << c << "\n";
}
```

```
int getAverage(int nNum1, int nNum2)
{
  return (nNum1 + nNum2) / 2;
}

void showInt(const char* pszMsg, int nNum)
{
  cout << pszMsg << nNum << "\n";
}

double getMean(double fX1, double fX2)
{
  return (fX1 + fX2) / 2;
}

void showDouble(const char* pszMsg, double fX)
{
  cout << pszMsg << fX << "\n";
}
```

Notice that functions **showChar**, **showInt**, and **showDouble** have the **void** return type instead of the **int** type. Moreover, the definition of each of these functions uses a single output statement—the **return 0;** a statement is not required by the new versions of these functions. Now that each **showXxxx** function contains a single statement, it is also suitable to be made an inline function!

Listing 5-6 also declares a new **void** function, namely, **newLine**. This function has no parameters, and its definition has a single statement, which emits a newline to the standard output stream.

RECURSIVE FUNCTIONS

Recursion is a method in which a function obtains its result by calling itself. Successive recursive calls must pass different arguments and must reach a limit or condition where the function stops calling itself. These two simple rules prevent a recursive function from indefinitely calling itself. Conceptually, recursion is a form of iteration that does not use the formal fixed or conditional loop. Many algorithms (such as calculating factorials and performing a quicksort) can be implemented using either recursive functions or straightforward loops. Some algorithms are easier to implement using recursion. An example is the algorithm for parsing and evaluating mathematical expressions. This is because an expression may contain smaller expressions and therefore recursion offers the best solution. In other words, the main expression may contain nested expressions. Here is an example:

```
Z = ((X + Y) * X) + (X * Y) / (1 + X);
```

The above statement contains the nested expressions **((X + Y) * X)**, **(X + Y)**, **(X * Y)**, and **(1 + X)**.

Here is a programming example that uses recursive and nonrecursive functions to yield the same results. Listing 5-7 shows the source code for the FN10.CPP program. This program performs the following tasks:

- Prompt you to enter an integer between 3 and 10
- Calculate the factorial of the input value using the recursive version of the factorial function. This function displays the arguments for the recursive calls to allow you to trace these calls.
- Display the input number and the factorial number obtained by the recursive function
- Display the input number and the factorial number obtained by the nonrecursive function
- Calculate the sum of integers from 1 to the input value using the recursive version of a summation function. This function displays the arguments for the recursive calls to allow you to trace these calls.
- Display the input number and the sum of integers obtained by the recursive summation function
- Display the input number and the sum of integers obtained by the nonrecursive summation function

Here is a sample session with the program in Listing 5-7:

```
Enter an integer (between 3 and 10) : 5

Testing recursive factorial function
Recursive call with argument 4
Recursive call with argument 3
Recursive call with argument 2
```

```
Recursive call with argument 1
Factorial of 5 = 120
Factorial of 5 = 120 (nonrecursive)



Testing recursive summation function
Recursive call with argument 4
Recursive call with argument 3
Recursive call with argument 2
Recursive call with argument 1
Sum of 1 to 5 = 15
Sum of 1 to 5 = 15 (nonrecursive)
```

Listing 5-7

The source code for the FN10.CPP program.

```cpp
// A C++ program that illustrates recursive functions

#include <iostream.h>

// declare the prototypes for recursive functions
double recFactorial(int nNum);
double recSumOfInts(int nNum);

// declare the prototypes for nonrecursive functions
double factorial(int nNum);
double sumOfInts(int nNum);

main()
{
  int nNum;
  double fX;

  // prompt user to enter integer in the range of 3 to 10
  do {
    cout << "Enter an integer (between 3 and 10) : ";
    cin >> nNum;
    cout << "\n";
  } while (nNum < 3 || nNum > 10);

  cout << "Testing recursive factorial function\n";
  fX = recFactorial(nNum);
  cout << "Factorial of " << nNum << " = "
       << fX << "\n";
  fX = factorial(nNum);
  cout << "Factorial of " << nNum << " = "
       << fX << " (nonrecursive)\n\n";

  cout << "Testing recursive summation function\n";
  fX = recSumOfInts(nNum);
  cout << "Sum of 1 to " << nNum << " = "
       << fX << "\n";
```

```
    fX = sumOfInts(nNum);
    cout << "Sum of 1 to " << nNum << " = "
        << fX << " (nonrecursive)\n";

    return 0;
}

double recFactorial(int nNum)
{
    if (nNum > 1) {
        cout << "Recursive call with argument "
            << (nNum - 1) << "\n";
        return nNum * recFactorial(nNum - 1);
    }
    else
        return 1.0;
}

double recSumOfInts(int nNum)
{
    if (nNum > 1) {
        cout << "Recursive call with argument "
            << (nNum - 1) << "\n";
        return nNum + recSumOfInts(nNum - 1);
    }
    else
        return 1.0;
}

double factorial(int nNum)
{
    double fResult = 1.;

    for (int i = 1; i <= nNum; i++)
        fResult *= (double)i;

    return fResult;
}

double sumOfInts(int nNum)
{
    double fSum = 0.;

    for (int i = 1; i <= nNum; i++)
        fSum += (double)i;

    return fSum;
}
```

Recursive calls

Listing 5-7 declares the prototypes for the recursive functions
recFactorial and **recSumOfInts** and the nonrecursive functions **factorial**
and **sumOfInts**.

The recursive function **recFactorial** implements the recursive algorithm
for calculating a factorial. The function has the return type **double** and the
single **int**-type parameter **nNum**. The function uses an **if** statement to
determine whether or not the argument for parameter **nNum** exceeds 1. If
this condition is true, the function displays the tracer message and then
makes the recursive call. The recursive call appears in the expression
nNum * recFactorial(nNum − 1). By contrast, if the tested condition is false,
the function **factorial** just returns 1. This part of the function provides the
response needed to end the recursive function calls.

The recursive function **recSumOfInts** implements the recursive algorithm
for calculating the sum of integers from 1 to a specified limit. The function
has the return type **double** and the single **int**-type parameter **nNum**. The
function uses an **if** statement to determine whether or not the argument for
parameter **nNum** exceeds 1. If this condition is true, the function displays
the tracer message and then makes the recursive call. This call appears in
the expression **nNum + recSumOfInts(nNum − 1)**. By contrast, if the tested
condition is false, the function **recSumOfInts** simply returns 1. This part of the
function offers the response required to terminate the recursive function calls.

The function **factorial** implements the nonrecursive algorithm for
calculating a factorial. The function has the return type **double** and the
single **int**-type parameter **nNum**. It declares the local **double**-type variable
fResult and initializes it with the value 1 and uses a fixed-iteration **for** loop to
obtain the factorial. Each loop iteration multiplies the value in variable
fResult with the value of the loop control variable **i**. The function returns the
value in variable **fResult**, which contains the factorial sought.

The function **sumOfInts** implements the nonrecursive algorithm for
adding integers between 1 and a specified limit. The function has the return
type **double** and the single **int**-type parameter **nNum**. It declares the local
double-type variable **fSum** and initializes it with the value 0. It uses a
fixed-iteration **for** loop to obtain the sum of integers. Each loop iteration
adds the value of the loop control variable **i** to the variable **fSum**. The

function returns the value in variable **fSum**, which contains the summation sought.

The function **main** declares the **int**-type variable **nNum** and the **double**-type variable **fX**. It prompts you to enter an integer between 3 and 10. To ensure that you comply with this range, function **main** uses a **do-while** loop. The loop statements store your input in the variable **nNum**.

The function **main** tests calculating the factorial using recursive and nonrecursive functions by performing the following tasks:

- Call the recursive function **recFactorial** and supply it with the argument **nNum**. The function **main** assigns the result of function **recFactorial** to the variable **fX**. The call to function **recFactorial** produces the lines of text that trace the recursive function calls.

- Display the input number and its factorial

- Call the nonrecursive function **factorial** and supply it with the argument **nNum**. The function **main** assigns the result of this function call to the function **fX**.

- Display the input number and its factorial

- Call the recursive function **recSumOfInts** and supply it with the argument **nNum**. The function **main** assigns the result of function **recSumOfInts** to the variable **fX**. The call to function **recSumOfInts** produces the lines of text that trace the recursive function calls.

- Display the range of added integers and their sum

- Call the nonrecursive function **sumOfInts** and supply it with the argument **nNum**. The function **main** assigns the result of this function call to the variable **fX**.

- Display the range of added integers and their sum

Exiting Functions

The **return** statement allows the program flow to exit a function. Simple non-**void** functions typically make the **return** statement the last statement. Therefore, exiting the function at the last statement makes sense. However, when you write a nontrivial function that checks its arguments and verifies other conditions, things may be more complicated. In these cases, the function may not be able to proceed normally due to illegal arguments or critical conditions. The solution for these cases is to have the function use additional **return** statements to support an early exit. Typically, such a function returns an error code using either the function's return value or a reference parameter. Programmers typically prefer using the function's return value as an error flag.

There are other cases in which a function does not need to proceed with its remaining statements because specific arguments lead to results that do not require much computational effort.

In the case of a **void** function, you can use a **return** statement (with no expression following the **return** keyword) to support an early exit from that function. Again, in the case of error, the **void** function should indicate the early exit by altering the value of a reference parameter.

Let's look at a programming example. Listing 5-8 shows the source code for the FN11.CPP program, which illustrates exiting functions. This program calculates the factorials of –1 though 5 and the values of the following infinite series polynomial, P(x), for x = 0 to 10:

```
P(x) = 1 - 1/x + 2/x² - 3/x³ + 4/x⁴ - …
```

Here is the output generated by the program in Listing 5-8:

```
Factorial of -1 = 1
Factorial of 0 = 1
Factorial of 1 = 1
Factorial of 2 = 2
Factorial of 3 = 6
Factorial of 4 = 24
Factorial of 5 = 120


P(0) = -1e+030
P(1) = -1e+030
P(2) = -3
P(3) = 0.25
P(4) = 0.703704
P(5) = 0.84375
P(6) = 0.904
P(7) = 0.935185
P(8) = 0.953353
P(9) = 0.964844
P(10) = 0.972565
```

Listing 5-8

The source code for the FN11.CPP program.

```cpp
// A C++ program that illustrates exiting functions

#include <iostream.h>
#include <math.h>

const double BAD_RESULT = -1.0e+30;

// declare the function prototypes
double polynomial(double x);
double factorial(int nNum);

main()
{
  const int FIRST_INT = -1;
  const int LAST_INT = 5;
  const double FIRST_DOUBLE = 0.0;
  const double LAST_DOUBLE = 10.0;
  const double INCREM_DOUBLE = 1.0;

  double fX;

  for (int i = FIRST_INT; i <= LAST_INT; i++)
    cout << "Factorial of " << i << " = "
         << factorial(i) << "\n";
  cout << "\n";

  fX = FIRST_DOUBLE;
  while (fX <= LAST_DOUBLE) {
    cout << "P(" << fX << ") = "
         << polynomial(fX) << "\n";
    fX += INCREM_DOUBLE;
  }

  return 0;
}

double polynomial(double x)
{
  const double TOLERANCE = 1.0e-8;
  double fTerm;
  double fSum = 1.0;
  double fChs = 1.0;

  // does x exceed 1?
  if (x > 1.0)
    // start loop
    for (int i = 1; ; i++) {
      // calculate term
      fTerm = i / pow(x, i);
      // is term too small?
      if (fTerm < TOLERANCE)
        return fSum; // return current sum
```

```
      // reverse sign for the current term
      fChs -= 1.;
      // update summation
      fSum += fChs * fTerm;
    }
  // function executes next statement only if x <= 1
  return BAD_RESULT;
}


double factorial(int nNum)
{
  double fResult = 1.0;

  // is argument less than 2?
  if (nNum < 2)
    return fResult; // return 1 for trivial argument

  // execute loop which calculates factorial
  // for nontrivial argument
  for (int i = 2; i <= nNum; i++)
    fResult *= i;

  return fResult;

}
```

Listing 5-8 declares the global constant **BAD_RESULT** and the prototypes for functions **polynomial** and **factorial**.

The function **polynomial** has the **double** return type and the single **double**-type parameter **x**. The function calculates the value of the polynomial P(x) by adding a number of terms. This addition stops when the absolute value of a term falls below a specific tolerance level. The function declares the local **double**-type constant **TOLERANCE**, which has the small tolerance level value of 10^{-8}. The function also declares the local **double**-type variables **fTerm**, **fSum**, and **fChs**. The function **polynomial** initializes both of the last two variables with the value 1.0. The function uses an **if** statement to determine whether or not the argument of parameter **x** exceeds 1. If this condition is true, the function proceeds with evaluating the polynomial for the argument **x**. This evaluation uses a **for** loop that performs the following tasks:

■ Calculate the current term for the polynomial and store that term in variable **fTerm**

■ Exit, using the **return fSum** statement, if the value in variable **fTerm** is less than the value of constant **TOLERANCE**. The **return** statement is the function's exit point for valid arguments for parameter **x**. The statement yields the value of the polynomial approximated using the tolerance level set in constant **TOLERANCE**.

- Toggle the value in variable **fChs** between 1 and −1
- Update the variable **fSum**, which stores the current polynomial value

The last statement in function **polynomial** is a **return** statement that yields the value in constant **BAD_RESULT**. The function executes this statement only if the argument for parameter **x** is 1 or less.

The function **polynomial** shows an example of a function that uses a **return** statement in the middle of the function's body to yield valid results. The code is also worthy of attention in that here the typical location of the **return** statement yields only a numeric error code.

The listing also declares the function **factorial**, which calculates factorials. The function has the return type **double** and has the single **int**-type parameter **nNum**. The function declares and initializes the local variable **fResult** and uses this variable to return the desired factorial value. The function **factorial** uses an **if** statement to determine if the argument for parameter **nNum** is less than 2. If this condition is true, the function exits using the statement **return fResult**. Thus, when the argument for parameter **x** is any value less than 2, the function returns the factorial value 1. By contrast, if the argument for parameter **x** is not less than 2, the function proceeds to calculate the factorial value using a **for** loop, which calculates the factorial value and stores it in variable **fResult**. The function returns the calculated result using the statement **return fResult**.

The function **main** declares a set of local constants and the variable **fX**. It then tests the function **factorial** using a **for** loop that displays the values of the factorials of −1 to 5. Each loop iteration calls the function **factorial**. The argument for this function call is the value of the loop control variable i.

The function **main** tests the function **polynomial** using a **while** loop. The variable **fX** controls the iterations of this loop. The function **main** initializes the variable **fX** before the **while** loop. The iterations alter the value in variable **fX** from 0 to 10 in increments of 1. Each loop iteration displays the value of polynomial P(x) with the variable **fX** as the argument. The loop also increments the value in variable **fX** to select the next argument for polynomial P(x).

New Features of Functions in C++

C++ offers new function features not found in its parent language C. These features allow you to assign default arguments and define functions that share the same name. The next subsections discuss these new features and also cover constant parameters.

DEFAULT ARGUMENTS

Have you ever written a function and supplied most of its parameters with the same arguments for different function calls? If you have, then you may have felt frustrated with having to feed the function call with the same values for some of the arguments. The good news is that C++ allows you to assign default arguments for parameters. The syntax for the default argument, which resembles that for the initialization of a variable, is:

```
parameterType parameterName = initialValue
```

C++ requires that you observe the following rules for declaring and using default arguments:

1. When you assign a default argument to a parameter, you must assign default arguments to all subsequent parameters.

2. You may assign default arguments to any or all parameters, as long as you obey rule number 1.

3. The default arguments feature divides the parameter list of a function into two parts. The first part contains parameters with no default arguments (this list may be empty if you assign default arguments to all parameters); the second part contains parameters with default arguments.

4. To use a default argument for a parameter, omit the argument for that parameter in a function call.

5. If you use a default argument for a parameter, you must use default arguments for all subsequent parameters. In other words, you cannot pick and choose the default arguments, because the compiler is unable to discern which argument goes to which parameter. (After all, this is programming and not black magic!)

Here are a few examples of functions with default arguments. First, here is the declaration of function **randomNumber**:

```
double randomNumber(double fSeed = 13.7);
```

This line declares the function **randomNumber** with a single **double**-type parameter **fSeed**. The declaration assigns the default argument of 13.7 to this parameter. Thus, you can use the function **randomNumber** in either of these ways:

```
double fRnd = randomNumber();
fRnd = randomNumber(fRnd);
```

The first call to function **randomNumber** has no argument. Therefore, the compiler resolves this call by using the default argument of 13.7 for parameter **fSeed**. By contrast, the second call to function **randomNumber** uses the argument **fRnd**.

Next, let's look at the declaration of function **myPower**:

```
double myPower(double fBase, int nExponent = 2);
```

The function **myPower** has the **double**-type parameter **fBase** and the **int**-type parameter **nExponent**. The latter parameter has the default argument of 2. Thus, you can use the function **myPower** in this fashion:

```
double fX = 12.5;
double fXSquared = myPower(fX);
double fXCubed = myPower(fX, 3);
```

The first call to function **myPower** has only one argument. The compiler resolves this call by using the default argument of 2 for parameter **nExponent**. Consequently, the function **myPower** returns the square of the first argument's value when you omit the argument for the exponent. By contrast, the second call to function **myPower** uses the arguments **fX** and 3. In this case, the compiler does not use the default argument for parameter **nExponent**, since it has been given both arguments explicitly.

Finally, let's look at the declaration of function **yourPower**:

```
double yourPower(double fBase,
                 double fExponent = 2.0,
                 double fErrorCode = -1.0e+30);
```

These statements declare the function **yourPower** with the three **double**-type parameters **fBase**, **fExponent**, and **fErrorCode**. The function assigns the default arguments of 2 and –1.0e+30 to the parameters **fExponent** and **fErrorCode**, respectively. Thus, you can use the function **yourPower** in these ways:

```
double fX = 12.5;
double fXSquared = yourPower(fX);
double fXCubed = yourPower(fX, 3);
double fXFourth = yourPower(fX, 4, -1.0e+40);
```

The first call to function **yourPower** has only one argument. The compiler resolves this call by using the default arguments for parameters **fExponent** and **fErrorCode**. Thus, the function **yourPower** returns a square value when using the default argument for parameter **fExponent**. The second call to function **yourPower** has two arguments. The compiler resolves this call by using the default argument for parameter **fErrorCode**. The last call to function **yourPower** has three arguments—one for each of the three parameters of the function.

Let's look at a programming example. Listing 5-9 contains the source code for the FN12.CPP program, which illustrates default arguments. The program uses a character display function with default arguments. The output of the program shows the effect of using the various default arguments of the character output function.

Here is the output generated by the program in Listing 5-9:

```
Call number 1 -> 'The letter is F'
Call number 2 -> 'G'Call number 3 -> '!'
Call number 4 -> 'H'
```

CODING NOTES

Default Argument Assignment Hint

Place the parameters with default arguments in the ascending order of the likelihood of using the default arguments. This approach allows you to make the best use of default arguments.

Listing 5-9

The source code for the FN12.CPP program.

```
// A C++ program that illustrates default arguments

#include <iostream.h>
#include <math.h>

// declare function prototype
void showChar(char c = '!', char* pszMsg = "", int nNewLine = 1);

main()
{
  char cLetter = 'F';

  // display text and letter
  showChar(cLetter++, "The letter is ");
  // display letter only
  showChar(cLetter++, "", 0);
  // emit a newline
  showChar();
  // display a letter and a newline
  showChar(cLetter++);

  return 0;
}

void showChar(char c, char* pszMsg, int nNewLine)
{
  static nCount = 1;
  cout << "Call number " << nCount++ << " -> '"
       << pszMsg << c << "'"
       << ((nNewLine == 1) ? "\n" : "");
}
```

Listing 5-9 declares the prototype of function **showChar**. The **void** function has the following parameters:

- The **char**-type parameter **c** passes the character to be displayed. This parameter has the exclamation character as a default argument.

- The **char***-type parameter passes the commenting string that appears before the argument of parameter **c**. This parameter has an empty string as a default argument.

- The **int**-type parameter **nNewLine** specifies whether or not to emit a newline after displaying the character argument of parameter **c**. This parameter has the default argument of 1. This value causes the function to emit a newline.

The definition of function **showChar** indicates that the function does some simple bookkeeping in addition to displaying output. The function uses the static local variable **nCount** to count the number of times you call it. The function **showChar** also displays the value in variable **nCount** followed by the string literal " -> '"; the argument of parameter **pszMsg**; the argument of parameter **c**; the string literal "'"; and either a newline or an empty string (depending on the argument of parameter **nNewLine**).

The function **main** declares the variable **cLetter** and initializes it with the character 'F'. It then makes the following calls to the function **showChar** (each function call that contains the argument **cLetter** increments the character in that variable):

- The first call to function **showChar** supplies two arguments. The compiler uses the default argument for parameter **nNewLine** to resolve this call. This function call displays the string "Call number 1 -> 'The letter is F'" on one line and then emits a newline.

- The second call to function **showChar** supplies three arguments. This call generates the string "Call number 2 -> 'G'" but emits no newline.

- The third call to function **showChar** supplies no arguments. The compiler uses the three default arguments to display the string "Call number 3 -> '!'" and to emit a newline.

- The fourth call to function **showChar** supplies only one argument—the variable **cLetter**. The compiler uses the default arguments for the parameter **pszMsg** and **nNewLine** to generate the string "Call number 4 -> 'H'" and a newline.

Notice that the definition of function **showChar** does not have the default arguments in the parameter list. These arguments are not needed because the prototype of function **showChar** has already defined them.

Constant Parameters

By default, a function can alter the data passed by the arguments to its parameters. If the parameter is a not a reference parameter, then the changes made to the argument are limited to the function's scope. By contrast, if the parameter is a reference parameter, then the changes made to the argument go beyond the function's scope. You can tell the compiler that the function should not alter the argument of a parameter by declaring that parameter as a constant parameter. The declaration uses the keyword **const** and has the following general syntax:

```
const parameterType[&] parameterName [= defaultArg]
```

Let me present a programming example. Listing 5-10 shows the source code for the FN13.CPP program, which illustrates constant parameters. I created this program by modifying the source code in program FN9.CPP (in Listing 5-6). The new source code declares all the parameters of all auxiliary functions as constant parameters. Here is a sample session with the program in Listing 5-10:

```
Enter a letter : S
Input character is S
Next character is T
Previous character is R



Enter first integer : 33
Enter second integer : 54
Average integer = 43



Enter first number : 5.43
Enter second number : 3.76
Average number = 4.595
```

Listing 5-10
The source code for the FN13.CPP program.

```cpp
// A C++ program that illustrates constant parameters

#include <iostream.h>

// declare function prototypes
char getNextChar(const char c);
char getPrevChar(const char c);
void showChar(const char* pszMsg, const char c);

int getAverage(const int nNum1, const int nNum2);
void showInt(const char* pszMsg, const int nNum);
```

```
double getMean(const double fX1, const double fX2);
void showDouble(const char* pszMsg, const double fX);

main()
{
  char cLetter;
  int nN1, nN2;
  double fX1, fX2;

  cout << "Enter a letter : ";
  cin >> cLetter;
  showChar("Input character is ", cLetter);
  showChar("Next character is ", getNextChar(cLetter));
  showChar("Previous character is ", getPrevChar(cLetter));
  cout << "\n";

  cout << "Enter first integer : ";
  cin >> nN1;
  cout << "Enter second integer : ";
  cin >> nN2;
  showInt("Average integer = ", getAverage(nN1, nN2));
  cout << "\n";

  cout << "Enter first number : ";
  cin >> fX1;
  cout << "Enter second number : ";
  cin >> fX2;
  showDouble("Average number = ", getMean(fX1, fX2));

  return 0;
}

char getNextChar(const char c)
{
  return c + 1;
}

char getPrevChar(const char c)
{
  return c - 1;
}

void showChar(const char* pszMsg, const char c)
{
  cout << pszMsg << c << "\n";
}


int getAverage(const int nNum1, const int nNum2)
{
  return (nNum1 + nNum2) / 2;
}
```

```
void showInt(const char* pszMsg, const int nNum)
{
  cout << pszMsg << nNum << "\n";
}

double getMean(const double fX1, const double fX2)
{
  return (fX1 + fX2) / 2;
}

void showDouble(const char* pszMsg, const double fX)
{
  cout << pszMsg << fX << "\n";
}
```

Listing 5-10 declares each of the functions **getNextChar** and **getPrevChar** with a **const char**-type parameter **c**. The listing declares the first and second parameters in functions **showChar**, **showInt**, and **showDouble** as constant parameters. In addition, the listing declares the parameters of functions **getAverage** and **getMean** as constant parameters. Making the parameters of these functions constant is valid since none of these functions alter the values of their arguments (or need to do so).

How do you know that the compiler protects the arguments of constant parameters from being changed? You can experiment with the source code in Listing 5-10 by writing, for example, the function **getAverage** like this:

```
// ERROR! Compiler will complain
int getAverage(const int nNum1, const int nNum2)
{
  nNum1 += nNum2;
  return nNum1 / 2;
}
```

The compiler will complain about the first statement in function **getAverage** and tells you that you are trying to change the value of a constant parameter.

FUNCTION OVERLOADING

The program FN13.CPP (in Listing 5-10) contains the functions **showChar**, **showInt**, and **showDouble**, which display a character, an integer, and a floating-point number, respectively. These functions essentially perform the same task but display different types of data. The name of each function indicates what it does and shows the client data type. C++ allows you to use the same function name to declare and define different versions of a function. This feature is called *function overloading*. C++ requires that you observe the following rules when declaring overloaded functions:

1. Each version of the overloaded function must have a different function *signature*. The signature of a function is defined by the number of parameters and their data types. The signature of a function does not include its return type, because C++ allows you to ignore the return type in a statement. It does, however, include the sequence of parameters that have different data types.

2. If the function has parameters with default arguments, the compiler does not include these parameters as part of the function's signature.

Let's look at an example of an overloaded function that obeys rule number 1:

```
double myPower(double fBase, double fExponent);
double myPower(double fBase, int nExponent);
double myPower(double fBase, double fExponent,
               double fErrorCode);
double myPower(double fBase, int nExponent,
               double fErrorCode);
```

This code snippet declares four versions of the overloaded function **myPower**. The signatures of the overloaded functions, in the order of their declaration, are (**double, double**), (**double, int**), (**double, double, double**), and (**double, int, double**). Since each one of these four signatures is unique, the compiler does not generate an error.

What about rule number 2? Let's look at another set of versions of function **myPower** that violates that rule:

```
// error! Functions have the same signatures
double myPower(double fBase, double fExponent = 2.0);
double myPower(double fBase, int nExponent = 2);
double myPower(double fBase, double fExponent = 2,
               double fErrorCode = -1.0E+30);
double myPower(double fBase, int nExponent = 2,
               double fErrorCode = -1.0E+30);
```

These versions of the overloaded function have the same signature, namely, (**double**). The compiler raises an error since it cannot resolve the call to function **myPower** when you use the default arguments.

Let's look at an example of successful use of overloaded functions. Listing 5-11 shows the source code for the FN14.CPP program, which illustrates overloading functions. I created this listing by modifying the FN13.CPP program (in Listing 5-10). I replaced the function **showChar**, **showInt**, and **showDouble** with three versions of the overloaded function **show**. I also reversed the parameters of the function **show** (from the inherited versions) and assigned a default argument to the parameter **pszMsg** in each function **show**.

Here is a sample session with the program in Listing 5-11:

```
Enter a letter : T
Input character is T
Next character is U
Previous character is S



Enter first integer : 345
Enter second integer : 873
Average integer = 609



Enter first number : 0.25
Enter second number : 0.75
Average number = 0.5
```

Listing 5-11
The source code for the FN14.CPP program.

```cpp
// A C++ program that illustrates overloading functions

#include <iostream.h>

// declare function prototypes
char getNextChar(const char c);
char getPrevChar(const char c);

int getAverage(const int nNum1, const int nNum2);
double getMean(const double fX1, const double fX2);

void show(const char c, const char* pszMsg = "");
void show(const int nNum, const char* pszMsg = "");
void show(const double fX, const char* pszMsg = "");
```

```
main()
{
  char cLetter;
  int nN1, nN2;
  double fX1, fX2;

  cout << "Enter a letter : ";
  cin >> cLetter;
  show(cLetter, "Input character is ");
  show(getNextChar(cLetter), "Next character is ");
  show(getPrevChar(cLetter), "Previous character is ");
  cout << "\n";

  cout << "Enter first integer : ";
  cin >> nN1;
  cout << "Enter second integer : ";
  cin >> nN2;
  show(getAverage(nN1, nN2), "Average integer = ");
  cout << "\n";

  cout << "Enter first number : ";
  cin >> fX1;
  cout << "Enter second number : ";
  cin >> fX2;
  show(getMean(fX1, fX2), "Average number = ");

  return 0;
}

char getNextChar(const char c)
{
  return c + 1;
}

char getPrevChar(const char c)
{
  return c - 1;
}

void show(const char c, const char* pszMsg)
{
  cout << pszMsg << c << "\n";
}


int getAverage(const int nNum1, const int nNum2)
{
  return (nNum1 + nNum2) / 2;
}

void show(const int nNum, const char* pszMsg)
{
  cout << pszMsg << nNum << "\n";
}
```

```
double getMean(const double fX1, const double fX2)
{
  return (fX1 + fX2) / 2;
}

void show(const double fX, const char* pszMsg)
{
  cout << pszMsg << fX << "\n";
}
```

Listing 5-11 declares the function prototypes and defines the function **main** and the auxiliary functions. The function **main** makes the following calls to the function **show**:

- The first call to function **show** has the arguments **cLetter** and a literal string. The compiler resolves this function call by invoking the function **show(const char, const char*)**, because the data types of the arguments and parameters (of the version of function **show** just given) match.

- The second call to function **show** has the arguments **getNextChar(cLetter)** (which returns a **char** type) and a literal string. The compiler resolves this function call by again invoking the function **show(const char, const char*)**, because the data types of the arguments and parameters match. The compiler then resolves the third call to function **show** in a similar manner.

- The fourth call to function **show** has the argument **getAverage(nN1, nN2)** (which returns an **int** type) and a literal string. The compiler resolves this function call by invoking the function **show(const int, const char*)**, because the data types of the arguments and parameters (of this version of function **show**) match.

- The last call to function **show** has the argument **getMean(fX1, fX2)** (which returns a **double** type) and a literal string. The compiler resolves this function call by invoking the function **show(const double, const char*)**, because the data types of the arguments and parameters (of this third version of function **show**) match.

Summary

This chapter discussed C++ functions and showed you various aspects of declaring them. You learned about the syntax for ordinary functions, recursive functions, and inline functions. You also learned about local automatic and static variables and when to use them. The chapter also discussed features related to parameters, such as reference parameters, constant parameters, and parameters with default arguments. It also discussed function overloading, a special C++ feature that allows you to use the same function name to declare different versions of a function. Each function must have a unique parameter list.

The next chapter introduces you to C++ classes. You will learn about the components of a class and how to declare classes that model real-world objects.

6 Object-Oriented Programming

Object-oriented programming fosters a new and exciting way to craft, maintain, update, and reuse software. Chapter 1 briefly discussed the basics of object-oriented programming (OOP). This chapter looks at how C++ supports OOP through classes. In this chapter you will learn about the basics of OOP: object and classes, messages and methods, inheritance, and polymorphism. The chapter will further show you how to declare base classes, distinguish the sections of a class, declare constructors and destructors, use **const** with member functions, and use C++ structures as special classes.

Basics of OOP

In the late eighties, programmers and software gurus got excited about artificial intelligence (AI). AI seemed very promising to programmers and end-users alike. The lure of very smart programs captured the imagination—smart files, smart directories, smart input, and so on seemed to intoxicate the software industry. However, AI did not deliver on the promise of super-intelligent software made by some gurus and hopeful software developers. AI proved to be a fad.

Following the widespread disillusionment with AI, the software industry focused its attention on another buzzword: object-oriented programming, or OOP for short. Like AI, object-oriented programming got the programmers and users dreaming again. However, unlike artificial intelligence, OOP offered more realistic goals and did not promise the moon!

The basics of OOP revolve around *objects* and *classes* (classes are the molds for objects). OOP looks at an object and defines it. The result of this definition is the class to which the object (and other similar objects) belongs. Object-oriented programming also supports a special way of looking at classes as they relate to each other (since their objects relate to each other). The result of all this object and class meddling is a new way to model objects and a powerful way to create robust and reusable software.

The next subsections discuss the components of object-oriented programming, using examples to clarify matters.

OBJECTS AND CLASSES

Since learning by example is a very effective way to teach, let me talk more about object-oriented programming using the example of a calculator that we first sketched in Chapter 1. Consider a simple four-function calculator, which I'll call ZX-01. This calculator has the buttons to enter the various digits and perform the four basic mathematical operations. The ZX-01 model represents a *class* of calculators. The internal registers of the ZX-01 parallel the *data members* of a class. These registers (or data members, if you like) store the operands, results, and other information related to the calculator's *state*. Collectively, these data members define the state of the calculator.

The buttons of the calculator parallel the *member functions* of the class. They allow you to perform calculations that alter the values in the internal registers. In other words, these buttons change the state of the calculator.

The individual ZX-01 calculators in use are examples of class *instances*. The various ZX-01 calculators share the same features and the same operations, as set by the calculator maker. However, each calculator has its own independent state. In other words, the operations of each ZX-01 calculator are independent of the operations of any other ZX-01 calculator.

MESSAGES AND METHODS

The OOP purists can look at the example of the ZX-01 calculator and say that when you push a calculator button you send a *message* to the calculator. The calculator (which is an object) responds by engaging its electronic circuits, which perform the requested task. In OOP terms, the engagement is the *method* of responding to the message. The message is more of an abstract command, whereas the method deals with the details of performing the requested operation. In C++ a method corresponds to the member function of a class. A message corresponds to invoking the name of a member function.

Why make the distinction between methods and messages? The answer lies in the fact that some object-oriented programming languages, such as C++, allow you to respond to a message using one of several methods. Therefore, messages and methods do not have a strict one-to-one relationship.

The notion of messages and methods affects the way we think about object-oriented programs. OOP encourages you to build applications that contain various objects communicating with each other. This model is similar to the employees of a company who communicate with each other and with the outside world using messages.

INHERITANCE

Inheritance is another important feature in object-oriented programming. This feature empowers you to declare a new class as a *descendant* (or *child*) class of existing ones. The descendant class brings refinements to the attributes and operations of the parent class. It inherits the data members (that is, the *attributes*) and member functions (that is, the *operations*) of the parent class, which in turn has inherited the data members and member functions of its own parent class, and so on. The descendant class additionally declares its own data members, new member functions, and member functions that override inherited ones. Thus, inheritance allows you to build a class hierarchy. The root of this hierarchy is called the *base* class. Each descendant class in the hierarchy supports more specialization than its parent class.

CODING NOTES

Methods and Messages

A message tells the object *what* action to take.

A method tells the object *how* to execute the message.

Let's look at the example of the ZX-01 calculator and how it fits in with the concept of inheritance. Suppose the makers of the ZX-01 calculator decide to create the ZX-11 scientific calculator. This new model performs the basic four mathematical operations (just like the ZX-01 model) and also supports various math functions, such as logarithmic and trigonometric functions. Instead of designing the ZX-11 from scratch, the calculator maker elects to use the design of the ZX-01 as a starting point. The calculator maker then adds registers, circuits, and buttons to support the new mathematical functions. In OOP terms, the ZX-11 calculator is a descendant of the ZX-01. The ZX-11 calculator has inherited the basic math operations of the ZX-01 and implemented additional features. The added registers, circuits, and buttons parallel new data members and member functions in a descendant class.

Suppose that the calculator maker next decides to design the ZX-100 programmable scientific calculator. Instead of designing the ZX-100 from scratch, the calculator maker chooses to use the design of the ZX-11 as a starting point. The calculator maker then adds even more registers, circuits, and buttons to support the keystroke programming feature. In OOP terms, the ZX-100 calculator is a descendant of the ZX-11. The ZX-100 calculator has inherited the basic math operations of the ZX-01 and the scientific operations of the ZX-11. The line of ZX-01, ZX-11, and ZX-100 calculators parallels a small hierarchy of classes.

C++ supports two inheritance schemes: *single* and *multiple* inheritance. Single inheritance creates hierarchies of classes such that each descendant class has only one parent class. The example of the calculators shows the single inheritance scheme. By contrast, multiple inheritance creates hierarchies of classes such that each descendant class has one or more parent classes.

POLYMORPHISM

Polymorphism is an important object-oriented programming feature that deals with the abstract response of class instances. The word *polymorphism* means assuming different shapes. Let me explain the concept of polymorphism using the calculator example. Suppose that you own one each of the ZX-01, ZX-11, and ZX-100 calculator models. All three models support the basic four math operations. You can pick up any one of these calculators and add two numbers, for example. In each case, pressing the + key performs the addition and displays the result. You really don't care about the exact low-level operations each calculator model performs to add the numbers. These low-level operations may be exactly the same or have some similarities (depending on what design the calculator maker uses). Thus, pressing the + key illustrates the polymorphic behavior of the calculator models.

Polymorphism is important in implementing the same kind of operation in a class hierarchy. For example, a class hierarchy that models geometric shapes has each class define a member function named **Draw**. The programs that use that class hierarchy send the message **Draw** to the various instances of the different classes without worrying about how these instances respond. Thus, supporting the member function **Draw** in each class empowers the hierarchy to offer a consistent and abstract response to the same message.

Declaring Base Classes

C++ supports declaring classes that encapsulate members. The members of a class are *data members* and *member functions*. The data members store values that represent the state of the class instances (that is, the objects that belong to the class). The member functions set and query the state of the class instances by manipulating the values in the data members. The general syntax for declaring a base class in C++ is this:

```
class className
{
  [public:
  // public constructors
  // public destructor
  // public data members
  // public member functions
  ]
```

```
 [protected:
// protected constructors
// protected destructor
// protected data members
// protected member functions
 ]


 [private:
// private constructors
// private destructor
// private data members
// private member functions
 ]
};
```

Declaring a class starts with the keyword **class** and is followed by the name of the class. The declarations of the class members are enclosed in a pair of open and closed braces and end with the semicolon character. The preceding syntax belongs to *base* classes. What is a base class, you may ask? A base class is one that is not a child of another class but that can have derived classes (whose syntax is described in Chapter 14, "Class Hierarchies").

The general syntax shows the sections **public**, **protected**, and **private**. The next section of this chapter discusses these sections of a class.

Let me present a few examples of declaring and using classes in the next subsections.

THE CLASS MYINT

Listing 6-1 shows the source code for the CLASS3.CPP program, which illustrates a class that encapsulates the **int** type. The class **myInt** is a simple wrapper for the predefined type **int**. The class declares two public constructors (more about constructors later in this chapter) and the public member functions **setInt**, **getInt**, and **show**. It also declares the protected data member **m_nInt**, which stores the integer value. Thus the state of each instance of class **myInt** is defined solely by the current value in data member **m_nInt**.

The program declares two instances of class **myInt** and uses the member functions **setInt**, **getInt**, and **show** to assign, query, and display the values of the first class instance, respectively. The program then creates the second instance using the first one. It queries and displays the value of the second instance using the member functions **getInt** and **show**. The program displays the value in each instance using two methods: The first involves sending the C++ message **show** to either instance, and the second stores a copy of the value of the instance in a separate **int**-type variable and then displays the value in that variable. Here is the output of the program in Listing 6-1:

```
Value of objInt1 is 10
Value of variable nNum (= objInt1) is 10
Value of objInt2 is 10
Value of variable nNum (= objInt2) is 10
```

Listing 6-1
The source code for the CLASS3.CPP program.

```cpp
// A C++ program that illustrates a simple class

#include <iostream.h>

class myInt
{
  public:
    // public constructor
    myInt();
    myInt(const myInt& anIntObj);
    void setInt(const int nNewNum);
    int getInt();
    void show(const char* pszMsg);

  protected:
    int m_nInt;
};

myInt::myInt()
{
  m_nInt = 0;
}

myInt::myInt(const myInt& anIntObj)
{
  m_nInt = anIntObj.m_nInt;
}

void myInt::setInt(const int nNewNum)
{
  m_nInt = nNewNum;
}
```

Constructors

Member functions

Data member

```
int myInt::getInt()
{
  return m_nInt;
}

void myInt::show(const char* pszMsg)
{
  cout << pszMsg << m_nInt << "\n";
}

main()
{
  int nNum;

  // create object objInt1 using void constructor
  myInt objInt1;
  objInt1.setInt(10);
  objInt1.show("Value of objInt1 is ");
  nNum = objInt1.getInt();
  cout << "Value of variable nNum (= objInt1) is "
       << nNum << "\n";

  // create object objInt2 using copy constructor
  myInt objInt2(objInt1);
  objInt2.show("Value of objInt2 is ");
  nNum = objInt2.getInt();
  cout << "Value of variable nNum (= objInt2) is "
       << nNum << "\n";

  return 0;
}
```

Listing 6-1 contains the declaration of class **myInt** as I described it earlier. The listing also shows the definitions of the constructors and the member functions, which are located after the class declaration. Notice that the name of each constructor and member function is qualified by the class name. This qualification uses the following syntax:

```
// definition of a constructor
className:className(parameterList)
{
  // statements
}
// definition of a member function
returnType className::memberFunctionName(parameterList)
{
  // statements
}
```

Notice that the definitions of the constructors and member functions of class **myInt** access the data member **m_nInt** without having to pass it as a parameter. This kind of automatic access to data members is a typical privilege that every member function has.

The first constructor simply assigns 0 to the data member **m_nInt**. The second constructor copies the value of the data member **m_nInt** of its parameter **anIntObj** into the data member **m_nInt**.

The member function **setInt** copies the value of the parameter **nNewNum** into the data member **m_nInt**.

The member function **getInt** simply returns the value of the data member **m_nInt**.

The member function **show** displays the value in data member **m_nInt**.

The function **main** declares the local **int**-type variable **nNum** and then declares the object **objInt1** as an instance of class **myInt**. This declaration uses the constructor **myInt()**. The function **main** then performs the following tasks with object **objInt1**:

- Assign the integer 10 to the object **objInt1** by sending that object the C++ message **setInt**. The argument for this message is the integer 10.

- Display the contents of object **objInt1** by sending that object the message **show**. The argument for this message is the string literal "Value in objInt1 is ."

- Copy the value of object **objInt1** into the variable **nNum**. This task sends the C++ message **getInt** to the object **objInt1**. The task assigns the result of the message to the targeted variable.

- Display the value in variable **nNum**

Next, the function **main** declares the object **objInt2** as an instance of class **myInt**. This declaration uses the constructor **myInt (const myInt&)** to create object **objInt2** as a copy of object **objInt1**. The function **main** then performs the following tasks with object **objInt2**:

- Display the contents of object **objInt2** by sending that object the message **show**. The argument for this message is the string literal "Value in objInt2 is ."

- Copy the value of object **objInt2** into the variable **nNum**. This task sends the C++ message **getInt** to the object **objInt2**. The task assigns the result of the message to the targeted variable.

- Display the value in variable **nNum**

This example illustrates the following points:

- The declaration of a class
- The definition of the constructors and member functions of a class
- The creation and manipulation of class instances

C++ allows you to define member functions *inside* the class declaration. Typically, such definitions involve one or two statements. In these cases, the compiler treats the member functions as inline functions. Listing 6-2 shows program CLASS3B.CPP, which is a version of Listing 6-1 that uses inline definitions—the class **myInt** defines the constructors and member functions inside the class declaration. The programs in Listings 6-1 and 6-2 perform the same tasks. The source code for function **main** in both listings is identical.

Listing 6-2
The source code for the CLASS3B.CPP program.

```
// A C++ program that illustrates a simple class
// with inline definitions of member functions

#include <iostream.h>

class myInt
{
  public:
    // public constructor
  myInt() { m_nInt = 0; }
  myInt(const myInt& anIntObj)
    { m_nInt = anIntObj.m_nInt; }
  void setInt(const int nNewNum)
    { m_nInt = nNewNum; }
  int getInt()
    { return m_nInt; }
  void show(const char* pszMsg)
      { cout << pszMsg << m_nInt << "\n"; }

  protected:
    int m_nInt;
};
```

```
main()
{
  int nNum;

  // create object objInt1 using void constructor
  myInt objInt1;
  objInt1.setInt(10);
  objInt1.show("Value in objInt1 is ");
  nNum = objInt1.getInt();
  cout << "Value in variable nNum (= objInt1) is "
       << nNum << "\n";

  // create object objInt2 using copy constructor
  myInt objInt2(objInt1);
  objInt2.show("Value in objInt2 is ");
  nNum = objInt2.getInt();
  cout << "Value in variable nNum (= objInt2) is "
       << nNum << "\n";

  return 0;
}
```

THE CLASS MYPOINT

Let's look at a second example of a class. Listing 6-3 shows the source code for the CLASS4.CPP program, which contains class **myPoint** that models two-dimensional coordinates. The class supports the following operations:

- Setting and querying the x-y coordinates of a point
- Calculating the distance between a point and the origin (0, 0)
- Calculating the distance between two points
- Copying the coordinates of one point into those of another

The program in Listing 6-3 performs these operations using two instances of class **myPoint**. Here is the program output:

```
Object 1 is at (10.5, 45.6)
Object 2 is at (24.15, 132.24)
Distance between object 1 and origin = 46.7933
Distance between object 2 and origin = 134.427
Distance between objects = 87.7087

Object 2 has moved to (10.5, 45.6)
New distance between objects = 0
```

Listing 6-3

The source code for the CLASS4.CPP program.

```cpp
// A C++ program that illustrates a simple class
// that models a two-dimensional coordinate system

#include <iostream.h>
#include <math.h>

inline double sqr(double x)
{ return x * x; }

class myPoint
{
  public:
    myPoint();

    void setXCoord(double fX)
      { m_fX = fX; }
    void setYCoord(double fY)
      { m_fY = fY; }
    void copyCoords(const myPoint& otherPoint);
    double getXCoord()
      { return m_fX; }
    double getYCoord()
      { return m_fY; }
    double getDistance(const myPoint& otherPoint)
      { return sqrt(sqr(m_fX - otherPoint.m_fX) +
                    sqr(m_fY - otherPoint.m_fY)); }
    double getDistanceFromOrigin()
      { return sqrt(sqr(m_fX) + sqr(m_fY)); }

  protected:
    double m_fX;
    double m_fY;
};

myPoint::myPoint()
{
  m_fX = 0.;
  m_fY = 0.;
}

void myPoint::copyCoords(const myPoint& otherPoint)
{
  m_fX = otherPoint.m_fX;
  m_fY = otherPoint.m_fY;
}

main()
{
  myPoint objPt1;
  myPoint objPt2;
```

```
double fX = 10.5;
double fY = 45.6;

// assign coordinates to object objPt1
objPt1.setXCoord(fX);
objPt1.setYCoord(fY);

// assign coordinates to object objPt2
objPt2.setXCoord(2.3 * fX);
objPt2.setYCoord(2.9 * fY);

// show coordinates of object objPt1
cout << "Object 1 is at ("
    << objPt1.getXCoord() << ", "
    << objPt1.getYCoord() << ")\n";

// show coordinates of object objPt2
cout << "Object 2 is at ("
    << objPt2.getXCoord() << ", "
    << objPt2.getYCoord() << ")\n";

// show distance between object objPt1 and origin
cout << "Distance between object 1 and origin = "
    << objPt1.getDistanceFromOrigin() << "\n";

// show distance between object objPt2 and origin
cout << "Distance between object 2 and origin = "
    << objPt2.getDistanceFromOrigin() << "\n";

// show distance between objects objPt1 and objPt2
cout << "Distance between objects = "
    << objPt1.getDistance(objPt2) << "\n\n";

// copy coordinates
objPt2.copyCoords(objPt1);

// show new coordinates of object objPt2
cout << "Object 2 has moved to ("
    << objPt2.getXCoord() << ", "
    << objPt2.getYCoord() << ")\n";

// show new distance between objects objPt1 and objPt2
cout << "New distance between objects = "
    << objPt1.getDistance(objPt2) << "\n";

    return 0;
}
```

Listing 6-3 declares the class **myPoint**. The declaration includes a constructor, member functions, and data members. The class declares the protected **double**-type data members **m_fX** and **m_fY**, which store the coordinates of a point.

The class declares the following inline member functions:

- The member function **setXCoord** assigns a new X coordinate to the data member **m_fX**.

- The member function **setYCoord** assigns a new Y coordinate to the data member **m_fY**.

- The member function **getXCoord** returns a copy of the value in the data member **m_fX**.

- The member function **getYCoord** returns a copy of the value in the data member **m_fY**.

- The member function **getDistance** returns the distance between the coordinates of a class instance and that of the parameter **otherPoint**. This parameter is also an instance of class **myPoint**.

- The member function **getDistanceFromOrigin** returns the distance between the coordinates of a class instance and that of the origin (0, 0).

The listing defines the constructor and member function **copyCoords** outside the class declaration. The constructor systematically assigns the coordinates (0, 0) to the class instances. When I discuss constructors later on in this chapter, I'll show you how to assign nondefault values to data members when you create class instances.

The function **copyCoords** copies the data members **m_fX** and **m_fY** of the **myPoint**-type parameter **otherPoint** to the data members **m_fX** and **m_fY** of a class instance.

The function **main** declares the objects **objPt1** and **objPt2** as instances of class **myPoint**. The function also declares and initializes the **double**-type variables **fX** and **fY**. The function **main** performs the following tasks:

- Assign new coordinates to object **objPt1**. This task involves sending the C++ messages **setXCoord** and **setYCoord** to the object **objPt1**. The arguments for the messages are **fX** and **fY**, respectively.

- Assign new coordinates to object **objPt2**. This task involves sending the C++ messages **setXCoord** and **setYCoord** to the object **objPt2**. The arguments for the messages are the expressions **2.3 * fX** and **2.9 * fY**, respectively.

- Display the coordinates of object **objPt1**. This task involves sending the C++ messages **getXCoord** and **getYCoord** to the object **objPt1**.

- Display the coordinates of object **objPt2**. This task involves sending the C++ messages **getXCoord** and **getYCoord** to the object **objPt2**.

- Display the distance between object **objPt1** and the origin. This task involves sending the C++ message **getDistanceFromOrigin** to the object **objPt1**.

- Display the distance between object **objPt2** and the origin. This task involves sending the C++ message **getDistanceFromOrigin** to the object **objPt2**.

- Display the distance between objects **objPt1** and **objPt2**. This task involves sending the C++ message **getDistance** to the object **objPt1**. The argument for this message is the object **objPt2**.

- Copy the coordinates of object **objPt1** into object **objPt2**. This task involves sending the C++ message **copyCoords** to object **objPt2**. The argument for this message is the object **objPt1**.

- Display the new coordinates of object **objPt2**. This task involves sending the C++ messages **getXCoord** and **getYCoord** to the object **objPt2**.

- Display the new distance between objects **objPt1** and **objPt2**. This task involves sending the C++ message **getDistance** to the object **objPt1**. The argument for this message is the object **objPt2**. Since the two objects have the same coordinates, the distance is 0.

The Sections of a Class

The classes in Listings 6-1 through 6-3 contain protected data members. You may have noticed that in each one of these listings, the function **main** does not directly access the data members of the class instances. Instead, the function relies on the member functions of the class to access the data members.

C++ supports the public, protected, and private sections to enforce different access privileges to class instances and class descendants. Using protected and private members allows the class to prevent class instances from accessing critical members. Such members include member functions that perform low-level operations (such as special memory management) to support other high-level member functions. As for accessing data members, the general rule is to declare them either protected or private. Using this rule means that a class must provide member functions to set or query the values in data members. The protected and private members are equally inaccessible to class instances. The difference between protected and private members affects how they are accessed by the member functions of descendant classes. More about this topic appears in Chapter 14, "Class Hierarchies."

C++ has the following rules for declaring and accessing the members of a class:

1. The public, protected, and private sections may appear in any sequence in a class declaration. The preferred style is to list the public, protected, and private sections in that order.

2. The default access level of a member is private.

3. The class declaration may contain multiple public, protected, and private sections.

4. A class declaration need not contain all three sections.

5. The instances of a class cannot access the protected and private members.

6. The access rules do not affect the member functions of the class itself.

7. All member functions of a class have automatic access to all of the data members of that class.

Hiding Data Members

C++ gurus stress the practice of making data members protected or private. Following this practice permits you to protect class instances from unauthorized or inappropriate access to data members.

Let's look at an example of a class that has protected data members and member functions. Listing 6-4 shows the source code for the CLASS5.CPP program, which illustrates a class with several protected members. The program contains a class that implements a number-guessing game. To play the game, *you* think of a secret number between 1 and 1000. The program makes several guesses for your secret number. Each time, the program displays a guess and requests that you enter an integer hint code. The program uses the codes 1, 0, and –1 if its last guess is higher than, matches, or is lower than the secret number, respectively. The guessing-game class uses a binary search to guess your secret number. Here is a sample session with the program in Listing 6-4, where my secret number is 550 (user input is underlilned):

```
Guess a number between 1 and 1000
At hint prompt enter one of the following:
 1 when my guess is high
 0 when my guess is correct
-1 when my guess is low

Guess is 500
Enter hint value : -1
Guess is 750
Enter hint value : 1
Guess is 625
Enter hint value : 1
Guess is 562
Enter hint value : 1
Guess is 531
Enter hint value : -1
Guess is 546
Enter hint value : -1
Guess is 554
Enter hint value : 1
Guess is 550
Enter hint value : 0
End of game!
```

Listing 6-4
The source code for the CLASS5.CPP program.

```
// A C++ program that illustrates a class with
// several protected member functions

#include <iostream.h>

const int MIN_NUM = 1;
```

```cpp
const int MAX_NUM = 1000;

class guessGame
{
  public:
    void play();

    protected:
      int m_nHi;
      int m_nLo;
      int m_nMedian;
      int m_nHint;

      void startGame();
      void showGuess();
      int playMore();

};

void guessGame::play()
{
  startGame();
  showGuess();
  while (playMore())
    showGuess();
}

void guessGame::startGame()
{
  cout << "Guess a number between " << MIN_NUM
       << " and " << MAX_NUM << "\n";
  cout << "At hint prompt enter one of the following:\n"
       << " 1 when my guess is high\n"
       << " 0 when my guess is correct\n"
       << "-1 when my guess is low\n\n";
  m_nLo = MIN_NUM;
  m_nHi = MAX_NUM;
  m_nMedian = (m_nLo + m_nHi) / 2;
}

void guessGame::showGuess()
{
  cout << "Guess is " << m_nMedian << "\n";
}


int guessGame::playMore()
{
  cout << "Enter hint value : ";
  cin >> m_nHint;
```

Protected data members

Protected member functions

```
    if (m_nHint == 0) {
      cout << "End of game!\n";
      return 0;
    }
    else if (m_nHint > 0)
      // set upper limit to last guess
      m_nHi = m_nMedian;
    else
      // set lower limit to last guess
      m_nLo = m_nMedian;

    // get new guess
    m_nMedian = (m_nLo + m_nHi) / 2;

    // double check player is not cheeting!
    if (m_nMedian == m_nLo || m_nMedian == m_nHi) {
      cout << "Your secret number must be " << m_nMedian << "\n";
      return 0;
    }
    else
      return 1;
  }


main()
{
  guessGame game;

  game.play();

  return 0;
}
```

Listing 6-5 declares the global constants MIN_NUM and MAX_NUM, which define the range of integers that contains the secret number. The listing then declares class guessGame, which contains the public member function play and several protected data members and member functions.

The class guessGame declares the following protected data members:

- The int-type members m_nLo and m_nHi, which store the current range of integers containing the secret number that you have thought of

- The int-type member m_nMedian, which contains the current guess for the secret number

- The int-type member m_nHint, which stores the hint code that you enter

The class declares the following protected member functions:

- The member function **startGame** displays the initial message, assigns the initial values to data members **m_nLo** and **m_nHi**, and calculates the first guess for the secret number.
- The member function **showGuess** displays the guess for the secret number.
- The member function **playMore** returns 1 if the class instance has not guessed the secret number and yields 0 otherwise. This function prompts you to enter the hint code to guide its guesses.

The class **guessGame** declares the public member function **play** to invoke these member functions. The function first invokes the member functions **startGame** and **showGuess** to display the greeting messages and show the first guess. It then uses a **while** loop to obtain the hint codes from you and to make more guesses. The condition of the **while** loop is the result of the member function **playMore**. The **while** loop contains the statement that invokes the member function **showGuess** to display the next guess.

The function **main** declares the object **game** as an instance of class **guessGame**. The function merely sends the C++ message **play** to the object **game** to play the game.

This example shows the class **guessGame**, which contains several protected member functions that perform different tasks. The class instance can only receive the C++ message **play**, because the member function **play** is the only public member function in the class.

CONSTRUCTORS

Constructors are special members that automatically initialize class instances. When you create a class instance, the program automatically invokes the constructor for that class. The general syntax for declaring a constructor in a class is:

```
class className
{
  public:
    // void constructor
```

```
    className();
    // copy constructor
    className(className& classNameObject);
    // additional constructor
    className(parameterList);
    // other members

};
```

C++ has the following rules about declaring and using constructors:

1. The name of the constructor must match the name of its class.

2. A constructor may have a parameter list to help fine-tune the creation of class instances.

3. A class may have multiple constructors to allow its instances to be initialized differently.

4. A constructor with no parameters (or with a parameter list that has default arguments for each parameter) is called the *void* or *default* constructor.

5. A constructor with one parameter that has the class type is called the *copy* constructor.

6. The declaration of an array of instances requires the use of the default constructor.

7. If the class does not declare a constructor, C++ creates a default constructor for that class.

8. C++ invokes a constructor when you create a class instance. The arguments of that instance select the appropriate constructor, if the class declares multiple constructors.

Here are examples of constructors:

```
class myComplex
{
 public:
  // constructors
  myComplex();
  myComplex(myComplex& complexObj);
  myComplex(double fReal, double fImag);
```

```
  // other members

 protected:
  double m_fReal;
  double m_fImag;

  // other members
};
```

The above example declares the class **myComplex**. The declaration has three constructors. The first one is the void constructor, since it has no parameters. The second constructor is the copy constructor, since it uses another class instance to initialize a new one. The third constructor is an additional constructor used to initialize the class instances with two **double**-type arguments.

Let me present an example of a class that uses multiple constructors to support different ways to initialize class instances. Listing 6-5 contains the source code for the CLASS6.CPP program, which illustrates a class with several constructors. The listing contains a new version of the class **myPoint**. This version contains three constructors: the default constructor, the copy constructor, and an additional constructor. The program creates three instances using each of the three constructors. The program then manipulates these instances using the member functions of the class. Here is a sample session with the program in Listing 6-5:

```
Object 1 is at (10.5, 45.6)
Object 2 is at (24.15, 132.24)
Object 3 is at (24.15, 132.24)
Distance between object 1 and origin = 46.7933
Distance between object 2 and origin = 134.427
Distance between object 3 and origin = 134.427
Distance between objects 1 and 2 = 87.7087
Distance between objects 1 and 3 = 87.7087
```

Listing 6-5
The source code for the CLASS6.CPP program.

```
// A C++ program that illustrates a class
// that uses multiple constructors

#include <iostream.h>
#include <math.h>

inline double sqr(double x)
{ return x * x; }
```

```
class myPoint
{
  public:
    myPoint();
    myPoint(const myPoint& otherPoint)
      { copyCoords(otherPoint); }
    myPoint(double fX, double fY);

    void setXCoord(double fX)
      { m_fX = fX; }
    void setYCoord(double fY)
      { m_fY = fY; }
    void copyCoords(const myPoint& otherPoint);
    double getXCoord()
      { return m_fX; }
    double getYCoord()
      { return m_fY; }
    double getDistance(const myPoint& otherPoint)
      { return sqrt(sqr(m_fX - otherPoint.m_fX) +
                    sqr(m_fY - otherPoint.m_fY)); }
    double getDistanceFromOrigin()
      { return sqrt(sqr(m_fX) + sqr(m_fY)); }

  protected:
    double m_fX;
    double m_fY;
};

myPoint::myPoint()
{
  m_fX = 0.;
  m_fY = 0.;
}

myPoint::myPoint(double fX, double fY)
{
  m_fX = fX;
  m_fY = fY;
}

void myPoint::copyCoords(const myPoint& otherPoint)
{
  m_fX = otherPoint.m_fX;
  m_fY = otherPoint.m_fY;
}

main()
{
  double fX = 10.5;
  double fY = 45.6;
  myPoint objPt1;
  myPoint objPt2(2.3 * fX, 2.9 * fY);
```

```
myPoint objPt3(objPt2);

// assign coordinates to object objPt1
objPt1.setXCoord(fX);
objPt1.setYCoord(fY);

// show coordinates of object objPt1
cout << "Object 1 is at ("
    << objPt1.getXCoord() << ", "
    << objPt1.getYCoord() << ")\n";

// show coordinates of object objPt2
cout << "Object 2 is at ("
    << objPt2.getXCoord() << ", "
    << objPt2.getYCoord() << ")\n";

// show coordinates of object objPt3
cout << "Object 3 is at ("
    << objPt3.getXCoord() << ", "
    << objPt3.getYCoord() << ")\n";

// show distance between object objPt1 and origin
cout << "Distance between object 1 and origin = "
    << objPt1.getDistanceFromOrigin() << "\n";

// show distance between object objPt2 and origin
cout << "Distance between object 2 and origin = "
    << objPt2.getDistanceFromOrigin() << "\n";

// show distance between object objPt3 and origin
cout << "Distance between object 3 and origin = "
    << objPt3.getDistanceFromOrigin() << "\n";

// show distance between objects objPt1 and objPt2
cout << "Distance between objects 1 and 2 = "
    << objPt1.getDistance(objPt2) << "\n";

// show distance between objects objPt1 and objPt3
cout << "Distance between objects 1 and 3 = "
    << objPt1.getDistance(objPt3) << "\n\n";

return 0;
}
```

The highlight of Listing 6-5 is the three constructors of class **myPoint**:

- The default constructor assigns zeros to the data members **m_fX** and **m_fY**.

- The copy constructor copies the values in the data members of parameter **otherPoint** to their counterparts in the initialized instance.

- The constructor **myPoint(double, double)** initializes the data members **m_fX** and **m_fY** using the arguments of parameters **fX** and **fY**, respectively.

The function **main** declares and initializes the local variables **fX** and **fY**. The function also declares the following instances of class **myPoint**:

- The object **objPt1**. The runtime system initializes this object using the void constructor, since the object's declaration has no parameters.

- The object **objPt2**. The runtime system initializes this object using the constructor **myPoint(double, double)**, since the declaration uses two **double**-type expressions.

- The object **objPt3**. The runtime system initializes this object using the copy constructor, because the argument of the declaration is the class instance **objPt2**.

The function **main** displays the coordinates of the three declared objects, as well as their distances from the origin and from each other.

CODING NOTES

Constructors Are Invoked Automatically

C++ automatically invokes a constructor for the class instance being created. This automatic invocation is foreign to such common programming languages as BASIC, Pascal, FORTRAN, and even C!

CODING
NOTES

Using Constructors for Type Conversion

You can use a constructor to convert a data type into one compatible with the class associated with the constructor. Here is an example:

```
class myDouble
{
  public:
    myDouble(double fX = 0)
      { m_fX = fX; }
    // other constructors
    // other members
  protected:
    double m_fX;
    // other members
};
main()
{
  myDouble Dbl;
  double fA = 3.124;
  // other declarations
  Dbl = myDouble(fA);
  // other statements
  return 0;
}
```

The function **main** uses the constructor of class **myDouble** to convert a **double**-type value (in variable **fA**) into a **myDouble**-type object.

Let's look at a program that illustrates the concept briefly discussed in the sidebar *Using Constructors for Type Conversion*. Listing 6-6 contains the source code for the CLASS7.CPP program, which illustrates using a constructor for type conversion. The program implements a special version of the class **myPoint**. It creates an instance of this class and then displays its coordinates, distance from the origin, and distance from the point (10, 10). Here is the output of the program in Listing 6-6:

```
Object 1 is at (10.5, 45.6)
Distance between object 1 and origin = 46.7933
Distance between objects 1 and (10, 10) = 35.6035
```

Listing 6-6

The source code for the CLASS7.CPP program.

```cpp
// A C++ program that illustrates a class
// that uses constructors for data conversion

#include <iostream.h>
#include <math.h>

inline double sqr(double x)
{ return x * x; }

class myPoint
{
  public:
    myPoint(double fX = 0., double fY = 0.);

    void setXCoord(double fX)
      { m_fX = fX; }
    void setYCoord(double fY)
      { m_fY = fY; }
    double getXCoord()
      { return m_fX; }
    double getYCoord()
      { return m_fY; }
    double getDistance(const myPoint& otherPoint)
      { return sqrt(sqr(m_fX - otherPoint.m_fX) +
                    sqr(m_fY - otherPoint.m_fY)); }
    double getDistanceFromOrigin()
      { return sqrt(sqr(m_fX) + sqr(m_fY)); }

  protected:
    double m_fX;
    double m_fY;
};

myPoint::myPoint(double fX, double fY)
{
  m_fX = fX;
  m_fY = fY;
}

main()
{
  double fX = 10.5;
  double fY = 45.6;
  myPoint objPt1(fX, fY);

  // show coordinates of object objPt1
  cout << "Object 1 is at ("
       << objPt1.getXCoord() << ", "
       << objPt1.getYCoord() << ")\n";
```

```
// show distance between object objPt1 and origin
cout << "Distance between object 1 and origin = "
     << objPt1.getDistanceFromOrigin() << "\n";

fX = 10.;
fY = 10.;
// show distance between objects objPt1 and (fX, fY)
cout << "Distance between objects 1 and ("
     << fX << ", " << fY << ") = "
     << objPt1.getDistance(myPoint(fX, fY)) << "\n";

return 0;
}
```

Listing 6-6 declares the class **myPoint** with a single constructor that has the two **double**-type parameter **fX** and **fY** with the default arguments 0 and 0, respectively. Using the two default arguments with the constructor makes it work as the default constructor.

The class **myPoint** in Listing 6-6 is a subset of the version in Listing 6-5. The version in Listing 6-6 declares the public member functions **setXCoord**, **setYCoord**, **getXCoord**, **getYCoord**, **getDistance**, and **getDistanceFromOrigin**. The class also declares the protected data members **m_fX** and **m_fY**.

The function **main** declares and initializes the **double**-type variables **fX** and **fY**. The function also declares the object **objPt1** and initializes it using the variables **fX** and **fY**. The function **main** then performs the following tasks:

- Display the coordinates of object **objPt1**. This task involves sending the C++ messages **getXCoord** and **getYCoord** to the object **objPt1**.

- Display the distance between object **objPt1** and the origin. This task involves sending the C++ message **getDistanceFromOrigin** to the object **objPt1**.

- Assign the value 10 to each of the variables **fX** and **fY**

- Display the distance between objects **objPt1** and the coordinates (**fX**, **fY**). This task involves sending the C++ message **getDistance** to the object **objPt1**. The argument for this message is the expression **myPoint(fX, fY)**. This expression converts the values in variables **fX** and **fY** into a temporary instance of class **myPoint** and then passes that instance as the argument of the message. This task shows how the class constructor converts data types.

DESTRUCTORS

Destructors are special member functions that uninitialize class instances when they reach the end of their scope. The general syntax for declaring a destructor in a class is:

```
class className
{
  public:
    // void constructor
    className();
    // other constructors
    // destructor
    ~className();
    // other members

};
```

C++ has the following rules about declaring and using destructors:

1. The name of the destructor must match the name of its class but must start with the tilde character ~.

2. A destructor has no parameter list.

3. A destructor has no return type.

4. A class has only one destructor.

5. If the class does not declare a destructor, C++ creates a default destructor for that class.

6. C++ automatically invokes a destructor when a class instance reaches the end if its scope.

You need to declare a destructor to perform cleanup operations for the class instances. Here are examples for such cleanup operations:

■ The class uses a constructor to create dynamic data. The destructor removes the memory space occupied by the data.

■ The class constructor opens a file for input or output. The destructor closes that file.

■ The destructor emits a message allowing you to trace the removal of class instances.

CODING NOTES

Destructors Are Invoked Automatically

C++ automatically invokes a destructor when a class instance reaches the end of its scope. This automatic invocation is unknown in common programming languages such as BASIC, Pascal, FORTRAN, and even C!

Let me present an example of a simple class that uses a destructor. Listing 6-7 shows the source code for the CLASS8.CPP. The program declares a class with a constructor and a destructor. The class basically stores long integers. To make the program more interesting, I chose to associate a name with each class instance to trace the creation and destruction of the instances. The constructor stores and displays the instance name, allowing the program to show you the names of the objects it creates. The destructor displays the name of the instance before the runtime system removes it, allowing the program to show you the names of the objects it destroys. The output of the constructor and destructor permit you to trace the lifespan of the object, so to speak. The program creates various instances of the class using nested blocks. Consequently, the runtime system does not sequentially remove all of the class instances, since some instances have more limited scopes than others. Here is the output of the program in Listing 6-7:

```
Creating instance obj1
obj1 stores 100
Creating instance obj2
obj2 stores 200
Creating instance obj3
Creating instance obj4
obj3 stores 300
obj4 stores 400
Removing instance obj4
Removing instance obj3
Creating instance obj5
Creating instance obj6
obj5 stores 500
obj6 stores 600
Removing instance obj6
Removing instance obj5
Removing instance obj2
Removing instance obj1
```

Listing 6-7

The source code for the CLASS8.CPP program.

```cpp
// A C++ program that illustrates a class destructor

#include <iostream.h>
#include <string.h>

class myObject
{
  public:
    myObject(const char* pszName, const long lValue = 0);
    ~myObject();
    void setValue(const long lNewValue = 0)
      { m_lVal = lNewValue; }
    long getValue()
      { return m_lVal; }

  protected:
    long m_lVal;
    char m_cName[30];
};

myObject::myObject(const char* pszName, const long lValue)
{
  // copy the object name to member m_cName
  strcpy(m_cName, pszName);
  cout << "Creating instance " << m_cName << "\n";
  m_lVal = lValue;
}

myObject::~myObject()
{
  cout << "Removing instance " << m_cName << "\n";
}

main()
{
  myObject obj1("obj1", 100);

  cout << "obj1 stores " << obj1.getValue() << "\n";

  { // block # 1
    myObject obj2("obj2", 200);

    cout << "obj2 stores " << obj2.getValue() << "\n";

    {  // block # 2
      myObject obj3("obj3", 300);
      myObject obj4("obj4", 400);
```

```
        cout << "obj3 stores " << obj3.getValue() << "\n";
        cout << "obj4 stores " << obj4.getValue() << "\n";
    }

    { // block # 3
      myObject obj5("obj5", 500);
      myObject obj6("obj6", 600);

      cout << "obj5 stores " << obj5.getValue() << "\n";
      cout << "obj6 stores " << obj6.getValue() << "\n";
    }
  }

  return 0;
}
```

Listing 6-7 declares the class **myObject**, which has public and protected members. The protected members are:

- The **long**-type data member **m_lVal**, which stores the long integer value of a class instance
- The **char**-type array member **m_cName**, which stores the name of the instance. You may remember from Chapter 1 that C++ treats strings as arrays of characters.

The class declares the following public members:

- The constructor, which has two parameters, **pszName** and **lValue**. The first parameter passes the name of the instance. The second parameter passes the initial long integer value.
- The destructor, which displays the name of the instance
- The member function **setValue**, which assigns a new value to the data member **m_lVal**
- The member function **getValue**, which obtains the value in data member **m_lVal**

The definition of the constructor uses the function **strcpy** (which is prototyped in file STRING.H) to copy the string passed by parameter **pszName** to the data member **m_cName**. The constructor displays the name of the instance and then assigns the value of parameter **lValue** to the data member **m_lVal**.

The definition of the destructor merely displays a message telling you that the runtime system is removing a class instance. The message states the instance's name using the characters in data member m_cName.

The function main creates six instances of class myObject. The function assigns a name and a value to each class instance and then displays the values in the instances. It creates the instance obj1 in the main block. The nested block #1 declares the instance obj2 and contains two other nested blocks. The nested block #2 declares the instances obj3 and obj4. When this block ends, the function main declares another nested block #3 (which is still inside block #1). The nested block #3 declares the instances obj5 an obj6. The program displays the constructor's output when the function main creates a class instance.

When program execution reaches the end of a nested block or the main block, the runtime system invokes the destructor for the instances whose scope is limited to the terminating block. The program displays the destructor's output when the runtime system removes a class instance.

If you examine the statements in function main and look at the program output, you can trace the creation and removal of each of the six class instances.

USING CONST WITH MEMBER FUNCTIONS

In the last chapter you learned that you can prevent a function from altering the argument of a parameter by declaring that parameter with the keyword const. How can you prevent a member function from altering the values of any data member? The answer lies in placing the keyword const after the parameter list. Here is the general syntax for using the keyword const with a member function:

```
returnType memberFunctionName(parameterList) const;
```

You may ask "Why use the const declaration?" Using the keyword const tells the C++ compiler that the definition of the associated member function cannot alter the value of a data member. This ensures that the member function does not *fiddle around*, so to speak, with the values of data members. This feature is useful especially when the class declaration and definition involve multiple programmers working as a team. Typically, the lead programmer declares the class and then asks the other programmers in the team to code the definitions of the member functions. The lead programmer can specify that certain member functions cannot alter the values of the data members in the class. If a programmer attempts to do otherwise, the C++ compiler flags an error during source code compilation.

C++ Structures as Public Classes

Like most popular programming languages, C++ enables you to define structures or records that contain logically grouped fields. C++ supports defining structures using the keyword struct (more about this in Chapter 12, "User-Defined Types"). C++ has inherited these structures from its parent language, C. However, C++ has another use for structures: They are equivalent to classes with default public members (compared to the default private members of formal classes). Thus structures may contain public, protected, and private members, and they may likewise declare constructors, destructors, member functions, and data members. The general syntax for declaring a class using the keyword struct is:

```
struct className
{
    [public:
   // public constructors
   // public destructor
   // public data members
   // public member functions
    ]

    [protected:
   // protected constructors
   // protected destructor
   // protected data members
   // protected member functions
    ]

    [private:
   // private constructors
   // private destructor
   // private data members
   // private member functions
    ]
};
```

C

The New Role of struct

Keep in mind that the **struct** keyword in C++ declares a special kind of class with default public members. A C++ structure with only data members is compatible with a C structure.

To illustrate that C++ structures are really public classes, I present Listing 6-8, which shows the source code of the STRUCT2.CPP program. I created this listing by modifying the source code of program CLASS8.CPP (in Listing 6-7). I replaced the keyword **class** with the keyword **struct**. Moreover, I removed the keyword **public**, to illustrate that members of a C++ structure are public by default. The result is a class defined using the keyword **struct** with a constructor, destructor, member functions, and data members. The programs in Listings 6-7 and 6-8 perform the same tasks. The outputs of these programs are identical.

Listing 6-8
The source code for the STRUCT2.CPP program, which illustrates declaring classes with the keyword struct.

```
// A C++ program that illustrates structures as classes

#include <iostream.h>
#include <string.h>                                    Structure

struct myObject
{
    myObject(const char* pszName, const long lValue = 0);   Public members
    ~myObject();
    void setValue(const long lNewValue = 0)
      { m_lVal = lNewValue; }
    long getValue()
      { return m_lVal; }

  protected:
    long m_lVal;
    char m_cName[30];
};

myObject::myObject(const char* pszName, const long lValue)
{
```

```
      // copy the object name to member m_cName
      strcpy(m_cName, pszName);
      cout << "Creating instance " << m_cName << "\n";
      m_lVal = lValue;
   }

   myObject::~myObject()
   {
      cout << "Removing instance " << m_cName << "\n";
   }

   main()
   {
      myObject obj1("obj1", 100);

      cout << "obj1 stores " << obj1.getValue() << "\n";

      { // block # 1
        myObject obj2("obj2", 200);

        cout << "obj2 stores " << obj2.getValue() << "\n";

        {  // block # 2
          myObject obj3("obj3", 300);
          myObject obj4("obj4", 400);

          cout << "obj3 stores " << obj3.getValue() << "\n";
          cout << "obj4 stores " << obj4.getValue() << "\n";
        }

        { // block # 3
          myObject obj5("obj5", 500);
          myObject obj6("obj6", 600);

          cout << "obj5 stores " << obj5.getValue() << "\n";
          cout << "obj6 stores " << obj6.getValue() << "\n";
        }
      }

      return 0;
   }
```

Summary

This chapter introduced you to the basics of object-oriented programming and presented C++ classes. The chapter discussed classes and objects, messages and methods, inheritance, and polymorphism. These topics form the cornerstone of object-oriented programming. You also learned how to declare base classes in C++ and how to create instances of these classes. The chapter also discussed using constructors and destructors to initialize and uninitialize class instances, respectively.

After this extensive look at objects and C++ classes, the next chapter focuses on a more dynamic aspect of C++ that is new to the language, managing stream input and output. You will learn, for instance, how to use the stream I/O objects to perform console I/O, as well as how to format stream output.

7 Managing Input and Output

C++ does not define console input and output statements as part of the language. Instead the language relies on libraries to perform console I/O. This chapter looks at managing input and output in C++ using the stream libraries. You will learn about formatted stream output, stream input, the **printf** function, and how to declare the operator **<<** for user-defined classes.

Formatted Stream Output

C++ offers a set of library files to support stream I/O. The basic libraries that handle console I/O use the header file IOSTREAM.H. This header file declares classes such as **ios**, **istream**, **ostream**, and **iostream**.

The **ios** stream class supports the lowest level of stream I/O. The classes **istream** and **ostream** are descendants of class **ios** and support input and output stream objects, respectively. The class **iostream** is a descendant of both classes **istream** and **ostream** and combines the operations of both parent classes.

The next subsections discuss the relevant classes, objects, operators, and member functions of the stream classes that support console I/O. Chapter 15, "Basic Stream File I/O," discusses how the C++ stream library supports stream file I/O.

BASIC

C++ and I/O Libraries

One of the main differences between BASIC and C++ is that C++ does not offer console and file I/O statements as part of the language. Rather, C++ (like its parent language C) depends on libraries to carry out console and file I/O. Thus, you can use both C++ and C I/O libraries in your C++ programs.

PASCAL

C++ and I/O Libraries

One of the major contrasts between Pascal and C++ is that C++ does not define console and file I/O statements as part of the language. Rather, C++ (like its parent language C) depends on libraries to perform console and file I/O. Thus, you may employ C++ and C I/O libraries in your C++ programs.

C

C++ Stream Libraries

C++ has stream libraries that are more flexible than the C I/O libraries. The main difference between C and C++ I/O libraries is that the C++ stream libraries are based on classes and work in a more integrated manner with user-defined classes.

STANDARD STREAM OBJECTS

C++ offers four standard streams, as shown in Table 7-1. These console objects support basic character-based input and output. This book relies on these console objects to present you with examples that run on different platforms. The C++ stream libraries support these objects. The objects **cout**, **cin**, and **cerr** are equivalent to the standard streams **stdout**, **stdin**, and **stderr** in C. I mention this correspondence because the C I/O libraries are also available to C++ programs.

Table 7-1
The Standard C++ Streams

Stream Object	Purpose
cout	Console output stream
cin	Console input stream
cerr	Console error stream (unbuffered)
clog	Console error stream (buffered)

STREAM OUTPUT OPERATORS

C++ supports the extractor operator <<, which allows the objects **cout**, **cerr**, and **clog** to output data. The stream classes define overloaded versions of the operator << to support the predefined data types that represent characters, integers, and floating-point numbers. In addition, the operator supports string literals and arrays of characters that store ASCIIZ strings.

Here are examples of using the extractor operator << with the objects **cout**, **cerr**, and **clog**:

```
cout << "Greetings everyone";
cerr << "Invalid input";
clog << "Bad filename";
```

You can chain the output using multiple << operators, as shown below:

```
cout << "Greetings " << "everyone!"
     << " How are" << " you?" << '\n';
```

This code snippet displays the string "Greetings everyone! How are you?" followed by a newline. Speaking of newlines, you may have wondered about the '\n' characters in previous programs. The '\n' character represents the newline character and is one of the special escape characters in C and C++. Table 7-2 shows the C and C++ escape characters.

Table 7-2

The Escape Characters

Character	Decimal Value	Hexadecimal Value	Comment
\a	7	0x07	Bell
\b	8	0x08	Backspace
\f	12	0x0C	Formfeed
\n	10	0x0A	Newline
\r	13	0x0D	Carriage return
\t	9	0x09	Horizontal tab
\v	11	0x0B	Vertical tab
\\	92	0x5C	Backslash
\'	44	0x2C	Apostrophe or single quote
\"	34	0x22	Double quote
\?	63	0x3F	Question mark
000			1 to 3 digits for an octal value
\X*hhh* and \x*hhh*			Hexadecimal value

THE IOS CLASS

The class **ios** declares enumerated values and member functions that fine-tune output. Table 7-3 lists the member functions of class **ios** that support console stream output. The next subsections discuss these member functions.

Table 7-3

The Member Functions of Class ios That Support Console Stream Output

Member Function	Purpose
flags	Sets or reads format flags.
setf	Sets format flags.
unsetf	Resets format flags.
width	Sets the output width.
fill	Sets or reads the padding character.
precision	Sets or reads the precision.

The Member Function flags

The member function **flags** sets and reads the format flags. There
are two overloaded versions of member function **flags**; they have the
following declarations:

```
long flags() const;
long flags(long lFlags);
```

The first version of member function **flags** returns the combined
formatting flags. The second version sets a new combination of the
formatting flags and yields the current formatting flags combination. The
parameter **lFlags** specifies the new format flags. Table 7-4 lists the format
flag settings of member function **flags**. The argument for parameter **lFlags**
may combine these settings using the bitwise-OR operator |.

Table 7-4

The Settings of Parameter lFlags for Member Function flags

Setting	Purpose
ios::dec	Formats numeric output as decimal numbers. This is the default numeric base.
ios::fixed	Displays floating-point values using the fixed form.
ios::hex	Formats numeric output as hexadecimal (base 16) numbers.
ios::internal	Adds fill characters right after the leading base of a sign character or characters.
ios::left	Aligns output to the left (uses a fill character to pad output).
ios::oct	Formats numeric output as octal (base 8) numbers.
ios::right	Aligns output to the right (uses a fill character to pad output). This is the default alignment setting.
ios::scientific	Displays floating-point values using scientific notation.
ios::showbase	Prefixes output with the base indicator (0 for octal, 0x for hexadecimal).
ios::showpoint	Formats floating-point values with decimal point and trailing zeros (based on the setting for precision).

continued

Table 7-4 (continued)

Setting	Purpose
ios::showpos	Displays the + sign with positive numbers.
ios::skipws	Skips input whitespace characters.
ios::stdio	Flushes stdio and sdterr after each insertion.
ios::unitbuf	Flushes the output stream after each insertion.
ios::uppercase	Displays hexadecimal values using uppercase characters.

Here are examples of using the formatting flags shown in Table 7-4:

```
// example 1
cout.flags(ios::hex | ios::uppercase);
cout << 15 << "\n"; // displays F
// example 2
cout.flags(ios::oct | ios::showbase);
cout << 8 << "\n";  // displays 010
// example 3
cout.flags(ios::hex | ios::uppercase | ios::showbase);
cout << 15 << "\n"; // displays 0xF
```

The first example sets the **hex** and **uppercase** flags to display the integer 15 as a hexadecimal number using uppercase characters to show the hexadecimal digit F. The second example sets the **oct** and **showbase** flags to display the integer 8 as the octal number 010. The output shows the base indicator 0. The third example sets the **hex**, **uppercase**, and **showbase** flags to display the integer 15 as a hexadecimal number 0xF. The output shows the base indicator 0x and the uppercase hexadecimal digit F.

Let's look at a programming example. Listing 7-1 shows the source code for the IO1.CPP program, which illustrates the member function **ios::flags**. The program performs the following tasks:

- Display the integer 16 in decimal, hexadecimal, and octal formats
- Display the number 355.113 using scientific and then fixed formats
- Display the current base for integer output

Here is the output of the program in Listing 7-1:

```
16 (base 10) = 0x10 (base 16) = 020 (base 8)
Floating-point number is +3.551130e+002
Floating-point number is +355.113000
Integer output uses base 8
```

Listing 7-1
The source code for the IO1.CPP program.

```
// A C++ program that illustrates
// the member function ios::flags

#include <iostream.h>

main()
{
  int nNum = 16;
  double fX = 355.113;
  long lFlags;

  cout << nNum << " (base 10) = ";
  cout.flags(ios::hex | ios::showbase);
  cout << nNum << " (base 16) = ";
  cout.flags(ios::oct | ios::showbase);
  cout << nNum << " (base 8)\n";

  cout.flags(ios::scientific | ios::showpos);
  cout << "Floating-point number is " << fX << "\n";

  cout.flags(ios::fixed | ios::showpos);
  cout << "Floating-point number is " << fX << "\n";

  lFlags = cout.flags(); // get flags
  if (lFlags & ios::dec)
    cout << "Integer output uses base 10\n";
  else if (lFlags & ios::hex)
    cout << "Integer output uses base 16\n";
  else
    cout << "Integer output uses base 8\n";

  return 0;
}
```

Listing 7-1 declares the function **main**, which tests the member function ios::**flags**. The function declares and initializes the **int**-type variable **nNum** and the **double**-type variable **fX**. The function also declares the **long**-type variable **lFlags**. The function **main** then performs the following tasks:

- Display the value in variable **nNum** using the default decimal base

- Set the format flags to display hexadecimal numbers that include the base indicator. This task sends the C++ message **flags** to object **cout**. The argument for this message is the expression ios::hex | ios::showbase.

- Display the value in variable **nNum** using the hexadecimal base

- Set the format flags to display octal numbers that include the base indicator. This task sends the C++ message **flags** to object **cout**. The argument for this message is the expression ios::oct | ios::showbase.

- Display the value in variable **nNum** using the octal base

- Sets the format to display floating-point numbers using the scientific format with the sign indicator. This task sends the C++ message **flags** to the object **cout**. The argument for this message is the expression ios::scientific | ios::showpos.

- Display the value in variable **fX** in scientific format

- Set the format to display floating-point numbers using the fixed format with the sign indicator. This task sends the C++ message **flags** to the object **cout**. The argument for this message is the expression ios::fixed | ios::showpos.

- Obtain the current format flags by sending the C++ message **flags** to object **cout**. This task stores the format flags in variable **lFlags**.

- Use an **if** statement to determine the numeric base of the flags stored in variable **lFlags**. The **if** clause uses the expression **lFlags & ios::dec** to determine if the decimal number flag is set. The **if else** clause uses the expression **lFlags & ios::hex** to determine if the hexadecimal number flag is set.

The Member Function setf

The member function **setf** sets the format flags. The stream library declares two versions of the overloaded member function **setf**. One version is masked, and the other is nonmasked. The nonmasked version of function **setf** handles format flags that have only one of two settings: *on* or *off.* The declaration of the nonmasked form is:

```
long setf(long lFlags);
```

The parameter **lFlags** specifies the combination of the format flags that are set on or off. The member function returns the current format settings. Table 7-5 shows the settings of parameter **lFlags** for the nonmasked version of member function **setf**.

Table 7-5
The Settings of Parameter **lFlags** *for the Nonmasked Version of Member Function* **setf**

Setting	Purpose
ios::showbase	Prefixes output with the base indicator (0 for octal, 0x for hexadecimal).
ios::showpoint	Formats floating-point values with a decimal point and trailing zeros (based on the setting of precision).
ios::showpos	Displays the + sign with positive numbers.
ios::skipws	Skips input whitespace characters.
ios::stdio	Flushes stdio and sdterr after each insertion.
ios::unitbuf	Flushes the output stream after each insertion.
ios::uppercase	Displays hexadecimal values using uppercase characters.

The masked version of member function **setf** handles format flags that have more than two settings. The **setf** member function has the following declaration:

```
long setf(long lFlags, long lMask);
```

The parameter **lFlags** specifies the combination of the format flags. The parameter **lMask** specifies the mask that corresponds to the format flags. The member function **setf** returns the current format settings. Table 7-6 shows the settings of parameter **lFlags** for the masked version of member function **setf**.

Table 7-6

The Settings of Parameter lFlags for the Masked Version of Member Function setf

Setting	Purpose
ios::dec	Formats numeric output as decimal numbers. This is the default numeric base.
ios::fixed	Displays floating-point values using the fixed form.
ios::hex	Formats numeric output as hexadecimal (base 16) numbers.
ios::internal	Adds fill characters right after the leading base of sign character(s).
ios::left	Aligns output to the left (uses fill character to pad output).
ios::oct	Formats numeric output as octal (base 8) numbers.
ios::right	Aligns output to the right (uses fill character to pad output). This is the default alignment setting.
ios::scientific	Displays floating-point values using scientific notation.

Table 7-7

The Settings of Parameter lMask for the Masked Version of Member Function setf

Setting	Purpose
ios::adjustfield	The mask for padding the flag bits (left, right, or internal).
ios::basefield	The mask for the radix flag bits (dec, hex, or oct).
ios::floatfield	The mask for the floating-point format flag bits (scientific or fixed).

Here are examples of using the member function **setf**:

```
cout.setf(ios::hex, ios::basefield); // masked version
cout.setf(ios::uppercase);           // nonmasked version
cout << 15 << "\n";                  // displays F
cout.setf(ios:showbase);             // nonmasked version
cout.setf(ios::oct, ios::basefield); // masked version
cout << 8 << "\n";                   // displays 010
cout.setf(ios::hex, ios::basefield); // masked version
cout << 15 << "\n";                  // displays 0xF
```

This code snippet first sets the hex flag by sending the C++ message **setf** to object **cout**. This message uses the masked version of member function **setf**. The arguments for this message are **ios::hex** (the format flag) and **ios::basefield** (the mask). The code then sets the uppercase flag by sending the C++ message **setf** to object **cout**. This message uses the nonmasked version of member function **setf**. The argument for this message is **ios::uppercase** (the format flag). The first output statement displays the number 15 as the hexadecimal integer F. The code snippet then sets the **showbase** flag by sending the C++ message **setf** to object **cout**. This message uses the nonmasked version of member function **setf**. The argument for this message is **ios::showbase**. Then, the code sets the **oct** flag by sending the C++ message **setf** to object **cout**. This message uses the masked version of member function **setf**. The arguments for this message are **ios::oct** (the format flag) and **ios::basefield** (the mask). The second output statement displays the number 8 as the octal integer 010. Next, the code sets the hex flag by sending the C++ message **setf** to object **cout**. This message uses the masked version of member function **setf**. The arguments for this message are **ios::hex** (the format flag) and **ios::basefield** (the mask). The second output statement displays the number 15 as the hexadecimal integer 0xF.

Let's look at a programming example. Listing 7-2 shows the source code for the IO2.CPP program, which illustrates the member function **setf**. The program performs the following tasks:

- Display the integer 16 in decimal, hexadecimal, and octal formats
- Display the number 355.113 using scientific and then fixed formats
- Display the current base for integer output

Here is the output of the program in Listing 7-2:

```
16 (base 10) = 0x10 (base 16) = 020 (base 8)
Floating-point number is +3.551130e+002
Floating-point number is +355.113000
Integer output uses base 8
```

Listing 7-2
The source code for the IO2.CPP program.

```
// A C++ program that illustrates
// the member function ios::setf

#include <iostream.h>

main()
{
  int nNum = 16;
  double fX = 355.113;
  long lFlags;

  cout << nNum << " (base 10) = ";
  cout.setf(ios::showbase);
  cout.setf(ios::hex, ios::basefield);
  cout << nNum << " (base 16) = ";
  cout.setf(ios::oct, ios::basefield);
  cout << nNum << " (base 8)\n";

  cout.setf(ios::showpos);
  cout.setf(ios::scientific, ios::floatfield);
  cout << "Floating-point number is " << fX << "\n";

  lFlags = cout.setf(ios::fixed, ios::floatfield);
  cout << "Floating-point number is " << fX << "\n";

  if (lFlags & ios::dec)
    cout << "Integer output uses base 10\n";
  else if (lFlags & ios::hex)
    cout << "Integer output uses base 16\n";
  else
    cout << "Integer output uses base 8\n";

  return 0;
}
```

Listing 7-2 declares the function **main**, which tests the member function **ios::setf**. The function declares and initializes the **int**-type variable **nNum** and the **double**-type variable **fX**. The function also declares the **long**-type variable **lFlags**. It then performs the following tasks:

- Display the value in variable **nNum** using the default decimal base

- Set the format flags to display hexadecimal numbers that include the base indicator. This task entails sending the C++ message **setf**, twice, to object **cout**. The first message invokes the nonmasked version of **setf**, whereas the second message invokes the masked version. The argument for first message is **ios::showbase**. This message sets the base indicator flag. The arguments for the second message are **ios::hex** (the format flag) and **ios::basefield** (the mask).

- Display the value in variable **nNum** using the hexadecimal base

- Set the format flags to display octal numbers that include the base indicator. This task involves sending the C++ message **setf** to object **cout**. The message invokes the masked version of member function **setf**. The arguments for this message are **ios::oct** and **ios::basefield**. This task need not send the message **setf(ios::showbase)** to object **cout**, since the base indicator flag is already set.

- Display the value in variable **nNum** using the octal base

- Set the format to display floating-point numbers using the scientific format along with the sign indicator. This task implies sending the C++ message **setf** twice to the object **cout**. The first message invokes the nonmasked version of **setf**, whereas the second message invokes the masked version. The argument for the first message is **ios::showpos**. This message sets the sign indicator flag. The arguments for the second message are **ios::scientific** (the format flag) and **ios::floatfield** (the mask).

- Display the value in variable **fX** in scientific format

- Set the format to display floating-point numbers using the fixed format and the sign indicator. This task involves sending the C++ message **setf** to the object **cout**. The message invokes the masked version of member function **setf**. The arguments for this message are **ios::fixed** (the format flag) and **ios::floatfield** (the mask). This task also assigns the result of the message to the local variable **lFlags**.

- Display the value in variable **fX** in fixed format.

- Use an **if** statement to determine the numeric base specified by the flags stored in variable **lFlags**. The **if** clause uses the expression **lFlags & ios::dec** to determine whether or not the decimal number flag is set. The **else if** clause uses the expression **lFlags & ios::hex** to determine whether or not the hexadecimal number flag is set.

The Member Function unsetf

The member function **unsetf** resets one or more format flags to their default values. The declaration for the member function **unsetf** is:

```
long unsetf(long lFlags);
```

The parameter **lFlags** specifies the flags to be reset to their default values. The member function returns the previous format flags. Previous Table 7-4 lists format flag settings that also apply to the member function **unsetf**. The argument for parameter **lFlags** may combine these settings using the bitwise-OR operator |.

Here are examples of using the formatting flags with member function **unsetf**:

```
cout.flags(ios::hex | ios::uppercase | ios::showbase);
cout << 15 << "\n"; // displays 0xF
cout.unsetf(ios::uppercase); // reset uppercase flag
cout << 15 << "\n"; // displays 0xf
cout.unsetf(ios::showbase);  // reset base flag
cout << 15 << "\n"; // displays f
```

This code snippet sets the **hex, uppercase,** and **showbase** flags. The first output statement displays the number 15 as 0xF. The code then sends the C++ message **unsetf** to object **cout** to reset the **uppercase** flag. The second output statement displays 0xf. The code then sends the C++ message **unsetf** to object **cout** to reset the **showbase** flag. The last output statement merely displays f.

Let's look at an example. Listing 7-3 shows the source code for the IO3.CPP program, which illustrates the member function **unsetf**. The program performs the following tasks:

- Display the number 16 as a decimal integer
- Set the base and hexadecimal flags and then display the number 16 as a hexadecimal integer
- Reset the hexadecimal flag and then display the number 16 as a decimal integer
- Set the scientific and sign indicator flags and then display the number 355.113 in scientific format (with a leading + sign)

- Reset the sign indicator flag and then display the number 355.113 in scientific format (without a leading + sign)

- Reset the scientific flag and then display the number 355.113 in fixed format

Here is the output of the program in Listing 7-3:

```
Number (in base 10) = 16
Number (in base 16) = 0x10
Number (in base 10) = 16
Number (in scientific format) = +3.551130e+002
Number (in scientific format) = 3.551130e+002
Number (in fixed format) = 355.113
```

Listing 7-3
The source code for the IO3.CPP program.

```
// A C++ program that illustrates
// the member function ios::unsetf

#include <iostream.h>

main()
{
  int nNum = 16;
  double fX = 355.113;

  cout << "Number (in base 10) = " << nNum << "\n";
  cout.flags(ios::hex | ios::showbase);
  cout << "Number (in base 16) = " << nNum << "\n";
  cout.unsetf(ios::hex);
  cout << "Number (in base 10) = " << nNum << "\n";

  cout.flags(ios::scientific|ios::showpos);
  cout << "Number (in scientific format) = "
       << fX << "\n";
  cout.unsetf(ios::showpos);
  cout << "Number (in scientific format) = "
       << fX << "\n";
  cout.unsetf(ios::scientific);
  cout << "Number (in fixed format) = "
       << fX << "\n";

  return 0;
}
```

Listing 7-3 declares the function **main**, which tests the member function ios::unsetf. The function declares and initializes the **int**-type variable **nNum** and the **double**-type variable **fX**. The function then performs the following tasks:

- Display the value in variable **nNum** using the default decimal base

- Set the hexadecimal and base indicator flags by sending the C++ message **flags** to the object **cout**. The argument for this message is the expression ios::hex | ios::showbase.

- Display the value in variable **nNum** as a hexadecimal integer with the 0x prefix

- Reset the hexadecimal flag by sending the C++ message **unsetf** to object **cout**. The argument for this message is ios::hex.

- Display the value in variable **nNum** using the default decimal base

- Set the scientific and sign indicator flags by sending the C++ message **flags** to the object **cout**. The argument for this message is the expression ios::scientific | ios::showpos.

- Display the value in variable **fX** using the scientific format. The output contains a leading + sign.

- Reset the sign indicator flag by sending the C++ message **unsetf** to object **cout**. The argument for this message is ios::showpos.

- Display the value in variable **fX** using the scientific format. This time, the output contains no leading + sign.

- Reset the scientific flag by sending the C++ message **unsetf** to object **cout**. The argument for this message is ios::scientific.

- Display the value in variable **fX** using the fixed format

The Member Function width

The member function **width** specifies the minimum width of a formatted field. It is offered in the C++ stream library, which has the following declaration for it:

```
int width(int nWidth = 0);
```

> **CODING NOTES**
>
> ## A Limitation of Member Function width
>
> The member function **width** affects the width of the next output only! Therefore, you need to use the member function **width** before each output, in a multiple-output statement, to control the width of that output.

The parameter **nWidth** specifies the new minimum width of a formatted field. The member function returns the current minimum width. The default argument for parameter **nWidth** specifies that the width be adequate to show the formatted value. Passing a negative value to parameter **nWidth** signals the member function to use an unlimited length to show the formatted value. The member function **width** sets the width for the next output only.

Here is an example of using the member function **width**:

```
// set width to 4 characters
cout.width(4);
cout << 15 << "\n"; // displays 15 with two leading spaces
cout << 15 << "\n"; // displays 15 with no leading spaces
```

This code snippet sets the width to four characters for the next output. Thus, the first output statement displays the number 15 with two leading spaces. By contrast, the second output statement displays the number 15 with no leading spaces, because the effect of member function **width** is limited to the first field in the first output statement.

Let's look at a programming example. Listing 7-4 shows the source code for the IO4.CPP program, which illustrates the member function **width**. The program displays the number 255 using different output widths. The program also demonstrates that the member function **width** affects only the output immediately following it.

Here is the output of the program in Listing 7-4:

```
Number is
        255
255

Number is    255
Number is         255
Number is             255
```

Listing 7-4

The source code for the IO4.CPP program.

```
// A C++ program that illustrates
// the member function ios::width

#include <iostream.h>

main()
{
  int i, nNum = 255;

  // set right-justified flag
  cout.flags(ios::right);
  cout << "Number is\n";
  // set width to 10 characters
  cout.width(10);
  cout << nNum << "\n";
  cout << nNum << "\n\n";

  for (i = 5; i < 20; i += 5) {
    cout << "Number is ";
    // set width to 'i' characters
    cout.width(i);
    cout << nNum << "\n";
  }

  return 0;
}
```

Listing 7-4 declares the function **main**. This function declares the local variables **i** and **nNum**, initializing **nNum** with the value 255. The function then performs the following tasks:

- Set the right flag by sending the C++ message **flags** to the object **cout**. The argument for this message is **ios::right**.

- Display the message "Number is" on a separate line

- Set the width for the next output to 10 characters. This task sends the C++ message **width** to object **cout**. The argument for this message is 10, the desired width value.

- Display the value in variable **nNum**. This output pads the number 255 with seven spaces (the space character is the default padding character).

- Display the value in variable **nNum**. This time, the number 255 appears with no leading spaces, because the message **width** affects only the previous output.

- Use a **for** loop to display the value in variable **nNum** using widths of 5, 10, and 15

The Member Function fill

The member function **fill** sets and reads the padding characters. The stream library offers two versions of this overloaded function. The declaration of the first version of member function **fill** is:

```
char fill(char cFill);
```

The parameter **cFill** specifies the new padding character. The member function returns the current padding character.

Here is an example of using the version just described of member function **fill**:

```
cout.fill('^');
cout.width(6);
cout << 20 << "\n"; // displays 20^^^^
```

This code snippet sets the padding character to '^' and specifies six characters for the next output. The output displays the integer 20 (which occupies two characters) and four padding characters.

The second version of the overloaded member function **fill** has the following declaration:

```
char fill() const;
```

This version of the function merely returns the padding character:

```
cout.fill('^');
cout.width(6);
cout << 20 << "\n"; // displays 20^^^^
  cout.fill() << "\n"; // displays ^
```

Let me present a programming example. Listing 7-5 contains the source code for the IO5.CPP program, which illustrates the member function fill. The program displays the number 255 three times. Each time, the output has a different kind of padding character. The program uses the padding characters '0', '*', and '+'.

Here is the output of the program in Listing 7-5:

```
Number is 0000000255
Number is *******255
Number is +++++++255
```

Listing 7-5

The source code for the IO5.CPP program.

```
// A C++ program that illustrates
// the member function ios::fill

#include <iostream.h>

main()
{
  int nNum = 255;

  // set right-justified flag
  cout.flags(ios::right);
  // set 0 as the padding character
  cout.fill('0');
  cout << "Number is ";
  // set width to 10 characters
  cout.width(10);
  cout << nNum << "\n";

  // set * as the padding character
  cout.fill('*');
  // set width to 10 characters
  cout << "Number is ";
  cout.width(10);
  cout << nNum << "\n";

  // set padding character to the next one
  cout.fill(char(cout.fill() + 1));
  cout << "Number is ";
  // set width to 10 characters
  cout.width(10);
  cout << nNum << "\n";

  return 0;
}
```

Listing 7-5 declares the function **main**, which tests the member function **ios::fill**. The function **main** declares and initializes the **int**-type variable **nNum**. The function then performs the following tasks:

- Set the right flag by sending the C++ message **flags** to the object **cout**. The argument for this message is **ios::right**.

- Set the padding character to '0' by sending the C++ message **fill** to the object **cout**. The argument for this message is the literal character '0'.

- Display the value in variable **nNum**. The output shows seven leading zeros.

- Set the padding character to '*' by sending the C++ message **fill** to the object **cout**. The argument for this message is the literal character '*'.

- Display the value in variable **nNum**. The output shows seven leading asterisks.

- Set the padding character to the character that comes after the '*'. This task sends the C++ message **fill** to the object **cout**. The argument for this message is the expression **char(cout.fill() + 1)**. This expression also sends the C++ message **fill** (which uses the second overloaded version of member function **fill**) to object **cout**.

- Display the value in variable **nNum**. The output shows seven leading plus signs.

The Member Function precision

The member function **precision** sets and reads the number of digits employed in formatting numeric values. In the case of floating-point values, this member function specifies the number of decimal places. The default value is six digits. The stream library offers two versions of the overloaded member function **precision**. The declaration of the first version is:

```
double precision(int nPrecision);
```

The parameter **nPrecision** specifies the new number of digits. The member function returns the current number of digits.

Here is an example of using the version just described of member function **precision**:

```
cout.precision(3);
cout << 20.1 << "\n"; // displays 20.100
```

This code snippet displays the value 20.100 by adding the two trailing zeros. These zeros appear because the member function **precision** specifies three decimals, while the output statement shows a floating-point number with one decimal place.

The second version of the overloaded member function **precision** has the following declaration:

```
int precision() const;
```

This version of member function **precision** merely returns the number of digits.

```
cout.precision(3);
cout << 20.1 << "\n"; // displays 20.100
cout.precision() << "\n"; // displays 3
```

Let me show you a programming example. Listing 7-6 contains the source code for the IO6.CPP program, which illustrates the member function **precision**. The program displays the number 355.678 six times. The first three times, the number appears in fixed format, using **precision** values of 1, 3, and 5. The second three times, the number appears in the scientific format, using **precision** values of 1, 3, and 5. The program rounds the output when using the **precision** values of 1 and 3. When the **precision** value is 5, the program displays trailing zeros.

Here is the output of the program in Listing 7-6:

```
Number = 355.7 (precision is 1)
Number = 355.678 (precision is 3)
Number = 355.67800 (precision is 5)
Number = 3.6e+002 (precision is 1)
Number = 3.557e+002 (precision is 3)
Number = 3.55678e+002 (precision is 5)
```

Listing 7-6
The source code for the IO6.CPP program.

```
// A C++ program that illustrates
// the member function ios::precision

#include <iostream.h>
```

```
main()
{
  double fX = 355.678;

  // display floating-point numbers in fixed format
  cout.flags(ios::fixed);
  cout.precision(1);
  cout << "Number = " << fX << " (precision is "
       << cout.precision() << ")\n";

  cout.precision(3);
  cout << "Number = " << fX << " (precision is "
       << cout.precision() << ")\n";

  cout.precision(5);
  cout << "Number = " << fX << " (precision is "
       << cout.precision() << ")\n";

  // display floating-point numbers in scientific format
  cout.flags(ios::scientific);
  cout.precision(1);
  cout << "Number = " << fX << " (precision is "
       << cout.precision() << ")\n";

  cout.precision(3);
  cout << "Number = " << fX << " (precision is "
       << cout.precision() << ")\n";

  cout.precision(5);
  cout << "Number = " << fX << " (precision is "
       << cout.precision() << ")\n";

  return 0;
}
```

Listing 7-6 declares the function **main**, which tests the member function **precision**. The function declares and initializes the **double**-type variable **fX**. The initializing value is 255.678. The function then performs the following tasks:

- Set the fixed-format flag by sending the C++ message **flags** to the object **cout**. The argument for this message is **ios::fixed**.

- Set the **precision** value to 1 by sending the C++ message **precision** to the object **cout**. The argument for this message is 1.

- Display the value in variable **fX**. The output, which is 355.7, shows that the object **cout** rounds up the value 355.678 to 355.7.

- Set the **precision** value to 3 by sending the C++ message **precision** to the object **cout**. The argument for this message is 3.
- Display the value in variable **fX**. The output is 355.678.
- Set the **precision** value to 5 by sending the C++ message **precision** to the object **cout**. The argument for this message is the number 5.
- Display the value in variable **fX**. The output is 355.67800. This output contains trailing zeros.
- Set the scientific format by sending the C++ message **flags** to the object **cout**. The argument for this message is **ios::scientific**.
- Set the **precision** value to 1 by sending the C++ message **precision** to the object **cout**. The argument for this message is the number 1.
- Display the value in variable **fX**. The output, which is 3.6e+002, shows that the object **cout** rounds up the value 355.678 to one decimal place in the scientific format.
- Set the **precision** value to 3 by sending the C++ message **precision** to the object **cout**. The argument for this message is 3.
- Display the value in variable **fX**. The output is 3.557e+002. The output shows that object **cout** rounds the number 355.678 to three decimal places in the scientific format.
- Set the **precision** value to 5 by sending the C++ message **precision** to the object **cout**. The argument for this message is the number 5.
- Display the value in variable **fX**. The output is 3.55678e+002. This output contains all the digits of the number 355.678.

USING MANIPULATORS

In addition to the member functions that I presented in the last subsection, the C++ stream library offers member functions that directly affect the stream output. In other words, you may use a *manipulator* with the operator << to avoid interrupting the chained output that uses a sequence of the operator <<. You need to include the header file IOMANIP.H to use the manipulators. Table 7-8 shows the parameterized manipulators. Table 7-9 shows the nonparameterized manipulators.

Table 7-8

The Parameterized Manipulators

Manipulator	Purpose
setw(int nWidth = 0)	Sets the minimum width of the next field (the default value is 0, which specifies adequate width for the output).
setbase(int nBase = 10)	Sets the base. The values 8, 10, and 16 select the octal, decimal, and hexadecimal bases, respectively. The default value is 10.
setfill(char cFill = ' ')	Sets the padding character. The default padding character is ' '.
setprecision(int nPrec = 6)	Sets the precision. The default value is 6.
setiosflags(long lFlags)	Sets the stream format flags.
resetiosflags(long lFlags)	Resets the stream format flags.

Table 7-9

The Nonparameterized Manipulators

Manipulator	Purpose
binary	Sets the stream mode to binary. Used with file I/O.
text	Sets the stream mode to text (default). Used with file I/O.
dec	Formats integers as decimal numbers.
hex	Formats integers as hexadecimal numbers.
oct	Formats integers as octal numbers.
ws	Whitespace extractor.
endl	Emits a newline.
ends	Ends a string with a null character.
flush	Flushes the output stream.

Here are examples of using the stream manipulators:

```
// example 1: display 011
cout << oct << setiosflags(ios::showbase) << 9 << endl;

// example 2: display 12.12
cout << setprecision(2) << 12.12345 << endl;
```

```
// example 3: display 0000125
cout << setw(7) << setfill('0') << 125 << endl;
```

The first example uses the manipulators **oct**, **setiosflags(ios::showbase)**, and **endl** to display the integer 9 as an octal number 011.

The second example uses the manipulators **setprecision** and **endl** to display the number 12.1234 to two decimal places. The argument of the manipulator is 2, the desired number of decimal places.

The third example uses the manipulators **setw** and **setfill** to specify an output that is seven characters wide and uses the 0 padding characters. The output statement displays the integer 125 as 0000125.

Let's look at a programming example. Listing 7-7 shows the source code for the IO7.CPP program, which illustrates selected stream manipulators. The program displays the following values:

- The integer 125 as a hexadecimal number with uppercase characters
- The integer 125 with leading zeros to fill in the gap in the 10-character output width
- The number 355.678 in scientific format with a single decimal place
- The number 355.678 in scientific format with three decimal places, a leading plus sign, and leading '*' characters as padding characters for the 30-character output width

Here is the output of the program in Listing 7-7:

```
Integer is 7D
Integer is 0000000125
Number is 3.6E+002
Number is *******************+3.557E+002
```

Listing 7-7
The source code for the IO7.CPP program.

```
// A C++ program that illustrates
// selected stream manipulators

#include <iostream.h>
#include <iomanip.h>
```

```
main()
{
  double fX = 355.678;
  int nNum = 125;

  cout << "Integer is "
       << hex               // hexadecimal format
       << setiosflags(ios::uppercase) // uppercase hex chars
       << nNum
       << endl;             // new line

  cout << "Integer is "
       << setfill('0')  // padding character is 0
       << setw(10)      // width is 10
       << dec           // decimal
       << nNum
       << endl;         // new line

  cout << "Number is "
       << setprecision(2)
       << fX
       << endl;         // new line

  cout << "Number is "
       << setfill('*')     // set padding characater to *
       << setprecision(3) // set precision to 3
       << setw(30)        // set width to 30 characters
       << setiosflags(ios::scientific |  // scientific format
                      ios::showpos    |  // show leading + sign
                      ios::right)         // right justify
       << fX
       << endl;         // new line

  return 0;
}
```

Listing 7-7 declares the function **main**, which tests selected stream
manipulators. It declares and initializes the **double**-type variable **fX** and the
int-type variable **nNum**. The initial values for these variables are 355.678 and
125, respectively. The function **main** then performs the following tasks:

- Display the value of variable **nNum** using the manipulators **hex**,
  setiosflags, and **endl**. The manipulator **hex** sets the hexadecimal flag. The
  manipulator **setiosflags** sets the **ios::uppercase** flag. The manipulator **endl**
  emits a newline. The **endl** manipulator replaces the string "\n" that I
  typically use in this book's programs.

- Display the value of variable **nNum** using the manipulators **setfill**, **setw**, **dec**, and **endl**. The manipulator **setfill** sets the padding character to 0. The manipulator **setw** sets the output width to 10 characters. The manipulator **dec** selects decimal output for integers. The manipulator **endl** emits a new line.

- Display the value in variable **fX** using the manipulators **setprecision** and **endl**. The manipulator **setprecision** sets the precision to 2.

- Display the value in variable **fX** using the manipulators **setfill**, **setprecision**, **setw**, **setiosflags**, and **endl**. The manipulator **setfill** sets the padding character to '*'. The manipulator **setprecision** sets the precision to 3. The manipulator **setw** sets the output width to 30 characters. The manipulator **setiosflags** sets the flags **ios::scientific**, **ios::showpos**, and **ios::right**. The output statement displays the value of variable **fX** as a right-justified scientific number with leading asterisks, a leading plus sign, and three decimal places.

Stream Input

C++ also supports the inserter operator **>>**, which permits the object **cin** to input data. The stream classes define overloaded versions of the operator **>>** to support the predefined data types that represent characters, integers, and floating-point numbers. The operator **>>** works with the **cin** input stream object. Here are examples of using the object **cin** and the operator **>>**:

```
// example 1
int nNum;
cout << "Enter an integer : ";
cin >> nNum;

// example 2
char cDrive;
cout << "Enter the drive letter : ";
cin >> cDrive;

// example 3
double fInterestRage;
cout << "Enter the interest rate : ";
cin >> fInterestRate;
```

Managing Input with Object cin

It is easier to manage stream input with object **cin** using a single statement for each input value.

The first example prompts you to enter an integer. The **cin** object stores the input in the **int**-type variable **nNum**. The second example prompts you to enter a character (which represents a drive letter). The **cin** object stores the input in the **char**-type variable **cDrive**. The third example prompts you to enter a floating-point number (which represents the interest rate). The **cin** object stores the input in the **double**-type variable **fInterestRate**.

The stream library offers the member function **getline**, which allows the object **cin** to input a string. The declaration of overloaded member function **getline** is:

```
istream& getline(char* pszStr, int nCount, char cDelim = '\n');
istream& getline(signed char* pszStr, int nCount,
                 char cDelim = '\n');
istream& getline(unsigned char* pszStr, int nCount,
                 char cDelim = '\n');
```

The parameter **pszStr** is a pointer to an ASCIIZ string. The parameter **nCount** specifies the maximum number of input characters, and the parameter **cDelim** specifies the string delimiter.

Here is an example of using the member function **getline**:

```
const int MAX = 30;
char cName[MAX + 1];
cout << "Enter your name : ";
cin.getline(cName, MAX);
cout << "Hello " << cName << "\n";
```

This example prompts you to enter your name. The input involves sending the C++ message **getline** to the object **cin**. The arguments for this message are the array of characters **cName** and the constant **MAX**. The array stores your input that does not exceed a **MAX** number of characters.

Let me present a programming example. Listing 7-8 contains the source code for the IO8.CPP program, which illustrates stream input using the object **cin**. The program performs the following tasks:

- Prompt you to enter a name, and then use the input to display a greeting message

- Prompt you to enter two numbers, separated by a space. The program then displays the input and the sum of the two numbers.

- Prompt you to enter two characters and then display the input characters

- Prompt you to enter a single character and then display that character

Here is a sample session with the program in Listing 7-8 (user input is underlined):

```
Enter your first name : John Smith
Hello John Smith. How are you?
Enter two numbers separated by a space : 25.2 14.8
25.2 + 14.8 = 40
Enter two characters : A U
You typed A and U
Enter a character : L
You entered L
```

Listing 7-8

The source code for the IO8.CPP program, which illustrates stream input using object cin.

```cpp
// A C++ program that illustrates stream input

#include <iostream.h>
#include <iomanip.h>

main()
{
  const int MAX = 30;
  double fX1, fX2;
  char cName[MAX+1];
  char cChar1, cChar2;
  char cChar[2];

  cout << "Enter your first name : ";
  cin.getline(cName, MAX);
  cout << "Hello " << cName << ". How are you?\n";

  cout << "Enter two numbers separated by a space : ";
  cin >> fX1 >> fX2;
  cout << fX1 << " + " << fX2
       << " = " << (fX1 + fX2) << endl;
```

```
    cout << "Enter two characters : ";
    cin >> cChar1 >> cChar2;
    cin.getline(cName, MAX);
    cout << "You typed " << cChar1
         << " and " << cChar2 << endl;

    cout << "Enter a character : ";
    cin.getline(cChar, 2);
    cout << "You entered " << cChar[0] << endl;

    return 0;
}
```

Listing 7-8 declares the function **main**. This function declares the constant **MAX**; the variables **fX1**, **fX2**, **cChar1**, **cChar2**; and the character arrays **cName** and **cChar**. The function then performs the following tasks:

- Prompt you to enter a name. This task stores your input by sending the C++ message **getline** to object **cin**. The arguments for this message are the character array **cName** and the constant **MAX**. Thus, the message **getline** stores up to **MAX** characters in the array **cName**.

- Prompt you to enter two numbers, separated by a space. This task uses the statement **cin >> fX1 >> fX2**; to obtain a sequence of two floating-point numbers.

- Display the input numbers and their sum

- Prompt you to enter two characters. You may separate the input characters with a space. This task uses the expression **cin >> cChar1 >> cChar2**; to obtain the sequence of two characters. This task stores the characters in variables **cChar1** and **cChar2**.

- Absorb the carriage return character that you enter after keying in the two characters. This task involves sending the C++ message **getline** to object **cin**. The arguments for this message are the character array **cName** (which acts as a dummy input buffer) and the constant **MAX**. If you omit the statement that supports this task, the carriage return character becomes an unwarranted input for the next prompted input!

- Prompt you to enter a character. This task sends the C++ message **getline** to object **cin** to obtain a string that consists of the input character and the carriage return. The arguments for this message are the two-character array **cChar** and the number 2. Thus, this task stores the input character in **cChar[0]** and the carriage return in **cChar[1]**.

- Display the input character that resides in **cChar[0]**

The printf Function

Both C and C++ libraries present you with a wealth of I/O functions to choose from. This section looks at the formatting features of the function **printf**, which is a part of the standard I/O library for C. The header file STDIO.H contains the prototype of function **printf**.

The **printf** function provides you with much power and presents appeallingly formatted output. The declaration of the function **printf** is:

```
int printf(const char *format [, argument]... );
```

The parameter **format** is a string that contains formatting instructions as well as text. The function **printf** supports a variable number of arguments. The general syntax for the individual formatting instruction is:

```
% [flags] [width] [.precision] [F |([F|N|h|])| h | l] <type character>
```

The **flags** options specify the output justification, numeric signs, decimal points, and trailing zeros. In addition, these flags specify the octal and hexadecimal prefixes. Table 7-10 lists the options for the flags in the format string of the function **printf**.

The **width** option indicates the minimum number of displayed characters. The function **printf** uses zeros and blanks to pad the output, if needed. When the **width** number begins with a 0, the **printf** function uses leading zeros instead of spaces for padding. When the '*' character appears instead of a width number, the **printf** function acquires the actual width number from the function's argument list. The argument that specifies the required width must come before the argument actually being formatted. The following is an example that displays the integer 4 using three characters, as specified by the third argument of **printf**:

```
printf("%*d", 4, 3);
```

The precision option specifies the maximum number of displayed characters. If you include an integer, the precision option defines the minimum number of displayed digits. When the '*' character is used in place of a precision number, the **printf** function obtains the actual precision from the argument list. The argument that specifies the required precision must come before the argument that is actually being formatted. The following is an example that displays the floating-point number 1.2345 using eight characters, as specified by the third argument of **printf**:

```
printf("%7.*f", 1.2345, 8);
```

The **F**, **N**, **h**, and **l** options are size options used to overrule the argument's default size. The **F** and **N** options work with far and near pointers, respectively. The **h** and **l** options indicate short int or long, respectively.

The **printf** function requires that you specify a data type character with each % format code. Table 7-10 shows the options for the flags in the format string of **printf**. Table 7-11 shows the data type characters used in the format string of **printf**.

Table 7-10
Options for the Flags in the Format String of the printf *Function*

Format Option	Result
–	Justifies to the left within the specified field.
+	Displays the plus or minus sign of a value.
[blank]	Displays a leading blank if the value is positive; displays a minus sign if the value is negative.
#	No effect on decimal integers; displays a leading 0X or 0x for hexadecimal integers; displays a leading zero for octal integers; displays the decimal point for reals.

Table 7-11
Data Type Characters Used in the Format String of printf

Category	Type Character	Result
Character	c	single character.
	d	signed decimal int.
	i	signed decimal int.
	o	unsigned octal int.
	u	unsigned decimal int.
	x	unsigned hexadecimal int (the set of numeric characters used is 0123456789abcdef).

continued

Table 7-11 (continued)

Format Option	Result	
	X	unsigned hexadecimal int (the set of numeric characters used is 0123456789ABCDEF).
Pointer	p	Displays only the offset for near pointers as *0000;* displays far pointers as *SSSS:0000.*
Pointer to int	n	Displays a pointer to an integer.
Real	f	Displays a signed value in the format [-]*dddd.dddd.*
	e	Displays a signed scientific value in the format [-]*d.dddde*[+I-]*ddd.*
	E	Displays a signed scientific value in the format [-]*d.dddd*E[+I-]*ddd.*
	g	Displays a signed value using either the f or e formats, depending on the value and the specified precision.
	G	Displays a signed value using either the f or E formats, depending on the value and the specified precision.
String pointer	s	Displays characters until the null terminator of the string is reached.

Here are examples of using the **printf** function:

```
// displays Count is 10
int nCount = 10;
printf("Count is %d\n", nCount);
// displays 5 * 4 = 20
double fX1 = 5.0, fX2 = 4.0;
printf(%g * %g = %g\n", fX1, fX2, fX1 * fX2);
// displays ASCII code of C is 67
char C = 'A';
printf("ASCII code of %c is %d\n", C, C);
// displays FF is decimal 255
int nNum = 255;
printf("%x is decimal %d\n", nNum. nNum);
// displays Hello! My name is Namir Shammas
char pszName = "Namir Shammas";
printf("Hello! My name is %s\n", pszName);
```

These simple examples show how the function **printf** uses the format string to display output. In some cases, the **printf** function displays the same value in two different ways—examples are the output "ASCII code of C is 67" and "FF is decimal 255."

CODING NOTES

Using the Function sprintf

You can use the function **sprintf** to format values and store these values in a string. The declaration of function **sprintf** is:

int sprintf(char *buffer*, const char *format [, argument] ...);

The parameter *buffer* accesses a string that stores the formatted results. The parameter format is the formatting string.

Here is an example:

```
char cOut[30];
double fX;
int nNum1 = 45, nNum = 34;
fX = double(nNum1 * nNum2);
sprintf(cOut, "%d * %d = %g\n", nNum1, nNum2, fX);
cout << cOut; // displays 45 * 34 = 1530
```

Let me present an example. Listing 7-9 shows the source code for the IO9.CPP program, which illustrates the **printf** function. The program uses the function **printf** to display the following items:

- The character A and its ASCII code using the %d and %c formats, respectively

- The integer 345 in decimal and hexadecimal forms using the %d and %x formats, respectively

- The long integer 1123456 in decimal and hexadecimal forms, using the %ld and %lx formats, respectively

- The unsigned integer 34 in decimal and octal forms, using the %u and %o formats, respectively

- The number 355.678 using the %lf format

- The number 355.678 using the %g format

- The number 355.678 using the %le format

- The name John Smith as a string using the %s format

Here is the output of the program in Listing 7-9:

```
Character A has ASCII code 65
Decimal integer 345 = hex 159
Decimal long integer 1123456 = hex 112480
Octal unsigned integer 34 = octal 42
Floating-point number is 355.678000 (using %lf format)
Floating-point number is 355.678 (using %g format)
Floating-point number is 3.556780e+002 (using %le format)
String is 'John Smith'
```

Listing 7-9

The source code for the IO9.CPP program.

```cpp
// A C++ program that illustrates
// the printf function

#include <iostream.h>
#include <stdio.h>
#include <iomanip.h>

main()
{
  char cChar = 'A';
  int nNum = 345;
  double fX = 355.678;
  long lNum = 1123456;
  unsigned uCount = 34;
  char* pszName = "John Smith";

  printf("Character %c has ASCII code %d\n", cChar, cChar);
  printf("Decimal integer %d = hex %x\n", nNum, nNum);
  printf("Decimal long integer %ld = hex %lx\n", lNum, lNum);
  printf("Octal unsigned integer %u = octal %o\n",
         uCount, uCount);
  printf("Floating-point number is %lf"
         " (using %%lf format)\n", fX);
  printf("Floating-point number is %g"
         " (using %%g format)\n", fX);
  printf("Floating-point number is %le"
         " (using %%le format)\n", fX);
  printf("String is '%s'\n", pszName);

  return 0;
}
```

Listing 7-9 declares the function **main**. The function declares and initializes local variables that have the **char**, **int**, **double**, **long**, **unsigned**, and **char*** types. The function then takes the following steps to display the values in the local variables:

- Display the character and ASCII code in variable **cChar**. This task uses the %c and %d formats to displays the character in variable **cChar** and its ASCII code. Notice that the second and third arguments to function **printf** are both **cChar**.

- Display the decimal and hexadecimal values in the **int**-type variable **nNum** using the %d and %x formats, respectively. Notice that the second and third arguments to function **printf** are both **nNum**.

- Display the decimal and hexadecimal values in the **long**-type variable **lNum** using the %ld and %lx formats, respectively. In this case, the second and third arguments to function **printf** are both **lNum**.

- Display the decimal and octal values in the **unsigned**-type variable **uCount** using the %u and %o formats, respectively. The last two arguments to function **printf** are both **uCount**.

- Display the value in the **double**-type variable **fX** using the %lf format. The output is 355.678000, which contains three trailing zeros, since the default output of format %lf has six decimal places.

- Display the value in the **double**-type variable **fX** using the %g format. The output of this general format is 355.678.

- Display the value in the **double**-type variable **fX** using the %le format. The output of this scientific format is 3.556780e+002. This format has the default of six decimal places.

- Display the string accessed by the character pointer **pszName** using the %s format

Declaring the << Operator for Classes

C++ allows a class to declare its own version of operator **<<**. This feature allows you to display some or all of the data members in a class. The general syntax for declaring the operator **<<** in a class is:

```
class className
{
  public:
  // public constructors
  // public destructor
  // public data members
  // public member functions
  friend ostream& operator <<(ostream& os, className& object);

  // other members

};
```

Notice that this syntax shows that the declaration of operator **<<** follows these rules:

1. The class must declare the operator << as a friend function, using the keyword **friend** (more about friend functions in Chapter 14, "Class Hierarchies").
2. The operator must return the reference type **ostream&**.
3. The first parameter of the operator **<<** must be a reference to type **ostream**. The second parameter should be a reference to the host class.

The definition of the operator **<<** emits the data members that you wish to display to the output stream parameter. The operator must return the output stream parameter. Here is an example of declaring the operator **<<** with the class **myComplex**:

```
class myComplex
{
  public:

  friend ostream& operator <<(ostream& os, myComplex& C);

  // other members
  protected:
```

```
        double m_fReal;
        double m_fImag;
   };
   ostream& operator <<(ostream& os, myComplex& C)
   {
     os << C.m_fReal << " +i " << C.m_fImag;
     return os;
   }
```

The class **myComplex** declares the data members **m_fReal** and **m_fImag**. The definition of the operator **<<** displays the values of these data members and also includes the string " +i " between the members. The operator accesses the data members of the class **myComplex** using the **myComplex**-type parameter **C**. The operator returns the output stream parameter **os**.

Let's look at an example. Listing 7-10 shows the source code for the CLASS9.CPP program, which illustrates defining the operator **<<** for a user-defined class. The program contains a class that models a two-dimensional point. The class declares the operator **<<** to display the coordinates of a point using the format (*X*, *Y*). The program performs the following tasks:

- Display the coordinates of two points

- Display the distance between the first point and the origin (0, 0)

- Display the distance between the second point and the origin (0, 0)

- Display the distance between the two points

Here is the output of the program in Listing 7-10:

```
Object 1 is at (10.5, 45.6)
Object 2 is at (22.05, 104.88)
Distance between object 1 and origin = 46.7933
Distance between object 2 and origin = 107.173
Distance between objects 1 and 2 = 60.3947
```

Listing 7-10
The source code for the CLASS9.CPP program.

```
// A C++ program that illustrates
// the use of the operator << with
// user-defined classes

#include <iostream.h>
```

```
#include <math.h>

inline double sqr(double x)
{ return x * x; }

class myPoint
{
  public:
    myPoint(double fX = 0., double fY = 0.);

    void setXCoord(double fX)
      { m_fX = fX; }
    void setYCoord(double fY)
      { m_fY = fY; }
    double getXCoord()
      { return m_fX; }
    double getYCoord()
      { return m_fY; }
    double getDistance(const myPoint& otherPoint)
      { return sqrt(sqr(m_fX - otherPoint.m_fX) +
                    sqr(m_fY - otherPoint.m_fY)); }
    double getDistanceFromOrigin()
      { return sqrt(sqr(m_fX) + sqr(m_fY)); }
     friend ostream& operator <<(ostream& os, myPoint& aPoint);

  protected:
    double m_fX;
    double m_fY;
};

myPoint::myPoint(double fX, double fY)
{
  m_fX = fX;
  m_fY = fY;
}

ostream& operator <<(ostream& os, myPoint& aPoint)
{
  os << "(" << aPoint.getXCoord() << ", "
     << aPoint.getYCoord() << ")";

  return os;
}

main()
{
  double fX = 10.5;
  double fY = 45.6;
  myPoint objPt1(fX, fY);
  myPoint objPt2(2.1 * fX, 2.3 * fY);

  // show coordinates of object objPt1
```

```
cout << "Object 1 is at " << objPt1 << "\n";

// show coordinates of object objPt2
cout << "Object 2 is at " << objPt2 << "\n";

// show distance between object objPt1 and origin
cout << "Distance between object 1 and origin = "
     << objPt1.getDistanceFromOrigin() << "\n";

// show distance between object objPt2 and origin
cout << "Distance between object 2 and origin = "
     << objPt2.getDistanceFromOrigin() << "\n";

// show distance between objects objPt1 and objPt2
cout << "Distance between objects 1 and 2 = "
     << objPt1.getDistance(objPt2) << "\n";

return 0;
}
```

Listing 7-10 declares the class **myPoint** (which is similar to the class **myPoint** that I presented in the last chapter). The class declares the protected data members **m_fX** and **m_fY**, which store the coordinates. The class also declares the following public members:

- The constructor, which initializes the data members
- The member functions **setXCoord** and **setYCoord**, which store new coordinates in the data members **m_fX** and **m_fY**, respectively
- The member functions **getXCoord** and **getYCoord**, which obtain the current coordinates in the data members **m_fX** and **m_fY**, respectively
- The member function **getDistance**, which returns the distance with two class instances
- The member function **getDistanceFromOrigin**, which yields the distance between a class instance and the origin
- The friend function operator **<<**, which displays the coordinates of a class instance

The definition of the operator **<<** displays the values in data members **m_fX** and **m_fY** of the **myPoint**-type parameter **aPoint**. Notice that the first statement uses the operator **<<** with the predefined type **double** to send the output to the stream object **os**. The operator **<<** returns the object **os**.

The function **main** declares and initializes the **double**-type variables **fX1** and **fX2**. The function also declares and initializes the objects **objPt1** and **objPt2** as instances of class **myPoint**. The function then performs the following tasks:

- Display the coordinates of object **objPt1**. This task uses the friend operator **<<** defined in class **myPoint**.
- Display the coordinates of object **objPt2**. This task also uses the friend operator **<<** defined in class **myPoint**.
- Display the distance between object **objPt1** and the origin. This task sends the C++ message **getDistanceFromOrigin** to the object **objPt1**.
- Display the distance between object **objPt2** and the origin. This task sends the C++ message **getDistanceFromOrigin** to the object **objPt2**.
- Display the distance between objects **objPt1** and **objPt2**. This task sends the C++ message **getDistance** to the object **objPt1**. The argument for this message is object **objPt2**.

Summary

This chapter has introduced you to the C++ stream I/O library. You learned about the standard I/O streams and about the console input and output operators and member functions. The chapter also discussed formatted stream output using various member functions of class **ios**. It also discussed using manipulators to fine-tune the stream output. You also learned about the **printf** function and its versatile formatting features. Finally you learned how to define the operator **<<** to support the output of data members in a user-defined class.

In the next chapter, we return to basic procedural features of C++, as we take a deeper look at the decision-making constructs (**if**, **else**, and **switch**) that the language has inherited from its predecessor, C.

8 Decision Making

*D*ecision-making constructs allow programs to examine conditions and take appropriate action. No respectable programming language lacks decision-making constructs. In this chapter you will learn about the decision-making constructs in C++. We will go over the simple **if** statement, the **if-else** statement, the multiple-alternative **if** statement, the **switch** statement, and the nested decision-making constructs.

The Simple if Statement

C++ offers the simple **if** statement to support single-alternative decision making. The general syntax for the simple **if** statement is:

```
// form 1
if (condition)
    statement;
// form 2
if (condition) {
    // sequence of statements
}
```

The **if** statement uses the keyword **if** followed by the parentheses that contain the tested condition. If that condition is true, the program executes the statement (see form 1) or the block of statements (see form 2) that come after the tested condition. Otherwise, the program bypasses this statement (or block of statements).

Here are examples of the single-alternative **if** statement:

```
// example 1
if (nNum < 0)
  cout << "Value is negative!\n";

// example 2
if (i > 0 && i < 100)
  cout << "Number is in range 1 to 100\n";

// example 3
if (nCount < 1)
  nCount = 1;
```

The first example uses the **if** statement to display a message if the value in variable **nNum** is negative. The second example employs the **if** statement to display a message when the variable **i** contains an integer in the range of 1 to 99. The third example assigns 1 to variable **nCount** if that variable contains a value that is less than 1.

BASIC

No Keyword then in an if Statement

C++ does not use the keyword then in an if statement. To compensate for the lack of the keyword then, C++ *requires* that you enclose the tested condition in parentheses. Moreover, C++ does not use any keyword similar to the ENDIF keyword used in some BASIC implementations.

In addition, C++ encloses a block of statements in a pair of open and close braces. By contrast, blocks of statements in BASIC are implicit.

PASCAL

No Keyword Then in an if Statement

C++ does not use the keyword Then in an if statement. To compensate for the lack of the keyword Then, C++ requires that you enclose the tested condition in parentheses.

In addition, C++ encloses a block of statements in a pair of open and close braces, instead of the BEGIN and END keywords used in Pascal.

PASCAL

Writing Conditions

The AND and OR Boolean operators in C++ have lower precedence than the relational operators. Therefore, you need not enclose the terms that use the relational operators in parentheses as you must in Pascal. Thus, for example, the following Pascal **If** statement:

```
If (nCout > 0) And (nNumElems > 0) Then
```

translates into the following C++ **if** statement:

```
if (nCout > 0 && nNumElems > 0)
```

Let me continue with a full example program. Listing 8-1 contains the source code for the IF3.CPP program, which illustrates the single-alternative **if** statement. The program uses a class that supports integer values that fall within a class-specified range. The program performs the following tasks:

- Create and initialize the integer-range object
- Display the value in the integer-range object
- Prompts you to enter an integer in the range used to create the integer-range object
- Determine whether or not your input is in the valid range. If it is not, the program displays a message to that effect.
- Display the current value in the integer-range object. If your input did not comply with the range of integers, the object maintains its previous value.

Here is a sample session with the program in Listing 8-1 (user input is underlined):

```
Object intObj stores 1
Enter an integer (between 1 and 100) : 555
Your input was out of range!
Object intObj stores 1
```

Listing 8-1

The source code for the IF3.CPP program.

```cpp
// A C++ program that demonstrates the
// single-alternative if statement

#include <iostream.h>

const int GOOD = 1;
const int BAD = 0;

class intRange
{
  public:
    intRange(int nFirst, int nLast);
    int setValue(int nNum);
    int getValue()
      { return m_nVal; }

  protected:
    int m_nFirst;
    int m_nLast;
    int m_nVal;
};

intRange::intRange(int nFirst, int nLast)
{
  // swap integers if nFirst > nLast
  if (nFirst > nLast) {
    int nSwap = nFirst;
    nFirst = nLast;
    nLast = nFirst;
  }

  m_nFirst = nFirst;
  m_nLast = nLast;
  m_nVal = m_nFirst;
}

int intRange::setValue(int nNum)
{
  int nResult = BAD;

  if (nNum >= m_nFirst && nNum <= m_nLast) {
    m_nVal = nNum;
    nResult = GOOD;
  }

  return nResult;
}

main()
{
```

```
    const int LO = 1;
    const int HI = 100;

    intRange intObj(LO, HI);
    int nNum;

    cout << "Object intObj stores "
         << intObj.getValue() << "\n";

    cout << "Enter an integer (between "
         << LO << " and " << HI << ") : ";
    cin >> nNum;

    if (intObj.setValue(nNum) == BAD)
      cout << "Your input was out of range!\n";

    cout << "Object intObj stores "
         << intObj.getValue() << "\n";

    return 0;
}
```

Listing 8-1 defines the global constants **GOOD** and **BAD**. The listing also declares the class **intRange**, which contains public and protected members. The protected members are:

- The **int**-type data members **m_nFirst** and **m_nLast**, which store the range of integers for a class instance

- The **int**-type data member **m_nVal**, which stores an integer value that must lie inside the range defined by the first pair of data members

The class **intRange** declares the following public members:

- The constructor, which sets the range of integers for each instance

- The member function **setValue**, which sets a new value for the data member **m_nVal** using the parameter **nValue**. The function returns the value of constant **GOOD** if the argument for the parameter is within the instance's valid range of integers. Otherwise, the member function yields the value of constant **BAD**.

- The member function **getValue**, which returns the value in data member **m_nVal**

The definition of the constructor uses a single-alternative **if** statement to swap the values of parameters **nFirst** and **nLast** when the former exceeds the latter. The **if** statement has a block of statements that swap the values of the two parameters.

The definition of member function **setValue** uses a single-alternative **if** statement to determine if the value of parameter **nNum** is inside the limits defined by data members **m_nFirst** and **m_nLast**. If this condition is true, the member function assigns the value of parameter **nNum** to data member **m_nVal**. The function also sets the local variable **nResult** to the value of constant **GOOD** (the member function initializes this variable using the value of constant **BAD**). The member function returns the value in the local variable **nResult**.

The function **main** declares the constants **LO** and **HI**, which define the range of integers. The function uses these constants in creating the object **intObj**, which is an instance of class **intRange**. The function also declares the local variable **nNum**. It then performs the following tasks:

- Display the value in object **intObj** by sending the C++ message **getValues** to that object

- Prompt you to enter an integer in the range defined by constants **LO** and **HI**. The function stores your input in variable **nNum**.

- Determine if your input lies within the specified range. This task uses a single-alternative **if** statement to compare the result of the C++ message **setValue** with the value of constant **BAD**. This task sends the C++ message **setValue** to object **intObj**. The argument for this message is the variable **nNum**, which contains your input.

- Display the current value in object **intObj** by sending the C++ message **getValue** to that object

The if-else Statement

C++ enables the if statement to support dual-alternative decision making. The general syntax for the dual-alternative if statement is:

```
if (condition)
  // statement or block of statements
else
  // statement or block of statements
```

The dual-alternative **if** statement uses the keyword **else** to separate the two sets of statements that offer the alternative actions. If the tested condition is true, the program executes the statement or statement block that comes after the tested condition. Otherwise, program execution resumes after the keyword **else** and executes the subsequent statement or statement block.

Here are examples of the dual-alternative **if** statement:

```
// example 1
if (nNum < 0)
  cout << "Value is negative\n";
else
  cout << "Value is 0 or greater\n"

// example 2
if (i > 0 && i < 100)
  j = i * i;
else
  j = 100;

// example 3
if (nCount < 1)
  nCount = 1
else
  nCount--;
```

The first example uses the **if** statement to determine whether or not the value in variable **nNum** is negative. If this condition is true, the **if** statement displays the message "Value is negative." Otherwise, the **if** statement executes the statement in the **else** clause to display the message "Value is 0 or greater."

The second example employs the **if** statement to determine if the variable i contains an integer in the range of 1 to 99. If this condition is true, the statement assigns the expression i * i to the variable j. Otherwise, the **if** statement executes the **else** clause statement to assign 100 to the variable j.

The third example uses the **if** statement to determine whether or not the value in variable **nCount** is less than 1. If this condition is true, the **if** statement assigns 1 to variable **nCount**. Otherwise, the **if** statement executes the **else** clause statement to decrement the value in variable **nCount**.

Let's look at a programming example. Listing 8-2 contains the source code for the IF4.CPP program, which illustrates the dual-alternative **if** statement. The program implements a class that finds the smaller and larger values of two integers. The program prompts you to enter two integers and then feeds your input to a class instance. The program then uses that instance to obtain the smaller and larger input values. If you enter two integers that are equal, the program displays a message to that effect.

Here is a sample session with the program in Listing 8-2:

```
Enter first integer : 67
Enter second integer : 55
Smaller integer is 55
Larger integer is 67
```

Listing 8-2
The source code for the IF4.CPP program.

```cpp
// A C++ program that illustrates
// the dual-alternative if statement

#include <iostream.h>

class minMaxFinder
{
  public:
    minMaxFinder();
    void setValues(int nNum1, int nNum2);
    int getMin()
      { return m_nMin; }
    int getMax()
      { return m_nMax; }

  protected:
    int m_nMin;
    int m_nMax;
};

minMaxFinder::minMaxFinder()
{
  m_nMin = -3768;
  m_nMax =  3767;
}
```

```
void minMaxFinder::setValues(int nNum1, int nNum2)
{
  if (nNum1 > nNum2) {
    m_nMin = nNum2;
    m_nMax = nNum1;
  }
  else {
    m_nMin = nNum1;
    m_nMax = nNum2;
  }
}

main()
{
  int nNum1, nNum2;
  minMaxFinder minMax;

  cout << "Enter first integer : ";
  cin >> nNum1;
  cout << "Enter second integer : ";
  cin >> nNum2;

  if (nNum1 != nNum2) {
    minMax.setValues(nNum1, nNum2);
    cout << "Smaller integer is " << minMax.getMin() << "\n";
    cout << "Larger integer is " <<  minMax.getMax() << "\n";
  }
  else
    cout << "Numbers are equal!";

  return 0;
}
```

Listing 8-2 declares the class **minMaxFinder**. The class has public and protected members. The protected members are the **int**-type data members **m_nMin** and **m_nMax**. These members store the smaller and larger values supplied to a class instance.

The class also declares the following public members:

- The constructor, which assigns the values –3768 and 3767 to the data members **m_nMin** and **m_nMax**, respectively.

- The member function **setValues**, which obtains the values to be compared. The parameters **nNum1** and **nNum2** pass these values to the function.

- The member function **getMin**, which returns the smaller value, stored in data member **m_nMin**.
- The member function **getMax**, which returns the bigger value, stored in data member **m_nMax**.

The definition of member function **setValues** uses a dual-alternative **if** statement to compare the values of the two parameters **nNum1** and **nNum2**. The condition of the **if** statement tests whether or not the value of parameter **nNum1** is greater than that of parameter **nNum2**. If this condition is true, the member function assigns the values of parameters **nNum2** and **nNum1** to the data members **m_nMin** and **m_nMax**, respectively. Otherwise, the member function uses the statements in the **else** clause to assign the values of parameters **nNum1** and **nNum2** to the data members **m_nMin** and **m_nMax**, respectively.

The function **main** declares the **int**-type variables **nNum1** and **nNum2**, along with the object **minMax**, which is an instance of class **minMaxFinder**. The function then performs the following tasks:

- Prompt you to enter two integers. This task stores your input in the variables **nNum1** and **nNum2**.
- Determine if the values in variables **nNum1** and **nNum2** are not equal. If this condition is true, the function **main** performs the remaining tasks. Otherwise, the function displays a message telling you that the two numbers are equal. This task uses a dual-alternative **if** statement. The **else** clause contains the output statement that comments on the equality of the input numbers.
- Assign the values of variables **nNum1** and **nNum2** to the object **minMax**. This task involves sending the C++ message **setValues** to the object **minMax**. The arguments for this message are the variables **nNum1** and **nNum2**.
- Display the smaller of the two input numbers. This task involves sending the C++ message **getMin** to the object **minMax**.
- Display the larger of the two input numbers. This task involves sending the C++ message **getMax** to the object **minMax**.

The Multiple-Alternative if Statement

C++ also permits the if statement to support multiple-alternative decision making. The general syntax for the multiple-alternative if statement is:

```
if (condition1)
  // statement #1 or block of statements #1
else if (condition2)
  // statement #2 or block of statements #2
else if (condition3)
  // statement #3 or block of statements #3
// other else if clauses
else
  // catch-all statement or catch-all block of statements
```

The multiple-alternative **if** statement allows a routine to test a battery of conditions and take one of multiple courses of action. The **if** statement tests the Boolean expressions **condition1**, **condition2**, **condition3**, and so on in that sequence. The first condition that is true causes the runtime system to execute its associated statements. Program execution resumes after the end of the **if** statement. If none of the tested conditions are true, the program executes the statements in the catch-all **else** clause (if one is used).

Here is an example of a multiple-alternative **if** statement:

```
if (N >= 0 && n < 10)
  cout << "Variable N is a single digit\n";
else if (N >= 10 && n < 100)
  cout << "Variable N has two digits\n";
else if (N >= 100 && n < 1000)
  cout << "Variable N has three digits\n";
else if (N >= 1000)
  cout << "Variable N has four or more digits\n";
else
  cout << "Variable N is negative\n";
```

This code snippet classifies the value in variable **N** as follows:

- The condition of the **if** clause determines whether or not the variable **N** contains an integer in the range of 0 to 9.

- The first **else if** clause determines whether or not the variable **N** contains an integer in the range of 10 to 99.

- The second **else if** clause determines whether or not the variable **N** contains an integer in the range of 100 to 999.

- The third else if clause determines whether or not the variable N contains an integer equal to or greater than 1000.

Each of the **if** and **else if** clauses displays a message reflecting the value in variable **N**. The catch-all **else** clause displays the message that the variable **N** contains a negative value.

Let's look at an example. Listing 8-3 shows the source code for the IF5.CPP program, which illustrates the multiple-alternative **if** statement. The program declares a class that takes an integer value between 0 and 9 and displays the English word for that digit. The class uses a special member function that allows you to trace the sequence of tested conditions.

Here is a sample session with the program in Listing 8-3. The output shows the tracer messages as well as the English word for the input digit:

```
Enter integer (0 to 9): 7
Comparing 7 with 0
Comparing 7 with 1
Comparing 7 with 2
Comparing 7 with 3
Comparing 7 with 4
Comparing 7 with 5
Comparing 7 with 6
Comparing 7 with 7
Digit is seven
```

CODING NOTES

When to Use the else Clause

Use the **else** clause to handle (or at least detect) the case when none of the tested conditions in an **if** statement are true.

CODING NOTES

Arranging the Tested Conditions

To speed up the execution of a multiple-alternative **if** statement, arrange the tested conditions in declining order of likelihood of being true. In other words, place the condition that is most likely to be true in the first **if** clause and the condition least likely to be true in the last **if else** clause.

Listing 8-3

The source code for the IF5.CPP program.

```cpp
// A C++ program that illustrates
// the multiple-alternative if statement

#include <iostream.h>

class sayDigit
{
  public:
    void sayIt(int nDigit);

  protected:
    int isEqual(int nVal1, int nVal2);
};

void sayDigit::sayIt(int nDigit)
{
  if (isEqual(nDigit, 0))
    cout << "Digit is zero\n";
  else if (isEqual(nDigit, 1))
    cout << "Digit is one\n";
  else if (isEqual(nDigit, 2))
    cout << "Digit is two\n";
  else if (isEqual(nDigit, 3))
    cout << "Digit is three\n";
  else if (isEqual(nDigit, 4))
    cout << "Digit is four\n";
  else if (isEqual(nDigit, 5))
    cout << "Digit is five\n";
  else if (isEqual(nDigit, 6))
    cout << "Digit is six\n";
  else if (isEqual(nDigit, 7))
    cout << "Digit is seven\n";
  else if (isEqual(nDigit, 8))
    cout << "Digit is eight\n";
  else if (isEqual(nDigit, 9))
    cout << "Digit is nine\n";
  else
    cout << "Multi-digit or negative integer!\n";
}

sayDigit::isEqual(int nVal1, int nVal2)
{
  cout << "Comparing " << nVal1 << " with " << nVal2 << "\n";
  return (nVal1 == nVal2) ? 1 : 0;
}

main()
{
  int nNum;
  sayDigit Digit;
```

```
cout << "Enter integer (0 to 9): ";
cin >> nNum;

if (nNum >= 0 && nNum < 10)
  Digit.sayIt(nNum);
else
  cout << "Your input is out of range!\n";

return 0;
}
```

Listing 8-3 declares the class **sayDigit**. This class declares the public member function **sayIt** and the protected member function **isEqual**.

The member function **isEqual** has the **int**-return type and two **int**-type parameters **nVal1** and **nVal2**. The function displays a message that it is comparing the values of the parameters and then returns 1 if they have equal values or yields 0 if they are not equal.

The member function **sayIt** uses the multiple-alternative **if** statement to determine if the value of the parameter is a single-digit integer. The **if** statement uses the member function **isEqual** to compare the value of parameter **nDigit** with a single-digit constant. Using the member function **isEqual** allows the program to trace the sequence of tested conditions—this way you don't have to take my word for it! The **if** statement has a catch-all **else** clause that displays a message telling you that the parameter has a multiple-digit or a negative value.

The function **main** declares the variable **nNum** and the object **Digit** as an instance of class **sayDigit**. The function prompts you to enter a digit, which it stores in variable **nNum**. The function then uses a dual-alternative **if** statement to determine if your input is a single-digit non-negative integer. If this condition is true, the function sends the C++ message **sayIt** to the object **Digit**. The argument for this message is the variable **nNum**. The message **sayIt** displays the tracer messages of member function **isEqual** and then displays the English word for the value in variable **nNum**.

The switch Statement

C++ offers the **switch** statement to support multiple-alternative decision making. The general syntax for the multiple-alternative **switch** statement is:

```
switch(expression)
{
  case constantExpression1:
    // statement set #1
    break;
  case constantExpression2:
    // statement set #2
    break;
. . .
[default:
  // catch-all statements]
}
```

The **switch** statement examines the value of the expression, which must be integer or integer-compatible (as are characters and enumerated types). The condition of the **switch** can be a variable, a function call, or an expression that includes constants, variables, and function calls.

The **switch** statement uses **case** labels for comparing the tested expression with different values. C++ has the following rules about the **case** labels:

1. The keyword **case** is followed by a single constant (either a literal constant or a constant expression), followed in turn by a colon.

2. You can include a sequence of more than one **case** label; all such labels end up executing the first sequence of statements that follows.

3. A **case** label cannot list a range of constant values. Each **case** label lists only one constant.

Program execution sequentially examines the values in the **case** labels. If a **case** label value matches the tested expression, the program executes the statements that come after the **case** label.

BASIC

Use the break Statement

Use the **break** statement at the end of each set of statements to resume program execution after the end of the **switch** statement. If you do not include the **break** statement, program execution examines the remaining case labels! Thus the default sequence of evaluation of case labels is radically different from that in the SELECT CASE statement in BASIC.

You may be surprised to read that the SELECT CASE statement in many recent BASIC implementations runs circles around the C++ **switch** statement! The rules for using the **case** labels indicate that the **switch** statement is suitable in examining a relatively limited set of values. You are better off using the multiple-alternative **if** statement to perform sophisticated decision making.

PASCAL

Use the break Statement

Use the **break** statement at the end of each set of statements to resume program execution after the end of the **switch** statement. If you do not include the **break** statement, program execution examines the remaining case labels! Thus the default sequence of evaluation the case labels is radically different from that in the CASE statement in Pascal.

You may be amazed to learn that the CASE statement in Pascal is much more flexible than the C++ **switch** statement. The rules for using the **case** labels imply that the **switch** statement is appropriate in examining a rather limited set of values. You are better off employing the multiple-alternative **if** statement to carry out involved decision-making.

A SAMPLE PROGRAM

Let me present a programming example. Listing 8-4 shows the source code for the SWITCH2.CPP program, which illustrates the multiple-alternative **switch** statement. The listing implements a version of the source code in Listing 8-3 that uses the **switch** statement instead of the **if** statement. However, the nature ofn the **switch** statement and its case labels prevents me from using a member function that traces the sequence of comparing the **switch** expression with the **case** labels. (This time you have to take my word for it!) The program prompts you to enter a single-digit integer and displays the English name of that digit.

Here is a sample session with the program in Listing 8-4:

```
Enter integer (0 to 9): 8
Digit is eight
```

Listing 8-4

The source code for the SWITCH2.CPP program.

```cpp
// A C++ program that illustrates
// the multiple-alternative switch statement

#include <iostream.h>

class sayDigit
{
  public:
    void sayIt(int nDigit);
};

void sayDigit::sayIt(int nDigit)
{
  switch (nDigit) {
    case 0:
      cout << "Digit is zero\n";
      break;

    case 1:
      cout << "Digit is one\n";
      break;

    case 2:
      cout << "Digit is two\n";
      break;

    case 3:
      cout << "Digit is three\n";
      break;

    case 4:
      cout << "Digit is four\n";
      break;

    case 5:
      cout << "Digit is five\n";
      break;
```

```
    case 6:
      cout << "Digit is six\n";
      break;

    case 7:
      cout << "Digit is seven\n";
      break;

    case 8:
      cout << "Digit is eight\n";
      break;

    case 9:
      cout << "Digit is nine\n";
      break;

    default:
      cout << "Multi-digit or negative integer!\n";
  }
}

main()
{
  int nNum;
  sayDigit Digit;

  cout << "Enter integer (0 to 9): ";
  cin >> nNum;

  if (nNum >= 0 && nNum < 10)
    Digit.sayIt(nNum);
  else
    cout << "Your input is out of range!\n";

  return 0;
}
```

Listing 8-4 declares the class **sayDigit**, which contains the public member function **sayIt**. This function has the **int**-type parameter **nDigit**. The definition of member function **sayIt** uses the **switch** statement to examine the value in parameter **nDigit**. The **switch** statement uses ten **case** labels to compare **nDigit** with the integers 0 through 9. Each **case** label has two statements: The first is an output statement that displays the English name of the digit, and the second is the **break** statement. The **switch** statement has the **default** clause, which displays a message telling you that the parameter **nDigit** is a multi-digit or negative integer.

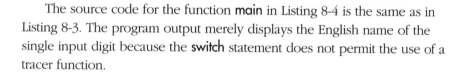

The source code for the function **main** in Listing 8-4 is the same as in Listing 8-3. The program output merely displays the English name of the single input digit because the **switch** statement does not permit the use of a tracer function.

A PROGRAM WITH NO BREAKS!

Let me present a version of program SWITCH2.CPP that does not use the **break** statement. Listing 8-5 shows the source code for the SWITCH3.CPP program. I created the source code for file SWITCH3.CPP by replacing the **break** statements in member function **sayIt** with the expression **nDigit++**. This expression increments the value of parameter **nDigit** (which is also used as the expression of the **switch** statement). This change causes the **switch** statement to display the output for the first constant that matches **nDigit** followed by the output of all subsequent constants. For example, if the argument of parameter **nDigit** is 5, then the **switch** statement displays the output of **case** labels 5 through 9 and the default clause. In other words, the **switch** statement generates cascaded output.

Here is a sample session with the program in Listing 8-5 (notice the cascaded output):

```
Enter integer (0 to 9): 0
Digit is zero
Digit is one
Digit is two
Digit is three
Digit is four
Digit is five
Digit is six
Digit is seven
Digit is eight
Digit is nine
Multi-digit or negative integer!
```

Listing 8-5

The source code for the SWITCH3.CPP program.

```cpp
// A C++ program that illustrates
// the multiple-alternative switch statement

#include <iostream.h>

class sayDigit
{
  public:
    void sayIt(int nDigit);
};

class sayDigit
{
  public:
    void sayIt(int nDigit);
};

void sayDigit::sayIt(int nDigit)
{
  switch (nDigit) {
    case 0:
      cout << "Digit is zero\n";

    case 1:
      cout << "Digit is one\n";

    case 2:
      cout << "Digit is two\n";

    case 3:
      cout << "Digit is three\n";

    case 4:
      cout << "Digit is four\n";

    case 5:
      cout << "Digit is five\n";

    case 6:
      cout << "Digit is six\n";

    case 7:
      cout << "Digit is seven\n";

    case 8:
      cout << "Digit is eight\n";

    case 9:
      cout << "Digit is nine\n";
```

```
      default:
        cout << "Multi-digit or negative integer!\n";
    }
}

main()
{
  int nNum;
  sayDigit Digit;

  cout << "Enter integer (0 to 9): ";
  cin >> nNum;

  if (nNum >= 0 && nNum < 10)
    Digit.sayIt(nNum);
  else
    cout << "Your input is out of range!\n";

  return 0;
}
```

THE IF STATEMENT IS BETTER THAN THE SWITCH STATEMENT

The earlier programming notes to BASIC and Pascal programmers mentioned that the **if** statement is better suited than the **switch** statement for dealing with a wide range of values. Let me present an example to illustrate how this is true. Listing 8-6 contains the source code for the SWITCH4.CPP program. The program prompts you to enter a character and then classifies the input as a lowercase, uppercase, digit, or punctuation character. The program uses two similar classes to generate the output. The first class discerns the category of the input character using a **switch** statement. The second class uses an **if** statement to classify the input character. If you examine the source code, you will realize that the class that uses the **switch** statement is not completely coded! Instead, it shows *sample* **case** labels to keep the listing short.

Here is a sample session with the program in Listing 8-6:

```
Enter a character : b
Character is a lowercase character (using a switch statement)
Character is a lowercase character (using an if statement)
```

Listing 8-6

The source code for the SWITCH4.CPP program.

```cpp
// A C++ program that illustrates that
// the if statement is more efficient than
// the switch statement for comparing
// an expression with a wide range of values

#include <iostream.h>

class sayChar
{
  public:
    void sayIt(char cChar);
};

class tellChar
{
  public:
    void sayIt(char cChar);
};

void sayChar::sayIt(char cChar)
{
  switch (cChar) {
    case 'a':
    case 'b':
    case 'c':
    // place other case labels
      cout << "a lowercase character";
      break;

    case 'A':
    case 'B':
    case 'C':
    // place other case labels
      cout << "an uppercase character";
      break;

    case '0':
    case '1':
    case '2':
    // place other case labels
      cout << "a digit";
      break;

    default:
      cout << "a punctuation character";
  }
  cout << " (using a switch statement)\n";
}

void tellChar::sayIt(char cChar)
```

Partial Case label list

```
{
  if (cChar >= 'a' && cChar <= 'z')
    cout << "a lowercase character";
  else if (cChar >= 'A' && cChar <= 'Z')
    cout << "an uppercase character";
  else if (cChar >= '0' && cChar <= '1')
    cout << "a digit";
  else
    cout << "a puncutation character";
  cout << " (using an if statement)\n";
}


main()
{
  char cChar;
  sayChar objChar1;
  tellChar objChar2;

  cout << "Enter a character : ";
  cin >> cChar;

  cout << "Character is ";
  objChar1.sayIt(cChar);

  cout << "Character is ";
  objChar2.sayIt(cChar);

  return 0;
}
```

Listing 8-6 declares the classes **sayChar** and **tellChar**. Each class declares its own version of member function **sayIt**.

The member function **sayChar::sayIt** uses a **switch** statement to examine the values of parameter **cChar**. The first set of **case** labels lists the character constants 'a', 'b', and 'c'. This list falls very short of recording the remaining lowercase characters. The second set of **case** labels lists the character constants 'A', 'B', and 'C'. Again, this list falls very short of recording the remaining uppercase characters. The third set of **case** labels lists the character constants '0', '1', and '2'. This list also falls short of recording the remaining digits. The default clause is supposed to handle punctuation characters. The current form of the listing ends up invoking the default clause for all the characters that are not listed in the **case** labels.

The member function **tellChar::sayIt** uses a multiple-alternative **if** statement to classify the value in parameter **cChar**. The **if** clause, the two **if else** clauses, and the **else** clause succeed in performing the classification task—no ifs and buts!

The function **main** declares the **char**-type variable **cChar** and the objects **objChar1** and **objChar2** as instances of classes **sayChar** and **tellChar**, respectively. The function prompts you to enter a character. The function **main** uses that input as the argument for the C++ message **sayIt**, which it sends to the objects **objChar1** and **objChar2**.

The example also shows you how to associate a set of statements with multiple **case** labels.

Nested Decision-Making Constructs

C++ allows you to nest decision-making constructs. Thus, you can nest **if** statements within **switch** statements and **switch** statements within **if** statements.

CODING NOTES

A Potential Problem with the Nested if Statement

There is a potential problem with a nested single-alternative **if** statement in a dual-alternative **if** statement. The problem may occur because the compiler may consider the **else** clause as part of the inner single-alternative **if** statement. Here is an example:

```
if (nCount >= 0)
   if (nCount == 0)
     nCount = 1;
 else
   nCount = nCountOld;
```

The indentation of the code snippet suggests that the first **if** statement is *meant* to own the **else** clause. However, the compiler regards the **else** clause as connected to the second **if** statement. In other words, the compiler thinks you meant this:

```
if (nCount >= 0)
   if (nCount == 0)
     nCount = 1;
   else
     nCount = nCountOld;
```

To solve this problem, enclose the nested **if** statement in a block, as shown below:

```
if (nCount >= 0) {
   if (nCount == 0)
     nCount = 1;
 }
 else
   nCount = nCountOld;
```

This form of the code snippet removes all ambiguity and compiles to give the correct logic.

Let's look at an example. Listing 8-7 shows the source code for the SWITCH5.CPP program, which illustrates a **switch** statement nested in an **if** statement. The program prompts you to enter a character. It then classifies the input as lowercase character, lowercase vowel, uppercase character, uppercase vowel, digit, or punctuation. The source code for the program uses **switch** statements inside the **if** statement to distinguish between vowels and nonvowels.

Here is a sample session with the program in Listing 8-7:

```
Enter a character : U
Character is an uppercase vowel
```

Listing 8-7
The source code for the SWITCH5.CPP program.

```cpp
// A C++ program that illustrates
// nested decision-making constructs

#include <iostream.h>

class sayChar
{
  public:
    void sayIt(char cChar);
};

void sayChar::sayIt(char cChar)
{
  if (cChar >= 'a' && cChar <= 'z')
    switch (cChar) {
      case 'a':
      case 'i':
      case 'o':
      case 'e':
      case 'u':
        cout << "a lowercase vowel\n";
        break;

      default:
        cout << "a lowercase character\n";
    }
```

```
   else if (cChar >= 'A' && cChar <= 'Z')
     switch (cChar) {
       case 'A':
       case 'I':
       case 'O':
       case 'E':
       case 'U':
         cout << "an uppercase vowel\n";
         break;

       default:
         cout << "an uppercase character\n";
     }
   else if (cChar >= '0' && cChar <= '9')
     cout << "a digit";
   else
     cout << "a puncutation character\n";
}

main()
{
  char cChar;
  sayChar objChar;

  cout << "Enter a character : ";
  cin >> cChar;

  cout << "Character is ";
  objChar.sayIt(cChar);

  return 0;
}
```

Listing 8-7 declares the class **sayChar**, which has the member function **sayIt**. This member function has the **char**-type parameter **cChar**. The member function uses a multiple-alternative **if** statement to classify the character in parameter **cChar** as lowercase, uppercase, digit, or punctuation. The **if** clause contains a **switch** statement that further examines the value of the parameter. The **switch** statement uses a set of **case** labels to determine if the parameter stores a lowercase vowel. If this condition is true, the program displays a message to that effect. Otherwise, the **switch** statement displays the output in the **default** clause.

The **if** statement uses the first **else if** clause to determine if the parameter stores an uppercase character. The **if else** clause contains a **switch** statement that further examines the value of the parameter. The **switch** statement uses a set of **case** labels to determine if the parameter stores an uppercase vowel. If this condition is true, the program displays a message to that effect. Otherwise, the **switch** statement displays the output in the **default** clause.

The preceding example shows you how nesting a **switch** statement in an **if** statement helps you zoom in on specific values in a wide range of values. The clauses of the **if** statement zoom in on general ranges, leaving the **switch** statement to home in on specific values.

Summary

This chapter presented the **if** and **switch** statements, which support decision making in C++. You learned about the various kinds of **if** statements: single-alternative, dual-alternative, and multiple-alternative. You also learned about the rules of using the **switch** statement. The chapter also discussed nesting decision-making constructs and pointed out a potential problem with nesting **if** statements.

The next chapter presents the C++ loops that allow your applications to repeat tasks. You will learn about fixed and conditional loops.

9

Loops

*L*oops enable programs to repeat tasks tirelessly. In fact the ability to repeat operations virtually endlessly (without fatigue-based errors) was among the most prominent features of the first computers. This chapter looks at the fixed and conditional loops in C++. You will learn about the for loop, the open-iteration for loop, the **do-while** loop, the **while** loop, exiting loops, skipping loop iterations, and nested loops.

The for Loop

C++ has inherited the fixed-iteration for loop from C and slightly improved on it. The C++ for loop is superior to FOR loops in other common programming languages such as BASIC and Pascal because it offers more control over initializing and incrementing the loop control variables. In addition, a C++ for loop supports better management of the loop's iterations. The general syntax for the for loop is:

```
for (initializationPart; iterationConditionPart, incrementPart);
```

The **for** loop contains the following three parts:

- The initialization part, which initializes the loop control variable(s). You can use single or multiple loop control variables.
- The iteration part, which contains a Boolean expression that causes the loop to iterate as long as the expression is true
- The increment part, which increments or decrements the loop control variable(s)

Here are examples of the **for** loop:

```
// example 1
for (i = 0; i < 10; i++)
  cout << i << "\n";

// example 2
for (i = 9; i >= 0; i -= 3)
  cout << (i*i) << "\n";

// example 3
for (int i = 1; i < 100; i++)
  cout << i << "\n";

// example 4
for (int i = 0, j = MAX; i < j; i++, j--)
  cout << (i + 2 * j) << "\n";
```

The first example initializes the loop control variable i to 0 and iterates as long as the value in variable i is less than 10. The loop increment part increases the value of variable i by 1. Thus the upward-counting loop iterates 10 times with the value in variable i changing from 0 to 9.

The second example shows a downward-counting loop that initializes the loop control variable i to 9. The loop iterates as long as the value in variable i is not negative. The loop increment part decreases the value of variable i by 3. Thus the loop iterates four times with the value in variable i having the sequence 9, 6, 3, and 0.

The third example shows an interesting C++ feature that is related to the **for** loop: This example declares the loop control variable i and also initializes it to 1. The loop iterates as long as the value in variable i is less than 100. The loop increment part increases the value of variable i by 1. Thus, the upward-counting loop iterates 99 times with the value in variable i changing from 1 to 99.

The fourth example shows that a C++ **for** loop can declare and initialize multiple loop control variables. The loop initializes the variables i and j to 0 and **MAX**, respectively. The loop iterates as long as the value in variable i is less than that in variable j. The loop increment part increases the value in each of the variables i and j by 1.

CODING NOTES

Declaring Loop Control Variables

When a **for** loop declares a loop control variable, that variable remains until the end of the scope that contains the **for** loop. Thus, the following code snippet contains valid statements:

```
for (int i = 0; i < 10; i++)
   cout << i << "\n";
cout << "Value of control variable "
     << "after loop ends is " << i << "\n";
```

BASIC

New for Loop Features

The two most relevant differences between FOR loops in BASIC and C++ are:

The C++ **for** loop uses a Boolean expression instead of an upper limit value to determine the extent of the iteration.

The C++ **for** loop can use multiple loop control variables.

PASCAL

New for Loop Features

The three most relevant differences between **for** loops in Pascal and those in C++ are:

The C++ **for** loop has an increment part that allows you to alter the value of the loop control variable by values other than 1.

The C++ **for** loop uses a Boolean expression instead of an upper limit value to decide the limit of the iteration.

The C++ **for** loop may utilize more than one loop control variable.

C

New for Loop Features

C++ **for** loops can declare their control variables.

A FOR LOOP TO GENERATE RANDOM NUMBERS

Let's look at an example that uses **for** loops. Listing 9-1 shows the source code for the FOR3.CPP program. The program declares a class that generates random numbers between 0 and 1 (exclusive). In addition, the class has a member function that calculates the statistical mean and standard deviation for a set of generated random numbers. The program emits samples of random numbers and then displays the statistical mean and standard deviation for samples of 100, 1000, and 10,000 random numbers. Statistical analysis tells us that equal-probability random number generators should yield mean and standard deviation values that are close to 0.5 and 0.28, respectively.

Here is a sample session with the program in Listing 9-1:

```
Sample of random numbers is:
0.708324
0.0629052
0.906369
0.329864
0.834571

Sample size    = 100
Mean           = 0.55095
Std. Deviation = 0.292456

Sample size    = 1000
Mean           = 0.507353
Std. Deviation = 0.287227

Sample size    = 10000
Mean           = 0.494396
Std. Deviation = 0.288884
```

Listing 9-1

The source code for the FOR3.CPP program.

```cpp
// A C++ program that illustrates the for loop

#include <iostream.h>
#include <math.h>

const double PI = 4 * atan(1);

class myRandomNumber
{
  public:
    myRandomNumber(double fInitSeed = 13);
    double getRandom();
    void testRandom(long lCount, double& fMean, double& fSdev);

  protected:
    double m_fSeed;

    double frac(double x);
    double sqr(double x);
    double cube(double x);
};

myRandomNumber::myRandomNumber(double fInitSeed)
{
  m_fSeed = fInitSeed;
}

double myRandomNumber::getRandom()
{
  m_fSeed = frac(cube(m_fSeed + PI));
  return m_fSeed;
}

void myRandomNumber::testRandom(long lCount, double& fMean,
                                double& fSdev)
{
  double fSumX = 0;
  double fSumXX = 0;
  double fX;

  if (lCount < 2)
    return;

  for (long i = lCount; i > 0; i--) {
    fX = getRandom();
    fSumX += fX;
    fSumXX += sqr(fX);
  }
  // calculate mean
  fMean = fSumX / lCount;
  // calculate std. deviation
  fSdev = sqrt((fSumXX - sqr(fSumX) / lCount) / (lCount - 1));
```

```
}

double myRandomNumber::frac(double x)
{
  int nInt = int(x);
  return x - nInt;
}

double myRandomNumber::sqr(double x)
{
  return x * x;
}


  double myRandomNumber::cube(double x)
  {
    return x * x * x;
  }


  main()
  {
    myRandomNumber RN;
    double fMean;
    double fSdev;

    cout << "Sample of random numbers is:\n";
    for (int i = 0; i < 5; i++)
      cout << RN.getRandom() << "\n";
    cout << "\n";

    for (long nNum = 100; nNum <= 10000; nNum *= 10) {
      RN.testRandom(nNum, fMean, fSdev);
      cout << "Sample size    = " << nNum << "\n"
           << "Mean           = " << fMean << "\n"
           << "Std. Deviation = " << fSdev << "\n\n";
    }

    return 0;
}
```

Listing 9-1 declares the class **myRandomNumber**. The class declares public and protected members. The protected members are:

- The **double**-type data member **m_fSeed**, which stores the last random number generated. The class also uses the value in this member to generate the next random number.

- The member function **frac**, which returns the fractional part of a floating-point number

- The member function **sqr**, which returns the squared value

- The member function **cube**, which returns the cubed value

The class **myRandomNumber** declares the following public members:

- The constructor, which initializes the data member **m_fSeed**. The parameter **fInitSeed** has a default argument.

- The member function **getRandom**, which returns the random number

- The member function **testRandom**, which tests the basic statistics for a set of **lCount** random numbers. The reference parameters **fMean** and **fSdev** return the mean and standard deviation statistics, respectively, to the caller.

The definition of member function **testRandom** declares the local variables **fSumX**, **fSumXX**, and **fX**. The function initializes the first two variables to 0 and uses them to add the values and squared values of the generated random numbers. The member function uses a downward-counting **for** loop to perform the following tasks:

- Generate a random number using member function **getRandom**. This task stores the number in variable **fX**.

- Add the value of variable **fX** to the variable **fSumX**

- Add the squared value of variable **fX** to variable **fSumXX**

The loop declares the **long**-type control variable **i** and initializes it using the value of **long**-type parameter **lCount**. The loop iterates as long as variable **i** contains a positive value. The loop increment part decreases the value of the control variable by 1. The statements following the **for** loop calculate the desired statistics and store them in the parameters **fMean** and **fSdev**.

The function **main** declares the object **RN** as an instance of class **myRandomNumber**. The function also declares the variables **fMean** and **fSdev**.

The function **main** displays a sample of five random numbers using the first **for** loop in that function. The upward-counting loop declares and uses the variable i. The loop iterates five times. Each loop iteration displays a random number. This task involves sending the C++ message getRandom to the object RN.

To obtain the basic statistics for the random number generator, the function main uses a second for loop. This loop declares and initializes the long-type variable nNum. The initial value of this variable is 100. The loop iterates as long as the value in variable nNum does not exceed 10,000. The loop increment value alters the value of variable nNum by multiplying it by 10. Thus the loop iterates three times, with the values of the loop control variable changing from 100, to 1000, and then to 10,000. The for loop shows you that you can increase the value of a loop control variable by multiplication (and not just addition). The first loop statement sends the C++ message testRandom to object RN. This message has the arguments nNum, fMean, and fSdev. The last two arguments yield the desired basic statistics. The loop's output statements display the results.

A FOR LOOP TO DISPLAY SUMMATIONS

Let's look at another example of for loops that increment their control variables by values other than 1. Listing 9-2 contains the source code for FOR4.CPP. The program displays the sum and sum of squares for a range of integers from 1 to 100. The program displays these summations in increments of 1 to 4. In other words, the first set of summations deals with the sequence 1, 2, 3, and so on, whereas the second set of summation deals with the sequence 1, 3, 5, and so on. Likewise, further sets select every third integer and every fourth integer.

Here is the output of the program in Listing 9-2:

```
For the range of 1 to 100
Sum of integers in increments of 1 = 5050
Sum of squared integers in increments of 1 = 338350

Sum of integers in increments of 2 = 2500
Sum of squared integers in increments of 2 = 171700

Sum of integers in increments of 3 = 1717
Sum of squared integers in increments of 3 = 116161

Sum of integers in increments of 4 = 1225
Sum of squared integers in increments of 4 = 88400
```

Listing 9-2

The source code for the FOR4.CPP program.

```cpp
// A C++ program that illustrates for loops
// that increment/decrement their control
// variables by more than 1

#include <iostream.h>

class SumOfNumbers
{
  public:
    void setLimits(const int nFirst,
                   const int nLast,
                   const int nStep = 1);
    double getSum();
    double getSumOfSquares();

  protected:
    int m_nFirst;
    int m_nLast;
    int m_nStep;

    double sqr(double x);
};

void SumOfNumbers::setLimits(const int nFirst,
                             const int nLast,
                             const int nStep)
{
  // verify sequence of range value
  // and assign the range to data members
  if (nFirst < nLast) {
    m_nFirst = nFirst;
    m_nLast = nLast;
  }
  else {
    m_nFirst = nLast;
    m_nLast = nFirst;
  }

  // verify step value and assign the step
  // to data member m_nStep
  if (nStep > 0)
    m_nStep = nStep;
  else
    m_nStep = 1;
}

double SumOfNumbers::getSum()
{
  double fSum = 0;
```

```
for (int i = m_nFirst; i <= m_nLast; i += m_nStep)          Upward-counting loop
    fSum += (double)i;

  return fSum;
}

double SumOfNumbers::getSumOfSquares()
{
  double fSum = 0;

  for (int i = m_nLast; i >= m_nFirst; i -= m_nStep)          Downward-counting loop
    fSum += sqr(double(i));

  return fSum;
}

double SumOfNumbers::sqr(double x)
{
  return x * x;
}

main()
{
  SumOfNumbers SON;
  int nFirst = 1;
  int nLast = 100;

  cout << "For the range of " << nFirst
       << " to " << nLast << "\n";
  for (int nIncr = 1; nIncr < 5; nIncr++) {
    SON.setLimits(nFirst, nLast, nIncr);
    cout << "Sum of integers in increments of "
         << nIncr << " = " << SON.getSum() << "\n";
    cout << "Sum of squared integers in increments of "
         << nIncr << " = " << SON.getSumOfSquares()
         << "\n\n";
  }

  return 0;
}
```

Listing 9-2 declares the class **SumOfNumbers**. This class declares public and protected members. The protected members are:

■ The **int**-type data members **m_nFirst** and **m_nLast**, which define the range of integers to process

- The int-type data member **m_nStep**, which stores the increment in the integer values

- The member function **sqr**, which returns the squared values

The class declares the following public members:

- The member function **setLimits**, which assigns values to the data members. These values define the range of integers and the increment in integer values.

- The member function **getSum** returns the sum of integers. The data members **m_nFirst** and **m_nLast** specify the range of integers. The data member **m_nStep** defines the increment in the value of the loop control variable.

- The member function **getSumOfSquares** yields the sum of squared integers. Again, the data members **m_nFirst** and **m_nLast** specify the range of integers, and the data member **m_nStep** defines the increment in the value of the loop control variable.

The member function **getSum** uses an upward-counting **for** loop to obtain the sum of integers. The loop declares the control variable **i** and initializes it with the value of data member **m_nFirst**. The loop iterates as long as the value in variable **i** does not exceeds the value in data member **m_nLast**. The increment part increases the value of the loop control variable by the value of the data member **m_nStep**. Each loop iteration adds the value of the loop control variable to the local variable **fSum**. The function **getSum** returns the value in that variable.

The member function **getSumOfSquares** uses a downward-counting **for** loop to obtain the sum of squared integers. The loop declares the control variable **i**, initializing it with the value of data member **m_nLast**. The loop iterates as long as the value in variable **i** does not fall below the value in data member **m_nFirst**. The increment part decreases the value of the loop control variable by the value of the data member **m_nStep**. Each loop iteration adds the squared value of the loop control variable to the local variable **fSum**. The function **getSumOfSquares** returns the value in variable **fSum**.

The function **main** declares the object **SON** as an instance of the class **SumOfNumbers**. The function also declares and initializes the variables **nFirst** and **nLast**. The function uses a **for** loop to display the summations in increments of 1 to 4. The loop declares and initializes the variable **nIncr** with the value of 1. The loop iterates as long as the value in the loop control variable is less than 5. The loop increment part increases the value in variable **nIncr** by 1. Each loop iteration sends the C++ message **setLimits** to the object **SON**. The arguments for this message are **nFirst**, **nLast**, and **nIncr**. The loop then displays the sum and sum of squares by sending the C++ messages **getSum** and **getSumOfSquares**, respectively, to the object **SON**.

ANOTHER EXAMPLE OF USING FOR LOOPS FOR SUMMATIONS

Let me present a programming example that uses multiple loop control variables. Listing 9-3 contains the source code for the FOR5.CPP program, which uses two such variables. The program calculates and displays the sum and sum of squares for integers in the range of 1 to 100. The program illustrates the use of two loop control variables to halve the number of loop iterations. I will discuss the loop control variables in more detail after Listing 9-3.

Here is the output of the program in Listing 9-3:

```
For the range of 1 to 100
Sum of integers   = 5050
Sum of squared integers = 338350
```

Listing 9-3

The source code for the FOR5.CPP program.

```
// A C++ program that illustrates a for loop
// that uses multiple loop control variables

#include <iostream.h>

class SumOfNumbers
{
  public:
    void setLimits(const int nFirst, const int nLast);
    double getSum();
    double getSumOfSquares();
```

```
  protected:
    int m_nFirst;
    int m_nLast;
    int m_nNumInts;

    double sqr(double x);
};

void SumOfNumbers::setLimits(const int nFirst,
                             const int nLast)
{
  // verify sequence of range value
  // and assign the range to data members
  if (nFirst < nLast) {
    m_nFirst = nFirst;
    m_nLast = nLast;
  }
  else {
    m_nFirst = nLast;
    m_nLast = nFirst;
  }

  m_nNumInts = m_nLast - m_nFirst + 1;
}

double SumOfNumbers::getSum()
{
  double fSum = 0;

  for (int i = m_nFirst, j = m_nLast;
       i < j;
       i++, j--)
    fSum += (double)i + double(j);

  // does the range of integers contain
  // an odd number of values
  if (m_nNumInts % 2 == 1)
    fSum += double(m_nFirst + m_nLast) / 2;

  return fSum;
}

double SumOfNumbers::getSumOfSquares()
{
  double fSum = 0;

  for (int i = m_nFirst, j = m_nLast;
       i < j;
       i++, j--)
    fSum += sqr(double(i)) + sqr(double(j));
```

```
    // does the range of integers contain
    // an odd number of values
    if (m_nNumInts % 2 == 1)
      fSum += sqr(double(m_nFirst + m_nLast)) / 2;

    return fSum;
}

double SumOfNumbers::sqr(double x)
{
    return x * x;
}

main()
{
    SumOfNumbers SON;
    int nFirst = 1;
    int nLast = 100;

    SON.setLimits(nFirst, nLast);
    cout << "For the range of " << nFirst
         << " to " << nLast << "\n";
    cout << "Sum of integers  = " << SON.getSum() << "\n";
    cout << "Sum of squared integers = "
         << SON.getSumOfSquares() << "\n";

    return 0;
}
```

Listing 9-3 declares a new version of class **SumOfNumbers**. This class has the members that are very similar to the ones in Listing 9-2 (the new version replaces data member **m_nStep** with **m_nNumInts**, which stores the number of integers to add). The new version uses **for** loops with two control variables in member functions **getSum** and **getSumOfSquares**.

The member function **getSum** contains a **for** loop that declares and initializes the control variables i and j. The initial values for these variables are **m_nFirst** and **m_nLast**, respectively. Thus, the variable i handles the lower-value integers, whereas variable j deals with the higher-value integers. The loop iterates as long as the value in variable i is less than that in variable j. The loop increment part increments and decrements variables i and j, respectively, by 1. Each loop iteration adds the typecasted values for variables i and j to the variable **fSum**. Thus, the **for** loop adds the sought-for numbers in about half the interactions of the **for** loop in Listing 9-2.

The member function **getSum** also determines if it is adding an odd number of integers. If this is true, the function needs to add in the median integer that was left out by the loop.

The member function **getSumOfSquares** uses a **for** loop that is similar to that of member function **getSum**. The loop adds the squared values of the control variables **i** and **j**.

The function **main** declares the object **SON** as an instance of the class **SumOfNumbers**. The function also declares and initializes the variables **nFirst** and **nLast**. The function then performs the following tasks:

- Set the range of integers by sending the C++ message **setLimits** to the object **SON**. The arguments for this message are the variables **nFirst** and **nLast**.

- Display the values in the variables **nFirst** and **nLast**

- Display the sum of integers by sending the C++ message **getSum** to object **SON**

- Display the sum of the integers squared by sending the C++ message **getSumOfSquares** to object **SON**

The Open-Iteration for Loop

By now you should be getting a feel of how versatile a **for** loop is in C++. The three parts of the loop offer you a lot of flexibility in setting up and managing its iterations. Interestingly, C++ (like C) allows any or all three parts of a **for** loop to be empty! For example, you can initialize a loop control variable *before* the loop's statement. You can also increment the loop control variable *inside* the loop's statements.

What happens when a **for** loop has all three parts empty? The answer is that you get an open-iteration loop. The source code needs to initialize, increment, and test the loop iteration outside the three parts of the **for** loop. Here is a code snippet that illustrates the open-iteration **for** loop's features:

```
int i = 0; // initialize variable
int j;
for (;;) {
  cout << i << " : ";
  // test loop condition and exit if i >= 10
  if (i >= 10)
    break;
  j = i + i * i - 5;
  i++; // increment loop control variable
  cout << j << "\n";
}
```

This snippet initializes the variable i and uses that variable to control the iterations of the **for** loop. The loop displays the value in variable i and then tests the loop's condition. If the value in variable i is equal to or greater than 10, the loop exits using the **break** statement (see the section "Exiting Loops" later in this chapter). The loop then calculates the value for variable j, increments variable i, and displays the value in variable j. The statement i++; increments the loop control variable and allows iteration to progress.

Let's look at a programming example. Listing 9-4 shows the source code for the FOR6.CPP program, which illustrates an open-iteration **for** loop. The program uses open-iteration loops for two purposes: first, to calculate factorials; and second, to obtain the factorials for integers from 1 up to the value whose factorial does not exceed 1000.

Here is the output of the program in Listing 9-4:

```
Factorial of 2 = 2
Factorial of 3 = 6
Factorial of 4 = 24
Factorial of 5 = 120
Factorial of 6 = 720
```

Listing 9-4
The source code for the FOR6.CPP program.

```
// A C++ program that illustrates an open-iteration for loop

#include <iostream.h>

double Factorial(const unsigned n);

main()
{
  const double HI = 1000.0;
  double fFact;
  unsigned nNum = 2;
```

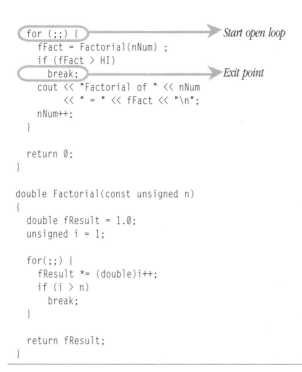

```
for (;;) {
    fFact = Factorial(nNum) ;
    if (fFact > HI)
        break;
    cout << "Factorial of " << nNum
         << " = " << fFact << "\n";
    nNum++;
}

return 0;
}

double Factorial(const unsigned n)
{
    double fResult = 1.0;
    unsigned i = 1;

    for(;;) {
        fResult *= (double)i++;
        if (i > n)
            break;
    }

    return fResult;
}
```

Start open loop

Exit point

Listing 9-4 declares the function **Factorial**, which uses an open-iteration **for** loop to calculate factorials. The function declares and initializes the local variables **fResult** and **i**. It uses the **double**-type variable **fResult** to store the calculated factorial and uses the **unsigned**-type variable **i** to control the iteration of the **for** loop. The open-iteration loop has two statements: The first updates the value of the factorial in variable **fResult** and also increments the variable **i**. The second compares the values of variable **i** and parameter **n**. If the variable **i** stores a value higher than that of parameter **n**, the loop exits using the **break** statement. The first loop statement handles incrementing the loop control variable, whereas the second statement deals with controlling the loop's iteration.

The function **main** declares the **double**-type constant **HI** and associates the value 1000.0 with it. The function also declares the **double**-type variable **fFact** and the **unsigned**-type variable **nNum**. It also initializes the variable **nNum** with the value 2.

The function **main** uses an open-iteration **for** loop to display factorials. The loop statements perform the following tasks:

- Calculate the factorial by calling the function **Factorial**. The argument for this call is the variable **nNum**. This task assigns the calculated factorial to the variable **fFact**.
- Determine if the value in variable **fFact** exceeds the value of constant **HI**. If this condition is true, the function executes the **break** statement. This task controls the loop's iteration.
- Display the values in variables **nNum** and **fFact**
- Increment the value in loop control variable **nNum**

The do-while Loop

C++ offers two conditional loops: the **do-while** loop and the **while** loop. The **do-while** loop iterates as long as a tested condition (located after the **while** clause) is true. The syntax for the **do-while** loop is:

```
do {
  // statements
} while (condition);
```

PASCAL

The do-while loop vs. the REPEAT-UNTIL Loop

The **do-while** loop is equivalent to a REPEAT-UNTIL loop in Pascal in which the tested condition contains a NOT operator. Here are the general syntax for the C++ **do-while** loop and that for the Pascal REPEAT-UNTIL loop:

```
// C++                          (* Pascal *)
do {                           REPEAT
  // statements                  (* statements *)
} while (condition);           UNTIL NOT condition;
```

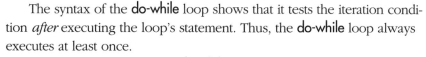

The syntax of the **do-while** loop shows that it tests the iteration condition *after* executing the loop's statement. Thus, the **do-while** loop always executes at least once.

Here is an example of the **do-while** loop:

```
do
   cout << "Enter a positive integer : ";
   cin >> nNum;
while (nNum < 1);
```

This example shows a **do-while** loop that iterates as long as the value in the variable **nNum** is less than 1.

Let me present a programming example. Listing 9-5 shows the source code for the DOWHILE2.CPP program, which illustrates the **do-while** loop. The program uses the **do-while** loop to enter non-negative numbers, calculate the square root, and calculate the cube root. The program contains a class that calculates the square and cube roots. The program prompts you, three times, to enter a non-negative number. Each time, the program displays the square and cube roots of the input value. If you enter a negative number, the program reprompts you.

Here is a sample session with the program in Listing 9-5 (user input is underlined):

```
Enter a positive number : -10
Enter a positive number : 100
Square root of 100 = 10
Cube root of 100 = 4.64159


Enter a positive number : 1000
Square root of 1000 = 31.6228
Cube root of 1000 = 10


Enter a positive number : 256
Square root of 256 = 16
Cube root of 256 = 6.3496
```

Listing 9-5

The source code for the DOWHILE2.CPP program.

```cpp
// A C++ program illustrates the do-while loop

#include <iostream.h>

const double DEF_TOLR = 1.0e-8;

  class myRoot
  {
    public:
      myRoot(double fTolerance = 1.0e-8)
        { setRootInfo(fTolerance); }
      void setRootInfo(double fTolerance = DEF_TOLR)
        { m_fTolerance = (fTolerance <= 0) ?
                DEF_TOLR : fTolerance; }
      double getSquareRoot(double fX);
      double getCubeRoot(double fX);

    protected:
      double m_fTolerance;

      double abs(double x)
        { return (x >= 0) ? x : -x; }
  };

  double myRoot::getSquareRoot(double fX)
  {
    double fDiff;
    double fGuess = fX / 2;

    do {
      fDiff = (fGuess * fGuess - fX) / (2 * fGuess);
      fGuess -= fDiff;
    } while (abs(fDiff) > m_fTolerance);

    return fGuess;
  }

  double myRoot::getCubeRoot(double fX)
  {
    double fDiff;
    double fGuess = fX / 2;
    double fSqr;

    do {
      fSqr = fGuess * fGuess;
      fDiff = (fSqr * fGuess - fX) / (3 * fSqr);
      fGuess -= fDiff;
    } while (abs(fDiff) > m_fTolerance);
```

```
    return fGuess;
  }

main()
{
  double fX;
  myRoot Root;

  for (int i = 0; i < 3; i++) {
    do {
      cout << "Enter a positive number : ";
      cin >> fX;
    } while (fX <= 0);
    cout << "Square root of " << fX << " = "
         << Root.getSquareRoot(fX) << "\n"
         << "Cube root of " << fX << " = "
         << Root.getCubeRoot(fX) << "\n\n";
  }

  return 0;

}
```

Listing 9-5 declares the class **myRoot**, which contains public and protected members. I wrote this class to work without any help from the standard math library routines prototyped in the header file MATH.H. The protected members are:

- The **double**-type data member **m_fTolerance**, which stores the tolerance for obtaining the square and cube roots
- The member function **abs**, which returns the absolute values

The class also declares the following public members:

- The constructor, which initializes the data member **m_fTolerance**
- The member function **setRootInfo**, which assigns a value to the data member **m_fTolerance**
- The member function **getSquareRoot**, which returns the square root of its parameter **fX**
- The member function **getCubeRoot**, which returns the cube root of its parameter **fX**

The member function **getSquareRoot** declares the local variables **fDiff** and **fGuess**. The function initializes the variable **fGuess**, which stores the guess for the square root, with the expression fX / 2. The function uses a do-while loop to refine the square root guess in variable fGuess. The loop stores the guess refinement in variable fDiff and then updates the value in variable fGuess. This loop iterates as long as the absolute value in variable fDiff exceeds the value in data member m_fTolerance. The function returns the value in variable fGuess, once the guess refinement ceases to exceed the tolerance level.

The member function getCubeRoot is similar to member function getSquareRoot. The function getCubeRoot also uses the do-while loop to define the guess for the cube root (which it stores in variable fGuess). The do-while loop iterates as long as the absolute value in variable fDiff exceeds the value in data member m_fTolerance. The function returns the value in variable fGuess.

If you are curious about the algorithms used in the member functions just described, they are based on Newton's root-seeking methods. This method solves for:

```
f(x) = 0
```

It uses the following algorithm that refines the guesses for x:

$$x_1 = x_0 - f(x_0) / f'(x_0)$$

—where f'(x) is the first derivative (that is, the slope) of function f(x) at x.

The function main declares the variable fX and the object Root as an instance of class myRoot. The function uses a for loop to perform the following tasks three times:

- Prompt you to enter a positive number and store your input in variable fX. This task uses a do-while loop to ensure that you comply with the needed value. The loop iterates as long as the value in variable fX is not positive.

- Display the square root by sending the object Root the C++ message getSquareRoot. The argument for this message is the variable fX.

- Display the cube root by sending the object Root the C++ message getCubeRoot. The argument for this message is the variable fX.

The while Loop

C++ offers the **while** loop as a control structure designed to iterate as long as a tested condition (located after the **while** clause) is true. The syntax for the **while** loop is:

```
while (condition)
   // statement or statement block
```

The syntax of the **while** loop shows that it tests the iteration condition *before* executing the loop's statement. Thus, the **while** loop will not execute if the tested condition is already false.

Here is an example of the **while** loop:

```
int i = 0;
while (i * i < 1000)
   i++;
```

This example has a **while** loop that iterates as long as the squared value of variable **i** is less than 1000.

Let me present a programming example. Listing 9-6 shows the source code for the WHILE2.CPP program, which illustrates the **while** loop. The program prompts you to enter a sum of integers from 1 to *n*. The program then calculates and displays the largest value of *n* whose sum is below the value you specified. The program also calculates the difference between the sum you specified and the sum of integers from 1 to *n*.

Here is a sample session with the program in Listing 9-6 (user input is underlined):

```
Enter sum of integers : -10
Enter sum of integers : 100
The sum of 1 to 14 = 91
Calculated sum falls short of target sum by 9
```

Listing 9-6
The source code for the WHILE2.CPP program.

```
// A C++ program that illustrates the while loop

#include <iostream.h>

void getLowestIntToSum(double fMySum, int& nInt, double& fSum);
```

```
main()
{
  double fMySum, fSum;
  int nInt;

  do {
    cout << "Enter sum of integers : ";
    cin >> fMySum;
  } while (fMySum < 1.0);

  getLowestIntToSum(fMySum, nInt, fSum);
  cout << "The sum of 1 to " << nInt
       << " = " << fSum << "\n";
  cout << "Calculated sum falls short of target sum by "
       << (fMySum - fSum) << "\n";

  return 0;
}

void getLowestIntToSum(double fMySum, int& nInt, double& fSum)
{
  fSum = 0;
  nInt = 1;

  while ((fSum + nInt) < fMySum)
    fSum += double(nInt++);
}
```

Listing 9-6 prototypes the function **getLowestIntToSum**, which returns the lowest integer (via the reference parameter **nInt**) that produces a sum (returned by the reference parameter **fSum**) that is the closest to the specified sum (passed by parameter **fMySum**). The function performs the following tasks:

- Initialize the parameters **fSum** and **nInt** with the values 0 and 1, respectively

- Use a **while** loop to iterate as long as the sum of values in parameters **fSum** and **nInt** is less than the value of parameter **fMySum**. Each loop iteration adds the value of parameter **nInt** to **fSum** and then increments **nInt**.

Exiting Loops

Earlier in this chapter when I presented the open-iteration loop, I showed you how to exit this loop using the **break** statement. You can also use the **break** statement to exit the **do-while** and **while** loops.

The **break** statement exits the current loop. Thus to exit nested loops (more about these loops later in this chapter), you need to use a **break** statement for each loop.

Here are examples of using the **break** statement with the **do-while** and **while** loops:

```
// exit from do-while loop example
double fY, fX = 1.0;
do {
  fY = fX * fX + 10;
  if (fY > 10000.0)
    break;
  cout << "f(" << fX << ") = " << fY << "\n";
} while (fX < 100.0);

// exit from while loop example
double fY, fX = 1.0;
while (fX > 0.0 && fX < 100.0) {
  fY = fX * fX - 30;
  cout << "f(" << fX << ") = " << fY << "\n";
  if (fY > 1000.0)
    break;
};
```

The first example has a **do-while** loop that iterates as long as the value in variable **fX** is less than 100. The loop contains a statement that determines whether or not the value in the variable **fY** (which is based on the value of variable **fX**) exceeds 10,000. If this condition is true, the loop exits by executing the **break** statement in the **if** statement.

The second example has a **while** loop that iterates as long as the value in variable **fX** is positive and less than 100. The loop contains an **if** statement that determines whether or not the value in the variable **fY** (which is based on the value of variable **fX**) exceeds 1000. If this condition is true, the loop exits by executing the **break** statement in the **if** statement.

Let's look at a programming example. Listing 9-7 shows the source code for the BREAK1.CPP program. The program evaluates the following mathematical polynomial:

$$P(x) = 1 + 1/x - 1/x^2 + 1/x^3 - 1/x^4 + \ldots$$

The program calculates the values of polynomial P(X) such that either of these conditions is true:

1. A maximum number of terms (each term is $1/X^n$) is reached.
2. A term is reached whose absolute value is smaller than a tolerance limit. The program uses the break statement to implement this condition.

Here is the output of the program in Listing 9-7:

```
P(1) = 2
P(2) = 1.33333
P(3) = 1.25
P(4) = 1.2
P(5) = 1.16667
```

Listing 9-7
The source code for the BREAK1.CPP program, which illustrates the exiting loops.

```cpp
// A C++ program that illustrates the break statement

#include <iostream.h>

const double DEF_TOLR = 1.0e-08;
const int MAX_TERMS = 100;
const double EPSILON = 1.0e-50;
const double BAD_RESULT = -1.0e+30;

class SumPoly
{
  public:
    SumPoly(const double fTolerance = DEF_TOLR,
            const int nMaxTerms = MAX_TERMS)
      { setParams(fTolerance, nMaxTerms); }
    void setParams(const double fTolerance = DEF_TOLR,
                   const int nMaxTerms = MAX_TERMS);
    double polynomial(double x);

  protected:
    double m_fTolerance;
    double m_nMaxTerms;

    double abs(double x)
      { return (x >= 0) ? x : -x; }
};
```

```
void SumPoly::setParams(const double fTolerance,
                        const int nMaxTerms)
{
  m_fTolerance = fTolerance;
  m_nMaxTerms = nMaxTerms;
}

double SumPoly::polynomial(double x)
{
  double fSum = 1;
  double fPow = 1;
  double fTerm;
  double fChs = 1;
  int nTerm = 1;

  if (abs(x) < EPSILON)
    return BAD_RESULT;

  do {
    // update power of x
    fPow *= x;
    // calculate term
    fTerm = fChs / fPow;
    // update summation
    fSum += fTerm;
    // is calculated term too small?
    if (abs(fTerm) < m_fTolerance)
      break;
    // toggle sign
    fChs *= -1.;
    // update counter for the number of terms
    nTerm++;
  } while (nTerm < m_nMaxTerms);

  return fSum;
}

main()
{
  const double LO = 1.0;
  const double HI = 5.0;
  SumPoly Poly;
  double fX = LO;

  while (fX <= HI) {
    cout << "P(" << fX << ") = "
         << Poly.polynomial(fX) << "\n";
    fX++;
  }

  return 0;
}
```

Listing 9-7 declares a set of global constants **DEF_TOLR, MAX_TERMS, EPSILON,** and **BAD_RESULT,** which specify the default tolerance, default maximum number of terms, small value, and bad function result, respectively. The listing also declares the class **SumPoly,** which contains public and protected members.

The protected members of the class **SumPoly** are:

- The **double**-type data member **m_fTolerance,** which stores the tolerance for a term ($1/X^n$) in polynomial P(X)

- The **int**-type data member **m_nMaxTerms,** which stores the maximum number of terms to be evaluated

- The member function **abs,** which returns the absolute value of a floating-point value

The class declares the following public members:

- The constructor, which initializes the data members

- The member function **setParams,** which assigns new values to the data members

- The member function **polynomial,** which calculates the polynomial values for the argument of parameter **x.** If the absolute value of the argument is less than the value of constant **EPSILON,** the function returns the value of constant **BAD_RESULT.**

The definition of member function **polynomial** declares a set of local variables to manage the sum of terms, term value, change in sign, and power of parameter **x.** The member function uses a **do-while** loop to calculate the terms of the polynomial P(X). The condition of the loop iterates as long as the term counter, variable **nTerm,** is less than the value of data member **m_nMaxTerms.** The loop iterations perform the following tasks:

- Update the power of X that is stored in the local variable **fPow**
- Calculate the term (as **fChs / fPow**) and store that value in variable **fTerm**
- Add the value of the calculated term to the variable **fSum.** This variable stores the polynomial value.

- Determine if the absolute value of the calculated term is smaller than the tolerance level (stored in data member m_fTolerance). If this condition is true, program flow exits the loop by executing the **break** statement. Thus, the function puts an *early* end to the loop's iteration (as opposed to ending the iteration when the loop's condition, nTerm < m_nMaxTerms, is false) using the **break** statement.

- Toggle the sign of the terms (stored in variable fChs)

- Increment the term counter (stored in variable nTerm)

The function **main** declares the local constants LO and HI, the variable fX, and the object Poly as an instance of class SumPoly. The function initializes the variable fX using the value of constant LO.

The function **main** uses a **while** loop to display the value of the polynomial for fX = 1, 2, 3, 4, and 5. Each loop iteration displays the polynomial value by sending the C++ message **polynomial** to the object Poly. The argument for this message is the variable fX.

Skipping Loop Iterations

C++ offers the **continue** statement to skip the remaining statements in a loop. Why skip the remaining loop statements? This condition arises when the loop statements examine a condition and conclude that the loop should not or need not proceed with executing the remaining statements. Here is an example of using the **continue** statement:

```
for (int i = -4; i < 5; i++) {
  if (i == 0)
  continue;
  double fX =  1.0 / i;
  cout << "1 / " << i << " = " << fX << "\n";
}
```

This code snippet shows a loop that displays reciprocal values. The loop has a control variable that changes values from −4 to 4, in increments of 1. The loop contains an **if** statement that determines whether or not the control variable contains 0. When this condition is true, the loop skips the remaining statements to *avoid* dividing by zero!

Let's look at a programming example. Listing 9-8 shows the source code for the CONTINU1.CPP program, which illustrates skipping loop iterations. The program calculates the value of a series polynomial defined by the following equation:

```
P(X, n1, n2) = Σᵢ Xⁱ / i² for i = n1 to n2, and i ≠ 0, and X ≠
```

The values of the parameters n1 and n2 may be negative. The program uses a class that implements the polynomial P(X) and calculates the values of P(X, n1, n2) for n1 = –3, n2 = 3, and X = 1 to 2 in increments of 0.25. The program also displays the equation for the polynomial P(X, n1, n2) being evaluated:

Here is the output of the program in Listing 9-8:

```
P(X) = X^(-3)/9 + X^(-2)/4 + X^(-1) + X + X^2/4 + X^3/9
```

```
P(1.000) = 2.722222
P(1.250) = 2.874528
P(1.500) = 3.248200
P(1.750) = 3.784904
P(2.000) = 4.465278
```

Listing 9-8

The source code for the CONTINU1.CPP program, which illustrates skipping loop iterations.

```cpp
// A C++ program that illustrates the continue statement

#include <iostream.h>
#include <stdio.h>
#include <math.h>

const double EPSILON = 1.0e-50;
const double BAD_RESULT = -1.0e+30;

class SumPoly
{
  public:
    SumPoly(const int nFirst, const int nLast)
      { setParams(nFirst, nLast); }
    void setParams(const int nFirst, const int nLast);

    double polynomial(double x);
```

```
  protected:
    int m_nFirst;
    int m_nLast;
};

void SumPoly::setParams(const int nFirst, const int nLast)
{
  if (nFirst < nLast) {
    m_nFirst = nFirst;
    m_nLast = nLast;
  }
  else {
    m_nFirst = nLast;
    m_nLast = nFirst;
  }
}

double SumPoly::polynomial(double x)
{
  double fSum = 0;
  double fTerm;

  if (fabs(x) < EPSILON)
    return BAD_RESULT;

  for (int i = m_nFirst; i <= m_nLast; i++) {
    if (i == 0)
      continue;
    // calculate term
    fTerm = pow(x, i) / (i * i);
    // update summation
    fSum += fTerm;
  }

  return fSum;
}

main()
{
  const double LO = 1.0;
  const double HI = 2.0;
  const double INCR = 0.25;
  const int FIRST = -3;
  const int LAST = 3;
  SumPoly Poly(FIRST, LAST);
  double fX = LO;
  char cFrmt[30];

  cout << "P(X) = ";
  for (int i = FIRST; i <= LAST; i++) {
```

```
    if (i == 0)
      continue;
    if (i > FIRST)
      cout << " + ";
    cout << "X";
    if (i != 1) {
      if (i > 0)
        cout << "^" << i;
      else
        cout << "^(" << i << ")";
    }
    if ((i * i) != 1)
      cout << "/" << (i * i);
  }
  cout << "\n\n";
  while (fX <= HI) {
    sprintf(cFrmt, "P(%5.3lf) = %lf\n", fX, Poly.polynomial(fX));
    cout << cFrmt;
    fX += INCR;
  }

  return 0;
}
```

Listing 9-8 declares the class **SumPoly**, which declares public and protected members. The protected members are the **int**-type data members **m_nFirst** and **m_nLast**, which store the values for polynomial parameters n1 and n2.

The class **SumPoly** declares the following public members:

■ The constructor, which initializes the data members by invoking the member function **setParams**

■ The member function **setParams**, which assigns the values of its parameters **nFirst** and **nLast** to the data members **m_nFirst** and **m_nLast**

■ The member function **polynomial**, which evaluates the polynomial P(X, n1, n2) for the argument of the parameter **x**

The definition of the member function **polynomial** uses a **for** loop that iterates in the range of values defined by data members **m_nFirst** and **m_nLast**. The first statement in the loop is an **if** statement that determines whether or not the loop control variable is 0. When this condition is true, the **if** statement executes the **continue** statement to skip the rest of the loop—the definition of the polynomial P(X, n1, n2) excludes the term with a zero index. The member function then calculates the value of the current term and stores it in the local variable **fTerm**. Next, the member function adds the value of variable **fTerm** to the variable **fSum**, which stores the polynomial value. The member function **polynomial** returns the value in variable **fSum**.

The function **main** declares a number of local constants and variables. Among the declared items is the object **Poly**, which is an instance of class **SumPoly**. The function **main** declares the object **Poly** using the arguments of **FIRST** and **LAST** (the local constants that define the values for the polynomial parameters n1 and n2).

The function **main** uses a **for** loop to display the equation of the evaluated polynomial. The first statement in the loop determines if the loop control variable is 0. When this condition is true, the **if** statement executes the **continue** statement to skip the rest of the loop—the definition of the polynomial P(X, n1, n2) excludes the term with a zero index.

The function **main** uses a **while** loop to vary the value in variable **fX** from 1.0 to 2.0 in steps of 0.25 (the values of constants LO, HI, and INCR, respectively). The first statement in the **while** loop uses the **sprintf** function to obtain a formatted string that has the image of the output. The second loop statement displays the contents of the formatted string, **cFrmt**.

Nested Loops

Like any other common programming languages, C++ allows you to nest loops in any combination. For example, you can nest **for** loops, as shown in the following code snippet:

```
double fSum = 0;
for (int i = 10; i < 100; i++)
  for (int j = 0; j < i; j++)
    fSum += double(j * i);
```

This code snippet shows two nested **for** loops used to obtain a summation.

You can also nest different kinds of loops. Here is a code snippet that shows you nested **while** and **do-while** loops:

```
double fSum = 0;
int i = 10;
int j;
while (i < 100) {
  j = 0;
  do {
    fSum += double(j++ * i);
  } while  (j < i);
  i++;
}
```

The nested loops obtain a summation, like the one in the example of the nested **for** loops.

Let's look at an example that contains nested loops. Listing 9-9 shows the source code for the LOOPS1.CPP program, which illustrates nesting a **for** loop and a **while** loop inside another **for** loop. The program generates random values and displays horizontal histograms using asterisk characters.

Here is a sample session with the program in Listing 9-9:

```
Sample histogram
*******************************         32.68
**********************************      35.51
*********                              9.33
************************                24.49
**********************************      35.08
***************************             28.78
******************                     18.88
*********                              9.47
****************************            29.34
****                                   4.02
```

Listing 9-9
The source code for the LOOPS1.CPP program.

```
// A C++ program that illustrates nested loops

#include <iostream.h>
#include <math.h>

const double EPSILON = 1.0e-50;
const double BAD_RESULT = -1.0e+30;
const double INIT_SEED = 113;
const int MAX_WIDTH = 40;
const double PI = 4 * atan(1);
```

```
class Histogram
{
  public:
    Histogram(double fSeed = INIT_SEED)
      { m_fSeed = fSeed; }
    void setParams(int nNumHisto, double fMax);
    void show();

  protected:
    double m_fSeed;
    double m_fMax;
    int m_nNumHisto;

    double random();
    double frac(double x)
      { return x - long(x); }
    double cube(double x)
      { return x * x * x; }
};

void Histogram::setParams(int nNumHisto, double fMax)
{
  m_nNumHisto = (nNumHisto > 2) ? nNumHisto : 3;
  m_fMax = (fMax > 0) ? fMax : 10;
}

void Histogram::show()
{
  double fX;
  int nVal;

  for (int i = 0; i < m_nNumHisto; i++) {
    fX = m_fMax * random() + 1;
    nVal = int(fX * m_fMax) / MAX_WIDTH;
    // nested for loop
    for (int j = 0; j < nVal; j++)
      cout << "*";
    // nested while loop
    while (nVal++ < MAX_WIDTH)
      cout << ' ';
    if (fX < 10.0) {
      cout << ' ';
      cout.width(4);
      cout.precision(3);
    }
    else {
      cout.width(5);
      cout.precision(4);
    }
    cout << fX << "\n";
  }
}
```

```
double Histogram::random()
{
  m_fSeed = frac(cube(m_fSeed + PI));
  return m_fSeed;
}

main()
{
  Histogram Histo;
  int nNumHisto = 10;
  double fMax = 40.0;

  Histo.setParams(nNumHisto, fMax);
  cout << "Sample histogram\n";
  Histo.show();

  return 0;
}
```

Listing 9-9 declares the class **Histogram**, which draws histograms. The class declares public and protected members. The protected members are:

- The **double**-type data member **m_fSeed**, which stores the last random number generated. The class uses this data member to generate subsequent random numbers.

- The **double**-type data member **m_fMax**, which stores the maximum histogram value

- The **int**-type **m_nNumHisto**, which stores the number of histograms to generate

- The member function **random**, which yields a random number between 0 and 1 (exclusive)

- The member functions **frac** and **cube**, which return the fractional part and the cubed value of a floating-point number, respectively

The class also declares the following public members:

- The constructor, which initializes the data member **m_fSeed**
- The member function **setParams**, which stores the values of the parameters **nNumHisto** and **fMax** into the data members **m_nNumHisto** and **m_fMax**, respectively
- The member function **show**, which displays a set of histograms

The definition of member function **show** indicates that it uses an outer **for** loop that contains a nested **for** loop and a nested **while** loop. The outer **for** loop uses the control variable **i** to draw the various histogram bars. Each loop iteration draws one histogram bar. The first two loop statements calculate the value of the histogram bar and the number of ' * ' characters to display. The nested **for** loop displays the ' * ' characters. The nested **while** loop displays spaces after the histogram bar to reach the right margin of **MAX_WIDTH** characters. The member function then displays the value of the histogram bar.

The function **main** declares local variables and the object **Histo** as an instance of class **Histogram**. The function initializes the histogram parameters by sending the C++ message **setParams** to the object **Histo**. The arguments for this message are the local variables **nNumHisto** and **fMax**. The function then displays a header followed by the histogram. To draw the latter, the function sends the C++ message **show** to the object **Histo**.

Summary

This chapter showed you the **for**, **do-while**, and **while** loops. You learned about the flexibility of the **for** loop, making it superior to other FOR loops in common programming languages. You also learned about using the conditional **do-while** and **while** loops. The text also discussed exiting loops, skipping loop iterations, and constructing nested loops.

In Chapter 10, we will take an in-depth look at how C++ handles another universal programming construct, the array.

10 Simple Arrays

*A*rrays are perhaps the simplest and yet most powerful data structures that are supported by many programming languages. If you have programmed in BASIC, Pascal, or C, just to name a few programming languages, you have most likely worked with arrays. C++ supports single-dimensional and multidimensional arrays. This chapter shows you how to declare, access, and initialize single-dimensional arrays. Moreover, you will learn how to declare arrays as function parameters. The chapter also discusses sorting arrays using the Shell sort, combsort, and quicksort methods. Finally, the chapter discusses searching array elements using the linear, binary, heuristic, and statistical search methods. The next chapter discusses multidimensional arrays.

Declaring Single-Dimensional Arrays

C++ requires that you declare an array before you use it. The general syntax for declaring an array is

```
type arrayName[numberOfElements];
```

This syntax shows the following aspects of the declaration:

- The declaration starts by stating the basic type associated with the array elements. You can use predefined or previously defined data types.

- The name of the array is followed by the number of elements. This number is enclosed in square brackets. The number of array elements must be a constant (literal or symbolic) or an expression that uses constants.

C

C++ Arrays Are Similar to C Arrays

Arrays in C++ and C are very similar. You may want to skip the sections that deal with declaring, using, and initializing arrays.

All arrays in C++ have indices that start at 0. Thus, the number of array elements is one larger than the index of the last array element.

Here are examples of declaring arrays:

```
// example 1
int nIntArr[10];
// example 2
const int MAX = 30;
char cName[MAX];
// example 3
const int MAX_CHARS = 40;
char cString[MAX_CHARS+1];
```

The first example declares the **int**-type array **nIntArr** with 10 elements. The declaration uses the literal constant 10. Thus the indices for the first and last array elements are 0 and 9, respectively. The second example declares the constant **MAX** and uses that constant to specify the number of elements of the **char**-type array **cName**. The third example declares the **char**-type array **cString**. The constant expression **MAX_CHARS + 1** defines the number of elements in the array **cString**.

BASIC

C++ Supports Zero-Index Arrays

C++ imposes the array indexing scheme that assigns the index 0 to the first array element. This indexing scheme differs from that of BASIC. In addition, declaring arrays in BASIC specifies the upper (and sometimes the lower) array index and not the number of elements.

Also keep in mind that C++ does not automatically initialize its arrays, as does BASIC.

PASCAL

C++ Supports Zero-Index Arrays

C++ imposes the array indexing scheme that assigns the index 0 to the first array element. This indexing scheme seems more rigid than that of Pascal, but it offers certain advantages. Arrays in Pascal are more commonly indexed in the range that starts with 1. Thus keep in mind that declaring a C++ array specifies the number of elements and not the upper array index.

Accessing Single-Dimensional Arrays

Once you declare an array, you can access its elements using the index operator []. The general syntax for accessing an element in an array is

```
arrayName[anIndex]
```

The index should be in the valid range of indices—between 0 and the number of array elements minus one.

Here are some examples of accessing array elements:

```
const int MAX = 10;
double fVector[MAX];
for (int i = 0; i < MAX; i++)
  fVector[i] = double(i) * i;
for (i = MAX - 1; i >= 0; i--)
  cout << fVector[i] << "\n";
```

This code snippet declares the constant MAX and uses that constant in declaring the **double**-type array fVector. Thus the array has elements with indices in the range of 0 to MAX – 1. The code uses the first **for** loop to assign values to the elements of array fVector. The loop statement accesses the elements of array fVector using the loop control variable i. The expression fVector[i] accesses element number i in array fVector. The code uses the second loop to display, in a descending order, the elements of array fVector. Again, the loop statement accesses the elements of array fVector using the loop control variable i.

Let's look at a programming example. Listing 10-1 shows the source code for the ARRAY1.CPP program, which illustrates declaring and accessing arrays. This example illustrates the following features:

- Declaring and accessing C++ arrays
- Declaring classes that support arrays. The example shows how to declare the operator [] that accesses the elements of an array in a class. What makes the example special is the fact that the operator [] makes accessing elements in the instances of the array-modeling class very similar to accessing C++ arrays.

The program performs the following tasks:

- Declare a C++ array and an array object
- Initialize a C++ array
- Assign the square root values of the C++ array elements to the elements of the array object
- Display the elements of the array object
- Double the values of the elements in the array object
- Display the elements of the array object

Here is the output of the program in Listing 10-1:

```
Initial array is:
1.4 1.7 2 2.2 2.4 2.6 2.8 3 3.2 3.3
After doubling values, array is:
2.8 3.5 4 4.5 4.9 5.3 5.7 6 6.3 6.6
```

Listing 10-1
The source code for the ARRAY1.CPP program.

```
// A C++ program that illustrates declaring
// and accessing array elements

#include <iostream.h>
#include <iomanip.h>
#include <math.h>

const int MAX_ELEMS = 10;
```

```
class myArray
{
  public:
    myArray(double fInitVal = 0);
    double& operator[](int nIndex)
      { return m_fArray[nIndex]; }
    void show(const char* pszMsg = "",
              const int nNumElems = MAX_ELEMS,
              const int bOneLine = 1);

  protected:
    double m_fArray[MAX_ELEMS];                              Array
};

myArray::myArray(double fInitVal)
{
  for (int i = 0; i < MAX_ELEMS; i++)
    m_fArray[i] = fInitVal;
}

void myArray::show(const char* pszMsg,
                   const int nNumElems,
                   const int bOneLine)
{
  cout << pszMsg << endl;
  if (bOneLine) {
    for (int i = 0; i < nNumElems; i++)
      cout << m_fArray[i] << ' ';
    cout << endl;
  }
  else {
    for (int i = 0; i < nNumElems; i++)
      cout << m_fArray[i] << endl;
    cout << endl;
  }
}

main()
{
  double fXArr[MAX_ELEMS];                                  Array
  myArray Array;

  // initialize array fXArr
  for (int i = 0; i < MAX_ELEMS; i++)
    fXArr[i] = 2.0 + (double)i;

  // assign values to object Array
  for (i = 0; i < MAX_ELEMS; i++)
    Array[i] = sqrt(fXArr[i]);

  cout.precision(2);
```

```
// show the array
Array.show("Initial array is:");

cout << endl;

// double the values in object Array
for (i = 0; i < MAX_ELEMS; i++)
  Array[i] += Array[i];

// show the array
Array.show("After doubling values, array is:");

return 0;
}
```

Listing 10-1 declares the constant **MAX_ELEMS**, which specifies the number of elements in the program's arrays. The listing declares class **myArray**, which has the protected data member **m_fArray**. This member is a **double**-type array that has **MAX_ELEMS** elements. The class declares the following public members:

- The constructor, which initializes the values of the elements of the data member **m_fArray**. The default argument of parameters **fInitVal** initializes the array elements to 0.

- The operator **[]**, which accesses the elements of data member **m_fArray**. Notice that the member function has the **double&** return type (instead of just **double**). Using a reference return type allows you to utilize the operator **[]** on both sides of the assignment operator, as shown in the last **for** loop in the listing. The parameter **nIndex** specifies the index of the accessed array element.

- The member function **show**, which displays some or all of the array elements. The parameter **nNumElems** specifies the number of array elements to display. The parameter **pszMsg** passes an accompanying message that appears before the function lists the array elements. The parameter **bOneLine** specifies whether or not to display the elements on the same line (when the argument of the parameter is 1) or in a column (when the argument of the parameter is 0).

The function **main** declares the **double**-type array **fXArr** and the object **Array** as an instance of class **myArray**. The declaration initializes the elements of the object **Array** to 0. By contrast, the elements of the C++ array **fXArr** have no initial values (except for the *arbitrary* values in their memory locations). The function **main** then performs the following tasks:

- Assign values to the elements of array **fXArr**. This task uses a **for** loop that iterates over all the elements of array **fXArr**. Each loop statement assigns the expression **2.0 + (double)i** to element number **i** of array **fXArr**. The array **fXArr** and the object **Array** have the same number of elements.

- Assign new values to the elements of the object **Array**. This task uses a **for** loop that iterates over the elements of object **Array**. Each loop iteration assigns the square root value of element **fXArr[i]** to element **Array[i]**. Notice that the loop's statement places **Array[i]** to the left side of the assignment operator. This feature shows you how an array-modeling class can provide you with array objects that syntactically behave like C++ arrays.

- Set the precision to 2 by sending the C++ message **precision** to object **cout**

- Display the elements in object **Array** by sending it the C++ message **show**. The argument for this message is the literal string "Initial array is:".

- Double the values in the elements of object **Array**. This task uses a **for** loop that iterates over the elements of object **Array**. Each loop iteration doubles the value of element **Array[i]** using the operator **+=**. Notice that the loop's statement places **Array[i]** to the left and right sides of the assignment operator. This feature confirms the flexibility of the operator **[]** in class **myArray**.

- Display the elements in object **Array** by sending it the C++ message **show**. The argument for this message is the literal string "After doubling values, array is:".

Initializing Single-Dimensional Arrays

C++ allows you to initialize some or all of the elements of an array. The general syntax for initializing an array is

```
type arrayName[numOfElems] = { value0 ,..., valueN };
```

You need to observe the following rules when you initialize an array:

1. The list of initial values appears in a pair of open and close braces and is comma-delimited. The list ends with a semicolon.

2. The list may contain a number of initial values that is equal to or less than the number of elements in the initialized array. Otherwise, the compiler generates a compile-time error.

3. The compiler assigns the first initializing value to the element at index 0, the second initializing value to the element at index 1, and so on.

4. If the list contains fewer values than the number of elements in the array, the compiler assigns zeros to the elements that do not receive initial values from the list.

5. If you omit the number of array elements, the compiler uses the number of initializing values in the list as the number of array elements.

Here are examples of initializing arrays:

```
// example 1
double fArr[5] = { 1.1, 2.2, 3.3, 4.4, 5.5 };
// example 2
int nArr[10] = { 1, 2, 3, 4, 5 };
// example 3
char cVowels[] = { 'A' , 'a', 'E', 'e', 'I', 'i', 'O',
                   'o', 'U', 'u' };
```

The code in example 1 declares the **double**-type array **fArr** to have 5 elements. The declaration also initializes all 5 elements with the successive values 1.1, 2.2, 3.3, 4.4, and 5.5. The second example declares the **int**-type array **nArr** to have 10 elements. The declaration also initializes only the first 5 elements with the values 1, 2, 3, 4, and 5. Therefore, the compiler assigns zeros to the elements at indices 5 through 9 of array **nArr**. The last example declares the **char**-type array **cVowels** and initializes the array elements with the lowercase and uppercase vowels. Since the declaration of array **cVowels** does not specify the number of elements, the compiler uses the number of initializing values, 10, as the number of elements in array **cVowels**.

Let me present a programming example. Listing 10-2 contains the source code for the ARRAY2.CPP program, which illustrates initializing arrays. The program illustrates the following features:

- Declaring and initializing C++ arrays. The program also demonstrates using the number of initializing values to establish the number of array elements.

- Initializing a data member that is a C++ array. C++ offers no syntax to directly initialize data members that are arrays.

The program declares and initializes two C++ arrays and an array object. The program performs the following tasks:

- Display the initial values in the array object
- Increment the values in the array object using the values in the two C++ arrays
- Display the new values in the array object

CODING NOTES

Calculating the Number of Array Elements

When you use a list of initializing values to implicitly set the number of elements in an array, you can calculate the number of array elements as sizeof(arrayName) / sizeof(arrayType). Here is an example:

```
char cVowels[] = { 'A' , 'a', 'E', 'e', 'I', 'i', 'O',
                   'o', 'U', 'u' };
int nArrayElems = sizeof(cVowels) / sizeof(char);
```

This code snippet calculates the number of elements in array **cVowels** by dividing the total byte size of the array by the byte size of an element's data type (**char**).

Here is the output of the program in Listing 10-2:

```
Initial array is:
0.1 0.2 0.3 0.4 0.5 0.6 0.7 0.8 0.9 1
New array is:
14.14 5.644 9.839 4.103 13.26 29.38 10.9 16.09 13.01 39.5
```

Listing 10-2
The source code for the ARRAY2.CPP program.

```cpp
// A C++ program that illustrates initializing array elements

#include <iostream.h>
#include <iomanip.h>

const int MAX_ELEMS = 10;

class myArray
{
  public:
    myArray(int bUseInitArray = 1, double fInitVal = 0);
    double& operator[](int nIndex)
      { return m_fArray[nIndex]; }
    void show(const char* pszMsg = "",
              const int nNumElems = MAX_ELEMS,
              const int bOneLine = 1);

  protected:
    double m_fArray[MAX_ELEMS];
};

myArray::myArray(int bUseInitArray, double fInitVal)
{
  // use initializing array
  if (bUseInitArray) {
    double fInitArr[] =
      { 0.1, 0.2, 0.3, 0.4, 0.5,
        0.6, 0.7, 0.8, 0.9, 1.0 };
    for (int i = 0; i < MAX_ELEMS; i++)
      m_fArray[i] = fInitArr[i];
  }
  else
    for (int i = 0; i < MAX_ELEMS; i++)
      m_fArray[i] = fInitVal;
}

void myArray::show(const char* pszMsg,
                   const int nNumElems,
                   const int bOneLine)
{
```

Initialized array (arrow pointing to the `double fInitArr[]` initialization)

```
      cout << pszMsg << endl;
      if (bOneLine) {
        for (int i = 0; i < nNumElems; i++)
          cout << m_fArray[i] << ' ';
        cout << endl;
      }
      else {
        for (int i = 0; i < nNumElems; i++)
          cout << m_fArray[i] << endl;
        cout << endl;
      }
   }

main()
{
      double fXArr1[MAX_ELEMS] = { 2.3, 4.5, 8.9, 7.4, 5.1,
                                   1.8, 8.7, 6.3, 3.6, 0.8 };
      double fXArr2[] = { 32.3, 24.5, 84.9, 27.4, 65.1,
                          51.8, 88.7, 96.3, 43.6, 30.8 };
      int nNumElems = sizeof(fXArr2) / sizeof(double);
      int nMinNum = (nNumElems > MAX_ELEMS) ?
                    MAX_ELEMS : nNumElems;
      myArray Array;


      cout.precision(4);

      // show the array
      Array.show("Initial array is:");

      // update values to object Array
      for (int i = 0; i < nMinNum; i++)
        Array[i] += fXArr2[i] / fXArr1[i];

      // show the array
      Array.show("New array is:");

      return 0;
   }
```

Initialized arrays

Listing 10-2 declares the constant **MAX_ELEMS**, which defines the size of the explicitly dimensioned arrays in the program. The listing declares the class **myArray**, which is similar to that in Listing 10-1. The main difference is that the new class version has a constructor that allows you to initialize the array in one of two ways. When the argument of the parameter **bUseInitArray** is 1 (which is the default argument) or any nonzero value, the constructor uses the local initialized C++ array **fInitArr** to provide the initializing values for the elements of data member **m_fArray**. The constructor declares the array **fInitArr** without explicitly specifying the number of elements. Instead, the number of initializing values (which must be equal to **MAX_ELEMS**) specifies the number of array elements. By contrast, if the parameter **bUseInitArray** is 0, the constructor assigns the value of parameter **fInitVal** to each element in the data member **m_fArray**.

The function **main** declares and initializes the C++ arrays **fXArr1** and **fXArr2**. The declaration of array **fXArr1** specifies the number of array elements. By contrast, the declaration of array **fXArr2** does not; it instead relies on the number of initializing values to set the number of elements. Of course, for the sake of compatibility, both arrays **fXArr1** and **fXArr2** have the same number of elements. The function **main** also declares the local variable **nNumElems** and assigns it the number of elements in array **fXArr2** using the **sizeof** operator. The function also declares the variable **nMinNum** and assigns it the least value of **nNumElems** and **MAX_ELEMS**. Using this variable enables the program to work if the number of initializing values for array **fXArr2** is not equal to **MAX_ELEMS**. The function **main** also declares the object **Array** as an instance of class **myArray**. The way the source code declares the object **Array** ends up using the default argument for the constructor of class **myArray**. Consequently, the runtime system initializes the data member **m_fArray** in object **Array** using the array **fInitArr**. The function **main** then performs the following tasks:

- Set the precision of the output to four digits
- Display the initial elements in the object **Array** by sending it the C++ message **show**. The argument for this message is the string literal "Initial array is:".
- Update the values in object **Array**. This task uses a **for** loop that iterates over the first **nMinNum** elements of the arrays. Each loop iteration increments the element **Array[i]** by the ratio of **fXArr2[i]** to **fXArr1[i]**.
- Display the new values of the elements in the object **Array** by sending it the C++ message **show**. The argument for this message is the string literal "New array is:".

Declaring Arrays as Function Parameters

C++ allows you to declare arrays as parameters to functions. The syntax for declaring such parameters is

```
// form 1: fixed parameter
type arrayParam[numberOfElements]
// form 2: open parameter
type openArrayParam[]
```

The first form specifies the number of elements. Use this form when you want an array of the specified size to be the argument for the parameter **arrayParam**. This kind of parameter is called a *fixed array* parameter. The second form does not specify the size of the array parameter, allowing the parameter to take arguments that are arrays of different sizes. This kind of parameter is called an *open array* parameter. In this case, you typically have an additional parameter that specifies the number of elements in the parameter **openArrayParam**.

Here are examples of declaring array parameters:

```
double mySum(double fMyArray[MAX_ELEMS]);
double theirSum(double fTheirArray[MAX_ELEMS],
                int nNumElems = MAX_ELEMS);
double yourSum(double fYourArray[], int nNumElems);
```

The function **mySum** declares the array parameter **fMyArray** and specifies the size of **MAX_ELEMS**. This kind of function expects the caller to pass a **double**-type array that has **MAX_ELEMS** number of elements. Since the function's parameter list does not have a parameter that passes the number of elements to process, it is safe to assume that function **mySum** processes all of the elements in parameter **fMyArray**.

The function **theirSum** has two parameters. The first is the array parameter **fMyArray** and specifies the size of **MAX_ELEMS**. The second is **nNumElems**. The parameters of the function **theirSum** suggest that the arguments for parameter **fTheirArray** must be **double**-type arrays with **MAX_ELEMS** elements. However, the presence of parameter **nNumElems** may suggest that the function can process a portion of the array **fTheirArray**.

The function **yourSum** declares the parameter **fYourArray**, which is an open **double**-type array. This function can take arguments that are **double**-type arrays of different sizes. The parameter **nNumElems** specifies the number of elements in the argument for parameter **fYourArray**. The argument for parameter **nNumElems** should be equal to or less than the number of elements in the argument for **fYourArray**. If not, the function risks accessing data that lie beyond the space occupied by the array argument.

Here are examples of calling the functions just described:

```
const int MAX_ELEMS = 10;
const int MAX_ARRAY = 20;

double fArray1[MAX_ELEMS];
double fArray2[MAX_ARRAY];
double fSum;
...
fSum = mySum(fArray1);
...
fSum = theirSum(fArray1);
...
fSum = theirSum(fArray1, MAX_ELEMS / 2);
...
fSum = yourSum(fArray1, MAX_ELEMS);
...
fSum = yourSum(fArray2, MAX_ARRAY);
```

This code snippet declares the constants **MAX_ELEMS** and **MAX_ARRAY**, which define the number of elements in the **double**-type arrays **fArray1** and **fArray2**, respectively. The code defines the **double**-type variable **fSum**. Then the code snippet makes the following calls to the tested functions:

- Call function **mySum** with the argument **fArray1**
- Call function **theirSum** with the argument **fArray1**. This function call uses the default argument of **MAX_ELEMS** for parameter **nNumElems**.
- Call function **theirSum** with the arguments **fArray1** and **MAX_ELEMS / 2**
- Call function **yourSum** with the arguments **fArray1** and **MAX_ELEMS**
- Call function **yourSum** with the arguments **fArray2** and **MAX_ARRAY**

The code snippet shows that function **yourSum** is very flexible, since it handles arrays of different sizes.

Let's look at a programming example. Listing 10-3 shows the source code for the ARRAY3.CPP program, which illustrates parameter arrays. The listing contains functions that sort, copy, and display arrays of integers. The program declares two C++ arrays (and initializes the first one) and performs the following tasks:

- Copy the values from the first array into the second array. Both arrays contain unsorted integers.

- Display the first unsorted array

- Sort the first array and then display its elements. This task uses a sorting function that has an array parameter with a fixed number of elements.

- Copy the values from the second array into the first array. The elements of the first array are once more unsorted.

- Sort the first array and then display its elements. This task uses a sorting routine that has an open array parameter.

- Sort the second array and then display its elements. This task also uses a sorting routine that has an open array parameter.

Here is the output of the program in Listing 10-3:

```
Unsorted array nArray1 is:
41 67 55 98 12 15 10 65 48 32
Sorted array nArray1 is:
10 12 15 32 41 48 55 65 67 98
Unsorted array nArray1 is:
41 67 55 98 12 15 10 65 48 32
Sorted array nArray1 is:
10 12 15 32 41 48 55 65 67 98
Sorted array nArray2 is:
10 12 15 32 41 48 55 65 67 98
```

Listing 10-3
The source code for the ARRAY3.CPP program, which illustrates parameter arrays.

```
// A C++ program that illustrates array parameters

#include <iostream.h>
#include <iomanip.h>
```

```
const int MAX_ELEMS = 10;
const int MAX_ARRAY = 20;

void bubbleSort1(int nArray[MAX_ELEMS],
                 int nNumElems = MAX_ELEMS);
void bubbleSort2(int nArray[], int nNumElems);
void copyArray(int nSourceArray[], int nTargetArray[],
               int nNumElems);
void showArray(const char* pszMsg, int nArray[], int nNumElems);

main()
{
  int nArray1[MAX_ELEMS] = { 41, 67, 55, 98, 12,
                             15, 10, 65, 48, 32 };
  int nArray2[MAX_ARRAY];

  // copy elements of array nArray1 into  nArray2
  copyArray(nArray1, nArray2, MAX_ELEMS);

  // display unsorted array nArray1
  showArray("Unsorted array nArray1 is:\n", nArray1, MAX_ELEMS);
  // sort array nArray1
  bubbleSort1(nArray1);
  // display sorted array nArray1
  showArray("Sorted array nArray1 is:\n", nArray1, MAX_ELEMS);

  // copy elements of array nArray2 into  nArray1
  copyArray(nArray2, nArray1, MAX_ELEMS);
  // display unsorted array nArray1
  showArray("Unsorted array nArray1 is:\n", nArray1, MAX_ELEMS);
  // sort array nArray1
  bubbleSort2(nArray1, MAX_ELEMS);
  // display sorted array nArray1
  showArray("Sorted array nArray1 is:\n", nArray1, MAX_ELEMS);
  // sort array nArray2
  bubbleSort2(nArray2, MAX_ELEMS);
  // display sorted array nArray2
  showArray("Sorted array nArray2 is:\n", nArray2, MAX_ELEMS);

  return 0;
}

void bubbleSort1(int nArray[MAX_ELEMS],
                 int nNumElems)
{
  for (int i = 0; i < (nNumElems - 1); i++)
    for (int j = i; j < nNumElems; j++)
      if (nArray[i] > nArray[j]) {
        int nSwap = nArray[i];
        nArray[i] = nArray[j];
        nArray[j] = nSwap;
      }
}
```

```
void bubbleSort2(int nArray[], int nNumElems)
{
  for (int i = 0; i < (nNumElems - 1); i++)
    for (int j = i; j < nNumElems; j++)
      if (nArray[i] > nArray[j]) {
        int nSwap = nArray[i];
        nArray[i] = nArray[j];
        nArray[j] = nSwap;
      }
}

void copyArray(int nSourceArray[], int nTargetArray[],
               int nNumElems)
{
  for (int i = 0; i < nNumElems; i++)
    nTargetArray[i] = nSourceArray[i];
}

void showArray(const char* pszMsg, int nArray[], int nNumElems)
{
  cout << pszMsg;
  for (int i = 0; i < nNumElems; i++)
    cout << nArray[i] << ' ';
  cout << endl;
}
```

Listing 10-3 declares the constants **MAX_ELEMS** and **MAX_ARRAY**, which are the sizes for two different kinds of integer arrays. The listing also declares the prototypes for the following functions:

- The function **bubbleSort1** sorts the arguments for parameter **nArray**. This is an array parameter that specifies **MAX_ELEMS** elements. The second parameter, **nNumElems**, specifies the number of elements to sort. This parameter has the default argument of **MAX_ELEMS**, used to sort the entire array.

- The function **bubbleSort2** sorts the arguments for the open array parameter **nArray**. The second parameter, **nNumElems**, specifies the number of elements to sort.

- The function **copyArray** copies the elements of one array into another. The first two parameters are the open array parameters **nSourceArray** and **nTargetArray**. These parameters represent the source and target arrays, respectively. The parameter **nNumElems** specifies the number of elements to copy.

- The function **showArray** displays the elements of the open array parameter **nArray**. The parameter **pszMsg** passes a leading message. The parameter **nNumElems** specifies the number of elements to display.

The declarations of these functions show that, with the exception of the function **bubbleSort1**, they use open array parameters to process integer arrays of various sizes. The listing includes the two versions of the sorting functions **bubbleSort1** and **bubbleSort2**. The source code illustrates that the latter function is more flexible than the former since it takes arguments that are arrays of different sizes.

The function **main** declares the **int**-type arrays **nArray1** and **nArray2**. These arrays have **MAX_ELEMS** and **MAX_ARRAY** elements, respectively. The function initializes the array **nArray1** with a list of unsorted integers. The function then performs the following tasks:

- Copy the elements of **nArray1** into **nArray2** by calling function **copyArray**. The arguments for this function call are **nArray1**, **nArray2**, and **MAX_ELEMS**. This means that the first **MAX_ELEMS** elements of array **nArray2** will contain copies of the values in the elements of array **nArray1**. The remaining elements of array **nArray2** are unchanged. In fact, by not using them, the program simulates many cases where arrays are not fully populated with meaningful data.

CODING NOTES

The Bubble Sort Method

The member functions **bubbleSort1** and **bubbleSort2** implement the bubble sort method. This is the simplest (and slowest) sorting method. The bubble sort method repeatedly compares immediately neighboring elements until the array is sorted. This method uses multiple passes to sort the array. The number of passes is equal to the number of array elements minus one. Each pass places one array element in its final location. The array elements tend to *bubble* up (hence the name of the method) to their final locations in the array. The next section in this chapter begins a discussion of more efficient sorting methods.

- Display the unsorted elements of array **nArray1** by calling the function **showArray**. The arguments for this function call are the literal string "Unsorted array nArray1 is:\n," the array **nArray1**, and the constant **MAX_ELEMS**.

- Sort the elements of array **nArray1** by calling the function **bubbleSort1**. The argument for this function call is array **nArray1**. The call uses the default argument of **MAX_ELEMS** for parameter **nNumElems**.

- Display the sorted elements of array **nArray1** by calling the function **showArray**. The arguments for this function call are the literal string "Sorted array nArray1 is:\n," the array **nArray1**, and the constant **MAX_ELEMS**.

- Copy the elements of **nArray2** into **nArray1** by calling the function **copyArray**. The arguments for this function call are **nArray2**, **nArray1**, and **MAX_ELEMS**. This task restores the values in the array **nArray1** to their original order.

- Display the unsorted elements of array **nArray1** by calling the function **showArray**. The arguments for this function call are the literal string "Unsorted array nArray1 is:\n," the array **nArray1**, and the constant **MAX_ELEMS**.

- Sort the elements of array **nArray1** by calling the function **bubbleSort2**. The arguments for this function call are the array **nArray1** and the constant **MAX_ELEMS**.

- Display the sorted elements of array **nArray1** by calling the function **showArray**. The arguments for this function call are the literal string "Sorted array nArray1 is:\n," the array **nArray1**, and the constant **MAX_ELEMS**.

- Sort the elements of array **nArray2** by calling the function **bubbleSort2**. The arguments for this function call are the array **nArray2** and the constant **MAX_ELEMS**.

- Display the sorted elements of array **nArray2** by calling the function **showArray**. The arguments for this function call are the literal string "Sorted array nArray2 is:\n," the array **nArray2**, and the constant **MAX_ELEMS**.

The function **main** uses the function **bubbleSort2** to sort the arrays **nArray1** and **nArray2**. Thus, the function **bubbleSort2** is a more general-purpose function than **bubbleSort1**.

Sorting and Searching Arrays

Sorting arrays and searching for data in arrays are among the most common nonnumerical array operations. Computer scientists have dedicated a lot of effort to perfecting the methods of sorting and searching. The next sections in this chapter present selected methods for these tasks. I offer these methods as a bonus, since you will most likely deal with sorting and searching arrays. Whether you are an old pro at this or not, it's worth looking at the C++ source code. The examples that I present deal with arrays of integers. You can easily modify the source code to work with other predefined or user-defined data types.

The next sections focus more on explicating the C++ code than on discussing in great detail the ins and outs of the algorithms used.

SORTING ARRAYS USING SHELL SORT

The Shell-Metzner sort method (or Shell sort for short) is one of the *in-place exchange sort* methods. Such methods sort array elements without the need for additional space or auxiliary arrays. The Shell sort method is also called a *diminishing increments* method.

Basically, the Shell sort method orders the elements of an array in cycles. Each cycle compares array elements that are distant from each other by a certain offset. Initially, the offset value is about a half or a third of the number of array elements. The initial offset value allows the Shell method to compare distant elements and perform long-range swaps, which enable array elements to quickly move near their final places in the sorted array.

Each cycle in the Shell sort consists of multiple passes. Each pass contributes to ordering array elements that are separated by the current offset value. When the last pass in a cycle orders the elements by the current offset, the Shell method reduces the offset value to start the next cycle. The new cycle compares elements that are closer to each other.

Eventually, the offset value becomes 1, leading to the comparison of immediately neighboring elements. When the last pass ends, the array elements are sorted.

The Shell sort method has an approximate order of $O(N (\lg N)^2)$, where N is the number of array elements and lg is the base 2 logarithm. The actual time for sorting or searching is proportional to the order of these methods. The algorithms for selecting the offset value are

```
H(i+1) = (H(i) - 1) / 2
H(i+1) = (H(i) - 1) / 3
```

—where H(0) is equal to the number of array elements. The first sequence of calculating H(i+1) is faster than the second sequence for arrays that exceed 500 elements.

Let me explain how the Shell sort method works using a concrete example. Consider the following array of integers:

```
45 87 12 33 54 48 23
```

The initial offset, H(1), is 2 (equals $(7 - 1) / 3$). The first cycle compares elements that are two indices apart. In other words, the cycle compares the elements as shown here:

```
45   87   12   33   54   48   23
└─────────┼─────────┼─────────┘
45   87   12   33   54   48   23
     └─────────┼─────────┘
```

Thus, the first cycle orders the array as:

```
12 33 23 48 45 87 54
```

Notice that the array has every other elements sorted. The second cycle has an offset value of 1. This offset compares neighboring elements. When the second cycle is finished, the array is sorted and has the following order:

```
12 23 33 45 48 54 87
```

Let me present a programming example. Listing 10-4 contains the source code for the ARRAY4.CPP program, which illustrates the Shell sort method. The program displays the unsorted elements of an array object, sorts these elements, and then displays the sorted elements of the array object.

Here is the output of the program in Listing 10-4:

```
Unsorted array is:
23 45 89 74 51 18 87 63 36 38
Sorted array is:
18 23 36 38 45 51 63 74 87 89
```

Listing 10-4
The source code for the ARRAY4.CPP program.

```
// A C++ program that illustrates
// the Shell sort algorithm

#include <iostream.h>
#include <iomanip.h>

const int MAX_ELEMS = 10;

class myArray
{
  public:
    myArray(int fInitVal = 0);
    int& operator[](int nIndex)
      { return m_nArray[nIndex]; }
    void show(const char* pszMsg = "",
              const int nNumElems = MAX_ELEMS,
              const int bOneLine = 1);
    void ShellSort(int nNumElems = MAX_ELEMS);

  protected:
    int m_nArray[MAX_ELEMS];
};

myArray::myArray(int fInitVal)
{
  for (int i = 0; i < MAX_ELEMS; i++)
    m_nArray[i] = fInitVal;
}

void myArray::show(const char* pszMsg,
                   const int nNumElems,
                   const int bOneLine)
{
  cout << pszMsg << endl;
  if (bOneLine) {
    for (int i = 0; i < nNumElems; i++)
      cout << m_nArray[i] << ' ';
    cout << endl;
  }
```

```
  else {
    for (int i = 0; i < nNumElems; i++)
      cout << m_nArray[i] << endl;
    cout << endl;
  }
}

void myArray::ShellSort(int nNumElems)
{
  int nOffset = nNumElems;
  int bSorted;

  if (nNumElems < 2)
    return;

  while (nOffset > 1) {
    nOffset = (nOffset - 1) / 3;
    nOffset = (nOffset < 1) ? 1 : nOffset;
    // arrange elements that are nOffset apart
    do {
      bSorted = 1; // set sorted flag
      // compare elements
      for (int i = 0, j = nOffset;
           i < (nNumElems - nOffset);
           i++, j++) {
        if (m_nArray[i] > m_nArray[j]) {
          // swap elements
          int nSwap = m_nArray[i];
          m_nArray[i] = m_nArray[j];
          m_nArray[j] = nSwap;
          bSorted = 0; // clear sorted flag
        }
      }
    } while (!bSorted);
  }
}

main()
{
  int nArr[MAX_ELEMS] = { 23, 45, 89, 74, 51,
                          18, 87, 63, 36, 38 };
  myArray Array;

  for (int i = 0; i < MAX_ELEMS; i++)
    Array[i] = nArr[i];

  Array.show("Unsorted array is:");
  Array.ShellSort();
  Array.show("Sorted array is:");

  return 0;
}
```

Listing 10-4 declares the class **myArray**, which resembles previous versions of the class **myArray**. The new version of class **myArray** supports arrays of integers instead of floating-point numbers. The class declares the protected data member **m_nArray**, which stores the array elements. The class also declares a constructor, the operator **[]**, and the member functions **show** and **ShellSort**.

The definition of member function **ShellSort** implements the algorithm that I discussed previously. The function uses a **while** loop to control the cycles. The first two statements inside the **while** loop update the offset value (stored in variable **nOffset**) using the second sequence of calculating the offset value (that is, $H(i+1) = (H(i) - 1) / 3$). The **while** loop contains a nested **do-while** loop that manages each pass. The **do-while** loop in turn contains a nested **for** loop that compares the elements that are **nOffset** indices apart.

The function **main** declares and initializes the C++ array **nArr**. The function also declares the object **Array** as an instance of class **myArray**. The function then performs the following tasks:

- Copy the values in array **nArr** into the object **Array**. This task uses a **for** loop to iterate over the elements in array **nArr**.

- Display the unsorted elements in object **Array** by sending it the C++ message **show**. The argument for this message is the literal string "Unsorted array is:".

- Sort the object **Array** by sending it the C++ message **ShellSort**

- Display the sorted elements in object **Array** by sending it the C++ message **show**. The argument for this message is the literal string "Sorted array is:".

SORTING ARRAYS USING COMBSORT

The combsort method also belongs to the category of in-place exchange sort methods. This relatively new method was developed by Richard Box and Stephen Lacey (see their article on the combsort method in the April 1991 issue of *Byte*). Box and Lacey presented the combsort method as a clever and efficient modification of the very slow bubble sort method.

However, when I studied their algorithm, I found out that it also happens to be a clever (though not intended) modification of the Shell sort method. The combsort method has an order of O(N lgN). Thus, the combsort method is faster than the Shell sort method except when you are sorting arrays that are already sorted in the reverse order. I noticed this fact by comparing the performance of the two methods.

The combsort method sorts an array by performing multiple passes of comparisons. Unlike Shell sort, combsort does not perform multiple cycles per pass. Initially, combsort compares distant elements that are apart by an offset value. Each pass reduces the offset value, which eventually reaches the value of 1. The combsort method then compares neighboring elements until the array is ordered.

Box and Lacey suggest the following sequence for calculating the offset value:

```
H(i+1) = (H(i) * 8) / 11
```

—where H(0) is equal to the number of array elements.

Let me present a programming example. Listing 10-5 contains the source code for the ARRAY5.CPP program, which illustrates the combsort method. The program displays the unsorted elements of an array object, sorts these elements, and then displays the sorted elements of the array object.

Here is the output of the program in Listing 10-5:

```
Unsorted array is:
23 45 89 74 51 18 87 63 36 38
Sorted array is:
18 23 36 38 45 51 63 74 87 89
```

Listing 10-5
The source code for the ARRAY5.CPP program.

```
// A C++ program that illustrates
// the combsort algorithm

#include <iostream.h>
#include <iomanip.h>

const int MAX_ELEMS = 10;
```

```
class myArray
{
  public:
    myArray(int fInitVal = 0);
    int& operator[](int nIndex)
      { return m_nArray[nIndex]; }
    void show(const char* pszMsg = "",
              const int nNumElems = MAX_ELEMS,
              const int bOneLine = 1);
    void CombSort(int nNumElems = MAX_ELEMS);

  protected:
    int m_nArray[MAX_ELEMS];
};

myArray::myArray(int fInitVal)
{
  for (int i = 0; i < MAX_ELEMS; i++)
    m_nArray[i] = fInitVal;
}

void myArray::show(const char* pszMsg,
                   const int nNumElems,
                   const int bOneLine)
{
  cout << pszMsg << endl;
  if (bOneLine) {
    for (int i = 0; i < nNumElems; i++)
      cout << m_nArray[i] << ' ';
    cout << endl;
  }
  else {
    for (int i = 0; i < nNumElems; i++)
      cout << m_nArray[i] << endl;
    cout << endl;
  }
}

void myArray::CombSort(int nNumElems)
{
  int nOffset = nNumElems;
  int bSorted;

  if (nNumElems < 2)
    return;

  do {
    nOffset = (nOffset * 8) / 11;
    nOffset = (nOffset < 1) ? 1 : nOffset;
    bSorted = 1; // set sorted flag
    // compare elements
    for (int i = 0, j = nOffset;
         i < (nNumElems - nOffset);
         i++, j++) {
```

```
      if (m_nArray[i] > m_nArray[j]) {
        // swap elements
        int nSwap = m_nArray[i];
        m_nArray[i] = m_nArray[j];
        m_nArray[j] = nSwap;
        bSorted = 0; // clear sorted flag
      }
    }
  } while (!bSorted || nOffset != 1);
}

main()
{
  int nArr[MAX_ELEMS] = { 23, 45, 89, 74, 51,
                          18, 87, 63, 36, 38 };
  myArray Array;

  for (int i = 0; i < MAX_ELEMS; i++)
    Array[i] = nArr[i];

  Array.show("Unsorted array is:");
  Array.CombSort();
  Array.show("Sorted array is:");

  return 0;
}
```

Listing 10-5 declares the class **myArray**, which resembles the class **myArray** in Listing 10-4. The new version of class **myArray** declares the member function **CombSort** instead of **ShellSort**.

The definition of member function **CombSort** implements the combsort algorithm. The function uses a **do-while** loop to control the cycles. The first two statements inside the **do-while** loop update the offset value (stored in variable **nOffset**). The **do-while** loop contains a nested **for** loop that compares the elements that are **nOffset** indices apart. The sorting stops when the sort flag (stored in variable **bSorted**) is not zero and the offset value is 1.

The function **main** declares and initializes the C++ array **nArr**. It also declares the object **Array** as an instance of class **myArray**. The function then performs the following tasks:

- Copy the values in array **nArr** into the object **Array**. This task uses a **for** loop to iterate over the elements in array **nArr**.

- Display the unsorted elements in object **Array** by sending it the C++ message **show**. The argument for this message is the literal string "Unsorted array is:".

- Sort the object **Array** by sending it the C++ message **CombSort**
- Display the sorted elements in object **Array** by sending it the C++ message **show**. The argument for this message is the literal string "Sorted array is:"

SORTING ARRAYS USING QUICKSORT

The quicksort method is the fastest sorting method, in most cases. This method, which has the order of O(N lgN), uses a clever divide-and-conquer approach to sorting arrays.

The basic approach of quicksort is to locate the median value of an array, divide the array into two subarrays, and then sort each subarray. The algorithm is recursive, since it deals with each subarray just as it does the main array. Thus, the quicksort method ends up dividing the main array into lots of little subarrays.

Let me present a programming example. Listing 10-6 contains the source code for the ARRAY6.CPP program, which illustrates the recursive quicksort method. The program displays the unsorted elements of an array object, sorts these elements, and then displays the sorted elements of the array object.

Here is the output of the program in Listing 10-6:

```
Unsorted array is:
23 45 89 74 51 18 87 63 36 38
Sorted array is:
18 23 36 38 45 51 63 74 87 89
```

Listing 10-6
The source code for the ARRAY6.CPP program.

```
// A C++ program that illustrates
// the quicksort algorithm

#include <iostream.h>
#include <iomanip.h>
```

```
const int MAX_ELEMS = 10;

class myArray
{
  public:
    myArray(int fInitVal = 0);
    int& operator[](int nIndex)
      { return m_nArray[nIndex]; }
    void show(const char* pszMsg = "",
              const int nNumElems = MAX_ELEMS,
              const int bOneLine = 1);
    void QuickSort(int nNumElems = MAX_ELEMS);

  protected:
    int m_nArray[MAX_ELEMS];

    void QSort(int nFirst, int nLast);
};

myArray::myArray(int fInitVal)
{
  for (int i = 0; i < MAX_ELEMS; i++)
    m_nArray[i] = fInitVal;
}

void myArray::show(const char* pszMsg,
                   const int nNumElems,
                   const int bOneLine)
{
  cout << pszMsg << endl;
  if (bOneLine) {
    for (int i = 0; i < nNumElems; i++)
      cout << m_nArray[i] << ' ';
    cout << endl;
  }
  else {
    for (int i = 0; i < nNumElems; i++)
      cout << m_nArray[i] << endl;
    cout << endl;
  }
}

void myArray::QuickSort(int nNumElems)
{
  if (nNumElems > 1)
    QSort(0, nNumElems - 1);
}
```

```
void myArray::QSort(int nFirst, int nLast)
{
  int i = nFirst, j = nLast;
  int nMedian;

  // obtain the median element
  nMedian = m_nArray[(nFirst + nLast) / 2];
  do {
    while (m_nArray[i] < nMedian)
      i++;
    while (nMedian < m_nArray[j])
      j--;
    if (i <= j) {
      // swap elements
      int nSwap = m_nArray[i];
      m_nArray[i++] = m_nArray[j];
      m_nArray[j--] = nSwap;
    }
  } while (i <= j);

  if (nFirst < j)
    QSort(nFirst, j);

  if (i < nLast)
    QSort(i, nLast);
}
```

→ *Workhorse routine*

```
main()
{
  int nArr[MAX_ELEMS] = { 23, 45, 89, 74, 51,
                          18, 87, 63, 36, 38 };
  myArray Array;

  for (int i = 0; i < MAX_ELEMS; i++)
    Array[i] = nArr[i];

  Array.show("Unsorted array is:");
  Array.QuickSort();
  Array.show("Sorted array is:");

  return 0;
}
```

Listing 10-6 declares the class **myArray**, which resembles the class **myArray** in Listing 10-5. The new version of class **myArray** declares the public and protected member functions **QuickSort** and **QSort**, to replace the member function **CombSort**.

The definition of member function **QuickSort** shows that its purpose is to trigger the recursive member function **QSort**. The arguments for invoking the member function **QSort** are 0 and **nNumElems** – 1. These arguments specify the indices for the first and last array elements, respectively.

The definition of member function **QSort** implements the heart of the quicksort algorithm. The function uses a **do-while** loop to locate the median value. The member function then uses the last two **if** statements to sort the subarrays. By declaring the member function as protected, we assure that the class instances cannot receive the **QSort** method. Instead, they must receive the C++ message **QuickSort**, which verifies the argument of the message before invoking **QSort**. Thus, the class **myArray** shows that the combination of the public member function **QuickSort** and the protected member function **QSort** guard the latter from erroneous invocations.

The function **main** declares and initializes the C++ array **nArr**. The function also declares the object **Array** as an instance of class **myArray**. It then performs the following tasks:

- Copy the values in array **nArr** into the object **Array**. This task uses a **for** loop to iterate over the elements in array **nArr**.

- Display the unsorted elements in object **Array** by sending it the C++ message **show**. The argument for this message is the literal string "Unsorted array is:".

- Sort the object **Array** by sending it the C++ message **QuickSort**

- Display the sorted elements in object **Array** by sending it the C++ message **show**. The argument for this message is the literal string "Sorted array is:".

LINEAR SEARCHES OF ARRAY ELEMENTS

The remaining sections in this chapter present methods for searching arrays. This section presents the linear search algorithm. The basic method is simple and straightforward—you examine every array element until you either find a match or exhaust the array elements. The linear search method works with sorted and unsorted arrays, although it does not take advantage of the order in sorted arrays. The method has a search order of O(N) for worst-case searches (where there is no matching element found). The order for successful searches is O(N/2).

Let's look at a programming example. Listing 10-7 contains the source code for the ARRAY7.CPP program, which illustrates the linear search method. The program displays the unsorted elements of an array object and then displays the results of searching for four values in the array object.

Here is the output of the program in Listing 10-7:

```
Array is:
23 45 89 74 51 18 87 63 36 38
Searching for 23 found match at index 0
Searching for 74 found match at index 3
Searching for 87 found match at index 6
Searching for 38 found match at index 9
```

Listing 10-7
The source code for the ARRAY7.CPP program.

```cpp
// A C++ program that illustrates
// the linear search algorithm

#include <iostream.h>
#include <iomanip.h>

const int MAX_ELEMS = 10;
const int NOT_FOUND = -1;

class myArray
{
  public:
    myArray(int fInitVal = 0);
    int& operator[](int nIndex)
      { return m_nArray[nIndex]; }
    void show(const char* pszMsg = "",
              const int nNumElems = MAX_ELEMS,
              const int bOneLine = 1);
    int linearSearch(int nKey,
                     int nLast = MAX_ELEMS - 1,
                     int nFirst = 0);

  protected:
    int m_nArray[MAX_ELEMS];
};
```

```
myArray::myArray(int fInitVal)
{
  for (int i = 0; i < MAX_ELEMS; i++)
    m_nArray[i] = fInitVal;
}

void myArray::show(const char* pszMsg,
                   const int nNumElems,
                   const int bOneLine)
{
  cout << pszMsg << endl;
  if (bOneLine) {
    for (int i = 0; i < nNumElems; i++)
      cout << m_nArray[i] << ' ';
    cout << endl;
  }
  else {
    for (int i = 0; i < nNumElems; i++)
      cout << m_nArray[i] << endl;
    cout << endl;
  }
}

int myArray::linearSearch(int nKey, int nLast, int nFirst)
{
  for (int i = nFirst; i <= nLast; i++)
    if (m_nArray[i] == nKey)
      break;
  return (i <= nLast) ? i : NOT_FOUND;
}

main()
{
  int j;
  int nArr[MAX_ELEMS] = { 23, 45, 89, 74, 51,
                          18, 87, 63, 36, 38 };
  myArray Array;

  for (int i = 0; i < MAX_ELEMS; i++)
    Array[i] = nArr[i];

  Array.show("Array is:");
  for (i = 0; i < MAX_ELEMS; i += 3) {
    cout << "Searching for " << nArr[i];
    j = Array.linearSearch(nArr[i]);
    if (j != NOT_FOUND)
      cout << " found match at index " << j << endl;
    else
      cout << " found no match\n";
  }
  return 0;
}
```

Listing 10-7 declares the class **myArray**, which resembles the class **myArray** in Listing 10-6. The new version of class **myArray** declares member function **linearSearch**, which conducts the linear search. This member function has the following parameters:

- The **int**-type parameter **nKey** is the search value.
- The **int**-type parameters **nFirst** and **nLast** define the range of search indices. The default arguments for these parameters are 0 and **MAX_ELEMS** – 1, respectively. These default arguments specify searching in the entire array (stored in data member **m_nArray**).

The definition of member function **linearSearch** uses a **for** loop to examine the array elements in the index range of **nFirst** to **nLast**. The loop uses an **if** statement to compare the search value with element **m_nArray[i]**. If the two values match, the **if** statement executes the **break** statement to stop the search. The member function either returns the index of the matching element or yields the value of the global constant **NOT_FOUND** if no match is found.

The function **main** declares and initializes the C++ array **nArr**. The function also declares the object **Array** as an instance of class **myArray**. The function then performs the following tasks:

- Copy the values in array **nArr** into the object **Array**. This task uses a **for** loop to iterate over the elements in array **nArr**.
- Display the unsorted elements in object **Array** by sending it the C++ message **show**. The argument is the literal string "**Array is:**".
- Search for the values in **nArr[0]**, **nArr[3]**, **nArr[6]**, and **nArr[9]** using a **for** loop. Each loop iteration displays the value of the search value and then sends the C++ message **linearSearch** to object **Array**. The argument for this message is the search value of **nArr[i]**. The loop assigns the result of the message to variable **j**. The loop uses an **if** statement to determine whether or not the search is successful. If it is, the code displays the index of the matching array element.

BINARY SEARCHES OF ARRAY ELEMENTS

The binary search method is the best general-purpose search method for sorted arrays. The method has an order of O(lg(N)).

The binary search method starts by comparing the search value with the value of the median array element. If the two values match, the search ends. If not, the method uses either half of the array (depending on how the search value compares with the value of the median array element) as the new subarray to search. The method treats the subarray just as it does the main array. The binary search repeats this process until it either finds a match or runs out of subarrays to examine.

Let's look at a programming example. Listing 10-8 contains the source code for the ARRAY8.CPP program, which illustrates the binary search method. The program displays the sorted elements of an array object and then displays the results of searching for four values in the array object.

Here is the output of the program in Listing 10-8:

```
Sorted array is:
18 23 36 38 45 51 63 74 87 89
Searching for 23 found match at index 1
Searching for 74 found match at index 7
Searching for 87 found match at index 8
Searching for 38 found match at index 3
```

Listing 10-8
The source code for the ARRAY8.CPP program.

```cpp
// A C++ program that illustrates
// the binary search algorithm

#include <iostream.h>
#include <iomanip.h>

const int MAX_ELEMS = 10;
const int NOT_FOUND = -1;
const int SORTED = 1;
const int UNSORTED = 0;
```

```
class myArray
{
  public:
    myArray(int fInitVal = 0);
    int& operator[](int nIndex)
      { return m_nArray[nIndex]; }
    void show(const char* pszMsg = "",
              const int nNumElems = MAX_ELEMS,
              const int bOneLine = 1);
    void QuickSort(int nNumElems = MAX_ELEMS);
    void clearSortFlag()
      { m_bSorted = UNSORTED; }
    int binarySearch(int nKey,
                     int nLast = MAX_ELEMS - 1,
                     int nFirst = 0);

  protected:
    int m_nArray[MAX_ELEMS];
    int m_bSorted;

    void QSort(int nFirst, int nLast);
};

myArray::myArray(int fInitVal)
{
  for (int i = 0; i < MAX_ELEMS; i++)
    m_nArray[i] = fInitVal;
  m_bSorted = UNSORTED;
}

void myArray::show(const char* pszMsg,
                   const int nNumElems,
                   const int bOneLine)
{
  cout << pszMsg << endl;
  if (bOneLine) {
    for (int i = 0; i < nNumElems; i++)
      cout << m_nArray[i] << ' ';
    cout << endl;
  }
  else {
    for (int i = 0; i < nNumElems; i++)
      cout << m_nArray[i] << endl;
    cout << endl;
  }
}

void myArray::QuickSort(int nNumElems)
{
  if (!m_bSorted && nNumElems > 1) {
    QSort(0, nNumElems - 1);
    m_bSorted = SORTED;
  }
```

```
    }

    void myArray::QSort(int nFirst, int nLast)
    {
      int i = nFirst, j = nLast;
      int nMedian;

      // obtain the median element
      nMedian = m_nArray[(nFirst + nLast) / 2];
      do {
        while (m_nArray[i] < nMedian)
          i++;
        while (nMedian < m_nArray[j])
          j--;
        if (i <= j) {
          // swap elements
          int nSwap = m_nArray[i];
          m_nArray[i++] = m_nArray[j];
          m_nArray[j--] = nSwap;
        }
      } while (i <= j);

      if (nFirst < j)
        QSort(nFirst, j);

      if (i < nLast)
        QSort(i, nLast);
    }

    int myArray::binarySearch(int nKey, int nLast, int nFirst)
    {
      int nMedian;

      if (!m_bSorted)
        return NOT_FOUND;

      do {
        nMedian = (nFirst + nLast) / 2;
        if (nKey < m_nArray[nMedian])
          nLast = nMedian - 1;
        else
          nFirst = nMedian + 1;
      } while (!(nKey == m_nArray[nMedian] || nFirst > nLast));

      return (nKey == m_nArray[nMedian]) ? nMedian : NOT_FOUND;

    }

    main()
    {
      int j;
      int nArr[MAX_ELEMS] = { 23, 45, 89, 74, 51,
                              18, 87, 63, 36, 38 };
```

```
myArray Array;

for (int i = 0; i < MAX_ELEMS; i++)
  Array[i] = nArr[i];

Array.QuickSort();
Array.show("Sorted array is:");
for (i = 0; i < MAX_ELEMS; i += 3) {
  cout << "Searching for " << nArr[i];
  j = Array.binarySearch(nArr[i]);
  if (j != NOT_FOUND)
    cout << " found match at index " << j << endl;
  else
    cout << " found no match\n";
}

  return 0;
}
```

Listing 10-8 declares the class **myArray**, which resembles the class **myArray** in Listing 10-7. The new version of class **myArray** declares the following new members:

- The protected **int**-type data member **m_bSorted**, which stores the sorted state. The class assigns the values of constants **SORTED** and **UNSORTED** to the data member.

- The member function **clearSortFlag**, which assigns **UNSORTED** to the data member **m_bSorted**

- The member functions **QuickSort** and **QSort**, which sort the elements of data member **m_nArray** using the quicksort method. The source code for the member function **QSort** is the same as in Listing 10-6. As for member function **QuickSort**, the new version uses the data member **m_bSorted** to determine if the array is not already sorted. In addition, the member function assigns the value of constant **SORTED** to data member **m_bSorted** after invoking the member function **QSort**.

- The member function **binarySearch**, which performs the binary search on the elements of data member **m_nArray**. This member function has the parameters **nKey**, **nLast**, and **nFirst**. These parameters play the same role as in member function **linearSearch** in Listing 10-7.

The definition of member function **binarySearch** first examines the value of data member **m_bSorted** to determine whether or not the array **m_nArray** is sorted. If that array is not sorted, the member function simply exits. Otherwise, the member function performs the binary search using a **do-while** loop. The loop statements determine the index of the median element in the current subarray. The loop then uses an **if** statement to compare the search key with this element. The outcome of this comparison determines the range of the new subarray. The loop iterates until it finds a match or until the value of parameter **nFirst** exceeds that of parameter **nLast**. The member function returns the index of the matching element or yields the value of the global constant **NOT_FOUND** if no match is found.

The function **main** declares and initializes the C++ array **nArr**. It also declares the object **Array** as an instance of class **myArray**. The function then performs the following tasks:

- Copy the values in array **nArr** into the object **Array**. This task uses a **for** loop to iterate over the elements in array **nArr**.

- Sort the object **Array** by sending it the C++ message **QuickSort**

- Display the sorted elements in object **Array** by sending it the C++ message **show**. The argument for this message is the literal string "Sorted array is:".

- Search for the values in **nArr[0]**, **nArr[3]**, **nArr[6]**, and **nArr[9]** using a **for** loop. Each loop iteration displays the search value and then sends the C++ message **binarySearch** to object **Array**. The argument for this message is the search value of **nArr[i]**. The loop assigns the result of the message to variable **j**. The loop uses an **if** statement to determine whether or not the search is successful. If it is, the code displays the index of the matching array element.

HEURISTIC SEARCHES OF ARRAY ELEMENTS

Suppose you have an application that uses an array such that you cannot sort it (for example, the application updates the array too frequently with new data), but you can swap a few array elements. How can you improve the search for this kind of unsorted array? The answer is the *heuristic* search method. This method moves the value of a matching array element using one of the following schemes:

- Move the matching value to the first array element. This scheme assumes that there is a very good chance the next queries will search for the value of the moved element.

- Swap the matching value with its lower-index neighbor. This scheme assumes that there is a reasonable chance the next queries will search for the value of the moved element. This scheme causes a repeatedly matching value to bubble to the front of the array.

- Move the matching value to the last array element. This scheme assumes that there is a very good chance the next queries will not search for the value of the moved element.

Let's look at a programming example. Listing 10-9 contains the source code for the ARRAY9.CPP program, which illustrates the heuristic search method. The program displays the unsorted elements of an array object and then displays the results of searching for the value 38, four times, in the array object. After each search, the program displays the new order of the elements in object **Array**.

Here is the output of the program in Listing 10-9:

```
Initial heuristic array is: 23 45 89 74 51 18 87 63 36 38
Searching for 38 found match at index 8
Heuristic array is: 23 45 89 74 51 18 87 63 38 36
Searching for 38 found match at index 7
Heuristic array is: 23 45 89 74 51 18 87 38 63 36
Searching for 38 found match at index 6
Heuristic array is: 23 45 89 74 51 18 38 87 63 36
Searching for 38 found match at index 5
Heuristic array is: 23 45 89 74 51 38 18 87 63 36
Searching for 38 found match at index 4
Heuristic array is: 23 45 89 74 38 51 18 87 63 36
```

Listing 10-9
The source code for the ARRAY9.CPP program.

```
// A C++ program that illustrates
// the heuristic search algorithm

#include <iostream.h>
#include <iomanip.h>
```

```
const int MAX_ELEMS = 10;
const int NOT_FOUND = -1;

class myArray
{
  public:
    myArray(int fInitVal = 0);
    int& operator[](int nIndex)
      { return m_nArray[nIndex]; }
    void show(const char* pszMsg = "",
              const int nNumElems = MAX_ELEMS,
              const int bOneLine = 1);
    int heuristicSearch(int nKey,
                        int nLast = MAX_ELEMS - 1,
                        int nFirst = 0);

  protected:
    int m_nArray[MAX_ELEMS];
};

myArray::myArray(int fInitVal)
{
  for (int i = 0; i < MAX_ELEMS; i++)
    m_nArray[i] = fInitVal;
}

void myArray::show(const char* pszMsg,
                   const int nNumElems,
                   const int bOneLine)
{
  cout << pszMsg;
  if (bOneLine) {
    for (int i = 0; i < nNumElems; i++)
      cout << m_nArray[i] << ' ';
    cout << endl;
  }
  else {
    for (int i = 0; i < nNumElems; i++)
      cout << m_nArray[i] << endl;
    cout << endl;
  }
}

int myArray::heuristicSearch(int nKey, int nLast, int nFirst)
{
  for (int i = nFirst; i <= nLast; i++)
    if (m_nArray[i] == nKey)
      break;
```

```
      if (i <= nLast) {
        if (i > 0) {
          // swap elements at indices i and i-1
          int nSwap = m_nArray[i];
          m_nArray[i] = m_nArray[i-1];
          m_nArray[-i] = nSwap;
        }
        return i;
      }
      else
        return NOT_FOUND;
    }

main()
{
  int j;
  int nLast = MAX_ELEMS - 1;
  int nArr[MAX_ELEMS] = { 23, 45, 89, 74, 51,
                          18, 87, 63, 36, 38 };
  myArray Array;

  for (int i = 0; i < MAX_ELEMS; i++)
    Array[i] = nArr[i];

  Array.show("Initial heuristic array is: ");

  for (i = 0; i < MAX_ELEMS / 2; i++) {
    cout << "Searching for " << nArr[nLast];
    j = Array.heuristicSearch(nArr[nLast]);
    if (j != NOT_FOUND)
      cout << " found match at index " << j << endl;
    else
      cout << " found no match\n";
    Array.show("Heuristic array is: ");
  }
  return 0;
}
```

Listing 10-9 declares the class **myArray**, which resembles the class **myArray** in Listing 10-7. The new version of class **myArray** declares member function **heuristicSearch**, which conducts the heuristic search. This member function has the same parameters as member function **linearSearch** in Listing 10-7.

The definition of member function **heuristicSearch** uses a **for** loop to examine the array elements in the index range of **nFirst** to **nLast**. The loop uses an **if** statement to compare the search data with element **m_nArray[i]**. If the two values match, the **if** statement executes the **break** statement to stop the search. The member function swaps the matching array element with its lower-index neighbor (unless the matching element is the first array element). The function returns the index of the matching element or yields the value of the global constant **NOT_FOUND** if no match is found.

The function **main** declares and initializes the C++ array **nArr**. It also declares the object **Array** as an instance of class **myArray**. It then performs the following tasks:

- Copy the values in array **nArr** into the object **Array**. This task uses a **for** loop to iterate over the elements in array **nArr**.

- Display the initial unsorted elements in object **Array** by sending it the C++ message **show**. The argument for this message is the literal string "Initial heuristic array is:".

- Search for the values in **nArr[nLast]** four times using a **for** loop. Each loop iteration displays the search value and then sends the C++ message **heuristicSearch** to object **Array**. The argument for this message is the search value of **nArr[i]**. The loop assigns the result of the message to variable **j**. The loop uses an **if** statement to determine whether or not the search is successful. If it is, the code displays the index of the matching array element. The last loop statement displays the new order of elements in object **Array** by sending it the C++ message **show**. The argument for this message is the string literal "Heuristic array is: ".

STATISTICAL SEARCHES OF ARRAY ELEMENTS

The heuristic method swaps array elements based on the general assumption that the application searches for certain array values more frequently than others. In other words, the probability of searching for an array element is not uniform. If this assumption is false (that is, the probability of searching for an array element *is* uniform), then the heuristic method does not offer a significant advantage. Instead of falling back on a linear search, you can use the statistical search method. This method is based on the following assumptions:

1. The probability of searching for an array element *is* uniform.

2. The average index of the matching array element is equal to the median index value.

The statistical search method searches the array in cycles using two indices. Each cycle uses the first and second indices to examine array elements above and below the median value, respectively. If the array contains an odd number of elements, the method starts by examining the median element first. Each cycle searches elements that are farther from the median. The search stops when the method finds a matching array element or when it has searched the entire array.

Let's look at a programming example. Listing 10-10 contains the source code for the ARRAY10.CPP program, which illustrates the statistical search method. The program displays the unsorted elements of an array object and then displays the results of searching for four values in the array object. The results also show the number of comparisons performed by the search method.

Here is the output of the program in Listing 10-10:

```
Array is: 23 45 89 74 51 18 87 63 36 38
Searching for 23 found match at index 0 (10 comparisons)
Searching for 74 found match at index 3 (4 comparisons)
Searching for 87 found match at index 6 (3 comparisons)
Searching for 38 found match at index 9 (9 comparisons)
```

Listing 10-10
The source code for the ARRAY10.CPP program.

```
// A C++ program that illustrates
// the statistical search algorithm

#include <iostream.h>
#include <iomanip.h>

const int MAX_ELEMS = 10;
const int NOT_FOUND = -1;
const int TRUE = 1;
const int FALSE = 0;
```

```
class myArray
{
  public:
    myArray(int fInitVal = 0);
    int& operator[](int nIndex)
      { return m_nArray[nIndex]; }
    void show(const char* pszMsg = "",
              const int nNumElems = MAX_ELEMS,
              const int bOneLine = 1);
    int statSearch(int nKey,
                   int nLast = MAX_ELEMS - 1,
                   int nFirst = 0);
    int getNumCompare()
      { return m_nNumCompare; }

  protected:
    int m_nArray[MAX_ELEMS];
    int m_nNumCompare;
};

myArray::myArray(int fInitVal)
{
  for (int i = 0; i < MAX_ELEMS; i++)
    m_nArray[i] = fInitVal;
}

void myArray::show(const char* pszMsg,
                   const int nNumElems,
                   const int bOneLine)
{
  cout << pszMsg;
  if (bOneLine) {
    for (int i = 0; i < nNumElems; i++)
      cout << m_nArray[i] << ' ';
    cout << endl;
  }
  else {
    for (int i = 0; i < nNumElems; i++)
      cout << m_nArray[i] << endl;
    cout << endl;
  }
}

int myArray::statSearch(int nKey, int nLast, int nFirst)
{
  int nNumElems, m, i, j, k, nCount, nShift;
  int notFound = TRUE;

  if (nFirst > nLast || nFirst >= MAX_ELEMS)
    return NOT_FOUND;

  nNumElems = nLast - nFirst + 1;
  m = nNumElems / 2;
  nCount = m;
  m_nNumCompare = 0;
```

```
      // is nNumElems an odd number?
      if ((nNumElems % 2) > 0) {
        m_nNumCompare++;
        // examine the median of an odd-number range
        if (m_nArray[m] == nKey) {
          nKey = m_nArray[m];
          return m;
        }
        nShift = 1;
      }
      else
        nShift = 0;
      k = 2 * m + nShift;
      // search around the median value
      while (notFound && nCount > 0) {
        // search above the median
        j = k - nCount;
        m_nNumCompare++;
        // m_nArray[j] matches search data?
        if (m_nArray[j] == nKey) {
          // save matching index in k
          k = j;
          notFound = FALSE;
        }

        // still not found a match
        if (notFound) {
          // search below the median and also
          // decrement nCount
          i = nCount- - 1;
          m_nNumCompare++;
          // m_nArray[i] matches search data?
          if (m_nArray[i] == nKey) {
            // save matching index in k
            k = i;
            notFound = FALSE;
          }
        }
      }

    return (notFound) ? NOT_FOUND : k;
}

main()
{
  int j;
  int nArr[MAX_ELEMS] = { 23, 45, 89, 74, 51,
                          18, 87, 63, 36, 38 };
  myArray Array;

  for (int i = 0; i < MAX_ELEMS; i++)
    Array[i] = nArr[i];
```

```
    Array.show("Array is: ");

    for (i = 0; i < MAX_ELEMS; i += 3) {
      cout << "Searching for " << nArr[i];
      j = Array.statSearch(nArr[i]);
      if (j != NOT_FOUND)
        cout << " found match at index "
             << j << " (" << Array.getNumCompare()
             << " comparisons)" << endl;
      else
        cout << " found no match\n";
    }
    return 0;
}
```

Listing 10-10 declares the class **myArray**, which resembles the class
myArray in Listing 10-7. The new version of class **myArray** declares member
function **statSearch**, which conducts the linear search. This member function
has the same parameters as member function **linearSearch** in Listing 10-7.

The definition of member function **statSearch** first determines if the
number of array elements is odd. If this condition is true, then the member
function compares the median array element with the search value. If the
two values match, the member function returns the index of the median
element. Otherwise, the function uses a **while** loop to examine the array
elements above and below the median, returning the index of the matching
element or yielding the value of the global constant **NOT_FOUND** if no
match is found. It uses the data member **nNumCompares** to keep track of
the number of comparisons. The class declares the member function
getNumCompare to obtain the value in data member **nNumCompare**.

The function **main** declares and initializes the C++ array **nArr**. It also
declares the object **Array** as an instance of class **myArray**. The function then
performs the following tasks:

- Copy the values in array **nArr** into the object **Array**. This task uses a **for**
  loop to iterate over the elements in array **nArr**.

- Display the unsorted elements in object **Array** by sending it the C++
  message **show**. The argument is the literal string "**Array is:**".

- Search for the values in **nArr[0]**, **nArr[3]**, **nArr[6]**, and **nArr[9]** using a **for**
  loop. Each loop iteration displays the value of the search value and then

sends the C++ message **statSearch** to object **Array**. The argument for this message is the search value of **nArr[i]**. The loop assigns the result of the message to variable **j**. The loop uses an **if** statement to determine whether or not the search is successful. If it is, the code displays the index of the matching array element and the number of comparisons performed by member function **statSearch**. The output statement sends the C++ message **getNumCompare** to obtain the number of comparisons.

Summary

This chapter discussed single-dimensional arrays. You learned about declaring, accessing, and initializing arrays. The chapter also discussed sorting and searching methods characteristically applied to arrays. You learned about the bubble sort, Shell sort, combsort, and quicksort methods, as well as the linear, binary, heuristic, and statistical search methods.

The next chapter looks at multidimensional arrays and discusses declaring, accessing, and initializing them. It also looks at ways of applying the combsort method and the linear and binary search methods to two-dimensional arrays.

11 Multidimensional Arrays

*A*rray support in C++ is not limited to single-dimensional arrays. Rather, it extends to multidimensional arrays. This chapter looks at declaring, accessing, and initializing multidimensional arrays. In addition, the chapter discusses declaring multidimensional arrays as function parameters. You will also learn about sorting multidimensional arrays using the combsort method, as well as searching multidimensional array elements using the linear and binary search methods.

Declaring Multidimensional Arrays

C++ requires that you declare a multidimensional array before you use it. The general syntax for declaring a multidimensional array is:

```
type arrayName[numberOfElement1][numberOfElement2]...
```

The above syntax shows the following aspects:

- The declaration starts by stating the basic type associated with the array elements. You can use predefined or previously defined data types.

- The name of the array is followed by a sequence of the number of elements for the various dimensions. These numbers appear in square brackets. Each number of elements must be a constant (literal or symbolic) or an expression that uses constants.

All multidimensional arrays in C++ have indices that start at 0. Thus, the number of array elements in each dimension is one value higher than the index of the last element in that dimension.

Here are examples of declaring multidimensional arrays:

```
// example 1
int nIntCube[20][10][5];
// example 2
const int MAX_ROWS = 50;
const int MAX_COLS = 20;
double fMatrix[MAX_ROWS][MAX_COLS];
// example 3
const int MAX_ROWS = 30;
const int MAX_COLS = 10;
char cNameArray[MAX_ROWS+1][MAX_COLS];
```

The first example declares the **int**-type three-dimensional array **nIntCube** with 20 by 10 by 5 elements. The declaration uses the literal constants 20, 10, and 5. Thus, the indices for the first dimension are in the range of 0 to 19, the indices for the second dimension are in the range of 0 to 9, and the indices for the third dimension are in the range of 0 to 4.

The second example declares the constants **MAX_ROWS** and **MAX_COLS** and uses these constants to specify the number of rows and columns of the **double**-type matrix **fMatrix**.

The third example declares the **char**-type matrix **cNameArray**. The constant expression **MAX_ROWS + 1** defines the number of rows in the array **cNameArray**. The constant **MAX_COLS** defines the number of columns in the array **cNameArray**.

Accessing Multidimensional Arrays

Once you declare a multidimensional array, you can access it elements using the index operator **[]**. The general syntax for accessing an element in a multidimensional array is:

```
arrayName[IndexOfDimension1][IndexOfDimension2]...
```

The indices for the various dimensions should be in the valid ranges— between 0 and the number of array elements for the dimension minus one. Here is an example of accessing multidimensional array elements:

```
const int MAX_ROWS = 10;
const int MAX_COLS = 20;
double fMatrix[MAX_ROWS][MAX_COLS];
for (int i = 0; i < MAX_ROWS; i++)
  for (int j = 0; j < MAX_COLS; j++)
    fMatrix[i][j] = double(2 + i 2 * j)
```

This code snippet declares the constants **MAX_ROWS** and **MAX_COLS** and uses these constants in declaring the **double**-type two-dimensional array **fMatrix**. Thus the array has rows with indices in the range of 0 to **MAX_ROWS – 1** and columns with indices in the range of 0 to **MAX_COLS – 1**. The code snippet uses nested **for** loops to initialize the elements of the array **fMatrix**. Notice that the last assignment statement uses the syntax **fMatrix[i][j]** and not **fMatrix[i, j]** or **fMatrix(i, j)** as is the case in Pascal and BASIC, respectively.

BASIC

Declaring and Accessing Multidimensional Arrays

C++ requires that you enclose *each* dimension in a pair of brackets. This style differs from BASIC's syntax, which places the comma-delimited list of dimensions in a single pair of parentheses.

Declaring and Accessing Multidimensional Arrays

C++ requires that you enclose *every* dimension in a pair of brackets. This style differs from Pascal's syntax, which places the comma-delimited list of dimensions in a single pair of brackets.

Let's look at a programming example. Listing 11-1 shows the source code for the MDARRAY1.CPP program, which illustrates declaring and accessing multidimensional arrays. This example illustrates the following features:

- Declaring and accessing C++ arrays
- Declaring classes that support multidimensional arrays

The example shows how you declare the operator () to access the elements of a multidimensional array in a class. Why use the operator () instead of the operator []? The answer is that C++ does not allow the operator [] to have more than one integer-compatible parameter. When you are storing and recalling array elements, then, the choice becomes either to use member functions or to use the operator (), which allows multiple indexing parameters. This operator is called the *iterator* operator; it is supposed to be used to sequentially access elements in data structures, such as lists.

The program performs the following tasks:

- Declare a C++ matrix and a matrix object
- Initialize a C++ matrix
- Assign the square root values of the C++ matrix elements to the elements of the matrix object
- Display the elements of the matrix object
- Double the values of the elements in the matrix object
- Display the elements of the matrix object

Here is the output of the program in Listing 11-1:

```
   Initial matrix is:
   1.4 1.4 1.4
   1.4 1.7 2.0
   1.4 2.0 2.4

   After doubling values, matrix is:
   2.8 2.8 2.8
   2.8 3.5 4.0
   2.8 4.0 4.9
```

Listing 11-1

The source code for the MDARRAY1.CPP program, which illustrates declaring and accessing multidimensional arrays.

```cpp
// A C++ program that illustrates declaring
// and accessing multidimensional matrix elements

#include <iostream.h>
#include <stdio.h>
#include <iomanip.h>
#include <math.h>

const int MAX_ROWS = 3;
const int MAX_COLS = 3;

class myMatrix
{
  public:
    myMatrix(double fInitVal = 0);
    double& operator()(int nRow, int nCol)
      { return m_fMatrix[nRow][nCol]; }
    void show(const char* pszMsg = "",
              const int nNumRows = MAX_ROWS,
              const int nNumCols = MAX_COLS);

  protected:
    double m_fMatrix[MAX_ROWS][MAX_COLS];               Matrix
};

myMatrix::myMatrix(double fInitVal)
{
  for (int i = 0; i < MAX_ROWS; i++)
    for (int j = 0; j < MAX_COLS; j++)
      m_fMatrix[i][j] = fInitVal;
}
```

```
void myMatrix::show(const char* pszMsg,
                    const int nNumRows,
                    const int nNumCols)
{
  char cString[10];

  cout << pszMsg << endl;
  for (int i = 0; i < nNumRows; i++) {
    for (int j = 0; j < nNumCols; j++) {
      sprintf(cString, "%3.1lf ", m_fMatrix[i][j]);
      cout << cString;
    }
    cout << endl;
  }
}

main()
{
  double fXMat[MAX_ROWS][MAX_COLS];              Matrix
  myMatrix Matrix;
  int i, j;

  // initialize matrix fXMat
  for (i = 0; i < MAX_ROWS; i++)
    for (j = 0; j < MAX_COLS; j++)
      fXMat[i][j] = 2.0 + (double)(i * j);

  // assign values to object Matrix
  for (i = 0; i < MAX_ROWS; i++)
    for (j = 0; j < MAX_COLS; j++)
      Matrix(i, j) = sqrt(fXMat[i][j]);

  // show the matrix
  Matrix.show("Initial matrix is:");

  cout << endl;

  // double the values in object Matrix
  for (i = 0; i < MAX_ROWS; i++)
    for (j = 0; j < MAX_COLS; j++)
      Matrix(i, j) += Matrix(i, j);

  // show the matrix
  Matrix.show("After doubling values, matrix is:");

  return 0;
}
```

Listing 11-1 declares the constants **MAX_ROWS** and **MAX_COLS**, which specify the number of rows and columns, respectively, in the program's matrices. The listing declares class **myMatrix**, which has the protected data

member **m_fMatrix**. This member is a **double**-type matrix that has
MAX_ROWS rows and MAX_COLS columns. The class declares the
following public members:

- The constructor, which initializes the values of the elements of the data
  member **m_fMatrix**. The default argument of parameter **fInitVal** initializes
  the matrix elements to 0.

- The operator **()**, which accesses the elements of data member
  m_fMatrix. Notice that the member function has the **double&** return type
  (instead of simply **double**). Using a reference return type allows you to
  utilize the operator **()** on either side of the assignment operator. The
  parameters **nRow** and **nCol** specify the row and column indices of the
  accessed matrix element.

- The member function **show**, which displays some or all of the matrix
  elements. The parameters **nNumRows** and **nNumCols** specify the
  number of matrix rows and columns, respectively, to display. The
  parameter **pszMsg** passes an accompanying message that appears
  before the function lists the matrix elements.

The function **main** declares the **double**-type matrix **fXMat** and the object
Matrix as an instance of class **myMatrix**. The declaration initializes the
elements of the object **Matrix** to 0. By contrast, the elements of the C++
matrix **fXMat** have no initial values (except for the arbitrary values in their
memory locations). The function **main** then performs the following tasks:

- Assign values to the elements of matrix **fXMat**. This task uses nested **for**
  loops, which iterate over all the elements of matrix **fXMat**. Each inner
  loop statement assigns the expression **2.0 + (double)(i + j)** to the element
  fXMat[i][j]. The matrix **fXMat** and the object **Matrix** have the same
  number of elements.

- Assign new values to the elements of the object **Matrix**. This task uses
  nested **for** loops, which iterate over the elements of object **Matrix**. Each
  inner loop iteration assigns the square root value of element **fXMat[i][j]**
  to element **Matrix(i, j)**. Notice that the loop's statement places **Matrix(i, j)**
  to the left side of the assignment operator.

- Display the elements in object **Matrix** by sending it the C++ message
  show. The argument for this message is the literal string "Initial matrix is:"

- Double the values in the elements of object **Matrix**. This task uses nested **for** loops, which iterate over the elements of object **Matrix**. Each inner loop iteration doubles the value of element **Matrix**(i, j) using the operator **+=**. Notice that the loop's statement places **Matrix**(i, j) to the left and right sides of the assignment operator.

- Display the elements in object **Matrix** by sending it the C++ message **show**. The argument for this message is the literal string "After doubling values, matrix is:".

Initializing Multidimensional Arrays

C++ allows you to initialize some or all of the elements of a multidimensional array. The general syntax for initializing a multidimensional array is:

```
type arrayName[numberOfElement1][numberOfElement2] = { value0 ,....,
                                                        valueN };
```

You need to observe the following rules when you initialize a multidimensional array:

1. The list of initial values appears in a pair of open and close braces and is comma-delimited.

2. The list may contain a number of initial values that is equal to or less than the total number of elements in the initialized array. Otherwise, the compiler generates a compile-time error.

3. The compiler assigns the initializing values in the sequence discussed in the sidebar "Initializing Multidimensional Arrays."

4. If the list contains fewer values than the number of elements in the array, the compiler assigns zeros to the elements that do not receive initial values from the list.

Initializing Multidimensional Arrays

How does the C++ compiler copy the items in a linear list of initializing values into the elements of a multidimensional array? The answer is that the compiler fills up the elements at the higher dimension number (represented by the index to the right) before the ones at the lower dimension number. Let me explain this storage scheme using the following example. Consider the array **fMat**, which has three rows and two columns:

```
double fMat[3][2];
```

The dimension for the rows is the low dimension number, whereas the dimension for the columns is the high dimension number. The element **fMat[0][0]** is the first array element. Thus, the compiler stores the first initializing value in element **fMat[0][0]**. The compiler then stores the second initializing value in element **fMat[0][1]**. The compiler stores the third initializing value in element **fMat[1][0]**, and so on. Here is the sequence of storing the initializing values in the matrix **fMat**:

```
fMat[0][0]
fMat[0][1]
fMat[1][0]
fMat[1][1]
fMat[2][0]
fMat[2][1]
```

You can apply the same rule to, say, the array **fCube[3][2][2]** and obtain the following sequence of initialized elements:

```
fCube[0][0][0]
fCube[0][0][1]
fCube[0][1][0]
fCube[0][1][1]
fCube[1][0][0]
fCube[1][0][1]
fCube[1][1][0]
fCube[1][1][1]
fCube[2][0][0]
fCube[2][0][1]
fCube[2][1][0]
fCube[2][1][1]
```

Here are examples of initializing multidimensional arrays:

```
// example 1
double fMat[3][2] = { 1.1, 2.2, 3.3, 4.4, 5.5, 6.6 };
// example 2
int nMat[5][2] = { 1, 2, 3, 4, 5 };
```

The code in example 1 declares the **double**-type two-dimensional array **fMat** to have three rows and two columns. The declaration also initializes all six elements with the values 1.1, 2.2, 3.3, 4.4, 5.5, and 6.6. The compiler stores these values sequentially in elements **fMat[0][0]**, **fMat[0][1]**, and so on. The second example declares the **int**-type matrix **nMat** to have five rows and two columns. The declaration also initializes only the first five elements (nMat[0][0], nMat[0][1], nMat[1][0], nMat[1][1], and nMat[2][0]) with the values 1, 2, 3, 4, and 5. Therefore, the compiler assigns zeros to the remaining matrix elements.

Let me present a programming example. Listing 11-2 contains the source code for the MDARRAY2.CPP program, which illustrates initializing multidimensional arrays. The program illustrates the following features:

- Declaring and initializing multidimensional arrays in C++. The program also demonstrates using the number of initializing values to establish the number of array elements.

- Initializing a data member that is a multidimensional C++ array. C++ offers no syntax to directly initialize data members that are arrays.

The program declares and initializes two C++ arrays and an array object. It performs the following tasks:

- Display the initial values in the array object
- Increment the values in the array object using the values in the two C++ arrays
- Display the new values in the array object

Here is the output of the program in Listing 11-2:

```
Initial matrix is:
1.9 2.3 7.6 3.2 6.7
2.9 3.8 8.7 7.5 4.5

New matrix is:
5.6 7.6 8.9 7.7 8.8
6.8 7.6 7.8 9.0 7.5
```

Listing 11-2

The source code for the MDARRAY2.CPP program, which illustrates initializing multidimensional arrays.

```
// A C++ program that illustrates initializing
// multidimensional matrix elements

#include <iostream.h>
#include <stdio.h>
```

```
#include <iomanip.h>
#include <math.h>

const int MAX_ROWS = 2;
const int MAX_COLS = 5;

class myMatrix
{
  public:
    myMatrix(int bUseInitArray = 1, double fInitVal = 0);
    double& operator()(int nRow, int nCol)
      { return m_fMatrix[nRow][nCol]; }
    void show(const char* pszMsg = "",
              const int nNumRows = MAX_ROWS,
              const int nNumCols = MAX_COLS);

  protected:
    double m_fMatrix[MAX_ROWS][MAX_COLS];
};

myMatrix::myMatrix(int bUseInitArray, double fInitVal)
{
  if (bUseInitArray) {
    double fInitMat[MAX_ROWS][MAX_COLS] =
      { 1.9, 2.3, 7.6, 3.2, 6.7,
        2.9, 3.8, 8.7, 7.5, 4.5 };
    for (int i = 0; i < MAX_ROWS; i++)
      for (int j = 0; j < MAX_COLS; j++)
        m_fMatrix[i][j] = fInitMat[i][j];
  }
  else
    for (int i = 0; i < MAX_ROWS; i++)
      for (int j = 0; j < MAX_COLS; j++)
        m_fMatrix[i][j] = fInitVal;
}

void myMatrix::show(const char* pszMsg,
                    const int nNumRows,
                    const int nNumCols)
{
  char cString[10];

  cout << pszMsg << endl;
  for (int i = 0; i < nNumRows; i++) {
    for (int j = 0; j < nNumCols; j++) {
      sprintf(cString, "%3.1lf ", m_fMatrix[i][j]);
      cout << cString;
    }
    cout << endl;
  }
}
```

Initialized matrix

```
main()
{
    double fXMat[2][MAX_ROWS][MAX_COLS] =
        { // data for sub-array fMat[0][][]
        19.9, 29.3, 87.6, 43.2, 76.7,
        32.9, 43.8, 88.7, 87.5, 64.5,
        // data for sub-array fMat[1][][]
        111.9, 222.3, 777.6, 333.2, 676.7,
        222.9, 333.8, 688.7, 787.5, 484.5 };

    myMatrix Matrix;

    // show the matrix
    Matrix.show("Initial matrix is:");

    cout << endl;

    // update matrix Matrix
    for (int i = 0; i < MAX_ROWS; i++)
      for (int j = 0; j < MAX_COLS; j++)
        Matrix(i, j) = fXMat[1][i][j] / fXMat[0][i][j];

    // show the matrix
    Matrix.show("New matrix is:");

    return 0;
}
```

Matrix →

Listing 11-2 declares the constants **MAX_ROWS** and **MAX_COLS**, which define the number of rows and columns of the matrices used in the program. The listing declares the class **myMatrix**, which is similar to that in Listing 11-1. The main difference is that the new class version has a constructor that allows you to initialize the matrix in one of two ways: When the argument of the parameter **bUseInitMatrix** is 1 (which is the default argument) or any nonzero value, the constructor uses the local initialized C++ matrix **fInitMat** to provide the initializing values for the elements of data member **m_fMatrix**. The constructor declares the matrix **fInitMat** to have **MAX_ROWS** rows and **MAX_COLS** columns. If the parameter **bUseInitMatrix** is 0, the constructor assigns the value of parameter **fInitVal** to each element in the data member **m_fMatrix**.

The function **main** declares and initializes the three-dimensional C++ matrix **fXMat**. This array conceptually models two matrices glued to each other. The declaration of matrix **fXMat** specifies a dual matrix with **MAX_ROWS** rows and **MAX_COLS** columns. The function **main** also declares the object **Matrix** as an instance of class **myMatrix**. The way the source code declares object **Matrix** ends up using the default argument for the constructor of class **myMatrix**. Consequently, the runtime system initializes data member **m_fMatrix** in object **Matrix** using the matrix **fInitMat**. The function **main** then performs the following tasks:

- Display the initial elements in the object **Matrix** by sending it the C++ message **show**. The argument for this message is the string literal "Initial matrix is:".

- Update the values in object **Matrix**. This task uses nested **for** loops, which iterate over the elements of the matrices. Each inner loop iteration assigns the ratio of **fXMat[1][i][j]** to **fXMat[0][i][j]**, to the element **Matrix(i, j)**.

- Display the new values of the elements in the object **Matrix** by sending it the C++ message **show**. The argument for this message is the string literal "New matrix is:".

Declaring Multidimensional Arrays as Function Parameters

C++ allows you to declare multidimensional arrays as parameters in functions. The programming language supports two syntaxes, one for fixed arrays and the other for open arrays:

```
// fixed array parameter
type parameterName[numberOfElement1][numberOfElement2]...
// open-array parameter
type parameterName[][numberOfElement2]...
```

The fixed-array parameter states the number of elements for each dimension. By contrast, the open array parameter lists the number of elements for the second dimension and up. In other words, the open parameter leaves the number of elements for the first dimension unspecified.

BASIC

Open Multidimensional Array Parameters

C++ puts restrictions on the level of generality of open multidimensional array parameters. Only the first dimension of the array is variable. Thus, C++ can allow you to write matrix manipulating functions that deal with matrices that have a variable number of rows but a fixed number of columns. This feature is more limited than that in modern implementations of BASIC that support truly general-purpose matrix parameters.

Here are examples of declaring multidimensional array parameters:

```
double mySum(double fMyMatrix[MAX_ROWS1][MAX_COLS]);
double theirSum(double fTheirMatrix[MAX_ROWS2][MAX_COLS],
                int nNumRows = MAX_ROWS1,
                int nNumCols = MAX_COLS);
double yourSum(double fYourMatrix[][MAX_COLS],
                int nNumRows, int nNumCols);
```

The function **mySum** declares the matrix parameter **fMyMatrix** and specifies that the parameter has **MAX_ROWS1** rows and **MAX_COLS** columns. This kind of function expects the caller to pass a **double**-type matrix that also has **MAX_ROWS1** rows and **MAX_COLS** columns. Since the function's parameter list does not have parameters that pass the number of rows and columns to process, it is safe to assume that function **mySum** processes all of the elements in parameter **fMyMatrix**.

The function **theirSum** has three parameters. The first one is the matrix parameter **fTheirMatrix** and specifies **MAX_ROWS2** rows and **MAX_COLS** columns. The second and third parameters, **nNumRows** and **nNumCols**, specify the number of rows and columns, respectively, to process. Thus, the first parameter suggests that the arguments for parameter **fTheirMatrix** must be **double**-type matrices with **MAX_ROWS2** rows and **MAX_COLS** columns. However, the presence of parameters **nNumRows** and **nNumCols** might suggest that the function can process a portion of the matrix **fTheirMatrix**.

The function **yourSum** declares the parameter **fYourMatrix**, which is an open **double**-type matrix. This function can take arguments that are **double**-type matrices of different numbers of rows. However, the arguments for the matrix parameter must have **MAX_COLS** columns. The parameters **nNumRows** and **nNumCols** specify the number of matrix rows and columns, respectively, to process. The argument for parameter **nNumRows** should be equal to or less than the number of rows in the argument for **fYourMatrix**. If not, the function risks accessing data that lie beyond the space occupied by the matrix argument.

Here are examples of calling these functions:

```
const int MAX_ROWS1 = 10;
const int MAX_ROWS2 = 10;
const int MAX_COLS = 20;

double fMatrix1[MAX_ROWS1][MAX_COLS];
double fMatrix2[MAX_ROWS2][MAX_COLS];
double fSum;
...
fSum = mySum(fMatrix1);
...
fSum = theirSum(fMatrix2);
...
fSum = theirSum(fMatrix2, MAX_ROWS2 / 2, MAX_COLS / 2);
...
fSum = yourSum(fMatrix1, MAX_ROWS1, MAX_COLS);
...
fSum = yourSum(fMatrix2, MAX_ROWS2, MAX_COLS);
```

This code snippet declares the constants **MAX_ROWS1**, **MAX_ROWS2**, and **MAX_COLS**, which define the number of rows and columns in the **double**-type matrices **fMatrix1** and **fMatrix2**, respectively. The code defines the **double**-type variable **fSum**. It then makes the following calls to the tested functions:

- Call function **mySum** with the argument **fMatrix1**

- Call function **theirSum** with the argument **fMatrix2**. This function call uses the default arguments of **MAX_ROWS2** and **MAX_COLS** for parameters **nNumRows** and **nNumCols**, respectively.

- Call function **theirSum** with the arguments **fMatrix2**, **MAX_ROWS2 / 2**, and **MAX_COLS / 2**

- Call function **yourSum** with the arguments **fMatrix1**, **MAX_ROWS1**, and **MAX_COLS**

- Call function **yourSum** with the arguments **fMatrix2**, **MAX_ROWS2**, and **MAX_COLS**

The code snippet shows that function **yourSum** is very flexible, since it handles matrices of different row sizes.

Let's look at a programming example. Listing 11-3 shows the source code for the MDARRAY3.CPP program, which illustrates parameter matrices. The listing contains functions that sort, copy, and display matrices of integers. The program declares two C++ matrices (initializing the first one) and performs the following tasks:

- Copy the values from the first matrix into the second matrix. Both matrices contain unsorted integers.

- Display the first unsorted matrix.

- Sort the first matrix, using the elements of the first column as the sorting key values, and then display its elements. This task uses a sorting function that has a matrix parameter with a fixed number of elements.

- Copy the values from the second matrix into the first matrix. The elements of the first matrix are now unsorted.

- Sort the first matrix, using the elements of the first column as the sorting key values, and then display its elements. This task uses a sorting routine that has an open matrix parameter.

- Sort the second matrix, using the elements of the first column as the sorting key values, and then display its elements. This task also uses a sorting routine that has an open matrix parameter.

Here is the output of the program in Listing 11-3:

```
Unsorted matrix nMatrix1 is:
41 67 55
98 12 15
10 65 48

Sorted matrix nMatrix1 is:
10 65 48
41 67 55
98 12 15

Unsorted matrix nMatrix1 is:
41 67 55
98 12 15
10 65 48
```

```
Sorted matrix nMatrix1 is:
10 65 48
41 67 55
98 12 15

Sorted matrix nMatrix2 is:
10 65 48
41 67 55
98 12 15
```

Listing 11-3
The source code for the MDARRAY3.CPP program.

```cpp
// A C++ program that illustrates
// multidimensional array parameters

#include <iostream.h>
#include <iomanip.h>

const int MAX_ROWS1 = 3;
const int MAX_ROWS2 = 10;
const int MAX_COLS = 3;

void bubbleSort1(int nMatrix[MAX_ROWS1][MAX_COLS],
                 int nSortColIndex = 0,
                 int nNumRows = MAX_ROWS1,
                 int nNumCols = MAX_COLS);
void bubbleSort2(int nMatrix[][MAX_COLS],
                 int nSortColIndex,
                 int nNumRows, int nNumCols = MAX_COLS);
void copyMatrix(int nSourceMatrix[][MAX_COLS],
                int nTargetMatrix[][MAX_COLS],
                int nNumRows, int nNumCols);
void showMatrix(const char* pszMsg,
                int nMatrix[][MAX_COLS],
                int nNumRows, int nNumCols);

main()
{
  int nMatrix1[MAX_ROWS1][MAX_COLS] =
    { 41, 67, 55, 98, 12, 15, 10, 65, 48 };
  int nMatrix2[MAX_ROWS2][MAX_COLS];
  int nColIndex = 0;

  // copy elements of array nMatrix1 into nMatrix2
  copyMatrix(nMatrix1, nMatrix2, MAX_ROWS1, MAX_COLS);
```

```
      // display unsorted matrix nMatrix1
      showMatrix("Unsorted matrix nMatrix1 is:\n",
              nMatrix1, MAX_ROWS1, MAX_COLS);
      // sort matrix nMatrix1
      bubbleSort1(nMatrix1);
      // display sorted matrix nMatrix1
      showMatrix("Sorted matrix nMatrix1 is:\n",
              nMatrix1, MAX_ROWS1, MAX_COLS);

      // copy elements of matrix nMatrix2 into  nMatrix1
      copyMatrix(nMatrix2, nMatrix1, MAX_ROWS1, MAX_COLS);
      // display unsorted matrix nMatrix1
      showMatrix("Unsorted matrix nMatrix1 is:\n",
              nMatrix1, MAX_ROWS1, MAX_COLS);
      // sort matrix nMatrix1
      bubbleSort2(nMatrix1, nColIndex, MAX_ROWS1, MAX_COLS);
      // display sorted matrix nMatrix1
      showMatrix("Sorted matrix nMatrix1 is:\n",
              nMatrix1, MAX_ROWS1, MAX_COLS);
      // sort matrix nMatrix2
      bubbleSort2(nMatrix2, nColIndex, MAX_ROWS1, MAX_COLS);
      // display sorted matrix nMatrix2
      showMatrix("Sorted matrix nMatrix2 is:\n",
              nMatrix2, MAX_ROWS1, MAX_COLS);

   return 0;
}

void bubbleSort1(int nMatrix[MAX_ROWS1][MAX_COLS],
                 int nSortColIndex,
                 int nNumRows, int nNumCols)
{
   int nSwap;

   for (int i = 0; i < (nNumRows - 1); i++)
     for (int j = i; j < nNumRows; j++)
       if (nMatrix[i][nSortColIndex] >
           nMatrix[j][nSortColIndex]) {
         for (int k = 0 ; k < nNumCols; k++) {
           nSwap = nMatrix[i][k];
           nMatrix[i][k] = nMatrix[j][k];
           nMatrix[j][k] = nSwap;
         }
       }
}

void bubbleSort2(int nMatrix[][MAX_COLS],
                 int nSortColIndex,
                 int nNumRows, int nNumCols)
{
   int nSwap;
```

```
    for (int i = 0; i < (nNumRows - 1); i++)
      for (int j = i; j < nNumRows; j++)
        if (nMatrix[i][nSortColIndex] >
            nMatrix[j][nSortColIndex]) {
          for (int k = 0 ; k < nNumCols; k++) {
            nSwap = nMatrix[i][k];
            nMatrix[i][k] = nMatrix[j][k];
            nMatrix[j][k] = nSwap;
          }
        }
}

void copyMatrix(int nSourceMatrix[][MAX_COLS],
                int nTargetMatrix[][MAX_COLS],
                int nNumRows, int nNumCols)
{
  for (int i = 0; i < nNumRows; i++)
    for (int j = 0; j < nNumCols; j++)
      nTargetMatrix[i][j] = nSourceMatrix[i][j];
}

void showMatrix(const char* pszMsg,
                int nMatrix[][MAX_COLS],
                int nNumRows, int nNumCols)
{
  cout << pszMsg;
  for (int i = 0; i < nNumRows; i++) {
    for (int j = 0; j < nNumCols; j++)
      cout << nMatrix[i][j] << ' ';
    cout << endl;
  }
  cout << endl;
}
```

Listing 11-3 declares the constants **MAX_ROWS1**, **MAX_ROWS2**, and **MAX_COLS**, which are the row and column sizes for two different kinds of integer matrices. The listing also declares the prototypes for the following functions:

- The function **bubbleSort1** sorts the arguments for parameter **nMatrix**. This is a multidimensional array parameter that specifies a matrix with **MAX_ROWS1** rows and **MAX_COLS** columns. The second parameter **nSortColIndex** specifies the index of the column to use for sorting. The last two parameters **nNumRows** and **nNumCols** specify the number of rows and columns to sort. These parameters have the default arguments of **MAX_ROWS1** and **MAX_COLS**, respectively, used to sort the entire matrix.

- The function **bubbleSort2** sorts the arguments for the open multidimensional array parameter **nMatrix**. The remaining parameters of this function are similar to those of function **bubbleSort1**. The main difference is that only the last parameter in function **bubbleSort2** has a default argument.

- The function **copyMatrix** copies the elements of one matrix into another. The first two parameters are the open multidimensional array parameters **nSourceMatrix** and **nTargetMatrix**, which represent the source and target matrices, respectively. The parameters **nNumRows** and **nNumCols** specify the number of rows and columns to copy.

- The function **showMatrix** displays the elements of the open multidimensional array parameter **nMatrix**. The parameter **pszMsg** passes a leading message. The parameters **nNumRows** and **nNumCols** specify the number of rows and columns to display.

The declarations of the functions just described show that, with the exception of function **bubbleSort1**, they use open multidimensional array parameters to process integer matrices of various row sizes. The listing includes the two versions of the sorting function, **bubbleSort1** and **bubbleSort2**. The source code illustrates that the latter function is more flexible than the former since it takes arguments that are matrices of different sizes.

The function **main** declares the **int**-type matrices **nMatrix1** and **nMatrix2**. These matrices have **MAX_ROWS1** and **MAX_ROWS2** rows, respectively, and both have **MAX_COLS** columns. The function initializes the matrix **nMatrix1** with a list of unsorted integers. It also declares and initializes the variable **nColIndex**, the sorting-column index. It then performs the following tasks:

- Copy the elements of **nMatrix1** into **nMatrix2** by calling function **copyMatrix**. The arguments for this function call are **nMatrix1**, **nMatrix2**, **MAX_ROWS1**, and **MAX_COLS**. These arguments indicate that the first **MAX_ROWS1** rows of matrix **nMatrix2** contain copies of the values in the elements of matrix **nMatrix1**. The remaining rows of matrix **nMatrix2** are unchanged. In fact, the program dispenses with them to simulate many cases where matrices are not fully populated with meaningful data.

- Display the unsorted elements of matrix **nMatrix1** by calling the function **showMatrix**. The arguments for this function call are the literal string "Unsorted matrix nMatrix1 is:\n," the matrix **nMatrix1**, and the constants **MAX_ROWS1** and **MAX_COLS**.

- Sort the elements of matrix **nMatrix1** by calling the function **bubbleSort1**. The argument for this function call is matrix **nMatrix1**. The call uses the default arguments of 0, **MAX_ROWS1**, and **MAX_COLS** for parameters **nSortColIndex**, **nNumRows**, and **nNumCols**, respectively.

- Display the sorted elements of matrix **nMatrix1** by calling the function **showMatrix**. The arguments for this function call are the literal string "Sorted Matrix nMatrix1 is:\n," the matrix **nMatrix1**, and the constants **MAX_ROWS1** and **MAX_COLS**.

- Copy the elements of **nMatrix2** into **nMatrix1** by calling function **copyMatrix**. The arguments for this function call are **nMatrix2**, **nMatrix1**, **MAX_ROWS1**, and **MAX_COLS**. This task restores the values in the matrix **nMatrix1** to their original order.

- Display the unsorted elements of matrix **nMatrix1** by calling the function **showMatrix**. The arguments for this function call are the literal string "Unsorted matrix nMatrix1 is:\n," the matrix **nMatrix1**, and the constants **MAX_ROWS1** and **MAX_COLS**.

- Sort the elements of matrix **nMatrix1** by calling the function **bubbleSort2**. The arguments for this function call are the matrix **nMatrix1**, the variable **nColIndex**, and the constants **MAX_ROWS1** and **MAX_COLS**.

- Display the sorted elements of matrix **nMatrix1** by calling the function **showMatrix**. The arguments for this function call are the literal string "Sorted matrix nMatrix1 is:\n," the matrix **nMatrix1**, and the constants **MAX_ROWS1** and **MAX_COLS**.

- Sort the elements of matrix **nMatrix2** by calling the function **bubbleSort2**. The arguments for this function call are the matrix **nMatrix2**, the variable **nColIndex**, and the constants **MAX_ROWS1** and **MAX_COLS**.

- Display the sorted elements of matrix **nMatrix2** by calling the function **showMatrix**. The arguments for this function call are the literal string "Sorted matrix nMatrix1 is:\n," the matrix **nMatrix2**, and the constants **MAX_ROWS1** and **MAX_COLS**.

The function **main** uses the function **bubbleSort2** to sort the matrices nMatrix1 and nMatrix2. Thus, function **bubbleSort2** is a more general-purpose function than **bubbleSort1**.

Sorting Multidimensional Arrays Using Combsort

The last chapter presented the Shell sort, combsort, and quicksort methods for sorting single-dimensional arrays. This section presents the combsort method for sorting two-dimensional arrays. While the basic sorting method is the same as for single-dimensional arrays, you need to keep in mind that the method uses the values of a selected column to sort the matrix. This means that the implementation should swap all rows during the sorting process. This swapping can slow down the implementation. I propose to use an array of indices that keeps track of the row order without actually swapping rows during the intermediate steps of the process. Once the intermediate comparisons of the array elements end, the method swaps the matrix rows to their final positions. Thus, the method swaps each row only once.

The process of swapping the rows involves using the array of indices used in sorting the matrix, along with an additional array of *inverse* indices. The array of indices determines what order the rows appear in. By contrast, the array of reverse indices specifies where each row will be moved to. The implementation of the combsort uses these arrays to determine quickly how to shuffle the rows around to obtain a sorted matrix. This approach allows the combsort method to swap rows *without* using an auxiliary array of rows.

Let me present a programming example. Listing 11-4 contains the source code for the MDARRAY4.CPP program, which illustrates the combsort method for sorting matrices. The program displays the unsorted elements of a matrix object, sorts these elements, and then displays them.

Here is the output of the program in Listing 11-4:

```
Unsorted matrix is:
53 45 89
74 51 18
87 63 36
38 15 33
67 93 83
```

```
Sorted matrix is:
38 15 33
53 45 89
67 93 83
74 51 18
87 63 36
```

Listing 11-4

*The source code for the MDARRAY4.CPP program, which illustrates sorting
multidimensional arrays using the combsort method.*

```cpp
// A C++ program that illustrates
// the combsort algorithm for matrices

#include <iostream.h>
#include <iomanip.h>

const int MAX_ROWS = 5;
const int MAX_COLS = 3;

class myMatrix
{
  public:
    myMatrix(int fInitVal = 0);
    int& operator()(int nRow, int nCol)
      { return m_nMatrix[nRow][nCol]; }
    void show(const char* pszMsg = "",
              const int nNumRows = MAX_ROWS,
              const int nNumCols = MAX_COLS);
    void CombSort(int nSortColIndex = 0,
                  int nNumRows = MAX_ROWS,
                  int nNumCols = MAX_COLS);

  protected:
    int m_nMatrix[MAX_ROWS][MAX_COLS];

    void swapRows(int nRow1, int nRow2,
                  int nNumCols = MAX_COLS);
};

myMatrix::myMatrix(int fInitVal)
{
  for (int i = 0; i < MAX_ROWS; i++)
    for (int j = 0; j < MAX_COLS; j++)
      m_nMatrix[i][j] = fInitVal;
}
```

```
void myMatrix::show(const char* pszMsg,
                    const int nNumRows,
                    const int nNumCols)
{
  cout << pszMsg << endl;
  for (int i = 0; i < nNumRows; i++) {
    for (int j = 0; j < nNumCols; j++)
      cout << m_nMatrix[i][j] << ' ';
    cout << endl;
  }
  cout << endl;
}

void myMatrix::CombSort(int nSortColIndex,
                        int nNumRows,
                        int nNumCols)
{
  int nOffset = nNumRows;
  int bSorted, i, j, ii, jj, nSwapBuffer;
  int nIndex[MAX_ROWS];
  int nRevIndex[MAX_ROWS];

  if (nNumRows < 2)
    return;

  // initialize array of indices
  for (i = 0; i < nNumRows; i++)
    nIndex[i] = i;

  do {
    nOffset = (nOffset * 8) / 11;
    nOffset = (nOffset < 1) ? 1 : nOffset;
    bSorted = 1; // set sorted flag
    // compare elements
    for (i = 0, j = nOffset;
         i < (nNumRows - nOffset);
         i++, j++) {
      ii = nIndex[i];
      jj = nIndex[j];
      if (m_nMatrix[ii][nSortColIndex] >
          m_nMatrix[jj][nSortColIndex]) {
        // swap indices
        nIndex[i] = jj;
        nIndex[j] = ii;
        bSorted = 0; // clear sorted flag
      }
    }
  } while (!bSorted || nOffset != 1);

  // set up the reverse indices
  for (i = 0; i < nNumRows; i++)
    nRevIndex[nIndex[i]] = i;
```

```
    // swap rows
    for (i = 0; i < (nNumRows - 1); i++) {
      // swap row number i?
      if (nIndex[i] != i) {
        swapRows(nIndex[i], i);
        ii = nIndex[nRevIndex[i]];
        nIndex[nRevIndex[i]] = nIndex[i];
        nSwapBuffer = nRevIndex[i];
        nRevIndex[i] = nRevIndex[ii];
        nRevIndex[ii] = nSwapBuffer;
      }
    }
}

void myMatrix::swapRows(int nRow1, int nRow2, int nNumCols)
{
  int nSwapBuffer;

  for (int j = 0; j < nNumCols; j++) {
    nSwapBuffer = m_nMatrix[nRow1][j];
    m_nMatrix[nRow1][j] = m_nMatrix[nRow2][j];
    m_nMatrix[nRow2][j] = nSwapBuffer;
  }
}

main()
{
  int nMat[MAX_ROWS][MAX_COLS] =
      { 53, 45, 89, // row 0
        74, 51, 18, // row 1
        87, 63, 36, // row 2
        38, 15, 33, // row 3
        67, 93, 83  // row 4
        };
  myMatrix Matrix;

  for (int i = 0; i < MAX_ROWS; i++)
    for (int j = 0; j < MAX_COLS; j++)
      Matrix(i, j) = nMat[i][j];

  Matrix.show("Unsorted matrix is:");
  Matrix.CombSort();
  Matrix.show("Sorted matrix is:");

  return 0;
}
```

Listing 11-4 declares the class **myMatrix**, which resembles the class **myMatrix** in Listing 11-3. The new version of class **myMatrix** declares the public member function **CombSort** and the protected member function **swapRows**. The member function **CombSort** uses the member function **swapRows** to swap the matrix rows.

The definition of member function **CombSort** implements the combsort algorithm for a matrix of integers. The function performs the following tasks:

- Initialize the local array **nIndex**, which stores the indices for the matrix rows

- Use a **do-while** loop to control the cycles of sorting the matrix rows (stored in data member **m_nMatrix**). The first two statements inside the loop update the offset value (stored in variable **nOffset**). The **do-while** loop contains a nested **for** loop, which compares the elements that are **nOffset** indices apart. The sorting stops when the sort flag (stored in variable **bSorted**) is not zero and the offset value is 1. Notice that the **for** loop uses the array **nIndex** to obtain the indices of the matrix rows. In addition, the **if** statement swaps the values in array **nIndex** instead of the matrix rows.

- Initialize the elements of the array **nRevIndex**, which stores the reverse indices

- Swap the matrix rows using the protected member function **swapRows**. This task uses a **for** loop that uses the information in the local arrays **nIndex** and **nRevIndex**. The loop statements update the values in these arrays after swapping the matrix rows.

The function **main** declares and initializes the C++ matrix **nMat**. The function also declares the object **Matrix** as an instance of class **myMatrix**. It then performs the following tasks:

- Copy the values in matrix **nMat** into the object **Matrix**. This task uses nested **for** loops to iterate over the elements in matrix **nMat**.

- Display the unsorted elements in object **Matrix** by sending it the C++ message **show**. The argument for this message is the literal string "Unsorted matrix is:".

- Sort the object **Matrix** by sending it the C++ message **CombSort**

- Display the sorted elements in object **Matrix** by sending it the C++ message **show**. The argument for this message is the literal string "Sorted matrix is:".

Linear Search of Multidimensional Array Elements

You can apply the linear search algorithms to search multidimensional arrays by rows, columns, or other higher dimensions. You can also implement the linear search algorithm to search in some or all of the multiple dimensions of an array. This flexibility comes from the fact that linear searching is not affected by the sorted order of the elements of multidimensional arrays.

The linear search method in multidimensional arrays is very similar to that in single-dimensional arrays. You simply search the elements by rows, columns, or other higher dimensions. The search ends by either finding a match or exhausting the elements of the searched dimension.

Let's look at a programming example. Listing 11-5 contains the source code for the MDARRAY5.CPP program, which illustrates the linear search method for integer matrices. The program displays the unsorted elements of a matrix object and then displays the results of searching for three values in the matrix object.

Here is the output of the program in Listing 11-5:

```
Matrix is:
23 45 89
74 51 18
87 63 36
38 15 33
67 93 83

Searching for 23 in column 0: found match at row 0
Searching for 87 in column 0: found match at row 2
Searching for 67 in column 0: found match at row 4
```

Listing 11-5

The source code for the MDARRAY5.CPP program, which illustrates linear searching in multidimensional arrays.

```
// A C++ program that illustrates
// the linear search algorithm for matrices

#include <iostream.h>
#include <iomanip.h>

const int MAX_ROWS = 5;
const int MAX_COLS = 3;
const int NOT_FOUND = -1;

class myMatrix
{
  public:
    myMatrix(int fInitVal = 0);
    int& operator()(int nRow, int nCol)
      { return m_nMatrix[nRow][nCol]; }
    void show(const char* pszMsg = "",
              const int nNumRows = MAX_ROWS,
              const int nNumCols = MAX_COLS);
    int linearSearch(int nKey,
                     int nColIndex = 0,
                     int nLastRow = MAX_ROWS - 1,
                     int nFirstRow = 0);

  protected:
    int m_nMatrix[MAX_ROWS][MAX_COLS];
};

myMatrix::myMatrix(int fInitVal)
{
  for (int i = 0; i < MAX_ROWS; i++)
    for (int j = 0; j < MAX_COLS; j++)
      m_nMatrix[i][j] = fInitVal;
}

void myMatrix::show(const char* pszMsg,
                    const int nNumRows,
                    const int nNumCols)
{
  cout << pszMsg << endl;
  for (int i = 0; i < nNumRows; i++) {
    for (int j = 0; j < nNumCols; j++)
      cout << m_nMatrix[i][j] << ' ';
    cout << endl;
    }
  cout << endl;
}
```

```
int myMatrix::linearSearch(int nKey, int nColIndex,
                           int nLastRow, int nFirstRow)
{
  for (int i = nFirstRow; i <= nLastRow; i++)
    if (m_nMatrix[i][nColIndex] == nKey)
      break;
  return (i <= nLastRow) ? i : NOT_FOUND;
}

main()
{
  int j, nColIndex = 0;
  int nMat[MAX_ROWS][MAX_COLS] =
      { 23, 45, 89, // row 0
        74, 51, 18, // row 1
        87, 63, 36, // row 2
        38, 15, 33, // row 3
        67, 93, 83  // row 4
      };

  myMatrix Matrix;

  for (int i = 0; i < MAX_ROWS; i++)
    for (int j = 0; j < MAX_COLS; j++)
      Matrix(i, j) = nMat[i][j];

  Matrix.show("Matrix is:");
  for (i = 0; i < MAX_ROWS; i += 2) {
    cout << "Searching for " << nMat[i][nColIndex]
         << " in column " << nColIndex << ": ";
    j = Matrix.linearSearch(nMat[i][nColIndex], nColIndex);
    if (j != NOT_FOUND)
      cout << "found match at row " << j << endl;
    else
      cout << "found no match\n";
  }
  return 0;
}
```

Listing 11-5 declares the class **myMatrix**, which resembles the class **myMatrix** in Listing 11-4. The new version of class **myMatrix** declares the member function **linearSearch**, which conducts the linear search. This member function has the following parameters:

- The **int**-type parameter **nKey** is the search value.
- The **int**-type parameter **nColIndex** is the index for the searched column.

- The int-type parameters **nFirstRow** and **nLastRow** define the range of rows to search. The default arguments for these parameters are 0 and MAX_ROWS − 1, respectively. These default arguments specify searching in all rows of the column **nColIndex**.

The definition of member function **linearSearch** uses a **for** loop to examine the matrix elements in the rows **nFirstRow** to **nLastRow** of column **nColIndex**. The loop uses an **if** statement to compare the search data with element **m_nMatrix[i][nColIndex]**. If the two values match, the **if** statement executes the **break** statement to stop the search. The member function returns the row index of the matching element or yields the value of the global constant **NOT_FOUND** if no match is found.

The function **main** declares and initializes the C++ matrix **nMat**. The function also declares the object **Matrix** as an instance of class **myMatrix**. In addition, the function declares and initializes the variable **nColIndex**, which stores the index of the search column. The function **main** then performs the following tasks:

- Copy the values in matrix **nMat** into the object **Matrix**. This task uses nested **for** loops to iterate over the elements in matrix **nMat**.

- Display the unsorted elements in object **Matrix** by sending it the C++ message **show**. The argument for this message is the literal string "Matrix is:".

- Search for the values in **nMat[0][0]**, **nMat[2][0]**, and **nMat[4][0]** using a **for** loop. Each loop iteration displays the search value and then sends the C++ message **linearSearch** to object **Matrix**. The arguments for this message are the search value of **nMat[i][nColIndex]** and the variable **nColIndex**. The loop assigns the result of the message to variable **j**. It uses an **if** statement to determine whether or not the search is successful. If it is, the code displays the row index of the matching matrix element.

Binary Search of Multidimensional Array Elements

You can extend the binary search method that I presented in the last chapter to work with multidimensional arrays. In the case of a multidimensional array, you must first sort the array using the values of a specific dimension (such as rows or columns). The binary search method then works with that dimension. As for the other dimensions, you need to use the linear search method. In case you want to search more than one dimension using a binary search, you should use auxiliary arrays to sort the multidimensional array. For example, you can have two arrays, one for rows and one for columns. You use these arrays to sort the multidimensional array by rows and columns (without actually rearranging the elements of the multidimensional array). Then you can use these arrays to guide the binary search method when applied to the rows or columns of the multidimensional array.

Let's look at a programming example. Listing 11-6 contains the source code for the MDARRAY6.CPP program, which illustrates the binary search method for integer matrices. The program displays the sorted elements of a matrix object and then displays the results of searching for three values in the matrix object.

Here is the output of the program in Listing 11-6:

```
Matrix is:
38 15 33
53 45 89
67 93 83
74 51 18
87 63 36

Searching for 53 in column 0: found match at row 1
Searching for 87 in column 0: found match at row 4
Searching for 67 in column 0: found match at row 2
```

Listing 11-6

The source code for the MDARRAY6.CPP program, which illustrates binary searching in multidimensional arrays.

```cpp
// A C++ program that illustrates
// the binary search algorithm for matrices

#include <iostream.h>
#include <iomanip.h>

const int MAX_ROWS = 5;
const int MAX_COLS = 3;
const int NOT_FOUND = -1;
const int SORTED = 1;
const int UNSORTED = 0;

class myMatrix
{
  public:
    myMatrix(int fInitVal = 0);
    int& operator()(int nRow, int nCol)
      { return m_nMatrix[nRow][nCol]; }
    void show(const char* pszMsg = "",
              const int nNumRows = MAX_ROWS,
              const int nNumCols = MAX_COLS);
    void clearSortFlag()
      { m_bSorted = UNSORTED; }
    void CombSort(int nSortColIndex = 0,
                  int nNumRows = MAX_ROWS,
                  int nNumCols = MAX_COLS);
    int binarySearch(int nKey,
                     int nLastRow = MAX_ROWS - 1,
                     int nFirstRow = 0);

  protected:
    int m_nMatrix[MAX_ROWS][MAX_COLS];
    int m_bSorted;
    int m_nSortColIndex;

    void swapRows(int nRow1, int nRow2,
                  int nNumCols = MAX_COLS);
};

myMatrix::myMatrix(int fInitVal)
{
  for (int i = 0; i < MAX_ROWS; i++)
    for (int j = 0; j < MAX_COLS; j++)
      m_nMatrix[i][j] = fInitVal;
  m_bSorted = UNSORTED;
}
```

```
void myMatrix::show(const char* pszMsg,
                    const int nNumRows,
                    const int nNumCols)
{
  cout << pszMsg << endl;
  for (int i = 0; i < nNumRows; i++) {
    for (int j = 0; j < nNumCols; j++)
      cout << m_nMatrix[i][j] << ' ';
    cout << endl;
  }
  cout << endl;
}

void myMatrix::CombSort(int nSortColIndex,
                        int nNumRows,
                        int nNumCols)
{
  int nOffset = nNumRows;
  int bSorted, i, j, ii, jj, nSwapBuffer;
  int nIndex[MAX_ROWS];
  int nRevIndex[MAX_ROWS];

  if (nNumRows < 2)
    return;

  // initialize array of indices
  for (i = 0; i < nNumRows; i++)
    nIndex[i] = i;

  do {
    nOffset = (nOffset * 8) / 11;
    nOffset = (nOffset < 1) ? 1 : nOffset;
    bSorted = 1; // set sorted flag
    // compare elements
    for (i = 0, j = nOffset;
         i < (nNumRows - nOffset);
         i++, j++) {
      ii = nIndex[i];
      jj = nIndex[j];
      if (m_nMatrix[ii][nSortColIndex] >
          m_nMatrix[jj][nSortColIndex]) {
        // swap indices
        nIndex[i] = jj;
        nIndex[j] = ii;
        bSorted = 0; // clear sorted flag
      }
    }
  } while (!bSorted || nOffset != 1);

  // set up the reverse indices
  for (i = 0; i < nNumRows; i++)
    nRevIndex[nIndex[i]] = i;
```

```
    // swap rows
    for (i = 0; i < (nNumRows - 1); i++) {
      // swap row number i?
      if (nIndex[i] != i) {
        swapRows(nIndex[i], i);
        ii = nIndex[nRevIndex[i]];
        nIndex[nRevIndex[i]] = nIndex[i];
        nSwapBuffer = nRevIndex[i];
        nRevIndex[i] = nRevIndex[ii];
        nRevIndex[ii] = nSwapBuffer;
      }
    }

  m_bSorted = SORTED;
  m_nSortColIndex = nSortColIndex;
}

int myMatrix::binarySearch(int nKey, int nLastRow, int nFirstRow)
{
  int nMedianRow;

  if (!m_bSorted)
    return NOT_FOUND;

  do {
    nMedianRow = (nFirstRow + nLastRow) / 2;
    if (nKey < m_nMatrix[nMedianRow][m_nSortColIndex])
      nLastRow = nMedianRow - 1;
    else
      nFirstRow = nMedianRow + 1;
  } while (!(nKey == m_nMatrix[nMedianRow][m_nSortColIndex] ||
             nFirstRow > nLastRow));

  return (nKey == m_nMatrix[nMedianRow][m_nSortColIndex]) ?
                                    nMedianRow : NOT_FOUND;
}

void myMatrix::swapRows(int nRow1, int nRow2, int nNumCols)
{
  int nSwapBuffer;

  for (int j = 0; j < nNumCols; j++) {
    nSwapBuffer = m_nMatrix[nRow1][j];
    m_nMatrix[nRow1][j] = m_nMatrix[nRow2][j];
    m_nMatrix[nRow2][j] = nSwapBuffer;
  }
}
```

```
main()
{
  int j, nColIndex = 0;
  int nMat[MAX_ROWS][MAX_COLS] =
      { 53, 45, 89, // row 0
        74, 51, 18, // row 1
        87, 63, 36, // row 2
        38, 15, 33, // row 3
        67, 93, 83  // row 4
      };

  myMatrix Matrix;

  // copy the matrix nMat to the matrix object
  for (int i = 0; i < MAX_ROWS; i++)
    for (int j = 0; j < MAX_COLS; j++)
      Matrix(i, j) = nMat[i][j];

  // sort the matrix object
  Matrix.CombSort(nColIndex);
  Matrix.show("Matrix is:");
  for (i = 0; i < MAX_ROWS; i += 2) {
    cout << "Searching for " << nMat[i][nColIndex]
         << " in column " << nColIndex << ": ";
    j = Matrix.binarySearch(nMat[i][nColIndex]);
    if (j != NOT_FOUND)
      cout << "found match at row " << j << endl;
    else
      cout << "found no match\n";
  }
  return 0;
}
```

Listing 11-6 declares the class **myMatrix**, which resembles the class **myMatrix** in Listing 11-5. The new version of class **myMatrix** declares the following new members:

- The protected **int**-type data member **m_bSorted**, which stores the sorted state. The class assigns the values of the global constants **SORTED** and **UNSORTED** to this data member.

- The protected **int**-type data member **m_nSortColIndex**, which stores the index of the sorting column

- The public member function **clearSortFlag**, which assigns the value of constant **UNSORTED** to the data member **m_bSorted**

- The public member function **CombSort**, which sorts the elements of data member **m_nMatrix** using the combsort method. The source code for this member function is similar to the version in Listing 11-4. The new version uses the data member **m_bSorted** to determine if the matrix is not already sorted. In addition, the member function assigns the values of constant **SORTED** and variable **nSortCollndex** to data members **m_bSorted** and **m_nSortCollndex**, respectively.

- The public member function **binarySearch**, which performs the binary search on the rows of column **m_nSortCollndex** in the data member **m_nMatrix**. This member function has the parameters **nKey**, **nLastRow**, and **nFirstRow**. These parameters play the same roles as in member function **linearSearch** in Listing 11-5.

- The protected member function **swapRows**, which swaps rows. Member function **CombSort** invokes member function **swapRows**.

The definition of member function **binarySearch** first examines the value of data member **m_bSorted** to determine whether or not the matrix **m_nMatrix** is already sorted. If that matrix is sorted, the member function simply exits. Otherwise, the member function performs the binary search using a **do-while** loop. The loop statements obtain the index of the median row in the sorting column. The loop then uses an **if** statement to compare the search key with the median element of the sorting column. The outcome of this comparison determines the new range of rows to search. The loop iterates until it finds a match or until the value of parameter **nFirstRow** exceeds that of parameter **nLastRow**. The member function then returns the index of the matching element or yields the value of the global constant **NOT_FOUND** if no match is found.

The function **main** declares and initializes the C++ matrix **nMat**. It also declares the object **Matrix** as an instance of class **myMatrix**. In addition, the function declares and initializes the variable **nCollndex**. It then performs the following tasks:

- Copy the values in matrix **nMat** into the object **Matrix**. This task uses nested **for** loops to iterate over the elements in matrix **nMat**.

- Sort the object **Matrix** by sending it the C++ message **CombSort**

- Display the sorted elements in object **Matrix** by sending it the C++ message **show**. The argument for this message is the literal string "Matrix is:".

- Search for the values in nMat[0][0], nMat[2][0], and nMat[4][0] using a for loop. Each loop iteration displays the value of the search value and then sends the C++ message binarySearch to object Matrix. The argument for this message is the search value of nMat[i][nColIndex]. The loop assigns the result of the message to variable j. The loop uses an if statement to determine whether or not the search is successful. If it is, the code displays the index of the matching matrix element.

Summary

This chapter discussed multidimensional arrays. You learned about declaring, accessing, and initializing multidimensional arrays. The chapter also discussed sorting and searching methods for two-dimensional arrays. You learned about the combsort method, the linear search method, and the binary search method.

The next chapter looks at user-defined types. Such types allow you to define enumerated lists and structures to represent multicomponent data.

III

Advanced C++ Components

*T*he third part of this book presents advanced C++ components. Chapter 12 discusses user-defined types and shows you how to define enumerated types, structures, and unions, as well as how to use these user-defined types as parameters in functions. Chapter 13 discusses pointers and shows you how to use them to access existing variables and objects as well as to manage dynamic memory. In addition the chapter discusses using pointers as parameters in functions and using pointers to functions. Chapter 14 presents class hierarchies and discusses inheritance schemes and how to construct class hierarchies. The chapter covers programming techniques that empower you to build robust class hierarchies.

User-Defined Types

*I*f you have worked with or studied various programming languages, you
have probably realized that the ability to declare user-defined types in a
language adds a significant flexibility to programming with that language.
C++, like most common programming languages, supports user-defined
types. This chapter discusses defining C++ alias types, enumerated types,
structures, unions, and reference variables. In addition you will learn how to
declare enumerated types, structures, references to enumerated types, and
references to structures as function parameters.

Defining C++ Types

You often employ the data types in a programming language, especially the
basic predefined ones, in different contexts. For example, the int type may
serve to define an array index, a counter for a number of items, pixel
coordinates, and even logical values, to name a few. C++, like its parent
language C, allows you to create alias types that make your source code
easier to read and comprehend. The **typedef** statement creates the data type
aliases and has the following syntax:

```
typedef oldType newType;
```

The *oldType* parameter represents a previously defined type (either a predefined data type or a user-data type). The *newType* parameter represents the new alias. Here are examples of using the **typedef** statement:

```
// example 1
typedef int Logical;
// example 2
typedef int ArrayIndexType;
// example 3
typedef int NumberOfElemsType;
// example 4
typedef double WeightType;
// example 5
typedef double SalaryType;
// example 6
typedef double AreaType;
```

Example 1 uses the **typedef** statement to create the **Logical** type as an alias type for **int**. Using the **Logical** type identifier is clearer than using **int** for variables and parameters that store logical data. For example, the prototype of function **show1** is a bit easier to read than that for function **show2**:

```
void show1(Logical bDisplayInOneLine);
void show2(int bDisplayInOneLine);
```

Example 2 employs the **typedef** statement to create the type **ArrayIndexType** as an alias for **int**. Again, using the **ArrayIndexType** is clearer than **int** for variables and parameters that represent array indices.

Example 3 utilizes the **typedef** statement to create the type **NumberOfElemsType** as an alias for **int**. Once more, using the **NumberOfElemsType** is clearer than **int** for variables and parameters that represent the number of elements in an array.

Similarly, examples 4, 5, and 6 use the **typedef** statement to create the types **WeightType**, **SalaryType**, and **AreaType** as aliases to the predefined type **double**. Using these alias types brings a clearer meaning to their related variables and parameters.

C++ allows you to create aliases for single- and multidimensional arrays. The general syntax for this kind of alias type is:

```
typedef basicElemType sdArrayType[numberOfElements];
typedef basicElemType mdArrayType[Elems1][Elems2]...;
```

CODING NOTES

The typedef Statement Does Not Create a New Type!

It is important to point out that the **typedef** statement does *not* create a new data type. Rather, it merely creates an alias. The alias type is still equivalent to its aliased type, as far as the compiler is concerned. Therefore, you cannot create overloaded functions and member functions that use alias data types and the original data types. For example, the compiler rejects the following overloaded functions:

```
// *** Error! Functions have the same signatures ***
typedef int Logical;
void show(Logical bDisplayInOneLine);
void show(int bDisplayInOneLine);
```

The compiler looks at the alias type **Logical** and sees **int**. Therefore, the two versions of function **show** have the (**int**) signature.

The **typedef** statement creates a single-dimensional array type by stating the type of the basic element of the array, the array name, and the number of elements. In the case of a multidimensional array, the **typedef** statement lists the size of each dimension.

PASCAL

Watch Out for the typedef Syntax for Arrays!

The syntax for creating alias array types may seem strange to you if you have been programming in Pascal. You may expect C++ to use the following syntax instead:

```
// Invalid syntax that uses Pascal-based style
typedef basicElemType[numberOfElements] sdArrayType;
typedef basicElemType[Elems1][Elems2]... mdArrayType;
```

Rather, C++ requires that the basic element type and the number of array elements be separated. C++ requests that you place the number of array elements after the alias array type identifier.

Here are examples of creating array type aliases:

```
// example 1
typedef int weekDays[7];
// example 2
const int MAX_ROWS = 25;
const int MAX_COLS = 80;
typedef char textScreen[MAX_ROWS][MAX_COLS];
```

Example 1 defines the alias array type **weekDays** as an **int**-type array of seven elements. Example 2 defines the alias matrix type **textScreen** as a **char**-type matrix of **MAX_ROWS** and **MAX_COLS**.

Defining variables and parameters using the alias array type merely requires using the name of the alias array type. You need not (and must not) include the number of array elements. Here are examples of using the alias types **weekDays** and **textScreen**:

```
main()
{
  weekDays theDays; // array of 7 int-type elements
  textScreen theScreen; // matrix of characters
  // other statements
}
```

Let me present a programming example. Listing 12-1 contains the source code for the TYPEDEF1.CPP program, which illustrates using the **typedef** statement. I created this program by editing the file ARRAY7.CPP (see Listing 10-7) by replacing the predefined data types with aliases that I created using the **typedef** statement. The program performs the following tasks:

- Display the unsorted elements of an array object
- Display the results of searching for four values in the array object, using the linear search method

Here is the output of the program in Listing 12-1:

```
Array is:
23 45 89 74 51 18 87 63 36 38
Searching for 23 found match at index 0
Searching for 74 found match at index 3
Searching for 87 found match at index 6
Searching for 38 found match at index 9
```

Listing 12-1

The source code for the TYPEDEF1.CPP program.

```
// A C++ program that illustrates
// using the typedef statement

#include <iostream.h>
#include <iomanip.h>

typedef int CountType;
const CountType MAX_ELEMS = 10;

typedef int IndexType;
typedef int ValueType;
typedef int Boolean;
typedef void Procedure;
typedef const char* MessageType;
typedef int IntArrayType[MAX_ELEMS];


const IndexType NOT_FOUND = -1;

class myArray
{
  public:
    myArray(ValueType fInitVal = 0);
    ValueType& operator[](IndexType nIndex)
      { return m_nArray[nIndex]; }
    Procedure show(MessageType pszMsg = "",
                   const CountType nNumElems = MAX_ELEMS,
                   const Boolean bOneLine = 1);
    IndexType linearSearch(ValueType nKey,
                           IndexType nLast = MAX_ELEMS - 1,
                           IndexType nFirst = 0);

  protected:
    IntArrayType m_nArray;
};

myArray::myArray(ValueType fInitVal)
{
  for (IndexType i = 0; i < MAX_ELEMS; i++)
    m_nArray[i] = fInitVal;
}

Procedure myArray::show(MessageType pszMsg,
                        const CountType nNumElems,
                        const Boolean bOneLine)
{
  cout << pszMsg << endl;
  if (bOneLine) {
    for (IndexType i = 0; i < nNumElems; i++)
      cout << m_nArray[i] << ' ';
    cout << endl;
  }
```

typedef aliases

```
    else {
      for (IndexType i = 0; i < nNumElems; i++)
        cout << m_nArray[i] << endl;
      cout << endl;
    }
}

IndexType myArray::linearSearch(ValueType nKey,
                                IndexType nLast,
                                IndexType nFirst)
{
  for (IndexType i = nFirst; i <= nLast; i++)
    if (m_nArray[i] == nKey)
      break;
  return (i <= nLast) ? i : NOT_FOUND;
}

main()
{
  IndexType j;
  IntArrayType nArr = { 23, 45, 89, 74, 51,
                        18, 87, 63, 36, 38 };
  myArray Array;

  for (IndexType i = 0; i < MAX_ELEMS; i++)
    Array[i] = nArr[i];

  Array.show("Array is:");
  for (i = 0; i < MAX_ELEMS; i += 3) {
    cout << "Searching for " << nArr[i];
    j = Array.linearSearch(nArr[i]);
    if (j != NOT_FOUND)
      cout << " found match at index " << j << endl;
    else
      cout << " found no match\n";
  }
  return 0;
}
```

Since Listing 12-1 is very similar to Listing 10-7, I will focus on how it uses the **typedef** statements to create the following alias types:

- The type **CountType** as an alias to type **int**
- The type **IndexType** as an alias to type **int**
- The type **ValueType** as an alias to type **int**
- The type **Boolean** as an alias to type **int**

- The type **Procedure** as an alias to type **void**
- The type **MessageType** as an alias to type **const char***. This alias includes the **const** keyword.
- The type **IntArrayType** as an alias to an array of **int** that has **MAX_ELEMS**. This **typedef** is an example of defining an array type alias.

The listing uses the alias types in the following parts of the source code:

- The declarations of the constants **MAX_ELEMS** and **NOT_FOUND** use the alias types **CountType** and **IndexType**, respectively.
- The constructor of class **myArray** has the **ValueType**-type parameter **fInitVal**.
- The operator **[ ]** has the **IndexType**-type parameter **nIndex** and the return value of **ValueType&**.
- The member function **show** has the return type **Procedure**. The parameters **pszMsg**, **nNumElems**, and **bOneLine** use the alias types **MessageType**, **CountType**, and **Boolean**, respectively.
- The member function **linearSearch** has the return alias type **IndexType**. The parameters **nKey**, **nLast**, and **nFirst** have the alias types **ValueType**, **IndexType**, and **IndexType**, respectively.
- The class declares the data member **m_nArray** using the alias array type **IntArrayType**. Notice that the declaration of this member does not require stating the number of array elements.
- The **for** loops in the constructor, in the member function **show**, and in the member function **linearSearch** all use the **IndexType**-type control variable **i**.
- The function **main** uses the alias types **IndexType**, **IntArrayType**, and **IndexType** to declare the variable **j**, the C++ array **nArr**, and the loop control variable **i** (used in the **for** loops).

If you compare Listings 10-7 and 12-1, you can see that the latter listing is easier to read because the alias types are more descriptive of how the source code uses their associated variables and parameters. For example, looking at the parameters of member function **linearSearch**, you can easily tell that the first parameter supplies a search value. You can also tell that the other two parameters are array indices. Trying to deduce the same information from **int**-type parameters in Listing 10-7 is not as easy as from the alias types in Listing 12-1.

Enumerated Types

You learned in Chapter 3 how to declare a single constant using the const keyword. C++ allows you to create a list of logically related constants that enumerate a set of values or states. This section discusses the enumerated types in C++.

BASIC ENUMERATED TYPES

C++ allows you to declare enumerated types using the following syntax:

```
enum enumeratedType { enumerator1, enumerator2, ... };
```

The declaration of an enumerated type starts with the keyword **enum** and is followed by the name of the enumerated type identifier and the list of *enumerators*. This comma-delimited list is enclosed in braces and ends with a semicolon.

What about the values associated with the enumerators? By default, the compiler assigns 0 to the first enumerator, 1 to the second one, and so on. The next subsection shows you how you can assign explicit values to some or all of the enumerators.

BASIC

Functions Can Return User-Defined Types

Unlike BASIC functions, C++ functions can return user-defined types. Thus, you need not completely rely on reference parameters to return values that are of user-defined types.

PASCAL

Functions Can Return User-Defined Types

Unlike most Pascal implementations (except the most recent ones from Borland), C++ functions can yield user-defined types. Thus, you need not completely rely on reference parameters to return values that are of user-defined types.

Here are examples of declaring enumerated types:

```
// example 1
enum weekDays { Sunday, Monday, Tuesday, Wednesday,
                Thursday, Friday, Saturday };
// example 2
enum colors { red, blue, green, yellow, brown };
// example 3
enum CPUtype { Intel_8086, Intel_80286,
               Intel_80386, Intel_80486, Intel_Pentium };
```

The first example declares the **weekDays** type with the names of the days of the week as the enumerators. The compiler assigns the value 0 to the enumerator **Sunday**, 1 to the enumerator **Monday**, and so on.

The second example declares the enumerated type **colors** and specifies the enumerators **red**, **blue**, **green**, **yellow**, and **brown**. The compiler assigns 0 to the enumerator **red**, 1 to the enumerator **blue**, and so on.

The last example declares the enumerated type **CPUtype** and lists the names of a number of Intel chips. The compiler assigns 0 to the enumerator **Intel_8086**, 1 to the enumerator **Intel_80286**, and so on.

Let's look at a programming example. Listing 12-2 shows the source code for the ENUM2.CPP program, which illustrates simple enumerated types. This program performs the following tasks:

- Generate three random integers between 0 and 6
- Translate the generated integer into a weekday enumerator
- Display the day name for that enumerated value as well as the names of the subsequent and preceding days

---

CODING NOTES

The Enumerators Are Unique Identifiers

The enumerators are unique identifiers. Duplicating enumerators in multiple enumerated types causes a compile-time error. Therefore, choose the names for the identifiers carefully. Use prefix characters to make the enumerators more distinct from other enumerators that have similar names. Here is an example:

```
enum ncsColors { ncsRed, ncsBlue, ncsGreen, ncsYellow, ncsBrown };
enum eprColors { eprRed, eprBlue, eprGreen, eprYellow, eprBrown };
```

The enumerated types **ncsColors** and **eprColors** essentially represent the same colors using enumerators with different prefix characters. The difference is good enough for the compiler!

PASCAL

C++ Enumerated Types Are Cool!

While both Pascal and C++ support enumerated types, you will find that C++ is more flexible than Pascal. The next subsection shows you how to assign values to the enumerators (something Pascal won't let you do!).

C

The enum Statement Defines a Type!

C++ uses the **enum** statement to define a new type and not just a tag! Therefore you need not use the keyword **enum** with the name of the enumerated data types.

Here is a sample session with the program in Listing 12-2:

```
Day # 1
Today is Tuesday
Tomorrow is Wednesday
Yesterday was Monday
```

```
Day # 2
Today is Sunday
Tomorrow is Monday
Yesterday was Saturday

Day # 3
Today is Wednesday
Tomorrow is Thursday
Yesterday was Tuesday
```

Listing 12-2

The source code for the ENUM2.CPP program.

```cpp
// A C++ program that illustrates simple enumerated types

#include <iostream.h>
#include <iomanip.h>
#include <stdlib.h>
#include <time.h>

const int TRUE = 1;
const int FALSE = 0;
typedef int Logical;

// declare enumerated type
enum weekDay { Sunday, Monday, Tuesday, Wednesday,
               Thursday, Friday, Saturday };

class myDay
{
  public:
    // constructor
    myDay(int nDayNum = 0)
      { setDay(nDayNum); }

    void show(const char* pszMsg = "",
              Logical bEmitCR = TRUE);
    void setDay(int nDayNum);
    weekDay getDay()
      { return m_eDay; }
    void getNext();
    void getPrevious();

  protected:
    weekDay m_eDay;
};
```

Enumerated type

```cpp
void myDay::show(const char* pszMsg, Logical bEmitCR)
{
  cout << pszMsg;
  switch (m_eDay) {
    case Sunday:
      cout << "Sunday";
      break;

    case Monday:
      cout << "Monday";
      break;

    case Tuesday:
      cout << "Tuesday";
      break;

    case Wednesday:
      cout << "Wednesday";
      break;

    case Thursday:
      cout << "Thursday";
      break;

    case Friday:
      cout << "Friday";
      break;

    case Saturday:
      cout << "Saturday";
      break;
  }

  if (bEmitCR)
    cout << endl;
}

void myDay::setDay(int nDayNum)
{
  // translate integer day number
  // into enumerated value
  switch (nDayNum) {
    case 0:
      m_eDay = Sunday;
      break;

    case 1:
      m_eDay = Monday;
      break;

    case 2:
      m_eDay = Tuesday;
      break;
```

```
    case 3:
      m_eDay = Wednesday;
      break;

    case 4:
      m_eDay = Thursday;
      break;

    case 5:
      m_eDay = Friday;
      break;

    case 6:
      m_eDay = Saturday;
      break;

    default:
      m_eDay = Sunday;
  }
}

void myDay::getNext()
{
  switch (m_eDay) {
    case Sunday:
      m_eDay = Monday;
      break;

    case Monday:
      m_eDay = Tuesday;
      break;

    case Tuesday:
      m_eDay = Wednesday;
      break;

    case Wednesday:
      m_eDay = Thursday;
      break;

    case Thursday:
      m_eDay = Friday;
      break;

    case Friday:
      m_eDay = Saturday;
      break;

    case Saturday:
      m_eDay = Sunday;
      break;
  }
}
```

```
void myDay::getPrevious()
{
  switch (m_eDay) {
    case Sunday:
      m_eDay = Saturday;
      break;

    case Monday:
      m_eDay = Sunday;
      break;

    case Tuesday:
      m_eDay = Monday;
      break;

    case Wednesday:
      m_eDay = Tuesday;
      break;

    case Thursday:
      m_eDay = Wednesday;
      break;

    case Friday:
      m_eDay = Thursday;
      break;

    case Saturday:
      m_eDay = Friday;
      break;
  }
}

main()
{
  const int MAX = 3;
  myDay makeMyDay;

  // reseed random-number generator
  srand((unsigned)time(NULL));
  for (int i = 0; i < MAX; i++) {
    // get random day number
    int n = rand() % 7;
    makeMyDay.setDay(n);
    // display today
    cout << "Day # " << (i+1) << endl;
    makeMyDay.show("Today is ");

    // display tomorrow
    makeMyDay.getNext();
    makeMyDay.show("Tomorrow is ");
```

```
    // display yesterday
    makeMyDay.getPrevious(); // back to today
    makeMyDay.getPrevious();
    makeMyDay.show("Yesterday was ");
    cout << endl;
  }

  return 0;
}
```

Listing 12-2 declares the enumerated type **weekDay**, which lists the names of the days of the week Sunday through Saturday. The compiler assigns 0 to the enumerator **Sunday**, 1 to the enumerator **Monday**, and so on. The listing also declares the class **myDay**, which manages the days of the week using the enumerated type **weekDay**. The class declares the protected data member **m_eDay**, which has the enumerated type **weekDay**. The class also declares the following public members:

- The constructor, which initializes the data member **m_eDay** using the value of the **int**-type parameter **nDayNum**. The default argument for this parameter is 0. Thus, the constructor sets the data member **m_eDay** to Sunday by default.

- The member function **show**, which displays the name of the current day stored in data member **m_eDay**

- The member function **setDay**, which sets the value of data member **m_eDay** using the **int**-type parameter **nDayNum**

- The member function **getDay**, which returns the enumerated value in the data member **m_eDay**

- The member functions **getNext** and **getPrevious**, which set the enumerated value in data member **m_eDay** to the next and previous days, respectively

The definition of member function **show** uses a **switch** statement to examine the enumerated value in data member **m_eDay**. The **case** labels use the enumerators of the type **weekDay** to display the name of the corresponding day.

The definition of member function **setDay** also uses a **switch** statement to map the value of the **int**-type parameter **nDayNum** into a **weekDay** enumerator. The **switch** statement uses **case** labels that have integer constants. Each **case** label has a statement that assigns an enumerator to the data member **m_eDay**. While this method seems long-winded, it is safer than using typecasting (which I discuss in the next subsection), because it does not rely on any data conversion.

The member functions **getNext** and **getPrevious** use **switch** statements to examine and update the value in data member **m_eDay**. The member function **getNext** sets the value in data member **m_eDay** to the next day. By contrast, the member function **getPrevious** sets the value in data member **m_eDay** to the previous day.

The function **main** declares the constant **MAX** and the object **makeMyDay** as an instance of class **myDay**. The function reseeds the random number generator and then uses a **for** loop to perform and repeat the following tasks:

- Obtain a random number in the range of 0 to 6 and store it in the local variable **n**

- Set the day in object **makeMyDay** by sending it the C++ message **setDay**. The argument for this message is the variable **n**. This message translates the integer value that represents the day number into an enumerator that is stored in the data member **makeMyDay.m_eDay**.

- Display the day count and the name of the current day. This task sends the C++ message **show** (with the string literal argument "Today is ") to the object **makeMyDay**.

- Set the object **makeMyDay** to the next day by sending it the C++ message **getNext**

- Display the name of the current day. This task sends the C++ message **show** (with the string literal argument "Tomorrow is ") to the object **makeMyDay**.

- Set the object **makeMyDay** two days earlier (to go back to the day before the initial day) by sending it the C++ message **getPrevious** twice

- Display the name of the current day. This task sends the C++ message **show** (with the string literal argument "Yesterday was ") to the object **makeMyDay**.

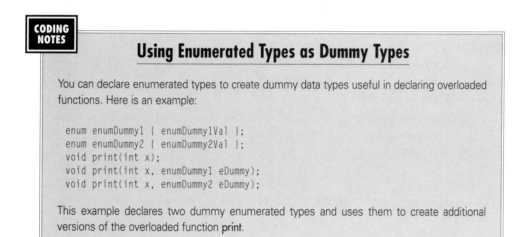

Using Enumerated Types as Dummy Types

You can declare enumerated types to create dummy data types useful in declaring overloaded functions. Here is an example:

```
enum enumDummy1 { enumDummy1Val };
enum enumDummy2 { enumDummy2Val };
void print(int x);
void print(int x, enumDummy1 eDummy);
void print(int x, enumDummy2 eDummy);
```

This example declares two dummy enumerated types and uses them to create additional versions of the overloaded function print.

TYPE CONVERSION AND ENUMERATED TYPES

You can select new enumerators by performing type conversions between the **int** type and enumerators. While this approach shortens the source code, you have to be careful to avoid converting integers to nonexistent enumerators. Here is an example of an erroneous conversion:

```
// *** Error! Bad conversion from int to enumerated type
enum weekDay { Sunday, Monday, Tuesday, Wednesday,
              Thursday, Friday, Saturday };
int nDayNum = 8;
weekDay eDay = weekDay(nDayNum);
```

The **int**-type variable **nDayNum** has the initial value of 8. The declaration of the enumerated variable **eDay** also initializes that variable using the typecast expression **weekDay(nDayNum)**. The error lies in the fact that the integer values associated with the enumerated type **weekDay** range from 0 to 6. Thus typecasting an integer value of 8 into a **weekDay** type is legal but undefined!

Let me present a version of program ENUM2.CPP that uses type conversion. Listing 12-3 shows the source code for the ENUM3.CPP program, which illustrates using type conversion to alter the values of the enumerated type **weekDay**. The program performs the same tasks as ENUM2.CPP, except that the source code uses type conversion instead of the **switch** statements.

C++ Does Not Support the Operators ++ and −− with Enumerated Types

Unlike C, C++ does not support the operators ++ and −− with enumerated types. The reason for this is that the integer values that are associated with enumerators are not necessarily contiguous.

Here is sample output from the program in Listing 12-3:

```
Day # 1
Today is Sunday
Tomorrow is Monday
Yesterday was Saturday

Day # 2
Today is Wednesday
Tomorrow is Thursday
Yesterday was Tuesday

Day # 3
Today is Friday
Tomorrow is Saturday
Yesterday was Thursday
```

Listing 12-3
The source code for the ENUM3.CPP program, which illustrates using type conversion to alter the values of enumerated types.

```
// A C++ program that illustrates enumerated types
// and uses type conversion to support changing
// the enumerators

#include <iostream.h>
#include <iomanip.h>
#include <stdlib.h>
#include <time.h>

const int TRUE = 1;
const int FALSE = 0;
typedef int Logical;

// declare enumerated type
enum weekDay { Sunday, Monday, Tuesday, Wednesday,
               Thursday, Friday, Saturday };
```

```
class myDay
{
  public:
    // constructor
    myDay(int nDayNum = 0)
      { setDay(nDayNum); }

    void show(const char* pszMsg = "",
              Logical bEmitCR = TRUE);
    void setDay(int nDayNum);
    weekDay getDay()
      { return m_eDay; }
    void getNext();
    void getPrevious();

  protected:
    weekDay m_eDay;
};

void myDay::show(const char* pszMsg, Logical bEmitCR)
{
  cout << pszMsg;
  switch (m_eDay) {
    case Sunday:
      cout << "Sunday";
      break;

    case Monday:
      cout << "Monday";
      break;

    case Tuesday:
      cout << "Tuesday";
      break;

    case Wednesday:
      cout << "Wednesday";
      break;

    case Thursday:
      cout << "Thursday";
      break;

    case Friday:
      cout << "Friday";
      break;

    case Saturday:
      cout << "Saturday";
      break;
  }

  if (bEmitCR)
    cout << endl;
}
```

```
void myDay::setDay(int nDayNum)
{
  if (nDayNum >= 0 && nDayNum < 7)
    m_eDay = weekDay(nDayNum);
  else
    m_eDay = Sunday;
}

void myDay::getNext()
{
  if (m_eDay != Saturday)
    m_eDay = weekDay(int(m_eDay) + 1);
  else
    m_eDay = Sunday;
}

void myDay::getPrevious()
{
  if (m_eDay != Sunday)
    m_eDay = weekDay(int(m_eDay) - 1);
  else
    m_eDay = Saturday;
}

main()
{
  const int MAX = 3;
  myDay makeMyDay;

  // reseed random-number generator
  srand((unsigned)time(NULL));
  for (int i = 0; i < MAX; i++) {
    // get random day number
    int n = rand() % 7;
    makeMyDay.setDay(n);
    // display today
    cout << "Day # " << (i+1) << endl;
    makeMyDay.show("Today is ");

    // display tomorrow
    makeMyDay.getNext();
    makeMyDay.show("Tomorrow is ");

    // display yesterday
    makeMyDay.getPrevious(); // back to today
    makeMyDay.getPrevious();
    makeMyDay.show("Yesterday was ");
    cout << endl;
  }

  return 0;
}
```

Listing 12-3 declares the enumerated type **weekDay** and the class **myDay**. The declarations of the enumerated type and the class match those of Listing 12-2. The main difference is in the definition of the following member functions:

- The member function **setDay** assigns the value of the int-type parameter **nDayNum** to the data member **m_eDay**. The member function first determines whether or not the argument for **nDayNum** is in the range 0 to 6. If it is, the member function **setDay** typecasts the argument into a **weekDay** value and assigns that value to the data member **m_eDay**. If the argument is out of range, the member function simply assigns the enumerator **Sunday** to the data member **m_eDay**.

- The member function **getNext** increments the enumerator stored in data member **m_eDay**. The member function first determines if data member **m_eDay** does not contain the enumerator **Saturday**. If this condition is true, the member function increments the enumerator. This process involves converting the value in **m_eDay** into an **int**, adding 1, and then converting the result back to the enumerated type **weekDay**. By contrast, if the tested condition is false, the member function assigns the enumerator **Sunday** to data member **m_eDay**. This assignment helps the member function select Sunday as the day succeeding Saturday.

- The member function **getPrevious** decrements the enumerator stored in data member **m_eDay**. The member function first determines if data member **m_eDay** does not contain the enumerator **Sunday**. If this condition is true, the member function decrements the enumerator. This process involves converting the value in **m_eDay** into an **int**, subtracting 1, and then converting the result back to the enumerated type **weekDay**. By contrast, if the tested condition is false, the member function assigns the enumerator **Saturday** to data member **m_eDay**. This assignment helps the member function select Saturday as the day preceding Sunday.

The source code for function **main** in Listing 12-3 matches that of Listing 12-2.

ENUMERATED TYPES WITH EXPLICIT VALUES

C++ allows you to assign integer values to enumerators. Make sure that the given constants resolve to integers between –32,768 and +32,767 (signed) or 0 and +65,535 (unsigned). Otherwise, the compiler will generate a warning.

C++ requires that you observe the following features and rules for assigning explicit values to enumerators:

1. The values must be within the valid ranges just given.

2. The values assigned to the enumerators need not be unique! Only the enumerator's identifiers need to be unique.

3. The values assigned need not follow any ascending or descending numeric pattern. You can assign numbers in an arbitrary manner.

4. The compiler assigns values to enumerators that have no explicit value. In this case, the value assigned to an enumerator equals one plus the value of the previous enumerator (or zero, if the enumerator is the first one).

Here are examples of enumerated types with explicit values:

```
enum weekDay { Sunday = 1, Monday, Tuesday, Wednesday,
               Thursday, Friday, Saturday };
enum digits { Five = 5, Four = 4, Three = 3, Zero = 0,
              One, Two, Six = 6, Seven, Eight, Nine };
```

The first example shows the enumerated type **weekDay** and assigns the value 1 to the enumerator **Sunday**. The compiler assigns the value 2 to the enumerator **Monday**, 3 to the enumerator **Tuesday**, and so on.

The second example shows a more elaborate use of the explicit values feature. The enumerated type **digits** explicitly assigns the integers 5, 4, 3, and 0 to the enumerators **Five**, **Four**, **Three**, and **Zero**, respectively. The compiler then assigns 1 and 2 to the enumerators **One** and **Two**, respectively. The declaration then assigns 6 to the enumerator **Six**. The compiler assigns 7, 8, and 9 to the enumerators **Seven**, **Eight**, and **Nine**, respectively.

Let me present a programming example. Listing 12-4 shows the source code for the ENUM4.CPP program, which illustrates using enumerated types with explicit values. The program uses an enumerated type to represent single digits and to perform the following tasks:

- Generate three random integers between 0 and 9
- Translate the generated integer into an enumerated digit value
- Display the current digit as well as the subsequent and preceding digits
- Display the outcome of comparing the current digit with the number 5

Here is the sample output of the program in Listing 12-4:

```
Digit # 1
Digit is 7
Next digit is 8
Previous digit is 6
Digit equals to 5? false

Digit # 2
Digit is 3
Next digit is 4
Previous digit is 2
Digit equals to 5? false

Digit # 3
Digit is 5
Next digit is 6
Previous digit is 4
Digit equals to 5? true
```

Listing 12-4
The source code for the ENUM4.CPP program.

```
// C++ program that illustrates using
// enumerated types with explicit values

#include <iostream.h>
#include <iomanip.h>
#include <stdlib.h>
#include <time.h>

const int TRUE = 1;
const int FALSE = 0;
typedef int Logical;

// declare enumerated type
enum digitEnum { Nine = 9, Eight = 8, Seven = 7, Six = 6,
                 Five = 5, Zero = 0, One, Two, Three, Four };
```

Enumerators with explicit values

```
class myDigit
{
  public:
    // constructor
    myDigit(int nDigit = 0)
      { setDigit(nDigit); }

    void show(const char* pszMsg = "",
              Logical bEmitCR = TRUE);
    void setDigit(int nDigit)
      { m_eDigit = digitEnum(nDigit); }
    digitEnum getDigit()
      { return m_eDigit; }
    void getNext();
    void getPrevious();
    Logical isEqual(int nDigit)
      { return (m_eDigit == nDigit) ? TRUE : FALSE; }

  protected:
    digitEnum m_eDigit;
};

void myDigit::show(const char* pszMsg, Logical bEmitCR)
{
  cout << pszMsg << int(m_eDigit);

  if (bEmitCR)
    cout << endl;
}


void myDigit::getNext()
{
  if (m_eDigit != Nine)
    m_eDigit = digitEnum(int(m_eDigit) + 1);
  else
    m_eDigit = Zero;
}

void myDigit::getPrevious()
{
  if (m_eDigit != Zero)
    m_eDigit = digitEnum(int(m_eDigit) - 1);
  else
    m_eDigit = Nine;
}

main()
{
  const int MAX = 3;
  const int HI_NUM = 10;
  myDigit OneDigit;
```

```
// reseed random-number generator
srand((unsigned)time(NULL));
for (int i = 0; i < MAX; i++) {
  // get random number
  int n = rand() % HI_NUM ;
  OneDigit.setDigit(n);
  // display digit
  cout << "Digit # " << (i+1) << endl;
  OneDigit.show("Digit is ");

  // display next digit
  OneDigit.getNext();
  OneDigit.show("Next digit is ");

  // display previous digit
  OneDigit.getPrevious(); // back to current digit
  OneDigit.getPrevious();
  OneDigit.show("Previous digit is ");
  OneDigit.getNext(); // back to "current" digit
  cout << "Digit equals to 5? "
       << (OneDigit.isEqual(HI_NUM / 2) ? "true" : "false")
       << "\n\n";
}

  return 0;
}
```

Listing 12-4 declares the enumerated type **digitEnum**, which lists the names of the single digits. The enumerators have been written in an arbitrary fashion, and explicit values have been assigned to the enumerators **Nine**, **Eight**, **Seven**, **Six**, **Five**, and **Zero**. The listing declares the class **myDigit**, which declares the protected data member **m_eDigit**. The class declares the following public members:

- The constructor assigns the value of the **int**-type parameter **nDigit** to the data member **m_eDigit**. The parameter has the default argument of 0.

- The member function **show** displays the integer that corresponds to the enumerator in data member **m_eDigit**.

- The member function **setDigit** sets the value of data member **m_eDigit** using the value of the **int**-type parameter **nDigit**. The inline code for this member function uses typecasting to convert the argument into an enumerator.

- The member function **getDigit** returns the enumerator stored in data member **m_eDigit**.

- The member functions **getNext** and **getPrevious** increment and decrement the enumerator stored in data member **m_eDigit**, respectively. These member functions wrap around the enumerator value when it reaches **Zero** and **Nine**.

- The member function **isEqual** compares the value in data member **m_eDigit** with the value of the **int**-type parameter **nDigit**. The member function returns the value of constant **TRUE** if the two values match. Otherwise, the function yields the value of the constant **FALSE**.

The definitions of member functions **show**, **getNext**, and **getPrevious** use typecasting to convert between the **int** type and the enumerated type **digitEnum**.

The function **main** declares the constants **MAX** and **HI_NUM** and also declares the object **OneDigit** as an instance of class **myDigit**. The function reseeds the random number generator and then uses a **for** loop to perform and repeat the following tasks:

- Obtain a random number in the range of 0 to 9 and store it in the local variable **n**

- Set the digit in object **OneDigit** by sending it the C++ message **setDigit**. The argument for this message is the variable **n**. This message translates the integer value that represents the random number into an enumerator that is stored in the data member **OneDigit.m_eDigit**.

- Display the digit count and the current digit. This task sends the C++ message **show** (with the string literal argument "Digit is ") to the object **OneDigit**.

- Set the object **OneDigit** to the next digit by sending it the C++ message **getNext**

- Display the current digit. This task sends the C++ message **show** with the string literal argument "Next digit is " to the object **OneDigit**.

- Set the object **OneDigit** to the two previous digits (to go back to the digit before the initial digit) by sending it the C++ message **getPrevious** twice

- Display the current digit. This task sends the C++ message **show** with the string literal argument "Previous digit is " to the object **OneDigit**.

- Set the digit to the next one (to go back to the original digit) by sending the object **OneDigit** the C++ message **getNext**.

- Display the outcome of comparing the digit with 5. This task sends the C++ message **isEqual** to object **OneDigit**. The argument for this message is the expression **HI_NUM / 2**. The outcome of the message yields either the string "true" or the string "false."

ANONYMOUS ENUMERATED TYPES

There are cases in which the name of an enumerated type is irrelevant. This kind of enumerated type is called *anonymous* or *untagged*. The general syntax for anonymous enumerated types is:

```
enum { enumerator1, enumerator2, ... };
```

This syntax shows that the keyword **enum** is immediately followed by the list of enumerators.

Why use anonymous enumerated type instead of formal constants? When integer constants are somewhat related, it may make more sense to group them in an anonymous enumerated type. Here are examples of anonymous enumerated types:

```
// example 1
enum { DaysPerYear = 365, MonthsPerYear = 12,
       WeeksPerYear = 52, DaysPerWeek = 7 };
// example 2
enum { Yes = 1, No = 0, DontCare = -1 };
```

The first example contains a list of enumerators that describe date-related constants, whereas the second example contains a list of enumerators that model Yes/No/Don't Care states.

Let me present a programming example. Listing 12-5 shows the source code for the ENUM5.CPP program, which illustrates using anonymous enumerated types. The program uses enumerators that describe time-related constants to perform the following tasks:

- Display the start time of noon
- Display the end time of 6:30:10 p.m.
- Display the number of seconds between noon and midnight

- Display the number of seconds between 6:30:10 p.m. and midnight
- Display the number of seconds between noon and 6:30:10 p.m.

The program displays the time in hh:mm:ss 24-hour format. Here is the output of the program in Listing 12-5:

```
Start time is 12:00:00
End time is 18:30:10
There are 43200 seconds between 12:00:00 and 00:00:00
There are 66610 seconds between 18:30:10 and 00:00:00
There are 23410 seconds between 18:30:10 and 12:00:00
```

Listing 12-5

The source code for the ENUM5.CPP program, which illustrates using anonymous enumerated types.

```
// A C++ program that illustrates untagged enumerated types

#include <iostream.h>
#include <iomanip.h>

enum Logical { FALSE, TRUE };                Untagged enumerated types
// declare untagged enumerated types
enum { SecondsPerMinute = 60,
       MinutesPerHour = 60,
       HoursPerDay = 24 };

class TimeCalc
{
  public:
    // constructor
    TimeCalc(int nHour = 0, int nMinute = 0, int nSecond = 0)
      { setTime(nHour, nMinute, nSecond); }

    Logical setTime(int nHour = 0,
                    int nMinute = 0,
                    int nSecond = 0);
    long getTime(int& nHour, int& nMinute, int& nSecond);
    long getTimeDiff(TimeCalc& TimeObj);
    void show(const char* pszMsg = "", Logical bEmitCR = TRUE);
    friend ostream& operator<<(ostream& os,
                               const TimeCalc& TimeObj);

  protected:
    int m_nSecond;
    int m_nMinute;
    int m_nHour;

    Logical validate(int nValue, int nMaxValue);
};
```

```
Logical TimeCalc::validate(int nValue, int nMaxValue)
{
  return (nValue >= 0 && nValue <= nMaxValue) ? TRUE : FALSE;
}

Logical TimeCalc::setTime(int nHour, int nMinute, int nSecond)
{
  if (validate(nHour, HoursPerDay - 1)          &&
      validate(nMinute, MinutesPerHour - 1)    &&
      validate(nSecond, SecondsPerMinute - 1)) {
      m_nHour = nHour;
      m_nMinute = nMinute;
      m_nSecond = nSecond;
      return TRUE;
  }
  else
    return FALSE;
}

long TimeCalc::getTime(int& nHour, int& nMinute, int& nSecond)
{
  long lResult;

  nHour = m_nHour;
  nMinute = m_nMinute;
  nSecond = m_nSecond;

  // calculate the total number of seconds
  // between midnight and the set time
  lResult = (long(m_nHour) * * MinutesPerHour + m_nMinute) *
            SecondsPerMinute + m_nSecond;

  return lResult;
}

long TimeCalc::getTimeDiff(TimeCalc& TimeObj)
{
  long lResult = TimeObj.m_nSecond - m_nSecond;

  lResult += (TimeObj.m_nMinute - m_nMinute) * SecondsPerMinute;
  lResult += (TimeObj.m_nHour - m_nHour) *
             MinutesPerHour * SecondsPerMinute;
  return lResult;
}

void TimeCalc::show(const char* pszMsg, Logical bEmitCR)
{
  cout << pszMsg;
  cout.fill('0');
  cout.flags(ios::right);
  cout.width(2);
```

```
    cout << m_nHour << ":";
    cout.width(2);
    cout << m_nMinute << ":";
    cout.width(2);
    cout << m_nSecond;
    if (bEmitCR)
      cout << endl;
}

ostream& operator<<(ostream& os, const TimeCalc& TimeObj)
{
  os.fill('0');
  os.flags(ios::right);
  os.width(2);
  os << TimeObj.m_nHour << ":";
  os.width(2);
  os << TimeObj.m_nMinute << ":";
  os.width(2);
  os << TimeObj.m_nSecond;
  return os;
}

main()
{
  const TimeCalc Midnight;
  int nHour, nMinute, nSecond;
  TimeCalc StartTime, EndTime;

  StartTime.setTime(12, 0, 0); // set start time to noon
  StartTime.getTime(nHour, nMinute, nSecond);
  // set EndTime to end after 6 hours, 30 minutes and 10 seconds
  EndTime.setTime(nHour + 6, nMinute + 30, nSecond + 10);
  StartTime.show("Start time is ");
  EndTime.show("End time is ");
  cout << "There are "
       << StartTime.getTime(nHour, nMinute, nSecond)
       << " seconds between "
       << StartTime << " and " << Midnight << endl;

  cout << "There are "
       << EndTime.getTime(nHour, nMinute, nSecond)
       << " seconds between "
       << EndTime << " and " << Midnight << endl;

  cout << "There are "
       << StartTime.getTimeDiff(EndTime)
       << " seconds between "
       << EndTime << " and " << StartTime << endl;

  return 0;
}
```

Listing 12-5 declares two untagged enumerated types: The first declares the enumerators **FALSE** and **TRUE**. The second declares the enumerators **SecondsPerMinute**, **MinutesPerHour**, and **HoursPerDay**. The first anonymous enumerated type groups **Boolean**-related enumerators, whereas the second enumerated type groups time-related enumerators.

The listing also declares the class **TimeCalc**, which supports the time. The class declares public and protected members. The protected members are:

- The **int**-type data members **m_nSecond**, **m_nMinute**, and **m_nHour**, which store the seconds, minutes, and hours, respectively
- The member function **validate**, which returns **TRUE** if the argument of the **int**-parameter **nValue** is between 0 and the value of **int**-type parameter **nMaxValue**. Otherwise, the member function yields **FALSE**.

The class **TimeCalc** declares the following public members:

- The constructor initializes the data members **m_nSecond**, **m_nMinute**, and **m_nHour**.
- The member function **setTime** sets a new time by assigning new values to the data members **m_nSecond**, **m_nMinute**, and **m_nHour**.
- The member function **getTime** returns the number of seconds between the current time (stored in the data members) and the previous midnight. The member function also returns the current count of hours, minutes, and seconds via the reference parameters **nHour**, **nMinute**, and **nSecond**, respectively.
- The member function **getTimeDiff** returns the number of seconds between the current time and the time specified by the **TimeCalc**-type parameter **TimeObj**.
- The member function **show** displays the current time in the 24-hour format.

The class also declares the friend operator **<<**, which displays the current time using the 24-hour format.

The function **main** declares the constant object **Midnight** as an instance of class **TimeCalc**. The function also declares the local variables **nHour**, **nMinute**, and **nSecond**. In addition, the function declares the objects **StartTime** and **EndTime** as instances of class **TimeCalc**. The function then performs the following tasks:

- Set the start time by sending the object **StartTime** the C++ message **setTime**. The arguments for this message are 12, 0, and 0.

- Obtain the time components of the **StartTime** object by sending it the C++ message **getTime**. The arguments for this message are the variables **nHour**, **nMinute**, and **nSecond**.

- Set the end time by sending the object **EndTime** the C++ message **setTime**. The arguments for this message are the expression **nHour + 6**, the expression **nMinute + 30**, and the expression **nSecond + 10**.

- Display the start time by sending the object **StartTime** the C++ message **show**. The argument for this message is the string literal "Start time is."

- Display the end time by sending the object **EndTime** the C++ message **show**. The argument for this message is the string literal "End time is."

- Display the number of seconds between the start time and midnight. This task sends the C++ message **getTime** to object **StartTime**. This task also displays the start time by using the friend operator **<<**.

- Display the number of seconds between the end time and midnight. This task sends the C++ message **getTime** to object **EndTime**. This task also displays the end time by using the friend operator **<<**.

- Display the number of seconds between the end and start times. This task sends the C++ message **getTimeDiff** to object **StartTime**. The argument for this message is object **EndTime**. This task also displays the start and end times by using the friend operator **<<**.

SCOPING ENUMERATED TYPES WITH CLASSES

One of the problems with using enumerators is that they have to be unique in the same scope. To solve this problem, you can use the ability to declare an enumerated type inside a class. The trick is to declare a class with only a public enumerated type, as shown in the following general syntax:

```
class className
{
  public:
    enum enumeratedType { enumerator1, enumerator2, ... };
};
```

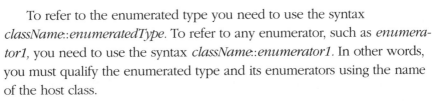

To refer to the enumerated type you need to use the syntax *className::enumeratedType*. To refer to any enumerator, such as *enumerator1*, you need to use the syntax *className::enumerator1*. In other words, you must qualify the enumerated type and its enumerators using the name of the host class.

Scoping enumerated types in classes enables you to use enumerators with the same names (but different qualifying classes) that are declared in different header files.

Here is an example of scoping enumerated types in classes:

```
// file BOOLCL1.H
class BooleanClass1
{
  public:
    enum boolean { false, true };
};


// file BOOCL2.H
class BooleanClass2
{
  public:
    enum boolean { false, true };
};


// main program file
#include <iostream.h>
#include <boolcl1.h>
#include <boolcl2.h>

main()
{
  BooleanClass1::boolean bIsOdd;
  BooleanClass2::boolean bDirectoryExist;
  int nNum = 11;
  // other declarations

  // other statements

  if ((nNum % 2) > 0)
    bIsOdd == BooleanClass1::true;
  else
    bIsOdd == BooleanClass1::false;

  // other statements

  bDirectoryExist = (fileExist("CALC.DAT")) ?
      BooleanClass2::true : BooleanClass2::false;
```

```
    // other statements

    return 0;
}
```

This code snippet declares the classes **BooleanClass1** and **BooleanClass2** in the header files BOOLCL1.H and BOOLCL2.H. Each class declares the enumerated type **boolean** with the enumerators **false** and **true**.

The function **main**, which includes the header files BOOLCL1.H and BOOLCL2.H, declares the variables **bIsOdd** to have the type **BooleanClass1::boolean**. The function also declares the variable **bDirectoryExist** to have the type **BooleanClass2::boolean**. The **if** statement assigns the values **BooleanClass1::true** or **BooleanClass1::false** to the variable **bIsOdd** depending on the value in the variable **nNum**. The function also assigns the values **BooleanClass2::true** or **BooleanClass2::false** to the variable **bDirectoryExist** depending on the result of calling function **fileExist**.

The code snippet shows that source code qualifies the name of each enumerated type (and its enumerators) using the name of its host class.

Let me present a programming example. Listing 12-6 shows the source code for the ENUM6.CPP program, which illustrates enumerated types qualified by skeleton classes. This program is based on the ENUM2.CPP program in Listing 12-2. The program models days of the week using two enumerated types, each nested in a class. The program also uses *twin* classes that model days. It displays four random days, along with their successor and predecessor days.

Here is sample output of the program in Listing 12-6:

```
Day # 1
Today is Monday
Tomorrow is Tuesday
Yesterday was Sunday

Day # 2
Today is Saturday
Tomorrow is Sunday
Yesterday was Friday

Day # 3
Today is Friday
Tomorrow is Saturday
Yesterday was Thursday

Day # 4
Today is Thursday
Tomorrow is Friday
Yesterday was Wednesday
```

Listing 12-6

The source code for the ENUM6.CPP program, which illustrates enumerated types qualified by skeleton classes.

```cpp
// A C++ program that illustrates
// enumerated types nested in classes

#include <iostream.h>
#include <iomanip.h>
#include <stdlib.h>
#include <time.h>

const int TRUE = 1;
const int FALSE = 0;
typedef int Logical;


class myWeekDays
{
  public:
    enum weekDays { Sunday, Monday, Tuesday, Wednesday,
                    Thursday, Friday, Saturday };
};

class yourWeekDays
{
  public:
    enum weekDays { Sunday, Monday, Tuesday, Wednesday,
                    Thursday, Friday, Saturday };
};

class myDay
{
  public:
    // constructor
    myDay(int nDayNum = 0)
      { setDay(nDayNum); }

    void show(const char* pszMsg = "",
              Logical bEmitCR = TRUE);
    void setDay(int nDayNum);
    myWeekDays::weekDays getDay()
      { return m_eDay; }
    void getNext();
    void getPrevious();

  protected:
    myWeekDays::weekDays m_eDay;
};
```

Untagged enumerated types

```
class yourDay
{
  public:
    // constructor
    yourDay(int nDayNum = 0)
      { setDay(nDayNum); }

    void show(const char* pszMsg = "",
              Logical bEmitCR = TRUE);
    void setDay(int nDayNum);
    yourWeekDays::weekDays getDay()
      { return m_eDay; }
    void getNext();
    void getPrevious();

  protected:
    yourWeekDays::weekDays m_eDay;
};

//
// Define members of class myDay
//

void myDay::show(const char* pszMsg, Logical bEmitCR)
{
  cout << pszMsg;
  switch (m_eDay) {
    case myWeekDays::Sunday:
      cout << "Sunday";
      break;

    case myWeekDays::Monday:
      cout << "Monday";
      break;

    case myWeekDays::Tuesday:
      cout << "Tuesday";
      break;

    case myWeekDays::Wednesday:
      cout << "Wednesday";
      break;

    case myWeekDays::Thursday:
      cout << "Thursday";
      break;

    case myWeekDays::Friday:
      cout << "Friday";
      break;

    case myWeekDays::Saturday:
      cout << "Saturday";
      break;
  }
```

```
   if (bEmitCR)
     cout << endl;
}

void myDay::setDay(int nDayNum)
{
  if ((nDayNum % 8) == 0)
    m_eDay = myWeekDays::weekDays(nDayNum);
  else
    m_eDay = myWeekDays::Sunday;
}

void myDay::getNext()
{
  if (m_eDay != myWeekDays::Saturday)
    m_eDay = myWeekDays::weekDays(int(m_eDay) + 1);
  else
    m_eDay = myWeekDays::Sunday;
}

void myDay::getPrevious()
{
  if (m_eDay != myWeekDays::Sunday)
    m_eDay = myWeekDays::weekDays(int(m_eDay) - 1);
  else
    m_eDay = myWeekDays::Saturday;
}

//
// Define members of class yourDay
//

void yourDay::show(const char* pszMsg, Logical bEmitCR)
{
  cout << pszMsg;
  switch (m_eDay) {
    case yourWeekDays::Sunday:
      cout << "Sunday";
      break;

    case yourWeekDays::Monday:
      cout << "Monday";
      break;

    case yourWeekDays::Tuesday:
      cout << "Tuesday";
      break;

    case yourWeekDays::Wednesday:
      cout << "Wednesday";
      break;
```

```
    case yourWeekDays::Thursday:
      cout << "Thursday";
      break;

    case yourWeekDays::Friday:
      cout << "Friday";
      break;

    case yourWeekDays::Saturday:
      cout << "Saturday";
      break;
  }

  if (bEmitCR)
    cout << endl;
}

void yourDay::setDay(int nDayNum)
{
  if ((nDayNum % 8) == 0)
    m_eDay = yourWeekDays::weekDays(nDayNum);
  else
    m_eDay = yourWeekDays::Sunday;
}

void yourDay::getNext()
{
  if (m_eDay != yourWeekDays::Saturday)
    m_eDay = yourWeekDays::weekDays(int(m_eDay) + 1);
  else
    m_eDay = yourWeekDays::Sunday;
}

void yourDay::getPrevious()
{
  if (m_eDay != yourWeekDays::Sunday)
    m_eDay = yourWeekDays::weekDays(int(m_eDay) - 1);
  else
    m_eDay = yourWeekDays::Saturday;
}

main()
{
  const int MAX = 4;
  myDay makeMyDay;
  yourDay makeYourDay;

  // reseed random-number generator
  srand((unsigned)time(NULL));
  for (int i = 0; i < MAX; i++) {
    // get random day number
    int n = rand() % 7;
```

```
    if (i < (MAX / 2)) {
      makeMyDay.setDay(n);
      // display today
      cout << "Day # " << (i+1) << endl;
      makeMyDay.show("Today is ");

      // display tomorrow
      makeMyDay.getNext();
      makeMyDay.show("Tomorrow is ");

      // display yesterday
      makeMyDay.getPrevious(); // back to today
      makeMyDay.getPrevious();
      makeMyDay.show("Yesterday was ");
    }
    else {
      makeYourDay.setDay(n);
      // display today
      cout << "Day # " << (i+1) << endl;
      makeYourDay.show("Today is ");

      // display tomorrow
      makeYourDay.getNext();
      makeYourDay.show("Tomorrow is ");

      // display yesterday
      makeYourDay.getPrevious(); // back to today
      makeYourDay.getPrevious();
      makeYourDay.show("Yesterday was ");
    }

    cout << endl;
  }

  return 0;
}
```

Listing 12-6 declares the classes myWeekDays, yourWeekDays, myDay, and yourDay. Each of the classes myWeekDays and yourWeekDays contains the nested enumerated type weekDays. The weekDays enumerated types in each class declare the same set of enumerators.

The listing declares the classes myDay and yourDay in a manner similar to class myDay in Listing 12-2. The main difference is that the classes myDay and yourDay qualify their associated enumerated type and enumerators with the names of classes myWeekDays and yourWeekDays, respectively. The fact that the classes myDay and yourDay are very similar is not very relevant to the example. I could have instead coded them to be more different.

The function **main** declares the objects **makeMyDay** and **makeYourDay** as instances of classes **myDay** and **yourDay**, respectively. The function manipulates the objects **makeMyDay** and **makeYourDay** much as object **makeYourDay** was manipulated in Listing 12-2. The function uses a **for** loop to manipulate object **makeMyDay** in the first two iterations and object **makeYourDay** in the last two iterations.

Structures

C++ supports user-defined structures. In Chapter 5 you learned that a C++ structure is really a class with default public members. However, in this section I present the C++ structures as placeholders for logically related data members. You can still take advantage of the ability to include constructors to initialize the data members of a structure.

DECLARING STRUCTURES

The general syntax for declaring a structure type is:

```
struct structureName
{
  type1 dataMember1;
  type2 dataMember2;
  // other data members
};
```

The structure declares its data members, which have either predefined data types or previously defined types (such as enumerated types, other structures, unions, or arrays). Here are examples of structures:

```
struct Point
{
  double m_fX;
  double m_fY;
};
```

```
struct Rectangle
{
  Point m_UpperLeftCorner;
  Point m_LowerRightCorner;
  double m_fLength;
  double m_fWidth;
};

struct Person
{
  char m_cFirstName[10];
  char m_cMiddleInitial;
  char m_cLastName[15];
  int m_BirthYear;
  double m_fWeight;
};
```

The structure **Point** has the two **double**-type data members **m_fX** and
m_fY. The structure **Rectangle** has the **Point**-type data members
m_UpperLeftCorner and **m_LowerRightCorner** and the **double**-type data
members **m_fLength** and **m_fWidth**. The structure **Rectangle** is an example of
a structure that contains data members that are themselves structures. The
structure **Person** has the following data members:

- The member **m_cFirstName**, which is an array of 10 characters that
  stores the first name
- The **char**-type member **m_cMiddleInitial**, which stores the middle initial
  character
- The member **m_cLastName**, which is an array of 15 characters that
  stores the last name
- The **int**-type member **m_BirthYear**, which stores the birth year
- The **double**-type member **m_fWeight**, which stores the weight

The structure **Person** is an example of a structure that contains data
members that are arrays.

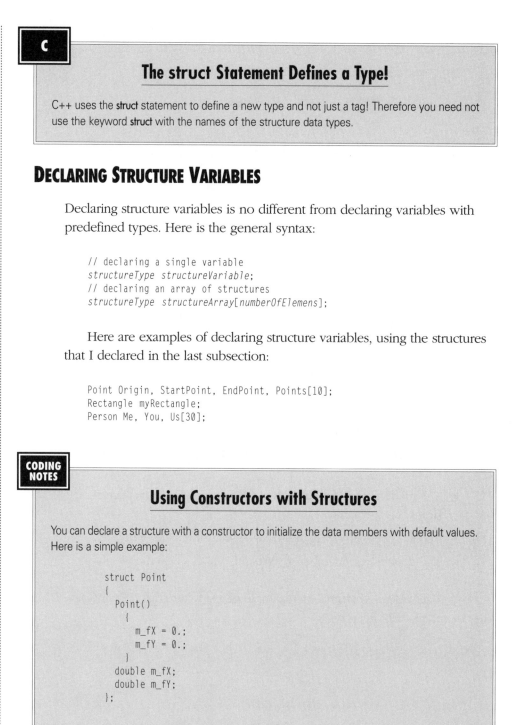

C

The struct Statement Defines a Type!

C++ uses the **struct** statement to define a new type and not just a tag! Therefore you need not use the keyword **struct** with the names of the structure data types.

DECLARING STRUCTURE VARIABLES

Declaring structure variables is no different from declaring variables with predefined types. Here is the general syntax:

```
// declaring a single variable
structureType structureVariable;
// declaring an array of structures
structureType structureArray[numberOfElemens];
```

Here are examples of declaring structure variables, using the structures that I declared in the last subsection:

```
Point Origin, StartPoint, EndPoint, Points[10];
Rectangle myRectangle;
Person Me, You, Us[30];
```

CODING NOTES

Using Constructors with Structures

You can declare a structure with a constructor to initialize the data members with default values. Here is a simple example:

```
struct Point
{
  Point()
    {
      m_fX = 0.;
      m_fY = 0.;
    }
  double m_fX;
  double m_fY;
};
```

This code snippet initializes the data members **m_fX** and **m_fY** to 0.

These examples declare the Point-type variables Origin, StartPoint, and EndPoint. The examples also declare the Point-type array Points to have 10 elements. They additionally declare the Rectangle-type variable myRectangle, the Person-type variables Me and You, and the Person-type array Us.

ACCESSING STRUCTURE MEMBERS

The data members of a structure are accessed by using the dot operator. The general syntax for accessing the data member of a structure is:

```
structureVariable.dataMember
```

Here are examples of accessing the data members of structures:

```
struct Point
{
  double m_fX;
  double m_fY;
};

struct Rectangle
{
  Point m_UpperLeftCorner;
  Point m_LowerRightCorner;
  double m_fLength;
  double m_fWidth;
};

Rectangle Shape;

// set the coordinates for the upper-left corner
Shape.m_UpperLeftCorner.m_fX = 10.5;
Shape.m_UpperLeftCorner.m_fY = 12.5;
// set the coordinates for the lower-right corner
Shape.m_LowerRightCorner.m_fX = 50.5;
Shape.m_LowerRightCorner.m_fY = 5.5;
Shape.m_fLength = Shape.m_UpperLeftCorner.m_fX -
                  Shape.m_LowerRightCorner.m_fX;
Shape.m_fWidth = Shape.m_LowerRightCorner.m_fY -
                 Shape.m_UpperLeftCorner.m_fY;
```

This code snippet declares the structure variable Shape and accesses its data members m_fLength and m_fWidth using the expressions Shape.m_fLength and Shape.m_fWidth, respectively. To access the nested data members **m_fX** and **m_fY**, each statement uses two dot operators, the first to access the data member **m_UpperLeftCorner** or **m_LowerRightCorner**, and the second to access the nested data member **m_fX** or **m_fY**.

Let me present a programming example. Listing 12-7 shows the source code for the STRUCT3.CPP program, which illustrates C++ structures. The program uses a structure to store an array of characters. The program performs the following tasks:

- Assign values to the structure variable
- Display the unsorted characters in the structure variable
- Sort the characters in the structure variable
- Display the sorted characters in the structure variable

Here is the output of the program in Listing 12-7:

```
Unsorted array is:
A x E t I P q s R G
Sorted array is:
A E G I P R q s t x
```

Listing 12-7
The source code for the STRUCT3.CPP program.

```
// A C++ program that illustrates C++ structures

#include <iostream.h>
#include <iomanip.h>

const int MAX_ELEMS = 100;

struct myArray                                    Structures
{
  char m_cArray[MAX_ELEMS];
  int m_nNumElems;
};

main()
{
  int cArr[] = { 'A', 'x', 'E', 't', 'I',
                'P', 'q', 's', 'R', 'G' };
  int nNumArr = sizeof(cArr) / sizeof(int);
  myArray Array;
```

```
// copy array cArr into structure Array
for (int i = 0; i < nNumArr; i++)
  Array.m_cArray[i] = cArr[i];
Array.m_nNumElems = nNumArr;

cout << "Unsorted array is:\n";
// display elements in structure Array
for (i = 0; i < Array.m_nNumElems; i++)
  cout << Array.m_cArray[i] << ' ';
cout << endl;

for (i = 0; i < (Array.m_nNumElems - 1); i++) {
  for (int j = i + 1; j < Array.m_nNumElems; j++)
    if (Array.m_cArray[i] > Array.m_cArray[j]) {
      char nSwapBuffer = Array.m_cArray[i];
      Array.m_cArray[i] = Array.m_cArray[j];
      Array.m_cArray[j] = nSwapBuffer;
    }
}

cout << "Sorted array is:\n";
// display elements in structure Array
for (i = 0; i < Array.m_nNumElems; i++)
  cout << Array.m_cArray[i] << ' ';
cout << endl;

return 0;
}
```

Listing 12-7 declares the global constant **MAX_ELEMS** and the structure **myArray**. This structure has the following members:

- The **char**-type data member **m_cArray**, which can store up to **MAX_ELEMS** characters
- The **int**-type data member **m_nNumElems**, which stores the number of elements in data member **m_cArray** that contain meaningful data

The function **main** declares and initializes the **char**-type array **cArr**. The function also declares and initializes the variable **nNumArr** (which stores the number of elements in array **cArr**) and the structure variable **Array**. It then performs the following tasks:

- Copy the characters in array **cArr** into the data member **m_cArray** of variable **Array**. This task uses a **for** loop to iterate over the elements of array **cArr**. Each loop iteration accesses an element of data member **m_cArray** using the expression **Array.m_cArray[i]**.

- Assign the value of variable **nNumArr** to the data member **m_nNumElems**. The assignment statement uses the dot operator to access the data member of variable **Array**.

- Display the unsorted characters in variable **Array**. This task uses a **for** loop to access elements of variable **Array** that contain the copied characters. The loop uses the data member **m_nNumElems** (minus one) of variable **Array** as the iteration upper limit. Each loop iteration displays the character in element **Array.m_cArray[i]**.

- Sort the array of characters in variable **Array**. This task uses nested **for** loops that implement the simple bubble sort method. The nested loops access the character using the dot operator with data member **m_cArray**. The loops use the data member **m_nNumElems** of variable **Array** in the loop continuation part.

- Display the sorted characters in variable **Array**. This task also uses a **for** loop to access elements of variable **Array**. The loop uses the data member **m_nNumElems** (minus one) of variable **Array** as the iteration upper limit. Each loop iteration displays the character in element **Array.m_cArray[i]**.

Initializing Structures

C++ allows you to initialize the data members of structures. This feature resembles initializing arrays and follows similar rules. The general syntax for initializing a structure variable is:

```
structureType structureVariable = { value1, value2, ...};
```

The compiler assigns *value1* to the first data member of the variable *structureVariable*, *value2* to the second data member of the variable *structureVariable*, and so on. You need to observe the following rules:

1. The assigned values should be compatible with their corresponding data members.

2. You can declare fewer initializing values than data members. The compiler assigns zeros to the remaining data members of the structure variable.

3. You cannot declare more initializing values than data members.

4. The initializing list sequentially assigns values to data members of nested structures.

5. The initializing list assigns values sequentially to data members that are arrays.

Keep in mind that the task of initializing structures is as simple or complex as the initialized structures themselves.

Here are examples of initializing structures:

```
struct Point
{
  double m_fX;
  double m_fY;
};

struct Rectangle
{
  Point m_UpperLeftCorner;
  Point m_LowerRightCorner;
  double m_fLength;
  double m_fWidth;
};

Point FocalPoint = { 12.4, 34.5 };
Rectangle Shape = { 100.0, 50.0, 200.0, 25.0 };

// calculate the length
Shape.m_fLength = Shape.m_UpperLeftCorner.m_fX -
                  Shape.m_LowerRightCorner.m_fX;
// calculate the width
Shape.m_fWidth = Shape.m_LowerRightCorner.m_fY -
                 Shape.m_UpperLeftCorner.m_fY;
```

This example declares the structures **Point** and **Rectangle**. The example also declares the **Point**-type variable **FocalPoint** and initializes its data members **m_fX** and **m_fY** with the values 12.4 and 34.5. The example further declares the **Rectangle**-type **Shape** and initializes the first two data members **m_UpperLeftCorner** and **m_LowerRightCorner**. Each one of these data members requires two initializing values since they have the type **Point**. Thus, the compiler assigns the values 100.0, 50.0, 200.0, and 25.0 to **Shape.m_UpperLeftCorner.m_fX, Shape.m_UpperLeftCorner.m_fY, Shape.m_LowerRightCorner.m_fX**, and **Shape.m_LowerRightCorner.m_fY**, respectively.

Let me present a programming example. Listing 12-8 shows the source code for the STRUCT4.CPP program, which illustrates initialized structures. This program is very similar to STRUCT3.CPP in Listing 12-7. The main difference is that program STRUCT4.CPP directly initializes the structure variable **Array**.

Here is the output of the program in Listing 12-8:

```
Unsorted array is:
A x E t I P q s R G
Sorted array is:
A E G I P R q s t x
```

Listing 12-8
The source code for the STRUCT4.CPP program.

```cpp
// A C++ program that illustrates initialized structures

#include <iostream.h>
#include <iomanip.h>

const int MAX_ELEMS = 100;

struct myArray
{
  int m_nNumElems;
  char m_cArray[MAX_ELEMS];
};

main()
{
  myArray Array = { 10, 'A', 'x', 'E', 't', 'I',
                        'P', 'q', 's', 'R', 'G' };

  cout << "Unsorted array is:\n";
  // display elements in structure Array
  for (int i = 0; i < Array.m_nNumElems; i++)
    cout << Array.m_cArray[i] << ' ';
  cout << endl;
```

Intialized Structure

```
    for (i = 0; i < (Array.m_nNumElems - 1); i++) {
      for (int j = i + 1; j < Array.m_nNumElems; j++)
        if (Array.m_cArray[i] > Array.m_cArray[j]) {
          char nSwapBuffer = Array.m_cArray[i];
          Array.m_cArray[i] = Array.m_cArray[j];
          Array.m_cArray[j] = nSwapBuffer;
        }
    }

    cout << "Sorted array is:\n";
    // display elements in structure Array
    for (i = 0; i < Array.m_nNumElems; i++)
      cout << Array.m_cArray[i] << ' ';
    cout << endl;

    return 0;
  }
```

Listing 12-8 is very similar to Listing 12-7. Notice that I declare the structure **myArray** by placing the **int**-type data member **m_nNumElems** *before* the array data member **m_cArray**. This order allows me to initialize the data member **m_nNumElems** and some of the elements in the array data member. Had I maintained the order in Listing 12-7, then I would have been obligated to initialize all the elements of data member **m_cArray** before I could initialize data member **m_nNumElems**.

The function **main** declares the structure variable **Array** and initializes it. The compiler assigns the first initializing value, 10, to the data member **m_nNumElems** of variable **Array**. It assigns the second initializing value, the character 'A', to the first element of array member **m_cArray** of variable **Array**. Likewise, the compiler assigns the remaining initializing values to elements 1 through 9 of the data member **m_cArray**. It then assigns null characters to the remaining elements of data member **m_cArray**.

The function **main** in Listing 12-8 manipulates the variable **Array** just as does Listing 12-7 (except that Listing 12-8 does not copy characters to the elements of data member **m_cArray**).

COPYING STRUCTURE VARIABLES

C++ permits the assignment operator to copy the values of one structure variable into another variable that has the same type. Thus, you can copy, in a single statement, multiple data members that include arrays and nested structures.

CODING NOTES

Potential Problems with Copying Structure Variables

The assignment operator performs what is called a *shallow copy* when applied to structure variables. A shallow copy involves copying, bit by bit, the values in the data members of the source variable to the corresponding data members in the target variable. The potential problem with this kind of copying arises when you have data members that are pointers (that is, variables that hold addresses) to other data. In this case, you have more than one structure variable with members that point to the same piece of information. What happens if you update the address held by one pointer variable but not the other? The answer is you end up with corrupted addresses! More about pointers and addresses comes in the next chapter.

Let me present a programming example. Listing 12-9 shows the source code for the STRUCT5.CPP program, which illustrates copying structure variables. Each variable stores an array of characters. The program performs the following tasks:

- Declare two structure variables and initialize only the first one
- Sort the characters in the first structure variable
- Display the characters in the first structure variable
- Copy the characters of the first structure variable into the second structure variable
- Display the characters in the second structure variable

Here is the output of the program in Listing 12-9:

```
Sorted array is:
A E G I P R q s t x
Copy of array is:
A E G I P R q s t x
```

Listing 12-9
The source code for the STRUCT5.CPP program.

```
// A C++ program that illustrates copying structure variables

#include <iostream.h>
#include <iomanip.h>
```

```
const int MAX_ELEMS = 100;

struct myArray
{
  int m_nNumElems;
  char m_cArray[MAX_ELEMS];
};

main()
{
  myArray Array = { 10, 'A', 'x', 'E', 't', 'I',
                        'P', 'q', 's', 'R', 'G' };
  myArray CopyArray;

  // sort the array
  for (int i = 0; i < (Array.m_nNumElems - 1); i++) {
    for (int j = i + 1; j < Array.m_nNumElems; j++)
      if (Array.m_cArray[i] > Array.m_cArray[j]) {
        char nSwapBuffer = Array.m_cArray[i];
        Array.m_cArray[i] = Array.m_cArray[j];
        Array.m_cArray[j] = nSwapBuffer;
      }
  }

  cout << "Sorted array is:\n";
  // display elements in structure Array
  for (i = 0; i < Array.m_nNumElems; i++)
    cout << Array.m_cArray[i] << ' ';
  cout << endl;

  // copy structures
  CopyArray = Array;

  cout << "Copy of array is:\n";
  // display elements in structure CopyArray
  for (i = 0; i < CopyArray.m_nNumElems; i++)
    cout << CopyArray.m_cArray[i] << ' ';
  cout << endl;

  return 0;
}
```

Listing 12-9 declares the structure **myArray** just as Listing 12-8 does. The function **main** declares and initializes the structure variable **Array**. The function also declares (but does not initialize) the structure variable **CopyArray**. It then performs the following tasks:

- Sort the characters in variable **Array**. This task uses nested **for** loops. The loops use the data member of variable **Array** to sort the characters in that variable.

- Display the sorted characters in the structure variable **Array**
- Copy the data members of structure variable **Array** into structure variable **CopyArray**. This task copies the values in data members **m_nNumElems** and **m_cArray**. Thus, the assignment statement copies in one swoop (and without using a loop) the array elements of variable **Array**.
- Display the characters in variable **CopyArray**. This task uses a **for** loop to display the first **CopyArray.m_nNumElems** elements in the array **CopyArray.m_cArray**.

Unions

Unions are special kinds of structures that overlay the space of their data members. The size of a union equals the size of its largest data member. C++ offers unions to be compatible with C. Unions were more popular in the days of limited memory resources. They serve two main purposes: first, to conserve memory space by storing different kinds of mutually exclusive information, and second, to perform data conversion using data members that access parts of other data members in the same union. The general syntax for declaring a union type is:

```
union unionName
{
  type1 dataMember1;
  type2 dataMember2;
  // other data members
};
```

The union declares its data members, which have either predefined data types or previously defined types (such as enumerated types, structures, other unions, or arrays). Here are examples of unions:

```
union XInt
{
  long m_lInt;
  int m_nInt[2];
};
```

```
union XFloat
{
  float m_fX;
  double m_lfX;
}
```

The first example declares the union **XInt**, which has the **long**-type data member **m_lInt** and the two-element array **int**-type data member **m_nInt**. Since the size of a **long** is equal to twice the size of an **int**, the size of union **XInt** is equal to **sizeof(long)** (which is also equal to **2 * sizeof(int)**).

The second example declares the union **XFloat** with its **float**-type and **double**-type data members **m_fX** and **m_lfX**, respectively. Since the **double** type occupies more space than the **float** type, the size of the union **XFloat** is equal to the size of the **double** type. The above two examples represent the two kinds of purposes for using unions.

Declaring union variables and accessing data members in unions is very similar to doing so with structures. Remember that the data members in unions do not complement each other as in structures. Instead, they store their data in the same location.

C++ regards unions, like structures, as special kinds of classes. You can include constructors in unions and use member functions to extract information from a union variable.

Let's look at a programming example. Listing 12-10 shows the source code for the UNION1.CPP program, which illustrates unions. The program uses a union that has a **long**-type data member and a two-element-array **unsigned**-type data member. The program performs the following tasks:

- Assign a value to the **long**-type data member
- Display the value of the **long**-type data member
- Display the values of the **unsigned**-type data member (which is a two-element array)
- Assign values to the **unsigned**-type data member
- Display the values of the **unsigned**-type data member
- Display the value of the **long**-type data member

The program illustrates how to access the lower and higher parts of a long integer using unsigned integers. If you use the **int** type instead, you get different results, because of the sign bit.

Here is the output of the program in Listing 12-10:

```
Assigning a value to data member m_lValue
Long integer is 65536
Low unsigned integer is 0
High unsigned integer is 1

Assigning a value to data member m_nValue
Low unsigned integer is 255
High unsigned integer is 255
Long integer is 16711935
```

Listing 12-10
The source code for the UNION1.CPP program.

```cpp
// A C++ program that illustrates unions

#include <iostream.h>
#include <iomanip.h>

union XInt                          // Union
{
  long m_lValue;
  unsigned m_uValue[2];
};

main()
{
  XInt myInt;

  // initialize the data member m_lValue of the union
  myInt.m_lValue = 65536;

  cout << "Assigning a value to data member m_lValue\n";
  cout << "Long integer is " << myInt.m_lValue << endl;
  cout << "Low unsigned integer is "
       << myInt.m_uValue[0] << endl;
  cout << "High unsigned integer is "
       << myInt.m_uValue[1] << endl;

  cout << endl;
  myInt.m_uValue[0] = 0xff;
  myInt.m_uValue[1] = 0xff;
  cout << "Assigning a value to data member m_uValue\n";
  cout << "Low unsigned integer is "
       << myInt.m_uValue[0] << endl;
```

```
    cout << "High unsigned integer is "
         << myInt.m_uValue[1] << endl;
    cout << "Long integer is " << myInt.m_lValue << endl;

    return 0;
}
```

Listing 12-10 declares the unions **XInt** with the following data members:

- The **long**-type data member **m_lValue**
- The **unsigned**-type array member **m_uValue**, which stores two elements

The function **main** declares the **XInt**-type variable **myInt** and performs the following tasks:

- Assign the integer 65536 to the data member **m_lValue** of variable **myInt**
- Display the value of data member **myInt.m_lValue**
- Display the value of data member **myInt.m_uValue[0]**. This number is the unsigned value of the lower part of data member **m_lValue**.
- Display the value of the data member **myInt.m_uValue[1]**. This number is the unsigned value of the higher part of data member **m_lValue**.
- Assign new values to the data member **m_uValue**
- Display the values in the data member **m_uValue**
- Display the equivalent **long**-type value using the data member **m_lValue**

Listing 12-10 allows you to directly access the data members of the union **XInt**. You can declare these data members as protected and define member functions that access the data members.

Listing 12-11 shows the source code for the UNION2.CPP program, which illustrates a union that uses member functions to access the values in its data members. The listing declares a new version of union **XInt**. This version declares the data members as protected and offers the member functions **setLong**, **setHighUnsigned**, **setLowUnsigned**, **getLong**, **getHighUnsigned**, and **getLowUnsigned** to access the data members. The program UNION2.CPP illustrates a level of abstraction that makes a union act more like a memory black box.

Here is the output of the program in Listing 12-11:

```
Assigning a value to data member m_lValue
Long integer is 65536
Low unsigned integer is 0
High unsigned integer is 1

Assigning a value to data member m_uValue
Low unsigned integer is 255
High unsigned integer is 255
Long integer is 16711935
```

Listing 12-11

The source code for the UNION2.CPP program, which illustrates a union that uses member functions.

```cpp
// A C++ program that illustrates
// unions that have member functions

#include <iostream.h>
#include <iomanip.h>

union XInt
{
  XInt(long lValue = 0)
    { m_lValue = lValue; }
  void setLong(long lValue)
   { m_lValue = lValue; }
  long getLong()
    { return m_lValue; }
  void setLowUnsigned(unsigned uValue)
    { m_uValue[0] = uValue; }
  void setHighUnsigned(unsigned uValue)
    { m_uValue[1] = uValue; }
  unsigned getLowUnsigned()
    { return m_uValue[0]; }
  unsigned getHighUnsigned()
    { return m_uValue[1]; }

  protected:
    long m_lValue;
    unsigned m_uValue[2];
};

main()
{
  XInt myInt;
```

```
// initialize the data member m_lValue of the union
myInt.setLong(65536);

cout << "Assigning a value to data member m_lValue\n";
cout << "Long integer is " << myInt.getLong() << endl;
cout << "Low unsigned integer is "
     << myInt.getLowUnsigned() << endl;
cout << "High unsigned integer is "
     << myInt.getHighUnsigned() << endl;

cout << endl;
myInt.setLowUnsigned(0xff);
myInt.setHighUnsigned(0xff);
cout << "Assigning a value to data member m_uValue\n";
cout << "Low unsigned integer is "
     << myInt.getLowUnsigned() << endl;
cout << "High unsigned integer is "
     << myInt.getHighUnsigned() << endl;
cout << "Long integer is " << myInt.getLong() << endl;


return 0;
}
```

Listing 12-11 shows that the function **main** performs the same tasks as in Listing 12-10, except that it sends C++ messages to the union variable **myInt**. These messages allow the function **main** to set and query the values in the data members of the union **XInt**.

Reference Variables

Reference variables are ali ases to existing variables and do not have their own storage allocated. C++ requires that the declaration of a reference variable include its initialization. It is important to point out that the initial value of a reference variable is permanent. You cannot make the reference variable an alias to another variable! The general syntax for declaring a reference variable is:

```
type& refVar = referencedVariable;
```

You can use a reference variable to access the value of a referenced variable. Here is an example of declaring and using a reference variable:

```
int nNum = 10;
int& rNum = nNum;

cout << rNum << "\n"; // displays 10
rNum++; // nNum is now 11
cout << nNum << "\n"; // displays 11
```

This example declares and initializes the **int**-type variable **nNum**. The example also declares the reference variable **rNum** and initializes it using the variable **nNum**. The first output statement displays the value of variable **nNum** using the reference variable **rNum**. The following statement applies the increment operator to the reference variable **rNum**, which has the effect of incrementing the value in variable **nNum**. The second output statement displays the new value in variable **nNum** (which is now 11).

Reference variables are more useful with class instances than with variables of predefined types. You can use a reference to a class together with typecasting to access the data of an object in a particular way.

Enumerated Types as Function Parameters

You can declare enumerated types as function parameters. To prevent the function from altering the argument of an enumerated type parameter, use the keyword const. Here is an example of using an enumerated type as a function parameter:

```
enum Logical { FALSE, TRUE };
showArray(int* nArray, const char* pszMsg = "",
          const Logical bOneLine = TRUE);
```

This example declares the enumerated type **Logical** and uses it in declaring the last parameter of function **showArray**. The constant parameter **bOneLine** has the enumerated type **Logical** and the default argument **TRUE**.

Let's look at a programming example. Listing 12-12 shows the source code for the ENUM7.CPP program, which illustrates passing enumerated types as function parameters. The program uses a class to model an object that moves at random. The program uses the random-walk object to move at random in any of the four directions (up, down, left, and right) and at a random vertical or horizontal distance of 1 to 100. The program displays the new coordinates along with the new distance and angle between the new coordinates and the origin (which are also the initial coordinates of the random-walk object).

Here is sample output of the program in Listing 12-12:

```
Object is at (62, 0)
Distance from starting point = 62
Angle = 0 degrees
Object is at (62, 74)
Distance from starting point = 96.5401
Angle = 50.0425 degrees
Object is at (62, 78)
Distance from starting point = 99.6393
Angle = 51.5198 degrees
Object is at (62, 144)
Distance from starting point = 156.78
Angle = 66.7054 degrees
Object is at (-36, 144)
Distance from starting point = 148.432
Angle = -75.9638 degrees
```

Listing 12-12

The source code for the ENUM7.CPP program, which illustrates passing enumerated types as function parameters.

```cpp
// A C++ program that illustrates enumerated types
// used as function parameters

#include <iostream.h>
#include <iomanip.h>
#include <stdio.h>
#include <stdlib.h>
#include <time.h>
#include <math.h>

const double PI = 4 * atan(1);
const double RAD2DEG = 180.0 / PI;
const double EPSILON = 1.0e-9;

inline double sqr(double x)
{
  return x * x;
}

enum Direction { Left, Right, Up, Down };
enum Logical { FALSE, TRUE };
```

```cpp
class Rover
{
  public:
    Rover(int nX = 0, int nY = 0);
    void Move(int nDisplacement, Direction eDir);
    void Show(const char* pszMsg = "", Logical bEmitCR = TRUE);
    double getDistanceTraveled()
      {
          return sqrt(sqr(m_nX - m_nX0) +
                      sqr(m_nY - m_nY0));
      }
    double getAngle();

  protected:
    int m_nX;
    int m_nY;
    int m_nX0;
    int m_nY0;
};

Rover::Rover(int nX, int nY)
{
  m_nX = nX;
  m_nY = nY;
  m_nX0 = nX;
  m_nY0 = nY;
}

void Rover::Move(int nDisplacement, Direction eDir)
{
  switch (eDir) {
    case Left:
      m_nX -= nDisplacement;
      break;

    case Right:
      m_nX += nDisplacement;
      break;

    case Down:
      m_nY -= nDisplacement;
      break;

    case Up:
      m_nY += nDisplacement;
      break;
  }
}

void Rover::Show(const char* pszMsg, Logical bEmitCR)
{
  cout << pszMsg;
```

```
    cout << "(" << m_nX << ", " << m_nY << ")";
    if (bEmitCR)
      cout << endl;
}

double Rover::getAngle()
{
  double fX = double(m_nX - m_nX0);
  double fY = double(m_nY - m_nY0);

  return (fabs(fX) > EPSILON) ?
         atan(fY / fX) * RAD2DEG : 90;
}


main()
{
  const int MAX = 5;
  const int MIN_DIST = 1;
  const int MAX_DIST = 100;
  Rover RollingStone;
  int nDist;
  Direction eDir;

  // reseed random-number generator
  srand((unsigned)time(NULL));

  for (int i = 0; i < MAX; i++) {
    nDist = rand() % MAX_DIST + MIN_DIST;
    eDir = Direction(rand() % 4);
    RollingStone.Move(nDist, eDir);
    RollingStone.Show("Object is at ");
    cout << "Distance from starting point = "
         << RollingStone.getDistanceTraveled() << endl
         << "Angle = "
         << RollingStone.getAngle()
         << " degrees\n";
  }

  return 0;
}
```

Listing 12-12 declares global constants, the inline function **sqr**, the enumerated types **Direction** and **Logical**, and the class **Rover**. The enumerated type **Direction** has the enumerators **Left**, **Right**, **Up**, and **Down**. The enumerated type **Logical** has the enumerators **FALSE** and **TRUE**.

The class **Rover** declares protected and public members. The protected members are:

- The int-type data members **m_nX** and **m_nY**, which store the current coordinates of the class instance

- The int-type data members **m_nX0** and **m_nY0**, which store the initial coordinates of the class instance

The class **Rover** declares the following public members:

- The constructor initializes the data members. The default arguments set the initial and current coordinates to (0, 0).

- The member function **Move** moves the class instance by **nDisplacement** units and in the direction specified by the **Direction**-type parameter **eDir**. Thus, the member function moves the class instance in one of the four directions.

- The member function **Show** displays the current coordinates. It uses the **Logical**-type parameter **bEmitCR** to determine whether or not to emit a carriage return after displaying the current coordinates. The default argument for parameter **bEmitCR** is **TRUE**.

- The member function **getDistanceTraveled** returns the distance between the current and initial coordinates.

- The member function **getAngle** returns the angle (in degrees) of the line drawn between the current and initial coordinates.

The definition of member function **Move** uses a **switch** statement to examine the value of the **Direction**-type parameter **eDir**. The **switch** statement updates the proper coordinate using the value of the parameter **nDisplacement**.

The function **main** declares the local constants **MAX**, **MIN_DIST**, and **MAX_DIST**. It also declares the int-type variable **nDist**, the **Direction**-type variable **eDir**, and the object **RollingStone** as an instance of class **Rover**. The function reseeds the random-number generator and then performs the following tasks for **MAX** number of times:

- Obtain a random number in the range of **MIN_DIST** and **MAX_DIST** and store it in variable **nDist**

- Obtain a random direction and store it in variable **eDir**

- Move the object **RollingStone** by sending it the C++ message **Move**. The arguments for this message are variables **nDist** and **eDir**. These variables provide the random distance and direction for moving object **RollingStone**.

- Display the current coordinates of object **RollingStone**

- Display the distance between the current and initial locations of object **RollingStone**. This task involves sending the C++ message **getDistanceTraveled** to the object **RollingStone**.

- Display the angle of the line drawn between the current and initial locations of object **RollingStone**. This task involves sending the C++ message **getAngle** to the object **RollingStone**.

Structures as Function Parameters

You can declare structures (and unions) as parameters of functions. To prevent a function from altering the argument of a structure parameter, use the keyword const. Passing a structure by value serves to supply the function with data. Here is an example of using a structure as a function parameter:

```
struct basicStat
{
  int nCount;
  double fSumX;
  double fSumXSqr;
};

double getMean(const basicStat Stats);
double getSdev(const basicStat Stats);
```

This example declares the structure **basicStat** and uses it to declare the parameter **Stats** in functions **getMean** and **getSdev**. The structure **basicStat** stores the number of observations, their sum, and the sum of their squares.

Let's look at a programming example. Listing 12-13 shows the source code for the STRUCT6.CPP program, which illustrates passing structures as function parameters. The program uses a structure that stores the number of observations, the sum of the observations, and the sum of the observations squared. The program generates random data and uses a statistical data structure to calculate the mean and standard deviation values.

Here is sample output for the program in Listing 12-13:

```
Number of observations = 300
Mean = 491.893
Standard deviation = 287.157
```

Listing 12-13
The source code for the STRUCT6.CPP program.

```cpp
// A C++ program that illustrates passing
// structures as function parameters

#include <iostream.h>
#include <stdlib.h>
#include <time.h>
#include <math.h>

const double BAD_RESULT = -1.0e+30;

inline double sqr(double x)
{ return x * x; }

// declare the structure for basic statistical data
struct BasicStat {
  int m_nNumData;
  double m_fSumX;
  double m_fSumXSqr;
};

// declare prototypes
BasicStat initBasicStat();
BasicStat addData(double fArray[], int nNumElems,
                  BasicStat BasStat);
double getMean(BasicStat BasStat);
double getSdev(BasicStat BasStat);

main()
{
  const int MAX_SETS = 3;
  const int MAX = 100;
  const int MIN_NUM = 1;
  const int MAX_NUM = 1000;
  double fData[MAX];
  double fMean, fSdev;
  int i;
```

```
    // declare a structure
    BasicStat StatData;

    // reseed random-number generator
    srand((unsigned)time(NULL));

    // initialize the structure variable StatData
    StatData = initBasicStat();

    for (int nDataSet = 0; nDataSet < MAX_SETS; nDataSet++) {
      // generate random data
      for (i = 0; i < MAX; i++)
        fData[i] = double(rand() % MAX_NUM + MIN_NUM);
      // update statistical summations
      StatData = addData(fData, MAX, StatData);
    }

    // calculate mean value
    fMean = getMean(StatData);
    // calculate standard deviation
    fSdev = getSdev(StatData);

    cout << "Number of observations = "
         << StatData.m_nNumData << "\n"
         << "Mean = " << fMean << "\n"
         << "Standard deviation = "
         << fSdev;

  return 0;
}

BasicStat initBasicStat()
{
  BasicStat BasStat = { 0, 0.0, 0.0 };
  return BasStat;
}

BasicStat addData(double fArray[], int nNumElems,
                  BasicStat BasStat)
{
  BasStat.m_nNumData += nNumElems;
  for (int i = 0; i < nNumElems; i++) {
    BasStat.m_fSumX += fArray[i];
    BasStat.m_fSumXSqr += sqr(fArray[i]);
  }
  return BasStat;
}

double getMean(BasicStat BasStat)
{
  if (BasStat.m_nNumData > 0)
    return BasStat.m_fSumX / BasStat.m_nNumData;
  else
    return BAD_RESULT;
}
```

```
double getSdev(BasicStat BasStat)
{
  if (BasStat.m_nNumData > 0)
    return sqrt((BasStat.m_fSumXSqr -
                 sqr(BasStat.m_fSumX) / BasStat.m_nNumData) /
                (BasStat.m_nNumData - 1));
  else
    return BAD_RESULT;
}
```

Listing 12-13 declares the structure **BasicStat**, which has the following data members:

- The **int**-type data member **m_nNumData**, which stores the number of observations

- The **double**-type data member **m_fSumX**, which stores the sum of the observations

- The **double**-type data member **m_fSumXSqr**, which stores the sum of the observations squared

The listing declares the following functions:

- The parameterless function **initBasicStat** returns an initialized **BasicStat** structure. The definition of this function declares, initializes, and returns a local **BasicStat** variable.

- The function **addData** updates the statistical summations in the structure **BasicStat**. The parameter **fArray** passes an array of **double**-type values. The **int**-type parameter **nNumElems** specifies the number of array elements. The **BasicStat**-type parameter **BasStat** supplies the input statistical summations structure. The function returns the updated value of the structure. The definition of this function updates the data members of the parameter **BasStat** and returns that parameter.

- The function **getMean** returns the mean value of the data supplied by the **BasicStat**-type parameter **BasStat**.

- The function **getSdev** returns the standard deviation of the data supplied by the same **BasicStat**-type parameter **BasStat**.

The function **main** declares a number of local constants, the **double**-type array **fData**, the **double**-type variables **fMean** and **fSdev**, the **int**-type variable **i**, and the **BasicStat**-type variable **StatData**. The function reseeds the random-number generator and then initializes the variable **StatData** by calling function **initBasicStat**. The statement assigns the result of this function call to the variable **StatData**. The function then uses a **for** loop to perform the following tasks for **MAX_SETS** number of times:

- Generate **MAX** number of random data in the range of **MIN_NUM** to **MAX_NUM**. This task uses a **for** loop to store the random numbers in the array **fData**.

- Update the statistical summations in variable **StatData**. This task calls the function **addData** and passes the arguments **fData**, **MAX**, and **StatData**. Thus, the function **addData** uses variable **StatData** as an argument and returns it as the result of the function call.

Once the loop terminates, function **main** calculates the mean and standard deviation statistics by calling functions **getMean** and **getSdev**, respectively. The argument for each function call is variable **StatData**. The function **main** stores the mean and standard deviation in variables **fMean** and **fSdev**, respectively. It then displays the number of observations and the mean and standard deviation statistics.

References to Enumerated Types as Function Parameters

You can use references to enumerated types as function parameters either to establish a two-way flow of data between a function and its caller or to return enumerators to the function caller. Here is an example of using references to enumerated types as function parameters:

```
enum weekDay { Sunday, Monday, Tuesday, Wednesday, Thursday,
               Friday, Saturday };
void next(weekday& eDay /* input and output */);
void nextAndPrevious(weekDay eToday, /* input */
                     weekDay& eTomorrow, /* output */
                     weekDay& eYesterday  /* output */);
```

This example shows the enumerated type **weekDay** and the declarations of functions **next** and **nextAndPrevious**. The function **next** has the reference enumerated-type parameter **eDay**, which passes the current day to the function and returns the next day to the function caller. The function **nextAndPrevious** has three enumerated-type parameters: The first parameter **eToday** passes a day enumerator to the function, whereas the reference parameters **eTomorrow** and **eYesterday** pass the enumerators for the next and previous days, respectively, to the caller of the function.

Let me present a programming example. Listing 12-14 shows the source code for the ENUM8.CPP program, which illustrates using reference enumerated types as function parameters. I developed this program by editing the ENUM3.CPP program. The program ENUM8.CPP performs the following tasks:

- Generate three random integers between 0 and 6
- Translate the generated integer into a **weekDay**-enumerated value
- Display the name of the day for that enumerated value as well as the names of the subsequent and preceding days

Here is sample output for the program in Listing 12-14:

```
Day # 1
Today is Friday
Tomorrow is Saturday
Yesterday was Thursday

Day # 2
Today is Tuesday
Tomorrow is Wednesday
Yesterday was Monday

Day # 3
Today is Thursday
Tomorrow is Friday
Yesterday was Wednesday
```

Listing 12-14

The source code for the ENUM8.CPP program.

```cpp
// A C++ program that illustrates using reference
// enumerated types as function parameters

#include <iostream.h>
#include <iomanip.h>
#include <stdlib.h>
#include <time.h>

const int TRUE = 1;
const int FALSE = 0;
typedef int Logical;

// declare enumerated type
enum weekDay { Sunday, Monday, Tuesday, Wednesday,
               Thursday, Friday, Saturday };

class myDay
{
  public:
    // constructors
    myDay(weekDay aDay)
      { setDay(aDay); }
    myDay(int nDayNum = 0)
      { setDay(nDayNum); }

    void show(const char* pszMsg = "",
              Logical bEmitCR = TRUE);
    void setDay(int nDayNum);
    void setDay(weekDay aDay)
      { m_eDay = aDay; }
    weekDay getDay()
      { return m_eDay; }
    void getNextAndPrevious(weekDay& eNextDay,
                            weekDay& ePrevDay);

  protected:
    weekDay m_eDay;
};

void myDay::show(const char* pszMsg, Logical bEmitCR)
{
  cout << pszMsg;
  switch (m_eDay) {
    case Sunday:
      cout << "Sunday";
      break;

    case Monday:
      cout << "Monday";
      break;
```

```
    case Tuesday:
      cout << "Tuesday";
      break;

    case Wednesday:
      cout << "Wednesday";
      break;

    case Thursday:
      cout << "Thursday";
      break;

    case Friday:
      cout << "Friday";
      break;

    case Saturday:
      cout << "Saturday";
      break;
  }

  if (bEmitCR)
    cout << endl;
}

void myDay::setDay(int nDayNum)
{
  if (nDayNum >= 0 && nDayNum < 7)
    m_eDay = weekDay(nDayNum);
  else
    m_eDay = Sunday;
}

void myDay::getNextAndPrevious(weekDay& eNextDay,
                              weekDay& ePrevDay)
{
  // get the next day
  if (m_eDay != Saturday)
    eNextDay = weekDay(int(m_eDay) + 1);
  else
    eNextDay = Sunday;

  // get the previous day
  if (m_eDay != Sunday)
    ePrevDay = weekDay(int(m_eDay) - 1);
  else
    ePrevDay = Saturday;
}
```

```
main()
{
  const int MAX = 3;
  myDay makeMyDay;
  weekDay eNextDay, ePrevDay;

  // reseed random-number generator
  srand((unsigned)time(NULL));
  for (int i = 0; i < MAX; i++) {
    // get random day number
    int n = rand() % 7;
    makeMyDay.setDay(n);
    // display today
    cout << "Day # " << (i+1) << endl;
    makeMyDay.show("Today is ");

    makeMyDay.getNextAndPrevious(eNextDay, ePrevDay);

    // display tomorrow
    makeMyDay.setDay(eNextDay);
    makeMyDay.show("Tomorrow is ");

    // display yesterday
    makeMyDay.setDay(ePrevDay);
    makeMyDay.show("Yesterday was ");
    cout << endl;
  }

  return 0;
}
```

Listing 12-14 declares the enumerated type **weekDay** and the class **myDay**. The declarations of the enumerated type and the class are very similar to those of Listing 12-3. The main difference is in the definitions of the following member functions:

- The class has two constructors. The first takes a **weekDay**-type parameter, whereas the second has an **int**-type parameter.

- The class has two versions of member function **setDay**. The first takes a **weekDay**-type parameter, whereas the second has an **int**-type parameter.

- The member function **getNextAndPrevious** has the two reference parameters **eNextDay** and **ePrevDay**, which return the next and previous day enumerators, respectively. The member function does not alter the value in data member **m_eDay**.

The function **main** declares the constant **MAX**, the object **makeMyDay** as an instance of class **myDay**, and the **weekDay**-type variables **eNextDay** and **ePrevDay**. The function reseeds the random number generator and then uses a **for** loop to perform and repeat the following tasks:

- Obtain a random number in the range of 0 to 6 and store it in the local variable **n**

- Set the day in object **makeMyDay** by sending it the C++ message **setDay**. The argument for this message is the variable **n**. This message translates the integer value that represents the day number into an enumerator that is stored in the data member **makeMyDay.m_eDay**.

- Display the day count and the name of the current day. This task sends the C++ message **show** (with the string literal argument "Today is ") to the object **makeMyDay**.

- Obtain the next and previous days by sending the C++ message **getNextAndPrevious** to the object **makeMyDay**. The arguments for this message are the variables **eNextDay** and **ePrevDay**, which obtain the next and previous day enumerators, respectively.

- Set the object **makeMyDay** to the next day by sending it the C++ message **setDay**. The argument for this message is the variable **eNextDay**.

- Display the name of the next day. This task sends the C++ message **show** with the string literal argument "Tomorrow is " to the object **makeMyDay**.

- Set the object **makeMyDay** to the previous day by sending it the C++ message **setDay**. The argument for this message is the variable **ePrevDay**.

- Display the name of the previous day. This task sends the C++ message **show** with the string literal argument "Yesterday was " to the object **makeMyDay**.

References to Structures as Function Parameters

You can use references to structures as function parameters either to establish a two-way flow of data between a function or its caller or to return information to the function caller. Here is an example of using references to structures as function parameters:

```
struct intRange
{
  int m_nMinVal;
  int m_nMaxVal;
  int m_nTheVal;
  int m_nErrorCode;
};

void setRange(int nMin, int nMax, intRange& anInt);
void setVal(int nNum, intRange& anInt);
```

This example declares the structure **intRange** to support a range of integers. The example also declares the prototypes for the functions **setRange** and **setVal**. These functions each have the reference parameter **anInt**, which supports two-way data flow between the function and its caller. The definition of the function **setRange** could show that it assigns the values of the parameters **nMin** and **nMax** to the data members **m_nMinVal** and **m_nMaxVal** of the parameter **anInt**. The function **setVal**, for its part, could assign the value of the parameter **nNum** to the data member **m_nTheVal** of parameter **anInt**, if that value lay in the range defined by data members **m_nMinVal** and **m_nMaxVal**. The latter function could also store the error code of its operation in the data member **m_nErrorCode**.

Let me present an example. Listing 12-15 shows the source code for the STRUCT7.CPP program, which illustrates using reference structures as function parameters. I created this program by modifying the source code of the STRUCT6.CPP program in Listing 12-13. The programs STRUCT6.CPP and STRUCT7.CPP perform the same tasks of generating the basic statistics for 300 random numbers.

Here is sample output for the program in Listing 12-15:

```
Number of observations = 300
Mean = 517.18
Standard deviation = 280.593
```

Listing 12-15
The source code for the STRUCT7.CPP program.

```cpp
// A C++ program that illustrates reference structures
// as function parameters

#include <iostream.h>
#include <stdlib.h>
#include <time.h>
#include <math.h>

const double BAD_RESULT = -1.0e+30;

inline double sqr(double x)
{ return x * x; }

// declare the structure for basic statistical data
struct BasicStat {
  int m_nNumData;
  double m_fSumX;
  double m_fSumXSqr;
};

// declare prototypes
void initBasicStat(BasicStat& BasStat);
void addData(double fArray[], int nNumElems,
             BasicStat& BasStat);
double getMean(const BasicStat& BasStat);
double getSdev(const BasicStat& BasStat);

main()
{
  const int MAX_SETS = 3;
  const int MAX = 100;
  const int MIN_NUM = 1;
  const int MAX_NUM = 1000;
  double fData[MAX];
  double fMean, fSdev;
  int i;
  // declare a structure
  BasicStat StatData;

  // reseed random-number generator
  srand((unsigned)time(NULL));

  // initialize the structure variable StatData
  initBasicStat(StatData);

  for (int nDataSet = 0; nDataSet < MAX_SETS; nDataSet++) {
    // generate random data
    for (i = 0; i < MAX; i++)
      fData[i] = double(rand() % MAX_NUM + MIN_NUM);
    // update statistical summations
    addData(fData, MAX, StatData);
  }
```

```
  // calculate mean value
  fMean = getMean(StatData);
  // calculate standard deviation
  fSdev = getSdev(StatData);

  cout << "Number of observations = "
       << StatData.m_nNumData << "\n"
       << "Mean = " << fMean << "\n"
       << "Standard deviation = "
       << fSdev;

  return 0;
}

void initBasicStat(BasicStat& BasStat)
{
  BasStat.m_nNumData = 0;
  BasStat.m_fSumX = 0.;
  BasStat.m_fSumXSqr= 0.;
}

void addData(double fArray[], int nNumElems,
             BasicStat& BasStat)
{
  BasStat.m_nNumData += nNumElems;
  for (int i = 0; i < nNumElems; i++) {
    BasStat.m_fSumX += fArray[i];
    BasStat.m_fSumXSqr += sqr(fArray[i]);
  }
}

double getMean(const BasicStat& BasStat)
{
  if (BasStat.m_nNumData > 0)
    return BasStat.m_fSumX / BasStat.m_nNumData;
   else
    return BAD_RESULT;
}

double getSdev(const BasicStat& BasStat)
{
  if (BasStat.m_nNumData > 0)
   return sqrt((BasStat.m_fSumXSqr -
                sqr(BasStat.m_fSumX) / BasStat.m_nNumData) /
                (BasStat.m_nNumData - 1));
  else
    return BAD_RESULT;

}
```

Listing 12-15 is very similar to Listing 12-13. The main differences are these:

- The function **initBasicStat** has the **BasicStat**-type reference parameter **BasStat**, which returns the initialized structure. The function has the **void** return type.
- The function **addData** has the **BasicStat**-type reference parameter **BasStat**, which supports a two-way data flow between the function and its caller. The function has the **void** return type.
- The functions **getMean** and **getSdev** declare their parameters using **const BasicStat&** instead of just **BasicStat**.

The function **main** in Listing 12-15 uses the new forms of functions **initBasicStat** and **addData** to initialize and update the statistical summations, respectively.

Summary

This chapter discussed creating alias types as well as defining enumerated types, structures, and unions. You also learned about assigning explicit values to the enumerators of an enumerated type, initializing the data members of a structure, and using member functions with unions. The chapter further discussed using enumerated types, structures, references to enumerated types, and references to structures as parameters of functions.

The next chapter presents pointers, which are a powerful component of C++.

CHAPTER

13 Pointers

*T*his chapter presents pointers, which are very special and powerful kinds of variables. You will learn the basics concerning the nature of pointers, including how to assign pointers to existing variables and the difference between pointers and references. You will then learn how to use pointers with more complex data types, as you work with pointers to arrays, pointers to structures, and pointers to classes. The chapter takes up some more advanced features of pointers (pointers and dynamic variables, constant pointers, and far pointers) and finally delves into the uses of pointers in conjunction with function calls: pointers to arrays as function parameters, pointers to enumerated types as function parameters, pointers to structures as function parameters, pointers to functions, and pointers to arrays of functions.

Overview

If you are a BASIC or FORTRAN programmer, then pointers are most likely new to you. If you approach the subject of pointers with a certain level of anxiety, then relax! The truth of the matter is that all programming languages use pointers. Some programming languages, such as BASIC and FORTRAN, however, use pointers only internally and do not make them available to programmers.

Pointers!

Remember these two important aspects of a pointer: A pointer stores an address of an item and knows about the data type of that item.

Programming the first computers was a real production! The programmers manipulated data in the computer's memory by directly specifying the memory address that contained the data. You can easily guess that direct memory manipulation did not make programming computers very endearing to programmers! The software developer community decided to develop programming languages, such as FORTRAN, where the programmer uses names for the memory locations (that is, variables) and let the compiler or interpreter worry about translating (or mapping, if you prefer) the names of the variables into their memory locations. In fact, this programming feature, which we now take for granted, also took memory management (a *very* delicate task) out of the hands of the programmer. Thus the name of a variable has an address and a data type associated with it. This association allows the compiler or interpreter to properly access and interpret the data in the computer's memory. In addition, the name of a function has an address associated with it that tells the compiler or interpreter where the function's executable code lies.

So, what is a pointer? A pointer is a special variable that stores the address of another variable or object. Knowing the address of a variable or object allows a pointer to access the data in that variable or object. In addition, a pointer has a data type associated with it. This association allows a pointer to interpret the data it accesses.

Declaring Pointers

As with ordinary variables, you must declare a pointer before you can use it. The general syntax for declaring a pointer is:

```
// form 1
type* pointerName;
// form 2
type *pointerName;
```

CODING NOTES

Void* Pointers

C++ permits you to declare the general-purpose **void*** pointer that allows you to access data chunks. To use that data, you need to typecast its address using a pointer to a non-**void** data type. In addition, C++ does not support pointer arithmetic with **void*** pointers since there is no specified data size.

This syntax declares a pointer and states the data type associated with the pointer. Keep in mind that this is *not* the type of the pointer itself but the type of the data *accessed* by the pointer. The two forms show that you need to place the * character either right after the type associated with the pointer or right before the name of the pointer.

Here are examples of declaring pointers:

```
int* pnCount;
char* pszName;
int *pnInt1, *pnInt2;
```

The first example declares the pointer **pnCount** as a pointer to an **int**-type variable. The second example declares the pointer **pszName** as a pointer to a **char**-type variable or an ASCIIZ string. The last example declares two pointers **pnInt1** and **pnInt2** as pointers to **int**-type variables. Notice that in the case of declaring multiple pointers, the * character appears before the name of each pointer. The following declaration is also valid:

```
int* pnInt1, *pnInt2;
```

What about the following declaration?

```
int* pnInt1, pnInt2;
```

The answer is that the latter example declares the **int**-type pointer **pnInt1** and the **int**-type variable whose name is **pnInt2**.

Since pointers store the address of other items, it is imperative to *properly initialize* pointers *before* using them. If you are new to pointers, then you need to keep this rule dear to your heart, or you will be courting the danger of crashing your system! The next sections show you how to initialize and use pointers with different kinds of items.

What if a pointer points nowhere particular? You can assign a null address (the value 0) to a C++ pointer and later test the pointer against a 0 (or null) value to determine whether or not it points to anywhere significant. Note that you must explicitly initialize pointers to null addresses before you compare their addresses with 0. Some functions, such as the operator **new**, return null addresses if their pointer-related operations fail.

POINTERS TO EXISTING VARIABLES

You can store the address of an existing variable in a pointer that has the same associated type. The general syntax for declaring a pointer and initializing it with the address of an existing variable is:

```
type variableName [= initialValue];
type* pointerName = &variableName;
```

This syntax uses the address-of operator **&** to obtain the address of the variable and assign it to the pointer. Here is an example:

```
int nCount = 0;
int* pnCount = &nCount;
```

The example declares and initializes the **int**-type variable **nCount** and also declares and initializes the **int**-type pointer **pnCount**. The initialization step stores the address of variable **nCount** in the pointer **pnCount**.

C++ allows you to defer initializing a pointer by assigning it the address of a variable in a statement separate from the declaration of the pointer. The general syntax for assigning an address to a pointer is:

```
type variableName;
type* pointerName;
// statements
pointerName = &variableName;
```

The address assignment uses the address-of operator **&**. Here is an example:

```
int nCount;
int* pnCount;

cin >> nCount;
pnCount = &nCount;
```

The example declares the int-type variable **nCount** and the int-type pointer **pnCount**. It then assigns a value to variable **nCount** from the input stream and finally stores the address of variable **nCount** in the pointer **pnCount**.

Once you assign the address of an existing variable to a pointer, you can access the data in that variable using the pointer. This access requires the indirection operator *, which should appear *before* the name of the pointer. Here is an example of using the indirection operator:

```
int nCount;
int* pnCount;

cin >> nCount;
pnCount = &nCount;
*pnCount += 10;
cout << *pnCout; // display value in variable nCount
```

The example assigns the address of the variable **nCount** to the pointer **pnCount**. Following this address assignment, the example increments the value in variable **nCount** by 10 and displays the current value, using the pointer **pnCount**. Notice the indirection operator, which appears before the name of the pointer in the last two statements.

Let's look at a programming example. Listing 13-1 shows the source code for the PTR1.CPP program, which uses a pointer to access existing variables. The program declares three int-type variables and a single pointer to the type int. The program initializes the first two variables, initializes the pointer to access the first variable, and then performs the following tasks:

- Double the value in the first variable using the pointer
- Display the value in the first variable twice, first using that variable directly and then using the pointer
- Assign the address of the second variable to the pointer
- Triple the value in the second variable using the pointer
- Display the value in the second variable twice, first using the variable directly and then using the pointer
- Assign the address of the third variable to the pointer

- Prompt you to enter an integer and store the input in the third variable using the pointer

- Display the value in the third variable twice, first using the variable directly and then using the pointer

Here is a sample session with the program in Listing 13-1 (user input is underlined):

```
Variable nNum1 stores 22 (direct access)
Variable nNum1 stores 22 (pointer access)
Variable nNum2 stores 66 (direct access)
Variable nNum2 stores 66 (pointer access)
Enter an integer : 55
Variable nNum3 stores 55 (direct access)
Variable nNum3 stores 55 (pointer access)
```

Listing 13-1

The source code for the PTR1.CPP program.

```cpp
// A C++ program that illustrates using pointers
// with existing variables

#include <iostream.h>
#include <iomanip.h>

main()
{
  int nNum1 = 11;
  int nNum2 = 22;
  int nNum3;
  int* pnNum = &nNum1;                    ────────▶ Declare and initialize a pointer

  // double the value in variable nNum1
  // using the pointer pnNum
  *pnNum *= 2;
  cout << "Variable nNum1 stores " << nNum1
       << " (direct access)\n";
  cout << "Variable nNum1 stores " << *pnNum
       << " (pointer access)\n";

  // assign address of variable nNum2 to pointer pnNum
  pnNum = &nNum2;                                          ────────▶ Pointer access
  // triple the value in variable nNum2
  // using the pointer pnNum
  *pnNum *= 3;
  cout << "Variable nNum2 stores " << nNum2
       << " (direct access)\n";
  cout << "Variable nNum2 stores " << *pnNum
       << " (pointer access)\n";
```

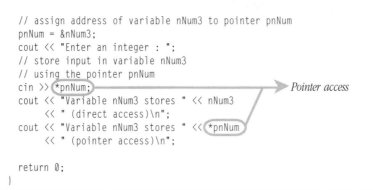

```
    // assign address of variable nNum3 to pointer pnNum
    pnNum = &nNum3;
    cout << "Enter an integer : ";
    // store input in variable nNum3
    // using the pointer pnNum
    cin >> *pnNum;                                          Pointer access
    cout << "Variable nNum3 stores " << nNum3
         << " (direct access)\n";
    cout << "Variable nNum3 stores " << *pnNum
         << " (pointer access)\n";

    return 0;
}
```

The function **main** in Listing 13-1 declares the **int**-type variables **nNum1**, **nNum2**, and **nNum3**, initializing the first two. It also declares the **int**-type pointer (that is, the pointer to an **int**-type) **pnNum** and initializes it with the address of variable **nNum1**. The function **main** performs the following tasks:

- Double the value in variable **nNum1** by using the pointer **pnNum** to access the contents of that variable

- Display the value in variable **nNum1** twice, using first the variable **nNum1** and then the expression ***pnNum**. This expression uses the indirection operator with the pointer **pnNum** to access the value in variable **nNum1**.

- Assign the address of variable **nNum2** to the pointer **pnNum**

- Triple the value in variable **nNum2** by using the pointer **pnNum** to access the contents of that variable

- Display the value in variable **nNum2** twice, using the variable **nNum2** and the expression ***pnNum**, which uses the indirection operator with the pointer **pnNum** to access the value in variable **nNum2**

- Assign the address of variable **nNum3** to the pointer **pnNum**

- Prompt you to enter an integer and store the input in the variable **nNum3** using the pointer **pnNum**. This task shows you that you can even store an input value in a variable by using a pointer to that variable.

- Display the value in variable **nNum3** twice, using the variable **nNum3** and the expression ***pnNum**, which uses the indirection operator with the pointer **pnNum** to access the value in variable **nNum3**

DIFFERENCE BETWEEN POINTERS AND REFERENCES

Reference variables (described in Chapter 12, "User-Defined Types") and pointers are somewhat similar and yet different. The differences are these:

- A reference variable must be initialized when declared. By contrast, you can declare a pointer without having to initialize it.

- You can assign the address of a variable to a pointer anywhere in the statements of a function. You cannot, however, assign a new reference to a reference variable.

- Using the pointer to access the data of its associated variable requires the indirection operator *. By contrast, a reference variable does not require the indirection operator *, since it is an alias to the referenced variable.

POINTERS TO POINTERS

C++ allows you to declare a pointer to another pointer. The general syntax for declaring a pointer to a pointer is:

```
type** pointerToPointerName;
```

Here are examples for declaring, initializing, and using pointers to pointers:

```
int nNum = 1;
int* pnNum = &nNum;
int** ppnNum = &pnNum;
cout << nNum << "\n"; // displays 1 using the variable nNum
cout << *pnNum << "\n"; // displays 1 using the pointer pnNum
cout << **ppnNum << "\n"; // displays 1 using the pointer-to-pointer
                          // ppnNum
```

The example declares the **int**-type variable **nNum**, the **int**-type pointer **pnNum**, and the **int**-type pointer-to-pointer **ppnNum**. The declarations in the example also include initializations. The example contains three output statements, which display the value in variable **nNum** using that variable, the pointer **pnNum**, and the pointer-to-pointer **ppnNum**.

CODING
NOTES

A Limitation in Initializing a Pointer to a Pointer

C++ does not allow you to apply the address-of operator & twice to assign an address of a pointer to a variable into a pointer to a pointer. Thus, for example, the compiler does not accept the latter statement shown here:

```
// Error! Illegal use of operator &
int nNum = 1;
int** ppnNum = &&nNum;
```

Let's look at a programming example. Listing 13-2 shows the source code for the PTR2.CPP program, which illustrates using a pointer to a pointer. The program prompts you to enter two integers and then displays your input along with the sum of integers. The program uses two int-type variables, two int-type pointers, and an int-type pointer-to-pointer (that is, a pointer to a pointer to an int) to access the input values.

Here is a sample session with the program in Listing 13-2:

```
Enter first integer : 100
Enter second integer : 200
100 + 200 = 300
```

Listing 13-2
The source code for the PTR2.CPP program.

```
// A C++ program that illustrates using pointers
// to pointers

#include <iostream.h>
#include <iomanip.h>

main()
{
  int nNum1;
  int nNum2;
  int* pnNum1 = &nNum1;
  int* pnNum2 = &nNum2;
  int** ppnNum;                                          ⟶ Declare pointer-to-pointer

  // assign address of pointer pnNum1 to ppnNum
  ppnNum = &pnNum1;
  cout << "Enter first integer : ";
  cin >> **ppnNum;                                       ⟶ Pointer-to-pointer access
```

```
// assign address of pointer pnNum2 to ppnNum
ppnNum = &pnNum2;
cout << "Enter second integer : ";
cin >> **ppnNum;                                        Pointer-to-pointer access

cout << nNum1 << " + " << nNum2 << " = "
     << (*pnNum1 + *pnNum2) << endl;

return 0;
}
```

The function **main** in Listing 13-2 declares the following variables and pointers:

- The int-type variables **nNum1** and **nNum2**

- The int-type pointers **pnNum1** and **pnNum2**. The function initializes these pointers with the addresses of the variables **nNum1** and **nNum2**, respectively.

- The int-type pointer-to-pointer **ppnNum**

The function **main** performs the following tasks:

- Assign the address of pointer **pnNum1** to the pointer-to-pointer **ppnNum**

- Prompt you to enter the first integer. This task stores your input in variable **nNum1** using the pointer-to-pointer **ppnNum**. The input statement uses the expression ****ppnNum** to access the variable **nNum1**.

- Assign the address of pointer **pnNum2** to the pointer-to-pointer **ppnNum**

- Prompt you to enter the second integer. This task stores your input in variable **nNum2** using the pointer-to-pointer **ppnNum**. The input statement uses the expression ****ppnNum** to access the variable **nNum2**.

- Display the input values and their sum. The function displays the input values using the variables **nNum1** and **nNum2**, and it displays the sum by using the expression (***pnNum1** + ***pnNum2**).

Thus the program in Listing 13-2 shows that you can access the data in a variable using the name of that variable, a pointer to that variable, or a pointer-to-pointer.

Pointers and Arrays

Pointers work well with accessing the elements of an array. This section looks at how pointers and arrays relate and how to use address arithmetic with pointers.

ARRAY NAMES ARE POINTERS, TOO!

C++, like its parent language C, regards the name of an array as a pointer to the first element in that array. Say, for example, you declare the following array:

```
char cName[30];
```

Here the name of the array, **cName**, is equivalent to the address of the first array element, **&cName[Ø]**. This feature presents you with a useful shorthand way for writing the address of the first element. Thus, you can assign the address of the first array element to a pointer by simply using the name of the array. Here is an example of this feature:

```
int nArr[30];
int *pnArr = nArr; // same as int *pnArr = &nArr[0];
```

The example declares the array **nArr** and the pointer **pnArr**. It initializes the pointer with the address of the first element in array **nArr** by simply assigning the name of the array to the pointer. You can replace **nArr** with the expression **&nArr[Ø]** to assign the same address to the pointer.

POINTER ARITHMETIC

One of the benefits from associating a data type with a pointer is pointer arithmetic, which increments or decrements the address in the pointer. What happens when you apply the **+**, **[−]**, **++**, and **[−][−]** operators to a pointer? Does the operation alter the address by bytes or by the size of the item pointed to? The answer is that these operators increment or decrement the address of a pointer by a multiple of item size. Here is an example that illustrates the feature just described:

```
const int MAX = 4;
int nArr[MAX] = { 1, 2, 3, 4 };
int* pnArr = nArr;

cout << *pnArr << endl; // displays nArr[0];
*pnArr++;
cout << *pnArr++ << endl; // displays nArr[1];
cout << *pnArr << endl; // displays nArr[2];
```

The example assigns the address of the first element in array **nArr** to the pointer **pnArr**. The first output statement displays the value in element **nArr[Ø]**. The next statement increments the address in pointer **pnArr**, which now points to the second element **nArr[1]**, as displayed by the second output statement. This statement also uses the postincrement operator **++** to increment the address in pointer **pnArr**, which now points to the third array element **nArr[1]**. The last output statement displays the value in element **nArr[2]**.

ACCESSING ARRAY ELEMENTS USING POINTERS

The last example also shows you that you can access the elements of an array using a pointer to the array elements. The process of systematically accessing the array elements using a pointer involves the following general steps:

1. Initialize the pointer with the first (or last) array element.

2. Use a loop to access each array element and increment (or decrement) the address in the pointer.

The general syntax for accessing an array element using a pointer is:

```
type* pointerName = arrayName;
*(pointerName + index) is equivalent to arrayName[index]
*(pointerName + index) is equivalent to pointerName[index]
```

Notice that C++ offers two forms for accessing the elements of an array using a pointer (and there are also two forms for using the pointer). Here is an example of accessing a single-dimensional array using a pointer:

```
const int MAX = 100;
double fArr[MAX];
double* pfArr = fArr;

for (int i = 0; i < MAX; i++)
  *(pfArr + i) = double(i * i - 3 * i + 3);

for (int i = 0; i < MAX; i++)
  pfArr[i] += 1.2 * pfArr[i] + 3.4;
```

The example declares the **double**-type array **fArr** and the **double**-type pointer **pfArr**. The example initializes the pointer with the address of the first array element. The example then uses the first **for** loop to initialize the array elements. The loop uses the pointer **pfArr** to access the array elements. (Notice that the expression ***(pfArr + i)** is equivalent to **fArr[i]**.) It then uses the second **for** loop to further manipulate the values in the array. Notice that this loop's statement uses the expression **pfArr[i]** instead of **fArr[i]** to access the array elements. I could have written the source code to use the expression ***(pfArr + i)** instead of **pfArr[i]**. Although the former expression uses the indirection operator *****, the latter is shorter to write.

Let's look at a programming example. Listing 13-3 shows the source code for the PTR3.CPP program, which uses pointers to access the elements of an array. The program displays an unsorted array of integers, sorts that array, and then displays the sorted array. It accesses the array elements in these operations using pointers only.

Here is the output of the program in Listing 13-3:

```
Unsorted array is:
8 6 1 2 5 4 7 3 0 9
Sorted array is:
0 1 2 3 4 5 6 7 8 9
```

Listing 13-3

The source code for the PTR3.CPP program.

```cpp
// A C++ program that illustrates using pointers
// to access single-dimensional arrays

#include <iostream.h>
#include <iomanip.h>

main()
{
  const int MAX = 10;
  int nArr[MAX] = { 8, 6, 1, 2, 5,
                    4, 7, 3, 0, 9 };
  int* pnArrI = nArr;
  int* pnArrJ = nArr;

  cout << "Unsorted array is:\n";
  for (int i = 0; i < MAX; i++) {
    cout << *pnArrI << ' ';
    pnArrI++;
  }
  cout << endl;

  // reset the address of the pointer
  // to access the first element
  pnArrI -= MAX;
  for (i = 0; i < (MAX - 1); i++) {
    for (int j = i + 1; j < MAX; j++)
      if ((*(pnArrI + i)) > (*(pnArrJ +j))) {
        int nSwapBuffer = *(pnArrI + i);
        *(pnArrI + i) = *(pnArrJ +j);
        *(pnArrJ + j) = nSwapBuffer;
      }
  }

  cout << "Sorted array is:\n";
  for (i = 0; i < MAX; i++) {
    cout << *pnArrI << ' ';
    pnArrI++;
  }
  cout << endl;

  return 0;
}
```

Pointer access to array elements

The function **main** in Listing 13-3 declares the local constant **MAX**, the **int**-type array **nArr**, and the **int**-type pointers **pnArrI** and **pnArrJ**. The function initializes the array **nArr** and initializes the two pointers with the address of the first element of array **nArr**. The function **main** performs the following tasks:

- Display the unsorted elements of array **nArr**. This task uses a **for** loop that contains two statements. The first statement displays an array element using the pointer **pnArrl** (remember that function **main** initializes this pointer to access the first array element). The second statement increments the address in the pointer to access the next array element. At the end of the loop, the pointer **pnArrl** points to the address that lies right after the array **nArr**.

- Reset the address of pointer **pnArrl** to access the first element of array **nArr**. This task subtracts the value of constant **MAX** (times **sizeof(int)**) from the address in the pointer. Because of the pointer arithmetic feature, this task actually subtracts **MAX * sizeof(int)** bytes and not just **MAX** bytes from the pointer **pnArrl**.

- Sort the array elements using nested **for** loops that implement the bubble sort method. These loops access the elements of the array numbered **i** and **j** using the expressions ***(pnArrl + i)** and ***(pnArrj + j)**, respectively.

- Display the sorted array elements using the pointer **pnArrl**. This task is very similar to the one that displays the unsorted array elements.

ACCESSING MATRIX ELEMENTS USING POINTERS

The preceding subsection shows you how to access the elements of a single-dimensional array using a pointer. What about accessing the elements of a matrix with a pointer? You have two alternatives. The first one uses an array of pointers to access the rows—each pointer accesses the elements in a single row. The second solution uses a single pointer-to-pointer.

The next program example shows you how to use an array of pointers and a pointer-to-pointer to access the elements of a matrix. Listing 13-4 contains the source code for the PTR4.CPP program, which accesses matrix elements using pointers. The program performs the following general tasks:

- Initialize the array of pointers
- Assign values to the matrix elements using the array of pointers
- Calculate the sum of the matrix elements

- Display the matrix elements
- Display the sum of the matrix elements

Here is the output of the program in Listing 13-4:

```
101 102 103 104 105
201 202 203 204 205
301 302 303 304 305
401 402 403 404 405
501 502 503 504 505
601 602 603 604 605
701 702 703 704 705
801 802 803 804 805
901 902 903 904 905

Sum of matrix elements = 22635
```

Listing 13-4
The source code for the PTR4.CPP program.

```cpp
// A C++ program that illustrates using pointers
// to access multidimensional arrays

#include <iostream.h>
#include <iomanip.h>

main()
{
  const int MAX_ROWS = 9;
  const int MAX_COLS = 5;
  double fMat[MAX_ROWS][MAX_COLS];
  double* pfMat[MAX_ROWS];
  double** ppfMat = pfMat;
  double fSum = 0;

  // initialize array of pointers
  for(int i = 0; i < MAX_ROWS; i++)
    pfMat[i] = &fMat[i][0];

  // assign values to the matrix elements
  for( i = 0; i < MAX_ROWS; i++)
    for(int j = 0; j < MAX_COLS; j++)
      *(*(pfMat + i) + j) = double(100 * (i+1) + (j+1));      Pointer access
                                                              to a matrix
  // add the values in the matrix
  for(i = 0; i < MAX_ROWS; i++)
    for(int j = 0; j < MAX_COLS; j++)
      fSum += *(*(ppfMat + i) + j);
```

```
// display the values in the matrix
for(i = 0; i < MAX_ROWS; i++) {
  for(int j = 0; j < MAX_COLS; j++)
    cout << fMat[i][j] << ' ';
  cout << endl;
}

// display the sum of matrix values
cout << endl << "Sum of matrix elements = "
     << fSum << endl;

return 0;
}
```

The function **main** in Listing 13-4 declares the constants **MAX_ROWS** and **MAX_COLS** to set the number of matrix rows and columns, respectively. The function also declares the following variables and pointers:

- The **double**-type matrix **fMat**, which has **MAX_ROWS** rows and **MAX_COLS** columns
- The **double**-type array of pointers **pfMat**, which has **MAX_ROWS** elements
- The **double**-type pointer-to-pointer **ppfMat**. The function initializes this pointer with the first element of the array of pointers **pfMat**.
- The **double**-type variable **fSum**. The function initializes this variable with Ø.

The function **main** then carries out its tasks in detail through the following steps:

- Initialize the array of pointers. This task uses a **for** loop to assign the address of the first element in each matrix row to an element in the array **pfMat**.
- Assign values to the matrix elements. This task uses nested **for** loops and the array of pointers **pfMat**. Notice that the loops assign the values to the matrix element **fMat[i][j]** using the expression ***(*(pfMat + i) + j)**. This expression uses the array of pointers **pfMat** along with two indirection operators.

- Add the values of the matrix to the variable **fSum**. This task uses nested **for** loops that access the element **fMat[i][j]** using the pointer-to-pointer **ppfMat**. The element access uses the expression ***(*(ppfMat + i) + j)**. Notice that the expressions using the pointer-to-pointer and the array of pointers have an identical syntax!
- Display the matrix elements. This task uses nested **for** loops and accesses the matrix elements using the variable **fMat**.
- Display the value in variable **fSum**

Pointers to Structures

You can declare pointers to structures and access the data members of these structures using the pointers. C++ requires that you use the pointer access operator **->** instead of the dot access operator. The general syntax for declaring a pointer to a structure variable is the same as the one for an ordinary variable.

Here is an example of declaring a pointer to a structure variable and using it to access the data members of that structure:

```
struct myComplex
{
  double m_fReal;
  double m_fImag;
};

main()
{
  myComplex ComplexVar = { 1.0, 2.0 };
  myComplex* pComplex = &ComplexVar;

  cout << "Complex number = "
       << pComplex->m_fReal
       << " + i "
       << pComplex->m_fImag;

  return 0;
};
```

The example declares the structure **myComplex** with its **double**-type data members **m_fReal** and **m_flmag**. The function **main** declares and initializes the structure variable **ComplexVar**. The function also declares the **myComplex**-type pointer **pComplex** and initializes it using the address of variable **ComplexVar**. The function then displays the values of the data members in variable **ComplexVar** using the pointer **pComplex**. Notice that the output statement uses the operator -> to access the data members **m_fReal** and **m_flmag** of the structure variable.

Let me present a programming example. Listing 13-5 shows the source code for the PTR5.CPP program, which uses a pointer to access the data members of a structure variable. The program declares a structure that contains matrix elements and their sum. The program declares a structure variable and its pointer and uses a pointer to perform the following general tasks:

- Assign values to the matrix elements
- Calculate the sum of matrix elements
- Display the matrix elements
- Display the sum of matrix elements

Here is the output of the program in Listing 13-5:

```
100 101 102 103 104
200 201 202 203 204
300 301 302 303 304
400 401 402 403 404
500 501 502 503 504
600 601 602 603 604
700 701 702 703 704
800 801 802 803 804
900 901 902 903 904

Sum of matrix elements = 22590
```

Listing 13-5

The source code for the PTR5.CPP program.

```cpp
// A C++ program that illustrates using pointers
// to structured variables

#include <iostream.h>
#include <iomanip.h>

const int MAX_ROWS = 9;
const int MAX_COLS = 5;

struct Matrix
{
  double m_fMat[MAX_ROWS][MAX_COLS];
  double m_fSum;
};

main()
{
  Matrix Mat;
  Matrix* pMat = &Mat;

  // assign values to the matrix elements
  for(int i = 0; i < MAX_ROWS; i++)
    for(int j = 0; j < MAX_COLS; j++)
      pMat->m_fMat[i][j] = double(100 * (i+1) + j);

  // add the values in the matrix
  for(i = 0; i < MAX_ROWS; i++)
    for(int j = 0; j < MAX_COLS; j++)
      pMat->m_fSum += pMat->m_fMat[i][j];        Pointer to structure access

  // display the values in the matrix
  for(i = 0; i < MAX_ROWS; i++) {
    for(int j = 0; j < MAX_COLS; j++)
      cout << pMat->m_fMat[i][j] << ' ';
    cout << endl;
  }

  // display the sum of matrix values
  cout << endl << "Sum of matrix elements = "
       << pMat->m_fSum << endl;                  Pointer to structure access

  return 0;
}
```

Listing 13-5 declares the global constants **MAX_ROWS** and **MAX_COLS**, which specify the number of matrix rows and columns, respectively. The listing also declares the structure type **Matrix**, which has the following data members:

- The **double**-type matrix data member **m_fMat**. This member has **MAX_ROWS** rows and **MAX_COLS** columns.
- The **double**-type data member **m_fSum**, which stores the sum of the matrix elements

The listing has function **main**, which declares the **Matrix**-type structured variable **Mat** and pointer **pMat**. The declaration of the pointer also initializes it using the address of the structured variable **Mat**. The function **main** performs the following tasks:

- Assign values to the matrix elements using nested **for** loops. Notice that the loops assign the values to the data member **m_fMat[i][j]** using the expression **pMat ->m_fMat[i][j]**. This expression uses the pointer **pMat** and the pointer access operator **->**.
- Add the values of the matrix to the variable **fSum**. This task uses nested **for** loops that access the data member **fMat[i][j]** using the pointer **pMat**. The loop's statement accesses the data members **m_fMat** and **m_fSum** using the operator **->**.
- Display the matrix elements. This task uses nested **for** loops and accesses the elements of the data member **m_fMat** using the pointer **pMat**.
- Display the value in the data member **m_fSum** using the pointer **pMat**

Pointers to Classes

C++ allows you to declare pointers to classes to access the various instances of a class. Declaration and address assignment of a pointer to a class work just as with simple variables.

Here is an example of using a pointer to a class:

```
#include <iostream.h>

class myComplex
{
  public:
    myComplex()
      { setComplex(0, 0); }
```

```
        void setComplex(double fReal, double fImag)
          {
             m_fReal = fReal;
             m_fImag = fImag;
          }
        double getReal()
          { return m_fReal; }
        double getImag()
          { return m_fImag; }

     protected:
        double m_fReal;
        double m_fImag;
   };

   main()
   {
     myComplex ComplexObj;
     myComplex* pComplex = &ComplexObj;

     pComplex->setComplex(1.2, 3.4);
     cout << "Complex number is "
          << pComplex->getReal()
          << " + i "
          << pComplex->getImag();
     return 0;
   }
```

The example declares the class **myComplex** with protected and public members. The class declares the **double**-type protected data members **m_fReal** and **m_fImag** to store the real and imaginary part of a complex number. The class declares a public constructor and the member functions **setComplex**, **getReal**, and **getImag**. The function **main** declares the object **ComplexObj** as an instance of class **myComplex** and also declares the pointer **pComplex** as a pointer to object **ComplexObj**. The function **main** assigns a new complex value by sending the C++ message **setComplex** to the object, using the pointer **pComplex**. Likewise, it displays the value in the object **ComplexObj** by sending the C++ messages **getReal** and **getImag** to that object, again using the pointer **pComplex**.

Let's look at a programming example. Listing 13-6 shows the source code for the PTR6.CPP program, which uses a pointer to a class. The program declares a class that models arrays and uses a pointer to that class to perform the following tasks on a class instance:

- Assign integers to an array object using a pointer to that object
- Display the unsorted values in the array object using the pointer to that object
- Sort the elements of the array object using the pointer
- Display the sorted values in the array object using the pointer

Here is the output of the program in Listing 13-6:

```
Unsorted array is:
23 45 89 74 51 18 87 63 36 38
Sorted array is:
18 23 36 38 45 51 63 74 87 89
```

Listing 13-6
The source code for the PTR6.CPP program.

```
// A C++ program that illustrates
// pointers to classes

#include <iostream.h>
#include <iomanip.h>

const int MAX_ELEMS = 10;

class myArray
{
  public:
    myArray(int fInitVal = 0);
    int& operator[](int nIndex)
      { return m_nArray[nIndex]; }
    void show(const char* pszMsg = "",
              const int nNumElems = MAX_ELEMS,
              const int bOneLine = 1);
    void ShellSort(int nNumElems = MAX_ELEMS);

  protected:
    int m_nArray[MAX_ELEMS];
};

myArray::myArray(int fInitVal)
{
  for (int i = 0; i < MAX_ELEMS; i++)
    m_nArray[i] = fInitVal;
}
```

```
void myArray::show(const char* pszMsg,
                   const int nNumElems,
                   const int bOneLine)
{
  cout << pszMsg << endl;
  if (bOneLine) {
    for (int i = 0; i < nNumElems; i++)
      cout << m_nArray[i] << ' ';
    cout << endl;
  }
  else {
    for (int i = 0; i < nNumElems; i++)
      cout << m_nArray[i] << endl;
    cout << endl;
  }
}

void myArray::ShellSort(int nNumElems)
{
  int nOffset = nNumElems;
  int bSorted;

  if (nNumElems < 2)
    return;

  while (nOffset > 1) {
    nOffset = (nOffset - 1) / 3;
    nOffset = (nOffset < 1) ? 1 : nOffset;
    // arrange elements that are nOffset apart
    do {
      bSorted = 1; // set sorted flag
      // compare elements
      for (int i = 0, j = nOffset;
           i < (nNumElems - nOffset);
           i++, j++) {
        if (m_nArray[i] > m_nArray[j]) {
          // swap elements
          int nSwap = m_nArray[i];
          m_nArray[i] = m_nArray[j];
          m_nArray[j] = nSwap;
          bSorted = 0; // clear sorted flag
        }
      }
    } while (!bSorted);
  }
}

main()
{
  int nArr[MAX_ELEMS] = { 23, 45, 89, 74, 51,
                          18, 87, 63, 36, 38 };
```

```
   myArray Array;
   myArray* pArray = &Array;              ──────► Declare and initialize a pointer to a class

   for (int i = 0; i < MAX_ELEMS; i++)
     pArray->operator[](i) = nArr[i];

   pArray->show "Unsorted array is:");
   pArray->ShellSort();                   ──────► Pointer to a class
   pArray->show "Sorted array is:");

   return 0;
}
```

Listing 13-6 declares the class **myArray**, which resembles previous versions of class **myArray** in program ARRAY4.CPP (Listing 10-4). The class **myArray** supports arrays of integers stored in the protected data member **m_nArray**. The class declares a constructor, the operator [], and the member functions **show** and **ShellSort**.

The function **main** declares and initializes the C++ array **nArr**. It also declares the object **Array** as an instance of class **myArray** and declares the pointer to that instance **pArray**. The function then performs the following tasks:

- Copy the values in array **nArr** into the object **Array** using the pointer **pArray**. This task uses a **for** loop to iterate over the elements in array **nArr**. Notice that the loop statement uses the expression **pArray-> operator[](i)** and not **pArray[i]** to access the targeted element in object **Array**.

- Display the unsorted elements in object **Array** by sending it the C++ message **show** using the pointer **pArray**. The argument for this message is the literal string "Unsorted array is:" This task accesses the member function **show** using the operator **->**.

- Sort the object **Array** by sending it the C++ message **ShellSort** using the pointer **pArray**. This task accesses the member function **ShellSort** using the operator **->**.

- Display the sorted elements in object **Array** by sending it the C++ message **show** using the pointer **pArray**. The argument for this message is the literal string "Sorted array is:" This task accesses the member function **show** using the operator **->**.

CODING NOTES

Accessing Operators Using Pointers

The general syntax for accessing a member function that is an operator is:

pointerToInstance->operator operatorSymbols(argumentList)

Here are examples:

```
pObject->operator[](nIndex) = 2; //
    access operator []
pObject->operator()(nRow, nCol) = 3;
    // access operator ()
```

The first example accesses the operator [] using a pointer to an object. The second example accesses the operator (), also by using a pointer to an object.

Pointers and Dynamic Variables

There are two basic types of variables and class instances as far as the runtime system is concerned: *static* and *dynamic*. The compiler preallocates the memory space for static variables and class instances (I am using the word *static* here as a term for something more general than the formal static variables in a function) *before* the program starts. By contrast, the runtime system allocates the space for *dynamic* variables and class instances, which allow programs to handle data in a custom-fit approach. For example, all of the array-manipulating programs that I have presented so far assume that the arrays have a number of elements determined at compile time. Although static arrays are fine in these examples, they are not always suitable for real-world applications where you cannot predetermine the number of array elements. Thus using dynamic arrays allows your programs to create arrays with the right sizes and to expand the arrays when needed. Other data structures, such as stacks, queues, lists, and trees, are typically implemented as dynamic data structures to greatly enhance their ability to deal with varying numbers of data items.

Concerning the management of dynamic variables you need to observe the following rules:

1. You must explicitly create and remove dynamic variables and objects.

2. Each dynamic variable and object must have at least one pointer to access it at all times. You can switch from one pointer to another.

3. C++ offers the operators **new** and **delete** to create and remove dynamic variables. The general syntax for allocating a single dynamic variable or class instance using operator **new** is:

```
pointerToVariable = new type;
```

The operator **new** returns the address of the dynamic variable to the associated pointer. If the allocation fails, the operator yields a null address. In the case of creating dynamic class instances, the runtime system invokes the constructor for the instance.

Here are examples of using the operator **new** to allocate dynamic variables:

```
class PC_Computer
{
  // members
};

int pNum;
double pX;
PC_Computer* pPC;

pNum = new int;
pX = new double;
pPC = new PC_Computer;
```

The examples declare the **int**-type pointer **pNum**, the **double**-type pointer **pX**, and the **PC_Computer**-type pointer **pPC**. The example allocates dynamic **int**-type and **double**-type variables and assigns their address to the pointers **pNum** and **pX**, respectively. The example also allocates a dynamic class instance and assigns its address to the pointer **pPC**.

BASIC

Dynamic Variables

BASIC does not support pointers and dynamic variables. The closest feature to dynamic variables in BASIC is the ability to redimension arrays at runtime using the REDIM statement.

Dynamic Variables

As a Pascal programmer you may be delighted to learn that C++ implements the operators new and delete (and allows you to avoid using the C functions malloc and free) to allocate and deallocate dynamic memory. These operators are similar to the Pascal intrinsics New and Delete.

The general syntax for allocating a dynamic array is:

```
pointerToArray = new type[numberOfElements];
```

The operator **new** assigns the address of the first array element to the associated pointer. Here is an example of creating a dynamic array:

```
class PC_Computer
{
  // members
};

const int MAX1 = 100;
const int MAX2 = 1000;
PC_Computer* pPC;

if (getNeededSize() < MAX2)
  pPC = new PC_Computer[MAX1];
else
  pPC = new PC_Computer[MAX2];
```

The example declares the class **PC_Computer** and a pointer to that class, **pPC**. The example allocates a dynamic array of **PC_Computer** instances whose size depends on the value returned by some function called **getNeededSize**. The example allocates a dynamic array with either **MAX1** or **MAX2** elements.

Dynamic Variables in C++

C++ uses the operators new and delete, instead of the functions malloc, calloc, and free, to allocate and deallocate dynamic memory. The operators new and delete are more aware of data types than the C memory-management functions. In addition, C++ allows you to define new versions of operators new and delete in a class!

The general syntax for deallocating a dynamic variable is:

```
delete pointerToVariable;
```

In the case of dynamic class instances, the operator **delete** also invokes the class destructor.

The general syntax for deallocating a dynamic array is:

```
delete [] pointerToArray;
```

The operator **delete** also works with null pointers. That is, you can apply the operator **delete** to a null pointer without raising a runtime error.

Here are examples for using the operator **delete** with single dynamic variables and dynamic arrays:

```
class PC_Computer
{
  // members
};

PC_Computer* pPC;
PC_Computer* pPCLab;

pPC = new PC_Computer; // single dynamic variable
pPCLab = new PC_Computer[10]; // dynamic array
// statements
delete pPC;
delete [] pPCLab;
```

CODING NOTES

Maintaining Dynamic Variables

Do not forget to deallocate the memory space of dynamic variables and arrays after you are done using them.

Do not assign a new address to a dynamic variable pointer *before* you either delete that variable or assign its address to another pointer. Failing to do so causes the program to have unaccessed dynamic variables in memory! This kind of poor programming practice is called *memory bleeding*.

The example declares the class **PC_Computer** and also declares the class pointers **pPC** and **pPCLab**. The example creates a single dynamic variable and assigns its address to the pointer **pPC**. It also creates an array of class instances and assigns the address of its first element to the pointer **pPCLab**. The last two statements use the operator **delete** to deallocate the memory space for the dynamic variable accessed by pointer **pPC** and the dynamic array accessed by pointer **pPCLab**. Notice that the last statement contains empty brackets after the operator **delete** to remove the memory of a dynamic array.

Let me present a programming example. Listing 13-7 shows the source code for the PTR7.CPP program, which illustrates pointers to dynamic variables and class instances. The program creates the following dynamic variables and objects:

- A dynamic array of integers
- A dynamic object that models a dynamic array of integers
- A dynamic variable that acts as a swap buffer

The program performs the following tasks:

- Create the dynamic array
- Assign values to the elements of the dynamic array
- Display the unsorted values in the dynamic array
- Sort the elements of the dynamic array in descending order. The sorting process uses a dynamic swap buffer to swap integers.
- Display the sorted values in the dynamic array
- Remove the dynamic array
- Create the object that models the dynamic array of integers
- Assign values to the elements of the object
- Display the unsorted values in the object
- Sort the elements of the object in ascending order
- Display the sorted values in the object
- Remove the dynamic object

Here is the output of the program in Listing 13-7:

```
Unsorted array:
23 45 89 74 51 18 87 63 36 38
Sorted array:
89 87 74 63 51 45 38 36 23 18


Unsorted array is:
23 45 89 74 51 18 87 63 36 38
Sorted array is:
18 23 36 38 45 51 63 74 87 89
```

Listing 13-7
The source code for the PTR7.CPP program.

```
// A C++ program that illustrates
// pointers to dynamic variables and class instances

#include <iostream.h>
#include <iomanip.h>

const int MAX_ELEMS = 10;

class myArray
{
  public:
    myArray(int nMaxElems = MAX_ELEMS, int fInitVal = 0);
    ~myArray()
      { delete [] m_pnArray; }                    Remove dynamic array
    int& operator[](int nIndex)
      { return m_pnArray[nIndex]; }
    void show(const char* pszMsg = "",
              const int nNumElems = MAX_ELEMS,
              const int bOneLine = 1);
    void ShellSort(int nNumElems = MAX_ELEMS);

  protected:
    int* m_pnArray;                               Pointer to dynamic array
    int m_nMaxElems;
};

myArray::myArray(int nMaxElems, int fInitVal)
{
  m_nMaxElems = (nMaxElems > 1) ? nMaxElems : 1;
  m_pnArray = new int[m_nMaxElems];
  for (int i = 0; i < m_nMaxElems; i++)
    m_pnArray[i] = fInitVal;
}
```

```cpp
void myArray::show(const char* pszMsg,
                   const int nNumElems,
                   const int bOneLine)
{
  cout << pszMsg << endl;
  if (bOneLine) {
    for (int i = 0; i < nNumElems; i++)
      cout << m_pnArray[i] << ' ';
    cout << endl;
  }
  else {
    for (int i = 0; i < nNumElems; i++)
      cout << m_pnArray[i] << endl;
    cout << endl;
  }
}

void myArray::ShellSort(int nNumElems)
{
  int nOffset = nNumElems;
  int bSorted;

  if (nNumElems < 2 ||
      nNumElems > m_nMaxElems)
    return;

  while (nOffset > 1) {
    nOffset = (nOffset - 1) / 3;
    nOffset = (nOffset < 1) ? 1 : nOffset;
    // arrange elements that are nOffset apart
    do {
      bSorted = 1; // set sorted flag
      // compare elements
      for (int i = 0, j = nOffset;
           i < (nNumElems - nOffset);
           i++, j++) {
        if (m_pnArray[i] > m_pnArray[j]) {
          // swap elements
          int nSwap = m_pnArray[i];
          m_pnArray[i] = m_pnArray[j];
          m_pnArray[j] = nSwap;
          bSorted = 0; // clear sorted flag
        }
      }
    } while (!bSorted);
  }
}
```

```
main()
{
  int nArr[MAX_ELEMS] = { 23, 45, 89, 74, 51,
                          18, 87, 63, 36, 38 };
  int* pnArray = new int[MAX_ELEMS];

  // copy array elements
  for (int i = 0; i < MAX_ELEMS; i++)
    pnArray[i] = nArr[i];

  cout << "Unsorted array:\n";
  for (i = 0; i < MAX_ELEMS; i++)
    cout << pnArray[i] << ' ';
  cout << endl;

  for (i = 0; i < (MAX_ELEMS - 1); i++)
    for (int j = i+1; j < MAX_ELEMS; j++)
      if (pnArray[i] < pnArray[j]) {
        // allocate dynamic swap buffer
        int* pnSwap = new int;
        *pnSwap = pnArray[i];
        pnArray[i] = pnArray[j];
        pnArray[j] = *pnSwap;
        // deallocate dynamic swap buffer
        delete pnSwap;
      }

  cout << "Sorted array:\n";
  for (i = 0; i < MAX_ELEMS; i++)
    cout << pnArray[i] << ' ';
  cout << endl << endl;

  delete [] pnArray;

  myArray* pArray =  new myArray;

  // copy array elements
  for (i = 0; i < MAX_ELEMS; i++)
    pArray->operator[](i) = nArr[i];

  pArray->show("Unsorted array is:");
  pArray->ShellSort();
  pArray->show("Sorted array is:");

  delete pArray;

  return 0;
}
```

Declare a pointer to a dynamic array and create the array

Delete dynamic array

Declare dynamic instance

Remove dynamic instance

Listing 13-7 declares the global constant **MAX_ELEMS** as the default array size. The listing also declares the class **myArray**, which models dynamic arrays of integers. The support for dynamic arrays makes this version of class **myArray** quite different from the previous ones that I've shown you. The class declares protected and public members. The protected members are:

- The data member **m_pnArray**, which is the pointer that accesses the dynamic array of integers
- The **int**-type data member **m_nMaxElems**, which stores the number of elements in the dynamic array

The class also declares the following public members:

- The constructor, which has two parameters, **nMaxElems** and **flnitVal**. The first parameter specifies the number of array elements, and the second parameter specifies the initial values for the elements in the dynamic array. The two parameters have the default arguments of **MAX_ELEMS** and 0, respectively.
- The destructor, which removes the memory of the dynamic array accessed by data member **m_pnArray**. Notice that the operator **delete** is followed by the empty brackets because the operator is deleting a dynamic array.
- The operator **[]**, which accesses the elements in the dynamic array
- The member function **show**, which displays the elements in the dynamic array
- The member function **ShellSort**, which sorts the elements in the dynamic array

The definition of the constructor shows that it performs the following tasks:

- Assign the number of elements to the data member **m_nMaxElems**. This task also ensures that the assigned value is at least 1.
- Allocate the dynamic memory for the array using the operator **new**. This task specifies **m_nMaxElems** elements.

- Initialize the elements of the dynamic array using a **for** loop. Each loop iteration assigns the value of parameter **fInitVal** to an element of the dynamic array.

The remaining member functions of class **myArray** resemble the ones that I presented in previous versions of this class. The main difference is that the member functions in the new class version access the elements of the dynamic array using the pointer data member **m_pnArray**.

The function **main** performs the following tasks:

- Declare and initialize the C++ array **nArr**, which has **MAX_ELEMS** elements

- Declare the **int**-type pointer **pnArray** and assign to it the address of a dynamic array of integers that has **MAX_ELEMS** elements

- Copy the values from the C++ array **nArr** to the dynamic array. This task uses a **for** loop that copies the element **nArr[i]** to the element of the dynamic array **pnArray[i]**.

- Display the unsorted elements in the dynamic array. This task uses a **for** loop to iterate over the elements of the dynamic array, accessed by pointer **pnArray**.

- Sort, in a descending order, the elements of the dynamic array using the bubble sort method. This method uses nested **for** loops that compare and swap the elements of the dynamic array. The **if** statement that compares and swaps array elements uses the local dynamic swap buffer **pnSwap**. The statement creates and removes the buffer using the operators **new** and **delete**, respectively.

- Display the sorted elements in the dynamic array. This task uses a **for** loop to iterate over the elements of the dynamic array, accessed by pointer **pnArray**.

- Remove the dynamic array using the operator **delete**. Notice that the deletion statement includes the empty brackets after the operator **delete**, because the statement deletes a dynamic array.

- Declare the pointer to class **myArray**, **pArray**, and assign it the address of a new class instance. This task uses the operator **new**, which invokes the default constructor for class **myArray** (that is, it uses the default arguments for the parameters of the constructor).

- Copy the values from the C++ array **nArr** to the dynamic array object. This task uses a **for** loop that copies the element **nArr[i]** to the corresponding element of the dynamic array. The source code uses the expression **pArray ->operator[](i)** to access the targeted element.

- Display the unsorted elements of the array object by sending the C++ message **show** to the dynamic object. The argument for this message is the string literal "Unsorted array is:" This task accesses the dynamic object using the pointer **pArray**.

- Sort the elements of the array object by sending the C++ message **ShellSort** to the dynamic object. This task accesses the dynamic object using the pointer **pArray**.

- Display the sorted elements of the array object by sending the C++ message **show** to the dynamic object. The argument for this message is the string literal "Sorted array is:" This task accesses the dynamic object using the pointer **pArray**.

- Delete the dynamic array object using the operator **delete**. Notice that the object's pointer comes right after the operator **delete**, since the operator deletes a single object. This task also triggers the destructor, which deletes the dynamic array accessed by data member **m_pnArray**.

Constant Pointers

You learned in the previous chapter that reference variables have a fixed association with the variables they refer to. You also learned in the previous sections that you can assign a new address to a pointer, making pointers more flexible than reference variables. C++ allows you to declare constant pointers such that the initial address they store remains fixed. In other words, the compiler generates an error if you attempt to store a new address in the constant pointer. Thus, constant pointers and reference variables are kissing cousins, so to speak. They differ in the syntax for using them, but they are otherwise functionally equivalent. The general syntax for declaring a constant pointer is:

```
const type* pointerName = address;
```

Here are examples of using constant pointers:

```
const char* pszName = "Namir Shammas";
int nNum = 12;
const int* pnNum = &nNum;
```

The first example is an interesting one. It declares a constant **char**-type pointer, **pszName**, and assigns it the address of a literal string. This example is rather typical of using constant pointers to access string literals. You can access and manipulate the string literal using another pointer. However, while the string literal is in scope, the pointer **pszName** accesses its address. The second example shows the constant **int**-type pointer **pnNum**, which stores the address of the **int**-type variable **nNum**.

Let me present a programming example. Listing 13-8 shows the source code for the PTR8.CPP program, which uses pointers and constant pointers to prompt you to enter two integers and to display the sum of these integers.

Here is a sample session with the program in Listing 13-8 (user input is underlined):

```
Enter first integer : 55
Enter second integer : 45
55 + 45 = 100
```

Listing 13-8
The source code for the PTR8.CPP program.

```
// A C++ program that illustrates using constant pointers

#include <iostream.h>
#include <iomanip.h>

main()
{
  const char* pszMsg1 = "Enter first integer : ";      Constant pointers
  const char* pszMsg2 = "Enter second integer : ";
  char* pStr;
  int nNum1;
  int nNum2;
```

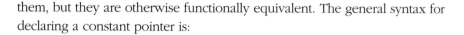

```
const int* pnNum1 = &nNum1;
int* pnN1 = (int*)pnNum1;
int* pnN2 = &nNum2;
const int* pnNum2 = pnN2;

// prompt for the first integer
cout << pszMsg1;
cin >> *((int*)pnNum1);

// prompt for the second integer
for (pStr = (char*)pszMsg2; *pStr != '\0'; pStr++)
  cout << *pStr; // display character
cin >> *((int*)pnNum2);

// display sum of integers
cout << *pnN1 << " + " << *pnN2 << " = "
     << (*pnNum1 + *pnNum2) << endl;

return 0;
}
```

The function **main** in Listing 13-8 declares the following variables and pointers:

- The constant **char**-type pointer **pszMsg1**, which stores the address of the string literal "Enter first integer : "

- The constant **char**-type pointer **pszMsg2**, which stores the address of the string literal "Enter second integer : "

- The **char**-type pointer **pStr**

- The **int**-type variables **nNum1** and **nNum2**

- The constant **int**-type pointer **pnNum1**, which stores the address of variable **nNum1**

- The **int**-type pointer **pnN1**, which stores the address of the constant pointer **pnNum1**. Notice that the initialization of pointer **pnN1** includes typecasting into **int***.

- The **int**-type pointer **pnN2**, which stores the address of variable **nNum2**

- The constant **int**-type pointer **pnNum2**, which stores the address in pointer **pnN2**. Notice that the initialization of the constant pointer does not require typecasting, because the compiler can automatically convert the address held by an ordinary pointer to one held by a constant pointer.

The function **main** performs the following tasks:

- Display the text for the first prompt using the constant pointer **pszMsg1**

- Input an integer and store it in variable **nNum1** using the constant pointer **pnNum1**. Notice that the input statement typecasts the constant pointer into an **int*** to accommodate the operator **>>**.

- Display the text of the second prompt message. This task uses, for the sake of illustration, a **for** loop that displays the text one character per iteration. The loop uses the pointer **pStr** to access the characters of the text. The loop initializes the pointer **pStr** using the typecast address of the constant pointer **pszMsg2**. The loop iterates as long as the character accessed by pointer **pStr** is not the null terminator.

- Input an integer and store it in the variable **nNum2** using the constant pointer **pnNum2**. Notice that the input statement typecasts the constant pointer into an **int*** to accommodate the operator **>>**.

- Display the input values and their sum. The output statement displays the input values using pointers **pnN1** and **pnN2**. The statement also displays the sum of the values using the constant pointers **pnNum1** and **pnNum2**.

Far Pointers

So far I have talked about pointers storing addresses. What about these addresses, you might ask? Some operating systems, such as the ones that run on Intel chips, use memory segments. To save space, the pointers we have described store only the *offset address* from the start of the current memory segment. This kind of pointer is called a *near* pointer. C++ supports another kind of pointer called the *far* pointer, which stores the entire address—both the *segment* and *offset* parts. Far pointers use more memory to store the segment and offset addresses. The general syntax for declaring near and far pointers is:

```
[const] type* near pointerName [= address];
[const] type* far pointerName [= address];
```

The declaration of pointers creates near pointers by default. Here are examples of far and near pointers:

```
int* far pNum1 = &nNum1;
int* far pNum2 = &nNum2;
const myArrayClass* far pArray;
const char* near pszMsg = "Hello There!";
```

The code snippet declares the far **int**-type pointers **pNum1** and **pNum2**. In addition, the code shows the declaration of a far pointer to a class and a near pointer to a string.

Let me present a programming example for these pointer types. Listing 13-9 shows the source code for the PTR9.CPP program, which uses near and far pointers to prompt you to enter two integers and to display the sum of these integers.

Here is a sample session with the program in Listing 13-9:

```
Enter first integer : 100
Enter second integer : 67
100 + 67 = 167
```

Listing 13-9
The source code for the PTR9.CPP program.

```
// A C++ program that illustrates using far pointers

#include <iostream.h>
#include <iomanip.h>

main()
{
    const char* near pszMsg1 = "Enter first integer : ";     ➤ Declare near pointers
    const char* near pszMsg2 = "Enter second integer : ";
    int nNum1;
    int nNum2;
    int* far pnNum1 = &nNum1;                                 ➤ Declare far pointers
    int* far pnNum2 = &nNum2;

    // prompt for the first integer
    cout << pszMsg1;
    cin >> *pnNum1;

    // prompt for the second integer
    cout << pszMsg2;
    cin >> *pnNum2;
```

```
    // display sum of integers
    cout << nNum1 << " + " << nNum2 << " = "
         << (*pnNum1 + *pnNum2) << endl;

    return 0;
}
```

The function **main** in Listing 13-9 declares the following variables and pointers:

- The constant **char**-type near pointer **pszMsg1**, which stores the address of the string literal "Enter first integer : "
- The constant **char**-type near pointer **pszMsg2**, which stores the address of the string literal "Enter second integer : "
- The **int**-type variables **nNum1** and **nNum2**
- The **int**-type far pointer **pnNum1**, which stores the address of variable **nNum1**
- The **int**-type far pointer **pnNum2**, which stores the address of variable **nNum2**

The function **main** performs the following tasks:

- Display the text for the first prompt using the constant pointer **pszMsg1**
- Input an integer and store it in the variable **nNum1** using the far pointer **pnNum1**
- Display the text of the second prompt message using the constant pointer **pszMsg2**
- Input an integer and store it in the variable **nNum2** using the far pointer **pnNum2**
- Display the input values and their sum. The output statement displays the input values using variable **nNum1** and **nNum2**. The statement also displays the sum of the values using the far pointers **pnNum1** and **pnNum2**.

Pointers as Function Parameters

Pointers have a variety of uses in passing arguments to functions, allowing the programmer great flexibility and avoiding needless overhead, as the examples that follow will show. You can use pointers to pass information to a function, from a function, and to and from a function (enabling two-way data flow between a function and its caller).

POINTERS TO ARRAYS AS FUNCTION PARAMETERS

You can use pointers to arrays as function parameters. Such pointers allow you to pass a static or dynamic array as an argument to a function. The general syntax for declaring a pointer to an array as a function parameter is:

```
[const] type* pointerToArray
```

Using the **const** keyword prevents the function from altering the values in the array. In other words, using the **const** keyword makes the values in the array read-only. Omitting the **const** keyword allows the function to alter the values in the array argument and submit the update back to the caller. Using pointers to arrays as function parameters enables you to write functions that handle arrays of varying sizes.

Here are examples of using pointers to arrays as function parameters:

```
struct myPersonnelData
{
  // members
};

void Sort(int* pnArray, int nNumberOfElements);
int LinearSearch(myPersonnelData* pData, int nNumberOfElements,
                 myPersonnelData searchData);
void Show(double* pfArray, int nNumElems);
```

The example shows the prototypes of functions **Sort**, **LinearSearch**, and **Show**. The function **Sort** sorts an array of integers — the first parameter **pnArray** is a pointer to an array of **int**-type. The function **LinearSearch** searches an array of **myPersonnelData** — the first parameter **pData** is a pointer to an array of **myPersonnelData**-type. The function **Show** displays an array of **double**-type—the first parameter **pfArray** is a pointer to an array of **double**-type. All of the functions in the example include a second parameter that passes the number of elements for the function to process.

Let's look at a programming example. Listing 13-10 shows the source code for the PTR10.CPP program, which contains pointers to arrays of integers as function parameters. The program declares two such functions, one to sort the array of integers and one to display it. The program declares two C++ arrays of different sizes and uses the functions to perform the following tasks on each array:

- Display the unsorted elements of the array
- Sort the array
- Display the sorted elements of the array

Here is the output for the program in Listing 13-10:

```
Unsorted first array is:
65 78 22 54 56 66
Sorted first array is:
22 54 56 65 66 78
Unsorted second array is:
265 378 522 354 156 766 888 123 111 433 445
Sorted second array is:
111 123 156 265 354 378 433 445 522 766 888
```

Listing 13-10
The source code for the PTR10.CPP program.

```
// A C++ program that illustrates using pointers
// to arrays as parameters in functions

#include <iostream.h>
#include <iomanip.h>

const int TRUE = 1;
const int FALSE = 0;

// prototype functions
void showIntArray(int* pnArray, int nNumElems,
                  const char* pszMsg = "");
void CombSort(int* pnArray, int nNumElems);
```

```
main()
{
  int nArray1[] = { 65, 78, 22, 54, 56, 66 };
  int nArray2[] = { 265, 378, 522, 354, 156, 766,
                    888, 123, 111, 433, 445 };
  int nSize1 = sizeof(nArray1) / sizeof(int);
  int nSize2 = sizeof(nArray2) / sizeof(int);

  // displays unsorted first array
  showIntArray(nArray1, nSize1, "Unsorted first array is:\n");
  // sort first array
  CombSort(nArray1, nSize1);
  // displays sorted first array
  showIntArray(nArray1, nSize1, "Sorted first array is:\n");


  // displays unsorted second array
  showIntArray(nArray2, nSize2, "Unsorted second array is:\n");
  // sort second array
  CombSort(nArray2, nSize2);
  // displays sorted second array
  showIntArray(nArray2, nSize2, "Sorted second array is:\n");

  return 0;
}

void showIntArray(int* pnArray, int nNumElems,
                  const char* pszMsg)
{
  cout << pszMsg;
  for (int i = 0; i < nNumElems; i++)
    cout << pnArray[i] << ' ';
  cout << endl;
}

void CombSort(int* pnArray, int nNumElems)
{
  int nOffset = nNumElems;
  int bSorted;

  if (nNumElems < 2)
    return;

  do {
    nOffset = (nOffset * 8) / 11;
    nOffset = (nOffset < 1) ? 1 : nOffset;
    bSorted = TRUE; // set sorted flag
    // compare elements
    for (int i = 0, j = nOffset;
         i < (nNumElems - nOffset);
         i++, j++) {
```

```
     if (pnArray[i] > pnArray[j]) {
       // swap elements
       int nSwap = pnArray[i];
       pnArray[i] = pnArray[j];
       pnArray[j] = nSwap;
       bSorted = FALSE; // clear sorted flag
     }
   }
 } while (!bSorted || nOffset != TRUE);
}
```

Listing 13-10 declares the prototypes of the functions **showIntArray** and **CombSort**. The function **showIntArray** displays the values in an array of integers and has the following parameters:

- The **int**-type pointer parameter **pnArray**, which accesses the array of integers to display
- The **int**-type parameter **nNumElems**, which specifies the number of array elements to display
- The constant **char**-type pointer **pszMsg**, which passes a message to display with the output

The function **CombSort** sorts the elements of an array of integers and has the following parameters:

- The **int**-type pointer parameter **pnArray**, which accesses the array of integers to sort
- The **int**-type parameter **nNumElems**, which specifies the number of array elements to sort

Both functions **showIntArray** and **CombSort** handle **int**-type arrays of different sizes. The definitions of these functions access the array elements using the pointer parameter **pnArray** (declared in each function). The source code uses the form **pnArray[*index*]** to access various array elements.

The function **main** declares and initializes the **int**-type arrays **nArray1** and **nArray2**. These arrays have different numbers of elements. The function also declares and initializes the variables **nSize1** and **nSize2**, which store the number of elements in arrays **nArray1** and **nArray2**, respectively. The function **main** performs the following tasks:

- Display the unsorted values in array **nArray1** by calling the function **showIntArray**. The arguments for this function call are **nArray1** (remember that the name of the array is a pointer to its first element), the variable **nSize1**, and the string literal "Unsorted first array is:\n."

- Sort the array by calling the function **CombSort**. The arguments for this function call are **nArray1** (the pointer to the array) and the variable **nSize1**.

- Display the sorted values in array **nArray1** by calling the function **showIntArray**. The arguments for this function call are **nArray1**, the variable **nSize1**, and the string literal "Sorted first array is:\n."

- Display the unsorted values in array **nArray2** by calling the function **showIntArray**. The arguments for this function call are **nArray2**, the variable **nSize2**, and the string literal "Unsorted second array is:\n."

- Sort the array by calling the function **CombSort**. The arguments for this function call are **nArray2** (the pointer to the array) and the variable **nSize2**.

- Display the sorted values in array **nArray2** by calling the function **showIntArray**. The arguments for this function call are **nArray2**, the variable **nSize2**, and the string literal "Sorted second array is:\n."

POINTERS TO ENUMERATED TYPES AS FUNCTION PARAMETERS

You can use pointers to enumerated types as function parameters. Such parameters serve either to pass an array of enumerators or to pass a single enumerator *back* to the function caller. You can use a reference parameter to perform the same task. The general syntax for declaring a pointer to an enumerated type as a function parameter is:

```
type* pointerToEnumeratedType
```

Here is an example of using pointers to enumerated types as function parameters:

```
enum Colors { Red, Blue, Green, Yellow };
void getScreenColors(Colors* pForegroundColor, /* output */
                     Colors* pBackgroundColor  /* output */);
```

The function **getScreenColors** returns the foreground and background colors to the function caller. The parameter **pForegroundColor** is the pointer to the foreground color, and the parameter **pBackgroundColor** is the pointer to the background color. Both parameters yield enumerators to the function caller.

Let's look at a sample program. Listing 13-11 shows the source code for the PTR11.CPP program, which illustrates using pointers to enumerated types as function parameters. The program declares the enumerated type **weekDay**, which lists the names of the days of the week. It generates three random days and displays the names of the days as well as the next and previous days. The program uses a function that returns the next and previous days, using pointers to enumerated types, for a given day.

Here is a sample run of the program in Listing 13-11:

```
Day # 1
Today is Tuesday
Tomorrow is Wednesday
Yesterday was Monday

Day # 2
Today is Saturday
Tomorrow is Sunday
Yesterday was Friday

Day # 3
Today is Monday
Tomorrow is Tuesday
Yesterday was Sunday
```

Listing 13-11
The source code for the PTR11.CPP program.

```cpp
// A C++ program that illustrates pointers to enumerated types
// used as function parameters

#include <iostream.h>
#include <iomanip.h>
#include <stdlib.h>
#include <time.h>

// declare enumerated type
enum weekDay { Sunday, Monday, Tuesday, Wednesday,
               Thursday, Friday, Saturday };
enum Logical { FALSE, TRUE };
```

```cpp
void showWeekDay(weekDay eDay,
                 const char* pszMsg = "",
                 Logical bEmitCR = TRUE);
void getNextAndPreviousDays(weekDay eDay,
                            weekDay* peNextDay,
                            weekDay* pePrevDay);


main()
{
  const int MAX = 3;
  weekDay Today, Tomorrow, Yesterday;

  // reseed random-number generator
  srand((unsigned)time(NULL));
  for (int i = 0; i < MAX; i++) {
    // get random day number
    int n = rand() % 7;
    Today = weekDay(n);
    // display today
    cout << "Day # " << (i+1) << endl;
    showWeekDay(Today, "Today is ");

    // display tomorrow
    getNextAndPreviousDays(Today, &Tomorrow, &Yesterday);
    showWeekDay(Tomorrow, "Tomorrow is ");

    // display yesterday
    showWeekDay(Yesterday, "Yesterday was ");
    cout << endl;
  }

  return 0;
}

void showWeekDay(weekDay eDay,
                 const char* pszMsg,
                 Logical bEmitCR)
{
  cout << pszMsg;
  switch (eDay) {
    case Sunday:
      cout << "Sunday";
      break;

    case Monday:
      cout << "Monday";
      break;

    case Tuesday:
      cout << "Tuesday";
      break;
```

```
    case Wednesday:
      cout << "Wednesday";
      break;

    case Thursday:
      cout << "Thursday";
      break;

    case Friday:
      cout << "Friday";
      break;

    case Saturday:
      cout << "Saturday";
      break;
  }

  if (bEmitCR)
    cout << endl;
}

void getNextAndPreviousDays(weekDay eDay,
                            weekDay* peNextDay,
                            weekDay* pePrevDay)
{
  switch (eDay) {
    case Sunday:
      *peNextDay = Monday;
      *pePrevDay = Saturday;
      break;

    case Monday:
      *peNextDay = Tuesday;
      *pePrevDay = Sunday;
      break;

    case Tuesday:
      *peNextDay = Wednesday;
      *pePrevDay = Monday;
      break;

    case Wednesday:
      *peNextDay = Thursday;
      *pePrevDay = Tuesday;
      break;

    case Thursday:
      *peNextDay = Friday;
      *pePrevDay = Wednesday;
      break;
```

```
   case Friday:
     *peNextDay = Saturday;
     *pePrevDay = Thursday;
     break;

   case Saturday:
     *peNextDay = Sunday;
     *pePrevDay = Friday;
     break;
  }
 }
```

Listing 13-11 declares the enumerated types **weekDay** and **Logical**. The enumerated type **weekDay** lists the names of the days of the week. The listing also contains the prototypes of functions **showWeekDay** and **getNextAndPreviousDays**. The first function displays the name of the day as specified by the **weekDay**-type parameter **eDay**. The second function yields the next and previous days for the day specified by an identical parameter. The function uses the **weekDay**-type pointer parameters **peNextDay** and **pePrevDay** to return the next and previous days to the function caller.

The function **main** declares the local constant **MAX** and the **weekDay**-type variables **Today**, **Tomorrow**, and **Yesterday**. The function reseeds the random number generator and then uses a **for** loop to perform the following tasks for **MAX** number of times:

- Generate a random number between 0 and 6 and store that number in the variable **n**

- Convert the random number into a **weekDay** enumerator and store that enumerator in the variable **Today**

- Display the enumerator in variable **Today** by calling function **showWeekDay**, whose arguments are the variable **Today** and the string literal "Today is "

- Obtain the next and previous days by calling the function **getNextAndPreviousDays**. The arguments for this function call are the variable **Today**, the address of variable **Tomorrow** (obtained by using the expression **&Tomorrow**), and the address of variable **Yesterday** (obtained by using the expression **&Yesterday**). I could have declared pointers to the variables **Tomorrow** and **Yesterday** and used these pointers. Using the address-of operator with the name of the variable, however, acts as a temporary pointer.

- Display the enumerator in variable **Tomorrow** by calling function **showWeekDay**. The arguments for this function call are the variable **Tomorrow** and the string literal "Tomorrow is ."

- Displays the enumerator in variable **Yesterday** by calling function **showWeekDay**. The arguments for this function call are the variable **Yesterday** and the string literal "Yesterday was ."

POINTERS TO STRUCTURES AS FUNCTION PARAMETERS

C++ allows you to use pointers to structures as function parameters. There are three typical uses for such pointers:

- Passing a pointer to a structure variable instead of a copy of that variable eliminates the overhead of making a copy of the variable for the function to use.

- Passing a pointer to a structure variable allows the pointer to support two-way data flow between the function and its caller.

- Passing a pointer to a structure type allows the function to process an array of structures.

The general syntax for declaring a pointer to a structure as a function parameter is:

```
[const] type* pointerToStructure
```

Using the **const** keyword prevents the function from altering the values in the structure. By the same token, omitting the **const** keyword allows the function to alter the values in the structure and submit the update back to the caller.

Here is an example of using a pointer to a structure as a function parameter:

```
struct ScreenChars
{
  // members
};
```

```
void LoadScreen(ScreenChars* pScreen /* input */);
void SaveScreen(ScreenChars* pScreen /* ouput */);
void UpdateScreen(ScreenChars* pScreen /* in/out */);
```

The example declares the structure **ScreenChars** and the prototypes of the functions **LoadScreen**, **SaveScreen**, and **UpdateScreen**. All three functions have the **ScreenChars**-type pointer parameter **pScreen**. The function **LoadScreen** uses the pointer **pScreen** to access a **ScreenChars**-type variable quickly. The function **SaveScreen** uses the pointer to output the screen's data to a **ScreenChars**-type variable. The function **UpdateScreen** uses the pointer **pScreen** to pass screen-related data to and from the function.

Let me present a programming example. Listing 13-12 shows the source code for the PTR12.CPP program, which illustrates using pointers to structures as function parameters. The program calculates the statistical mean and standard deviation for each of two sets of random numbers. The program declares a structure that has data members to store the statistical summations, mean, and standard deviation. The functions in the program initialize data memebers and variables, update the summations, and obtain the mean and standard deviation, using parameters that are pointers to the structure.

Here is a sample output for the program in Listing 13-12:

```
Number of observations in set # 1 = 100
Mean = 593.71
Standard deviation = 274.943

Number of observations in set # 2 = 200
Mean = 460.235
Standard deviation = 280.823
```

Listing 13-12
The source code for the PTR12.CPP program.

```
// A C++ program that illustrates pointers to structures
// used as function parameters

#include <iostream.h>
#include <stdlib.h>
#include <time.h>
#include <math.h>
```

```
// declare the structure for basic statistical data
struct BasicStat {
  int m_nNumData;
  double m_fSumOfX;
  double m_fSumOfXSqr;
  double m_fMean;
  double m_fSdev;
};

// declare function prototypes
void initBasicStat(BasicStat* pStatData);
void addData(double* pfArray, int nNumElems,
             BasicStat* pStatData);
void calcBasicStat(BasicStat* pStatData);


main()
{
  const int MAX1 = 100;
  const int MAX2 = 2 * MAX1;
  const int MIN_NUM = 1;
  const int MAX_NUM = 1000;
  double fData1[MAX1];
  double fData2[MAX2];
  // declare a structure
  BasicStat StatData1, StatData2;
  // declare pointers to structures StatData1 and StatData2
  BasicStat* pStatData1 = &StatData1;
  BasicStat* pStatData2 = &StatData2;

  // reseed random-number generator
  srand((unsigned)time(NULL));

  // assign data to array fData1
  for (int i = 0; i < MAX1; i++)
    fData1[i] = double(rand() % MAX_NUM + MIN_NUM);

  // assign data to array fData2
  for (i = 0; i < MAX2; i++)
    fData2[i] = double(rand() % MAX_NUM + MIN_NUM);


  // initialize structures
  initBasicStat(pStatData1);
  initBasicStat(pStatData2);

  // update statistical summations
  addData(fData1, MAX1, pStatData1);
  addData(fData2, MAX2, pStatData2);

  // calculate basic stats for the two structures
  calcBasicStat(pStatData1);
  calcBasicStat(pStatData2);
```

```
    cout << "Number of observations in set # 1 = "
         << StatData1.m_nNumData << "\n"
         << "Mean = " << StatData1.m_fMean << "\n"
         << "Standard deviation = "
         << StatData1.m_fSdev << "\n\n";

    cout << "Number of observations in set # 2 = "
         << StatData2.m_nNumData << "\n"
         << "Mean = " << StatData2.m_fMean << "\n"
         << "Standard deviation = "
         << StatData2.m_fSdev;

    return 0;
}

void initBasicStat(BasicStat* pStatData)
{
    // initialize some of the data members
    pStatData->m_nNumData = 0;
    pStatData->m_fSumOfX = 0;
    pStatData->m_fSumOfXSqr = 0;
}

void addData(double* pfArray, int nNumElems,
             BasicStat* pStatData)
{
    pStatData->m_nNumData += nNumElems;
    // obtain statistical summations
    for (int i = 0; i < nNumElems; i++) {
        pStatData->m_fSumOfX += pfArray[i];
        pStatData->m_fSumOfXSqr += pfArray[i] * pfArray[i];
    }
}

void calcBasicStat(BasicStat* pStatData)
{
    if (pStatData->m_nNumData < 2)
        return;
    // calculate mean value
    pStatData->m_fMean = pStatData->m_fSumOfX / pStatData->m_nNumData;
    // calculate standard deviation
    pStatData->m_fSdev =
        sqrt((pStatData->m_fSumOfXSqr -
              pStatData->m_fSumOfX * pStatData->m_fSumOfX /
              pStatData->m_nNumData) /
              (pStatData->m_nNumData - 1));

}
```

Listing 13-12 declares the structure BasicStat, which has the following data members:

- The int-type data member m_nNumData stores the number of observations.
- The double-type data member m_fSumOfX stores the sum of observations.
- The double-type data member m_fSumOfXSqr stores the sum of observations squared.
- The double-type data member m_fMean stores the statistical mean.
- The double-type data member m_fSdev stores the statistical standard deviation.

The listing declares the prototypes of the functions initBasicStat, addData, and calcBasicStat.

The function initBasicStat initializes the data members m_nNumData, m_fSumOfX, and m_fSumOfXSqr of the structure accessed by the BasicStat-type pointer pStatData. Thus, the pointer serves to output data back to the function caller.

The function addData adds the values in the double-type array (accessed by the double-type pointer parameter pfArray) to the BasicStat structure variable accessed by the pointer pStatData. Thus the pointer supports two-way data flow between the function and its caller.

The function calcBasicStat calculates the statistical mean and standard deviation for the structure variable accessed by pointer pStatData. Thus the pointer supports two-way data flow between the function and its caller.

The definitions of these functions use the BasicStat-type pointers to access the structure's data members. The source code uses the operator --> with the pointer parameter pStatData.

The function main declares a number of local constants and the arrays fData1 and fData2. These arrays have different sizes. The function also declares the BasicStat-type variables StatData1 and StatData2. Moreover, the function declares the BasicStat-type pointers pStatData1 and pStatData2 and initializes them with the addresses of variables StatData1 and StatData2, respectively.

The function main performs the following tasks:

- Reseed the random number generator
- Assign random values to the arrays **fData1** and **fData2**
- Initialize the member variables of **StatData1** by calling the function **initBasicStat**. The argument for this function call is the pointer **pStatData1**, which accesses variable **StatData1**.
- Initialize the members of **StatData2** by calling the function **initBasicStat** once again. The argument for this function call is the pointer **pStatData2**, which accesses variable **StatData2**.
- Update the summations in variable **StatData1** by calling the function **addData**. The arguments for this function call are the array **fData1**, the constant **MAX1**, and the pointer **pStatData1**.
- Update the summations in variable **StatData2** by calling the function **addData** a second time. The arguments for this function call are the array **fData2**, the constant **MAX2**, and the pointer **pStatData2**.
- Calculate the statistical mean and standard deviation for variable **StatData1** by calling the function **calcBasicStat**. The argument for this function call is the pointer **pStatData1**.
- Similarly calculate the statistical mean and standard deviation for variable **StatData2**, again by calling the function **calcBasicStat**. The argument for this function call is the pointer **pStatData2**.
- Display the number of observations and statistical mean and standard deviation for variable **StatData1**. The output statement uses the variable **StatData1** to access the data members **m_nNumData**, **m_fMean**, and **m_fSdev**.
- Perform a similar display for variable **StatData2**.

Pointers to Functions

C++, like C, allows you to declare and use pointers to functions. Such a pointer stores the address of a function (that is, the location of the first executable statement). You can use pointers to functions to invoke the functions. The general syntax for declaring a pointer to a function is:

```
type (*pointerToFunction)(parameterList) [= functionAddress];
```

When you initialize a pointer to a function, you must use the name of a function whose return type and parameter list match the pointer declaration. This condition is also true when you assign the address of a function to a pointer. The general syntax for this kind of assignment is:

```
type functionName(parameterList);
type (*pointerToFunction)(parameterList);
pointerToFunction = functionName;
```

The general syntax for invoking a function using its pointer is:

```
(*pointerToFunction)(argumentList)
```

Here is an example of declaring and using pointers to functions:

```
// prototype function
int LinearSearch(int* pnArray, int nNumArray, int nSearchVal);
int StatSearch(int* pnArray, int nNumArray, int nSearchVal);

main()
{
  int nArray[100] = { 44, 55, 66, 77, 32, 12 };
  int nCount = 6;
  int nSearchVal = nArray[1];
  int nIndex;
  // declare pointer to function
  int (*Search)(int*, int , int);

  // assign address of function LinearSearch to pointer Search
  Search = LinearSearch;
  // other statements
  // invoke LinearSearch
  nIndex = (*Search)(nArray, nCount, nSearchVal);
  // other statements
  // assign address of function StatSearch to pointer Search
  Search = StatSearch;
  // other statements
  // invoke StatSearch
  nIndex = (*Search)(nArray, nCount, nSearchVal);
  // other statements

  return 0;
}
```

BASIC

Pointers to Functions

Just when you thought that pointers to variables, arrays, and object were tough to grasp, C++ throws pointers to functions at you! Pointers to functions may sound very bizarre to BASIC programmers. However, such point-ers open a new door for writing functions that use pointers to other functions as param-eters. More about this feature later in this chapter.

PASCAL

Pointers to Functions

Pointers to functions resemble procedural parameters in Pascal.

The example declares the functions **StatSearch** and **LinearSearch**. The function **main** declares the function pointer **Search**. Notice that the return type and parameter list for this pointer match those in functions **StatSearch** and **LinearSearch**. The function **main** first assigns the address of function **LinearSearch** to pointer **Search** and then uses that pointer to invoke function **LinearSearch**. The arguments for this invocation are the array **nArray**, the variable **nCount**, and the variable **nSearchVal**. These arguments match the parameter list of the function pointer (and the function it points to). The function **main** then assigns the address of function **StatSearch** to pointer **Search** and then uses that pointer to invoke function **StatSearch**. The arguments for this invocation are the array **nArray**, the variable **nCount**, and the variable **nSearchVal**.

Let me present a programming example. Listing 13-13 shows the source code for the PTR13.CPP program, which uses function pointers. The program processes two arrays of integers and performs the following tasks on each array:

- Display the unsorted elements of the array
- Sort the array using one of two sorting functions. This task involves a function pointer.
- Display the sorted elements of the array

Here is the output of the program in Listing 13-13:

```
Unsorted first array is:
38 75 148 123 85 30 145 105 60 63
Sorted first array is:
30 38 60 63 75 85 105 123 145 148
Unsorted second array is:
34 67 133 111 76 27 130 94 54 57
Sorted second array is:
27 34 54 57 67 76 94 111 130 133
```

Listing 13-13
The source code for the PTR13.CPP program.

```cpp
// A C++ program that illustrates pointers to functions

#include <iostream.h>
#include <iomanip.h>

const int MAX_ELEMS = 10;

enum Logical { FALSE, TRUE };

// declare prototypes
void ShellSort(int* pnArray, int nNumElems);
void CombSort(int* pnArray, int nNumElems);
void showIntArray(int* pnArray,
                  const int nNumElems,
                  const char* pszMsg = "" );

main()
{
  int nArr[MAX_ELEMS] = { 23, 45, 89, 74, 51,
                          18, 87, 63, 36, 38 };
  int nArray1[MAX_ELEMS];
  int nArray2[MAX_ELEMS];
  // declare pointer to function
  void (*pSort)(int*, int);
```
Declare pointer to sorting function

```
        // assign values to array nArray1 and nArray2
        // based on the values in array nArr
        for (int i = 0; i < MAX_ELEMS; i++) {
          nArray1[i] = (5 * nArr[i]) / 3;
          nArray2[i] = (3 * nArr[i]) / 2;
        }

        showIntArray(nArray1, MAX_ELEMS, "Unsorted first array is:");
        // assign the address of the CombSort to function pointer pSort
        pSort = CombSort;                                              Assign function address
        (*pSort)(nArray1, MAX_ELEMS);                                 Invoke function using pointer
        showIntArray(nArray1, MAX_ELEMS, "Sorted first array is:");

        showIntArray(nArray2, MAX_ELEMS, "Unsorted second array is:");
        // assign the address of the CombSort to function pointer pSort
        pSort = ShellSort;
        (*pSort)(nArray2, MAX_ELEMS);
        showIntArray(nArray2, MAX_ELEMS, "Sorted second array is:");

        return 0;
      }

      void ShellSort(int* pnArray, int nNumElems)
      {
        int nOffset = nNumElems;
        int bSorted;

        if (nNumElems < 2)
          return;

        while (nOffset > 1) {
          nOffset = (nOffset - 1) / 3;
          nOffset = (nOffset < 1) ? 1 : nOffset;
          // arrange elements that are nOffset apart
          do {
            bSorted = TRUE; // set sorted flag
            // compare elements
            for (int i = 0, j = nOffset;
                 i < (nNumElems - nOffset);
                 i++, j++) {
              if (pnArray[i] > pnArray[j]) {
                // swap elements
                int nSwap = pnArray[i];
                pnArray[i] = pnArray[j];
                pnArray[j] = nSwap;
                bSorted = FALSE; // clear sorted flag
              }
            }
          } while (!bSorted);
        }
      }
```

```
void CombSort(int* pnArray, int nNumElems)
{
  int nOffset = nNumElems;
  int bSorted;

  if (nNumElems < 2)
    return;

  do {
    nOffset = (nOffset * 8) / 11;
    nOffset = (nOffset < 1) ? 1 : nOffset;
    bSorted = TRUE; // set sorted flag
    // compare elements
    for (int i = 0, j = nOffset;
         i < (nNumElems - nOffset);
         i++, j++) {
      if (pnArray[i] > pnArray[j]) {
        // swap elements
        int nSwap = pnArray[i];
        pnArray[i] = pnArray[j];
        pnArray[j] = nSwap;
        bSorted = FALSE; // clear sorted flag
      }
    }
  } while (!bSorted || nOffset != TRUE);
}

void showIntArray(int* pnArray,
                  const int nNumElems,
                  const char* pszMsg)
{
  cout << pszMsg << endl;
  for (int i = 0; i < nNumElems; i++)
    cout << pnArray[i] << ' ';
  cout << endl;
}
```

Listing 13-13 declares the prototypes of the functions **ShellSort**, **CombSort**, and **showIntArray**. The first two functions sort arrays of integers and have matching parameter lists. The third function displays arrays of integers.

The function **main** declares the arrays **nArr**, **nArray1**, and **nArray2**, which have the same numbers of elements. The function initializes only the first array. It also declares the function pointer **pSort**, whose return type and parameter list match those of functions **ShellSort** and **CombSort**. The function **main** then performs the following tasks:

- Assign values to the arrays **nArray1** and **nArray2**, which are based on the values of the array **nArr**
- Display the unsorted elements of array **nArray1** by calling the function **showIntArray**. The arguments for this function call are array **nArray1**, constant **MAX_ELEMS**, and the string literal "Unsorted first array is:".
- Assign the address of function **CombSort** to the function pointer **pSort**
- Sort the array **nArray1** with function **CombSort** using the function pointer **pSort**. The arguments for this invocation are the array **nArray1** and the constant **MAX_ELEMS**.
- Display the sorted elements of array **nArray1** by calling the function **showIntArray**. The arguments for this function call are array **nArray1**, constant **MAX_ELEMS**, and the string literal "Sorted first array is:".
- Display the unsorted elements of array **nArray2** by calling the function **showIntArray**. The arguments for this function call are array **nArray2**, constant **MAX_ELEMS**, and the string literal "Unsorted second array is:".
- Assign the address of function **ShellSort** to the function pointer **pSort**
- Sort the array **nArray2** with function **ShellSort** using the function pointer **pSort**. The arguments for this invocation are the array **nArray2** and the constant **MAX_ELEMS**.
- Display the sorted elements of array **nArray2** by calling the function **showIntArray**. The arguments for this function call are array **nArray2**, constant **MAX_ELEMS**, and the string literal "Sorted second array is:".

POINTERS TO ARRAYS OF FUNCTIONS

In addition to declaring individual function pointers, C++ allows you to declare an array of function pointers. Each pointer in this kind of array stores the address of a function. The general syntax for declaring an array of function pointers is:

```
type (*pointerToFunction[numberOfPointers])(parameterList);
```

The syntax shows that declaring an array of function pointers is similar to declaring a single function pointer. The main difference is that the name of the array must be followed by the number of pointers, enclosed in square brackets.

When you assign the address of a function to an element in an array of function pointers, you must include the element's index, as shown in this general syntax:

```
type functionName(parameterList);
type (*pointerToFunction[numElems])(parameterList);
pointerToFunction[nIndex] = functionName;
```

The general syntax for invoking a function using its pointer is:

```
(*pointerToFunction[nIndex])(argumentList)
```

Here is an example of declaring and using an array of function pointers:

```
// prototype function
void StatSearch(int* pnArray, int nNumArray, int nSearchVal);
void LinearSearch(int* pnArray, int nNumArray, int nSearchVal);

main()
{
  int nArray[100] = { 44, 55, 66, 77, 32, 12 };
  int nCount = 6;
  int nSearchVal = nArray[1];
  // declare pointer to function
  void (*Search[2])(int*, int, int);

  // assign address of function LinearSearch to pointer Search
  Search[0] = LinearSearch;
  // assign address of function StatSearch to pointer Search
  Search[1] = StatSearch;
  // other statements
  // invoke LinearSearch
  (*Search[0])(nArray, nCount, nSearchVal);
  // other statements
  // invoke StatSearch
  (*Search[1])(nArray, nCount, nSearchVal);
  // other statements

  return 0;
}
```

The example declares the functions **StatSearch** and **LinearSearch**. The function **main** declares the array of function pointers **Search** to have two elements. The return type and parameter list for this pointer match those in functions **StatSearch** and **LinearSearch**. The function **main** first assigns the addresses of functions **LinearSearch** and **StatSearch** to pointers **Search[∅]** and **Search[1]**, respectively. The function then uses pointer **Search[∅]** to invoke function **LinearSearch** and pointer **Search[1]** to invoke function **StatSearch**. The arguments for each invocation are the array **nArray**, the variable **nCount**, and the variable **nSearchVal**.

Let's look at a programming example. Listing 13-14 shows the source code for the PTR14.CPP program. I created this program by modifying the source code in program PTR13.CPP, changing the function pointer **pSort** into a two-element array of function pointers. Using an array of function pointers allows the new program version to assign the addresses of functions **CombSort** and **ShellSort** to elements 0 and 1, respectively, before displaying and sorting the two arrays.

Here is the output of the program in Listing 13-14:

```
Unsorted first array is:
38 75 148 123 85 30 145 105 60 63
Sorted first array is:
30 38 60 63 75 85 105 123 145 148
Unsorted second array is:
34 67 133 111 76 27 130 94 54 57
Sorted second array is:
27 34 54 57 67 76 94 111 130 133
```

Listing 13-14
The source code for the PTR14.CPP program.

```cpp
// A C++ program that illustrates pointers
// to arrays of functions

#include <iostream.h>
#include <iomanip.h>

const int MAX_ELEMS = 10;

enum Logical { FALSE, TRUE };

// declare prototypes
void ShellSort(int* pnArray, int nNumElems);
void CombSort(int* pnArray, int nNumElems);
void showIntArray(int* pnArray,
                  const int nNumElems,
                  const char* pszMsg = "" );

main()
{
  int nArr[MAX_ELEMS] = { 23, 45, 89, 74, 51,
                          18, 87, 63, 36, 38 };
```

```
    int nArray1[MAX_ELEMS];
    int nArray2[MAX_ELEMS];
    // declare pointer to function
    void (*pSort[2])(int*, int);                    ➤ Declare pointer to array of sorting function

    // assign values to array nArray1 and nArray2
    // based on the values in array nArr
    for (int i = 0; i < MAX_ELEMS; i++) {
      nArray1[i] = (5 * nArr[i]) / 3;
      nArray2[i] = (3 * nArr[i]) / 2;
    }

    // assign addresses of sorting functions to the array
    // of function pointers
    pSort[0] = CombSort;                             ➤ Assign function addresses to
    pSort[1] = ShellSort;                              array of pointer

    showIntArray(nArray1, MAX_ELEMS, "Unsorted first array is:");
    // invoke function pointer at index 0
    (*pSort[0])(nArray1, MAX_ELEMS);
    showIntArray(nArray1, MAX_ELEMS, "Sorted first array is:");
                                                    ➤ Invoke
    showIntArray(nArray2, MAX_ELEMS, "Unsorted second array is:");   function
    // invoke function pointer at index 1                            using pointer
    (*pSort[1])(nArray2, MAX_ELEMS);
    showIntArray(nArray2, MAX_ELEMS, "Sorted second array is:");

    return 0;
}

void ShellSort(int* pnArray, int nNumElems)
{
    int nOffset = nNumElems;
    int bSorted;

    if (nNumElems < 2)
      return;

    while (nOffset > 1) {
      nOffset = (nOffset - 1) / 3;
      nOffset = (nOffset < 1) ? 1 : nOffset;
      // arrange elements that are nOffset apart
      do {
        bSorted = TRUE; // set sorted flag
        // compare elements
        for (int i = 0, j = nOffset;
             i < (nNumElems - nOffset);
             i++, j++) {
          if (pnArray[i] > pnArray[j]) {
            // swap elements
            int nSwap = pnArray[i];
            pnArray[i] = pnArray[j];
```

```
                pnArray[j] = nSwap;
                bSorted = FALSE; // clear sorted flag
              }
            }
        } while (!bSorted);
    }
}

void CombSort(int* pnArray, int nNumElems)
{
    int nOffset = nNumElems;
    int bSorted;

    if (nNumElems < 2)
        return;

    do {
        nOffset = (nOffset * 8) / 11;
        nOffset = (nOffset < 1) ? 1 : nOffset;
        bSorted = TRUE; // set sorted flag
        // compare elements
        for (int i = 0, j = nOffset;
             i < (nNumElems - nOffset);
             i++, j++) {
          if (pnArray[i] > pnArray[j]) {
            // swap elements
            int nSwap = pnArray[i];
            pnArray[i] = pnArray[j];
            pnArray[j] = nSwap;
            bSorted = FALSE; // clear sorted flag
          }
        }
    } while (!bSorted || nOffset != TRUE);
}

void showIntArray(int* pnArray,
                  const int nNumElems,
                  const char* pszMsg)
{
    cout << pszMsg << endl;
    for (int i = 0; i < nNumElems; i++)
      cout << pnArray[i] << ' ';
    cout << endl;
}
```

Since Listings 13-13 and 13-14 are very similar, I will focus on the differences between them. Notice the following aspects of function **main** in Listing 13-14:

- The function declares the array of function pointers **pSort** as **void** **(*pSort[2])(int*, int)**.
- The function assigns the address of function **CombSort** to **pSort[Ø]**.
- The function assigns the address of function **ShellSort** to **pSort[1]**.
- The function **main** invokes the function **CombSort** using the pointer **pSort[Ø]**. The arguments for this call are array **nArray1** and constant **MAX_ELEMS**.
- The function **main** invokes the function **ShellSort** using the pointer **pSort[1]**. The arguments for this call are array **nArray2** and constant **MAX_ELEMS**.

POINTERS TO FUNCTIONS AS PARAMETERS

After learning about function pointers, you may ask whether or not C++ allows such pointers to be function parameters. The answer is yes! C++ allows you to declare function parameters that are pointers to other functions. This is a very powerful programming language feature that allows a function to use other functions that are selected at runtime instead of compile time.

The declaration of a function pointer as a parameter uses the same syntax as the declaration of a function pointer as a variable.

Here is an example of declaring and using function pointers as function parameters:

```
// prototype function
void StatSearch(int* pnArray, int nNumArray, int nSearchVal);
void LinearSearch(int* pnArray, int nNumArray, int nSearchVal);
void SearchAndSave(int* pnArray, int nNumArray,
                   int nSearchVal,
                   void (*pSort)(int*, int),
                   const char* pszFilename);

main()
{
  const char* pszFilename = "ARRAY.DAT";
  int nArray[100] = { 44, 55, 66, 77, 32, 12 };
  int nCount = 6;
  int nSearchVal = nArray[1];
```

```
// declare pointer to function
void (*Search)(int*, int, int);

// assign address of function LinearSearch to pointer Search
Search = LinearSearch;
// other statements
// invoke LinearSearch and save data to a file
SearchAndSave(nArray, nCount, nSearchVal,
              (*Search)(nArray, nCount, nSearchVal), pszFilename);
// other statements
// assign address of function StatSearch to pointer Search
Search = StatSearch;
// invoke StatSearch
SearchAndSave(nArray, nCount, nSearchVal,
              (*Search)(nArray, nCount, nSearchVal), pszFilename);
// other statements

return 0;
}
```

The example declares the functions StatSearch, LinearSearch, and SearchAndSave. The last-named function has a function pointer parameter (pSort) whose return type and parameter list match those of functions LinearSearch and StatSearch. The function main declares the function pointer Search, whose return type and parameter list also match those for functions StatSearch and LinearSearch. The function main first assigns the address of function LinearSearch to pointer Search. Then the function calls function SearchAndSave to search the array nArray using the LinearSearch function. The arguments for this invocation are the array nArray, the variable nCount, the variable nSearchVal, the function pointer Search, and the constant pointer pszFilename. The function main then assigns the address of function StatSearch to pointer Search and calls function SearchAndSave a second time. The arguments for this function call match those of the first call to function SearchAndSave.

Let's look at a programming example. Listing 13-15 shows the source code for the PTR15.CPP program, which illustrates function pointers as function parameters. I created this program by modifying program PTR13.CPP, changing the function showIntArray in Listing 13-13 into function SortAndShow. The program declares two arrays of integers, sorts these arrays, and displays their ordered elements.

Here is the output of the program in Listing 13-15:

```
Sorted first array is:
30 38 60 63 75 85 105 123 145 148
Sorted second array is:
27 34 54 57 67 76 94 111 130 133
```

Listing 13-15

The source code for the PTR15.CPP program.

```cpp
// A C++ program that illustrates pointers to functions
// as function parameters

#include <iostream.h>
#include <iomanip.h>

const int MAX_ELEMS = 10;

enum Logical { FALSE, TRUE };

// declare prototypes
void ShellSort(int* pnArray, int nNumElems);
void CombSort(int* pnArray, int nNumElems);
void SortAndShow(int* pnArray,
                 const int nNumElems,
                 void (*pSort)(int*, int),
                 const char* pszMsg = "" );

main()
{
  int nArr[MAX_ELEMS] = { 23, 45, 89, 74, 51,
                          18, 87, 63, 36, 38 };
  int nArray1[MAX_ELEMS];
  int nArray2[MAX_ELEMS];
  // declare pointer to function
  void (*pSort)(int*, int);

  // assign values to array nArray1 and nArray2
  // based on the values in array nArr
  for (int i = 0; i < MAX_ELEMS; i++) {
    nArray1[i] = (5 * nArr[i]) / 3;
    nArray2[i] = (3 * nArr[i]) / 2;
  }

  // assign the address of the CombSort to function pointer pSort
  pSort = CombSort;
  SortAndShow(nArray1, MAX_ELEMS, pSort, "Sorted first array is:");

  // assign the address of the CombSort to function pointer pSort
  pSort = ShellSort;
  SortAndShow(nArray2, MAX_ELEMS, pSort, "Sorted second array is:");

  return 0;
}

void ShellSort(int* pnArray, int nNumElems)
{
  int nOffset = nNumElems;
  int bSorted;
```

```
        if (nNumElems < 2)
          return;

      while (nOffset > 1) {
        nOffset = (nOffset - 1) / 3;
        nOffset = (nOffset < 1) ? 1 : nOffset;
        // arrange elements that are nOffset apart
        do {
          bSorted = TRUE; // set sorted flag
          // compare elements
          for (int i = 0, j = nOffset;
               i < (nNumElems - nOffset);
               i++, j++) {
            if (pnArray[i] > pnArray[j]) {
              // swap elements
              int nSwap = pnArray[i];
              pnArray[i] = pnArray[j];
              pnArray[j] = nSwap;
              bSorted = FALSE; // clear sorted flag
            }
          }
        } while (!bSorted);
      }
    }

    void CombSort(int* pnArray, int nNumElems)
    {
      int nOffset = nNumElems;
      int bSorted;

      if (nNumElems < 2)
        return;

      do {
        nOffset = (nOffset * 8) / 11;
        nOffset = (nOffset < 1) ? 1 : nOffset;
        bSorted = TRUE; // set sorted flag
        // compare elements
        for (int i = 0, j = nOffset;
             i < (nNumElems - nOffset);
             i++, j++) {
          if (pnArray[i] > pnArray[j]) {
            // swap elements
            int nSwap = pnArray[i];
            pnArray[i] = pnArray[j];
            pnArray[j] = nSwap;
            bSorted = FALSE; // clear sorted flag
          }
        }
      } while (!bSorted || nOffset != TRUE);
    }
```

```
void SortAndShow(int* pnArray,
                 const int nNumElems,
                 void (*pSort)(int*, int),
                 const char* pszMsg )
{
  // sort the array
  (*pSort)(pnArray, nNumElems);
  // display the array
  cout << pszMsg << endl;
  for (int i = 0; i < nNumElems; i++)
    cout << pnArray[i] << ' ';
  cout << endl;
}
```

Listing 13-15 declares the prototypes of functions **ShellSort**, **CombSort**, and **SortAndShow**. The last of these functions has the following parameters:

- The **int**-type pointer parameter **pnArray**, which accesses the array of integers

- The constant **int**-type parameter **nNumElems**, which passes the number of array elements to sort and display

- The function pointer parameter **pSort**, which passes the address of the sorting function

- The constant **char**-type pointer **pszMsg**, which passes the message preceding the list of array elements in the output

The function **main** declares the arrays **nArr**, **nArray1**, and **nArray2**, which have the same numbers of elements. The function initializes only the first array. It also declares the function pointer **pSort**. The return type and parameter list of this function pointer match those of functions **ShellSort** and **CombSort**. The function **main** then performs the following tasks:

- Assign values to the arrays **nArray1** and **nArray2**; these values are based on the values of the array **nArr**

- Assign the address of function **CombSort** to the function pointer **pSort**

- Sort and display the array **nArray1** by calling function **SortAndShow**. The arguments for this invocation are the array **nArray1**, the constant **MAX_ELEMS**, the function pointer **pSort** (which has the address of function **CombSort**), and the string literal "Sorted first array is:\n."

- Assign the address of function **ShellSort** to the function pointer **pSort**
- Sort and display the array **nArray2** by calling function **SortAndShow**. The arguments for this invocation are the array **nArray2**, the constant **MAX_ELEMS**, the function pointer **pSort** (which has the address of function **ShellSort**), and the string literal "Sorted second array is:\n."

The definition of function **SortAndShow** uses the pointer parameter **pSort** to invoke a sorting function.

POINTERS TO ARRAYS OF FUNCTIONS AS PARAMETERS

C++ allows you to declare function parameters that are arrays of pointers. The syntax for declaring this kind of pointer is the same as that for declaring a C++ array of function pointers. Likewise, invoking the functions through the array of pointers uses the same syntax as with C++ arrays of function pointers.

Here is an example of declaring and using an array of function pointers as function parameters:

```
// prototype function
void StatSearch(int* pnArray, int nNumArray, int nSearchVal);
void LinearSearch(int* pnArray, int nNumArray, int nSearchVal);
void SearchAndSave(int* pnArray, int nNumArray,
                   int nSearchVal,
                   void (*pSearch[2])(int*, int),
                   int nSearchFunctionIndex,
                   const char* pszFilename);

main()
{
  const char* pszFilename = "ARRAY.DAT";
  int nArray[100] = { 44, 55, 66, 77, 32, 12 };
  int nCount = 6;
  int nSearchVal = nArray[1];
  // declare pointer to function
  void (*Search[2])(int*, int, int);

  // assign address of function LinearSearch to pointer Search[0]
  Search[0] = LinearSearch;
  // assign address of function StatSearch to pointer Search[1]
  Search[1] = StatSearch;
  // other statements
```

```
// invoke LinearSearch and save data to a file
SearchAndSave(nArray, nCount, nSearchVal,
              (*Search)(nArray, nCount, nSearchVal),
              0, pszFilename);
// other statements
// invoke StatSearch
SearchAndSave(nArray, nCount, nSearchVal,
              (*Search)(nArray, nCount, nSearchVal),
              1, pszFilename);
// other statements

return 0;
}
```

The example declares the functions **StatSearch**, **LinearSearch**, and **SearchAndSave**. The third function is similar to the one in the last example, except that it uses the array of function pointers **Search** and a new parameter, **nSearchFunctionIndex**, which selects which pointer in the array parameter **pSearch** to invoke. The function **main** declares the array of function pointers **Search** to have two elements. The return type and parameter list for this pointer match those in functions **StatSearch** and **LinearSearch**. The function **main** first assigns the addresses of functions **LinearSearch** and **StatSearch** to pointers **Search[Ø]** and **Search[1]**, respectively. The function then invokes function **SearchAndSave** twice to search and save the array. The arguments for each invocation are the array **nArray**, the variable **nCount**, the variable **nSearchVal**, the array of pointers parameter **Search**, the integer 0 (1 for the second call), and the pointer **pszFilename**. The first call searches the array using function **LinearSearch**, whereas the second call searches the array using function **StatSearch**.

Let me present a programming example. Listing 13-16 shows the source code for the PTR16.CPP program, which illustrates using arrays of pointers as function parameters. I created the source code in Listing 13-16 by modifying Listing 13-15. The new version of function **SortAndShow** uses an array of pointers as parameter **pSort** and has an additional parameter **nFunctionIndex**. This parameter selects which element of parameter **pSort** to invoke (and consequently, which sorting function to use).

Here is the output of the program in Listing 13-16:

```
Sorted first array is:
30 38 60 63 75 85 105 123 145 148
Sorted second array is:
27 34 54 57 67 76 94 111 130 133
```

Listing 13-16

The source code for the PTR16.CPP program.

```cpp
// A C++ program that illustrates using arrays of
// function pointers as parameters

#include <iostream.h>
#include <iomanip.h>

const int MAX_ELEMS = 10;
const int MAX_FUN = 2;

enum Logical { FALSE, TRUE };

// declare prototypes
void ShellSort(int* pnArray, int nNumElems);
void CombSort(int* pnArray, int nNumElems);
void SortAndShow(int* pnArray,
                 const int nNumElems,
                 void (*pSort[MAX_FUN])(int*, int),
                 int nFunctionIndex = 0,
                 const char* pszMsg = "" );

main()
{
  int nArr[MAX_ELEMS] = { 23, 45, 89, 74, 51,
                          18, 87, 63, 36, 38 };
  int nArray1[MAX_ELEMS];
  int nArray2[MAX_ELEMS];
  // declare pointer to function
  void (*pSort[MAX_FUN])(int*, int);

  // assign values to array nArray1 and nArray2
  // based on the values in array nArr
  for (int i = 0; i < MAX_ELEMS; i++) {
    nArray1[i] = (5 * nArr[i]) / 3;
    nArray2[i] = (3 * nArr[i]) / 2;
  }

  // assign the address of the sorting functions pointer pSort
  pSort[0] = CombSort;
  pSort[1] = ShellSort;

  SortAndShow(nArray1, MAX_ELEMS, pSort,
              0, "Sorted first array is:");
  SortAndShow(nArray2, MAX_ELEMS, pSort,
              1, "Sorted second array is:");

  return 0;
}

void ShellSort(int* pnArray, int nNumElems)
{
  int nOffset = nNumElems;
  int bSorted;
```

```
    if (nNumElems < 2)
      return;

  while (nOffset > 1) {
    nOffset = (nOffset - 1) / 3;
    nOffset = (nOffset < 1) ? 1 : nOffset;
    // arrange elements that are nOffset apart
    do {
      bSorted = TRUE; // set sorted flag
      // compare elements
      for (int i = 0, j = nOffset;
           i < (nNumElems - nOffset);
           i++, j++) {
        if (pnArray[i] > pnArray[j]) {
          // swap elements
          int nSwap = pnArray[i];
          pnArray[i] = pnArray[j];
          pnArray[j] = nSwap;
          bSorted = FALSE; // clear sorted flag
        }
      }
    } while (!bSorted);
  }
}

void CombSort(int* pnArray, int nNumElems)
{
  int nOffset = nNumElems;
  int bSorted;

  if (nNumElems < 2)
    return;

  do {
    nOffset = (nOffset * 8) / 11;
    nOffset = (nOffset < 1) ? 1 : nOffset;
    bSorted = TRUE; // set sorted flag
    // compare elements
    for (int i = 0, j = nOffset;
         i < (nNumElems - nOffset);
         i++, j++) {
      if (pnArray[i] > pnArray[j]) {
        // swap elements
        int nSwap = pnArray[i];
        pnArray[i] = pnArray[j];
        pnArray[j] = nSwap;
        bSorted = FALSE; // clear sorted flag
      }
    }
  } while (!bSorted || nOffset != TRUE);
}
```

```
void SortAndShow(int* pnArray,
                 const int nNumElems,
                 void (*pSort[MAX_FUN])(int*, int),
                 int nFunctionIndex,
                 const char* pszMsg )
{
  // sort the array
  (*pSort[nFunctionIndex])(pnArray, nNumElems);
  // display the array
  cout << pszMsg << endl;
  for (int i = 0; i < nNumElems; i++)
    cout << pnArray[i] << ' ';
  cout << endl;
}
```

Listing 13-16 is similar to Listings 13-15 and 13-14. Notice the following aspects of function **main** in Listing 13-16:

- The function **main** declares the array of function pointers **pSort**.
- It assigns the addresses of functions **CombSort** and **ShellSort** to the two elements of pointer **pSort**.
- It invokes the function **SortAndShow** to sort and display the elements of array **nArray1**. The arguments for this function call are array **nArray1**, constant **MAX_ELEMS**, array of pointers **pSort**, the integer 0, and the string literal "Sorted first array is:" The fourth argument causes function **SortAndShow** to use element **pSort[∅]** to invoke function **CombSort**.
- It next invokes the function **SortAndShow** to sort and display the elements of array **nArray2**. The arguments for this function call are array **nArray2**, constant **MAX_ELEMS**, array of pointers **pSort**, the integer 1, and the string literal "Sorted second array is:" The fourth argument causes function **SortAndShow** to use element **pSort[1]** to invoke function **ShellSort**.

The definition of function **SortAndShow** uses the value of parameter **nFunctionIndex** to invoke the corresponding element of array of pointers **pSort**.

Summary

This chapter discussed C++ pointers. You learned about pointers to existing variables, arrays, structures, and classes. You also learned how to use pointers to create and remove dynamic variables. The chapter also discussed constant pointers, near pointers, and far pointers. You also learned about using pointers to arrays, enumerated types, and structures as function parameters. The last part of the chapter discussed pointers to functions, arrays of function pointers, and how to use these special kinds of pointers as function parameters.

The next chapter discusses class hierarchies and shows you how to create descendant classes that enhance the operations of their parent classes.

14

Class
Hierarchies

*T*his chapter looks at declaring and using class
hierarchies to build classes that support different
objects. You will learn about single and multiple inheritance,
declaring a class hierarchy, constructors for child classes,
virtual functions and the rules governing them, virtual
destructors, friend functions, operators, friend operators,
multiple inheritance, containment, and friend classes.

Single and Multiple Inheritance

Object-oriented programming permits you to declare new
classes that are descendants of existing classes. The feature
of *inheritance* allows descendant classes to offer more
specialized operations than do their parent classes.

C++ is an object-oriented programming language that
supports two inheritance schemes: *single inheritance* and
multiple inheritance. Single inheritance derives a descendant
class from a single parent class. Multiple inheritance, by
contrast, derives a descendant class from two or more
parent classes. The subject of multiple inheritance has stirred
a lot of debate among C++ programmers. Most programmers prefer using single inheritance and bill it as the sound
way for building class hierarchies. These same programmers

foresee many design problems with multiple inheritance. Most of this chapter focuses on single inheritance hierarchies.

What is the basic conceptual difference between class hierarchies that use single and multiple inheritance? Using single inheritance, you create a descendant class that *"is a"* refinement of its parent class. This *"is a"* relationship is a characteristic of class hierarchies that are built using single inheritance. For example, if you create a class hierarchy for geometric shapes, then each descendant class *"is a"* geometric shape that supports special attributes and operations.

In contrast, by using multiple inheritance, you create a descendant class that *"has the"* attributes and operations of its parent classes. In other words, the descendant class has the summation of the attributes and operations of its parent classes. For example, you can declare a class that models a car as a descendant of classes that model the engine, the car's body, the electrical system, the air-conditioning system, and so on. These parent classes need not be part of the same hierarchy, but they do contribute to creating a car-modeling class. Thus, a car class is not an engine, or a body, or an electrical system. Instead, the car class is the summation of the parent classes — the car has an engine, has an electrical system, and so on.

Declaring a Class Hierarchy

C++ allows you to declare a descendant class from a parent class. The general syntax for declaring a descendant class that uses the single inheritance scheme is:

```
class className : [public] parentClassName
{
  [public:
  // public constructors
  // public destructor
  // public data members
  // public member functions
  ]

  [protected:
  // protected constructors
  // protected destructor
```

```
    // protected data members
    // protected member functions
    ]

    [private:
    // private constructors
    // private destructor
    // private data members
    // private member functions
    ]
};
```

A declaration for a descendant class starts with the keyword **class** and is followed by:

- The name of the class
- The colon character
- The optional keyword **public**
- The name of the parent class

The keyword **public** allows the class instances to access the public members of the parent class. Without this keyword, only the member functions of the descendant class can access the parent's members.

C++ enforces the following rules regarding the public, protected, and private sections of a descendant class:

1. All of the member functions can access all data members in a class regardless of which section they appear in.
2. The class instances can access only the public members.
3. The member functions of a descendant class can access only public and protected members of the parent class. Thus, the private members of a class cannot be accessed by the member functions of a descendant class.

Here is an example for declaring a descendant class:

```
class Rectangle
{
  public:
    Rectangle(double fLength = 0, double fWidth = 0)
      { setDimensions(fLength, fWidth); }
```

```
        void setDimensions(double fLength = 0, double fWidth = 0)
          {
            m_fLength = fLength;
            m_fWidth = fWidth;
          }
        double getLength()
          { return m_fLength; }
        double getWidth()
          { return m_fWidth; }
        double getArea()
          { return m_fLength * m_fWidth; }

    protected:
      double m_fLength;
      double m_fWidth;
  };

class Solid : public Rectangle
{
    public:
      Solid(double fLength = 0, double fWidth = 0,
            double fHeight = 0)
        { setDimensions(fLength, fWidth, fHeight); }
      void setDimensions(double fLength = 0, double fWidth = 0,
            double fHeight = 0)
          {
            m_fLength = fLength;
            m_fWidth = fWidth;
            m_fHeight = fHeight;
          }
      double getHeight()
        { return m_fHeight; }
      double getVolume()
        { return m_fHeight * getArea(); }

    protected:
      double m_fHeight;
  };
```

This example declares the base class **Rectangle** and its descendant class
Solid. The class **Rectangle** declares the protected **double**-type data members
m_fLength and **m_fWidth**. These data members store the length and width of
a rectangle, respectively. The class declares the following public members:

- The constructor, which initializes the data members

- The member function **setDimensions**, which assigns new values to the
  data members

- The member function **getLength**, which returns the value in data
  member **m_fLength**

- The member function **getWidth**, which returns the value in data member **m_fWidth**

- The member function **getArea**, which returns the area of the rectangle, calculated using the data members

The example declares the class **Solid** as a public descendant of class **Rectangle**. The descendant class declares the protected **double**-type data members **m_fHeight**, which stores the height of the solid. The class inherits the protected data members **m_fLength** and **m_fWidth** and ends up with three data members. The class **Solid** also declares the following public members:

- The constructor, which initializes the data members

- The member function **setDimensions**, which assigns new values to the data members. This member function is a new version that assigns values to the inherited and declared data members.

- The member function **getHeight**, which returns the value in data member **m_fHeight**

- The member function **getVolume**, which returns the volume of the solid shape, calculated using data member **m_fHeight** and the result from the inherited member function **getArea**

The class **Solid** inherits the member functions **setDimensions(double, double)** (the one that assigns values to the inherited data members), **getLength**, **getWidth**, and **getArea**. The definition of member function **getVolume** uses the inherited member function **getArea**.

Let me present two programming examples. The first creates a new class as a public descendant of its parent class. The second creates a new class as a nonpublic descendant of its parent class. The first example shows how the descendant class adds new operations to those of the parent class. By contrast, the second example shows how the members of the parent class support the *internal* operations of the descendant class.

THE EXAMPLE OF THE SORTED ARRAY

Let's look at the first example. Listing 14-1 shows the source code for the DESCLS1.CPP program, which illustrates the descendant of public classes. The program declares the class **myArray**, which supports basic integer arrays, and its descendant class **mySortedArray**, which supports sorted integer arrays. The program creates an instance of the descendant class and performs the following tasks:

- Assign integers to the class instance
- Display the unsorted integers stored in the class instance
- Sort the array elements of the class instance
- Display the sorted integers stored in the class instance

Here is the output of the program in Listing 14-1:

```
Unsorted array is:
23 45 89 74 51 18 87 63 36 38
Sorted array is:
18 23 36 38 45 51 63 74 87 89
```

Listing 14-1
The source code for the DESCLS1.CPP program.

```
// A C++ program that illustrates creating a new class
// as a public descendant of a parent class

#include <iostream.h>
#include <iomanip.h>

const int MAX_ELEMS = 10;

enum Logical { FALSE, TRUE };

class myArray                              ────────►  Base class
{
  public:
    myArray(int nNumElems = MAX_ELEMS, int fInitVal = 0);
    ~myArray()
      { delete [] m_pnArray; }
    int& operator[](int nIndex)
      { return m_pnArray[nIndex]; }
    void show(const char* pszMsg = "",
              const int nNumElems = MAX_ELEMS);
```

```
   protected:
     int* m_pnArray;
     int m_nNumElems;
};

class mySortedArray : public myArray                    Child class
{
   public:
     void CombSort(int nNumElems);

};

myArray::myArray(int nNumElems, int fInitVal)
{
   m_nNumElems = (nNumElems > 0) ? nNumElems : 1;
   m_pnArray = new int[m_nNumElems];
   for (int i = 0; i < m_nNumElems; i++)
     m_pnArray[i] = fInitVal;
}

void myArray::show(const char* pszMsg,
                   const int nNumElems)
{
   cout << pszMsg << endl;
   for (int i = 0; i < nNumElems; i++)
     cout << m_pnArray[i] << ' ';
   cout << endl;
}

void mySortedArray::CombSort(int nNumElems)
{
   int nOffset = nNumElems;
   Logical bSorted;

   if (nNumElems < 2)
     return;

   do {
     nOffset = (nOffset * 8) / 11;
     nOffset = (nOffset < 1) ? 1 : nOffset;
     bSorted = TRUE; // set sorted flag
     // compare elements
     for (int i = 0, j = nOffset;
          i < (nNumElems - nOffset);
          i++, j++) {
       if (m_pnArray[i] > m_pnArray[j]) {
         // swap elements
         int nSwap = m_pnArray[i];
         m_pnArray[i] = m_pnArray[j];
         m_pnArray[j] = nSwap;
         bSorted = FALSE; // clear sorted flag
       }
     }
   } while (!bSorted || nOffset != 1);
}
```

```
main()
{
  int nArr[MAX_ELEMS] = { 23, 45, 89, 74, 51,
                          18, 87, 63, 36, 38 };
  mySortedArray Array;

  for (int i = 0; i < MAX_ELEMS; i++)
    Array[i] = nArr[i];

  Array.show("Unsorted array is:");
  Array.CombSort(MAX_ELEMS);
  Array.show("Sorted array is:");

  return 0;
}
```

Listing 14-1 declares the enumerated type **Logical** and the classes **myArray** and **mySortedArray**. The class **myArray** supports simple dynamic arrays of integers. It declares protected and public members. The protected members are:

- The **int***-type data member **m_pnArray**, which accesses the dynamic array of integers
- The int-type data member m_nNumElems, which stores the number of elements in the dynamic array

The class declares the following public members:

- The constructor, which allocates the space for the dynamic array (using the operator **new**) and initializes the array elements using the argument of parameter **fInitVal**. The int-type parameter **nNumElems** specifies the number of elements in the dynamic array.
- The destructor, which deallocates the space for the dynamic array using the operator **delete**
- The operator [], which accesses an element in the dynamic array
- The member function **show**, which displays the values in the dynamic array

The definitions of the constructor, operator [], and member function **show** access the array elements using the format **m_pnArray[***index***]**.

The listing also declares the class **mySortedArray** as a public descendant of class **myArray**. The descendant class declares the member function **CombSort** to sort the array elements. The class inherits the data members **m_pnArray** and **m_nNumElems** as well as the constructor, operator [], and member function **show**. The member function **CombSort** sorts the elements of the dynamic array using the inherited data member **m_pnArray**.

The function **main** declares and initializes the C++ array **nArr**. The function also declares the object **Array** as an instance of class **mySortedArray**. It then performs the following tasks:

- Copy the values in array **nArr** into the object **Array**. This task uses a **for** loop to iterate over the elements in array **nArr**.

- Display the unsorted elements in object **Array** by sending it the C++ message **show**. The argument for this message is the literal string "Unsorted array is:".

- Sort the object **Array** by sending it the C++ message **CombSort**

- Display the sorted elements in object **Array** by sending it the C++ message **show**. The argument for this message is the literal string "Sorted array is:".

THE EXAMPLE OF THE ARRAY-BASED STACK

The second example shows you how to create a descendant class from a nonpublic class. In other words, the descendant supports a new kind of object based on the attributes and operations of the parent class. While the descendant class is still *technically* a special version of the parent class, the descendant class uses the parent class mainly for basic support. The next example illustrates how this concept works. Listing 14-2 shows the source code for the DESCLS2.CPP program, which creates a descendant class of a nonpublic class. The program declares the classes **myArray** and **myStack**. The class **myArray** supports a dynamic array of integers. The class **myStack**, which is a descendant of class **myArray**, supports a fixed stack of integers. The number of array elements and the size of the stack are fixed at runtime and not at compile time. This feature leaves some flexibility for sizing the instances of both classes. The program creates an instance of class **myStack** and performs the following tasks:

- Push integers onto the stack
- Display the height of the stack
- Pop integers off the stack until the stack is empty
- Display the height of the stack (which should be zero)

Here is the output of the program in Listing 14-2:

```
Pushing 23 onto the stack
Pushing 45 onto the stack
Pushing 89 onto the stack
Pushing 74 onto the stack
Pushing 51 onto the stack

Stack has 5 elements

Popping 51 off the stack
Popping 74 off the stack
Popping 89 off the stack
Popping 45 off the stack
Popping 23 off the stack

Stack has 0 elements
```

Listing 14-2
The source code for the DESCLS2.CPP program.

```cpp
// A C++ program that illustrates
// creating a new class as a nonpublic
// descendant of a parent class

#include <iostream.h>
#include <iomanip.h>

const int MAX_ELEMS = 5;

enum Logical { FALSE, TRUE };

class myArray                                    Base class
{
  public:
    myArray(int nNumElems = MAX_ELEMS, int fInitVal = 0);
    ~myArray()
      { delete [] m_pnArray; }
    int& operator[](int nIndex)
      { return m_pnArray[nIndex]; }
    void show(const char* pszMsg = "",
              const int nNumElems = MAX_ELEMS);

  protected:
    int* m_pnArray;
```

```
    int m_nNumElems;
};

class myStack : myArray                    Child of non-public parent class
{
  public:
    myStack(int nMaxHeight = 10)
      : myArray(nMaxHeight, 0)
      { clear(); }
    Logical push(int nNum);
    Logical pop(int& nNum);
    int getHeight()
      { return m_nHeight; }
    void clear()
      { m_nHeight = 0; }

  protected:
    int m_nHeight;
};

myArray::myArray(int nNumElems, int fInitVal)
{
  m_nNumElems = (nNumElems > 0) ? nNumElems : 1;
  m_pnArray = new int[m_nNumElems];
  for (int i = 0; i < m_nNumElems; i++)
    m_pnArray[i] = fInitVal;
}

void myArray::show(const char* pszMsg,
                   const int nNumElems)
{
  cout << pszMsg << endl;
  for (int i = 0; i < nNumElems; i++)
    cout << m_pnArray[i] << ' ';
  cout << endl;
}

Logical myStack::push(int nNum)
{
  if (m_nHeight < m_nNumElems) {
    m_pnArray[m_nHeight++] = nNum;
    return TRUE;
    }
    else
      return FALSE;
  }

  Logical myStack::pop(int& nNum)
  {
    if (m_nHeight > 0) {
      nNum = m_pnArray[-m_nHeight];
      return TRUE;
    }
    else
      return FALSE;
  }
```

```
main()
{
  int nArr[MAX_ELEMS] = { 23, 45, 89, 74, 51 };
  int nVal;
  myStack Stack(MAX_ELEMS);

  for (int i = 0; i < MAX_ELEMS; i++) {
    cout << "Pushing " << nArr[i] << " onto the stack\n";
    if (!Stack.push(nArr[i]))
      cout << "Stack overflow at i = " << i << endl;
  }

  cout << endl;
  cout << "Stack has " << Stack.getHeight() << " elements\n";
  cout << endl;

  while (Stack.pop(nVal))
    cout << "Popping " << nVal << " off the stack\n";

  cout << endl;
  cout << "Stack has " << Stack.getHeight() << " elements";

  return 0;
}
```

Listing 14-2 declares the classes **myArray** and **myStack**. The class
myArray is identical to the version in Listing 14-1. The listing declares the
class **myStack** as a nonpublic descendant of class **myArray**. This means that
the instances of class **myStack** cannot access any member of the class
myArray—not even the public members of the parent class! The class
myStack declares the protected data member **m_nHeight** to store the current
stack height. The class declares the following public members:

- The constructor, which allocates the dynamic array of integers that
  supports the stack. The constructor also sets data member **m_nHeight** to
  zero by invoking the member function **clear**.

- The member function **push**, which pushes the value of parameter **nNum**
  into the stack. If the stack is not full, the member function stores the
  value of **nNum** in the next available element of the dynamic array,
  increments the stack height, and returns **TRUE**. By contrast, if the stack is
  full, the member function yields the enumerator **FALSE** and does not
  push the value of **nNum** in the stack.

- The member function **pop**, which pops an element off the top of the stack and returns that value using the reference parameter **nNum**. The function yields **TRUE** if the stack is not empty and returns **FALSE** otherwise. When the member function returns **FALSE**, the value returned by parameter **nNum** is not relevant.

- The member function **getHeight**, which returns the current height of the stack

- The member function **clear**, which resets the stack height to zero

The definitions of the member functions **push** and **pop** access the supporting dynamic array using the inherited data member **m_pnArray**. The member function **push** also uses the inherited data member **m_nNumElems** to determine whether or not the stack is full.

The function **main** declares and initializes the C++ array **nArr**, declares the variable **nVal**, and declares the object **Stack** as an instance of class **myStack**. The declaration of this object specifies a maximum stack size of **MAX_ELEMS** elements. The initialization of object **Stack** creates a dynamic array with **MAX_ELEMS** elements. The function performs the following tasks:

- Push the values in array **nArr** onto the object **Stack**. This task uses a **for** loop to iterate over the elements of array **nArr**. Each loop iteration pushes the element **nArr[i]** onto the object **Stack** by sending the C++ message **push** to that object. The argument for this message is the array element **nArr[i]**. The loop displays a warning message in case the stack of object **Stack** overflows.

- Display the height of the stack in object **Stack**. This task involves sending the C++ message **getHeight** to the object **Stack**.

- Pop the elements from the object **Stack**. This task uses a **while** loop to pop all of the stack elements. The loop's condition is the result of sending the C++ message **pop** to the object **Stack**. The argument for this message is the variable **nVal**, which obtains the popped value. The loop iteration displays the value in variable **nVal**.

- Display the height of the stack in object **Stack**. This task involves sending the C++ message **getHeight** to the object **Stack**. The program displays 0, because the **while** loop emptied the stack.

Constructors for Child Classes

You learned in Chapter 6 that constructors are special members that automatically initialize class instances. In the case of a base class, the runtime system merely invokes the constructor for that class. In the case of descendant classes, you need to invoke the constructor for the parent class before you initialize the data members of the descendent class. When you apply this scheme in a multiple class hierarchy, the constructor of the descendant class ends up invoking the constructor of the base class first and the constructor of the parent class last. The general syntax for this cascaded constructor invocation is:

```
constructor(parameterList1) :
    constructorOfParentClass(parameterList2)
    {
      // initializing statements
    }
```

Here is an example of invoking the constructors of parent classes:

```
class A
{
  A()
   {
     // statements
   }
  // declarations of members
};

class B : public A
{
  B() : A()
   {
     // statements
   }
  // declarations of members
};

class C : public B
{
  C() : B()
   {
     // statements
   }
  // declarations of members
};
```

This example shows a small class hierarchy made up of classes A, B, and C. Class A is the base class, and classes B and C are descendant classes. The constructor of class B invokes the constructor of the parent class A before carrying out any initialization. Likewise, the constructor of class C invokes the constructor of the parent class B (which in turn invokes the constructor of class A) before carrying out any initialization.

Let me present a programming example. Listing 14-3 shows the source code for the DESCLS3.CPP program, which illustrates the constructors of descendant classes. The program declares a small hierarchy of trivial classes: classA, classB, and classC. These classes store integers. The constructors of these classes store the integer values and display tracer messages. Each class has a member function that displays the values of the integers stored in a class instance.

Here is the output of the program in Listing 14-3 (notice the cascaded tracer messages generated by the constructor of classes classB and classC):

```
Invoking constructor of class classA
Object A stores 1

Invoking constructor of class classA
Invoking constructor of class classB
Object B stores 10, 20

Invoking constructor of class classA
Invoking constructor of class classB
Invoking constructor of class classC
Object C stores 100, 200, 300
```

Listing 14-3
The source code for the DESCLS3.CPP program.

```cpp
// A C++ program that illustrates
// invoking the constructors of parent classes

#include <iostream.h>
#include <iomanip.h>

class classA
{
  public:
    classA(int nA)
      { m_nA = nA;
        cout << "Invoking constructor of class classA\n";
      }
```

```
      void show(const char* pszMsg = "")
        { cout << pszMsg << m_nA << endl; }

  protected:
    int m_nA;
};

class classB : public classA
{
  public:
    classB(int nA, int nB)
     : classA(nA)
      { m_nB = nB;
        cout << "Invoking constructor of class classB\n";
      }
    void show(const char* pszMsg = "")
      { cout << pszMsg << m_nA
            << ", " << m_nB << endl;
      }

  protected:
    int m_nB;
};


class classC : public classB
{
  public:
    classC(int nA, int nB, int nC)
     : classB(nA, nB)
      { m_nC = nC;
        cout << "Invoking constructor of class classC\n";
      }
    void show(const char* pszMsg = "")
      { cout << pszMsg << m_nA
            << ", " << m_nB
            << ", " << m_nC
            << endl;
      }

  protected:
    int m_nC;
};

main()
{
  classA objectA(1);
  objectA.show("Object A stores ");
  cout << endl;
  classB objectB(10, 20);
  objectB.show("Object B stores ");
  cout << endl;
```

Constructor of child class

```
classC objectC(100, 200, 300);
objectC.show("Object C stores ");

return 0;
}
```

Listing 14-3 declares the class classA, which has the protected int-type data member m_nA and the following public members:

- A constructor that assigns the value of parameter nA to data member m_nA and emits a tracer message
- The member function show, which displays the value in data member m_nA

The listing also declares the class classB, which is a descendant of class classA. This class has the protected int-type data member m_nB and the following public members:

- A constructor that invokes the constructor of the parent class (and passes the value of parameter nA to that constructor), assigns the value of parameter nB to data member m_nB, and emits a tracer message
- The member function show, which displays the value in data members m_nA (inherited from the parent class) and m_nB

The listing also declares the class classC, which is a descendant of class classB. This class has the protected int-type data member m_nC and the following public members:

- A constructor that invokes the constructor of the parent class (and passes the values of parameters nA and nB to that constructor), assigns the value of parameter nC to data member m_nC, and emits a tracer message
- The member function show, which displays the value in data members m_nA, m_nB (both are inherited from the parent class), and m_nC.

The function **main** performs the following tasks:

- Declare the object **objectA** as an instance of class **classA**. This declaration initializes the class instance with the integer 1 and invokes the constructor of class **classA**. This constructor assigns the value 1 to data member **m_nA** and emits a tracer message.

- Display the value in object **objectA** by sending the C++ message **show** to that object with the string literal argument "Object A stores "

- Declare the object **objectB** as an instance of class **classB**. This declaration initializes the class instance with the integers 10 and 20 and invokes the constructor of class **classB**. This constructor invokes the constructor of the parent class (and passes the value 10 to it), assigns the value 20 to data member **m_nB**, and emits a tracer message. Thus, creating object **objectB** ends up sending two tracer messages—one from the constructor of the **classA** and the other from the constructor of **classB**.

- Display the value in object **objectB** by sending the C++ message **show** to that object with the string literal argument "Object B stores "

- Declare the object **objectC** as an instance of class **classC**. This declaration initializes the class instance with the integers 100, 200, and 300 and invokes the constructor of class **classC**. This constructor invokes the constructor of the parent class (and passes the values 100 and 200 to it), assigns the value 300 to data member **m_nC**, and emits a tracer message. Thus, creating object **objectC** ends up sending three tracer messages—one from each class constructor.

- Display the value in object **objectC** by sending the C++ message **show** to that object with the string literal argument "Object C stores "

Virtual Functions

Examine the following code snippet:

```
class A
{
  public:
    int doA()
```

```
        { return doA1() * doA2(); }
      int doA1()
        { return 2; }
      int doA2()
        { return 10; }

};

class B : public A
{
  public:
    int doA1()
      { return 20; }
};

main()
{
  B objB;

  cout << objB.doA();

  return 0;
}
```

This example declares the class **A** and its descendant class **B**. The class **A** contains the member functions **doA**, **doA1**, and **doA2**. The member function **doA** returns a value that is the product of invoking the member functions **doA1** and **doA2**. The class **B** declares its own version of member function **doA1** and inherits member functions **doA** and **doA2**. When function **main** sends the C++ message **doA** to object **objB** (an instance of class **B**), what value does that message yield? Because class **B** declares its own version of member function **doA1**, you expect the C++ message **doA** to wind up invoking member function **B::doA1** and **A::doA2**, yielding the value 200. However, the output statement in function **main** displays 20, because the C++ message **doA** ends up invoking member functions **A::doA1** and **A::doA2**! In other words, the compiler does not get the hint, so to speak, that you wish to invoke member function **B::doA1** when you send the C++ message **doA** to the instances of class **B**.

To solve this problem, C++ allows you to declare *virtual functions*. The general syntax for declaring a virtual member function is:

```
virtual returnType functionName(parameterList);
```

Applying this syntax to the classes **A** and **B**, I can generate the following code that works correctly:

```
class A
{
  public:
    int doA()
      { return doA1() * doA2(); }
    virtual int doA1()
      { return 2; }
    int doA2()
      { return 10; }

};

class B : public A
{
  public:
    virtual int doA1()
      { return 20; }
};

main()
{
  B objB;

  cout << objB.doA();

  return 0;
}
```

Notice that the code snippet declares the member function **doA1** as virtual in both classes **A** and **B**. When function **main** sends the C++ message **doA** to object **objB**, it invokes the member functions **B::doA1** and **A::doA2**, yielding the correct result of 200.

Let's look at a programming example. Listing 14-4 contains the source code for the DESCLS4.CPP program, which illustrates virtual functions. The program uses a hierarchy of classes that test various kinds of random number generators. The base class provides the operations that initialize the statistical summations, accumulate random numbers in these summations, and calculate the mean and standard deviation. The base class declares the random number generating function as virtual. The program also declares two descendant classes that implement their own versions of the random number generator function, which they also declare as virtual. Thus, each class is able to test the random number generator.

The test program declares an instance for each class and tests the random number generator for that class. The output for each class instance includes the count for the random numbers, the mean value, and the standard deviation.

Here is sample output for the program in Listing 14-4 (the output shows that the three random number generators are close enough to the expected values of 0.5 and 0.288 for the mean and standard deviation, respectively):

```
Testing the random number generator # 1
Number of observations = 1000
Mean value            = 0.512695
Standard deviation    = 0.296554

Testing the random number generator # 2
Number of observations = 1000
Mean value            = 0.489244
Standard deviation    = 0.290478

Testing the random number generator # 3
Number of observations = 1000
Mean value            = 0.486501
Standard deviation    = 0.288077
```

Listing 14-4
The source code for the DESCLS4.CPP program.

```cpp
// A C++ program that illustrates
// declaring and using virtual functions

#include <iostream.h>
#include <iomanip.h>
#include <math.h>

const double PI = 4 * atan(1);

class BasicStat1
{
  public:
    BasicStat1()
      { clearSums(); }
    void clearSums();
    void addRandData(int nNumObs);
    void getStat(int& nSum, double& fMean, double& fSdev);
    virtual double random();                              // ─────► Virtual function

  protected:
    int m_nSum;
    double m_fSumX;
    double m_fSumXX;
    double m_fSeed;
```

Virtual function

```
    double sqr(double x)
      { return x * x; }
    double frac(double x)
      { return x - int(x); }
};

class BasicStat2 : public BasicStat1
{
  public:
    BasicStat2()
      { clearSums(); }
    virtual double random();

  protected:
    double cube(double x)
      { return x * x * x; }
};

class BasicStat3 : public BasicStat2
{
  public:
    BasicStat3()
      { clearSums(); }
    virtual double random();

  protected:
    double fourth(double x)
      { return sqr(x) * sqr(x); }
};

void BasicStat1::clearSums()
{
  m_nSum = 0;
  m_fSumX = 0;
  m_fSumXX = 0;
  m_fSeed = 0.123456789;
}

void BasicStat1::addRandData(int nNumObs)
{
  for (int i = 0; i < nNumObs; i++) {
    double x = random();
    m_fSumX += x;
    m_fSumXX += sqr(x);
  }
  if (nNumObs > 0)
    m_nSum += nNumObs;
}

void BasicStat1::getStat(int& nSum, double& fMean, double& fSdev)
{
  nSum = m_nSum;
```

Virtual function

```
  if (m_nSum > 0) {
    fMean = m_fSumX / m_nSum;
    fSdev = sqrt((m_fSumXX - sqr(m_fSumX) / m_nSum)/(m_nSum - 1));
  }
}
```

```
double BasicStat1::random()
{
  m_fSeed = frac(sqr(PI + m_fSeed));
  return m_fSeed;
}
```

```
double BasicStat2::random()
{
  m_fSeed = frac(cube(PI + m_fSeed))
  return m_fSeed;
}
```                                    *Definition of virtual function*

```
double BasicStat3::random()
{
  m_fSeed = frac(fourth(PI + m_fSeed));
  return m_fSeed;
}
```

```
main()
{
  const int MAX = 1000;

  int nSum;
  double fMean;
  double fSdev;
  BasicStat1 BasStat1;
  BasicStat2 BasStat2;
  BasicStat3 BasStat3;

  cout << "Testing the random number generator # 1\n";
  BasStat1.addRandData(MAX);
  BasStat1.getStat(nSum, fMean, fSdev);
  cout << "Number of observations = " << nSum << endl
       << "Mean value             = " << fMean << endl
       << "Standard deviation     = " << fSdev << endl
       << endl;

  cout << "Testing the random number generator # 2\n";
  BasStat2.addRandData(MAX);
  BasStat2.getStat(nSum, fMean, fSdev);
  cout << "Number of observations = " << nSum << endl
       << "Mean value             = " << fMean << endl
       << "Standard deviation     = " << fSdev << endl
       << endl;

  cout << "Testing the random number generator # 3\n";
```

```
BasStat3.addRandData(MAX);
BasStat3.getStat(nSum, fMean, fSdev);
cout << "Number of observations = " << nSum << endl
     << "Mean value           = " << fMean << endl
     << "Standard deviation   = " << fSdev << endl;

return 0;
}
```

Listing 14-4 declares the classes **BasicStat1**, **BasicStat2**, and **BasicStat3**. The class **BasicStat1** is the base class for the small class hierarchy. This class declares protected and public members. The protected members are:

- The data members **m_nSum**, **m_fSumX**, and **m_fSumXX**, which store the number of observations, the sum of the observations, and the sum of the observations squared, respectively

- The **double**-type data member **m_fSeed**, which stores the last random number, used to generate the next random number

- The member functions **sqr** and **frac**, which return the square and fractional part of a floating-point argument, respectively

The class **BasicStat1** declares the following public members:

- The constructor, which invokes the member function **clearSums** to clear the statistical summations and to assign a new seed value to the data member **m_fSeed**

- The member function **clearSums**, whose purpose has just been stated

- The member function **addRandData**, which adds random numbers to the statistical summations. The **int**-type parameter **nNumObs** specifies the number of observations to add.

- The member function **getStat**, which obtains the number of observations, the mean value, and the standard deviation through the reference variables **nSum**, **fMean**, and **fSdev**, respectively

- The virtual member function **random**, which returns a random number between 0 and 1 (exclusive)

The listing declares the class **BasicStat2** as a public descendant of class **BasicStat1**. The descendant class declares the protected member function **cube** (which yields the cube value), the public constructor, and the virtual member function **random**. The constructor invokes the inherited member function **clearSums** to initialize the statistical summations and the seed value. The virtual member function **random** returns the random value implemented in the class **BasicStat2**, using the protected member function **cube** to calculate random numbers.

The listing further declares the class **BasicStat3** as a public descendant of class **BasicStat2**. The descendant class declares the protected member function **fourth** (which yields the fourth power), the public constructor, and the virtual member function **random**. The constructor invokes the inherited member function **clearSums** to initialize the statistical summations and the seed value. The virtual member function **random** returns the random value implemented in the class **BasicStat3**, again using the protected member function **fourth** to calculate random numbers.

I declared class **BasicStat3** as a descendant of class **BasicStat2** to show the effect of virtual member functions in a class hierarchy. I could have instead declared **BasicStat3** as a descendant of class **BasicStat1**. In the case of this example it would make no functional difference in the program's output.

Virtual Destructors

Although C++ allows you to inherit destructors, many C++ programmers strongly recommend that you declare destructors as virtual. This kind of declaration ensures that each class instance is properly disposed of. A *virtual destructor* of a descendant class invokes the destructors of the parent class.

Here is an example of using virtual destructors:

```
class City
{
  public:
    City();
    virtual ~City();
    // declarations of other members
};
```

```
class State : public City
{
  public:
    State();
    virtual ~State();
    // declarations of other members
};

class Country : public State
{
  public:
    Country();
    virtual ~Country();
    // declarations of other members
};
```

The example declares the classes **City**, **State**, and **Country** as a miniature class hierarchy. The example declares the destructor of each class as virtual to ensure that the instances of these classes are properly removed. Thus, the destructor of class **Country** also invokes the destructors of classes **State** and **City**.

Let's look at a programming example. Listing 14-5 shows the source code for the DESCLS5.CPP program, which illustrates virtual destructors. The program has a two-class hierarchy that creates, removes, and manipulates dynamic integers. The destructors of the classes are virtual.

The output of the program in Listing 14-5 is:

```
Integer in Int1 is 1
Integer 1 in Int2 is 100
Integer 2 in Int2 is 200
Invoking destructor ~TwoInts
Invoking destructor ~OneInt
Invoking destructor ~OneInt
```

Listing 14-5

The source code for the DESCLS5.CPP program.

```
// A C++ program that illustrates
// declaring virtual destructors

#include <iostream.h>
#include <iomanip.h>

class OneInt
{
  public:
    OneInt()
      { m_pnInt1 = new int; }
    virtual ~OneInt()
      {
        delete m_pnInt1;
        cout << "Invoking destructor ~OneInt\n";
      }
    void setInt1(int nInt)
      { *m_pnInt1 = nInt; }
    int getInt1()
      { return *m_pnInt1; }

  protected:
    int* m_pnInt1;
};

class TwoInts : public OneInt
{
  public:
    TwoInts() : OneInt()
      { m_pnInt2 = new int; }
    virtual ~TwoInts()
      {
        delete m_pnInt2;
        cout << "Invoking destructor ~TwoInts\n";
      }
    void setInt2(int nInt)
      { *m_pnInt2 = nInt; }
    int getInt2()
      { return *m_pnInt2; }

  protected:
    int* m_pnInt2;
};

main()
{
  OneInt Int1;
  TwoInts Int2;

  Int1.setInt1(1);
  Int2.setInt1(100);
```

Virtual destructors

```
    Int2.setInt2(200);

    cout << "Integer in Int1 is " << Int1.getInt1() << endl;
    cout << "Integer 1 in Int2 is " << Int2.getInt1() << endl;
    cout << "Integer 2 in Int2 is " << Int2.getInt2() << endl;

    return 0;
}
```

Listing 14-5 declares the class **OneInt** and its public descendant **TwoInts**. The class **OneInt** declares the protected data member **m_pInt1**. This class also has a constructor, a virtual destructor, and the member functions **setInt1** and **getInt1**. The constructor creates a dynamic integer and assigns its address to the data member **m_pnInt1**. The destructor deallocates the space for the dynamic integer.

The listing also declares the class **TwoInts** as a descendant of class **OneInt**. The class **TwoInts** declares the protected data member **m_pInt2** and also includes a constructor, a virtual destructor, and the member functions **setInt2** and **getInt2**. The descendant class inherits the members of class **OneInt**. The constructor creates the dynamic integers and assigns their addresses to the data members **m_pnInt1** and **m_pInInt2**. The virtual destructor deallocates the space for the second dynamic integer and then invokes the destructor of the parent class to remove the space for the first dynamic integer.

The function **main** creates the objects **Int1** and **Int2** as instances of classes **OneInt** and **TwoInts**, respectively. The relevant part of this program is when the objects are out of scope. In the case of object **Int1** the program invokes the virtual destructor **~OneInt**. In the case of object **Int2**, the program invokes the destructor **~TwoInts** (to deallocate the second dynamic integer) and then the destructor **~OneInt** (to deallocate the first dynamic integer).

Rules for Virtual Functions

C++ requires that you observe the following rules when working with virtual member functions:

1. A virtual member function can override a nonvirtual member function inherited from a parent class.

2. You can override a virtual member function only by using another virtual member function in a descendant class (this rule is sometimes called *once virtual always virtual*). The overriding member function must have the same parameter list and return type as the one being overridden.

3. You may overload a virtual member function with a nonvirtual member function in a class. However, the descendants of that class can inherit only the virtual member function!

Friend Functions

Friend functions are special nonmember functions that you declare in a class. A friend function has the same access privileges as a member function. As the sidebar "Friendship in C++" suggests, friend functions may violate the true spirit of object-oriented programming to offer you convenient coding! What are friend functions used for? you may ask. A friend function is a regular function that you call (that is, it is not a C++ message that you send to a class instance) such that one of its arguments must be an instance of the host class (or the *befriended* class, if you prefer). Thus, the friend function's first parameter can have a type other than that of the befriended class.

The general syntax for declaring a friend function in a class is:

```
class className
{
  // declaration of members
  friend returnType functionName(parameterList);
};
```

Notice that you declare a **friend** function by placing the keyword **friend** before the function's return type. The definition of a friend function does not require using the keyword **friend**. The parameter list of a friend function may have any number and type of parameters as long as one of the parameters has the type of the befriended class.

Here is an example of a class declaring friend functions:

```
class myComplex
{
 public:
  myComplex();
  // declaration of other members

  friend myComplex DivideComplex(myComplex& C, double fReal);
  friend myComplex DivideComplex(double fReal, myComplex& C);

  // declaration of other members
};
```

The example shows the class **myComplex** with the overloaded friend function **DivideComplex**. The first version of this friend function has the **myComplex&**-type parameter **C** and the **double**-type parameter **fReal**. The second version of the function declares these parameters in the reverse sequence. The friend function **DivideComplex** returns the type **myComplex**. Notice that the second version of function **DivideComplex** has a **double**-type first parameter and not a **myComplex&**-type parameter.

Let's look at a programming example. Listing 14-6 contains the source code for the DESCLS6.CPP program, which illustrates friend functions. The program declares a string class containing friend functions that compare string objects with each other and with ASCIIZ strings. The program declares string objects and ASCIIZ string variables, assigns characters to these objects and variables, and then compares them. The output first identifies the string objects and variables and then displays the outcomes of the comparisons.

Here is the output of the program in Listing 14-6:

```
String object 1 is ABCDEFG
String object 2 is 1234567890
ASCIIZ string 1 is ABCDEFG
ASCIIZ string 2 is 1234567890

String objects are not equal
String object 1 and ASCIIZ string 1 equal
String object 1 and ASCIIZ string 2 not equal
String object 2 and ASCIIZ string 1 not equal
String object 2 and ASCIIZ string 2 not equal
```

CODING
NOTES

Friendship in C++

Friendship of functions, operators, and classes with other classes is a special relationship that C++ supports. The OOP purists are not too thrilled about the concept of a nonmember function having access privileges to the members of the befriended class. However, friend functions, operators, and classes support a convenient and direct way to code functions, operators, and classes. Without friendship, certain features in C++ become either very convoluted or downright unavailable.

Listing 14-6

The source code for the DESCLS6.CPP program.

```cpp
// A C++ program that illustrates
// declaring and using friend functions

#include <iostream.h>
#include <string.h>

class myString
{
  public:
    myString(int nSize = 10)
      { m_pszString = new char[m_nSize = nSize]; }
    ~myString()
      { delete [] m_pszString; }
    void assign(const char* pszString);
    void show(const char* pszMsg = "");
    friend int compare(myString& aString1, myString aString2);
    friend int compare(const char* pszString1, myString aString2);
    friend int compare(myString aString1, const char* pszString2);

  protected:
    char* m_pszString;
    int m_nSize;
};

void myString::assign(const char* pszString)
{
  // source string small enough to copy?
  if (strlen(pszString) < unsigned(m_nSize))
    strcpy(m_pszString, pszString);
  else
    // copy first m_nSize characters
    strncpy(m_pszString, pszString, m_nSize);
}
```

Friend functions

```
void myString::show(const char* pszMsg)
{
  cout << pszMsg << m_pszString << "\n";
}

int compare(myString& aString1, myString aString2)
{
  return strcmp(aString1.m_pszString, aString2.m_pszString);
}

int compare(const char* pszString1, myString aString2)
{
  return strcmp(pszString1, aString2.m_pszString);
}

int compare(myString aString1, const char* pszString2)
{
  return strcmp(aString1.m_pszString, pszString2);
}

main()
{
  const int MAX_CHARS = 81;
  myString aString1(MAX_CHARS);
  myString aString2(MAX_CHARS);

  char cString1[] = "ABCDEFG";
  char cString2[] = "1234567890";

  aString1.assign(cString1);
  aString2.assign(cString2);

  aString1.show("String object 1 is ");
  aString2.show("String object 2 is ");
  cout << "ASCIIZ string 1 is " << cString1 << "\n";
  cout << "ASCIIZ string 2 is " << cString2 << "\n\n";

  cout << "String objects are ";
  if (compare(aString1, aString2) != 0)
    cout << "not ";
  cout << "equal\n";

  cout << "String object 1 and ASCIIZ string 1 ";
  if (compare(aString1, cString1) != 0)
    cout << "not ";
  cout << "equal\n";

  cout << "String object 1 and ASCIIZ string 2 ";
  if (compare(aString1, cString2) != 0)
    cout << "not ";
  cout << "equal\n";
```

```
  cout << "String object 2 and ASCIIZ string 1 ";
  if (compare(cString1, aString2) != 0)
    cout << "not ";
  cout << "equal\n";

  cout << "String object 2 and ASCIIZ string 2 ";
  if (compare(cString2, aString2) != 0)
    cout << "not ";
  cout << "equal\n";

  return 0;
}
```

Listing 14-6 declares the class **myString**, which supports minimal dynamic strings. The class has the protected data members **m_nSize** and **m_pszString**, which manage the dynamic string created with each instance. The class declares the following public members:

- A constructor that allocates the space for the dynamic string
- A destructor that removes the space of the dynamic string
- The member function **assign**, which assigns a new string to the dynamic string
- The member function **show**, which displays the contents of the dynamic string

The class **myString** further declares three versions of the overloaded friend class **compare**: The first version compares instances of class **myString**, and each of the other two versions compares an instance of class **myString** with an ASCIIZ string. The overloaded functions return an **int**-type value that reflects how their arguments compare. The definitions of these functions call the function **strcmp**.

The function **main** declares the objects **aString1** and **aString2** as instances of class **myString**. The function also declares and initializes the ASCIIZ string variables **cString1** and **cString2**. The function then performs the following tasks:

- Assign the ASCIIZ string variables **cString1** and **cString3** to objects **aString1** and **aString2**, respectively. Each assignment involves sending the C++ message **assign** to a string object. The argument for each message is an ASCIIZ string variable.

- Display the contents of objects **aString1** and **aString2** by sending the C++ message **show** to each object. The argument for each message is a string literal that identifies that object.

- Display the contents of the ASCIIZ string variables **cString1** and **cString2**. The output includes string literals that identify the string variables.

- Compare the objects **aString1** and **aString2** by calling the friend function **compare**. The arguments for this function call are the compared objects. The output identifies the objects compared and shows the outcome of the comparison.

- Similarly compare the object **aString1** and the string variable **cString1**

- Similarly compare the object **aString1** and the string variable **cString2**

- Similarly compare the object **aString2** and the string variable **cString1**

- Similarly compare the object **aString2** and the string variable **cString2**

Operators

One of the many reasons I really like C++ is that it allows you to declare operators in a class. These operators are essentially member functions that have a special declaration and usage syntax. The C++ operators empower you to support more abstract and natural syntax. For example, you can create a string class and define the operators = and +=, which assign and concatenate strings and characters, respectively. The general syntax for declaring an operator in a class is:

```
class className
{
  // declaration of members
  className& operator operatorSymbol(parameterList);
};
```

The declaration of an operator uses the keyword **operator** followed by the operator's symbol. The general syntax for defining an operator is:

```
className& className::operator operatorSymbol(parameterList)
{
  // statements
  return *this;
};
```

The definition of an operator also uses the keyword **operator**. C++ enforces rules on the number of parameters and the general categories of their types. Here is a list of examples for the rules:

- The operator [] can have only one integer-compatible parameter.
- The assignment operators =, +=, −=, /=, *=, %=, and so on can have only one parameter. There is no restriction on the type of the parameter, as long as you can convert that type to the host class.
- The operator () can have any number and types of parameters.

Here is an example of a class declaring operators:

```
class myComplex
{
 public:
  myComplex();
  // declaration of other members

  myComplex& operator =(myComplex& C);
  myComplex& operator =(double fReal);
  myComplex& operator +=(myComplex& C);
  myComplex& operator +=(double fReal);
  // declaration of other members
 protected:
   double m_fReal;
   double m_fImag;
};

myComplex& operator =(myComplex& C)
{
  m_fReal = C.m_fReal;
  m_fImag = C.m_fImag;
  return *this;
}
```

The example shows the class **myComplex** with the overloaded operators = and +=. The first version of operator = has a **myComplex&**-type parameter, allowing it to assign one class instance to another. The second version assigns a **double**-type value to a class instance. Similarly, the overloaded operators += add class instances and floating-point numbers to already-existing class instances. The example also shows the definition of the **operator =(myComplex)**. Notice that the definition has the **return *this** statement, which returns the reference to the targeted class.

The this pointer

C++ offers the keyword **this** as a self-reference pointer to the host class. The OOP languages use the keyword **me** or **self**. Use the expression ***this** in the **return** statement of an operator to return the updated data members of the class instance.

Let me present a programming example. Listing 14-7 shows the source code for the DESCLS7.CPP program, which illustrates operators. The program uses a new version of the string class that employs the operators = and += to assign and append string objects, ASCIIZ strings, and characters to string objects. The program first tests using the operators = and += to assign and append string objects, ASCIIZ strings, and characters to string objects and then displays the results of using these operators.

Here is the output of the program in Listing 14-7:

```
String object 1 is ABCDEFG
String object 2 is ABCDEFG
String object 3 is !
New string object 1 is 1234567890ABCDEFG!
```

Listing 14-7
The source code for the DESCLS7.CPP program.

```
// A C++ program that illustrates
// declaring and using operators

#include <iostream.h>
#include <string.h>

class myString
{
  public:
    myString(int nSize = 10)
      { m_pszString = new char[m_nSize = nSize]; }
    ~myString()
      { delete [] m_pszString; }
    int getLen()
      { return strlen(m_pszString); }
    int getMaxLen()
      { return m_nSize; }
    myString& operator =(myString& aString);
    myString& operator =(const char* pszString);
```

→ *Operators*

```
    myString& operator =(const char cChar);
    myString& operator +=(myString& aString);
    myString& operator +=(const char* pszString);         Operators
    myString& operator +=(const char cChar);
    void show(const char* pszMsg = "");

  protected:
    char* m_pszString;
    int m_nSize;
};

myString& myString::operator =(myString& aString)
{
  // source string small enough to copy?
  if (strlen(aString.m_pszString) < unsigned(m_nSize))
    strcpy(m_pszString, aString.m_pszString);
  else
    // copy first m_nSize - 1 characters
    strncpy(m_pszString, aString.m_pszString, m_nSize - 1);
  return *this;
}

myString& myString::operator =(const char* pszString)
{
  // source string small enough to copy?
  if (strlen(pszString) < unsigned(m_nSize))
    strcpy(m_pszString, pszString);
  else
    // copy first m_nSize - 1 characters
    strncpy(m_pszString, pszString, m_nSize - 1);
  return *this;
}

myString& myString::operator =(const char cChar)
{
  if (m_nSize > 1) {
    m_pszString[0] = cChar;
    m_pszString[1] = '\0';
  }
  return *this;
}

myString& myString::operator +=(myString& aString)
{
  // source string small enough to copy?
  if (strlen(aString.m_pszString) + strlen(m_pszString) <=
      unsigned(m_nSize))
    strcat(m_pszString, aString.m_pszString);
  else
    // copy first m_nSize characters
    strncat(m_pszString, aString.m_pszString,
            m_nSize - strlen(m_pszString));
  return *this;
}
```

```
myString& myString::operator +=(const char* pszString)
{
  // source string small enough to copy?
  if (strlen(pszString) + strlen(m_pszString) <=
      unsigned(m_nSize))
    strcat(m_pszString, pszString);
  else
    // copy first m_nSize characters
    strncat(m_pszString, pszString,
            m_nSize - strlen(m_pszString));
  return *this;
}

myString& myString::operator +=(const char cChar)
{
  int nWorkSize = strlen(m_pszString);

  // source string small enough to copy?
  if (nWorkSize + 1 <= m_nSize) {
    m_pszString[nWorkSize] = cChar;
    m_pszString[nWorkSize + 1] = '\0';
  }
  return *this;
}

void myString::show(const char* pszMsg)
{
  cout << pszMsg << m_pszString << "\n";
}

main()
{
  const int MAX_CHARS = 81;
  myString aString1(MAX_CHARS);
  myString aString2(MAX_CHARS);
  myString aString3(MAX_CHARS);

  char cString1[] = "ABCDEFG";
  char cString2[] = "1234567890";
  char cChar = '!';

  aString1 = cString1;
  aString2 = aString1;
  aString3 = cChar;

  aString1.show("String object 1 is ");
  aString2.show("String object 2 is ");
  aString3.show("String object 3 is ");

  aString1 = ""; // clear string object 1
  aString1 += cString2; // append ASCIZZ string
```

```
    aString1 += aString2; // append string object
    aString1 += cChar; // apend a character
    aString1.show("New string object 1 is ");

    return 0;
}
```

Listing 14-7 declares a new version of class **myString**. This version contains three versions of the operators = and +=. These versions assign and append class instances, ASCIIZ strings, and characters. Notice that each operator returns a reference to the class **myString**. The definitions of these operators use the functions **strcpy**, **strncpy**, **strcat**, and **strncat** to assign and append some or all of the characters from the source strings to the dynamic string (accessed by data member **m_pszString**). The last statement that defines the operators = and += in each instance is **return *this**.

The function **main** declares the objects **aString1**, **aString2**, and **aString3** as instances of class **myString**. These instances can store the same number of characters, as specified by the local constant **MAX_CHARS**. The function also declares and initializes the string variables **cString1** and **cString2**, as well as the **char**-type variable **cChar**. The function performs the following tasks:

- Assign the string variable **cString1** to the object **aString1** using the operator =. The assignment statement is really a C++ message that invokes the member **myString::operator =(const char*)**. The argument for this message is the string variable **cString1**.

- Assign the object **aString1** to object **aString2** using the operator =. This statement invokes the member **myString::operator =(myString&)**.

- Assign the character in variable **cChar** to object **aString3** using the operator =. This statement invokes the member **myString::operator =(const char)**.

- Display the contents of objects **aString1**, **aString2**, and **aString3** by sending the C++ message **show** to each object. The argument for each message is a string literal that identifies the object.

- Assign an empty string literal to the object **aString1** by using the operator =

- Append the characters in the string variable **cString2** to object **aString1** using the operator **+=**. This statement invokes the member **myString::operator +=(const char*)**.

- Append the characters in the object **aString2** to object **aString1** using the operator **+=**. This statement invokes the member **myString::operator +=(myString&)**.

- Append the character in the variable **cChar** to the same object using the operator **+=**. This statement invokes the member **myString::operator +=(const char)**.

- Display the new string in object **aString1**. This task involves sending the C++ message **show** (with the string literal argument "New string object 1 is ") to the object **aString1**.

Friend Operators

In addition to friend functions, C++ supports *friend operators*. These friend operators have the advantage of allowing the first parameter to be of a type other than the befriended class. Let me illustrate the limitation of member operators by showing the following code example:

```
class myComplex
{
 public:
  myComplex();
  // declaration of other members

  myComplex& operator =(myComplex& C);
  myComplex& operator =(double fReal);
  myComplex& operator +(myComplex& C);
  myComplex& operator +(double fReal);
  // declaration of other members
};
```

The example declares the overloaded versions of operator **+** as members (and not as friends) of class **myComplex**. Using either version of the operator **+** requires that the left operand be an instance of class **myComplex**. The right argument can be either another class instance or a double-type value. What if you needed or simply wanted to have an expression in which the left operand is a **double**-type value? You can't! Here is where friend operators come in very handy.

The general syntax for declaring a friend operator is:

```
class className
{
  // declaration of members
  friend returnType operator operatorSymbol(parameterList);
};
```

The declaration of an operator uses the keywords **friend** and **operator** followed by the operator's symbol. As with friend functions, the parameter list of a friend operator must include a parameter that has the befriended class. The general syntax for defining an operator is:

```
returnType operator operatorSymbol(parameterList)
{
  // statements
  return *this;
};
```

The definition of an operator only uses the keyword **operator**; it does not require the name of the befriended class to qualify it.

Applying the friend operator to the last version of class **myComplex** generates the following declaration:

```
class myComplex
{
 public:
  myComplex();
  // declaration of other members

  myComplex& operator =(myComplex& C);
  myComplex& operator =(double fReal);
  friend myComplex operator +(myComplex& C1, myComplex& C2);
  friend myComplex operator +(myComplex& C, double fReal);
  friend myComplex operator +(double fReal, myComplex& C);
  // declaration of other members
};
```

The example shows that the class **myComplex** declares three versions of the overloaded friend operator **+** to handle all possible combinations of adding class instances and **double**s. Each friend operator has at least one parameter that is a class instance.

Let me present a programming example. Listing 14-8 contains the source code for the DESCLS8.CPP program, which illustrates friend operators. The program declares a special version of the string class that declares and uses the friend operator **+** to concatenate string objects, ASCIIZ strings, and characters. The program uses the overloaded versions of the friend operator **+** to assign a string expression to a string object and then display the assigned characters.

Here is the output of the program in Listing 14-8:

```
String object 3 is !||ABCDEFG..567890
```

Listing 14-8
The source code for the DESCLS8.CPP program.

```cpp
// A C++ program that illustrates
// declaring and using friend operators

#include <iostream.h>
#include <string.h>

const int MIN_SIZE = 30;

class myString
{
  public:
    myString(int nSize = MIN_SIZE)
      { m_pszString = new char[m_nSize = nSize]; }
    myString(unsigned nSize)
      { m_pszString = new char[m_nSize = int(nSize)]; }
    myString(myString& aString);
    myString(const char* pszString);
    myString(const char cChar);
    ~myString()
      { delete [] m_pszString; }
    int getLen()
      { return strlen(m_pszString); }
    int getMaxLen()
      { return m_nSize; }
    myString& operator =(myString& aString);
    myString& operator =(const char* pszString);
    myString& operator =(const char cChar);
    myString& operator +=(myString& aString);
    myString& operator +=(const char* pszString);
    myString& operator +=(const char cChar);
    friend myString operator +(myString& aString1,
                               myString& aString2);
    friend myString operator +(myString& aString1,
                               const char* pszString2);
```

→ *Friend operators*

```
    friend myString operator +(const char* pszString1,
                                myString& aString2);
    friend myString operator +(myString& aString,
                                const char cChar);
    friend myString operator +(const char cChar,
                                myString& aString);
    void show(const char* pszMsg = "");

  protected:
    char* m_pszString;
    int m_nSize;
};

myString::myString(myString& aString)
{
  m_pszString = new char[m_nSize = aString.m_nSize];
  strcpy(m_pszString, aString.m_pszString);
}


myString::myString(const char* pszString)
{
  m_pszString = new char[m_nSize = strlen(pszString) + 1];
  strcpy(m_pszString, pszString);
}


myString::myString(const char cChar)
{
  m_pszString = new char[m_nSize = MIN_SIZE];
  m_pszString[0] = cChar;
  m_pszString[1] = '\0';
}


myString& myString::operator =(myString& aString)
{
  // source string small enough to copy?
  if (strlen(aString.m_pszString) < unsigned(m_nSize))
    strcpy(m_pszString, aString.m_pszString);
  else
    // copy first m_nSize - 1 characters
    strncpy(m_pszString, aString.m_pszString, m_nSize - 1);
  return *this;
}


myString& myString::operator =(const char* pszString)
{
  // source string small enough to copy?
  if (strlen(pszString) < unsigned(m_nSize))
    strcpy(m_pszString, pszString);
  else
    // copy first m_nSize - 1characters
    strncpy(m_pszString, pszString, m_nSize - 1);
  return *this;
}
```

Friend operators

```
myString& myString::operator =(const char cChar)
{
  if (m_nSize > 1) {
    m_pszString[0] = cChar;
    m_pszString[1] = '\0';
  }
  return *this;
}

myString operator +(myString& aString1, myString& aString2)
{
  myString Result(strlen(aString1.m_pszString) +
                  strlen(aString2.m_pszString) + 1);
  strcpy(Result.m_pszString, aString1.m_pszString);
  strcat(Result.m_pszString, aString2.m_pszString);
  return Result;
}

myString operator +(myString& aString1, const char* pszString2)
{
  myString Result(strlen(aString1.m_pszString) +
                  strlen(pszString2) + 1);
  strcpy(Result.m_pszString, aString1.m_pszString);
  strcat(Result.m_pszString, pszString2);
  return Result;
}

myString operator +(const char* pszString1, myString& aString2)
{
  myString Result(strlen(aString2.m_pszString) +
                  strlen(pszString1) + 1);
  strcpy(Result.m_pszString, pszString1);
  strcat(Result.m_pszString, aString2.m_pszString);
  return Result;
}

myString operator +(myString& aString, const char cChar)
{
  int len = strlen(aString.m_pszString);
  myString Result(len + 2);

  strcpy(Result.m_pszString, aString.m_pszString);
  Result.m_pszString[len] = cChar;
  Result.m_pszString[len+2] = '\0';
  return Result;
}

myString operator +(const char cChar, myString& aString)
{
  int len = strlen(aString.m_pszString);
  myString Result(len + 2);
```

```
    strcpy(Result.m_pszString, aString.m_pszString);
    Result.m_pszString[0] = cChar;
    Result.m_pszString[1] = '\0';
    strcat(Result.m_pszString, aString.m_pszString);
    return Result;
}

myString& myString::operator +=(myString& aString)
{
  // source string small enough to copy?
  if (strlen(aString.m_pszString) + strlen(m_pszString) <=
      unsigned(m_nSize))
    strcat(m_pszString, aString.m_pszString);
  else
    // copy first m_nSize characters
    strncat(m_pszString, aString.m_pszString,
            m_nSize - strlen(m_pszString) - 1);
  return *this;
}

myString& myString::operator +=(const char* pszString)
{
  // source string small enough to copy?
  if (strlen(pszString) + strlen(m_pszString) <=
      unsigned(m_nSize))
    strcat(m_pszString, pszString);
  else
    // copy first m_nSize characters
    strncat(m_pszString, pszString,
            m_nSize - strlen(m_pszString) - 1);
  return *this;
}

myString& myString::operator +=(const char cChar)
{
  int nWorkSize = strlen(m_pszString);

  // source string small enough to copy?
  if (nWorkSize + 1 <= m_nSize) {
    m_pszString[nWorkSize] = cChar;
    m_pszString[nWorkSize + 1] = '\0';
  }
  return *this;
}

void myString::show(const char* pszMsg)
{
  cout << pszMsg << m_pszString << "\n";
}
```

```
main()
{
  const int MAX_CHARS = 81;
  myString aString1(MAX_CHARS);
  myString aString2(MAX_CHARS);
  myString aString3(MAX_CHARS);

  char cString1[] = "ABCDEFG";
  char cString2[] = "567890";
  char cChar = '!';

  aString1 = "||";
  aString2 = "..";

  aString3 = cChar     +      // character
             aString1 +      // string object
             cString1 +      // ASCIIZ string
             aString2 +      // string object
             cString2;       // ASCIIZ string

  aString3.show("String object 3 is ");

  return 0;
}
```

Listing 14-8 declares a new version of class **myString**. This version has multiple constructors. The last two constructors convert from ASCIIZ strings and characters to class instances. The class declares five overloaded versions of the friend operator **+**. These versions handle concatenating class instances with other instances, ASCIIZ strings, and characters. These friend operators return the **myString** type. The definitions of these friend operators use the functions **strlen**, **strcat**, and **strncat** and employ a local instance of class **myString** to return the operator's result.

The function **main** declares the objects **aString1**, **aString2**, and **aString3** as instances of class **myString**. These instances can store the same number of characters, as specified by the local constant **MAX_CHARS**. The function also declares and initializes the string variables **cString1** and **cString2** and the **char**-type variable **cChar**. The function performs the following tasks:

- Assign the string literal "||" to object **aString1** using the operator **=**

- Assign the string literal ".." to object **aString2** using the operator **=**

- Assign a string expression the object **aString3** using the different versions of the friend operator **+**. The expression concatenates a character, a string object, an ASCIIZ string, another string object, and another ASCIIZ string. Notice that every other item in the expression is an instance of class **myString**. To concatenate two consecutive items that are not instances of class **myString**, you need to typecast one of these items using a constructor. The employed constructor must have a parameter that matches or that is compatible with the typecasted value.

- Display the new string in object **aString3**. This task involves sending the C++ message **show** (with the string literal argument "String object 3 is ") to the object **aString3**.

Multiple Inheritance

Earlier in this chapter I introduced you to multiple inheritance. C++ allows you to declare a descendant class from multiple parent classes using the following general syntax:

```
class className : [virtual] [public] parentClassName1,
                  [virtual] [public] parentClassName2,
                  [other classes]
{
   [public:
   // public constructors
   // public destructor
   // public data members
   // public member functions
   ]

   [protected:
   // protected constructors
   // protected destructor
   // protected data members
   // protected member functions
   ]

   [private:
   // private constructors
   // private destructor
   // private data members
   // private member functions
   ]
};
```

Declaring a descendant class starts with the keyword **class** and is followed by:

- The name of the class
- The colon character
- The name of the first parent class preceded by the optional keywords **virtual** and **public**
- The name of the second parent class, preceded by a comma character and the optional keywords **virtual** and **public**
- The names of other parent classes, each preceded by a comma and the optional keywords **virtual** and **public**

The keyword **virtual** alerts the compiler to the fact that the descendant class has parent classes that share a common ancestor class and so permits it to anticipate common class ancestry. The keyword **public** allows the class instances to access the public members of the parent class. Without this keyword, only the member functions of the descendant class can access the parent's members. C++ allows you to declare the descendant class as a public or nonpublic descendant of the various parent classes.

Here is an example of declaring a descendant class from independent parent classes:

```
class Salary
{
  // declaration of members
};

class Person
{
  // declaration of members
};

class Employee : public Person, public Salary
{
  // declaration of members
};
```

The example shows the skeleton declarations of three classes: **Salary**, **Person**, and **Employee**. The first two classes are nondescendant classes, whereas the class **Employee** is a public descendant of both classes **Person** and **Salary**.

Suppose the classes **Salary** and **Person** were descendants of some basic class—call it **CObject**. The declarations of the classes just described, which now share a common ancestor class, become:

```
class CObject
{
  // declaration of members
};

class Salary : virtual public CObject
{
  // declaration of members
};

class Person : virtual public CObject
{
  // declaration of members
};

class Employee : virtual public Person, virtual public Salary
{
  // declaration of members
};
```

These declarations use the keyword **virtual** in declaring all descendant classes, because these classes share the same base class, **CObject**. If you omit the keyword **virtual**, you get a compiler error.

The next subsections present examples of creating a descendant class from multiple parent classes. In the first example, the parent classes do not share a common ancestor class. In the second example, by contrast, the parent classes do share such a class.

THE SEARCH SIMULATION EXAMPLE

Let's look at an example of creating a descendant class from disjoint parent classes. Listing 14-9 shows the source code for the DESCLS9.CPP program. The program declares the following classes:

- The class **Random**, which generates random numbers between 0 and 1 (exclusive)

- The class **Distance**, which manages the coordinates of two points, calculates the distance between them, and calculates the angle of the line joining the two points

■ The class **Rescue**, a descendant of classes **Random** and **Distance**, which simulates rescuing a person (how nice!)

The program simulates searching for a lost person in a grid whose X and Y coordinates range from 1 to 1000. The program searches for the missing person in cycles. In each cycle the program displays the distance between you and the missing person and displays the angle of the line joining your location with that of the lost person. The program prompts you to enter your move in the X and Y directions. To make it more interesting, the program takes into account that both you and the missing person are moving at the same time. If your final coordinates in a move are within a critical distance from the person's final move, you locate the person and the simulation ends. If not, the program carries out another search cycle.

Here is a sample session with the program in Listing 14-9 (user input is underlined):

```
Current distance = 363.24
Current angle = 38.8381 degrees
Enter shift in X coordinates : 100
Enter shift in Y coordinates : 100
Current distance = 254.502
Current angle = 41.0509 degrees
Enter shift in X coordinates : 100
Enter shift in Y coordinates : 100
Current distance = 135.06
Current angle = 32.6166 degrees
Enter shift in X coordinates : 100
Enter shift in Y coordinates : 80
Current distance = 83.8832
Current angle = -5.62709 degrees
Enter shift in X coordinates : 80
Enter shift in Y coordinates : -10
Current distance = 136.34
Current angle = -38.6735 degrees
Enter shift in X coordinates : 0
Enter shift in Y coordinates : 0


Sorry you gave up!
```

Listing 14-9

The source code for the DESCLS9.CPP program.

```
/*

    A C++ program that illustrates the following
    small class hierarchy, which uses multiple
    inheritance:


        Distance        Random
           |               |
           |               |
           |               |
           |               |
           |               |
           \------/-----/
                   |
                   |
                Rescue

*/

#include <iostream.h>
#include <math.h>
#include <string.h>

const double PI = 4 * atan(1);
const double RAD2DEG = 180.0 / PI;
const double INIT_SEED = 113;
const double MIN_XY = 1.0;
const double MAX_XY = 1000.0;
const double CRITIC_DIST = 10.0;
const double EPSILON = 1.0e-8;
const double INFINITY = 1.0e+50;

enum Logical { FALSE, TRUE };

double sqr(double x)
{
  return x * x;
}

double cube(double x)
{
  return x * x * x;
}

double frac(double x)
{
  return x - (long)x;
}
```

```
class Random                                    → First parent class
{
  public:
    Random(double fSeed = INIT_SEED)
      { m_fSeed = fSeed; }

    double getRandom();

  protected:
    double m_fSeed;
};

class Distance                                  → Second parent class
{
  public:
    Distance(double fX1, double fY1,
             double fX2, double fY2);
    void setPoint1(double fX, double fY);
    void setPoint2(double fX, double fY);
    double getDeltaX()
      { return m_fX2 - m_fX1; }
    double getDeltaY()
      { return m_fY2 - m_fY1; }
    double getDistance()
      { return sqrt(sqr(m_fX2 - m_fX2) +
                    sqr(m_fY2 - m_fY1)); }
    double getAngle();

  protected:
    double m_fX1;
    double m_fX2;
    double m_fY1;
    double m_fY2;
    double m_fDeltaX;
    double m_fDeltaY;
};

class Rescue : public Random, public Distance   → Descendant class
{
  public:
    Rescue(double fMin, double fMax,
           double fCriticalDistance);

    void initRescue();
    Logical searchMore();
    void getCoords();

  protected:
    double m_fMin;
    double m_fMax;
    double m_fShift;
```

```
    double m_fCriticalDistance;

    double calcRandCoord()
      { return getRandom() * m_fMax + m_fMin; }
    double calcRandShift()
      { return (0.5 - getRandom()) * m_fShift; }
    double checkCoord(double fX)
      { return (fX >= m_fMin && fX <= m_fMax) ?
                fX : m_fMin + m_fMax / 2.; }
};

double Random::getRandom()
{
  m_fSeed = frac(cube(m_fSeed + PI));
  return m_fSeed;
}

Distance::Distance(double fX1, double fY1,
                   double fX2, double fY2)
{
  setPoint1(fX1, fY1);
  setPoint2(fX2, fY2);
}

void Distance::setPoint1(double fX, double fY)
{
  m_fX1 = fX;
  m_fY1 = fY;
}

void Distance::setPoint2(double fX, double fY)
{
  m_fX2 = fX;
  m_fY2 = fY;
}

double Distance::getAngle()
{
  double fDeltaY = m_fY2 - m_fY1;

  return (fabs(fDeltaY) > EPSILON) ?
    RAD2DEG * atan((m_fX2 - m_fX1) / fDeltaY) :
    INFINITY;
}

Rescue::Rescue(double fMin, double fMax,
               double fCriticalDistance)
          : Random(), Distance(0, 0, 0, 0)
{
  m_fMin = fMin;
  m_fMax = fMax;
  m_fShift = (fMax - fMin + 1) / 10.;
```

```
    m_fCriticalDistance = fCriticalDistance;
    initRescue();
}

void Rescue::initRescue()
{
    double fX = calcRandCoord();
    double fY = calcRandCoord();

    setPoint1((m_fMin + m_fMax) / 2, (m_fMin + m_fMax) / 2);
    setPoint2(fX, fY);
}

Logical Rescue::searchMore()
{
    if (fabs(m_fDeltaX) < 1.0 || fabs(m_fDeltaY) < 1.0 ||
        getDistance() < m_fCriticalDistance)
        return FALSE;
    else
        return TRUE;
}

void Rescue::getCoords()
{

    cout << "Current distance = "
         << getDistance() << "\n"
         << "Current angle = "
         << getAngle() << " degrees\n";

    // calculate the random movement of lost person
    m_fDeltaX = calcRandShift();
    m_fDeltaY = calcRandShift();
    setPoint2(checkCoord(m_fX2 + m_fDeltaX),
              checkCoord(m_fY2 + m_fDeltaY));

    // prompt for movement of rescuer
    cout << "Enter shift in X coordinates : ";
    cin >> m_fDeltaX;
    if (m_fDeltaX > m_fShift) // verify limit
        m_fDeltaX = m_fShift;
    cout << "Enter shift in Y coordinates : ";
    cin >> m_fDeltaY;
    if (m_fDeltaY > m_fShift) // verify limit
        m_fDeltaY = m_fShift;
    setPoint1(checkCoord(m_fX1 + m_fDeltaX),
              checkCoord(m_fY1 + m_fDeltaY));
}

//
// test classes
//
```

```
main()
{
  Rescue R(MIN_XY, MAX_XY, CRITIC_DIST);

  R.getCoords();
  while (R.searchMore())
    R.getCoords();

  cout << "\n\n";
  if (R.getDistance() <= CRITIC_DIST)
    cout << "Congratulations for the rescue!";
  else
    cout << "Sorry you gave up!";

  return 0;
}
```

Listing 14-9 declares a set of global constants that set the general parameters for the search simulation. The listing also declares the global functions **sqr**, **cube**, and **frac** to return the square, cube, and fractional values of floating-point numbers. As for classes, the listing declares the classes **Random**, **Distance**, and **Rescue**.

The Class Random

The class **Random** declares the protected **double**-type data member **m_fSeed**, which stores the last random number. The class uses this data member to generate the next random number. The class **Random** declares a constructor that initializes the data member **m_fSeed** and the member function **getRandom**, which returns a random number between 0 and 1 (exclusive).

The Class Distance

The class **Distance** manages the distance between two points and declares protected and public members. The protected members are:

- The **double**-type data members **m_fX1**, **m_fY1**, **m_fX2**, and **m_fY2**, which store the coordinates of two points
- The **double**-type data members **m_fDeltaX** and **m_fDeltaY**, which store the differences in the X and Y coordinates of the two points

The class Distance also declares the following public members:

- The constructor, which initializes the data members **m_fX1**, **m_fY1**, **m_fX2**, and **m_fY2**, which store the coordinates of two points
- The member functions **setPoint1** and **setPoint2**, which store new coordinates for the first and second point, respectively
- The member function **getDeltaX**, which returns the difference in the X coordinates
- The member function **getDeltaY**, which returns the difference in the Y coordinates
- The member function **getDistance**, which returns the distance between the two points
- The member function **getAngle**, which returns the angle (in degrees) of the line that connects the two points

The Class Rescue

The listing declares the class **Rescue** as a public descendant of classes **Random** and **Distance**. The descendant class declares protected and public members. The protected members are:

- The **double**-type data members **m_fMin** and **m_fMax**, which define the range of X and Y coordinates
- The **double**-type data member **m_fShift**, which stores the maximum change in X and Y coordinates for the lost person
- The **double**-type data member **m_fCriticalDistance**, which stores the maximum distance considered for locating the lost person
- The member function **calcRandCoord**, which returns a random value for the X or Y coordinate
- The member function **calcRandShift**, which returns a random value for the shift in the X or Y coordinate
- The member function **checkCoord**, which verifies that the argument for the **double**-type parameter **fX** lies in the range of coordinates. If that argument is outside the defined range, the function returns the value of the expression **m_fMin + m_fMax / 2**.

The class **Rescue** declares the following public members:

- The constructor, which initializes the data members and invokes the member function **InitRescue**

- The member function **initRescue**, which sets up your initial coordinates and the coordinates of the lost person

- The member function **searchMore**, which determines whether or not you found the lost person, or if you quit the search

- The member function **getCoords**, which displays and prompts for the various coordinates

The definition of member function **getCoords** supports the following tasks:

- Display the current distance between you and the lost person

- Display the angle of the line connecting your location with that of the lost person

- Calculate the random movement of the lost person and update her/his coordinates

- Prompt you to enter the move in the X and Y directions. The member function verifies that your input is within the limit of **m_fShift**.

- Set your new coordinates

The Function main

The function **main** declares the object **R** as an instance of class **Rescue**. The function creates this instance using the constants **MIN_XY, MAX_XY**, and **CRITIC_DIST** to set the grid range and critical distance. The function **main** performs the following tasks:

- Display the initial distance and angle and prompt you for your first move. This task involves sending the C++ message **getCoords** to the object **R**.

- Perform the simulated search for the lost person using a **while** loop. The loop examines the Boolean value returned by sending the C++ message **searchMore** to the object **R**. This message determines whether or not you found the lost person (or quit the search). Each loop iteration sends the C++ message **getCoords** to the object **R**. This message displays the current distance and angle and prompts you for your next move.

■ Determine whether you found the lost person or quit the search. This task involves sending the C++ message **getDistance** to the object. The function uses an **if** statement to compare the result of this message with the constant **CRITIC_DIST**. The function **main** displays a message "Congratulations for the rescue!" if you found the person or the message "Sorry you gave up!" if you stopped searching.

THE CALCULATOR EXAMPLE

The next example shows a set of classes that have a common base class. Listing 14-10 shows the source code for the DESCLS10.CPP program. The classes in the program model the computing engines of simple algebraic calculators. The base class of the hierarchy is class **ALCalc01** (where "AL" stands for algebraic logic); it has the descendants **ALCalc100**, **ALCalc120**, and **ALCalc200**.

The Class ALCalc01 in Brief

The class **ALCalc01**, which is the parent of the descendant classes **ALCalc100** and **ALCalc200**, models the engine of a simple four-function calculator. This calculator engine contains the following components:

■ The mathematical registers X and Y, which store the operands

■ The mathematical register Z, which stores the results of mathematical operations

■ The Boolean error flag register, which stores the error state of the last operation

■ The character-type register, which stores the name of the last operation

The calculator supports the following operations:

■ Perform the four basic math operations

■ Set new values to the X and Y registers

- Query the value in the Z register
- Query the error state
- Clear the registers
- Display the value in the register Z
- Display the last operands, operator, and result

The Class ALCalc100 in Brief

The class ALCalc100, a child of class AlCalc01, supports the emulation of memory registers. The class instances enable you to specify the number of memory registers at runtime. The class supports the following operations:

- Store numbers in the memory registers, accessed by numeric indices
- Recall numbers from the memory registers
- Clear the contents of the memory registers by assigning zeros to them

The Class ALCalc200 in Brief

The class ALCalc200, the other child of class ALCalc01, supports the following operations:

- Undertake a limited set of operations that include calculating the square root, square, natural log, and common log functions. These operations allow the class to implement a limited scientific calculator.
- Display the last mathematical function evaluated, the argument of the function, and the result
- Clear the memory registers

In order to display the last mathematical function executed, the class has a special data member emulating a register that stores the name of the last function.

The Class ALCalc120 in Brief

The class ALCalc120 is a child of classes ALCalc100 and ALCalc200. The descendant class merely inherits the combined operations of its parent classes.

Here is the output of the program in Listing 14-10:

```
Testing class ALCalc01
55 + 13 = 68
123 - 55 = 68
0.55 * 13 = 7.15
355 * 113 = 3.14159

Testing class ALCalc100
55 + 13 = 68
123 - 55 = 68
68 * 68 = 4624

Testing class ALCalc120
55 + 13 = 68
123 - 55 = 68
68 * 68 = 4624
Ln(68) = 4.21951
Sqr(68) = 4624

Testing class ALCalc200
Ln(13) = 2.56495
Sqr(13) = 169
```

Listing 14-10
The source code for the DESCLS10.CPP program.

```
/*

A C++ program that illustrates the following
small class hierarchy that uses multiple
inheritance with a common base class:


                    ALCalc01
                       |
                       |
                       |
            /-------------\
            |             |
            |             |
            |             |
            |             |
        ALCalc100     ALCalc200
            |             |
            |             |
            |             |
            \-------------/
                  |
                  |
                  |
              ALCalc120

*/
```

```
#include <iostream.h>
#include <math.h>
#include <string.h>

const double BAD_RESULT = -1.0e+30;
const double EPSILON = 1.0e-50;

enum Logical { FALSE, TRUE };

class ALCalc01                                    ─────────►  Base class
{
  public:
    ALCalc01(double fRegX = 0., double fRegY = 0.);

    // set new register values
    void setRegX(double fRegX)
      { m_fRegX = fRegX; }
    void setRegY(double fRegY)
      { m_fRegY = fRegY; }
    double getRegZ()
      { return m_fRegZ; }
    Logical getError();

    void add(Logical bShowResult = TRUE,
             const char* pszMsg = "");
    void sub(Logical bShowResult = TRUE,
             const char* pszMsg = "");
    void mult(Logical bShowResult = TRUE,
              const char* pszMsg = "");
    void div(Logical bShowResult = TRUE,
             const char* pszMsg = "");
    void showRegZ(const char* pszMsg = "");
    void showOperation(const char* pszMsg = "");
    void clearRegs();

  protected:
    double m_fRegX;
    double m_fRegY;
    double m_fRegZ;
    char m_cOp;
    Logical m_bErr;

};
```

```
class ALCalc100 : virtual public ALCalc01          First descendant class
{
  public:
    ALCalc100(int nMaxMem = 10,
              double fRegX = 0.,
              double fRegY = 0.);
    ~ALCalc100();
    void stoMem(int nIndex, double x);
    void rclMem(int nIndex, double& x);
    void clearMem();

  protected:
    double* m_pfMem;
    int m_nMaxMem;
};

class ALCalc200 : virtual public ALCalc01          Second descendant class
{
  public:
    ALCalc200(double fRegX = 0., double fRegY = 0.)
      : ALCalc01(fRegX, fRegY)
    {
      strcpy(m_cFunc, "");
    }

    void Sqrt(Logical bShowResult = TRUE,
              const char* pszMsg = "");
    void Sqr(Logical bShowResult = TRUE,
             const char* pszMsg = "");
    void Ln(Logical bShowResult = TRUE,
            const char* pszMsg = "");
    void Log(Logical bShowResult = TRUE,
             const char* pszMsg = "");
    void showFunction(const char* pszMsg = "");
    void clearRegs(); // override inherited function

  protected:
    char m_cFunc[10];
};

class ALCalc120 : virtual public ALCalc100,        Child of descendant classes
                  virtual public ALCalc200
{
  public:
    ALCalc120(int nMaxMem = 10, double fRegX = 0.,
              double fRegY = 0.)
      : ALCalc100(nMaxMem, fRegX, fRegY)
    {
      strcpy(m_cFunc, "");
    }
};
```

```
//
// define member functions of class ALCalc01
//

ALCalc01::ALCalc01(double fRegX, double fRegY)
{
  m_fRegX = fRegX;
  m_fRegY = fRegY;
  m_fRegZ = 0.0;
  m_cOp = ' ';
  m_bErr = FALSE;
}

Logical ALCalc01::getError()
{
  Logical bTemp = m_bErr;
  m_bErr = FALSE;
  return bTemp;
}

void ALCalc01::add(Logical bShowResult, const char* pszMsg)
{
  m_fRegZ = m_fRegY + m_fRegX;
  m_cOp = '+';
  m_bErr = FALSE;
  if (bShowResult)
    cout << pszMsg << m_fRegZ;
}

void ALCalc01::sub(Logical bShowResult, const char* pszMsg)
{
  m_fRegZ = m_fRegY - m_fRegX;
  m_cOp = '-';
  m_bErr = FALSE;
  if (bShowResult)
    cout << pszMsg << m_fRegZ;
}

void ALCalc01::mult(Logical bShowResult, const char* pszMsg)
{
  m_fRegZ = m_fRegY * m_fRegX;
  m_cOp = '*';
  m_bErr = FALSE;
  if (bShowResult)
    cout << pszMsg << m_fRegZ;
}

void ALCalc01::div(Logical bShowResult, const char* pszMsg)
{
  if (fabs(m_fRegY) > EPSILON) {
    m_cOp = '*';
    m_bErr = FALSE;
```

```
      m_fRegZ = m_fRegY / m_fRegX;
      if (bShowResult)
        cout << pszMsg << m_fRegZ;
  }
  else {
    m_fRegZ = BAD_RESULT;
    m_cOp = ' ';
    m_bErr = TRUE;
  }
}

void ALCalc01::showRegZ(const char* pszMsg)
{
  cout << pszMsg << m_fRegZ;
}

void ALCalc01::showOperation(const char* pszMsg)
{
  cout << pszMsg << m_fRegY << " " << m_cOp << " "
       << m_fRegX << " = " << m_fRegZ << "\n";
}

void ALCalc01::clearRegs()
{
  m_fRegX = 0.0;
  m_fRegY = 0.0;
  m_fRegZ = 0.0;
  m_cOp = ' ';
  m_bErr = FALSE;
}


//
// define member functions of class ALCalc100
//

ALCalc100::ALCalc100(int nMaxMem,
             double fRegX, double fRegY)
    : ALCalc01(fRegX, fRegY)
{
  m_pfMem = new double[m_nMaxMem = nMaxMem];
  for (int i = 0; i < m_nMaxMem; i++)
    m_pfMem[i] = 0.;
}

ALCalc100::~ALCalc100()
{
  delete [] m_pfMem;
}

void ALCalc100::stoMem(int nIndex, double x)
{
  if (nIndex >= 0 && nIndex < m_nMaxMem) {
```

```
    m_pfMem[nIndex] = x;
    m_bErr = FALSE;
  }
  else
    m_bErr = TRUE;
}


void ALCalc100::rclMem(int nIndex, double& x)
{
  if (nIndex >= 0 && nIndex < m_nMaxMem) {
    x = m_pfMem[nIndex];
    m_bErr = FALSE;
  }
  else
    m_bErr = TRUE;
}


void ALCalc100::clearMem()
{
  for (int i = 0; i < m_nMaxMem; i++)
    m_pfMem[i] = 0.;
}


//
// define member functions of class ALCalc200
//

void ALCalc200::Sqrt(Logical bShowResult, const char* pszMsg)
{ if (m_fRegX >= 0.) {
    m_fRegZ = sqrt(m_fRegX);
    m_bErr = FALSE;
    strcpy(m_cFunc, "Sqrt(");
    if (bShowResult)
      cout << pszMsg << m_fRegZ;
  }
  else {
    m_fRegZ = BAD_RESULT;
    m_bErr = TRUE;
    strcpy(m_cFunc, "");
  }
}

void ALCalc200::Sqr(Logical bShowResult, const char* pszMsg)
{
  m_fRegZ = m_fRegX * m_fRegX;
  m_bErr = FALSE;
  strcpy(m_cFunc, "Sqr(");
  if (bShowResult)
    cout << pszMsg << m_fRegZ;
}
```

```
void ALCalc200::Ln(Logical bShowResult, const char* pszMsg)
{
  if (m_fRegX > 0.) {
    m_fRegZ = log(m_fRegX);
    m_bErr = FALSE;
    strcpy(m_cFunc, "Ln(");
    if (bShowResult)
      cout << pszMsg << m_fRegZ;
  }
  else {
    m_fRegZ = BAD_RESULT;
    m_bErr = TRUE;
    strcpy(m_cFunc, "");
  }
}

void ALCalc200::Log(Logical bShowResult, const char* pszMsg)
{
  if (m_fRegX > 0.) {
    m_fRegZ = log10(m_fRegX);
    m_bErr = FALSE;
    strcpy(m_cFunc, "Log10(");
    if (bShowResult)
      cout << pszMsg << m_fRegZ;
  }
  else {
    m_fRegZ = BAD_RESULT;
    m_bErr = TRUE;
    strcpy(m_cFunc, "");
  }
}

void ALCalc200::showFunction(const char* pszMsg)
{
  cout << pszMsg << m_cFunc << m_fRegX
       << ") = " << m_fRegZ << "\n";
}

void ALCalc200::clearRegs()
{
  ALCalc01::clearRegs();
  strcpy(m_cFunc, "");
}

//
// test classes
//

main()
{
  {
```

```
   ALCalc01 calculator;

   cout << "Testing class ALCalc01\n";

   // test addition
   calculator.setRegX(13.0);
   calculator.setRegY(55.0);
   calculator.add(FALSE);
   calculator.showOperation();

   // test subtraction
   calculator.setRegX(55.0);
   calculator.setRegY(123.0);
   calculator.sub(FALSE);
   calculator.showOperation();

   // test multiplication
   calculator.setRegX(13.0);
   calculator.setRegY(0.55);
   calculator.mult(FALSE);
   calculator.showOperation();

   // test division
   calculator.setRegX(113.0);
   calculator.setRegY(355.0);
   calculator.div(FALSE);
   calculator.showOperation();
}
cout << "\n";
{
   ALCalc100 calculator;
   double fX;

   cout << "Testing class ALCalc100\n";

   // test addition
   calculator.setRegX(13.0);
   calculator.setRegY(55.0);
   calculator.add(FALSE);
   calculator.showOperation();
   fX = calculator.getRegZ();
   calculator.stoMem(0, fX);

   // test subtraction
   calculator.setRegX(55.0);
   calculator.setRegY(123.0);
   calculator.sub(FALSE);
   calculator.showOperation();
   fX = calculator.getRegZ();
   calculator.stoMem(1, fX);
```

```
        // test multiplication
        calculator.rclMem(0, fX);
        calculator.setRegX(fX);
        calculator.rclMem(1, fX);
        calculator.setRegY(fX);
        calculator.mult(FALSE);
        calculator.showOperation();
    }
    cout << "\n";
    {
        ALCalc120 calculator;
        double fX;

        cout << "Testing class ALCalc120\n";

        // test addition
        calculator.setRegX(13.0);
        calculator.setRegY(55.0);
        calculator.add(FALSE);
        calculator.showOperation();
        fX = calculator.getRegZ();
        calculator.stoMem(0, fX);

        // test subtraction
        calculator.setRegX(55.0);
        calculator.setRegY(123.0);
        calculator.sub(FALSE);
        calculator.showOperation();
        fX = calculator.getRegZ();
        calculator.stoMem(1, fX);

        // test multiplication
        calculator.rclMem(0, fX);
        calculator.setRegX(fX);
        calculator.rclMem(1, fX);
        calculator.setRegY(fX);
        calculator.mult(FALSE);
        calculator.showOperation();

        // test ln(x)
        calculator.Ln(FALSE);
        calculator.showFunction();

        // test square function
        calculator.Sqr(FALSE);
        calculator.showFunction();
    }
    cout << "\n";
    {
        ALCalc200 calculator;
```

```
    cout << "Testing class ALCalc200\n";

    // test addition
    calculator.setRegX(13.0);

    // test ln(x)
    calculator.Ln(FALSE);
    calculator.showFunction();

    // test square function
    calculator.Sqr(FALSE);
    calculator.showFunction();
  }

  return 0;
}
```

Listing 14-10 declares the global double-type constants **BAD_RESULT** and **EPSILON**, as well as the enumerated type **Logical**. The next subsections discuss the various classes that appear in the listing.

The Class ALCalc01 in Detail

The class **ALCalc01** declares public and protected members. The protected members are:

- The **double**-type data members **m_fRegX** and **m_fRegY**, which emulate the registers X and Y in the calculator. These registers store the operands.
- The **double**-type data member **m_fRegZ**, which emulates the register Z in the calculator. This register stores the result of a mathematical operation.
- The **char**-type data member **m_cOp**, which stores a character that represents the last operation
- The **Logical**-type data member **m_bErr**, which stores the state of the error for the last operation

The class declares the following public members:

- The constructor, which initializes the data members
- The member functions **setRegX** and **setRegY**, which store new operands in the data members **m_fRegX** and **m_fRegY**, respectively

- The member function **getRegZ**, which returns the value in the data member **m_fRegZ**

- The member function **getError**, which returns (and resets) the value in the data member **m_bErr**

- The member functions **add**, **sub**, **mult**, and **div**, which perform the addition, subtraction, multiplication, and division operations. These member functions use the operands in data members **m_fRegX** and **m_fRegY** and store the result in data member **m_fRegZ**. The functions reset the value in data member **m_bErr** and assign the character that represents the operation in data member **m_cOp**. The member function **div** tests for division by zero. The function sets the data member **m_bErr** to true if the operation attempts to divide by a number whose absolute value is smaller than the value of the constant **EPSILON**.

- The member function **showRegZ**, which displays the value in data member **m_fRegZ**

- The member function **showOperation**, which displays the most recent operands, operation, and result

- The member function **clearRegs**, which resets the values in all of the data members

The Class ALCalc100 in Detail

The class **ALCalc100** is a virtual descendant of class **ALCalc01**. This class declares public and protected members to support the emulated memory registers feature. The class declares the following protected members:

- The data member **m_pfMem**, which is a pointer to the dynamic array of doubles. This array emulates the memory registers. The class instances use this member to access the elements of the dynamic array.

- The int-type data member **m_nMaxMem**, which contains the number of dynamic array elements

The class declares the following public members:

- The constructor, which allows you to specify the number of memory registers (that is, the number of elements in the supporting dynamic array) and the initial values in the registers X and Y (that is, the inherited data members **m_fRegX** and **m_fRegY**)

- The member function **stoMem**, which stores the value of parameter **x** at the memory register specified by the index **nIndex**. If you specify an out-of-range index, the function sets the inherited data member **m_bErr** to true. The function uses the data member **m_pfMem** to access the targeted element of the dynamic array.

- The member function **rclMem**, which recalls the value of the memory register specified by the index **nIndex**. The reference parameter **x** passes the sought value. If you specify an out-of-range index, the function sets the inherited data member **m_bErr** to true. The function uses the data member **m_pfMem** to access the targeted element of the dynamic array.

- The member function **clearMem**, which clears the memory registers by assigning zeros to the elements of the dynamic array

The Class ALCalc200 in Detail

The class **ALCalc200** is a virtual descendant of class **ALCalc01**. The class declares a single protected data member **m_cFunc**, which stores the name of the last mathematical function evaluated.

The class declares the following public members:

- The constructor, which initializes the inherited data members (by invoking the constructor of the parent class) and initializes the data member **m_cFunc** with an empty string

- The member functions **Sqrt**, **Sqr**, **Ln**, and **Log**, which evaluate the square root, square, natural logarithm, and common logarithm. These functions use the value in data member **m_fRegX** as the argument and store the result in data member **m_fRegZ**. The square root and logarithm functions check the value in data member **m_fRegX** before performing the mathematical function evaluation.

- The member function **showFunction**, which displays the name of the most recent mathematical function evaluated, its argument, and its result

- The member function **clearRegs**, which overrides the inherited member function. This function invokes the inherited member function and then resets the value in data member **m_cFunc**.

The Class ALCalc120 in Detail

The class **ALCalc120** is a virtual descendant of classes **ALCalc100** and **ALCalc200**. This class supports the same operations as classes **ALCalc01**, **ALCacl100**, and **ALCalc200** combined. Declaring class **ALCalc120** as a virtual descendant of multiple classes enables the compiler to resolve the redundancy in the lineage of this class.

The Function main

The function **main** tests the four classes in nested blocks. Each block declares the object calculator as an instance of an **ALCalcxxxx** class. The function **main** performs various operations on each class instance.

Containment

Containment is a programming technique that uses class instances or pointers to classes as data members of other classes. In other words, you declare a class that contains data members that are themselves instances of other classes or pointers to other classes. The contained classes need not be (and are usually not) related to the host class by common ancestor classes. With containment, the host class has access to the public members of the contained classes.

Some C++ gurus prefer using containment to using multiple inheritance, because initializing contained classes involves fewer possible ambiguities than initializing multiple-inheritance classes.

Using Pointers to Classes

Use pointers to classes as contained data members when these classes do not have default constructors or when you want to initialize these data members in a particular way.

Don't forget to create and remove the dynamic class instances (accessed by the pointer-to-class data members) by means of the constructor and destructor, respectively.

Here is a simple example of contained classes:

```
class Array
{
  // declaration of members
};
class Matrix
{
  // declaration of members
};

class LinearEquationSystem
{
  public:
    // declaration of members
  protected:
   Array m_Array;
   Matrix m_Matrix;
   // declaration of other members

};
```

The example declares the classes **Array**, **Matrix**, and **LinearEquationSystem**. The example declares the last-named class as having the data members **m_Array** and **m_Matrix**, which are instances of classes **Array** and **Matrix**, respectively.

Let's look at a programming example. Listing 14-11 shows the source code for the DESCLS11.CPP program, which illustrates containment. I created this program by modifying the source code in Listing 14-9 (the rescue simulation program). The new program interacts in the same way with you, but it uses containment instead of multiple inheritance.

Listing 14-11
The source code for the DESCLS11.CPP program.

```
/*

    A C++ program that illustrates the following
    small class hierarchy, which uses containment:
```

```
             Distance          Random
                |                 |
                |                 |
                |                 |
             data members of
                |                 |
                \-------------/
                        |
                        |
                     Rescue

*/

#include <iostream.h>
#include <math.h>
#include <string.h>

const double PI = 4 * atan(1);
const double RAD2DEG = 180.0 / PI;
const double INIT_SEED = 113;
const double MIN_XY = 1.0;
const double MAX_XY = 1000.0;
const double CRITIC_DIST = 10.0;
const double EPSILON = 1.0e-8;
const double INFINITY = 1.0e+50;

enum Logical { FALSE, TRUE };

double sqr(double x)
{
  return x * x;
}

double cube(double x)
{
  return x * x * x;
}

double frac(double x)
{
  return x - (long)x;
}

class Random
{
  public:
    Random(double fSeed = INIT_SEED)
      { m_fSeed = fSeed; }

    double getRandom();

  protected:
    double m_fSeed;
};
```

```
class Distance
{
  public:
    Distance(double fX1, double fY1,
             double fX2, double fY2);
    void setPoint1(double fX, double fY);
    void setPoint2(double fX, double fY);
    double getDeltaX()
      { return m_fX2 - m_fX1; }
    double getDeltaY()
      { return m_fY2 - m_fY1; }
    double getDistance()
      { return sqrt(sqr(m_fX2 - m_fX2) +
                    sqr(m_fY2 - m_fY1)); }
    double getAngle();
    void setDeltaX(double fDeltaX)
      { m_fDeltaX = fDeltaX; }
    void setDeltaY(double fDeltaY)
      { m_fDeltaY = fDeltaY; }
    double getX1()
      { return m_fX1; }
    double getX2()
      { return m_fX2; }
    double getY1()
      { return m_fY1; }
    double getY2()
      { return m_fY2; }

  protected:
    double m_fX1;
    double m_fX2;
    double m_fY1;
    double m_fY2;
    double m_fDeltaX;
    double m_fDeltaY;
};

class Rescue
{
  public:
    Rescue(double fMin, double fMax,
           double fCriticalDistance);
    ~Rescue();
    void initRescue();
    Logical searchMore();
    void getCoords();
    double getDistance()
      { return m_pDistance->getDistance(); }

  protected:
    double m_fMin;
```

```
    double m_fMax;
    double m_fShift;
    double m_fCriticalDistance;
    // declare pointers to contained classes
    Distance* m_pDistance;
    Random* m_pRandom;
```

Pointers to contained class

```
    double calcRandCoord()
      { return m_pRandom->getRandom() * m_fMax + m_fMin; }
    double calcRandShift()
      { return (0.5 - m_pRandom->getRandom()) * m_fShift; }
    double checkCoord(double fX)
      { return (fX >= m_fMin && fX <= m_fMax) ?
                 fX : m_fMin + m_fMax / 2.; }
};

double Random::getRandom()
{
  m_fSeed = frac(cube(m_fSeed + PI));
  return m_fSeed;
}


Distance::Distance(double fX1, double fY1,
                   double fX2, double fY2)
{
  setPoint1(fX1, fY1);
  setPoint2(fX2, fY2);
}

void Distance::setPoint1(double fX, double fY)
{
  m_fX1 = fX;
  m_fY1 = fY;
}

void Distance::setPoint2(double fX, double fY)
{
  m_fX2 = fX;
  m_fY2 = fY;
}

double Distance::getAngle()
{
  double fDeltaY = m_fY2 - m_fY1;

  return (fabs(fDeltaY) > EPSILON) ?
    RAD2DEG * atan((m_fX2 - m_fX1) / fDeltaY) :
    INFINITY;
}

Rescue::Rescue(double fMin, double fMax,
               double fCriticalDistance)
```

```
{
  m_fMin = fMin;
  m_fMax = fMax;
  m_fShift = (fMax - fMin + 1) / 10.;
  m_fCriticalDistance = fCriticalDistance;
  m_pDistance = new Distance(0, 0, 0, 0);
  m_pRandom = new Random;
  initRescue();
}

Rescue::~Rescue()
{
  delete m_pDistance;
  delete m_pRandom;
}


void Rescue::initRescue()
{
  double fX = calcRandCoord();
  double fY = calcRandCoord();

  m_pDistance->setPoint1((m_fMin + m_fMax) / 2,
                         (m_fMin + m_fMax) / 2);
  m_pDistance->setPoint2(fX, fY);
}

Logical Rescue::searchMore()
{
  if (fabs(m_pDistance->getDeltaX()) < 1.0 ||
      fabs(m_pDistance->getDeltaY()) < 1.0 ||
        m_pDistance->getDistance() < m_fCriticalDistance)
    return FALSE;
  else
    return TRUE;
}

void Rescue::getCoords()
{
  int fX, fY;

  cout << "Current distance = "
       << m_pDistance->getDistance() << "\n"
       << "Current angle = "
       << m_pDistance->getAngle() << " degrees\n";

  // calculate the random movement of lost person
  m_pDistance->setDeltaX(calcRandShift());
  m_pDistance->setDeltaY(calcRandShift());
  m_pDistance->setPoint2(
      checkCoord(m_pDistance->getX2() +
                 m_pDistance->getDeltaX()),
      checkCoord(m_pDistance->getY2() +
                 m_pDistance->getDeltaY())
      );
```

```
      // prompt for movement of rescuer
      cout << "Enter shift in X coordinates : ";
      cin >> fX;
      m_pDistance->setDeltaX(fX);
      if (m_pDistance->getDeltaX() > m_fShift) // verify limit
        m_pDistance->setDeltaX(m_fShift);
      cout << "Enter shift in Y coordinates : ";
      cin >> fY;
      m_pDistance->setDeltaY(fY);
      if (m_pDistance->getDeltaY() > m_fShift) // verify limit
        m_pDistance->setDeltaY(m_fShift);
      m_pDistance->setPoint1(
          checkCoord(m_pDistance->getX1() +
                     m_pDistance->getDeltaX()),
          checkCoord(m_pDistance->getY1() +
                     m_pDistance->getDeltaY())
          );
}


//
// test classes
//

main()
{
  Rescue R(MIN_XY, MAX_XY, CRITIC_DIST);

  R.getCoords();
  while (R.searchMore())
    R.getCoords();

  cout << "\n\n";
  if (R.getDistance() <= CRITIC_DIST)
    cout << "Congratulations for the rescue!";
  else
    cout << "Sorry you gave up!";

  return 0;
}
```

Listing 14-11 declares the classes **Random**, **Distance**, and **Rescue**. The class **Rescue** resembles the version in Listing 14-9. Notice the following differences in the new class version:

- The protected data member **m_pDistance**, which is a pointer to the class **Distance**

- The protected data member **m_pRandom**, which is a pointer to the class **Distance**

- The modified constructor, which creates dynamic instances of classes Random and Distance to be accessed by the data members m_pDistance and m_pRandom, respectively

The listing also includes the additional member functions (getX1, getY1, getX2, and getY2) in class Distance to access the data members m_fX1, m_fY1, m_fX2, m_fY2 and to assign new values to the data members m_fDeltaX and m_fDeltaY. The member functions Rescue::searchMore and Rescue::getCoords use these member functions to access the data members of class Distance. Thus, you learn that a contained class should declare all the member functions needed by the host class.

The code for the function main is the same in Listing 14-11 as in Listing 14-9.

Friend Classes

C++ allows you to declare *friend classes*. Such classes have access to all the members of the befriended classes. While friendship between classes is not a genuine part of object-oriented programming, it does reduce the software red tape, so to speak.

The general syntax for declaring a friend class is:

```
class className
{
    friend friendClassName;
    // declaration of other members
};
```

Declaring a friend class involves the keyword friend followed by the name of that class.

Declarations of friend classes typically appear in a set of classes that you design simultaneously. You cannot declare friend classes as an add-on feature. Friend classes serve in two main categories of situations:

- The friend classes access the members of the befriended classes in function parameters or as local instances declared in member functions.

- The friend classes are also contained in other classes. The friendship between the contained and host classes allows the latter to directly access data members of the friend classes without the overhead of accessing member functions.

Let me present a programming example. Listing 14-12 shows the source code for the DESCLS12.CPP program, which illustrates friend classes. I created this program by modifying the source code of Listing 14-11. The new listing declares the class **Rescue** as a friend to classes **Random** and **Distance**. This friendship allows the class **Rescue** to access the data members of classes **Random** and **Distance** without accessing member functions. Consequently, the code in Listing 14-12 does away with the member functions **getX1**, **getY1**, **getX2**, **getY2**, **setPoint1**, and **setPoint2** (found in Listing 14-11). Thus, the program in Listing 14-12 is a bit more efficient than the one in Listing 14-11 because the friendship between the classes eliminates the need for member functions that access data members.

Listing 14-12
The source code for the DESCLS12.CPP program.

```
/*

    A C++ program that illustrates the following
    small class hierarchy, which uses containment:

        Distance        Random
           |               |
           |               |
           |               |
        data members of
           |               |
        \-------------/
                |
                |
            Rescue

*/

#include <iostream.h>
#include <math.h>
#include <string.h>

const double PI = 4 * atan(1);
const double RAD2DEG = 180.0 / PI;
const double INIT_SEED = 113;
```

```
const double MIN_XY = 1.0;
const double MAX_XY = 1000.0;
const double CRITIC_DIST = 10.0;
const double EPSILON = 1.0e-8;
const double INFINITY = 1.0e+50;

enum Logical { FALSE, TRUE };

double sqr(double x)
{
  return x * x;
}

double cube(double x)
{
  return x * x * x;
}

double frac(double x)
{
  return x - (long)x;
}

class Random
{
  public:
    friend class Rescue;

    Random(double fSeed = INIT_SEED)
      { m_fSeed = fSeed; }

    double getRandom();

  protected:
    double m_fSeed;
};

class Distance
{
  public:
    friend class Rescue;                                    Friend class

    Distance(double fX1, double fY1,
             double fX2, double fY2);
    void setPoint1(double fX, double fY);
    void setPoint2(double fX, double fY);
    double getDeltaX()
      { return m_fX2 - m_fX1; }
    double getDeltaY()
      { return m_fY2 - m_fY1; }
```

```
        double getDistance()
          { return sqrt(sqr(m_fX2 - m_fX2) +
                        sqr(m_fY2 - m_fY1)); }
        double getAngle();

    protected:
        double m_fX1;
        double m_fX2;
        double m_fY1;
        double m_fY2;
        double m_fDeltaX;
        double m_fDeltaY;
};

class Rescue
{
    public:
        Rescue(double fMin, double fMax,
               double fCriticalDistance);
        ~Rescue();
        void initRescue();
        Logical searchMore();
        void getCoords();
        double getDistance()
          { return m_pDistance->getDistance(); }

    protected:
        double m_fMin;
        double m_fMax;
        double m_fShift;
        double m_fCriticalDistance;
        // declare pointers to contained classes
        Distance* m_pDistance;
        Random* m_pRandom;

        double calcRandCoord()
          { return m_pRandom->getRandom() * m_fMax + m_fMin; }
        double calcRandShift()
          { return (0.5 - m_pRandom->getRandom()) * m_fShift; }
        double checkCoord(double fX)
          { return (fX >= m_fMin && fX <= m_fMax) ?
                    fX : m_fMin + m_fMax / 2.; }
};

double Random::getRandom()
{
    m_fSeed = frac(cube(m_fSeed + PI));
    return m_fSeed;
}

Distance::Distance(double fX1, double fY1,
                   double fX2, double fY2)
```

```
{
  setPoint1(fX1, fY1);
  setPoint2(fX2, fY2);
}

void Distance::setPoint1(double fX, double fY)
{
  m_fX1 = fX;
  m_fY1 = fY;
}

void Distance::setPoint2(double fX, double fY)
{
  m_fX2 = fX;
  m_fY2 = fY;
}

double Distance::getAngle()
{
  double fDeltaY = m_fY2 - m_fY1;

  return (fabs(fDeltaY) > EPSILON) ?
    RAD2DEG * atan((m_fX2 - m_fX1) / fDeltaY) :
    INFINITY;
}

Rescue::Rescue(double fMin, double fMax,
               double fCriticalDistance)
{
  m_fMin = fMin;
  m_fMax = fMax;
  m_fShift = (fMax - fMin + 1) / 10.;
  m_fCriticalDistance = fCriticalDistance;
  m_pDistance = new Distance(0, 0, 0, 0);
  m_pRandom = new Random;
  initRescue();
}

Rescue::~Rescue()
{
  delete m_pDistance;
  delete m_pRandom;
}

void Rescue::initRescue()
{
  double fX = calcRandCoord();
  double fY = calcRandCoord();

  m_pDistance->setPoint1((m_fMin + m_fMax) / 2,
                         (m_fMin + m_fMax) / 2);
  m_pDistance->setPoint2(fX, fY);
}
```

```
Logical Rescue::searchMore()
{
  if (fabs(m_pDistance->m_fDeltaX) < 1.0 ||
      fabs(m_pDistance->m_fDeltaY) < 1.0 ||
        m_pDistance->getDistance() < m_fCriticalDistance)
    return FALSE;
  else
    return TRUE;
}

void Rescue::getCoords()
{

  cout << "Current distance = "
       << m_pDistance->getDistance() << "\n"
       << "Current angle = "
       << m_pDistance->getAngle() << " degrees\n";

  // calculate the random movement of lost person
  m_pDistance->m_fDeltaX = calcRandShift();
  m_pDistance->m_fDeltaY = calcRandShift();
  m_pDistance->setPoint2(
      checkCoord(m_pDistance->m_fX2 +
                 m_pDistance->m_fDeltaX),
      checkCoord(m_pDistance->m_fY2 +
                 m_pDistance->m_fDeltaY)
      );

  // prompt for movement of rescuer
  cout << "Enter shift in X coordinates : ";
  cin >> m_pDistance->m_fDeltaX;
  if (m_pDistance->m_fDeltaX > m_fShift) // verify limit
    m_pDistance->m_fDeltaX = m_fShift;
  cout << "Enter shift in Y coordinates : ";
  cin >> m_pDistance->m_fDeltaY;
  if (m_pDistance->m_fDeltaY > m_fShift) // verify limit
    m_pDistance->m_fDeltaY = m_fShift;
  m_pDistance->setPoint1(
      checkCoord(m_pDistance->m_fX1 +
                 m_pDistance->m_fDeltaX),
      checkCoord(m_pDistance->m_fY1 +
                 m_pDistance->m_fDeltaY)
      );
}

//
// test classes
//

main()
{
  Rescue R(MIN_XY, MAX_XY, CRITIC_DIST);
```

```
    R.getCoords();
    while (R.searchMore())
      R.getCoords();

    cout << "\n\n";
    if (R.getDistance() <= CRITIC_DIST)
      cout << "Congratulations for the rescue!";
    else
      cout << "Sorry you gave up!";

    return 0;
}
```

Summary

This chapter discussed the basic aspects of class hierarchies. You learned about single and multiple inheritance and the conceptual meaning of each type of inheritance. You also learned about declaring a class hierarchy, declaring constructors for child classes, declaring virtual functions, and using virtual destructors. The text also discussed the rules of virtual functions and showed you how to declare and use friend functions, operators, friend operators, and friend classes. The chapter also discussed multiple inheritance, containment, and the difference between the two.

The next chapter discusses the basic file I/O streams. You will learn to read and write files using text and binary file streams.

IV

Advanced C++ Topics

*T*he last part of this book, which includes Chapters 15 through 18, presents advanced topics in C++ programming. Chapter 15 presents basic stream file I/O. The chapter discusses the stream library functions that allow you to support text file I/O, binary file I/O, and random access file I/O. Chapter 16 presents exception (runtime error) handling and discusses the C++ metaphor of throwing and catching exceptions. The chapter presents the C++ syntax for these operations and shows you how to manage exceptions. Chapter 17 presents templates and shows you how to use function templates and class templates to write generic functions and classes, respectively. The chapter discusses the syntax for declaring function templates and also illustrates how to declare class templates, define their member functions, and instantiate the classes. Chapter 18 covers new development in C++. These include the

Standard C++ Libraries, such as the Standard Template Library (STL). You will learn about new features such as the new include format, namespaces, and template parameter arguments.

15 Basic Stream File I/O

*T*his chapter looks at the basic file stream I/O in C++. In Chapter 7, "Managing Input and Output," you learned that C++ does not have I/O statements that are built into the language. Instead, C++ (like its parent C) relies on libraries to perform I/O. Chapter 7 introduced you to the C++ stream library and covered console I/O. This chapter looks at file I/O as supported by the stream library. You will learn about file I/O basics in the C++ stream library, common stream I/O functions, sequential text file stream I/O, sequential binary file stream I/O, and random access file stream I/O.

The C++ Stream Library

The C++ stream library contains the class **ios** that I presented in Chapter 7. This class declares identifiers that set the file stream mode. Table 15-1 shows the file modes supported by class **ios**.

The C++ stream library has the classes **ifstream**, **ofstream**, and **fstream** to support input file streams, output file streams, and both input and output file streams. Typically you use the class **fstream** to create file stream objects.

Table 15-1
The File Modes in Class ios

Identifier	Meaning
ios::app	Opens stream to append data
ios::ate	Sets stream pointer to the end of the file
ios::binary	Opens in binary mode
ios::in	Opens stream for input
ios::nocreate	Generates an error if the file does not already exist
ios::noreplace	Generates an error if the file does already exist
ios::out	Opens stream for output
ios::trunc	Truncates the file size to 0 if it already exists

Common Stream I/O Functions

The C++ stream library offers a set of member functions common to all file stream I/O operations. This section presents these member functions.

THE FUNCTION OPEN

The member function **open**, as the name might suggest, opens the file stream for input, output, append, and both input and output. The member function allows you to specify whether the file stream I/O is in text or binary mode. The declaration of the member function **open** is:

```
void open(const char* szName, int nMode,
        int nProt = filebuf::openprot);
```

The parameter **szName** is the name of the file to open. The parameter **nMode** is an integer that contains the mode bits defined as **ios** enumerators that can be combined with the bitwise OR operator (|). Table 15-1 shows these enumerators. The parameter **nProt** is the file protection specification; it has a default argument of **filebuf::openprot**.

Here are examples of using the member function **open**:

```
// example 1
char cAutoExec = "\\AUTOEXEC.BAT";
fstream f;
// open for input
f.open(cAutoExec, ios::in);

// example 2
fstream f;
// open for output
f.open("MYDATA.DAT", ios::out);

// example 3
fstream f;
// open for random access I/O
f.open("RECORDS.DAT", ios::in | ios::out | ios::binary);
```

The first example opens the file AUTOEXEC.BAT for text input, the second example opens the file MYDATA.DAT for text output, and the last example opens the file RECORDS.DAT for binary input and output (which is really random access mode).

THE FUNCTION CLOSE

The member function **close** flushes any awaiting output and closes the file stream buffer. The declaration for this member function is:

```
void close( );
```

Here is an example of using the member function **close**:

```
char cAutoExec = "\\AUTOEXEC.BAT";
fstream f;
// open for input
f.open(cAutoExec, ios::in);
// I/O statements
f.close(); // close file stream buffer
```

The example opens the file AUTOEXEC.BAT for input, performs input operations (not shown in the code), and then closes the file stream buffer.

OTHER MEMBER FUNCTIONS

In addition to member functions **open** and **close**, the C++ stream library offers the following member functions and operators:

- The member function **good**, which returns a nonzero value if there is no error in a stream operation. The declaration of this member function is:

```
int good();
```

- The member function **fail**, which returns a nonzero value if there is an error in a stream operation. The declaration of this member function is:

```
int fail();
```

- The member function **eof**, which returns a nonzero value if the stream has reached the end of the file. The declaration of this member function is:

```
int eof();
```

- The overloaded operator **!**, which determines the error status. This operator takes a stream object as an argument.

Sequential Text Stream I/O

The C++ stream library offers the operators **<<** and **>>** and the member function **getline** to support text stream I/O. The declaration of member function **getline** is:

```
istream& getline(char* pszStr, int nCount, char cDelim = '\n');
istream& getline(signed char* pszStr, int nCount,
                 char cDelim = '\n');
istream& getline(unsigned char* pszStr, int nCount,
                 char cDelim = '\n');
```

The parameter **pszStr** is a pointer to an ASCIIZ string. The parameter **nCount** specifies the maximum number of input characters. The parameter **cDelim** specifies the string delimiter.

Here is an example of using the member function **getline** as part of file I/O:

```
const int MAX_CHARS = 81;
char aLine[MAX_CHARS];
fstream f;
f.open("README.DOC", ios::in);
while (!f.eof()) {
  f.getline(aLine, MAX_CHARS);
  cout << aLine << endl;
}
f.close();
```

The example opens the file README.DOC for text input. The code snippet contains a **while** loop that reads each line in the file and displays it on the console. The input operation uses the member function **getline**.

Let's look at a programming example. Listing 15-1 shows the source code for the FIO1.CPP program, which illustrates text file stream I/O. The program basically translates a character in a file and writes the resulting text to another file. The program performs the following tasks:

- Prompt you to enter the input filename
- Prompt you to enter the output filename
- Prompt you to enter the character to find (which I'll also call the search character)
- Prompt you to enter the character to replace the search character
- Open the input and output files
- Read the lines from the input files, translate the occurrences of the character that you specify, write the processed lines to output file, and echo the output to the console
- Close the input and output file buffers

To test the program, I stored the following lines in the text file FIO1.DAT:

```
This is line # 1
This is line # 2
This is line # 3
This is line # 4
```

Here is a sample session with the program in Listing 15-1 (user input is underlined):

```
Enter input filename : fio1.dat
Enter output filename : fio1.out
Enter character to find : #
Enter character to replace : @
This is line @ 1
This is line @ 2
This is line @ 3
This is line @ 4



Translation successful!
```

Listing 15-1
The source code for the FIO1.CPP program.

```cpp
// A C++ program that illustrates
// text file stream input and output

#include <fstream.h>
#include <iomanip.h>
#include <string.h>

const int LINE_SIZE = 90;
const int FILENAME_SIZE = 64;

enum Logical { FALSE, TRUE };

class Translator
{
  public:
    Translator();
    void getInputFilename();
    void getOutputFilename();
    void getFindChar();
    void getReplChar();
    Logical Translate();

  protected:
    char m_cInputFilename[FILENAME_SIZE + 1];
    char m_cOutputFilename[FILENAME_SIZE + 1];
    char m_cFind;
    char m_cRepl;
};
```

```
Translator::Translator()
{
  strcpy(m_cInputFilename, "");
  strcpy(m_cOutputFilename, "");
  m_cFind = '\0';
  m_cRepl = '\0';
}

void Translator::getInputFilename()
{
  cout << "Enter input filename : ";
  cin.getline(m_cInputFilename, FILENAME_SIZE);
}

void Translator::getOutputFilename()
{
  cout << "Enter output filename : ";
  cin.getline(m_cOutputFilename, FILENAME_SIZE);
}

void Translator::getFindChar()
{
  cout << "Enter character to find : ";
  cin >> m_cFind;
}

void Translator::getReplChar()
{
  cout << "Enter character to replace : ";
  cin >> m_cRepl;
}

Logical Translator::Translate()
{
  fstream fin, fout;
  char cLine[LINE_SIZE + 1];

  if (strcmp(m_cInputFilename, "") == 0  ||
      strcmp(m_cOutputFilename, "") == 0 ||
      m_cFind == '\0'                    ||
      m_cRepl == '\0')
    return FALSE;

  // open input file stream
  fin.open(m_cInputFilename,  ios::in);
  // open failed?
  if (!fin)
    return FALSE;
  // open output file stream
  fout.open(m_OutputFilename,  ios::out);
  if (!fout) {
```

Open stream for input

Open stream for output

```
    fin.close();
    return FALSE;
  }

  while (!fin.eof()) {
    fin.getline)cLine,   LINE_SIZE):                      Input line from stream
    for (int i = 0; i < int(strlen(cLine)); i++)
      if (cLine[i] == m_cFind)
        cLine[i] = m_cRepl;
    // write to output file
    fout << cLine << endl;                                Output line to stream
    // echo to console
    cout << cLine << endl;
  }
  // close file stream buffers
  fin.close();
  fout.close();                                           Close streams
  return TRUE;
}

main()
{
  Translator TR;

  TR.getInputFilename();
  TR.getOutputFilename();
  TR.getFindChar();
  TR.getReplChar();
  if (TR.Translate())
    cout << "\n\nTranslation successful!\n";
  else
    cout << "Translation failed\n";

  return 0;
}
```

Listing 15-1 declares the class **Translator**, which has protected and public members. The protected members are:

- The string data member **m_cInputFilename**, which stores the input filename

- The string data member **m_cOutputFilename**, which stores the output filename

- The **char**-type data member **m_cFind**, which stores the character to find

- The **char**-type data member **m_cRepl**, which stores the replacement character

The class declares the following public members:

- The constructor, which assigns empty strings to the string data members and assigns null characters to the **char**-type data members
- The member function **getInputFilename**, which prompts you for the input filename and stores it in the data member **m_cInputFilename**
- The member function **getOutputFilename**, which prompts you for the output filename and stores it in the data member **m_cOutputFilename**
- The member function **getFindChar**, which prompts you for the character to find and stores it in data member **m_cFind**
- The member function **getReplChar**, which prompts you for the replacement character and stores it in data member **m_cRepl**
- The **Logical** member function **Translate**, which conducts the character translation that involves the input and output files

The definition of the member function **Translate** declares the **fstream** objects **fin** and **fout** as the input and output file stream objects—instances of class **fstream**. The member function also declares the string variable **cLine** and performs the following tasks:

- Exit, returning the enumerator **FALSE**, if any one of the four data members retains its initial value (assigned to them by the constructor)
- Open the input file stream by sending the C++ message **open** to the object **fin**. The arguments for this message are the data member **m_cInputFilename** and the enumerator **ios::in**.
- Exit, returning **FALSE**, if the preceding task fails. This task uses the operator **!** with the object **fin** to test for error.
- Open the output file stream by sending the C++ message **open** to the object **fout**. The arguments for this message are the data member **m_cOutputFilename** and the enumerator **ios::out**.
- Exit, returning **FALSE**, if the preceding task fails. This task uses the operator **!** with the object **fout** to test for errors. This task also closes the input file stream by sending the C++ message **close** to the object **fin**.

- Translate the characters in the input file stream. This task uses a **while** loop. The first statement in the loop sends the C++ message **getline** to the object **fin**. This message, which obtains the next input line, has the arguments **cLine** and **LINE_SIZE**. The statement stores the input in the string variable **cLine**. The second statement is a nested **for** loop that examines the characters in the string variable **cLine**. The **for** loop uses an **if** statement to detect and translate the characters that match data member **m_cFind**. After the **for** loop ends its iterations, the **while** loop writes the string variable **cLine** to the output file stream using the operator **<<**. The last loop statement echoes the output to object **cout**.

- Close the input and output file streams by sending the C++ message **close** to the file stream objects

The function **main** declares the object **TR** as an instance of class **Translator**. The function performs the following tasks:

- Prompt you for the input filename by sending the C++ message **getInputFilename** to the object **TR**

- Prompt you for the output filename by sending the C++ message **getOutputFilename** to the object **TR**

- Prompt you for the search character by sending the C++ message **getFindChar** to the object **TR**

- Prompt you for the replacement character by sending the C++ message **getReplChar** to the object **TR**

- Translate the character you specified in the input file and write the result to the output file. This task involves sending the C++ message **Translate** to the object **TR**. The function uses the result of this message in an **if** statement to determine whether to display a confirmation message or an error message.

Sequential Binary File Stream I/O

The C++ stream library offers the member functions **read** and **write** to read from and write to file streams.

THE FUNCTION WRITE

The class **ostream** declares the member function **write** as:

```
ostream& write(const char* pch, int nCount);
ostream& write(const unsigned char* puch, int nCount);
ostream& write(const signed char* psch, int nCount);
```

The parameters **pch**, **puch**, and **psch** are pointers to a character array, and the parameter **nCount** specifies the number of characters to be written. The member function inserts the specified number of bytes from a buffer into the stream. If the underlying file was opened in text mode, additional carriage return characters may be inserted. The member function **write** works mainly for binary stream output.

Here is an example of using the member function **write**:

```
const int MAX_CHARS = 80;
char cName[MAX_CHARS + 1] = "Namir Shammas";
int nNumChars = strlen(cName) + 1;
fstream f;
f.open("MYDATA.DAT:, ios::out | ios::binary);
// write the number of characters
f.write((const unsigned char*)&nNumChars, sizeof(nNumChars));
// write the characters
f.write((const unsigned char*)cName, nNumChars);
f.close();
```

The example opens the file MYDATA.DAT for binary output by sending the C++ message **open** to the object **f** (an instance of class **fstream**). The last two executable statements write the number of output characters and then the characters themselves by sending the C++ message **write** to the object **f**. The arguments for the first **write** message are the typecasted address of the variable **nNumChars** and the expression **sizeof(nNumChars)**. The arguments for the second **write** message are the string variable **cName** and the variable **nNumChars**.

THE FUNCTION READ

The class **istream** declares the member function **read** as:

```
istream& read(char* pch, int nCount);
```

```
istream& read(unsigned char* puch, int nCount);
istream& read(signed char* psch, int nCount);
```

The parameters **pch**, **puch**, and **psch** are pointers to a character array, and the parameter **nCount** specifies the maximum number of characters to read. The member function extracts bytes from the stream until the limit **nCount** is reached or until the end of file is reached. The member function **read** is useful for binary stream input.

Here is an example of using the member function **read**:

```
const int MAX_CHARS = 80;
char cName[MAX_CHARS + 1] = "Namir Shammas";
int nNumChars = strlen(cName) + 1;
fstream f;
f.open("MYDATA.DAT:, ios::out | ios::binary);
// read the number of characters
f.read((const unsigned char*)&nNumChars, sizeof(nNumChars));
// read the characters
f.read((const unsigned char*)cName, nNumChars);
f.close();
```

The example opens the file MYDATA.DAT for binary input by sending the C++ message **open** to the object **f** (an instance of class **fstream**). The last two executable statements read the number of input characters and then the characters themselves by sending the C++ message **read** to the object **f**. The arguments for the first **read** message are the typecasted address of the variable **nNumChars** and the expression **sizeof(nNumChars)**. The arguments for the second **read** message are the string variable **cName** and the variable **nNumChars**.

Let's look at a programming example. Listing 15-2 shows the source code for the FIO2.CPP program, which illustrates binary stream I/O. The program performs the following tasks:

- Open a file stream for binary output
- Write a set of four strings. The output for each string is preceded by the number of characters in that string.
- Close the file stream
- Open a file stream for binary input
- Read the strings in the input file

- Display the strings
- Close the file stream

Here is the output of the program in Listing 15-2:

```
This is line number 1
This is line number 2
This is line number 3
This is line number 4
```

Listing 15-2
The source code for the FIO2.CPP program.

```
// A C++ program that illustrates
// binary file stream input and output

#include <fstream.h>
#include <iomanip.h>
#include <stdio.h>
#include <string.h>

main()
{
  const int LINE_SIZE = 80;
  const int MAX_LINES = 4;

  char cImg[LINE_SIZE + 1];
  unsigned len;
  fstream f;

  // open stream for output
  f.open("MYDATA.DAT", ios::out | ios::binary);
  for (int i = 1; i <= MAX_LINES; i++) {
    sprintf(cImg, "This is line number %d", i);
    len = strlen(cImg) + 1;
    // write the number of characters
    f.write((const char*)&len, sizeof(len));            Output to binary file
    // write the characters
    f.write((const char*)cImg, len);                    Output to binary file
  }
  // close output file stream
  f.close();

  // open stream for input
  f.open("MYDATA.DAT", ios::in | ios::binary);
  while (!f.eof()) {
    // read the number of characters
    f.read((char*)&len, sizeof(len));                   Input from binary file
    if (f.eof())
      break;
```

```
   // read the characters
   f.read((char*)cImg, len);
   cout << cImg << endl;
 }
 // close output file stream
 f.close();

 return 0;
}
```

Input from binary file

Listing 15-2 defines the function **main**, which declares the constants **LINE_SIZE** and **MAX_LINES** to specify the maximum size of a text line and the maximum number of output lines, respectively. The function also declares the string variable **cImg**, the **unsigned**-type variable **len**, and the object **f** as an instance of class **fstream**. The function **main** then performs the following tasks:

- Open the file stream object **f** for binary output by sending the C++ message **open** to that object. The arguments for this message are the string literal "MYDATA.DAT," which specifies the output filename, and the expression **ios::out | ios::binary**, which specifies the I/O mode.

- Write the lines to the output file stream. This task uses a **for** loop to write **MAX_LINES** lines. The loop's statements create a string using the function **sprintf** and store it in variable **cImg**. The loop also stores the number of characters in variable **cImg**, plus one, in the variable **len**. The **for** loop contains two file stream output statements: The first one writes the value in variable **len** to the stream, and the second one writes the string variable **cImg** to the stream. The arguments for the first **write** message are **&len** and **sizeof(len)**; the arguments for the second are the variables **cImg** and **len**.

- Close the file stream by sending the C++ message **close** to the object **f**

- Open the file stream object **f** for binary input by sending the C++ message **open** to that object. The arguments for this message are the string literal "MYDATA.DAT," which specifies the input filename, and the expression **ios::in | ios::binary**, which specifies the binary input I/O mode.

- Read the lines from the input file stream, using a **while** loop. The loop includes two file stream input statements: The first one reads a value into variable **len** from the stream, and the second one reads the string into variable **clmg**. The arguments for the first **read** message are **&len** and **sizeof(len)**, and the arguments for the second are the variables **clmg** and **len**.

■ Close the file stream by sending the C++ message **close** to the object **f**

Random Access File Stream I/O

Random access file stream I/O uses the member functions **write**, **read**, and **seekg**. The last-named member function allows you to move the stream pointer to the location of the next input or output. The declaration of member function **seekg** in class **istream** is:

```
istream& seekg(streampos pos);
istream& seekg(streamoff off, ios::seek_dir dir);
```

The parameter **pos** is the new position value (the type **streampos** is a typedef equivalent to the predefined type **long**). The parameter **off** specifies the new offset value (the type **streamoff** is also a typedef equivalent to the predefined type **long**). The parameter **dir** specifies the seek direction and must be one of the following enumerators:

■ The enumerator **ios::beg**, which seeks from the beginning of the stream

■ The enumerator **ios::cur**, which seeks from the current position in the stream

■ The enumerator **ios::end**, which seeks from the end of the stream

Here is an example of using the member function **seekg**:

```
const int MAX_CHARS = 80;
char cName[MAX_CHARS + 1] = "Namir Shammas";
int nRecordNumber = 2;
int nNumChars = strlen(cName) + 1;
```

```
fstream f;
f.open("MYDATA.DAT:, ios::out | ios:in | ios::binary);
// seek a specific record
f.seekg(nRecordNumber * MAX_CHARS);
// read the characters
f.read((const unsigned char*)cName, MAX_CHARS);
f.close();
```

The example opens the file MYDATA.DAT for binary input and output by sending the C++ message **open** to the object **f** (an instance of class **fstream**). The example sets the stream pointer to read record number **nRecordNumber**. The argument for the **seekg** message is the expression **nRecordNumber*MAX_CHARS** — each record is **MAX_CHARS** bytes long.

Let's look at a programming example. Listing 15-3 shows the source code for the FIO3.CPP program, which illustrates random access file stream I/O. The program has a class that models an array that stores its elements in a random access file stream. The program assigns unsorted values to the file-based array, displays the unsorted array elements, sorts the array elements, and then displays the sorted array elements.

Here is the output of the program in Listing 15-3:

```
Unsorted array is:
23 45 89 74 51 18 87 63 36 38
Sorted array is:
18 23 36 38 45 51 63 74 87 89
```

Listing 15-3
The source code for the FIO3.CPP program.

```
// A C++ program that illustrates
// random access files

#include <fstream.h>
#include <iomanip.h>

enum Logical { FALSE, TRUE };

const int BAD_VALUE = -32678;

class myArray
{
  public:
    myArray(const char* pszFilename, int nSize, int nInitVal = 0);
    ~myArray()
      { m_f.close(); }
```

```
      void store(int nVal, int nIndex);
      int recall(int nIndex);
      void show(const char* pszMsg,
                const int nNumElems,
                const int bOneLine = TRUE);
      void CombSort(int nNumElems);

   protected:
      fstream m_f;
      int m_nSize;
};

myArray::myArray(const char* pszFilename, int nSize, int nInitVal)
{
   m_f.open(pszFilename, ios::in | ios::out | ios::binary);
   m_nSize = nSize;
   for (int i = 0; i < m_nSize; i++)
      m_f.write((const char*)&nInitVal, sizeof(nInitVal));
}

void myArray::show(const char* pszMsg,
                   const int nNumElems,
                   const int bOneLine)
{
   int nVal;

   // set stream pointer to beginning of file
   m_f.seek(0);                                          Seek byte in binary file
   cout << pszMsg << endl;
   if (bOneLine) {
      for (int i = 0; i < nNumElems; i++) {
         m_f.read((char*)&nVal, sizeof(nVal));
         cout << nVal << ' ';
      }
      cout << endl;
   }
   else {
      for (int i = 0; i < nNumElems; i++) {
         m_f.read((char*)&nVal, sizeof(nVal));
         cout << nVal << endl;
      }
      cout << endl;
   }
}

void myArray::store(int nVal, int nIndex)
{
   if (nIndex < m_nSize) {
      m_f.seekg(Index * sizeof(int))                     Seek byte in binary file
      m_f.write((const char*)&nVal, sizeof(nVal));
   }
}
```

```
int myArray::recall(int nIndex)
{
  int nVal = BAD_VALUE;

  if (nIndex < m_nSize) {
    m_f.seekg(Index * sizeof(int));          ────────►  Seek byte in binary file
    m_f.read((char*)&nVal, sizeof(nVal));
  }
  return nVal;
}


void myArray::CombSort(int nNumElems)
{
  int nOffset = nNumElems;
  int bSorted;
  int elemI, elemJ;

  if (nNumElems < 2)
    return;

  do {
    nOffset = (nOffset * 8) / 11;
    nOffset = (nOffset < 1) ? 1 : nOffset;
    bSorted = TRUE; // set sorted flag
    // compare elements
    for (int i = 0, j = nOffset;
         i < (nNumElems - nOffset);
         i++, j++) {
      m_f.seekg(i * sizeof(int));
      m_f.read((char*)&elemI, sizeof(elemI));
      m_F.seekg(j * sizeof(int));
      m_f.read((char*)&elemJ, sizeof(elemJ));
      if (elemI > elemJ) {
        // swap elements
        m_f.seekg(i * sizeof(int));
        m_f.write((const char*)&elemJ, sizeof(elemJ));
        m_f.seekg(j * sizeof(int));
        m_f.write((const char*)&elemI, sizeof(elemI));
        bSorted = FALSE; // clear sorted flag
      }
    }
  } while (!bSorted || nOffset != TRUE);
}

main()
{
  const int MAX_ELEMS = 10;
  int nArr[MAX_ELEMS] = { 23, 45, 89, 74, 51,
                          18, 87, 63, 36, 38 };
  myArray Array("RAND.DAT", MAX_ELEMS);
```

```
    for (int i = 0; i < MAX_ELEMS; i++)
      Array.store(nArr[i], i);

    Array.show("Unsorted array is:", MAX_ELEMS);
    Array.CombSort(MAX_ELEMS);
    Array.show("Sorted array is:", MAX_ELEMS);

    return 0;
  }
```

Listing 15-3 declares the class **myArray**, which models arrays that store their data in a random access file stream. The class declares protected and public members. The protected members are:

- The data member **m_f**, which is an object of class **fstream**. This member is the handle to the random file stream.

- The **int**-type data member **m_nSize**, which stores the number of array elements

  The class declares the following public members:

- The constructor, which opens the file stream, assigns the argument of parameter **nSize** to data member **m_nSize**, and initializes the array using the argument of parameter **nInitVal**. The constructor opens the file stream by sending the C++ message **open** to the data member **m_f**. The arguments for this message are the parameter **pszFilename** and the expression **ios::in | ios::out | ios::binary**.

- The destructor, which closes the file stream by sending the C++ message **close** to the data member **m_f**

- The member function **store**, which stores the argument of parameter **nVal** at the array index specified by parameter **nIndex**. The member function verifies the argument of **nIndex** and then writes the stored value. Writing the value involves sending the C++ messages **seekg** and then **write** to data member **m_f**. The argument for the message **seekg** is the expression **nIndex * sizeof(int)**. The arguments for the message **write** are the address of parameter **nVal** and the expression **sizeof(nVal)**.

- The member function **recall**, which returns the value of the array element at index **nIndex**. If the index is out of range, the member function yields the value of the global constant **BAD_VALUE**. Otherwise the member function reads the sought array element. As before, reading that value involves sending the C++ messages **seekg** and then **read** to data member **m_f**. The argument for the message **seekg** is the expression **nIndex * sizeof(int)**. The arguments for the message **read** are the address of parameter **nVal** and the expression **sizeof(nVal)**.

- The member function **show**, which displays the elements in the array. This member function sends the C++ message **seekg** to data member **m_f** to set the stream pointer to the first byte in the stream. The member function then sends the C++ message **read** to data member **m_f** to sequentially read the array elements.

- The member function **CombSort**, which sorts the elements of the array. The member function sends the C++ messages **seekg**, **read**, and **write** to seek, read, and write array elements, respectively.

The function **main** declares the local constant **MAX_ELEMS**, the C++ array **nArr**, and the object **Array** as an instance of class **myArray**. The function creates this object by specifying that it uses file RAND.DAT and has **MAX_ELEMS** elements. The function **main** then performs the following tasks:

- Copy the elements of array **nArr** into the object **Array**. This task uses a **for** loop to iterate over the elements of array **nArr**. Each loop iteration sends the C++ message **store** to the object **Array**. The arguments for this message are **nArr[i]** and **i**.

- Display the unsorted array elements by sending the C++ message **show** to the object **Array**. The arguments for this message are the string literal "Unsorted array is:" and the constant **MAX_ELEMS**.

- Sort the array elements by sending the C++ message **CombSort** to the object **Array**. The argument for this message is the constant **MAX_ELEMS**.

- Display the sorted array elements by sending the C++ message **show** to the object **Array**. The arguments for this message are the string literal "Sorted array is:" and the constant **MAX_ELEMS**.

Summary

This chapter discussed basic file stream I/O. You learned about the member functions of the C++ stream library that assist in this capacity. These member functions include **open**, **close**, **eof**, **good**, and **fail**, as well as the operator **!**. The chapter also discussed using the operators **<<** and **>>** and the member function **getline** to support sequential text stream I/O. The text presented the member functions **read** and **write** as means to support sequential binary file stream I/O. You also learned to use the member functions **read**, **write**, and **seekg** to perform random access file stream I/O.

The next Chapter discusses exception hankling and how to manage runtime errors..

16

Exception Handling

*T*his chapter looks at managing runtime errors, called *exceptions*. You will learn about exceptions in general, exception classes, standard exceptions, throwing an exception, catching exceptions, the **try** block, **catch** clauses, nested **try** blocks, rethrowing an exception, unexpected exceptions, and uncaught exceptions.

What Is an Exception?

The more complex a program is, the more prone it is to experiencing runtime errors. How do you handle runtime errors? The answer depends on the programming language you are using. In languages like C, the programmer needs to resort to *defensive programming* techniques. Many C functions return error codes if they cannot perform their task (such as opening a file for I/O operations). These kinds of functions allow you to test the waters, so to speak, *before* you proceed. Other languages such as Microsoft MS-BASIC and Visual Basic have formal error handling features. These kinds of features allow the program flow to jump to another part of a routine if an error occurs.

C++ supports *exceptions* and *exception handing* to detect and manage runtime errors. The word *exception* comes from the *exceptional program flow* that occurs during a runtime error.

C++ makes use of classes and objects in handling exceptions. The metaphor used in C++ to handle exceptions is *throwing* and *catching* exceptions. Either the runtime library or your code throws exceptions. To handle the thrown exceptions, you need to catch them.

Exception Classes

C++ makes use of classes to represent and encapsulate exceptions. There are two general kinds of classes that model exceptions:

- *Skeleton classes*. These classes have no members, because their names are sufficient to refer to and handle the exceptions.

- *Classes with data members*. These classes declare data members that allow them to better describe the exception.

  Here are examples of exception classes:

```
class badInputException {};
class badRangeException {};
class badFileException
{
  public:
    char m_pszFilename[31];
};
```

The first two examples are skeleton classes that model exceptions handling input and a range of values. These classes have no members. The last example declares an exception class that has the data member **m_pszFilename**. The class uses this data member to describe which file failed a file I/O operation.

Standard Exceptions

C++ defines a set of basic exception classes that represent the most common runtime errors. Table 16-1 lists these exceptions and also indicates their lineage.

Table 16-1

The Standard Exceptions

Exception Class	Parent Class	Purpose
exception	[none]	The base class for all of the exceptions thrown by the C++ standard library
logic_error	exception	Reports logical program errors that can be detected before the program proceeds with executing subsequent statements
runtime_error	exception	Reports runtime errors that are detected when the program executes certain statements
ios::failure	exception	Reports stream I/O errors
domain_error	logic_error	Reports an infraction of a condition
invalid_argument	logic_error	Signals that the argument of a function is not valid
length_error	logic_error	Signals that an operation attempts to create an object with a length that exceeds or is equal to NPOS (the biggest value of the type **size_t**)
out_of_range	logic_error	Signals that an argument is out of range
bad_cast	logic_error	Reports an invalid dynamic cast expression during runtime identification
bad_typeid	logic_error	Reports a null pointer in a type-identifying expression
range_error	runtime_error	Signals an invalid postcondition
overflow_error	runtime_error	Signals arithmetic overflow
bad_alloc	runtime_error	Signals a failure of dynamic allocation

Throwing an Exception

C++ offers the **throw** statement to throw an exception (which is a predefined data item, or an instance of an **exception** class). The general syntax for the **throw** statement is:

```
throw exceptionObject;
```

The **exceptionObject** can be a predefined type or an **exception** class instance. The latter can be a previously declared instance or a temporary instance created using the constructor of the **exception** class.

Here are examples of throwing exceptions:

```
class badValueException
{
  public:
    badValueException(int nVal = 0)
      { cout << nVal << " is a bad value\n"; }
};

int nBadVal;

throw badValueException(100);
throw nBadVal;
```

The code snippet shows two **throw** statements: The first one throws an instance of an **exception** class, and the second throws an **int**-type variable. Please keep in mind that I have not yet introduced you to the **try** statement that should contain the **throw** statements. Also, I have not yet introduced you to the **catch** statement that catches the exceptions.

The Try Block

Throwing an exception occurs in a **try** block, which causes the compiler to pay special attention to generating code for handling exceptions. The general syntax for the **try** block is:

```
try {
  // statements that may throw one or more exceptions
}
```

The **try** block contains any statement that may raise an exception, including **throw** statements. Here is an example of a **try** block:

```
class badValueException
{
  public:
    badValueException(int nVal = 0)
      { cout << nVal << " is a bad value\n"; }
};
```

```
main()
{
  int nBadVal;

  try {
    throw badValueException(100);
  }
  // statements to handle the exception
  return 0;
}
```

The code snippet shows a **try** block that contains a **throw** statement. The statements that follow the **try** block handle the exceptions that it raises. The next section discusses the exception-handing **catch** handler.

The Catch Clauses

C++ offers the **catch** clauses (or handlers) to work with the **try** block. The **catch** handlers have a logic similar to that of the **case** clauses of a **switch** statement. The general syntax for a **catch** handler is:

```
catch(exceptionType [exceptionObject]) {
  // statements that handle or rethrow the exception
}
```

A **catch** clause declares an exception type and an optional exception parameter. You need this parameter to pass additional information related to the exception. You can use multiple catch handlers as well as the special **catch(...)** clause to catch and handle exceptions as shown in the following general syntax:

```
catch(exceptionType1 [exceptionObject1]) {
  // statements that handle or rethrow exceptionType1
}
catch(exceptionType2 [exceptionObject2]) {
  // statements that handle or rethrow the exceptionType2
}
catch(exceptionType3 [exceptionObject3]) {
  // statements that handle or rethrow the exceptionType3
}
catch(...) {
  // statements that handle or rethrow the all other exceptions
}
```

CODING NOTES

Use the catch(...) Handler Very Carefully!

Use the **catch(...)** handler very carefully, since, unlike the **else** or **default** clauses of an **if** or **switch** statement, it can trap errors that you did not anticipate!

Here is an example of using the **try** block with **catch** clauses:

```
class myError1 {};
class myError2
{
  public:
   myError2(int nError)
     { m_nError = nError; }
   int m_nError;
};

main()
{
  int nVal = -1;

  try {
    throw myError1(nVal);
  }
  catch(int nError) {
    cout << "Hanlding int exception\n";
    cout << nError << " is invalid\n";
  }
  catch(myError1) {
    cout << "Handling myError1 exception\n";
  }
  catch(myError2 errObj) {
    cout << "Handling myError2 exception\n";
    cout << errObj.m_nError << " is invalid\n";
  }
  catch(...) {
    cout << "Handling other errors\n";
  }

  return 0;
}
```

This example declares the exception classes **myError1** and **myError2**. The first exception class is a skeleton class, whereas the second class has the public data member **m_nError** and a constructor that initializes it. The function **main** declares and initializes the **int**-type variable **nVal**. The function has a **try** block containing a **throw** statement that throws a **myError1** exception (using the value in the variable **nVal**). The function **main** has the following **catch** clauses:

- The **catch(int nError)** clause that catches exceptions that have the **int** type. This clause displays a message and the value of the parameter **nError**.

- The **catch(myError1)** clause that catches **myError1** exceptions. This clause has no parameters and simply displays a message.

- The **catch(myError2 errObj)** clause that catches **myError2** exceptions. This clause displays a message and then displays the data member **errObj.m_nError**. It shows you how to use the exception parameter.

- The **catch(...)** clause that catches all other exceptions

Let's look at a programming example. This program uses exceptions that are of a predefined type, a skeleton exception class, and two nonskeleton exception classes. The program has several **try** blocks that test each kind of exception.

Here is the output of the program in Listing 16-1:

```
Testing throwing an int
123 is not a valid int
Testing throwing an error1 exception
Handling error1 exception
Testing throwing an error2 exception
Handling error2 exception
100 is not a valid int
Testing throwing an error3 exception
Handling error3 exception
123 is not a valid int
```

Listing 16-1

The source code for the ERROR1.CPP program.

```cpp
// A C++ program that illustrates
// exception classes, throwing exceptions,
// and catching exceptions

#include <iostream.h>

// declare a skeleton exception class
class error1 {};

// declare a nonskeleton exception class
class error2
{
  public:
    error2(int nCode)
      { m_nCode = nCode; }
    int m_nCode;
};

// declare a nonskeleton exception class
class error3
{
  public:
    error3()
      { m_nCode = 0; }
    void setCode(int nCode)
      { m_nCode = nCode; }
    int getCode()
      { return m_nCode; }
  protected:
    int m_nCode;
};

main()
{
  int nNum = 123;
  error2 errorObj2(100);
  error3 errorObj3;

  // test throwing a predefined-type object
  cout << "Testing throwing an int\n";
  try {
    throw nNum;
  }
  catch (int nCode)
  {
    cout << nCode << " is not a valid int\n";
  }
```

Try block

Catch clause

```
catch (char cCode)
{
   cout << cCode << " is not a valid char\n";
}
catch (long lCode)
{
   cout << lCode << " is not a valid long\n";
}
```

Catch clauses

```
// test throwing an error1 exception
cout << "Testing throwing a error1 exception\n";
try {
   throw error1();
}
catch (error1)
{
   cout << "Handling error1 exception\n";
}
catch (char cCode)
{
   cout << cCode << " is not a valid char\n";
}
catch (long lCode)
{
   cout << lCode << " is not a valid long\n";
}

   // test throwing error2 class
cout << "Testing throwing an error2 exception\n";
try {
   throw errorObj2;
}
catch (error2 err)
{
   cout << "Handling error2 exception\n";
   cout << err.m_nCode << " is not a valid int\n";
}
catch (char cCode)
{
   cout << cCode << " is not a valid char\n";
}
catch (long lCode)
{
   cout << lCode << " is not a valid long\n";
}

   // test throwing an error3 exception
cout << "Testing throwing an error3 exception\n";
try {
   errorObj3.setCode(nNum);
   throw errorObj3;
}
```

```
catch (error3 err)
{
  cout << "Handling error3 exception\n";
  cout << err.getCode() << " in not a valid int\n";
}
catch (char cCode)
{
  cout << cCode << " is not a valid char\n";
}
catch (long lCode)
{
  cout << lCode << " is not a valid long\n";
}

return 0;
}
```

Listing 16-1 declares the exception classes **error1**, **error2**, and **error3** and defines the function **main**.

THE CLASS ERROR1

The listing declares the class **error1** as a skeleton exception class. The class has no members and relies on its name to throw and catch an exception.

THE CLASS ERROR2

The class **error2** is an exception class that has the public data member **m_nCode**, along with a constructor that initializes the data member. Making that member public simplifies assigning values to it and retrieving them. The source code for the class **error2** suggests that you *may* throw temporary instances of that class.

THE CLASS ERROR3

The class **error3** is an exception class that has the protected data member **m_nCode**, as well as a constructor that initializes the data member and member functions **setCode** and **getCode** to access it. The source code for the class **error3** suggests that you *may* throw nontemporary instances of that class.

THE FUNCTION MAIN

The function **main** declares the **int**-type variable **nNum** and the objects **errObj2** and **errObj3** as instances of classes **error2** and **error3**, respectively. The function performs the following tasks:

- Throw the variable **nNum** in a **try** block. This **try** block is followed by three catch clauses that handle **int**-type, **char**-type, and **long**-type exceptions. Each clause has a parameter and displays the value of that parameter. The program invokes the first **catch** clause to handle the int-type exception.

- Throw the **error1** exception in a **try** block. This **try** block is followed by three catch clauses that handle **error1**-type, **char**-type, and long-type exceptions. The first **catch** clause handles the **error1** exception and has no parameters. This clause simply displays an error message. Each of the next two clauses has a parameter and displays the value of that parameter. The program invokes the first **catch** clause to handle the **error1**-type exception.

- Throw the **errorObj2** object to trigger an **error2**-type exception in a **try** block. This **try** block is followed by three **catch** clauses that handle **error2**-type, **char**-type, and **long**-type exceptions. The first **catch** clause handles the **error2** exception and has the parameter **err**. This clause displays an error message and the value of the data member **err.m_nCode**. Each of the next two clauses has a parameter and displays the value of that parameter. The program invokes the first **catch** clause to handle the **error2**-type exception.

- Assign a value to the object **errObj3** (using the value in variable **nNum**) and then throw the **errorObj3** object to trigger an error3-type exception in a **try** block. This **try** block is followed by three **catch** clauses that handle error3-type, **char**-type, and **long**-type exceptions. The first **catch** clause handles the **error3** exception and has the parameter **err**. This clause displays an error message and the value of the data member **err.m_nCode** (by sending the C++ message **getCode** to object **err**). Each of the last two clauses has a parameter and displays the value of that parameter. The program invokes the first **catch** clause to handle the error3-type exception.

Nested Try-Catch Blocks

In handling really sophisticated exceptions, you may inquire about the ability to nest **try** blocks and **catch** clauses inside other **catch** clauses. C++ allows you to nest **try** blocks. In other words, you can throw a new exception while handling a previous one. The nature of such an action depends on the first exception you are handling.

Let's look at a simple programming example. Listing 16-2 shows the source code for the ERROR2.CPP program, which illustrates nested **try** blocks. The program throws a main exception and then throws a secondary error in the catch clause that handles the main exception. This clause contains a nested **try** block and nested **catch** clauses. The **catch** clauses display messages telling about the exception they are handling.

Here is the output of program 16-2:

```
Throwing the main exception
Handling main exception
Handling exception error3
```

Listing 16-2
The source code for the ERROR2.CPP program.

```
// A C++ program that illustrates
// nested try blocks

#include <iostream.h>

// declare skeleton exception classes
class mainError {};
class error1 {};
class error2 {};
class error3 {};
```

```
main()
{
  int nNum = 123;

  // throw an exception
  cout << "Throwing the main exception\n";
  try {
    throw mainError();
  }
  catch (mainError)
  {
    cout << "Handling main exception\n";
    try {
      if (nNum < 10)
        throw error1();
      else if (nNum < 100)
        throw error2();
      else if (nNum < 1000)
        throw error3();
    }
    catch (error1)
    {
      cout << "Handling exception error1";
    }
    catch (error2)
    {
      cout << "Handling exception error2";
    }
    catch (error3)
    {
      cout << "Handling exception error3";
    }
    catch (...)
    {
      cout << "Handling other errors\n";
    }
  }
  catch (int nCode)
  {
    cout << nCode << " is not a valid int\n";
  }
  catch (char cCode)
  {
    cout << cCode << " is not a valid char\n";
  }
  catch (long lCode)
  {
    cout << lCode << " is not a valid long\n";
  }

  return 0;
}
```

Nested try block

Catch all clause

Listing 16-2 declares the skeleton exception classes **mainError**, **error1**, **error2**, and **error3**. The listing defines function **main**, which declares and initializes the **int**-type variable **nNum**. The function displays a message and then throws the exception **mainError** in a **try** block, which is followed by four **catch** clauses that handle exceptions of the **mainError**, **int**, **char**, and **long** types. The first **catch** clause displays an error message and then executes the multiple-alternative **if** statement inside a nested **try** block. This **if** statement throws the **error1**, **error2**, or the **error3** exception depending on the value in variable **nNum**. The nested **try** block is followed by four **catch** clauses that handle **error1** exceptions, **error2** exceptions, **error3** exceptions, and all other exceptions. Each **catch** clause simply displays an error message.

Rethrowing an Exception

C++ allows you to rethrow an exception after partially handling it or after determining that the exception handler cannot deal with it at all. Rethrowing an exception preserves its state and passes it to a higher level of exception handlers. Typically, you rethrow an exception in a function that is called by another function. Consequently, the caller must then handle the rethrown exception. The syntax for rethrowing an exception is:

```
throw;
```

That's all!

Here is a simple programming example that shows you how to rethrow an exception. Listing 16-3 shows the source code for the ERROR3.CPP program, which illustrates rethrowing exceptions. The program declares the functions **main** and **solver**, each with **try** blocks and **catch** clauses. The function **main** calls function **solver**. The latter function handles one kind of exception and rethrows all other kinds to the caller, **main**. Function **main** handles all exceptions rethrown by function **solver**.

Here is the output of the program in Listing 16-3:

```
Handling main exception in function solver
Cannot handle secondary exception in function solver
Handling secondary exception in function main
```

Listing 16-3

The source code for the ERROR3.CPP program.

```cpp
// A C++ program that illustrates
// rethrowing exceptions

#include <iostream.h>

// declare skeleton exception classes
class mainError {};
class secError {};

void solver(int nCode)
{
  try {
    if (nCode >= 0)
      throw mainError();
    else
      throw secError();
  }
  catch(mainError)
  {
    cout << "Handling main exception "
         << "in function solver\n";
  }
  catch(...)
  {
    cout << "Cannot handle secondary exception "
         << "in function solver\n";
    // rethrow exception to caller
    throw;
  }
}

main()
{
  // throw an exception
  try {
    solver(1);
    solver(-1);
  }
  catch (mainError)
  {
    cout << "Handling main exception in function main\n";
  }
  catch (secError)
  {
    cout << "Handling secondary exception in function main\n";
  }
  catch(...)
  {
```

Rethrow exception

```
    cout << "This is the last resort to "
         << "solve your problems!\n";
  }

  return 0;
}
```

Listing 16-3 declares the skeleton exception classes **mainError** and **secError**. It then defines the functions **solver** and **main**.

THE FUNCTION SOLVER

The function **solver** has an **int**-type parameter **nCode**. The function throws a **mainError** exception when the value of that parameter is nonnegative. Otherwise, the function throws the **secError** exception. The **try** block in function **solver** is followed by the **catch(mainError)** and **catch(...)** clauses. The first **catch** clause handles the exception by displaying an error message. The second **catch** clause displays a message and then rethrows the exception using the **throw;** statement.

THE FUNCTION MAIN

The function **main** calls function **solver** twice, inside a **try** block. The first call has the argument 1, and the second call has the argument [nd]1. Thus, the first call results in function **solver** throwing and handling the exception **mainError**. By contrast, the second call results in function **solver** throwing exception **secError**, partially handling it, and then rethrowing that exception to function **main**. Function **main** has three **catch** clauses to handle the **mainError** exception, the **secError** exception, and all other unspecified exceptions. The second call to function **solver** causes program flow to jump to the **catch(secError)** clause, which displays the string literal "Handling secondary exception in function main."

Associating Exceptions and Functions

By default, a function can raise *any* known exception. That's a lot of exceptions to anticipate. C++ allows you to prototype functions in a way that lists the exceptions that are raised by that function. The syntax for this kind of function prototype is:

```
returnType functionName(parameterList) throw(listOfExceptions);
```

The above syntax shows that the function prototype includes the keyword **throw** (after the function's parameter list), which declares the comma-delimited list of exceptions raised by the function. Here is an example:

```
void solver(int nCode) throw(mainError, secError);
```

The above example declares the function **solver**, which can throw the exceptions **mainError** and **secError**. Thus, the following **try** block and **catch** clauses can safely deal with the exceptions raised by function **solver**:

```
try {
  solver(-11);
}
catch(mainError)
{
  cout << "Handling mainError exception\n";
}
catch(secError)
{
  cout << "Handling secError exception\n";
}
```

This code snippet does not need the **catch(...)** clause, since the exceptions raised by function **solver** are known.

To declare that a function does not throw *any* exceptions, use the following general syntax:

```
returnType functionName(parameterList) throw();
```

The above syntax shows that the function prototype includes the keyword **throw** with an empty list of exceptions. Here is an example:

```
void superSolver(int nCode) throw();
```

The above example declares the function **superSolver**, which throws no exceptions. (This is the kind of function you wish all software libraries to offer.)

Let's look at a programming example. Listing 16-4 shows the source code for the ERROR4.CPP program, which illustrates associating exceptions with functions. The program declares the functions **solver** and **main**. The prototype of function **solver** lists the exceptions raised by that function.

Here is the output of the program in Listing 16-4:

```
Handling main exception
```

Listing 16-4
The source code for the ERROR4.CPP program.

```
// A C++ program that illustrates
// associating exceptions with functions

#include <iostream.h>

// declare skeleton exception classes
class mainError {};
class secError {};

void solver(int nCode) throw(mainError, secError);

main()
{
  // throw an exception
  try {
      solver(1);
  }
  catch (mainError)
  {
    cout << "Handling main exception\n";
  }
  catch (secError)
  {
    cout << "Handling secondary exception\n";
  }

  return 0;
}

void solver(int nCode) throw(mainError, secError)
{
  if (nCode >= 0)
    throw mainError();
  else
    throw secError();
}
```

Listing 16-4 declares the skeleton exception classes **mainError** and **secError**. The listing also declares the prototype of function **solver**, which indicates that the function raises the exceptions **mainError** and **secError**. The definition of the function **solver** raises either kind of exception based on the value of its **int**-type parameter **nCode**. The function **main** calls function **solver** inside a **try** block. The former function has two **catch** clauses that handle the **mainError** and **secError** exceptions that are raised by function **solver**.

Handling Unexpected Exceptions

Handling exceptions can be a tricky business. As much as you plan to handle exceptions, you may still be faced with the possibility of unexpected exceptions. Using the **catch(...)** clause is one way to handle such exceptions. C++ offers another route. The header file EXCEPT.H declares the functions **unexpected** and **set_unexpected**. By default, the runtime system calls the function **unexpected** if you do not use the **catch(...)** clause after a **try** block. The function **set_unexpected** allows you to replace the standard function **unexpected** with your own function. To use the function **set_unexpected**, call it and pass the name of your own function as the sole argument.

Here is a programming example that illustrates how and when to use the function **set_unexpected** to set up your own catchall exception handler. Listing 16-5 shows the source code for the ERROR5.CPP program, which illustrates handling unexpected exceptions. The program declares the functions **badNews**, **solver**, and **main**. The prototype of function **solver** lists the exceptions raised by that function. However, this function ends up raising an unexpected exception when it calls function **badNews**.

Here is the output of the program in Listing 16-5:

```
Handling unexpected exception!
```

Listing 16-5
The source code for the ERROR5.CPP program.

```
// A C++ program that illustrates
// handling unexpected exceptions

#include <iostream.h>
#include <except.h>
#include <stdlib.h>
```

```
// declare skeleton exception classes
class mainError {};
class secError {};
class Kaboom {};

void badNews()
{
  throw Kaboom();
}

void solver(int nCode) throw(mainError, secError)
{
  if (nCode > 0)
    throw mainError();
  else if (nCode < 0)
    throw secError();
  badNews();
}

void myUnexpected()
{
  cout << "Handling unexpected exception!\n";
  exit(1); // exit with error code 1
}
```

Define custom function

```
main()
{
  set_unexpected(myUnexpected);
  // throw an exception
  try {
      solver(0);
  }
  catch (mainError)
  {
    cout << "Handling main exception\n";
  }
  catch (secError)
  {
    cout << "Handling secondary exception\n";
  }

  return 0;
}
```

Set custom function

Listing 16-5 includes the header files IOSTREAM.H, EXCEPT.H (needed to use function **set_unexpected**), and STDLIB.H (needed to use function **exit**). The listing declares the skeleton exception classes **mainError**, **secError**, and **Kaboom**. The listing further declares the functions **badNews**, **solver**, **myUnexpected**, and **main**.

THE FUNCTION badNEWS

The function **badNews** has the sole task of ruining your day by throwing a **Kaboom** exception. That's all this disruptive little function does!

THE FUNCTION SOLVER

The function **solver** declares that it throws the exceptions **mainError** and **secError**. The function uses the value of parameter **nCode** to determine which exception to throw. If **nCode** passes a positive value, the function throws exception **mainError**. By contrast, if **nCode** passes a negative value, the function throws exception **secError**. If **nCode** is zero, the function throws no exceptions and instead calls function **badNews**. The latter function ends up throwing exception **Kaboom**.

THE FUNCTION MYUNEXPECTED

The function **myUnexpected** simply displays an error message and then calls the function **exit** (declared in STDLIB.H). The argument for function **exit** is the program exit code (0 means there is no error, and any other value represents an error code).

THE FUNCTION MAIN

The function **main** invokes the function **set_unexpected** and passes it the address of function **myUnexpected**. The function **main** then calls function **solver**, in a **try** block, and supplies that function with the argument 0. This value ends up calling function **badNews**, which in turn raises the **Kaboom** exception. The function **main** does not handle that exception (after all, function **solver** had already promised that it only emits exceptions **mainError** and **secError**). Consequently, the runtime system ends up invoking the function **myUnexpected**.

Uncaught Exceptions

Despite the bravest efforts in handling exceptions, there are cases when you have to terminate program execution. Recovery from such an exception (and a fatal one at that) is impossible. C++ allows you to use the functions **terminate** and **set_terminate**. The header file EXCEPT.H declares these functions. The function **terminate** conducts default program termination. You can specify your own termination function by calling function **set_terminate** and passing it the address of your function.

Here is a programming example that illustrates how and when to use the function **set_terminate** to end a program. Listing 16-6 shows the source code for the ERROR6.CPP program, which illustrates uncaught exceptions. The program declares the functions **badNews**, **solver**, and **main**. The prototype of function **solver** lists the exceptions raised by that function. However, this function ends up raising a terminate exception when it calls function **badNews**. The program reacts to this exception by terminating its execution.

Here is the output of the program in Listing 16-6:

```
Terminating program. That's all folks!
```

Listing 16-6
The source code for the ERROR6.CPP program.

```
// A C++ program that illustrates
// handling uncaught exceptions

#include <iostream.h>
#include <except.h>
#include <stdlib.h>

// declare skeleton exception classes
class mainError {};
class secError {};
class Kaboom {};

void badNews()
{
  throw Kaboom();
}
```

```
void solver(int nCode) throw(mainError, secError)
{
  if (nCode > 0)
    throw mainError();
  else if (nCode < 0)
    throw secError();
  badNews();
}

void myTerminate()
{
  cout << "Terminating program. That's all folks!\n";
  exit(1);
}
```
→ *Define custom function*

```
main()
{
  set_terminate(myTerminate);
```
→ *Set custom function*
```
  // throw an exception
  try {
      solver(0);
  }
  catch (mainError)
  {
    cout << "Handling main exception\n";
  }
  catch (secError)
  {
    cout << "Handling secondary exception\n";
  }

  return 0;
}
```

Listing 16-6 is very similar to Listing 16-5. I created the new listing by replacing the functions **set_unexpected** and **myUnexpected** with functions **set_terminate** and **myTerminate**. I also changed the message emitted by the latter function. While Listings 16-5 and 16-6 are similar, the actions they take are profoundly different. Listing 16-5 handles unexpected exceptions, whereas Listing 16-6 formally gives up on resuming program execution and terminates it.

Summary

This chapter has looked at managing runtime errors, called exceptions. You've learned about exceptions in general and how C++ uses the model of throwing and catching exceptions. You learned about exception classes and the standard exceptions supported by C++. The chapter discussed the syntax and statements for throwing an exception and catching exceptions. You learned about the **try** block, the **catch** clauses, and nested **try** blocks. You also learned about rethrowing an exception and how to deal with unexpected exceptions and uncaught exceptions.

The next chapter discusses templates. You will learn about general-purpose function templates and class templates. Templates represent a powerful tool for developing truly generic functions and classes.

17

Templates

*T*he template concept is a feature that was added to C++ a few years ago to support creating function templates and class templates. These functions and classes are not tied to specific data types. Instead, they represent generic versions of functions and classes. You can think of templates as sophisticated macros. In this chapter you will learn about function templates, class template declaration, class template implementation, class template instances, template parameters, and class derivation and templates.

Overview of Templates

Have you ever found yourself creating new versions of functions for new data types by using existing functions that support other data types? The process of cutting and pasting source code, so to speak, can get out of hand if you need to create, for example, functions that sort and search data for every predefined data type and every user-defined type that you employ. Worse yet, what happens if you want to update the code for a *replicated* function to make it more efficient? You have to go back and edit *every* version of that function to provide the improvement to support all of the data types. This kind of programming is not very productive.

C++ offers a solution to the problem we have described—*templates*. Using this programming feature, you can create general-purpose functions and classes that are not tied to a specific data type. Instead, these templates use template parameters that represent general data types. When the compiler encounters a function template or a class template, it switches to a learning mode and memorizes the template source code, among other actions. To use a function template or a class template, you *instantiate* that template. This process involves associating the template parameters with defined data types. When the compiler instantiates a template, it generates code and verifies that code. Consequently, the instantiation may cause the compiler to generate error messages if it cannot instantiate the template due to insufficient information.

Chapter 18 will present the Standard Template Library (STL), which implements class templates for popular data structures. (The C++ ANSI committee is working to standardize this library.) The remainder of the present chapter will provide you with the overview that will prepare you to use such a library.

Function Templates

C++ allows you to declare and define function templates. The general syntax for declaring a function template is:

```
template <class T[, other template types]>
returnType functionName(parameterList);
```

The declaration of a function template contains the following components:

- The keyword **template**, which tells the compiler that you are declaring a function template

- The comma-delimited list of template parameters enclosed in angle brackets. Each class template parameter starts with the keyword **class** followed by an identifier (which is typically **T**, or **Type**). Typically this list contains one template parameter. It is important to point out that the keyword **class** refers to classes as well as predefined data types. It is also important to point out that in the case of multiple template parameters, the first template parameter must have the **class** keyword, although the other template parameters may use predefined or previously defined data types. Here is an example that uses the type **int** for the second template parameter:

```
template <class T, int arraySize>
class Array
{
  // declarations of members
};
```

- The function's return type
- The name of the function
- The parameter list

The general syntax for defining a function template is:

```
template <class T> returnType functionName(parameterList)
{
  // statements
}
```

Here is an example of declaring and defining a function template that swaps values in single variables:

```
template <class T> void swap(T& data1, T& data2);

main()
{
  int nNum1 = 1;
  int nNum2 = 2;
  char cLetter1 = 'A';
  char cLetter2 = 'a';

  // swap integers
  swap(nNum1, nNum2);
  // swap character
  swap(cLetter1, cLetter2);

  return 0;
}

template <class T>
void swap(T& data1, T& data2)
{
  T Buffer = data1;
  data1 = data2;
  data2 = Buffer;
}
```

The example declares the function template **swap**, which has the **void** return type and the T-type parameters **data1** and **data2**. The function swaps the values of these parameters. The definition of the function declares the local variable **Buffer**, which also has the template type **T**.

The example also shows how the function **main** uses the function template **swap**. To instantiate a function template, simply call it and provide arguments that use known data types. The function **main** calls the function template twice: once with **int**-type arguments and the second time with **char**-type arguments. Each call instantiates the function template with a predefined data type.

Let me present a programming example. Listing 17-1 shows the source code for the TMPLT1.CPP program, which illustrates function templates. The program declares a function template that returns the minimum of two values. The program applies this function to arguments that have an **int**-type and others that belong to a user-defined class (that encapsulates integers).

Here is the output of the program in Listing 17-1:

```
Integer 1 is 100
Integer 2 is 22
The smaller integer is 22
Integer object 1 is 100
Integer object 2 is 22
The smaller integer object is 22
```

Listing 17-1
The source code for the TMPLT1.CPP program.

```cpp
// A C++ program that illustrates
// function templates

#include <iostream.h>
#include <iomanip.h>

class myInt
{
  public:
    myInt(int nInt = 0)
      { m_nInt = nInt; }
    myInt& operator =(myInt& intObj);
    myInt& operator =(int nInt);
    friend int operator >(myInt& intObj1, myInt& intObj2)
      { return (intObj1.m_nInt > intObj2.m_nInt) ? 1 : 0; }
```

```
    int getInt()
      { return m_nInt; }
    void show(const char* pszMsg = "")
      { cout << pszMsg << m_nInt << endl; }

  protected:
    int m_nInt;
};

myInt& myInt::operator =(myInt& intObj)
{
  m_nInt = intObj.m_nInt;
  return *this;
}

myInt& myInt::operator =(int nInt)
{
  m_nInt = nInt;
  return *this;
}

template <class T>
T getMin(T& Value1, T& Value2)
{
  return (Value1 > Value2) ? Value2 : Value1;
}
```

Declare template function

```
main()
{
  int nNum1 = 100;
  int nNum2 = 22;
  int nNum3;

  myInt intObj1, intObj2, intObj3;

  intObj1 = nNum1;
  intObj2 = nNum2;
  // get the smallest int using function template
  nNum3 = getMin(nNum1, nNum2);
  // get the smallest integer object using function template
  intObj3 = getMin(intObj1, intObj2);

  cout << "Integer 1 is " << nNum1 << endl;
  cout << "Integer 2 is " << nNum2 << endl;
  cout << "The smaller integer is " << nNum3 << endl;

  intObj1.show("Integer object 1 is ");
  intObj2.show("Integer object 2 is ");
  intObj3.show("The smaller integer object is ");

  return 0;
}
```

Use template function

Listing 17-1 declares the class **myInt**, the function template **getMin**, and the function **main**. The highlight of the listing is function **getMin**. This function has the template parameter T as the return type and two parameters that are references to the template parameter T. The function uses the operator > to compare the values of the parameters **Value1** and **Value2**, and it returns the smaller value. Thus, to instantiate this function template with a user-defined class, that class *must* define a friend operator >. Otherwise, the compiler cannot instantiate the function template with that class!

The listing declares the class **myInt**, which encapsulates the **int** type. The class has a constructor, the member functions **getInt** and **show**, two versions of the overloaded operator =, and the friend operator >. The function template **getMin** needs the instantiating classes to have the friend operator >. The operator = allows you to assign the result of the function **getMin** to an instance of class **myInt**.

The function **main** declares the **int**-type variables **nNum1**, **nNum2**, and **nNum3**, initializing the first two variables. It also declares the objects **intObj1**, **intObj2**, and **intObj3** as instances of class **myInt**. The function then performs the following tasks:

- Assign the value in variable **nNum1** to object **intObj1**. This task uses **operator =(int)**.
- Assign the value in variable **nNum2** to object **intObj2**. This task also uses **operator =(int)**.
- Assign the smaller of the values in variables **nNum1** and **nNum2** to variable **nNum3**. This task involves calling the function template, which is instantiated with the predefined type **int**. The arguments for this function call are variables **nNum1** and **nNum2**.
- Assign the smaller of the values in objects **intObj1** and **intObj2** to object **intObj3**. This task invokes calling the function template, which is instantiated with the class **myInt**. The arguments for this function call are objects **intObj1** and **intObj2**.
- Display the values in variables **nNum1**, **nNum2**, and **nNum3**
- Display the values in objects **intObj1**, **intObj2**, **intObj3**. This task involves sending the C++ message **show** to each object. The argument for each message is a string literal that identifies the associated object.

Class Template Declaration

C++ allows you to declare class templates to represent objects whose exact data types are defined during instantiation. In other words, class templates are more abstract than ordinary classes. Class templates are commonly used to build generic data structures such as arrays, stacks, queues, lists, trees, and hash tables, just to name a few.

The general syntax for declaring a base class template is:

```
template <class T[, other template types]>
class className
{
  // declarations of nested structures, enumerated types,
  // classes, and friend classes

  public:
  // public constructors
  // public destructor
  // public member functions
  // public data members

  protected:
  // protected constructors
  // protected destructor
  // protected member functions
  // protected data members

  private:
  // private constructors
  // private destructor
  // private member functions
  // private data members
};
```

The syntax shows that declaring a base class template is not really that different from declaring an ordinary base class. Class templates must follow the same rules as ordinary classes.

The syntax of the class template shows that its declaration starts with the keyword **template** and is followed by the list of template parameters enclosed in angle brackets. This list enumerates one or more template parameters. You can use the keyword **class** or any other predefined type with these template parameters. When you use the keyword **class**, you tell the compiler that you can instantiate the template class with user-defined classes, structures, and predefined types. By contrast, when you specify a predefined type, you specify that the argument for that template parameter must be a compatible type.

Most of the class templates you see or write yourself have one template parameter. Here is the skeleton declaration of a typical sample class template:

```
template <class T>
class myTemplateList
{
  // declarations of members
};
```

The class **myTemplateList** uses the single template parameter T. Here is the skeleton declaration of a sample class template that uses two template parameters:

```
template <class ValueType, class NodeType>
class myTemplateHashTable
{
  // declarations of members
};
```

The class **myTemplateHashTable** uses the template parameters **ValueType** and **NodeType**. Here is another example of using class and nonclass template parameters:

```
template <class T, int arraySize>
class myTemplateArray
{
  // declarations of members
};
```

The class **myTemplateArray** uses the **class T** and **int arraySize** template parameters.

Class Template Implementation

C++ requires the following syntax for defining the member functions of class templates:

```
template <class T, ...>
returnType classTemplate<T, ...>::memberFunction(parameterList)
{
  // statements
}
```

Notice the following aspects of the general syntax:

- The definition of the member function starts with the keyword **template** and is followed by the angle brackets that contain the list of template parameters.
- The name of the class template is followed by the angle brackets that contain the list of template parameter identifiers. In fact, C++ requires that you use this syntax with all of the references to the class template!

Here is an example of a class template declaration and the definition of one of its member functions:

```
template <class T, int arraySize>
class myTemplateArray
{
  // declarations of members
  T& operator[](int nIndex);
  // declarations of other members
  T* m_pData;
};

template <class T, int arraySize>
T& myTemplateArray<T, arraySize>::operator [](int nIndex)
{
  return m_pData[nIndex];
}
```

The class **myTemplateArray** (which is the same class presented earlier in this section) declares the operator **[]**. Notice that the definition of the operator starts with **template <class T, int arraySize>**. In addition, the definition uses the class name **myTemplateArray<T, arraySize>::** and not just **myTemplateArray::**.

Where Do You Store Templates?

You can list the declaration of a class template in a header file and define its member functions in a .CPP file. However, since the compiler does not compile template code, you must include the .CPP file (instead of the header file) in the source code of client .CPP files. An alternative to this approach is to declare and define the class template in a header file and then include the header file in the source code of client .CPP files.

Class Template Instances

Instantiating class templates is easy. You declare an instantiated class template by specifying the actual types for the template parameters. Here is an example:

```
class Rectangle
{
  // declarations
};

main()
{
  myTemplateArray<int, 10> intArray;
  myTemplateArray<char, 30> charArray;
  myTemplateArray<double, 100> dblArray;
  myTemplateArray<long, 10> longArray;
  myTemplateArray<Rectangle, 50> rectangleArray;

  // statements

  return 0;
}
```

The example instantiates the class **myTemplateArray** with the types **int**, **char**, **double**, **long**, and **Rectangle**, respectively. The first four types are predefined types, whereas the last type is a user-defined class.

Let's look at a programming example. Listing 17-2 shows the source code for the TMPLT2.CPP program, which illustrates template classes. The program models a class template that supports generic arrays. It declares the class template **myArray** and the class **myString**. The program uses the class template to create dynamic arrays of integers, characters, and strings (using the class **myString**) and to perform the following tasks for each kind of array:

- Assign values to the array elements
- Display the unsorted array elements
- Sort the elements of the array
- Display the sorted array elements

Here is the output of the program in Listing 17-2:

```
Unsorted array is:
23 45 89 74 51 18 87 63 36 38

Sorted array is:
18 23 36 38 45 51 63 74 87 89
Unsorted array is:
a W Q y H L J M d D
Sorted array is:
D H J L M Q W a d y
Unsorted array is:

Virginia
Michigan
California
New York
Maryland
Oregon
Idaho
Nevada
Arizona
Alaska
Sorted array is:
Alaska
Arizona
California
Idaho
Maryland
Michigan
Nevada
New York
Oregon
Virginia
```

Listing 17-2
The source code for the TMPLT2.CPP program.

```cpp
// A C++ program that illustrates
// the template classes

#include <iostream.h>
#include <iomanip.h>
#include <string.h>

const int MIN_SIZE = 30;

enum Logical { FALSE, TRUE };

template <class T>
class myArray
{
  public:
    myArray(int nSize, T InitVal);
    ~myArray()
      { delete [] m_pArray; }
    T& operator[](int nIndex)
      { return m_pArray[nIndex]; }
    void show(const int nNumElems,
              const char* pszMsg = "",
              const Logical bOneLine = TRUE);
    void CombSort(int nNumElems);

  protected:
    T* m_pArray;
    int m_nSize;
};

template <class T>
myArray<T>::myArray(int nSize, T InitVal)
{
  m_nSize = (nSize > 1) ? nSize : 1;
  m_pArray = new T[m_nSize];
  for (int i = 0; i < m_nSize; i++)
    m_pArray[i] = InitVal;
}

template <class T>
void myArray<T>::show(const int nNumElems,
                      const char* pszMsg,
                      const Logical bOneLine)
{
  cout << pszMsg << endl;
  if (bOneLine) {
    for (int i = 0; i < nNumElems; i++)
      cout << m_pArray[i] << ' ';
```

 ➤ *Declare template class*

```
      cout << endl;
    }
    else {
      for (int i = 0; i < nNumElems; i++)
        cout << m_pArray[i] << endl;
      cout << endl;
    }
}

template <class T>
void myArray<T>::CombSort(int nNumElems)
{
  int nOffset = nNumElems;
  Logical bSorted;

  // check argument of parameter nNumElems
  if (nNumElems < 2)
    return;

  do {
    nOffset = (nOffset * 8) / 11;
    nOffset = (nOffset < 1) ? 1 : nOffset;
    bSorted = TRUE; // set sorted flag
    // compare elements
    for (int i = 0, j = nOffset;
         i < (nNumElems - nOffset);
         i++, j++) {
      if (m_pArray[i] > m_pArray[j]) {
        // swap elements
        T nSwap = m_pArray[i];
        m_pArray[i] = m_pArray[j];
        m_pArray[j] = nSwap;
        bSorted = FALSE; // clear sorted flag
      }
    }
  } while (!bSorted || nOffset != 1);
}

class myString                                    Declare non-template class
{
  public:
    myString(int nSize = MIN_SIZE)
      { m_pszString = new char[m_nSize = nSize]; }
    myString(myString& aString);
    myString(const char* pszString);
    myString(const char cChar);
    ~myString()
      { delete [] m_pszString; }
    int getLen()
      { return strlen(m_pszString); }
    int getMaxLen()
      { return m_nSize; }
```

```
    myString& operator =(myString& aString);
    myString& operator =(const char* pszString);
    myString& operator =(const char cChar);
    friend int operator >(myString& aString1, myString& aString2)
      { return (strcmp(aString1.m_pszString,
                       aString2.m_pszString) > 0) ? 1 : 0; }
    friend ostream& operator <<(ostream& os, myString& aString);

  protected:
    char* m_pszString;
    int m_nSize;
};

myString::myString(myString& aString)
{
  m_pszString = new char[m_nSize = aString.m_nSize];
  strcpy(m_pszString, aString.m_pszString);
}

myString::myString(const char* pszString)
{
  m_pszString = new char[m_nSize = strlen(pszString) + 1];
  strcpy(m_pszString, pszString);
}

myString::myString(const char cChar)
{
  m_pszString = new char[m_nSize = MIN_SIZE];
  m_pszString[0] = cChar;
  m_pszString[1] = '\0';
}

myString& myString::operator =(myString& aString)
{
  // source string small enough to copy?
  if (strlen(aString.m_pszString) < unsigned(m_nSize))
    strcpy(m_pszString, aString.m_pszString);
  else
    // copy first m_nSize - 1 characters
    strncpy(m_pszString, aString.m_pszString, m_nSize - 1);
  return *this;
}

myString& myString::operator =(const char* pszString)
{
  // source string small enough to copy?
  if (strlen(pszString) < unsigned(m_nSize))
    strcpy(m_pszString, pszString);
  else
    // copy first m_nSize - 1 characters
    strncpy(m_pszString, pszString, m_nSize - 1);
  return *this;
}
```

```
myString& myString::operator =(const char cChar)
{
  if (m_nSize > 1) {
    m_pszString[0] = cChar;
    m_pszString[1] = '\0';
  }
  return *this;
}

ostream& operator <<(ostream& os, myString& aString)
{
  os << aString.m_pszString;
  return os;
}

main()
{
  const int MAX_ELEMS = 10;
  int nArr[MAX_ELEMS] = { 23, 45, 89, 74, 51,
                          18, 87, 63, 36, 38 };
  int cArr[MAX_ELEMS] = { 'a', 'W', 'Q', 'y', 'H',
                          'L', 'J', 'M', 'd', 'D' };

  myArray<int> IntegerArray(MAX_ELEMS, 0);
  myArray<char> CharArray(MAX_ELEMS, ' ');
  myArray<myString> StringArray(MAX_ELEMS, "");
```

Use template class with
predefined class types

```
  // assign integers to elements of array IntegerArray
  for (int i = 0; i < MAX_ELEMS; i++)
    IntegerArray[i] = nArr[i];
  // assign characters to elements of array CharArray
  for (i = 0; i < MAX_ELEMS; i++)
    CharArray[i] = cArr[i];
  // assign strings to elements of array stringArray
  StringArray[0] = "Virginia";
  StringArray[1] = "Michigan";
  StringArray[2] = "California";
  StringArray[3] = "New York";
  StringArray[4] = "Maryland";
  StringArray[5] = "Oregon";
  StringArray[6] = "Idaho";
  StringArray[7] = "Nevada";
  StringArray[8] = "Arizona";
  StringArray[9] = "Alaska";

  // test array IntegerArray
  IntegerArray.show(MAX_ELEMS, "Unsorted array is:");
  IntegerArray.CombSort(MAX_ELEMS);
  IntegerArray.show(MAX_ELEMS, "Sorted array is:");
  cout << "\n\n";
```

```
// test array CharArray
CharArray.show(MAX_ELEMS, "Unsorted array is:");
CharArray.CombSort(MAX_ELEMS);
CharArray.show(MAX_ELEMS, "Sorted array is:");
cout << "\n\n";

StringArray.show(MAX_ELEMS, "Unsorted array is:", FALSE);
StringArray.CombSort(MAX_ELEMS);
StringArray.show(MAX_ELEMS, "Sorted array is:", FALSE);

return 0;
}
```

Listing 17-2 declares the class template **myArray**, the class **myString**, and the function **main**. The next subsections discuss these program components in more detail.

The Class Template myArray

The listing declares the class template **myArray** to have the template parameter **T**, which represents the type of each array element. The class template declares protected and public members. The protected members are:

- The data member **m_pArray**, which is a pointer to the template parameter **T**. This member accesses the dynamic array.
- The **int**-type data member **m_nSize**, which stores the number of elements in the dynamic array

The class template declares the following public members:

- The constructor, which creates the dynamic array and initializes it using the **T**-type parameter **InitVal**
- The destructor, which removes the space of the dynamic array
- The operator **[]**, which accesses the elements of the dynamic array. The operator returns a reference to the template parameter **T**.
- The member function **show**, which displays the elements of the dynamic array. This member function requires that you define the operator **<<** for the instantiating data type.

- The member function **CombSort**, which sorts the elements of the dynamic array. Using this member function requires that you define the operators **=** and **>** for the instantiating data types.

The definition of each member function follows the general syntax that I mentioned in the last section—the definitions start with the keywords **template <class T>** and use **myArray<T>::** (instead of just **myArray::**) to qualify the name of the member function.

Using the class template **myArray** requires that you define the operators **<<**, **>**, and **=** for the instantiating data types.

THE CLASS MYSTRING

The listing declares the class **myString**, which models a string class that instantiates the class template **myArray**. The class **myString** declares constructors, a destructor, the member function **getLen**, the member function **getMaxLen**, the operator **=**, the friend operator **>**, and the friend operator **<<**. The class needs the least three operators to work with the member functions **CombSort** and **show** in the class template.

THE FUNCTION MAIN

The function **main** declares and initializes the **int**-type array **nArr** and the char-type array **cArr**. The function also declares the following objects:

- The object **IntegerArray**, which instantiates the class template **myArray** with the predefined type **int**. The function creates **MAX_ELEMS** elements and initializes them with zeros.

- The object **CharArray**, which instantiates the class template **myArray** with the predefined type char. The function creates **MAX_ELEMS** elements and initializes them with the space character.

- The object **StringArray**, which instantiates the class template **myArray** with the class **myString**. The function creates **MAX_ELEMS** elements and initializes them to null strings.

The function **main** performs the following tasks:

- Assign integers to the elements of array **IntegerArray**. This task uses a **for** loop to copy the elements of array **nArr** into the elements of array **IntegerArray**.

- Assign characters to the elements of array **CharArray**. This task uses a **for** loop to copy the elements of array **cArr** into the elements of array **CharArray**.

- Assign string literals to the elements of array **StringArray**. This task uses a series of assignment statements.

- Display the unsorted elements in object **IntegerArray** by sending the C++ message **show** to that object. The arguments for the message are the constant **MAX_ELEMS** and the string literal "Unsorted array is:"

- Sort the elements in the object **IntegerArray** by sending the C++ message **CombSort** to that object. The argument for the message is the constant **MAX_ELEMS**.

- Display the sorted elements in object **IntegerArray** by sending the C++ message **show** to that object. The arguments for the message are the constant **MAX_ELEMS** and the string literal "Sorted array is:"

- Display the unsorted elements in object **CharArray** by sending the C++ message **show** to that object. The arguments for the message are the constant **MAX_ELEMS** and the string literal "Unsorted array is:"

- Sort the elements in the object **CharArray** by sending the C++ message **CombSort** to that object. The argument for the message is the constant **MAX_ELEMS**.

- Display the sorted elements in object **CharArray** by sending the C++ message **show** to that object. The arguments for the message are the constant **MAX_ELEMS** and the string literal "Sorted array is:"

- Display the unsorted elements in object **StringArray** by sending the C++ message **show** to that object. The arguments for the message are the constant **MAX_ELEMS** and the string literal "Unsorted array is:"

- Sort the elements in the object **StringArray** by sending the C++ message **CombSort** to that object. The argument for this message is the constant **MAX_ELEMS**.

- Display the sorted elements in object **StringArray** by sending the C++ message **show** to that object. The arguments for the message are the constant **MAX_ELEMS** and the string literal "Sorted array is:"

Template Parameters

The general syntax for declaring class templates shows that you can declare a class template with multiple template parameters. When you use the keyword **class** to declare a template parameter, that parameter can be instantiated using a user-defined class or a predefined class. You can also replace the keyword **class** with the name of a predefined or previously defined data type. This kind of template parameter helps in fine-tuning the design of the class template.

Let me present a programming example that declares a class template with two template parameters. Listing 17-3 shows the source code for the TMPLT3.CPP program. I created this program by editing Listing 17-2. The new program declares a new version of the class template **myArray**. This class has the template parameters **class T** and **int nSize**; the second parameter defines the size of the array maintained by the class. The program uses the class template **myArray** to manipulate arrays of integers and characters in a manner identical to Listing 17-2. To shorten Listing 17-3, I eliminated the class **myString**, the object **StringArray**, and any code related to that class and its instances.

Here is the output of the program in Listing 17-3:

```
Unsorted array is:
23 45 89 74 51 18 87 63 36 38
Sorted array is:
18 23 36 38 45 51 63 74 87 89


Unsorted array is:
a W Q y H L J M d D
Sorted array is:
D H J L M Q W a d y
```

Listing 17-3
The source code for the TMPLT3.CPP program.

```cpp
// A C++ program that illustrates
// the template parameters

#include <iostream.h>
#include <iomanip.h>

enum Logical { FALSE, TRUE };

template <class T, int nSize>
class myArray
{
  public:
    myArray(T InitVal);
    T& operator[](int nIndex)
      { return m_Array[nIndex]; }
    void show(const int nNumElems,
              const char* pszMsg = "",
              const Logical bOneLine = TRUE);
    void CombSort(int nNumElems);

  protected:
    T m_Array[nSize];
    int m_nSize;
};

template <class T, int nSize>
myArray<T, nSize>::myArray(T InitVal)
{
  m_nSize = nSize;
  for (int i = 0; i < m_nSize; i++)
    m_Array[i] = InitVal;
}

template <class T, int nSize>
void myArray<T, nSize>::show(const int nNumElems,
                            const char* pszMsg,
                            const Logical bOneLine)
{
  cout << pszMsg << endl;
  if (bOneLine) {
    for (int i = 0; i < nNumElems; i++)
      cout << m_Array[i] << ' ';
    cout << endl;
  }
  else {
    for (int i = 0; i < nNumElems; i++)
      cout << m_Array[i] << endl;
    cout << endl;
  }
}
```

→ *Declare template class with multiple template parameters*

```
template <class T, int nSize>
void myArray<T, nSize>::CombSort(int nNumElems)
{
  int nOffset = nNumElems;
  Logical bSorted;

  // check argument of parameter nNumElems
  if (nNumElems < 2)
    return;

  do {
    nOffset = (nOffset * 8) / 11;
    nOffset = (nOffset < 1) ? 1 : nOffset;
    bSorted = TRUE; // set sorted flag
    // compare elements
    for (int i = 0, j = nOffset;
         i < (nNumElems - nOffset);
         i++, j++) {
      if (m_Array[i] > m_Array[j]) {
        // swap elements
        T nSwap = m_Array[i];
        m_Array[i] = m_Array[j];
        m_Array[j] = nSwap;
        bSorted = FALSE; // clear sorted flag
      }
    }
  } while (!bSorted || nOffset != 1);
}

main()
{
  const int MAX_ELEMS = 10;
  int nArr[MAX_ELEMS] = { 23, 45, 89, 74, 51,
                          18, 87, 63, 36, 38 };
  int cArr[MAX_ELEMS] = { 'a', 'W', 'Q', 'y', 'H',
                          'L', 'J', 'M', 'd', 'D' };

  myArray<int, MAX_ELEMS> IntegerArray(0);
  myArray<char, MAX_ELEMS> CharArray(' ');

  // assign integers to elements of array IntegerArray
  for (int i = 0; i < MAX_ELEMS; i++)
    IntegerArray[i] = nArr[i];
  // assign characters to elements of array CharArray
  for (i = 0; i < MAX_ELEMS; i++)
    CharArray[i] = cArr[i];

  // test array IntegerArray
  IntegerArray.show(MAX_ELEMS, "Unsorted array is:");
  IntegerArray.CombSort(MAX_ELEMS);
  IntegerArray.show(MAX_ELEMS, "Sorted array is:");
  cout << "\n\n";
```

```
// test array CharArray
CharArray.show(MAX_ELEMS, "Unsorted array is:");
CharArray.CombSort(MAX_ELEMS);
CharArray.show(MAX_ELEMS, "Sorted array is:");
cout << "\n\n";

return 0;
}
```

Listing 17-3 declares the class **myArray** with the template parameters **class T** and **int nSize**. The new version of the class template uses the template parameter to declare the array data member **m_Array**. In other words, the new version does not use dynamic allocation and deallocation. Instead, it relies on the template parameter to create the internal array during instantiation.

The source code shows that each member function starts with the keywords template **<class T, int nSize>** and uses **myArray<T, nSize>::** to qualify itself. The statements inside the member functions (except the constructor) are identical to their counterparts in Listing 17-2.

The source code for function **main** is a subset of that in Listing 17-2—I eliminated the creation and use of the object **StringArray** from Listing 17-3.

Here is another programming example. Listing 17-4 shows the source code for the TMPLT4.CPP program, which illustrates use of multiple class-type template parameters in a class template. I created Listing 17-4 by modifying Listing 17-3. The new program declares a new class template **myArray**, which has the template parameters **class T, class IDX**, and **int nSize**. I inserted the second template parameter to provide a type used for indexing. This template parameter enables you to instantiate the class template **myArray** with such types as **short, int, long, unsigned**, and **char**. You are no longer limited to using the predefined type **int** to index the array elements. The constructor and member functions **show** and **CombSort** use the template parameter **IDX** as the type for the loop control variables.

Here is the output of the program in Listing 17-4:

```
Unsorted array is:
23 45 89 74 51 18 87 63 36 38
Sorted array is:
18 23 36 38 45 51 63 74 87 89

Unsorted array is:
23 45 89 74 51 18 87 63 36 38
Sorted array is:
18 23 36 38 45 51 63 74 87 89
```

Listing 17-4

The source code for the TMPLT4.CPP program.

```cpp
// A C++ program that illustrates
// the template parameters

#include <iostream.h>
#include <iomanip.h>

enum Logical { FALSE, TRUE };

template <class T, class IDX, int nSize>
class myArray
{
  public:
    myArray(T InitVal);
    T& operator[](IDX nIndex)
      { return m_Array[nIndex]; }
    void show(const int nNumElems,
              const char* pszMsg = "",
              const Logical bOneLine = TRUE);
    void CombSort(int nNumElems);

  protected:
    T m_Array[nSize];
    int m_nSize;
};

template <class T, class IDX, int nSize>
myArray<T, IDX, nSize>::myArray(T InitVal)
{
  m_nSize = nSize;
  for (IDX i = 0; i < m_nSize; i++)
    m_Array[i] = InitVal;
}

template <class T, class IDX, int nSize>
void myArray<T, IDX, nSize>::show(const int nNumElems,
                                  const char* pszMsg,
                                  const Logical bOneLine)
{
  cout << pszMsg << endl;
  if (bOneLine) {
    for (IDX i = 0; i < nNumElems; i++)
      cout << m_Array[i] << ' ';
    cout << endl;
  }
```

Declare template class with multiple template parameters

```
    else {
      for (IDX i = 0; i < nNumElems; i++)
        cout << m_Array[i] << endl;
      cout << endl;
    }
}

template <class T, class IDX, int nSize>
void myArray<T, IDX, nSize>::CombSort(int nNumElems)
{
  int nOffset = nNumElems;
  Logical bSorted;

  // check argument of parameter nNumElems
  if (nNumElems < 2)
    return;

  do {
    nOffset = (nOffset * 8) / 11;
    nOffset = (nOffset < 1) ? 1 : nOffset;
    bSorted = TRUE; // set sorted flag
    // compare elements
    for (IDX i = 0, j = nOffset;
         i < (nNumElems - nOffset);
         i++, j++) {
      if (m_Array[i] > m_Array[j]) {
        // swap elements
        T nSwap = m_Array[i];
        m_Array[i] = m_Array[j];
        m_Array[j] = nSwap;
        bSorted = FALSE; // clear sorted flag
      }
    }
  } while (!bSorted || nOffset != 1);
}

main()
{
  const int MAX_ELEMS = 10;
  int nArr[MAX_ELEMS] = { 23, 45, 89, 74, 51,
                          18, 87, 63, 36, 38 };

  myArray<int, int, MAX_ELEMS> IntegerArray(0);
  myArray<int, char, MAX_ELEMS> CharArray(' ');

  // assign values to elements of array IntegerArray
  for (int i = 0; i < MAX_ELEMS; i++)
    IntegerArray[i] = nArr[i];
  // assign values to elements of array CharArray
  for (char c = 0; c < MAX_ELEMS; c++)
    CharArray[c] = nArr[int(c)];
```

```
// test array IntegerArray
IntegerArray.show(MAX_ELEMS, "Unsorted array is:");
IntegerArray.CombSort(MAX_ELEMS);
IntegerArray.show(MAX_ELEMS, "Sorted array is:");
cout << "\n\n";

// test array CharArray
CharArray.show(MAX_ELEMS, "Unsorted array is:");
CharArray.CombSort(MAX_ELEMS);
CharArray.show(MAX_ELEMS, "Sorted array is:");
cout << "\n\n";

return 0;
}
```

In addition to the changes to the class template that I mentioned earlier, the function **main** declares the two arrays of integers **IntegerArray** and **CharArray** as follows:

- The object **IntegerArray** instantiates the class template **myArray** with the type **int** twice to create an array of integers whose elements are indexed using the type **int**. The function **main** assigns values to this object using a **for** loop that uses an **int**-type loop control variable.

- The object **CharArray** instantiates the class template **myArray** with the types **int** and **char** to create an array of integers whose elements are indexed using the type **char**. The function **main** assigns values to this object using a **for** loop that uses a **char**-type loop control variable.

As for displaying and sorting the objects, the statements in Listing 17-4 match those in Listing 17-3.

Class Derivation and Templates

C++ allows you to declare descendants of class templates. The general syntax for declaring a descendant class template is:

```
template <class T, ...>
class className : [public] parentClass [, otherParentClasses]
```

```
{
  // declarations of nested structures, enumerated types,
  // classes, and friend classes

  public:
  // public constructors
  // public destructor
  // public member functions
  // public data members

  protected:
  // protected constructors
  // protected destructor
  // protected member functions
  // protected data members

  private:
  // private constructors
  // private destructor
  // private member functions
  // private data members
};
```

C++ requires that you observe the same rules that apply to ordinary descendant classes when you create descendant class templates. In fact, C++ permits you to create an ordinary descendant class from a class template. You can also create abstract class templates. Thus, C++ allows you to implement powerful class templates that significantly reduce the number of classes needed to perform the same tasks on different data types.

Here is an example of declaring a descendant class template:

```
template <class T>
class myTemplateArray
{
  // declarations of members
};

template <class T>
class myTemplateRamArray : public myTemplateArray<T>
{
  // declarations of members
};
```

The example declares the class template **myTemplateArray** and its descendant class **myTemplateRamArray**. Notice that the reference to the parent class uses **public myTemplateArray<T>** instead of **public** myTemplateArray. This syntax conforms to the rule that requires stating the template parameter identifiers when referencing the class template.

Let me present a programming example. Listing 17-5 shows the source code for the TMPLT5.CPP program, which illustrates descendant class templates. I created this program by editing program TMPLT3.CPP in Listing 17-3. The listing declares the class templates **myArray** and **mySortedArray**. The latter class is the descendant of the former class. The class **myArray** supports indexing and displaying array elements. The descendant class template **mySortedArray** supports sorting the array elements. The program instantiates the class template **mySortedArray** to create, initialize, display, sort, and redisplay arrays of integers and characters.

Here is the output of the program in Listing 17-5:

```
Unsorted array is:
23 45 89 74 51 18 87 63 36 38
Sorted array is:
18 23 36 38 45 51 63 74 87 89

Unsorted array is:
a W Q y H L J M d D
Sorted array is:
D H J L M Q W a d y
```

Listing 17-5
The source code for the TMPLT5.CPP program.

```cpp
// A C++ program that illustrates
// descendant class templates

#include <iostream.h>
#include <iomanip.h>

enum Logical { FALSE, TRUE };

template <class T, int nSize>          ──▶ Base class
class myArray
{
  public:
    myArray(T InitVal);
    T& operator[](int nIndex)
      { return m_Array[nIndex]; }
    void show(const int nNumElems,
              const char* pszMsg = "",
              const Logical bOneLine = TRUE);
```

```
   protected:
     T m_Array[nSize];
     int m_nSize;
};

template <class T, int nSize>
class mySortedArray : public myArray<T, nSize>
{
  public:
    mySortedArray(T InitVal)
      : myArray<T, nSize>(InitVal) {}
    void CombSort(int nNumElems);
};

template <class T, int nSize>
myArray<T, nSize>::myArray(T InitVal)
{
  m_nSize = nSize;
  for (int i = 0; i < m_nSize; i++)
    m_Array[i] = InitVal;
}

template <class T, int nSize>
void myArray<T, nSize>::show(const int nNumElems,
                            const char* pszMsg,
                            const Logical bOneLine)
{
  cout << pszMsg << endl;
  if (bOneLine) {
    for (int i = 0; i < nNumElems; i++)
      cout << m_Array[i] << ' ';
    cout << endl;
  }
  else {
    for (int i = 0; i < nNumElems; i++)
      cout << m_Array[i] << endl;
    cout << endl;
  }
}

template <class T, int nSize>
void mySortedArray<T, nSize>::CombSort(int nNumElems)
{
  int nOffset = nNumElems;
  Logical bSorted;

  // check argument of parameter nNumElems
  if (nNumElems < 2)
    return;
```

→ *Descendant class*

```
  do {
    nOffset = (nOffset * 8) / 11;
    nOffset = (nOffset < 1) ? 1 : nOffset;
    bSorted = TRUE; // set sorted flag
    // compare elements
    for (int i = 0, j = nOffset;
         i < (nNumElems - nOffset);
         i++, j++) {
      if (m_Array[i] > m_Array[j]) {
        // swap elements
        T nSwap = m_Array[i];
        m_Array[i] = m_Array[j];
        m_Array[j] = nSwap;
        bSorted = FALSE; // clear sorted flag
      }
    }
  } while (!bSorted || nOffset != 1);
}

main()
{
  const int MAX_ELEMS = 10;
  int nArr[MAX_ELEMS] = { 23, 45, 89, 74, 51,
                          18, 87, 63, 36, 38 };
  int cArr[MAX_ELEMS] = { 'a', 'W', 'Q', 'y', 'H',
                          'L', 'J', 'M', 'd', 'D' };

  mySortedArray<int, MAX_ELEMS> IntegerArray(0);
  mySortedArray<char, MAX_ELEMS> CharArray(' ');

  // assign integers to elements of array IntegerArray
  for (int i = 0; i < MAX_ELEMS; i++)
    IntegerArray[i] = nArr[i];
  // assign characters to elements of array CharArray
  for (i = 0; i < MAX_ELEMS; i++)
    CharArray[i] = cArr[i];

  // test array IntegerArray
  IntegerArray.show(MAX_ELEMS, "Unsorted array is:");
  IntegerArray.CombSort(MAX_ELEMS);
  IntegerArray.show(MAX_ELEMS, "Sorted array is:");
  cout << "\n\n";

  // test array CharArray
  CharArray.show(MAX_ELEMS, "Unsorted array is:");
  CharArray.CombSort(MAX_ELEMS);
  CharArray.show(MAX_ELEMS, "Sorted array is:");
  cout << "\n\n";

  return 0;
}
```

Listing 17-5 declares the class template **myArray** with the template parameters **class T** and **int nSize**. The listing also declares the descendant class template **mySortedArray** with the same template parameters. Notice that the declaration of the descendant class template refers to the parent class template as **myArray<T, nSize>** and not just **myArray**. The class template **myArray** declares a constructor, the operator **[]**, and the member function **show**. The descendant class template declares a constructor and the member function **CombSort**.

The function **main** creates the object **IntegerArray** and **CharArray** by instantiating the class template **mySortedArray** using the **int** and **char** types (for the first template parameters), respectively. The source code for assigning values to these objects and manipulating them is very similar to that in Listing 17-3.

Summary

This chapter has presented templates. You learned about declaring and defining general-purpose function templates. You also learned how to declare, implement, and instantiate class templates. The chapter also discussed template parameters and how to use them to fine-tune the design of class templates. Finally, the chapter discussed the creation of hierarchies for class templates.

The next chapter is a roundup of the lastest features in C++ as it continues to evolve. Among these features is a new set of libraries known as the C++ Standard Libraries, which include the Standard Template Library (STL), an implementation of class templates for popular data structures.

18

C++: The Next Generation

*T*he ANSI C++ Committee is working on standardizing C++. Thus, C++ continues to evolve. Your journey into the world of C++ ends with a look at new aspects of the language. The last major changes in C++, which occurred a few years ago, brought new features such as templates and exception handling. This chapter covers new features such as the new **#include** format, the type **bool**, new reserved words, namespaces, template parameter arguments, the new C++ standard libraries, and the new Standard Template Library (STL).

The New #include Format

C++ is evolving away from C. One example is the new **#include** format. The new format states the name of the library instead of the name of the header file. Thus, the new **#include** format supports library names that are longer than the names of header files (which are limited by some operating systems, such as MS-DOS). The compiler has the task of relating the library name to its filename. Here is an example that uses the **#include** directive to include the familiar stream library declared in the IOSTREAM.H file:

```
#include <iostream>

main()
{
  cout << "C++: the next generation\n";
  return 0;
}
```

Looking at the above listing, you can immediately tell that it is C++ source code, because of the new **#include** format.

The bool Type

Well, the ANSI C++ Committee finally did it! Responding to the frustration of many C++ programmers, the committee has adopted the Boolean type **bool** as a predefined type with the enumerators **false** and **true**. These enumerators have the values of 0 and 1, respectively. Thus, the next generation of C++ compilers translate the **int**-type values that have been used so far into **bool** types. This conversion affects the following language components:

- The results of the relational operators
- The results of the logical operators
- The condition tested in a conditional operator (the ()?:)
- The conditions tested in **if, while, do-while**, and **for** statements

New Reserved Words

The ANSI C++ Committee has recommended reserving a new set of keywords, shown in Table 18-1, to represent logical and bitwise operators. These new keywords help international programmers who work with keyboards that lack characters such as '∧', '&', and '|'.

Table 18-1
New Reserved Keywords

Keyword	Equivalent Character	Purpose
and	&&	Logical AND
or	||	Logical OR
not	!	Logical NOT

Keyword	Equivalent Character	Purpose
not_eq	!=	Logical not equal
bitand	&	Bitwise AND
and_eq	&=	Bitwise AND assignment
bitor	|	Bitwise OR
or_eq	|=	Bitwise OR assignment
xor	^	Bitwise XOR
xor_eq	^=	Bitwise XOR assignment
compl	~	Ones complement

Namespaces

One of the weaknesses in C is that there is only one *namespace* for the identifiers in an application. This means that you have to avoid duplicating the names of identifiers that share the same scope. One example that stands out immediately is enumerated types. Nesting enumerated types, structures, and even classes inside other classes may be a programming trick that works for some programmers, although other programmers may see this trick as complicating matters.

The new C++ compilers will support the namespace feature that allows you to declare the names of identifiers inside a namespace. The general syntax for a namespace is:

```
namespace myNameSpace {
  // declarations
}
```

Notice that the above syntax does not end the declaration of a namespace with a semicolon. C++ requires that you observe the following rules when using namespaces:

1. You can define a namespace only at the global level. In other words, you cannot create a namespace inside a function or a class.

2. You can declare nested namespaces.

3. You can extend the namespace in multiple header files.

4. You can create a name that is an alias to a namespace.

5. You cannot create namespace instances.

6. You must qualify the items declared in the namespace using the name of the host namespace.

7. You may use the **using** directive to avoid the preceding rule, as long as it does not lead to ambiguity.

Here is an example of a simple usage of a namespace:

```
#include <iostream>
#include <cstring>

namespace Namir {
  class Shammas {
    public:
      Shammas()
        { strcpy(m_pszName, "Namir Shammas") };
      void show ();
    protected:
      char m_pszName[30];
  };
}

void Namir::Shammas::show()
  { cout << m_pszName << "\n"; }

main()
{
  Namir::Shammas Me;

  Me.show();

  return 0;
}
```

This example declares the namespace **Namir**, which declares the class **Shammas**. This class has a constructor (which initializes the string data member **m_pszName**) and the member function **show** (which displays the characters in the data member). Notice that the example defines the member function **show** outside the class and the namespace. Consequently, the definition qualifies the name of the member function with **Namir::Shammas::** instead of just **Shammas::**. The function **main** declares the

object **Me** as an instance of class **Namir::Shammas**. The function sends the
C++ message **show** to object **Me** to display the characters in data member
m_pszName.

Using the namespace feature, I can declare two versions of class
Shammas in two different namespaces. Here is an example:

```
#include <iostream>
#include <cstring>

namespace Namir {
  class Shammas {
    public:
     Shammas()
       { strcpy(m_pszName, "Namir Shammas") };
      void show ();
     protected:
       char m_pszName[30];
  };
}

namespace Joseph {
  class Shammas {
    public:
     Shammas()
       { strcpy(m_pszName, "Joseph Shammas") };
      void show ();
     protected:
       char m_pszName[30];
  };
}


void Namir::Shammas::show()
  { cout << m_pszName << "\n"; }

void Joseph::Shammas::show()
  { cout << m_pszName << "\n"; }

main()
{
  Namir::Shammas Me;
  Joseph::Shammas MySon;

  Me.show();
  MySon.show();

  return 0;
}
```

This example declares the namespaces **Namir** and **Joseph**. Each namespace declares its own version of class **Shammas**. The two classes are very similar. The example defines the member functions **Namir::Shammas::show** and **Joseph::Shammas::show** outside the namespaces. The function **main** declares the objects **Me** and **MySon** as instances of classes **Namir::Shammas** and **Joseph::Shammas**. The function sends the C++ message **show** to each object.

The **using** directive allows you to omit referring to a namespace. I can rewrite the above example with the **using** directive:

```
#include <iostream>
#include <cstring>

namespace Namir {
  class Shammas {
    public:
     Shammas()
       { strcpy(m_pszName, "Namir Shammas") };
     void show ();
    protected:
      char m_pszName[30];
  };
}

namespace Joseph {
  class Shammas {
    public:
     Shammas()
       { strcpy(m_pszName, "Joseph Shammas") };
     void show ();
    protected:
      char m_pszName[30];
  };
}


void Namir::Shammas::show()
  { cout << m_pszName << "\n"; }

void Joseph::Shammas::show()
  { cout << m_pszName << "\n"; }

main()
{
  using Namir; // use the Namir namespace
  Shammas Me;
  Joseph::Shammas MySon;
```

```
  Me.show();
  MySon.show();

  return 0;
}
```

Notice that function **main** has the **using Namir;** statement that tells the compiler that the class **Shammas** refers to **Namir::Shammas**. The example shows that the reference to class **Joseph::Shammas** must still be explicit to avoid ambiguous references to the class **Shammas**. I can rewrite the function **main** as follows to employ the **using** directive for each namespace:

```
main()
{
  using Namir; // use the Namir namespace
  Shammas Me;

  Me.show();

  using Joseph; // use the Joseph namespace
  Shammas MySon;

  MySon.show();

  return 0;
}
```

The code snippet shows that I can switch automatic references to the class **Shammas** anywhere in a function.

Finally, I can include both namespaces **Namir** and **Joseph** inside another namespace, as shown in the source code below:

```
#include <iostream>
#include <cstring>

namespace Family {
  // first nested namespace
  namespace Namir {
    class Shammas {
      public:
        Shammas()
          { strcpy(m_pszName, "Namir Shammas") };
        void show ();
      protected:
        char m_pszName[30];
    };
  }
```

```
      // second nested namespace
      namespace Joseph {
        class Shammas {
          public:
           Shammas()
             { strcpy(m_pszName, "Joseph Shammas") };
           void show ();
          protected:
            char m_pszName[30];
        };
      }
    }

    void Family::Namir::Shammas::show()
      { cout << m_pszName << "\n"; }

    void Family::Joseph::Shammas::show()
      { cout << m_pszName << "\n"; }

    main()
    {
      Family::Namir::Shammas Me;
      Family::Joseph::Shammas MySon;

      Me.show();
      MySon.show();

      return 0;
    }
```

The current example declares the namespace **Family** to contain the
nested namespaces **Namir** and **Joseph**. Thus, the example qualifies the
names of the two member functions **show** using **Family::Namir::Shammas::**
and **Family::Joseph::Shammas::**. The function **main** uses the qualifier class
names **Family::Namir::Shammas** and **Family::Joseph::Shammas** to declare the
objects **Me** and **MySon**, respectively.

Template Parameter Arguments

The new versions of C++ compilers should support default arguments for
template parameters. These arguments parallel in syntax and purpose the
default arguments of a function. The general syntax for the default arguments for template parameters is:

```
template <class T1[, class T2 = value, ...]>
class className
{
  // declarations of members
};
```

The syntax shows that you can assign a default argument to a template parameter. Once you do, you must assign default arguments to all subsequent template parameters. To use a default argument, omit the argument for that template parameter during instantiation. Here is an example of declaring and using a template class with default arguments:

```
template <class T, int nArraySize = 10>
class Array
{
  public:
    // constructors
    Array() {}
    Array(T InitVal)
      { for (int i = 0; i < nArraySize; i++)
          m_Array[i] = InitVal;
      }
      T& operator [](int nIndex)
        { return m_Array[nIndex]; }
  protected:
    T m_Array[nArraySize];
};

main()
{
  const int MAX = 100;
  Array<int, MAX> Array1;
  Array<int> Array2;

  // statements

  return 0;
}
```

The above example declares the class template **Array** with the template parameter **class T** and **int nArraySize**. The declaration assigns the default argument of 10 to the second template parameter. The function **main** declares the objects **Array1** and **Array2** as instantiations of class **Array**. The declaration of object **Array1** instantiates the class **Array** with the arguments **int** and **MAX**, but the declaration of object **Array2** instantiates the class **Array** with the argument **int** and therefore uses the default argument of 10 for the template parameter **nArraySize**. Thus, object **Array1** has **MAX** elements, whereas object **Array2** has 10 elements.

The C++ Standard Libraries

In addition to using the existing C libraries, the ANSI C++ Committee is promoting a new set of libraries. The following subsections introduce you to these new and reorganized libraries.

THE LANGUAGE SUPPORT LIBRARY

The language support library supports the C++ language itself. Table 18-2 lists the categories in this library and shows their related header files. The categories support such aspects as value limits, dynamic allocation, exception handling, and runtime type identification (RTTI).

Table 18-2
The Categories in the Language Support Library and Their Related Header Files

Category	Header file(s)
Types	<cstddef>
Implementation properties	<limits>, <climits>, and <cfloat>
Start and termination	<cstdlib>
Dynamic memory management	<new>
Type identification	<typeinfo>
Exception handling	<exception>
Miscellaneous runtime support	<cstdarg>, <csetjmp>, <ctime>, <csignal>, and <cstdlib>

THE DIAGNOSTICS LIBRARY

The diagnostics library supports detecting and reporting error conditions. Table 18-3 lists the categories in this library and shows their related header files.

Table 18-3
The Categories in the Diagnostics Library and Their Related Header Files

Category	*Header file(s)*
Exception classes	<stdexcept>
Assertions	<cassert>
Error numbers	<cerrno>

THE GENERAL UTILITIES LIBRARY

The general utilities library supports other components of the standard C++ library as well as the Standard Template Library (STL). Table 18-4 lists the categories in this library and shows their related header files. This library contains components such as templatized relational operators, function objects that assist the STL classes, and memory allocation used by the STL classes.

Table 18-4
The Categories in the General Utilities Library and Their Related Header Files

Category	*Header file(s)*
Utility components	<utility>
Function objects	<functional>
Memory	<memory>
Date and time	<ctime>

THE STRING LIBRARY

The string library supports string classes that handle the **char** and **wchar_t** (multibyte characters) data types, as well as user-defined character types. Table 18-5 lists the categories in this library and shows their related header files. This library contains components such as the classes **basic_string** and the descendant classes **string** and **wstring**. The class **basic_string** supports such common string operations as assigning, appending, inserting, removing, copying, searching, and comparing characters in string objects.

Table 18-5

The Categories in the String Library and Their Related Header Files

Category	Header file(s)
String classes	<string>
Null-terminated sequence utilities	<cctype>, <cwctype>, <cstring>, <cwchar>, and <cstdlib>

THE LOCALIZATION LIBRARY

The localization library supports localizing software for different countries and cultures. Such support includes:

- Internationalization of character classification and string collation
- Numeric, monetary, and date/time formatting and parsing
- Message retrieval

Table 18-6 lists the categories in this library and shows their related header files.

Table 18-6
The Categories in the Localization Library and Their Related Header Files

Category	Header file(s)
Locales	<locale>
Standard local categories	
C library locales	<clocal>

THE CONTAINERS LIBRARY

The containers library is an alias to the Standard Template Library (STL), which I cover in the next major section. Table 18-7 lists the categories in this library and shows their related header files. These files offer templatized classes that model generic sets, lists, queues, stacks, arrays, and maps.

Table 18-7
The Categories in the Containers Library and Their Related Header Files

Category	Header file(s)
Sequences	<bitset>, <deque>, <list>, <queue>, <stack>, and <vector>
Associative containers	<map> and <set>

THE ITERATORS LIBRARY

The iterators library supports iterations over STL containers (stacks, queues, lists, and so on), streams, and stream buffers. The header file **<iterator>** contains the templatized components of the iterators.

THE ALGORITHMS LIBRARY

The algorithms library supports algorithmic operations on STL containers and other sequences. Table 18-8 lists the algorithms in this library and shows their related header files. These files offer templatized components that support such operations as searching, sorting, comparing, and merging.

Table 18-8
The Categories in the Algorithms Library and Their Related Header Files

Category	Header file(s)
Nonmodifying sequence operations	<algorithm>
Mutating sequence operations	
Sorting and related operations	
C library algorithms	<cstdlib>

THE NUMERICS LIBRARY

The numerics library supports efficient numerical operations. Table 18-9 lists the numerics in this library and shows their related header files. The highlight of this library is the support for complex numbers using **float**, **double**, and **long double** types.

Table 18-9
The Categories in the Numerics Library and Their Related Header Files

Category	Header file(s)
Complex numbers	<complex>
Numeric arrays	<valarray>
Generalized numeric operations	<numeric>
C library	<cstdlib>

The C++ Standard Template Library

Class templates allow you to develop generic data structures to support arrays, stacks, queues, lists, trees, maps, sets, hash tables, and so on. Since nontrivial applications often use a common data structure, such as an array, the ANSI C++ Committee has sponsored and supported the Standard Template Library. This library of templatized classes supports common data structures and provides you with a time-saving set of classes. Table 18-10 lists the templatized classes in the STL. The iterators library provides the iterators that allow you to sequentially and randomly access the elements in the various containers. The companion CD-ROM contains the file STL.ZIP, which is an archive file that holds the STL header files.

Table 18-10
The STL Classes That Support Common Data Structures

Class	Purpose
deque	Double-queue that supports random-access iteration, persistent-time insertion/removal from either end of the queue, and linear-time insertion/removal in the middle of the queue
list	Doubly-linked list with forward/backward element access and persistent-time insertion/ removal of elements in any list location
map	Associative container with unique access keys
multimap	Associative container with possible duplicate access keys
multiset	Set with duplicate members
priority_queue	Priority queue that supports random-access iteration. Also supports stack-like operations. Created using **vector** or **deque**.
queue	Queue that inserts elements at the head and removes them from the tail. Created using **list** or **deque**.
set	Set with unique members
stack	Stack that is created using a **vector**, **list**, or **deque**
vector	Array that supports random-access iterations, persistent-time insertion/removal at the array's extremes, and linear-time insertion/ removal inside the array

Summary

This chapter ends your journey into C++ by offering what's new in the next versions of C++ compilers. You learned about the new **#include** format, the Boolean type **bool**, the new reserved words, the namespace feature, template parameter arguments, the new C++ standard libraries, and the new Standard Template Library (STL).

Where do you go from here? Well, for starters, write lots of programs. The examples and the insight into the foundations of object-oriented programming presented in this book are meant to give you a solid basis on which to write C++ programs, from the simple to the more complex. So go ahead and exercise these concepts in your own programs. Additionally, read lots of programs to examine their style and structure and enhance your understanding of C++ foundations. Check out the Resource Center, located at the back of this book, for brief but useful listings of publications, vendors, and other books associated with the C++ language. And look for more advanced C++ titles wherever IDG and other programming books are sold. The study of programming can never be exhausted, so you can bet that I will continue to write books on the subject. Perhaps we'll take a few more steps in the C++ journey together once again.

Resource Center

List of Publications

- *Dr. Dobb's Journal (DDJ)*, published by Miller Freeman:
  411 Borel Avenue
  San Mateo, CA 94402

- *C/C++ Users Journal*, published by Miller Freeman:
  1601 W. 23rd Street, Suite 200
  Lawrence, KS 66046-2700
  Phone 913-841-1631
  Fax 913-810-2624

- *Microsoft Systems Journal (MSJ)*, published by Miller Freeman:
  P.O.Box 56621
  Boulder, CO 80322-6621
  Phone 800-666-1084
  Fax 303-661-1994

- *C++ Report*, published by SIGS Publications:
  71 West 32nd Street, Third Floor
  New York, NY 10010
  Phone 800-361-1279
  Fax 615-370-4845

List of Books

Here is a list of some worthwhile C++ books. There are many more C++ books out there. Consult your local bookstore for the availability of older and newer C++ books.

- ANSI X3J16/IS WG21 Joint Technical Committee, *Working Paper for Draft Proposal International Standard for Information Systems—Programming Language C++*, Washington, DC: CBEMA (1995).

- Eckel, Bruce (editor), *Black Belt C++*, New York, NY: M&T Books (1994).

- Eckel, Bruce, *Thinking in C++*, Englewood Cliffs, NJ: Prentice Hall (1995).

- Ellis, Margaret A. and Bjarne Stroustrup, *The Annotated C++ Reference Manual*, Reading, MA: Addison-Wesley (1992).

- Gamma, Erich et al., *Design Patterns*, Reading, MA: Addison-Wesley (1995).

- Lippman, Stanley B., *C++ Primer*, Reading, MA: Addison-Wesley (1991).

- Martin, Robert C., *Designing Object-Oriented C++ Applications Using the Booch Method*, Englewood Cliffs, NJ: Prentice Hall (1995).

- Nelson, Mark, *C++ Programmer's Guide to the Standard Template Library*, Foster City, CA: IDG Books Worldwide, Inc. (1995).

- Rudd, Anthony, *C++ Complete*, New York, NY: Wiley (1994).

- Sedgewick, Robert, *Algorithms in C++*, Reading, MA: Addison-Wesley (1992).

- Shammas, Namir C., *Advanced C++*, Indianapolis, IN: SAMS Publishing (1992).

- Stroustrup, Bjarne, *The C++ Programming Language*, Reading, MA: Addison-Wesley (1993).

- Stroustrup, Bjarne, *The Design and Evolution of C++*, Reading, MA: Addison-Wesley (1994).

- Yao, Paul and Joseph Yao, *Foundations of Visual C++ Programming for Windows 95*, Foster City, CA: IDG Books Worldwide, Inc. (1995).

List of C++ Vendors

Here is a list of the main C++ compiler vendors. Contact them or contact your local software dealers or a mail order company.

- Microsoft Corporation: Visual C++

     One Microsoft Way
     Redmond, WA 98052
     (contact local dealers or mail order dealers)

- Borland International: Borland C++

     100 Borland Way
     Scotts Valley, CA 95066
     Phone 408-431-1000, 800-331-0877

- Watcom: Watcom C++

     415 Phillip Street
     Waterloo, Ontario N2L 3X2, Canada
     Phone 519-886-3700, 800-265-4555
     Fax 519-747-4971

- Symantec: Symantec C++

     10201 Torre Avenue
     Cupertino, CA 95014
     Phone 800-628-4777

IDG Books Worldwide License Agreement

versions. Each shareware program has its own use permissions and limitations. These limitations are contained in the individual license agreements that are on the software discs. The restrictions include a requirement that after using the program for a period of time specified in its text, the user must pay a registration fee or discontinue use. By opening the package which contains the software disc, you will be agreeing to abide by the licenses and restrictions for these programs. Do not open the software package unless you agree to be bound by the license agreements.

4. Limited Warranty. IDG warrants that the Software and disc are free from defects in materials and workmanship for a period of sixty (60) days from the date of purchase of this Book. If IDG receives notification within the warranty period of defects in material or workmanship, IDG will replace the defective disc. IDG's entire liability and your exclusive remedy shall be limited to replacement of the Software, which is returned to IDG with a copy of your receipt. This Limited Warranty is void if failure of the Software has resulted from accident, abuse, or misapplication. Any replacement Software will be warranted for the remainder of the original warranty period or thirty (30) days, whichever is longer.

5. No Other Warranties. To the maximum extent permitted by applicable law, IDG and the author disclaim all other warranties, express or implied, including but not limited to implied warranties of merchantability and fitness for a particular purpose, with respect to the Software, the programs, the source code contained therein and/or the techniques described in this Book. This limited warranty gives you specific legal rights. You may have others which vary from state/jurisdiction to state/jurisdiction.

6. No Liability For Consequential Damages. To the extent permitted by applicable law, in no event shall IDG or the author be liable for any damages whatsoever (including without limitation, damages for loss of business profits, business interruption, loss of business information, or any other pecuniary loss) arising out of the use of or inability to use the Book or the Software, even if IDG has been advised of the possibility of such damages. Because some states/jurisdictions do not allow the exclusion or limitation of liability for consequential or incidental damages, the above limitation may not apply to you.

7. U.S.Government Restricted Rights. Use, duplication, or disclosure of the Software by the U.S. Government is subject to restrictions stated in paragraph (c) (1) (ii) of the Rights in Technical Data and Computer Software clause of DFARS 252.227-7013, and in subparagraphs (a) through (d) of the Commercial Computer—Restricted Rights clause at FAR 52.227-19, and in similar clauses in the NASA FAR supplement, when applicable.

How To Use the CD

The accompanying CD contains the entire text of *Foundations of C++ and Object-Oriented Programming* in easy-to-use hypertext form. It also contains copies of all the source code used in the book.

Installation Instructions

To install the CD, follow these steps:

Put the CD in your CD drive.

From Windows Program Manager (or File Manager) select File | Run.

Enter *d*:SETUP (where *d* is the drive letter of your CD drive).

This creates a program group "IDG Books" and the *Foundations of C++ and Object-Oriented Programming* icon. To use the CD, put it in the CD drive and double-click on the icon.

Source Code

Source code is organized on the CD by chapter. You can load these programs, your compiler directly from the CD to or you can copy them to your hard disk.

Viewer Documentation

The viewer used for this CD is the Microsoft Multimedia Viewer, which is used in many multi-media products, such as Microsoft Bookshelf. On the viewer's toolbar are the following buttons. To select an option, click on the appropriate button or press the underlined letter.

Contents	Move to the contents page.
Index	Display a list of key words and phrases.
Go Back	Return to the previously viewes page.
History	Display a list of most recently viewed pages and select one to return to.
Search	Perform a ful-text search for any word or phrase
<<	View previous page.
>>	View next page.

Text References

Within the text, certain words and phrases are highlighted in red or blue.

A red highlight means there is a glossary definition for the term. When you click on the term, a "pop-up" window appears that contains the definition. When you click anywhere else or press Esc, the pop-up window disappears. (You may also use the Tab key to select a high-lighted term and press Enter to display the reference.)

A blue highlight is a reference to another page in the document. When you click on a reference to a figure, table, or listing, a new window opens that contains the figure, table, or listing. When you click on a reference to a chapter or sidebar, the screen changes to the first page of the chapter or sidebar.

Search

When you select the Search button, a dialog box appears. Using this dialog box, you may search all of the book, or selected sections, for any word or phrase. To search the entire book, simply type the word or phrase in the "Search by Word" box and press Enter or click OK.

To search only specific sections, select the parts to search in the "Topic Groups" box.

You can do more complex searches by using the keywords "AND," "OR," "NEAR," and "NOT" to narrow down the search; click the "Hints" button for some samples.

To limit the search to the topics selected on a previous search, select the "Options" button and check "List of Previous Topics Found."

To limit the search to topic titles only, select the "Options" button and check "Topic Titles Only."

Search Results

When a search has completed, the "Search Results" dialog box is displayed. You can use this dialog box to review all the "finds" of your search. All topics containing the searched text are listed. You can scroll through this list to look for likely areas to view.

Click the "Go To" button to display the topic. The Search Results dialog box stays open on top of the document so that you can move easily from place to place within the list, reviewing all references to the searched text. In the document, the text found is highlighted wherever it appears.

The "Previous Match" and "Next Match" buttons move within a topic, stopping at each highlighted find.

The "To Search" button returns to the Search dialog box.

The "Cancel" button closes the Search Results box, leaving the current topic on display.

Index

The Index box provides a list of all indexed key words and phrases. Type the first character or characters of a word or phrase, and the list will move to the first entry that matches the characters entered. Click OK to select a key word.

If only one topic contains a reference for the key word selected, that topic will be displayed immediately. If more than one topic is referenced, a dialog box listing all related topics is displayed. Select the topic desired and click OK. Click "To Index" to return to the index list or "Cancel" to close the dialog.

Index

(continued)

(continued)

(continued)

● **E** ●

• F •

(continued)

(continued)

Listings Quick Reference

O R D E R   F O R M

5/8/95

Order Center: **(800) 762-2974** *(8 a.m.–6 p.m., EST, weekdays)*

Quantity	ISBN	Title	Price	Total

Shipping & Handling Charges

	Description	First book	Each additional book	Total
Domestic	Normal	$4.50	$1.50	$
	Two Day Air	$8.50	$2.50	$
	Overnight	$18.00	$3.00	$
International	Surface	$8.00	$8.00	$
	Airmail	$16.00	$16.00	$
	DHL Air	$17.00	$17.00	$

*For large quantities call for shipping & handling charges.
**Prices are subject to change without notice.

Ship to:

Name _____

Company _____

Address _____

City/State/Zip _____

Daytime Phone _____

Payment: ☐ Check to IDG Books (US Funds Only)

☐ VISA ☐ MasterCard ☐ American Express

Card # _____ Expires _____

Signature _____

Subtotal _____

CA residents add
applicable sales tax _____

IN, MA, and MD
residents add
5% sales tax _____

IL residents add
6.25% sales tax _____

RI residents add
7% sales tax _____

TX residents add
8.25% sales tax _____

Shipping _____

Total _____

Please send this order form to:

IDG Books Worldwide
7260 Shadeland Station, Suite 100
Indianapolis, IN 46256

*Allow up to 3 weeks for delivery.
Thank you!*

IDG BOOKS WORLDWIDE REGISTRATION CARD

RETURN THIS REGISTRATION CARD FOR FREE CATALOG

Title of this book: Foundations of C++ and Object Oriented Programming

My overall rating of this book: ❑ Very good [1] ❑ Good [2] ❑ Satisfactory [3] ❑ Fair [4] ❑ Poor [5]

How I first heard about this book:

❑ Found in bookstore; name: [6]

❑ Advertisement: [8]

❑ Word of mouth; heard about book from friend, co-worker, etc.: [10]

❑ Book review: [7]

❑ Catalog: [9]

❑ Other: [11]

What I liked most about this book:

What I would change, add, delete, etc., in future editions of this book:

Other comments:

Number of computer books I purchase in a year: ❑ 1 [12] ❑ 2-5 [13] ❑ 6-10 [14] ❑ More than 10 [15]

I would characterize my computer skills as: ❑ Beginner [16] ❑ Intermediate [17] ❑ Advanced [18] ❑ Professional [19]

I use ❑ DOS [20] ❑ Windows [21] ❑ OS/2 [22] ❑ Unix [23] ❑ Macintosh [24] ❑ Other: [25]_____
(please specify)

I would be interested in new books on the following subjects:
(please check all that apply, and use the spaces provided to identify specific software)

❑ Word processing: [26]

❑ Data bases: [28]

❑ File Utilities: [30]

❑ Networking: [32]

❑ Other: [34]

❑ Spreadsheets: [27]

❑ Desktop publishing: [29]

❑ Money management: [31]

❑ Programming languages: [33]

I use a PC at (please check all that apply): ❑ home [35] ❑ work [36] ❑ school [37] ❑ other: [38] _____

The disks I prefer to use are ❑ 5.25 [39] ❑ 3.5 [40] ❑ other: [41]_____

I have a CD ROM: ❑ yes [42] ❑ no [43]

I plan to buy or upgrade computer hardware this year: ❑ yes [44] ❑ no [45]

I plan to buy or upgrade computer software this year: ❑ yes [46] ❑ no [47]

Name: _____ Business title: [48] _____ Type of Business: [49] _____

Address (❑ home [50] ❑ work [51]/Company name: _____)

Street/Suite# _____

City [52]/State [53]/Zipcode [54]: _____ Country [55] _____

❑ **I liked this book!** You may quote me by name in future
IDG Books Worldwide promotional materials.

My daytime phone number is _____

IDG BOOKS

THE WORLD OF
COMPUTER
KNOWLEDGE

❑ YES!

Please keep me informed about IDG's World of Computer Knowledge.
Send me the latest IDG Books catalog.